Crossing Borders
An International Reader

Crossing Borders
An International Reader

Anna Joy
Sacramento City College

Harcourt College Publishers

Fort Worth   Philadelphia   San Diego   New York   Orlando   Austin   San Antonio
Toronto   Montreal   London   Sydney   Tokyo

Publisher	Earl McPeek
Acquisitions Editor	Julie McBurney
Project Editor	Laurie Bondaz
Art Director	April Eubanks
Production Manager	Cindy Young

Cover credit: Lamberto Alvarez

ISBN: 0-15-505325-6

Library of Congress Catalog Card Number: 99-61039

Copyright © 2000 by Harcourt, Inc.

All rights reserved. No part of this publication may be reproduced or transmitted in any form or by any means, electronic or mechanical, including photocopy, recording, or any information storage and retrieval system, without permission in writing from the publisher.

Requests for permission to make copies of any part of the work should be mailed to: Permissions Department, Harcourt, Inc., 6277 Sea Harbor Drive, Orlando, FL 32887-6777.

Unless otherwise noted, the Web Site Domain Names (URLs) provided are not published by Harcourt, Inc., and the Publisher can accept no responsibility or liability for the content of these sites. Because of the dynamic nature of the Internet, Harcourt cannot in any case guarantee the continued availability of third party Web sites.

Copyrights and Acknowledgments appear on pages 633–638, which constitute a continuation of the copyright page.

Address for Domestic Orders: Harcourt College Publishers, 6277 Sea Harbor Drive, Orlando, FL 32887-6777. 800-782-4479

Address for International Orders: International Customer Service, Harcourt, Inc., 6277 Sea Harbor Drive, Orlando, FL 32887-6777. 407-345-3800, (fax) 407-345-4060, (e-mail) hbintl@harcourtbrace.com

Address for Editorial Correspondence: Harcourt College Publishers, 301 Commerce Street, Suite 3700, Fort Worth, TX 76102

Web Site Address: http://www.hbcollege.com

Printed in the United States of America

9 0 1 2 3 4 5 6 7 8   066   9 8 7 6 5 4 3 2 1

Harcourt College Publishers

To Chuck, Sarah, and Rachel, with love.

PREFACE

> Undoubtedly philosophers are in the right when they tell us that nothing is great or little otherwise than by comparison.
>
> Jonathan Swift
> *Gulliver's Travels*

Marshall McLuhan predicted in 1964 that everyone on the planet would soon be living in a "global village" created by mass media. The accuracy of his prediction is borne out by the presence of Western pop culture in all but the most inaccessible countries of the world. Pictures of even the remotest corners of the globe appear routinely on our television sets. Anyone with a radio or television set can learn about or view conflicts anywhere on earth. In the past decade, the United States has sent troops to Africa, Asia, Latin America, Europe, and the Middle East. Multinational corporations and economic alliances worldwide have internationalized trade. Our connection to the rest of the world is so immediate and inevitable that we need to acquire at least a minimal understanding of world geography, history, social and political systems, and general culture in order to join the world community.

Crossing Borders: An International Reader focuses on multicultural issues as examined in provocative international readings. An important goal of the book is to help students appreciate the complex, interconnected world in which we live. The book is also intended to introduce students to the richness and variety of human cultures and to the depth and quality of writing produced by authors outside of the United States.

UNIQUE ASPECTS OF THIS BOOK

This book is characterized by several features that are unique and that differentiate it from other multicultural and international readers. Other readers often rely heavily on personal narratives, resulting in a shortage of rhetorical and analytical models. In this book, two out of three readings consist of objective analyses and can serve as examples of expository writing. Of those selections that use narrative, most are short fiction; other narrative pieces use detailed explanations to make a point.

Selections in this reader also give students practice reading across the disciplines. Authors' experiences and expertise in history, psychology, sociology, and anthropology shape their discussions. Chapter 4, for example, includes an analysis of children in

Balinese culture by Margaret Mead, one of the United States' most widely recognized anthropologists. Other writers, like novelist and essayist Barbara Kingsolver, are also well represented. The interdisciplinary aspect of the readings make it possible to combine college composition with courses across the disciplines, including anthropology, psychology, sociology, and history.

Finally, in addition to its emphasis on models other than narrative and its attention to interdisciplinary readings, this book offers writing instruction that sets it apart from other anthologies with an international focus. Chapter 1 offers guidelines for reading texts that may challenge the student's sense of cultural norms. Students are introduced to ideas about culture and ways to examine cultural attitudes and subjects that may seem foreign to them. Guidelines for careful reading help students evaluate a writer's assumptions about family, politics, social issues, and human behavior, assumptions that are often determined by the writer's culture. Students are also invited to examine their own biases about these subjects. Chapter 1 also includes instructions for writing a summary, a sample summary and summary abstract, and a practice exercise on summary writing. Chapter 2 discusses the reading journal and covers writing a response paper. In chapter 3 students are invited to write comparative essays. The chapter discusses readings that compare cultures, offers suggestions for writing a paper comparing two texts, and provides a sample comparative paper. Chapter 4 shows students how to write an investigative paper that draws on information from several texts. Exercises and topics in chapters 2 through 4 permit students to practice what they have learned about writing response papers, comparative essays, and information papers.

ORGANIZATION

Part 1, the book's first four chapters, guides students through the writing tasks entailed in composing summaries and various types of essays and papers. Part 2, a thematically organized anthology, is composed of approximately forty readings of varying length that have been arranged in chapters focusing on eight different themes. Each chapter begins with a "First Thoughts" section of epigraphs or longer quotations designed to help students start thinking about the chapter's theme or ideas raised within the chapter.

READING SELECTIONS

The readings in this book introduce students to a variety of styles, genres, and cultural contexts. Genres include essays, autobiographies, professional studies, informed analyses, and a sprinkling of poems and short stories. The authors and their subjects cover 27 countries and 22 distinct cultural or religious groups, 12 from the United States. Six selections focus on either global or regional concerns. In addition to its international readings, each chapter contains at least one selection about the United

States, and other readings offer comparisons between situations in the United States and those in other countries.

Many of the writers represented in this text are internationally known; several are Nobel laureates. Important contributors include Czeslaw Milosz, Aung San Suu Kyi, Pablo Neruda, Salman Rushdie, Naguib Mahfouz, Franz Kafka, Sembene Ousmane, and Federico Garcia Lorca. Writers from various academic disciplines and cultural groups in this country are represented by such well-known authors as Audre Lorde, Connie May Fowler, Gish Jen, Margaret Mead, Gloria Anzaldúa, Neil Postman, and Barbara Kingsolver.

Thematically arranged readings, which begin in chapter 5, focus on themes common to human experience: the family, rites of passage, working, custom and gender roles, the individual and the group, immigrants and exiles, the artist in society, and the spiritual life. Although many of the readings have not appeared in other anthologies, each has been tested in the classroom and proven to be engaging and challenging for students.

OTHER FEATURES OF THE TEXT

Each major reading selection in this volume is preceded by information about the author, and many readings are introduced with a section entitled "Facts about . . . ," which introduces the region or culture treated in the selection. This information gives students a context for interpreting points of view and themes. A map at the back of the book indicates the location of countries represented by readings in the book.

Each main reading selection is accompanied by four types of apparatus:

- "Writing before Reading" entries precede the readings and encourage students to write about issues related to the readings and to examine feelings they have about particular subjects.
- "Reading for Meaning" questions provide students with prompts to help them evaluate a text, to connect ideas in the text to their own experience, and to examine assumptions they might bring to the readings.
- "Comparing Texts" exercises encourage students to compare authors' perspectives and approaches.
- Topics included in the "Ideas for Writing" sections give students the opportunity to write about their observations about cultures. Entries ask students to analyze ideas and styles of writing and to write reader-response papers and short research projects using resources in this textbook or outside sources.

All of these questions and topics for writing are useful for class discussion, for study groups, and as writing prompts. Additional readings sometimes appear in the "Comparing Texts" sections following the main reading selections (such readings, and others in the "Ideas for Writing" sections, are marked with an asterisk in the table of contents). These texts provide numerous possibilities for comparison. In the "Comparing Texts" section following Connie May Fowler's "No Snapshots in the Attic: A

Granddaughter's Search for a Cherokee Past," for example, Fowler's essay is linked with several related texts. One comparative exercise contains excerpts from William Wood's *New England's Prospect* and Thomas Morton's *New England Canaan,* texts written in two of the early English settlements in North America. In this exercise, students are asked to analyze the assumptions the authors make about the native people they encountered in the "New World." The intent of such exercises is to offer additional perspectives on historical, social, political, or ethical issues discussed in the main readings.

One reading, the first chapter of Mary Wollstonecroft's *Vindication of the Rights of Women* appears as an appendix at the back of this book. The second appendix offers suggestions for using the Internet to gather information and to communicate with people interested in cross-cultural issues, while the third appendix contains a useful bibliography arranged by chapter themes. Other helpful items at the back of the book include a geographical index, a rhetorical index, and a thematic index.

ANCILLARIES

An Instructor's Manual to accompany *Crossing Borders: An International Reader* includes an overview of the themes in each chapter, approaches to teaching the reading selections, a sample course outline, suggested answers to "Reading for Meaning" entries, and considerations for discussing exercises and topics in the sections "Comparing Texts" and "Ideas for Writing."

ACKNOWLEDGMENTS

My appreciation goes to my friend and editor, Helen Triller-Yambert, for her excellent sense of what this book is about and for her sound advice about how to improve it. I am also indebted to the editorial and production staff at Harcourt who have offered their expert guidance and generous support all along the way. Special thanks to Julie McBurney, Laurie Bondaz, Cindy Young, and April Eubanks.

I would also like to thank the following reviewers for their useful suggestions and comments: Beverly Chin, University of Montana; Sherrie Gradin, Portland State University; Erika Hartman, South Suburban College, Illinois; Maureen Hoag, Wichita State University; James McDonald, University of Southwestern Louisiana; Fran O'Connor, Nassau Community College; Gary Olson, University of South Florida.

Most of all, I wish to thank the writers who have contributed to this book, many of whom write at great risk to themselves. The world is a richer place because of them.

Anna Joy

BRIEF CONTENTS

PART 1 Reading Texts and Comparing Cultures

Chapter 1   Reading about Culture
What Is "Natural"?
The Importance of Questioning What We Regard as Natural
Preparing to Read about Culture
Cultural Analysis
An Introduction to Cultural Analysis
Understanding Ideas
Writing a Summary

Chapter 2   Responding to Texts
A Note on Texts
The Writer's Stance
Examining the Writer's Stance
Writing a Response
The Reading Journal
Responding to Texts about Culture
Writing a Response Paper
Responding to the Text

Chapter 3   Making Comparisons
Perspectives on Culture
Writing to Compare

Chapter 4   Exploring Ideas from Several Cultures
The Investigation or Information Paper
Investigating: Using Information from Several Texts
Investigating: Sample Research Paper

Part 2   Readings for Cultural Analysis and Comparison

Chapter 5   The Family

Chapter 6   Rites of Passage

Chapter 7   Working

Chapter 8   Custom and Gender Roles

Chapter 9   The Individual and the Group

Chapter 10 Immigrants and Exiles

Chapter 11 The Artist in Society

Chapter 12 The Spiritual Life

APPENDIX A
Mary Wollstonecroft, Chapter 1: *Vindication of the Rights of Women*

APPENDIX B
Internet

APPENDIX C
Bibliography

GEOGRAPHICAL INDEX

RHETORICAL INDEX

THEMATIC INDEX

INDEX OF AUTHORS AND TITLES

CONTENTS

PART 1 Reading Texts and Comparing Cultures 1

Chapter 1   Reading about Culture 3
What Is "Natural"? 4
The Importance of Questioning What We Regard as "Natural" 4
Preparing to Read about Culture 5
Cultural Analysis 6
An Introduction to Cultural Analysis 7

> Writing before Reading 7
> **Raymonde Carroll** Introduction to *Cultural Misunderstandings* 8
> *This essay introduces the author's study of French and American perspectives on a variety of subjects and offers an introduction to cultural analysis, providing important information about the cultural contexts for the varieties of human behavior.*
> Reading for Meaning 17

Understanding Ideas 17
Writing a Summary 18
> Reading Actively 18
> **Sample Summary** Summary of Raymonde Carroll's Introduction to *Cultural Misunderstandings* 19
> **Sample Summary Abstract** Summary Abstract of Raymonde Carroll's Introduction to *Cultural Misunderstandings* 21

Conclusions about Summary Writing 22
Practice Exercise 22

Chapter 2   Responding to Texts 23
A Note on Texts 24
The Writer's Stance 25
Examining the Writer's Stance 25
Writing a Response 28
The Reading Journal 28
Responding to Texts about Culture 29

> Writing before Reading 29
> **Marvin Harris** Small Things 29
> *The author explains that cultural biases in various locations worldwide about eating or not eating insects stem from practical considerations involving scarcity of other sources of protein.*

Sample Two Column Journal	**38**
Reading for Meaning	40
Writing a Response Paper	**41**
Finding Main Points	41
Responding to the Text	**42**
Sample Response Paper Response Paper for "Small Things"	42
Ideas for Writing	45

Chapter 3   Making Comparisons   46
Perspectives on Culture   47

Writing before Reading	47
Nikita Pokrovsky The Land of Meaningless Courtesy	48
In an article written for Russian businessmen, Nikita Pokrovsky provides a Russian view of American business protocol and critiques the American way of doing business.	
Reading for Meaning	51
Comparing Texts	52
Ideas for Writing	52
Writing before Reading	52
Czeslaw Milosz Looking to the West	52
Polish immigrant and Nobel Prize winner Czeslaw Milosz provides an analysis of the Central and Eastern European mind and the history that produced it.	
Reading for Meaning	63
Comparing Texts	64
Ideas for Writing	64
Writing to Compare	**65**
Sample Essay Examining the West: A Comparison of "The Land of Meaningless Courtesy" and "Looking to the West"	68
Organizing Comparative Essays	75

Chapter 4   Exploring Ideas from Several Cultures   77
The Investigation or Information Paper   78

Writing before Reading	78
Barbara Kingsolver Somebody's Baby	78
Kingsolver's essay compares attitudes toward children in Spain with those held in the United States.	
Reading for Meaning	84
Comparing Texts	84
Ideas for Writing	84

Writing before Reading	85
Raymonde Carroll Parents and Children	85
Carroll compares French and American assumptions about parenting.	
Reading for Meaning	100
Comparing Texts	100
Ideas for Writing	101
Writing before Reading	101
Margaret Mead Children and Ritual in Bali	101
Mead's essay examines the rituals that protected as well as frightened children in pre-World War II Bali.	
Reading for Meaning	113
Comparing Texts	114
Ideas for Writing	114
Investigating: Using Information from Several Texts	**115**
Sample Research Paper Bringing Up Baby: Growing Up in Spain, France, the United States, and Bali	116

PART 2 Readings for Cultural Analysis and Comparison — 127

Chapter 5 The Family — 129

Writing before Reading	131
Li Zhai Role Reversal: The Kind Father and Stern Mother	131
The author's essay examines the changing roles of men and women in Chinese families.	
Reading for Meaning	134
Comparing Texts	134
*Nicholas Bornoff excerpt from Pink Samurai	135
Bornoff describes the lives of a Japanese couple and their children, especially with reference to the role of each family member.	
Ideas for Writing	135
Writing before Reading	136
Connie May Fowler No Snapshots in the Attic: A Granddaughter's Search for a Cherokee Past	136
The author describes her quest to sort out myths and facts about her family's history.	
Reading for Meaning	143
Comparing Texts	143

*Asterisked items are briefer readings (sometimes quite brief), often intended for comparative purposes, that appear in the apparatus for lengthier selections.

William Wood New England's Prospect 144
Wood describes Native Americans in 1634.

Thomas Morton New English Caanan 145
A visitor to New England describes Native Americans in 1637.

Ideas for Writing 148

Connie May Fowler excerpt from *River of Hidden Dreams* 149
In an excerpt from her novel, Fowler describes her grandmother's forced removal from her Native American family.

Writing before Reading 150
Gish Jen The Water-Faucet Vision 151
In this short story, which takes place in the United States, a little girl believes she can use miracles to correct what goes wrong in her family.

Reading for Meaning 158
Comparing Texts 158
Ideas for Writing 159

Writing before Reading 159
Nancie Solien Gonzalez Household and Family in the Caribbean: Some Definitions and Concepts 159
Anthropologist Gonzalez defines Black Caribbean notions of family and explores European-American misunderstandings of consanguine households.

Reading for Meaning 167
Comparing Texts 167
Ideas for Writing 167

Writing before Reading 168
David Elkind WAAAH!!: Why Kids Have a Lot to Cry About 168
Elkind examines the basic instability of American families, and the benefits and costs to the children and to the culture.

Reading for Meaning 176
Comparing Texts 176
Ideas for Writing 177

Chapter 6 Rites of Passage 178

Writing before Reading 180
Susan Orlean Debuting: Phoenix, Arizona 180
The author describes the quinceañera, or coming-of-age party in one Latino community in Phoenix, Arizona.

Reading for Meaning 192
Comparing Texts 192
Ideas for Writing 192

Writing before Reading	193
Horace Miner Body Ritual among the Nacirema	193
Anthropologist Miner offers a parody of cultural studies in this spoof on the "magical beliefs and practices" of the Nacirema (American spelled backwards).	
Reading for Meaning	198
Comparing Texts	198
Ideas for Writing	198
Writing before Reading	199
Martin King Whyte Choosing Mates—The American Way	199
Whyte studies the culture of dating and mating in the United States and concludes that living together before marriage does not necessarily lead to long-term commitment and successful marriages.	
Reading for Meaning	210
Comparing Texts	210
Ideas for Writing	210
Writing before Reading	211
Nicholas Bornoff The Marriage-Go-Round	211
The author follows a case study of an arranged marriage in Japan, noting that the custom gives parents virtual control over the choice of their child's spouse.	
Reading for Meaning	220
Comparing Texts	221
Ideas for Writing	221
Writing before Reading	221
Nahid Toubia Women and Health in Sudan	221
Physician Toubia offers a serious argument against Islamic practices that endanger women's health, if not their lives.	
Reading for Meaning	233
Comparing Texts	233
Ideas for Writing	234

Chapter 7 Working 236

Writing before Reading	238
Betsy Jacobson and Beverly Kaye Balancing Act	238
The authors discuss ways that our work defines us yet competes with our need for a rich personal life.	
Reading for Meaning	243
Comparing Texts	243
Ideas for Writing	244
Writing before Reading	244

Paul Harrison The Barefoot Businessman: Traditional and
Small-Scale Industry 245
> *Writer and journalist Harrison analyzes the "informal sector" of self-employed vendors and service people in various Third World nations.*

Reading for Meaning 255
Comparing Texts 255
Ideas for Writing

    *Robert Kaplan excerpts from "The Coming Anarchy" and from *The Ends of the Earth: A Journey at the Dawn of the 21st Century* 256
> *Kaplan uses Sierra Leone as a microcosm of what is occurring throughout West Africa and much of the underdeveloped world in terms of the demise of central governments, the rise of regionalism, the spread of disease, and the growing pervasiveness of war.*

Writing before Reading 256
Naguib Mahfouz Respected Sir 257
> *In a segment from Mahfouz's novel, an Egyptian petty bureaucrat looks forward to a promotion with religious fervor.*

Reading for Meaning 262
Comparing Texts 262
Ideas for Writing 263

Writing before Reading 263
Hugh Williamson China's Toy Industry Tinderbox 263
> *Williamson examines dangerous working conditions in some of China's toy factories.*

Reading for Meaning 269
Comparing Texts 270
Ideas for Writing 270

Writing before Reading 270
J. E. Thomas Culture and the Communal Organisation 270
> *A British educator discusses the corporate, communal culture and its historical roots in Japan.*

Reading for Meaning 283
Comparing Texts 284

    *Ross and Kathryn Petras excerpt on International Business Machines (IBM) from *Inside Track: How to Get into and Succeed in America's Prestigious Companies* 284
> *Writing to help prospective employees in their job search, authors Petras and Petras trace the company history and describe the labor force at IBM.*

Ideas for Writing 287

Writing before Reading	287
Robert Levine with Ellen Wolff Social Time: The Heartbeat of Culture	288
Psychology professor Levine and writer Wolff examine "clock time" and "social time" in Brazil and in cultures elsewhere.	
Reading for Meaning	293
Comparing Texts	294
Ideas for Writing	294

Chapter 8 Custom and Gender Roles 295

Writing before Reading	296
Gordon Murray Picking on the Little Guy: In Boyhood and in the Battlefields	297
On the basis of personal experience, instructor and psychotherapist Gordon Murray examines the way boys learn to be bullies both in childhood and later as adults.	
Reading for Meaning	302
Comparing Texts	302
Ideas for Writing	302
Writing before Reading	303
Octavio Paz Mexican Masks	303
Nobel Prize–winning Mexican author Octavio Paz examines the need to create a false self in the intensely masculine or "macho" culture of Mexico.	
Reading for Meaning	315
Comparing Texts	315
Ideas for Writing	316
Writing before Reading	316
Sembene Ousmane The *Bilal's* Fourth Wife	316
In this short story, Ousmane provides a humorous debunking of polygyny as a village Mosque's caretaker marries his fourth wife, who outwits her husband and works the patriarchal legal system to her advantage.	
Reading for Meaning	324
Comparing Texts	324
Ideas for Writing	324
Writing before Reading	325
Nawal El Saadawi Growing Up Female in Egypt	325
Physician Nawal El Saadawi's quasi-fictional memoirs reveal her humiliation and suffering as a female in a fiercely male-dominated society in Egypt.	
Reading for Meaning	333
Comparing Texts	334

*Nawal El Saadawi excerpts from "The Political
Challenges Facing Arab Women at the End of the
20th Century"   334
   *The author examines the role that religious fundamentalism
   has played in eroding women's rights in Arab countries
   and concludes that the burden of change falls entirely on
   women.*

  Ideas for Writing   335

  Writing before Reading   336
  Nira Yuval-Davis Front and Rear: The Sexual Division of
  Labour in the Israeli Army   336
   *A sociology lecturer in Great Britain, Yuval-Davis examines ideology
   and its effects on male/female roles in the military in Israel.*
  Reading for Meaning   351
  Comparing Texts   352
  Ideas for Writing   352

  Writing before Reading   352
  James M. Dubik An Officer and a Feminist   352
   *U.S. Army ranger Dubik discusses how being a parent and having
   daughters changed his perspective on women's role in the military.*
  Reading for Meaning   355
  Comparing Texts   355
  Ideas for Writing   356

Chapter 9 The Individual and the Group   357

  Writing before Reading   359
  Aung San Suu Kyi Freedom from Fear   359
   *A prodemocracy party leader in Myanmar, the former Burma, Suu
   Kyi discusses her faith that the spirit of a people can challenge a
   corrupt, repressive government.*
  Reading for Meaning   364
  Comparing Texts   364
  Ideas for Writing   365

  Writing before Reading   365
  Andrea Malin Mother Who Won't Disappear   365
   *Andrea Malin reports on the resistance offered by mothers of
   prisoners jailed by the totalitarian government in Argentina.*
  Reading for Meaning   374
  Comparing Texts   374
  Ideas for Writing   374

  Writing before Reading   375

Neil Postman Defending against the Indefensible ... 375
  Critic and communications expert Postman describes the way an individual can be manipulated by language and instructs readers in ways to recognize when someone is using language in order to mislead.
  Reading for Meaning ... 384
  Comparing Texts ... 385
  *****George Orwell** excerpt from "Politics and the English Language" ... 385
  In this classic essay (from which Neil Postman took the title of his essay), Orwell focuses on the distortions of political language.
  Ideas for Writing ... 385

  Writing before Reading ... 386
  Dorothy D. Lee An Anthropologist Learns from the Hopi ... 386
  Dorothy Lee explains how the culture of the classroom can overwhelm the individual and offers as an alternative the Hopi way of balancing the needs of the individual with the needs of the group.
  Reading for Meaning ... 397
  Comparing Texts ... 398
  Ideas for Writing ... 398

  Writing before Reading ... 398
  Pablo Neruda excerpt from *The Heights of Macchu Picchu* ... 398
  Chilean poet Neruda's poem explores the individual's need to belong somewhere and to find a connection with a group for whom he or she feels a strong connection.
  Reading for Meaning ... 403
  Comparing Texts ... 403
  *****Carl Jung** excerpt from, *Modern Man in Search of a Soul* ... 403
  Jung characterizes people who are truly "modern" as cut off from the past and from the sense of human community.
  *****William Wordsworth** excerpt from *Preface* to the *Lyrical Ballads* ... 404
  Wordsworth describes the blunted nature of human perception and his faith that it can be revived.
  Ideas for Writing ... 404

Chapter 10 Immigrants and Exiles ... 405

  Writing before Reading ... 407
  Salman Rushdie Imaginary Homelands ... 408

Pakistani writer Salman Rushdie discusses the dilemma of writers-in-exile who know that the country they have left exists only in memory.

Reading for Meaning — 418
Comparing Texts — 418
    *Richard Wright excerpt from *Native Son* — 418
    In the opening paragraphs excerpted from his novel Native Son, Wright describes an incident in the home of a poor Black family.
Ideas for Writing — 421
    *Salman Rushdie excerpt from *Midnight's Children* — 421
    In the opening paragraph from his novel, Rushdie deals with "imaginative truth."

Writing before Reading — 422
Jenefer Shute Sport, African Cultures, Value for Money: A Return to South Africa — 422
    South African writer Jenefer Shute returns to her native country after the dismantling of apartheid and finds that needed changes have not taken place.
Reading for Meaning — 432
Comparing Texts — 433
Ideas for Writing — 433
    *Alan Paton excerpt from *Cry, The Beloved Country* — 434
    Novelist Alan Paton describes conditions in post–World War II "Shanty Town," the blacks' section of Johannesburg, later to become part of Soweto.

Writing before Reading — 435
David Mura Fictive Fragments of a Father and Son — 436
    David Mura, a third-generation Japanese American, examines his father's history, his passive acceptance of being interned, and Mura's own feelings about his father's choice to assimilate into the larger Anglo European culture.
Reading for Meaning — 442
Comparing Texts — 442
    *Franz Kafka excerpt from *The Trial* — 442
    In this passage from his novel, Kafka describes the character K.'s arguments in his own defense when charged with an unstipulated crime.
Ideas for Writing — 444

Writing before Reading — 445
Ruxana Meer Razia Begum in London — 445

In this short story, Pakistani American writer and teacher Ruxana Meer explores the intergenerational conflicts in an immigrant Pakistani family.

Reading for Meaning	449
Comparing Texts	449
Ideas for Writing	449
Writing before Reading	449
Francis Fukuyama Immigrants and Family Values	450

Public policy professor Francis Fukuyama argues that the fears that newly arrived immigrants threaten the American way of life are unfounded—and indeed, that immigrants often staunchly uphold such values.

Reading for Meaning	463
Comparing Cultures	463
***Henry Louis Gates, Jr.** excerpt from "It's Not Just Anglo-Saxon"	463

Harvard humanities professor Henry Louis Gates, Jr., defends a multicultural curriculum, especially at the university level.

Ideas for Writing	464
Writing before Reading	465
Gloria Anzaldúa La Conciencia de la Mestiza: Towards a New Consciousness	465

In this excerpt from her book Borderlands/La Frontera, editor and author Anzaldúa explores the meaning of her mixed Spanish and Native American heritage, celebrating the mestiza (literally, the woman of "mixed" ancestry) as a rich New World product.

Reading for Meaning	478
Comparing Texts	479
Ideas for Writing	479

Chapter 11 The Artist in Society 480

Writing before Reading	482
André Brink The Artist as Insect	482

South African novelist André Brink analyzes the vital role the artist plays in awakening the masses who have suffered under repressive governments to the possibilities of democracy and freedom.

Reading for Meaning	486
Comparing Texts	487
Ideas for Writing	487
Writing before Reading	487

Audre Lorde The Transformation of Silence into Language and Action — 487

Black lesbian poet Audre Lorde's conference paper defends the role of the writer as a warrior who speaks out against daily tyrannies.

Reading for Meaning — 491
Comparing Texts — 491
Ideas for Writing — 491

Writing before Reading — 492
Franz Kafka A Hunger Artist — 492

Kafka's short story explores the artist's connection to his art and to the audiences who try in various ways to understand him.

Reading for Meaning — 500
Comparing Texts — 500
    *****Lawrence Ferlinghetti** Constantly Risking Absurdity — 500

Poet Ferlinghetti describes his view of the artist and his purpose.

    *****Edmund Wilson** excerpt from *Philoctetes* — 501

Wilson discusses his interpretation of Sophocles' story of the Greek archer Philoctetes, who symbolizes for Wilson the paradoxical necessity and discomfort inherent in the relationship between the artist and his community.

Ideas for Writing — 502

Writing before Reading — 502
Jane M. Young The Power of Image and Place — 503

Anthropologist Jane Young explores the meaning of art and ritual among the Zuni of western New Mexico.

Reading for Meaning — 511
Comparing Texts — 512
    *****H. A. Frankfort** excerpt from *The Intellectual Adventure of Ancient Man* — 512

Frankfort describes the "speculative thinking" typical of ancient peoples.

Ideas for Writing — 512

Writing before Reading — 513
Connie Stephens Marriage in the Hausa *Tatsuniya* Tradition: A Cultural and Cosmic Balance — 513

Author Stephens analyzes elements in the stories of the Hausa women of northwest Africa that give women some measure of self-worth in the male-dominated Islamic culture in which they live.

Reading for Meaning — 524
Comparing Texts — 524

	***Italo Calvino** excerpt from "The Canary Prince"	525
	In this excerpt from Calvino's modern fairy tale, a princess imprisoned by an evil stepmother escapes to save the life of her prince.	
	Ideas for Writing	527

Chapter 12 The Spiritual Life — 528

	Writing before Reading	531
	John Garvey A Different Kind of Knowing: For Those with Ears to Hear	531
	John Garvey argues that religion alone, and not art, provides the spiritual training that enables human beings to make ethical, moral decisions.	
	Reading for Meaning	534
	Comparing Texts	534
	***Rainer Maria Rilke** excerpt from "The First Elegy" in *Duino Elegies*	535
	Rilke's First Elegy, referenced by Garvey as representative of the great power of art to bring readers into the presence of beauty, examines the role of man in the universe.	
	***James Joyce** excerpt from "The Dead"	536
	Joyce's concluding paragraph from this short story is used by Garvey as another example of the power and limitations of art.	
	Ideas for Writing	536
	Writing before Reading	537
	Malidoma Patrice Somé Slowly Becoming	537
	Shaman or holy man of the Dagara people of the Burkina Faso area of coastal West Africa, Somé describes the role of his grandfather in his spiritual development.	
	Reading for Meaning	556
	Comparing Texts	556
	Ideas for Writing	556
	Writing before Reading	557
	Rigoberta Menchú The Bible and Self-Defense: The Examples of Judith, Moses, and David	557
	Guatemalan Quiché Indian Rigoberta Menchú writes about the parallels she and her people found between their Indian ancestors and the biblical heroes Judith, Moses, and David.	
	Reading for Meaning	566
	Comparing Texts	566
	Ideas for Writing	567

Writing before Reading	567
Wang Bin Two Great Traditions	567
Wang Bin writes about assumptions that distinguish Christian thinking from the Chinese-Confucian understanding of life.	
Reading for Meaning	573
Comparing Texts	573
***Confucius** excerpts from the *Analects*	573
*excerpts from *The Gospel According to St. Matthew*	574
Ideas for Writing	575
*excerpts from the *Tao-Te Ching*	575
Writing before Reading	576
Federico García Lorca Gacela of the Dead Child	576
García Lorca, Spanish poet and dramatist, argues in this poem for a cosmic significance to human pain and suffering.	
Reading for Meaning	578
Comparing Texts	579
***Pablo Neruda** excerpt from *The Heights of Macchu Picchu*	579
Ideas for Writing	580
Writing before Reading	580
Will Herberg The Religion of Americans and American Religion	580
Author and professor of religious studies, Will Herberg, argues that Americans, regardless of their stated religion, share a common belief in the "American Way of Life," which constitutes an "American religion."	
Reading for Meaning	599
Comparing Texts	599
Ideas for Writing	600

APPENDIX A
Mary Wollstonecroft, Chapter 1: *Vindication of the Rights of Women*   **601**

APPENDIX B
Internet   **608**

APPENDIX C
Bibliography   **612**

GEOGRAPHICAL INDEX   **617**

RHETORICAL INDEX   **619**

THEMATIC INDEX   **625**

INDEX OF AUTHORS AND TITLES   **629**

PART 1
READING TEXTS AND COMPARING CULTURES

CHAPTER 1
Reading about Culture

CHAPTER 2
Responding to Texts

CHAPTER 3
Making Comparisons

CHAPTER 4
Exploring Ideas from Several Cultures

CHAPTER 1
READING ABOUT CULTURE

First Thoughts

Premières impressions

Man tends to regard the order he lives in as *natural.* The houses he passes on his way to work seem more like rocks rising out of the earth than like products of human hands. He considers the work he does in his office or factory as essential to the harmonious functioning of the world. The clothes he wears are exactly what they should be, and he laughs at the idea that he might equally well be wearing a Roman toga or medieval armor. He respects and envies a minister of state or a bank director, and regards the possession of a considerable amount of money as the main guarantee of peace and security. . . . He is accustomed to satisfying those of his physiological needs which are considered private as discreetly as possible, without realizing that such a pattern of behavior is not common to all human societies. In a word, he behaves a little like Charlie Chaplin in *The Gold Rush,* bustling about in a shack poised precariously on the edge of a cliff.

Czeslaw Milosz
Looking to the West

A man of Sung, who sold ceremonial caps, went to Yueh, but the people of Yueh cut their hair short and decorated their bodies, so [they] had no use for them.

Chang-Tzu

WHAT IS "NATURAL"?

However observant we fancy ourselves, however careful, attentive, and well intended we may be, the obvious sometimes eludes us. In the classic tale, "The Emperor's New Clothes" an entire country, including the emperor himself, agree that the naked emperor is wearing the finest clothes any tailor ever made. Each citizen denies what he or she actually sees—the unclothed emperor—in favor of the only possible sight: the emperor magnificently clothed. The tale illustrates how people can become convinced that an agreed-upon reality is actually what they see, or at least what they *should* see if they are not to be declared insane or incompetent.

In many ways, this children's tale is an apt allegory of most people's lives. We don't bother questioning what we see until something startles us into seeing things as if for the first time. François Molière wrote a humorous version of this awakening in his comedy, *The Middle-Class Gentleman*. In this play, Jourdain, a comic social climber, discovers, much to his amazement, that he has been speaking prose all his life. In the everyday world, we aren't particularly conscious of the patterns of behavior that are routine for us. We take our way of life for granted, and as long as nothing seems to threaten it, we pay no attention to the fact that, as Czelaw Milosz says in the citation that opens this chapter, our "pattern of behavior is not common to all human societies." To put it another way, when things are going well in our lives—we are able to pay the rent, we have a steady job, boyfriends, girlfriends, partners, spouses, or children seem healthy and reasonably happy—we are free to assume that our world is based on a solid, unshakable foundation, and we can't imagine that anything might upset the order of our universe. During these times, "man tends to regard the order he lives in as *natural*," says Czeslaw Milosz. Occasionally disturbing events may lead to our filing for a divorce or to our losing a job. Some other upset might make us question our purpose in life and the very meaning of what we do. At that moment our way of life seems much more tenuous, and we realize that, like the character in the Charlie Chaplin movie, our house has always been "poised precariously on the edge of a cliff."

THE IMPORTANCE OF QUESTIONING WHAT WE REGARD AS "NATURAL"

Not being aware of the ways our own culture shapes our ideas and assumptions about the world sets us up for disappointments, misunderstandings, and painful embarrassments. As the Chinese philosopher Chang-Tzu points out in the parable that begins this chapter, when we fail to understand that other people don't necessarily act, dress, or think like we do, we may arrive in a new situation and discover that we have come with a great many assumptions that no longer have meaning. We can guard against such disappointments by making fewer presumptions about what is "normal" and by keeping an open mind about other ways of behaving.

There are plenty of historical examples that suggest how dangerous cultural blindness can be and how important it is to question the established order of things, the status quo into which we are born. In 1792, when Mary Wollstonecraft wrote *The Vindication of the Rights of Women,* she understood the immense task women faced in trying to change the prevailing attitude, usually one held by women themselves, that they were "naturally" inferior to men. Moreover, women were thought incapable of higher reasoning, and, it was believed, they were best kept away from the difficulties of commerce, employment, and politics. To the argument that women were by nature the lesser sex, Wollstonecraft offered a simple solution: "Strengthen the female mind by enlarging it, and there will be an end to blind obedience." Wollstonecraft was painfully aware, however, that female subservience was not something that men would easily relinquish: "But, as blind obedience is ever sought for by [the] power[ful], tyrants and sensualists are in the right when they endeavour to keep women in the dark, because the former only want slaves, the latter a play-thing." Wollstonecraft appreciated how difficult it would be to change such assumptions about women. It often takes a tremendous collective effort, extraordinary people, and just the right moment in history to change what people have presumed for years to be true.

More than 150 years after Wollstonecraft published the *Vindication of the Rights of Women,* Martin Luther King and hundreds of others who participated in the Civil Rights movement in the United States risked their lives by actively opposing the racist Jim Crow laws that kept blacks and whites separate. Dr. King knew exactly why it would take a long time and require the utmost patience to overturn those laws: "Freedom is never voluntarily given by the oppressor; it must be demanded by the oppressed." Like the attitudes that kept women in their place in the eighteenth and nineteenth centuries, these apartheid laws, which were rigorously enforced in the southern United States, were accepted as part of the natural order of things.

These examples argue for the importance of examining ways that the culture into which we were born has shaped our beliefs about what is "normal" and "natural." Such self-awareness helps us see that our assumptions are just that—a set of culturally determined ideas among a seemingly infinite number of ideas and possible ways to be. A fuller picture of ourselves as part of a larger, diverse human community is also useful in avoiding the disappointments, misunderstandings, and painful embarrassments that result from ignorance of other people's cultural norms.

PREPARING TO READ ABOUT CULTURE

These same ideas about reserving judgment about the behavior of others within our own culture apply when we are reading about other cultures. When reading about value systems and behavior unlike our own, it is helpful to recognize that each of us is stamped indelibly with the culture that produced us. As the writer James Joyce noted, we bring our family and cultural history, our language and sensibility to everything we do and observe, and in the end, for all our pretense at objectivity, we are simply "reading the book of ourselves." In other words, we see our values, assumptions, points of view, and judgments reflected in the objects and people we observe.

We are aware of this cultural envelope from the moment we are born. Our family's patterns of speech, body language, and ways of touching, as well as their judgments of others and their expectations of us, become part of the assumptions we make about ourselves and our world. Raymonde Carroll, a cultural anthropologist, sums it up this way: "My culture is the logic by which I give order to the world." In other words, I see what I am used to seeing, and I interpret my experiences in ways that are comfortable to me.

CULTURAL ANALYSIS

When examining behavior that lies outside our experience or when reading about ideas that give a different meaning to activities than we ordinarily do, we are performing what Raymonde Carroll calls "cultural analysis." Cultural analysis is the process by which we can explore people's communication in a cultural context that may be very different from our own. The purpose of such analysis, Carroll adds, is "to discover what things—whether a mode of conduct, an expectation, or a pattern of discourse—mean." Through this process, the meaning of a particular behavior that seems strange to us actually makes sense within the culture that produced it. This degree of open-mindedness allows us to see the normalcy of all behavior. Such a stance should be the goal we always aim for. But how do we achieve it?

Again, Raymonde Carroll can be of some help. She calls "cultural analysis" or investigation of other cultures "an act of humility by which I temporarily try to forget my way of seeing the world (the only way I have learned to consider valid) and briefly replace it with another way of conceiving this world, a way which by definition I cannot adopt (even if I wanted to) but the validity of which I assert by this act." Becoming open-minded about what we read also involves what Samuel Taylor Coleridge calls exercising "a willing suspension of disbelief." In other words, we should not discount a particular activity as ridiculous or unfounded simply because it is obviously different from the way we do things. Instead, we should develop the attitude to which Raymonde Carroll aspires when she encounters people whose values and ideas are foreign to her: "I must imagine a universe in which the "shocking" act can take place and seem normal, can take on meaning without even being noticed." She concludes, "I must try to enter, for an instant, the cultural imagination of the other." Carroll recommends a few steps that will make this process easier.

An important step in preparing to read about other cultures is to acknowledge that we are part of at least one culture, and sometimes several cultures have produced our view of ourselves and the world we live in. The same is true of authors whose works we will read. It is natural, then to look for what is familiar to us when we read and to distrust or even reject the unfamiliar. One effective technique for focusing as objectively as possible on the material we are reading or the activity we are observing is to see the experience or ideas in slow motion and in detail. Then we can study the ideas, behavior, thoughts, words, and the larger patterns of discourse. This method helps us focus more on the subject we wish to examine and less on ourselves.

Developing a curiosity about other cultures is one of the more effective ways of bypassing our native thinking long enough to appreciate others' ways of thinking and behaving. A genuine interest in what other people think, how they react, what they expect in certain situations, or what other cultural patterns of speech and behavior might mean is a way of looking beyond ourselves and appreciating cultural differences.

AN INTRODUCTION TO CULTURAL ANALYSIS

What follows is Raymonde Carroll's introduction to her book, *Cultural Misunderstandings,* a study of French and American perspectives on a variety of subjects. This essay also offers a more complete introduction to cultural analysis and provides important information about the cultural contexts for the varieties of human behavior. With a better understanding of how the values and beliefs of a culture shape people's ideas and behavior, we may have an easier time decoding gestures and speech, and recognizing our own cultural assumptions.

Like other selections in this book, Carroll's introduction is preceded by a brief biography of the author, the circumstances or motivation for writing, and a description of the country or culture the author discusses. Ideas about what was happening when the selection was written, where and for whom it was written, and why the author wrote it provide you with a context for reading that can enrich your understanding of the text.[1] Before you read the background information on the author and culture, you will find a topic or two under the heading, "Writing before Reading" for each selection in this textbook. These topics for freewriting and discussion ask you to explore your background and knowledge of the subject, and to discover your own cultural assumptions before you read what the writer has to say. "Reading for Meaning" is a section that follows Carroll's "Introduction" as well as the other readings in this textbook. Questions and prompts in this section are designed to help you get more involved with the readings and to think more deeply about what you have read.

Writing before Reading

Discuss a misunderstanding you had with someone based on cultural differences. Briefly describe what happened. Then explain your thinking at the time, and show how it differed from the perceptions of the person with whom you disagreed.

---

[1] The term *text* refers to written or printed words and what they are about.

INTRODUCTION TO *CULTURAL MISUNDERSTANDINGS*

Raymonde Carroll

Raymonde Carroll was born in Tunisia, North Africa, attended school in France and the United States, and has taught French language and literature in several American universities. Currently she teaches at Oberlin College in Ohio. Her husband is an American anthropologist, and Carroll herself has been involved in anthropological studies and research for some years. She lived for three years on a Polynesian atoll in the Pacific while collecting legends of Micronesia for her book Nukuoro Stories. *For her work,* Cultural Misunderstandings (Evidence Invisible) *(1988), Carroll spent ten summers interviewing "French people of all sorts, from a famous writer to a ninety-year-old former waitress," as well as French people living in the United States. She has been gathering information about Americans and their views during the twenty years she has lived in the United States.*

1   In the following series of essays I have attempted to discover the sources of some frequent cultural misunderstandings which occur between the French and Americans in several important areas of interpersonal relationships. My intention is to provide a point of departure, to indicate a pathway for those who would like to understand what separates us. This study is far from exhaustive. By its very nature, in fact, this type of study can never be complete. Nothing illustrates this fact better, in my opinion, than the story that Clifford Geertz relates in his book, *The Interpretation of Cultures*:

> There is an Indian story—at least I heard it as an Indian story—about an Englishman who, having been told that the world rested on a platform which rested on the back of an elephant which rested in turn on the back of a turtle, asked (perhaps he was an ethnographer; it is the way they behave), What did the turtle rest on? Another turtle. And that turtle? "Ah, Sahib, after that it is turtles all the way down."

This is indeed the way cultural analysis presents itself. The more one does, the more there is to do and, more important, the more one wants to do, forever seeking the turtle beneath the turtle.

2   Of what does this cultural analysis consist? This question brings to my mind a Raymond Devos sketch in which he complains of the absence of an announcer and of the difficulty of introducing oneself, because "if I tell them my name, they'll say they already know it, and if I don't tell them, they'll say 'Who's he?'" I have the same feeling concerning cultural analysis. I will, nonetheless, risk an explanation.

3   There may be as many definitions of cultural analysis as there are anthropologists. I am therefore not going to get entangled in the history of

cultural analysis or in a comparative study of the French and American conceptions of it. I will simply explain as clearly as possible what I mean by it. Very plainly, I see cultural analysis as a means of perceiving as "normal" things which initially seem "bizarre" or "strange" among people of a culture different from one's own. To manage this, I must imagine a universe in which the "shocking" act can take place and seem normal, can take on meaning without even being noticed. In other words, I must try to enter, for an instant, the cultural imagination of the other.

4   The road leading to this point, however, is long and tricky. From the start, we are caught in what seems to be an insolvable problem. On the one hand, since we know more about the world (thanks to anthropology, travel, cinema, television, tourism, immigration, wars of independence, and ethnic and civil rights movements), we are aware of differences, and we fight for the right to maintain these differences. On the other hand, the (justified) fear of racism and its hideous consequences incites us to maintain forcefully that we are all the same, universal human beings. We constantly fall into the trap of wanting to reconcile these two truths; we are caught between the desire to deny differences (we are all human) and the desire to emphasize them (the right to be different). Yet this problem exists only from an ethical perspective. It is indeed when we try to make both of these truths fit into the hierarchy of our value system that we find ourselves in a difficult position.

5   The problem disappears, however, from the perspective of cultural analysis, which does not concern itself with value judgements. Of course, we are all human. But we speak thousands of different languages, which makes us no less human, and do not find it inconceivable to learn a variety of "foreign" languages. Yet we refuse to accept the idea that we communicate with others through something similar to language, "languages" of which we are unaware—our cultures—despite the fact that we speak a great deal today about cultural differences. Indeed, if I am a cultural being, where is my individuality? Where is my free will? Am I a conditioned and completely predictable being, like a laboratory rat? In order to rid ourselves of these anxieties, we must accept, once and for all, the truth of the following statement: the fact that we are cultural beings in no way implies that we are mere numbers in a series, in no way denies our differences within a common cultural frame of reference. Just as we may speak the same language but never in the same way, so can we participate in a particular cultural milieu and maintain our individuality and our personality.

6   Indeed, my culture is the logic by which I give order to the world. And I have been learning this logic little by little, since the moment I was born, from the gestures, the words, and the care of those who surrounded me; from their gaze, from the tone of their voices; from the noises, the colors, the smells, the body contact; from the way I was raised, rewarded, punished, held, touched, washed, fed; from the stories I was told, from the books I read, from the songs I sang; in the street, at school, at play; from the relationships I witnessed between others, from the judgments I

heard, from the aesthetics embodied everywhere, in all things right down to my sleep and the dreams I learned to dream and recount. I learned to breathe this logic and to forget that I had learned it. I find it natural. Whether I produce meaning or apprehend it, it underlies all my interactions. This does not mean that I must agree with all those who share my culture: I do not necessarily agree with all those who speak the same language as I do. But as different as their discourse may be from mine, it is for me familiar territory, it is recognizable. The same is true, in a certain sense, of my culture.

7   Part of this logic is tacit, invisible, and this is the most important part. It consists in the premises from which we constantly draw our conclusions. We are not conscious of these premises because they are, for us, verities. They are everything which "goes without saying" for us and which is therefore transparent.

8   Cultural analysis is necessary only because my culture is not the only one in the world. As soon as there is contact with another culture (and this has always been the case), there is potential for conflict. Indeed, when I meet someone from a culture different from my own, I behave in the way that is natural to me, while the other behaves in the way that is natural to him or her. The only problem is that our "natural" ways do not coincide. Most of the time, though, we get along well, because the fact that our "verities" do not coincide does not mean that they necessarily conflict. The problem only arises, in fact, when there is a conflict. But since it is in the very nature of a verity to be self-evident and not to be challenged, I will not attribute the uneasiness or hurt I feel in a conflict situation to an erroneous interpretation on my part. Instead, I will attribute this difficulty to one, or some, of the other's inherent characteristics. That is to say, following an intercultural experience which bothered or annoyed me without my truly knowing why, or even without my being aware of my discomfort, I will have a tendency to say things like, "The French are ..." or "Americans are ..." In other words, if stereotypes are hardy, it is not because they contain a grain of truth but rather because they express and reflect the culture of those who espouse them. Thus when I—a French person—say, "American children are spoiled and impolite," I am not expressing a basic truth but referring rather to the French conception of child raising, which I unconsciously learned to regard as truth, whereas it is merely my (French) truth. When I—an American—say, "French people are rude, they don't let you get a word in edgewise, they interrupt you all the time," I am merely referring to the implicit rules of American conversation. But in order to understand this, I must first become aware of my reading, of the interpretation I bring to the cultural text, of the filter through which I learned to perceive the world. In other words, before learning to understand the culture of the other, I must become aware of my own culture, of my cultural presuppositions, of the implicit premises that inform my interpretation, of my verities. Only after

taking this step, which is in fact the most difficult one, can I begin to understand the cultural presuppositions of the other, the implicit premises which inform a formerly opaque text.

9 The idea that my gaze transforms what I see is very familiar today, almost a cliché. Unfortunately there is a great distance between knowing that my gaze transforms and becoming aware of the ways in which my gaze transforms. Moreover, even if I am ready to recognize the filter which my gaze (taken in its broadest sense) inserts between the world and myself, I will probably attribute it to my artistic sense, or my originality, or my "style," or my way of looking at the world (traits with which I am pleased), or even to my mood (conceiving of it therefore as temporary), thereby affirming and confirming my individuality.

10 The difficult thing for me to accept is that my gaze is also deeply French (or American) and is therefore similar to other French gazes and recognizable as such. Of course, I know that French table manners are different from those of the Americans or the Chinese. I know that in certain societies it is polite to burp after a meal, I know that in other societies breasts go uncovered but not thighs. I've read, I've seen, I've traveled, I've heard—in short I am a daughter (or son) of this century. But even with that, I have a long road to travel before I can accept that I am a cultural being in my way of loving (not only of making love) and of hating, in my friendships, my dreams, my fantasies, my anger, in all that makes me a human being like all other human beings.

11 Along this road, two major obstacles. The first, mentioned earlier, is the fear of thinking that I am controlled by an exterior force (which I take to be the culture), that I am transformed into an automation. This fear is dispelled as soon as I realize (a) that my culture is not something external to me, I create it just as it creates me; it is no more outside me than my thoughts; it produces me and I produce it; (b) and that cultural propositions, the premises of which are invisible to me, exist at such a level of abstraction as to allow for and include a very wide range of variations at the level of experience. In other words, two people can act in very different ways and at the same time reaffirm the same cultural proposition at the level of production of meaning.

12 The second obstacle is completely different from the first. Indeed, it is no longer a matter of resistance but of technique: assuming that I want to become aware of the cultural being that I am, that I want to become aware of my "invisible verities" in order to understand those of the other and to avoid intercultural misunderstandings, how can I go about it? How can I actually do a cultural analysis?

13 Several anthropologists, Gregory Bateson, Vern Carroll, and Clifford Geertz in particular, have provided models for cultural analysis to which I subscribe, although these models differ on many points. Those who would like to acquire further knowledge of such a theoretical anthropological

orientation should read their works. For those who simply (!) want to avoid intercultural misunderstandings, I provide a recipe which is effective yet easy to follow.

14   The first step consists of clearing the deck, so to speak. I must, above all, avoid all attempts at discovering the deep-seated reasons for the cultural specificity of such-and-such a group. That is to say that I must avoid the temptation of psychological or psychoanalytic explanations ("because American mothers...," "because French people can't stand authority...") I must also avoid the temptation of explanations that are ecological ("because the Xs lack protein"), geographical ("because they live in the thin mountain air"); meterological ("because of the abundance of rain"), or demographic ("because of the opposition between city and country"). I must avoid the temptation of economic explanations ("because they are capitalists"), of religious explanations ("the French Catholics," "the American Puritans"), of historical explanations (the role of invasions, wars), or even of sociological explanations ("the American family is such because people move around a lot"), and so on. This is not to suggest that these explanations, or different types of analyses, are inferior to cultural analysis. It simply means that they do not deal with culture, that they belong to another domain, as closely connected as that domain may be to culture. Indeed, I am not using cultural analysis to find out why things are as they are or to uncover their deep-rooted nature ("what they are"). Rather, I seek to understand the system of communication by which meaning is produced and received within a group. I seek to discover what things—whether a mode of conduct, an expectation, or a pattern of discourse—mean. I'll come back to this.

15   The second step consists of being on the lookout. I must, in fact, listen to my own discourse and learn to recognize the value judgments I include when I (sincerely) believe I am simply describing something. The easiest ones to recognize take the form mentioned above: "The French (the Americans/the Japanese) are..." followed by an adjective ("arrogant," "vulgar," "cold"). When I do this (and we do it at an incredible pace), I am not describing something but assigning characteristics of my choosing to the other. It is, in fact, the same thing as saying "I find the Xs to be like this or like that," but the assertion "The Xs are..." takes the convincing form of a general truth.

16   Once I can easily identify sentences like these, I must watch out for phrases like "The French (the Indians/the Americans) have no sense of...," "don't know how to...," or other negative expressions which suggest a lack. Indeed, in this case, the only shortcoming for which I am reproaching these Xs is the absence of my culture. What I am saying, in fact, is that the Xs do not have "my" sense of whatever it is.

17   As soon as we are consciously ready to do so, it becomes easier and easier to notice these statements. The process actually winds up becoming automatic.

18 Once I become accustomed to operating at this level of awareness, I can turn to the analysis of a cultural text. What cultural text? It can take almost any form. Linguistic difficulties aside, I am faced with a cultural text when I get a "strange" feeling upon being confronted with an opacity that I cannot dissipate without falling back on the explanation "The Xs are . . . ," which, as we have seen, is anything but an explanation. This can happen to me upon seeing a foreign film, or it can pop up in my daily life, be part of a lived experience. How, then, can I discover the logic that will render this opacity transparent?

19 First of all, by remembering the experience in detail, by seeing "in slow motion." This requires some effort, because we are generally used to remembering the broad features of an experience, and for the most part we remember them as we have already interpreted them. In the beginning, it might be useful to jot everything down, thereby enhancing memory and allowing for greater detachment. It is even more effective to set aside for a while the "text" thus constructed and to pick it up again later, allowing more and more details to be remembered.

20 Now that I have the text before my eyes (whether literally or not), it is clearer to me why I found the experience bizarre or unpleasant (it may even have been painful). Putting all that aside, I must try to imagine a context in which this experience is no longer shocking or unpleasant, try to imagine a universe in which what was "bizarre" becomes "normal." Of course, it is not a matter of finding just any interpretation that comes to my mind and which is different from the original one. I must find an interpretation the validity of which can be verified, that is to say, a cultural proposition that is asserted elsewhere in the same culture, though perhaps in a very different form.

21 Here is an example. One day in Nukuoro, I gave my neighbor a gift: a beautiful piece of cloth. This neighbor was an old woman who was important in the community because of her knowledge of traditions, tales, and legends, and of the native medicine. There was nothing surprising about my action; all kinds of gifts are exchanged almost every day. I will never forget, however, the way in which my gift was received on this occasion. The woman threw my beautiful piece of fabric aside, then began literally to "bawl me out" for having given it to her. I went back to my house, very shaken and close to tears. A present which I had taken such care in choosing, thousands of miles from this island where all I thought one could buy was copra . . . My first reaction was to wonder why she was upset with me, what I had done to anger her, in what serious way I had transgressed common practice (with which I thought I was well acquainted). Then I decided that my reaction was probably ethnocentric, that I had to look elsewhere. At that point, I could have imagined all kinds of explanations different from my first interpretation—for example, that she had not eaten yet that day and that she was in a bad mood. Yet it is obvious that this type of explanation would be purely fanciful, difficult to justify, and, moreover, not useful.

22   I saw this old woman's daughter, one of my principal informants, shortly after this incident, and she put me on the right track. She had already seen my gift at her mother's house (it is a very small village, and the incident occurred thirty or forty yards from my house). Upon mentioning the gift, which according to her was very beautiful, she asked me if her mother had bawled me out (the Nukuoro expression would be the equivalent of "boiled over") and, without waiting for a reply, told me not to worry if she had, that her mother liked the fabric very much, and that she would most certainly wear it to church the following Sunday (proof that she had appreciated the gift and that she wanted other people to see it).

23   Why, then, had she screamed at me? It obviously wasn't because of me, or because of my taste. I therefore had to examine the meaning given exchange and gifts in Nukuoro. Who gives gifts to whom? In what circumstances? What type of gifts? As I asked myself these questions, it became more and more clear that by offering a gift, I had put myself in a position of "superiority," if only temporarily, to the extent that I was the one who was giving and she receiving. (The analysis should be much more detailed and refined, but this should suffice here as an example.) Basically, we can say that by screaming and becoming indignant, she was reestablishing the former order: she had no need of this cloth, which she treated as if it were insignificant, and she accepted it, in a sense, to make me happy, because by refusing it she would have insulted me and cut off the nearly familial ties we had established and which she obviously wanted to maintain since she had accepted the gift. When I thought back over the old woman's discourse, I also remembered that she had said something like, "Why are you giving me this? Is it because I told you the legend of Vave? Is it because I brought you some taro?" and so on. By reciting a long list, she reminded me that I hadn't exhausted my debt to her, that I was therefore still her "inferior" (as a child would be), that I was still tied to her. And this conduct was obviously "normal" for a person from Nukuoro, as I later verified, although no one else had acted in such an extreme fashion.

24   The preceeding is an example, an extremely abridged example, of the way cultural analysis functions. By finding my interpretation in the meaning of the gift, I gave myself the possibility of verifying the validity of this interpretation in other areas of this culture.

25   The next step in cultural analysis consists of trying to discover, by analyzing other experiences, written texts (newspapers, novels, advertisements, civil codes), or oral texts (tales and legends, films, conversations), other domains in which the same cultural proposition seems to be confirmed, but in an apparently different fashion. Thus, the preceding interpretation of the meaning of gift giving was confirmed in a variety of contexts, including, for example, the manner in which a biblical legend had been (unknowingly) transformed by the local church.

26   Once I become familiar with the technique of analysis, I have only to practice this continual back and forth—"your culture," "my culture"—until it comes easily.

27   One warning. We are often intimidated by the idea of attempting such a foray into the cultural imaginary of the other, of confidently propelling ourselves into cultural analysis, because we are convinced, deep down, that this constitutes an act of arrogance on our part. Indeed, how can I claim to understand Japanese or German culture if I cannot really understand my neighbor, my parents, my children? Nevertheless, cultural analysis is not an act of arrogance but, quite the contrary, an act of humility by which I temporarily try to forget my way of seeing the world (the only way I have learned to consider valid) and briefly replace it with another way of conceiving this world, a way which by definition I cannot adopt (even if I want to) but the validity of which I assert by this act.

28   It is easier to understand the nature and goal of cultural analysis, as I understand it, if one thinks of translation. In order to understand a foreign language, I need, metaphorically speaking, a grammar book and a dictionary. Yet these tools are not enough to allow me to penetrate the mysteries of the foreign language: I need to know the meaning of words arranged in a certain way in a certain context. The better I know how to use these two tools, this "grammar book" and this "dictionary," the less I will misinterpret the meaning of the text. And the better I know a language, the more I will be aware not only of the nuances but also of the difficulties, the opacities which previously had not been apparent. All this is nothing new. We all agree on this point, which is why I mention it here. What we accept from translation, which is a difficult but fortunately far from impossible exercise, we have no reason not to accept from cultural analysis. As for translation, the principle is simple (to understand what the foreigner means to say, in his or her own way), though the practice may be ambitious and difficult. As with translation, if I want to make fewer and fewer mistakes in my interpretation of foreigners, I must constantly practice cultural analysis and accept the idea that the more I do, the more I will have to do (and will want to do), and, especially, I must resign myself (and this is the most troubling part) to the fact that I will never attain "the" truth, but "a" truth.

29   What may require the most practice is the ability to determine where the opacity lies. Because not everything is opaque; on the contrary, the vast majority of intercultural exchanges occur without a hitch. Just as it is possible to "get by" in a foreign language, even to speak it "fluently" but remain totally incapable of producing a good translation of a text in this language, it is also possible to learn all sorts of explicit rules and to respect them (even while doing violence to one's own feelings). One can live for a long time in a foreign country, speak the language, and make many "friends," without ever really understanding their culture, without ever really ridding oneself of a certain division between "them"

(that is, those who are "bizarre" in some way) and "us" (adaptable, but guardians of a better system). This tendency is visible among immigrants who arrive in a country as a couple or a family and develop a *modus vivendi* between the home culture and the exterior culture. This juxtaposition is not only possible but frequent when only some members of the family (breadwinners or young children) shuttle back and forth between the two cultural worlds. But as soon as I remove these (protective?) barriers from my daily life, whether I encounter this other culture in my work, in my friendships, in my romantic relationships, in my neighborhood, my market, my temple, or in the education of my children, I have thousands of occasions to experience intercultural misunderstanding, to interpret in my own way an act or a discourse that pertains to a different way of doing things and that requires a different filter; thousands of occasions to treat an opacity as it if it were transparent. Hence, the small (and sometimes deep) wounds, which are all the more painful as we do not know to attribute them to an intercultural misunderstanding; we therefore attribute them to the other's faults or to our own inadequacies. It is indeed within the realm of interpersonal relationships where one feels the most secure, the least guarded— among friends, among lovers, among colleagues, among those closest to us—that cultural misunderstanding has the greatest chance of arising. This is so because we erroneously think that in this domain we are all basically the same—Americans, French, all universal beings. We are, in fact, not the same, but this is far from catastrophic. Indeed, one of the greatest advantages of cultural analysis, aside from that of expanding our horizons, is that of transforming our cultural misunderstandings from a source of occasionally deep wounds into a fascinating and inexhaustible exploration of the other.

30   As soon as I become aware of all the preceding, what is left (the practice) demands patience and a great deal of intellectual discipline, but it is not difficult from a methodological point of view. It is, nonetheless, a strenuous, sometimes exhausting undertaking from an emotional point of view. Cultural analysis can be more painful than psychoanalysis, as painful as the latter may be. It occurs through a questioning of the very tissue of my being, and it demands an effort which is all the more difficult as I am perfectly integrated into my group and function within it without difficulty. It is also an undertaking which I must accept with the knowledge that I can never completely change my way of being and thinking, which has become entirely involuntary and necessary to me, like breathing. This means that, like it or not, I may find certain traits in myself which I have noticed in other members of my culture; that I may also discover a relationship, which I will find despicable, between certain members of my culture whom I disapprove of or even hate, and myself. This also

means that I am, in a sense, going to alienate myself from myself, examine myself when I least expect it.

31   But these anxieties should not be blown out of proportion. Whatever I do, I will continue to react as I have always reacted. The only difference is that I will be better able to understand my "spontaneity" without in doing so losing it. And when it comes to understanding quickly a misunderstanding that hurt me, made me angry, or disappointed me, cultural analysis is a great advantage. When it comes to discovering the imaginary worlds of others, to discovering other worlds, it offers an enrichment I wish for everyone.

Reading for Meaning

Questions that follow are designed to help you think more deeply about ideas and writing techniques that Raymonde Carroll uses in her discussion of cultural misunderstandings. You will find them useful for class discussion and for preparing to do the kind of cultural analysis required for most readings in this book.

1. Paraphrase Raymonde Carroll's definition of cultural analysis.
2. Carroll asserts, "My culture is the logic by which I give order to the world." Explain what she means by this statement. Think of examples from your own experience that illustrate this idea.
3. According to Raymonde Carroll, what makes cultural analysis important?
4. What is one source of stereotyping? Can you think of others?
5. Identify an important step involved in cultural analysis. What, specifically, would this step require you to do?
6. Choose a situation from your own life, and employ a few of the techniques for performing cultural analysis that Carroll describes to arrive at some conclusion about this experience.
7. Why does Carroll find the sympathetic examination of another culture an "exhausting undertaking"?

UNDERSTANDING IDEAS

Becoming aware of the varieties of human culture and our own unique place within one culture puts us in a position to record our observations and, perhaps, share them with others. The number of possible responses we will discuss in this and the next three chapters varies from the simple summary of a writer's ideas to the complex task of using information in several texts to write an information paper. The first of these projects, writing a summary, is introduced in this chapter. Writing critical response papers and comparisons are explained in chapters 2 and 3. Chapter 4 contains a discussion of papers that rely on information from several sources. Explanations of writing tasks in these first four chapters include sample papers.

WRITING A SUMMARY

A summary is a restatement of the main ideas in a text. Learning to write effective summaries will help you understand what you read and prepare you to read and write critically. Writing summaries gives you practice distinguishing important general points from more specific support. Because summarizing invites you to paraphrase a writer's ideas (the reader uses his or her own phrasing to restate the writer's points), writing summaries provides an excellent test of whether you have understood what is important to the author and what is not, and whether you can interpret the nuances of a text. Our understanding is never quite complete, however, until we can respond to a text in some way. We will discuss this more responsive way to interact with texts in chapters 2, 3, and 4.

READING ACTIVELY

The more thorough the reading, the better the reader's understanding of a text. To begin, it's a good idea to prepare yourself for reading. Be sure to read any background material provided about the author, the subject, the country where the text was written, and the occasion for writing. Think about the title of the selection and what it implies about the subject and the author's approach. Then jot down in a journal, or in the margin of the text, your initial reactions to the title. Freewrite about your own experiences or assumptions about the subject. Exercises in this book entitled "Writing before Reading" will help you discover what you know or think about the subject of each reading selection prior to reading about it. After completing one or two of these exercises, read the text itself several times. For your initial reading, skim the text quickly, reading just the introduction, headings, if included, the first sentence or two of each paragraph, and the conclusion. This first reading provides you with an overview of the text that will help you distinguish general points from detailed support. This reading also allows you to focus on main ideas without getting lost in minor details.

The second time through, read more slowly, taking time to underline key phrases, note significant ideas in the margins, and write out questions you have or objections to the author's ideas. The importance of this second, more active reading cannot be overestimated. Much of what you learn and retain from your reading, and much of your intellectual growth, comes as a result of questioning, agreeing with, or responding to texts in some way.

Before writing a summary or an analytical paper, go through the text a third time. For this reading, note main points you have underlined or mentioned in marginal notes. Also examine how the text is organized. This is best done by breaking the essay into sections according to the major ideas that each section discusses. This exercise, in effect, gives you an outline of the writer's ideas, ideas that you can then select for your summary.

SAMPLE SUMMARY

The following short paper is a summary of Raymonde Carroll's essay.

```
                                                    Brown 1
Wendell Brown

Ms. Ginzberg

English 1A

12 September 1999

           Summary of Raymonde Carroll's

    Introduction to Cultural Misunderstandings

   Raymonde Carroll's introduction to her book

Cultural Misunderstandings is a defense of cultural

analysis and a guide for analyzing cultures other than

our own.

   In the beginning of her discussion, Carroll

admits that no inquiry into cultural differences is

ever quite complete (1-2).² Nevertheless, she

attempts the task armed with her own belief that

cultural analysis is a way of normalizing practices

that at first seem alien to us (3). According to

Carroll, it is of utmost importance that we not make

"value judgments," and the first step in

establishing a relatively objective view of the

"other" is to realize how much we use the precepts

of our own culture to make sense of our experience

(5-10).
```

---

[2] Numbers refer to paragraphs in Carroll's text. You may omit paragraph numbers in summaries that you write.

To understand what certain behavior means within a particular culture, Carroll suggests following a few procedures. First, she advises that we not use psychology, economics, history, or religion to explain behavior (14). In addition, we must realize that the judgments we make about behavior reflect our own cultural norms (15-17). With these things in mind, we can read the "text" or behavior of people in another culture and, again, follow steps Carroll outlines. She recommends we try to see things "in slow motion" and figure out what "context" or set of assumptions makes what we have witnessed normal and acceptable (19-20). She illustrates this procedure with an example of gift giving (21-24) and adds that we can confirm our interpretation of an experience by comparing it to similar occurrences and by studying the folklore and writings of the culture involved (24).

Raymonde Carroll assures us that cultural analysis may be difficult and demand much self-scrutiny, but it is guaranteed to replace the pain of misunderstandings with a richer, deeper understanding of others (28-31).

Sample Summary Abstract

The summary abstract is a much shorter collection of the main ideas in a reading. Summary abstracts precede articles in professional journals and may be required for papers written in various disciplines. (For a sample abstract that appears in a published text, see the first paragraph of Jane M. Young's "The Power of Image and Place," page 503. The opening paragraph serves as a summary of the article.) A sample summary abstract follows.

```
                                                   Chan 1
    Trudy Chan

    Mr. Prince

    English 1

    10 September 1999

            Summary Abstract of Raymonde Carroll's

         Introduction to Cultural Misunderstandings

      In the introduction to her book Cultural

    Misunderstandings, Raymonde Carroll explains how

    cultural analysis works. Carroll cautions the reader

    not to make "value judgments" or offer academic

    approaches to a subject. Instead, she suggests that

    we examine the cultural context that might cause

    certain behavior. The rewards of patient inquiry are

    greater knowledge and understanding of others.
```

> **CONCLUSIONS ABOUT SUMMARY WRITING**
>
> We can draw these conclusions about the form and content of summaries.
>
> - Summaries refer to the author and title of the selection, usually in the first sentence.
> - The beginning of a summary also includes a statement of the author's thesis or controlling idea. This practice not only ensures that the reader understands the overall point of the reading but also gives the summary its own focus and direction.
> - Summaries are a compilation of the writer's main points.
> - Details, examples, statistics, or other data are not usually included in a summary.
> - Words or phrases borrowed from the author are enclosed in quotation marks.
> - The better summaries favor paraphrase over direct quotation. A reader who can paraphrase what he or she has read is more likely to have understood the writer's meaning than the reader who includes lengthy, undigested quotes in a summary. In addition, by paraphrasing, the reader can condense a longer article to a few central points.
> - Summaries may include transitional phrases such as "according to the author" or "the writer says" in order to attribute ideas mentioned in the summary to their authors.
> - Readers do not write about themselves or their opinions of what they have read when writing a summary. That element must wait until the student writes a more interpretative paper. The response essay is one form of writing that includes students' reactions to what they have read.

PRACTICE EXERCISE

Read the article, "Somebody's Baby," by Barbara Kingsolver (page 79). Use the techniques discussed in this chapter to preview and annotate this selection; then write a summary of the main ideas in Kingsolver's essay.

CHAPTER 2
RESPONDING TO TEXTS

First Thoughts

Primeras impresiones

One day six blind men learned that a king was camped near their village. This king, most formidable in battle, brought with him a mighty elephant. The six blind men, who knew nothing of elephants, wanted to touch it, thinking to gain some knowledge of it. So it was that each man found the elephant and felt some small piece of it. Later that day they came together to share what they had learned. The man who had felt the leg declared it to be solid and strong, like a pillar. The one who had felt the trunk said it was a long snake with rough skin. He who had touched a tusk of the elephant found it to be a long, sharp spear. "It is a high cliff," said he who had felt the forehead of the beast. The man who had touched the elephant's ear described it as wide, flat, and rough in texture, like a rug. "It's nothing but a rope," declared the one who had felt the elephant's tail. Each man understood a small part of the animal. Only together did they have true wisdom and the understanding that comes from knowing the whole.

"The Blind Men and the Elephant"
A Sufi folktale

Th[e] perpetual dealing with people very different from myself caused a shattering in me of preconceptions I scarcely knew I held. The writer is meeting in Europe people who are not American, whose sense of reality is entirely different from his own. They may love or hate or admire or fear or envy this country— they see it, in any case, from another point of view, and this forces the writer to reconsider many things he had always taken for granted. This reassessment, which can be very painful, is also very valuable. . . . Even the most incorrigible maverick has to be born somewhere.

> He may leave the group that produced him—he may be forced to—but nothing will efface his origins, the marks of which he carries with him everywhere. I think it is important to know this and even find it a matter for rejoicing, as the strongest people do, regardless of their station. On this acceptance, literally, the life of a writer depends.
>
> James Baldwin
> *The Price of the Ticket*

Reading texts that express points of view and values quite unlike your own can be as disorienting as living in Paris was for James Baldwin. Like Baldwin, you may find yourself reassessing ideas you have taken for granted up to this point. On the whole, though, you may also discover that this meeting of cultures can be a valuable experience that will deepen your understanding of yourself and other people.

This chapter and chapters 3 and 4 introduce several additional methods of reading and writing across cultures. Chapter 2 introduces techniques for understanding and responding to texts that reflect ideas and cultural values that may be different from your own. Discussion of the process for responding to readings is followed by a sample essay of this type of writing. In the process of reading and responding to texts in this and subsequent chapters, you are encouraged to examine the cultural assumptions that inform your responses.

A NOTE ON TEXTS

Before discussing ways to interpret and respond to a writer's "text," it is helpful to clarify in a bit more detail what this term means. Literally, the "text" refers to written or printed words and what they are about. "Text" is sometimes used more broadly to include virtually any human product—a work of art, a shard of pottery, a complex situation—anything that can be interpreted or "read" in some way. For the purposes of this book, "text" refers to its original meaning—any printed or written collection of words and what the words are about, with the additional considerations of how those words make meaning.

When we analyze a text, in effect, we isolate certain of its elements—such as ideas, organization, tone or style, audience, and the purpose for writing—in order to discuss the text or to produce our own written response to it. Although it is important to be able to analyze texts in this way, it is also important to remember that authors do not ordinarily begin with these pieces and somehow cobble them together. On the contrary, effective texts work holistically, with purpose, audience, tone, organizational strategies, ideas, and supporting arguments bound together seamlessly.

THE WRITER'S STANCE

The meaning of a text has much to do with the perspective or stance the writer takes toward his subject and toward the reader. Tone and style help the writer convey his or her stance. "Tone" literally refers to tone of voice, the attitude (defensive, sad, judgmental) we convey about our subject when we speak. The concept of "tone" applies to the attitude a writer conveys through his or her words and phrasing. Reading for tone is useful in discovering the emotional shadings of a text.

"Style," a related idea, is the collection of features an author uses that constitutes his or her unique way of writing. Kurt Vonnegut calls style "revelations, accidental or intentional" that writers make about themselves. In other words, authors assume a "writing personality" that they reveal, either unintentionally or by design, through the words they use. A writer's words disclose a cultural personality as well—a point of view, attitude, or assumptions—that has to do with the cultural environment in which he or she lives and writes. Learning to "read" clues to this cultural environment helps readers appreciate an author's culture and analyze ways that environment informs the writer's ideas and opinions. Equally important is the realization that interpretations of the writer's text depend largely on the reader's own culturally influenced perspective and assumptions. A reconsideration of what one has heretofore taken for granted can, as James Baldwin learned, "be very painful," yet it can be a sign of strength to accept the fact that "nothing will efface [our] origins."

EXAMINING THE WRITER'S STANCE

To fully appreciate the dynamic between the writer-and-culture, and the reader-and-culture, careful examination of words, phrasing, ideas, point of view, and the overall effect of each of these on the reader is essential. We will discuss elements of the writer's stance in three excerpts from texts that present aspects of cultures in Bali and in areas of West Africa. The first two texts are written by authors who are not part of the culture they are examining. The third is written by an African shaman about the culture that produced him. These samples show not only the writers' relative distances from their subjects but also the assumptions they make about the culture and their relative involvement in it.

Excerpt 1 from "Children and Ritual in Bali," Margaret Mead

The Balinese move easily in a group. A whole village may make a pilgrimage of two or three days to make offerings at the seaside or in the high mountains. A troupe of Balinese went to the Paris Exposition in 1931, and a troupe visited New York in 1952. But one Balinese, isolated from those he knows and taken to a strange place, wilts and sickens; people say it is because he is *paling*—disoriented—the word used for trance, insanity, for being drunk, confused, or lost. And the Balinese are mortally afraid of drunkenness, where the clues to the direction, the calendar, the caste system, the framework of life . . . are lost or blurred.

Following the children as they grow up reveals that, even within the simultaneity of ritual satisfaction and individual fear, the capacity to enjoy such rituals, to dance the lovely dances and fill the air with music, has been—in the case of the Balinese—developed at certain costs. The culture contains—or did contain . . . ritual solutions for the instabilities it created, and the people, on their little island, were safe. But it was the safety of a tightrope dance, beautiful and precarious.

ANALYSIS

We may note to begin with that Margaret Mead is sensitive to the culture that she examines. She describes Balinese dancing as "lovely" and finds the culture balanced in a way that is "beautiful and precarious." She also judges that problems caused by the culture are also solved by it. Beyond this level of sympathy, Mead draws conclusions that she offers as fact, as clear-cut judgments based soundly on her observations and obvious sympathy for the Balinese people and their way of life. She uses Balinese terms for conditions that are uniquely Balinese—*paling,* for example—and has studied the culture over a span of some years, as evidenced by her mention of the tours conducted by Balinese dancers in 1931 and 1952. Hers is the voice of a sensitive observer who has a deep appreciation of the culture but whose touchstone for cultural assumptions lies outside it.

EXCERPT 2 FROM "THE MAN WHO COULD TURN INTO AN ELEPHANT: SHAPE-SHIFTING AMONG THE KURANKO OF SIERRA LEONE," MICHAEL JACKSON

This article about "shape-shifting," like "Children and Ritual in Bali," is also written by an anthropologist. Michael Jackson's point of view, however, is different from Margaret Mead's. This writer is interested in revealing how his own perspective was changed by an encounter with a people whose beliefs are quite unlike his own. His honest subjectivity succeeds in recording not the pretense of objectivity, but the interplay between two very different sets of assumptions about the way the world works.

> For a long time my image of shape-shifters, like my image of witches, was conditioned by what Kuranko told me and by what I imagined, remembering nights alone in the dark forests of my native New Zealand when the inexplicable crack of a dead branch, the soughing of the wind, or an ominous shadow at the edge of a clearing would make my heart race and bring to mind childhood tales of hobgoblins and genies. . . . Steeped in ideas about shape-shifting from early childhood, one would be prone to interpret such ambiguous images in this way. The idea of shape-shifting was born and bolstered, I assumed, in such moments of panic and by such tricks of the night—like UFOs in our own popular imagination. The problem was, however, that this conjecture left unexplained the absence of any skeptical attitude towards

shape-shifting among the Kuranko with whom I discussed it. Furthermore, it became clear to me that beliefs about shape-shifting were not reducible to fugitive images and haphazard observations: they were conditioned by a complex of shared assumptions and ideas which required careful ethnographic elucidation. . . .

Rather than pursue the problem of how these beliefs may be justified from our point of view, I want to examine the grounds on which Kuranko accept them as true.

Analysis

Whereas Margaret Mead simply describes beliefs and child-rearing practices among the Balinese, leaving the reader to judge whether the events she describes are plausible, Michael Jackson identifies the preconceptions he held prior to his inquiry into the shape-shifting practices of the Kuranko. For example, he mentions how he brought his own childhood imaginings to bear on his investigation. He soon discovered, however, that it was not important to establish the "truth" or "falsehood" of the Kuranko beliefs. Instead, he found it more valuable to analyze the cultural context that produced such beliefs. Jackson's attitude toward his task is much like the one that Raymonde Carroll defends in her discussion of cultural analysis. Carroll advises that we keep an open mind during our inquiry in order to discover why a particular behavior seems normal to the people who have adopted it.

Excerpt 3 from "Slowly Becoming,"
Malidoma Patrice Somé

The third and final excerpt is taken from the opening chapter of Malidoma Patrice Somé's autobiographical work, *Of Water and Spirit: An African Shaman's Initiation*. A fuller text of that chapter appears in chapter 12: The Spiritual Life. In this passage, Somé describes his relationship with his grandfather and the general nature of the relationship between grandfathers and grandsons among members of his tribe.

> My grandfather had been my confident interlocutor for as long as I can remember. There is a close relationship between grandfathers and grandchildren. The first few years of a boy's life are usually spent, not with his father, but with his grandfather. What the grandfather and grandson share together—that the father cannot—is their close proximity to the cosmos. The grandfather will soon return to where the grandson came from, so therefore the grandson is bearer of news the grandfather wants. The grandfather will do anything to make the grandson communicate the news of the ancestors before the child forgets, as inevitably happens. My grandfather obtained this news through hypnosis, putting me to sleep in order to question me.
>
> It is not only to benefit the grandfather that this relationship with his grandson must exist. The grandfather must also transmit the "news" to the grandson using the protocol secret to grandfathers and grandsons. He must communicate to this new member of the community the hard tasks ahead on the bumpy road of existence.
>
> For the Dagara, every person is an incarnation, that is, a spirit who has taken on a body. So our true nature is spiritual. This world is where one comes to carry out

specific projects. A birth is therefore the arrival of someone, usually an ancestor that somebody already knows, who has important tasks to do here. . . . Elders become involved with a new life practically from the moment of conception because that unborn child has just come from the place they are going to.

ANALYSIS

Somé makes generalizations about the cultural practices he describes, as do the two other writers. However, the pronoun "our" in Somé's work sets his point of view apart. As an inheritor of the Dagara culture, he does not question his people's beliefs about the spiritual connection between grandfathers and their grandsons. Nor does he look for reasons why the Dagara people believe in reincarnation or for explanations of their beliefs. Like the writers of the other two selections, Somé assumes that the reader is an observer, an outsider who knows little about the Dagara people. While Somé wants to convey the beliefs of a culture to people who know nothing about it, as do Margaret Mead and Michael Jackson, Somé is also a spokesperson for that culture, a writer who believes in and is part of the way of life he describes.

WRITING A RESPONSE

Writing a critical response to a text involves an awareness of words, phrases, ideas, tone, point of view, structure, and other considerations that make up the content and texture of a text. Initially, your responses may amount to impressions as you declare that an essay is "interesting" or as you find yourself disliking something you have read. Although these reactions are valid and may lead you to a deeper analysis, for a critical response to convey something about the text or the way it is put together, it must contain detailed support for the conclusions you have reached. In other words, you need to communicate to your readers some understanding of what the writer says, his or her purpose for writing, how well the writer achieves that purpose, the writer's assumptions, and how those ideas or assumptions correspond to or contradict your own. Ultimately, your purpose for writing should be to deepen your own and your reader's understanding of the text.

THE READING JOURNAL

Accomplished readers can identify a writer's main points and thesis, and can also use the text to draw out their experience, observations, background, and opinions. Such deep reading is an important part of interpreting a text and may prompt questions about a writer's meaning, background, purpose for writing, or cultural assumptions. By keeping a journal—usually written in a bound or loose-leaf notebook of some kind—you can record your ideas and reactions to a text. The reading journal is particularly useful when you are preparing to write papers based on the ideas and writing strategies you discover in a text. A sample of the two-column journal, with one column for the writer's ideas and another for your responses, follows the next essay, "Small Things," an analysis of the practice of eating insects in non-Western countries. Read the essay first, and then examine the sample two-column journal entry.

RESPONDING TO TEXTS ABOUT CULTURE

Read the biographical introduction and the essay, "Small Things," by Marvin Harris. The questions, responses, and sample paper that follow this reading will prepare you to write your own response papers. A new section entitled "Ideas for Writing" appears for the first time as well. This section offers ideas for writing papers and is included after each of the subsequent readings that appear in this book.

Writing before Reading

1. Take a minute or two to write about your associations with insects, such as lice, grasshoppers, cockroaches, and insect larvae. What do such insects remind you of? Do you look more favorably on some species of insects than you do on others? Are there circumstances under which you might consider eating certain insects?

2. How can you account for the attitude toward insects you have just described? In other words, what in your experience or memory has shaped your opinion of insects? Is your attitude typical of people you know?

SMALL THINGS

Marvin Harris

Marvin Harris is the author of sixteen books, several of which focus on cultural practices. He has also written articles for The New York Times Magazine, Natural History, *and* Psychology Today. *He was chair of the Anthropology Department at Columbia University before joining the faculty at the University of Florida, Gainesville. Harris's research has taken him to Brazil, Mozambique, Ecuador, and Kerala, India. The following essay is taken from* Good to Eat: Riddles of Food and Culture *(1985), a book that explores what makes certain foods acceptable in some cultures and unacceptable in others. In his essay on "small things," Harris examines possible causes for the Western bias against eating insects.*

1   Ask Europeans or Americans why they don't eat insects, and you can count on the answer: "Insects are disgusting, and full of germs. Ugh!" The object of this chapter is not to try to change anyone's feelings about eating insects. All I want to do is to offer a better explanation. I think we have the whole thing backward. The European and American rejection of insects as food has little to do with insects as disease carriers or their association with dirt and filth. The reason we don't eat them is not that they are dirty and loathsome; rather, they are dirty and loathsome because we don't eat them.

2   Back in the days when I was teaching introductory anthropology at Columbia College, I used to pass around open cans of Japanese fried grasshoppers to get students in the mood for thinking about cultural differences: "Don't be greedy. Take some but leave a few for your neighbor." I thought it was a great way to identify potential field-workers until my chairman pointed out that if anyone got sick they could take me and the whole university to court. Given the large number of students who did show signs of impending illness, I had to accept the advice. Groans of disgust gave way to hostile glares and an evident lack of interest in the point I was trying to make. Pressed for their reaction, they didn't mince words: "I don't care what you say. Anyone who would eat these things isn't normal. It's unnatural to want to eat insects."

3   But one thing I'm sure of is that none of us has an instinctive aversion to eating small invertebrates, be they insects, spiders, or earthworms. First of all, if our ancestry is a guide to our nature, we have to accept the fact that we are descended from a long line of insect eaters.... Most living species of contemporary great apes and monkeys eat significant quantities of insects. Even monkeys which do not actively pursue insects as prey consume them in copious amounts in the form of adventitious or sought-after bonuses wrapped up in leaves or buried inside fruit. Monkeys also spend a good part of the time searching each other's hair for lice, not altogether as an expression of pure altruism; the searchers get to eat all the lice they want, as well as an assurance that the little rascals have been sent to a place where they can do no further harm.

4   Chimpanzees—our closest relatives among the great apes—pursue insect game as avidly as they pursue baby bushpigs and baboons. In their eagerness to dine on termites and ants they even manufacture a special tool—a strong, supple twig stripped of leaves. To catch termites, they insert the twig into the ventilation shafts of a termite mound. They wait a few seconds for the residents to swarm over the twig, then they pull it out and lick off the prey with their tongue. In "fishing" for a species of aggressive driver ants which can inflict painful bites, the procedure is similar but requires greater skill and determination. Upon finding the ants' subterranean nest, the chimps insert their special tool into the entrance. Hundreds of infuriated ants swarm up the twig. William McGrew

tells what happens next: "The Chimpanzee watches their progress and when the ants have almost reached its hand, the tool is quickly withdrawn. In a split second the opposite hand rapidly sweeps the length of the tool—catching the ants in a jumbled mass between thumb and forefinger. These are then popped into the open, waiting mouth in one bite and chewed furiously."

5   All this insectivory among monkeys and apes is to be expected given the likelihood that the whole primate order probably evolved from a primitive shrew which belonged to the mammalian order known as the insectivores. In shaping humankind's primate ancestry, natural selection favored precisely those traits which were useful for the pursuit and capture of insects and other small invertebrates in tropical arboreal habitats. An animal that subsists by hunting for insects on the limbs, branches, or leaves of trees needs a special set of traits: keen stereoscopic vision rather than a keen sense of smell; an agile body; fingers that can grasp and pick up tidbits and bring them close to its eyes for inspection prior to putting them in the mouth; and, above all, a complex, alert mind capable of monitoring the movements of prey amid the light-dappled, wind-blown, rain-spattered arboreal canopy. In this sense, insectivory laid the basis for the further evolution of manual dexterity, differentiation of hands from feet, and the extra braininess that define *Homo*'s distinct place in the great chain of being.

6   With insectivorous ancestors so prominent in our family tree, we should not be surprised that the abomination of insects and other small invertebrates by Europeans and Americans is the exception rather than the rule. Franz Bodenheimer, father of entomology in modern Israel, was the first scholar to document the extent of humankind's appetite for insects. (He is also known for his demonstration that the manna from heaven of the Old Testament was a crystalized excretion of surplus sugar from a species of scale insect that inhabits the Sinai Peninsula.) Bodenheimer presents evidence of insectivory on all the inhabited continents. People around the globe seem to be especially fond of locusts, grasshoppers, crickets, ants, termites, and the larvae and pupae of large moths, butterflies, and beetles. In some societies insects rival vertebrates as a source of animal protein and fat.

7   Before there were European settlements in California, for example, the native peoples lacked agriculture or domesticated animals other than dogs, and depended heavily on insects for their basic subsistence. They especially sought the young, fat larvae of bees, wasps, ants, crane flies, and moths. In late summer the pupae of a small fly *(Ephydra hians)* washed ashore along the beaches of California and Nevada's brackish lakes, forming windrows which made it easy for the Indians to harvest huge numbers at a time. They also caught copious quantities of locusts by beating the ground and driving hordes of these insects in a contracting circle onto beds of hot coals. To capture pandora moth

caterpillars the Indians built smudge fires under the pine trees and waited for the two-and-a-half-inch creatures to become stupefied and plop to the ground. Women, children, and old men killed and dried these caterpillars in a bed of hot ashes. They also laid tons of dried locusts and moth larvae aside for the winter months when even insects became scarce.

8   Many indigenous peoples of the Amazon basin seem to be especially keen on insect fare. According to a study carried out among the Tatuya Indians who live near the border of Colombia and Brazil, about twenty different species of insects are consumed. The comprehensiveness of this study is unique, but I only have permission to cite the quantitative results in preliminary form. About 75 percent of the insects were consumed in their fat larval stage; the rest were divided between winged sexuals—also fat in preparation for flight and mating—plus the soldier castes of ants and termites whose large heads make tempting tidbits if you can bite them faster than they can bite you (remember the chimpanzees chewing furiously). An important finding is that insect consumption is more significant for women than for men. This fits in nicely with the generalization I have already drawn attention to, that women in Amazonia have less access than men to animal food. In the case of the Tatuya, women seem to make up for some of this disparity by eating more insects proportionate to fish and meat. At certain times of the year, insects counted for about 14 percent of the women's average per capita protein intake from all sources.

9   But I don't want to give the impression that only band and village peoples find small things good to eat. Many of the world's most sophisticated civilizations consume insects as part of their daily fare. The Chinese, for example, until recently at least, ate silkworm pupae, cicadas, crickets, giant water beetles *(Lethocerus indicus)*, stinkbugs, cockroaches *(Periplaneta americana* and *P. australasie)*, and fly maggots. China's insectivorous foodways may have stemmed in part from a gourmet interest in exotic dishes. But the biggest consumers of insects were the poor and destitute classes who lacked alternative sources of animal proteins and fats. The peasants of traditional China did not participate in the great haute cuisine of the gentry and the imperial court. Instead they were noted for making "judicious use of every kind of edible vegetable, and insects as well as offal." In keeping with their frugal dietary regimen, China's peasants consumed large quantities of silkworms, especially in the silk-producing provinces. The young women who unwound the cocoons dropped each silkworm into a pot of hot water, kept at the ready for the unreeling, thereby assuring themselves a supply of freshly cooked food throughout the day. "They seem to eat off and on all day long since they work rapidly for long hours at a stretch, and the cooked morsels are constantly before them. One gets a pleasant odour of food being cooked, when passing through a reeling

factory." In several silkworm districts farmers cropped their silkworm cocoons during the busy spring planting season, but had to wait until the summer before they had enough time to unwind the silk. To kill the pupae and preserve the silk, they either baked the cocoons or pickled them in brine. After they unwound the cocoons, the farmers dried the salted worms in the sun to preserve them for the leaner months. When the time came for them to be eaten, they were soaked in water and taken out and fried with onions or mixed with eggs, if the farmer had laying hens.

10   In contemplating the enjoyment of insect foods by non-Westerners, the extreme lack of animal proteins and fats in the diet of preindustrial peasant population must be kept in mind. Coolies in the nineteenth century in north China, for example, ate "sweet potatoes three times a day, every day, all through the year with small amounts of salted turnips, bean curd, and pickled beans." For these unfortunate souls, cockroaches and water bugs were luxuries.

11   The peoples of Southeast Asia rivaled the Chinese in their intense insect-eating foodways. Laotians, Vietnamese, and Thais all seem to have gone in for giant water bugs. In addition, the Laotians ate fried cockroach eggs and several species of large spiders (not insects of course, but equally small and ill-reputed as food among Westerners). In the early 1930s W. S. Bristowe gave a detailed account of Laotian foodways, insisting that the people ate insects and arachnids as well as other arthropods such as scorpions not merely to ward off starvation but because they liked the taste. I see no contradiction here: people might very well be expected to acquire a taste for something that wards off starvation. Bristowe himself tried eating spiders, dung beetles, water bugs, crickets, grasshoppers, termites, and cicadas and found:

> none distasteful, a few quite palatable, notably the giant waterbug. For the most part they were insipid, with a faint vegetable flavour, but would not anyone tasting bread, for instance, for the first time, wonder why we eat such a flavourless food? A toasted dungbeetle or soft-bodied spider has a nice crisp exterior and soft interior of soufflé consistency which is by no means unpleasant. Salt is usually added, sometimes chili or the leaves of scented herbs, and sometimes they are eaten with rice or added to sauces or curry. Flavour is exceptionally hard to define, but lettuce would, I think, best describe the taste of termites, cicadas and crickets; lettuce and raw potato that of the giant *Nephila* spider, and concentrated Gorgonzola cheese that of the giant waterbug *(Lethocerus indicus)*. I suffered no ill effects from the eating of these insects.

12   More about those spiders. Bristowe describes how he went spider hunting with a Lao companion and in one hour collected six *Melpoeus albostriatus* weighing a total of half a pound. Other notable spider eaters include New Caledonians, the Kamchatka, the San of the Kalahari, the

Caribs of the West Indies, and the inhabitants of Madagascar. The Guaharibo and Piaroa Indians of South America display a special fondness for tarantulas.

13   Before the invention of soap and insecticides, lice afflicted humans much as they afflict other primates; family members picked them out one by one from each other's hair and cracked their bodies between their teeth. Many human lice-pickers solve the problem of making sure that the elusive creatures will not reinfest them by cracking the lice between their teeth and swallowing them, monkey-style. Bodenheimer cites a nineteenth-century naturalist's account of lice eating among the nomadic Kirghiz.... "I was witness of a touching, if barbarous scene of wifely devotion. Our host's son was deep in sleep.... Meanwhile his affectionate and devoted wife profited the opportunity to clean his shirt of the vermin [lice] swarming in it.... She systematically took every fold and seam in the shirt and passed it between her glistening white teeth, nibbling rapidly. The sound of the continuous cracking could be heard clearly."

14   In brief, my personal observation and my reading of available accounts of insect eating, supplemented by inquiries addressed to anthropological colleagues, convinces me that the overwhelming majority of human cultures until recent times regarded at least some insects as good to eat. But I cannot attest to the true extent of insectivory in the world today because the loathing in which insectivory is held by Europeans and Americans has been communicated to the food experts of less developed countries, and this has made them reluctant to study the contribution of insects to national diet, or even to admit that their compatriots eat any insects at all. A further complication is that insectivory may actually be on the wane in countries like China and Japan. But even if this is the case, it does not diminish the puzzle of why insectivory should ever be spurned since it was or still is an accepted foodway in hundreds of cultures.

15   Another thing is clear: The majority of the world's cultures still do not share the loathing expressed toward insects in European and Euro-American foodways. What makes this loathing particularly interesting is that not so long ago (anthropologically speaking) Europeans themselves practiced insectivory. Aristotle, for example, was familiar enough with the consumption of cicadas to state that they tasted best in the nymph stage before the last molt and that among the adult forms "first males were better to eat, but after copulation the females, which are then full of white eggs." Aristophanes call grasshoppers "four winged fowl" and implies that they were eaten by the poorer classes of Athens. Pliny's *Natural History* attests to the fact that the Romans also ate insects; especially a bark-dwelling grub called *cossus*, which was served in what Pliny called "the most delicate dishes." From medieval times onward, aside from a few references to German soldiers in Italy eating

fried silkworms, or gourmets consuming the larvae of the cockchafer beetle—rolled in flour and bread crumbs—even the French abstained from insect fare. In fact, during the nineteenth century, while some scientists and men of letters were trying to get the French to eat horsemeat, others were trying with less success to get them to eat insects. At least one elegant insect banquet was held at a fancy Paris restaurant in the 1880s (shades of the horsemeat banquets a few years earlier) whose *pièce de résistance* was white cockchafer larvae. During an 1878 debate in the French parliament over a law aimed at eradicating insect pests, a member of the Senate, M. W. de Fonvielle, published a recipe for making soup out of maybugs. Meanwhile the vice-president of the Insect Society of Paris illustrated a lecture on his "absorption" theory of insect control by swallowing a handful of maybugs accompanied by "signs of high satisfaction."

16   Like the advocates of horsemeat, some European insectivory enthusiasts embraced their cause in the name of providing cheap meat to the working classes. Outraged by insects that ate up "every blessed green thing that do grow," the English squire V. H. Holt, for example, published a book in 1885 entitled "Why Not Eat Insects?" If farm laborers would diligently collect wireworms, leather jackets, maybug larvae, and chafer-grubs, not only would the wheat crop be twice as big, but children would be kept out of mischief, and the poor would no longer have to complain that they can't afford to eat meat. "In these days of agricultural depression we should do all we can to alleviate the suffering of our starving labourers. Ought we not to exert our influence towards pointing out to them a neglected food supply?" This sounds like a rational proposition, but it was doomed to failure.

17   From a nutritional standpoint, insect flesh is almost as nourishing as red meat or poultry. One hundred grams of African termites contains 610 calories, 38 grams of protein, and 46 grams of fat. By comparison 3.5 ounces (100 grams) cooked medium-fat hamburger contains only 245 calories, 21 grams of protein, and 17 grams of fat. An equal portion of moth larvae contains almost 375 calories, 46 grams of protein, and 10 grams of fat. By dry weight, locusts range from 42 percent to 76 percent protein and from 6 percent to 50 percent fat. Lowly housefly pupae contain 63 percent protein and 15 percent fat while bee pupae when dried consist of over 90 percent protein and 8 percent fat. The only unfavorable comparison that one could make between insects and red meat, poultry, or fish concerns the quality of their protein as measured in terms of the essential amino acids, but some insects have amino acid scores that are almost as good as beef or chicken. Like other flesh foods, insects are rich in lysine, which tends to be the amino acid in shortest supply in most grains and tubers. Most importantly, perhaps, the combination of high fat content with high protein has the "protein-saving" effect, which is nutritionally desirable for people who are faced with

chronic shortages of both proteins and calories. In this regard, insects would seem to be a better food bargain than high-protein, low-fat arthropods such as shrimp, crabs, lobsters, and other crustaceans (which are close relatives of insects) and of low-calorie, low-fat clams, oysters, and other molluscs. One would have to eat 7.3 pounds (3,300 grams) of shrimp versus a mere 1.1 pounds (500 grams) of winged termites to satisfy daily calorie needs.

18   A possible drawback of insects is that they are covered with a hard substance known as chitin, which humans cannot digest. The thought of having to crunch through the chitinous spiny legs, wings, and bodies of creatures like grasshoppers and beetles alarms those not accustomed to insectivorous foodways, but the indigestibility of chitin cannot be used to explain the Euro-American rejection of insects as food any more than one could explain a reluctance to eat lobster or shrimp because of the indigestibility of their "shells" which, as it happens, are also made of chitin. The solution to the chitin problem is quite simple: eat insects in their pupal and larval stages before they grow legs and wings and before their skin gets thick and hard; or pull off the legs and wings of adult forms and consume only the softer parts. True, even the soft, immature forms contain a small amount of chitin, but this might even be advantageous since the chitin acts as roughage which... is in short supply in other kinds of meat.

19   This brings us to the number one rationalization given by Euro-Americans for their loathing of insect flesh: bugs carry and transmit dreadful diseases. No one would deny that insects carry or harbor fungi, viruses, bacteria, protozoans, and worms which can adversely affect human health. But... in the absence of scientific sanitary animal husbandry, so do cattle, sheep, pigs, chickens, and every other familiar barnyard animal. There is usually a simple solution to the problem of contaminated flesh: cook it. And since there is no reason why insects cannot be cooked, the same advice applies to the problem of contaminated insect flesh. Humans probably do not usually eat insects raw any more than they usually eat meat raw. With the exception of the honey ant, whose honey-swollen abdomen is bitten off and swallowed whole, or an occasional locust, grub, or similar tidbit, most insects are fried or roasted, which rids them of hairs and spines and gives them a crisp exterior. Adult forms may also be roasted or boiled, making it easy to detach and winnow the offending wings and legs. Giant water bugs, roaches, beetles, and crickets are boiled and then soaked in vinegar. The object is not to gulp them down raw, but to pick them apart cooked, with slivers of bamboo, much as one picks meat out of a boiled crab or lobster. Actually, it is not as morsels of food that insects endanger human health. Even roaches or houseflies—to take the worst cases—are far more dangerous crawling over plates, utensils, and foods that are ready to be served, than boiled in a soup or fried in oil.

20   Scientists have recently discovered that some beetles and cockroaches may produce or contain carcinogens and that some people have allergic reactions to cockroaches, meal moths, flour beetles, rice weevils, and grain borers. But scientists have also recently discovered that everything from mushrooms to charcoal-broiled steak presents carcinogenic risks, and as for allergic reactions, wheat, strawberries, and shellfish contain some of the most potent allergens known.

21   One might at this point wish to resort to a bad-to-think argument. Granting that insects can be eaten without harmful effects, nonetheless the fact remains that many creeping, crawling creatures are associated with dirt and filth, which in turn are associated with disease. It is this mental association, whether true or false in the actual case, which makes insect eating so unappetizing for most Euro-Americans. But why should anyone associate dirtiness with clean-leaving locusts, beetle larvae, silkworms, termites, moth larvae, and hundreds of other insect species which spend their lives in the great outdoors, far from humans, eating grass, leaves, and wood? If anything, most insects are as clean as most products of fields and barnyards. Was not European agriculture historically based on raising crops fertilized with the excrement of cows, horses, pigs, and other animal droppings? If all it takes for a food species to fall into ill repute is an association with dirt, humankind would have starved to death long ago. Besides, the European pattern of rejecting insects as food was already firmly established long before disease was linked to dirt and before the lack of sanitation came to be seen as a danger to public health. . . .

22   What I am suggesting boils down to this: If a habitat is rich in insect fauna—especially large and/or swarming species—*and* if it is at the same time poor in large wild or domesticated vertebrate animal species, diets will tend to be highly insectivorous. But if a habitat is poor in insect fauna—especially large and/or swarming species—*and* if it is at the same time rich in domesticated or wild species of large vertebrates, diets will tend to exclude insects. Actually, there are four rather than just two types of situations which should be kept in mind. A simple "two-by-two" square shows what I mean:

	Large Vertebrates Absent	Large Vertebrates Present
Swarming Insects Present	1	2
Swarming Insects Absent	3	4

Cell 1 represents the situation in which the consumption of "small things" is likely to be more intense, as in Amazonia or in the tropical forest area of Africa: lots of swarming insect species, few large vertebrate species. Cell 4 represents the situation in which the eating of "small things" is likely to be least intense, as in Europe or the United States and Canada: few swarming insects and lots of large vertebrates. Cells 2 and 3 represent two different situations, each likely to be associated with intermediate levels of the consumption of "small things": lots of both large vertebrates and swarming insects; and a paucity of both large vertebrates and of swarming insects.

23   One loose end remains: the peculiar loathing which accompanies the European and American rejection of insects as food. The interesting fact is that most Westerners not only refrain from insectivory but the mere thought of eating a grub or a termite—not to mention a roach!—makes many people sick to their stomachs. And to touch an insect—or worse, to have one crawl on you—is itself a disgusting event. Insects, in other words, are to Americans and Europeans as pigs are to Moslems and Jews. They are pariah species. The standard claim that insects *are* dirty and disgusting makes no more sense than the standard claim of Jews and Moslems that pigs *are* dirty and disgusting. I have already formulated a theory . . . for predicting when a species that is not good to eat will become a pariah or a deity. Let me apply it here.

24   A species will be apotheosized or abominated depending on its residual utility or harmfulness. A Hindu cow not eaten provides oxen, milk, and dung. It is apotheosized. A horse not eaten wins battles and plows fields. It is a noble creature. A pig not eaten is useless—it neither plows fields, gives milk, nor wins wars. Therefore it is abominated. Insects not eaten are worse than pigs not eaten. They not only devour crops in the field, they eat the food right off your plate, bite, sting, make you itch, and suck your blood. If you don't eat them, they'll eat you. They're all harm and nothing good. The few useful species such as insects that eat other insects or that pollinate plants do not compensate for the uncountable hosts of noxious cousins.

25   To make themselves even more loathsome to Westerners, insects lead a furtive existence in close proximity to humans; they penetrate houses, closets, and cabinets, hiding during the day and emerging only at night. Small wonder many of us react phobically to them. Since we don't eat them we are free to identify them with the quintessential evil—enemies who attack us from within—and to make of them icons of dirt, fear, and loathing.

SAMPLE TWO-COLUMN JOURNAL

In a two-column reading journal, passages from a text appear next to comments and reactions to that text. Using the reading journal this way helps you focus on points a writer makes or techniques he or she may employ. One of the benefits of keeping this journal is that these initial responses may become the focus for an essay or supply supporting details.

Harris's "Small Things"	My Responses
Taste rather than nutrition is behind Southeast Asians' enjoyment of spiders and insects.	What is going on in the mind of someone who munches on "toasted dung-beetle" or a "giant water-bug"? How is it that people can look at identical phenomena and pronounce them either inviting or repulsive? What is in my mind that is not in theirs that allows them to gleefully devour a fried fly pupae? Conversely, what is in my mind that is not in theirs? Good illustration of the power of human culture to determine what is acceptable to us and what is not.
In the 1930s a Westerner, W. S. Bristowe, studied "Laotian foodways" and recorded his impressions of the small things they like to eat. He found	Harris's observations about Bristowe add a subtle twist to his discussion. The fact that one intrepid explorer can adjust to such folkways

Harris	My Responses
(continued)	(continued)
"none distasteful" and "quite a few palatable." As if to validate Harris's claim that Westerners who get sick when they eat insects do so for psychosomatic reasons, Bristowe writes, "I suffered no ill effects from the eating of these insects."	with apparent ease contradicts the idea that culture is as powerful a determiner as I assumed when I wrote my last observations. After all, Bristowe, who sounds a bit fussy, seems to have had no problem whatsoever enjoying the "nice crisp exterior and soft interior of soufflé consistency" which he finds typical of the "soft-bodied spider."

Reading for Meaning

If you are having trouble generating ideas about a reading, an effective way to explore what you think, know, or have experienced is to ask yourself a series of questions about the subject, point of view, opinions, organization, tone, or style presented in the text. The following questions ask you to respond to ideas in Marvin Harris's "Small Things."

1. Do you find it comforting that our primate ancestors as well as human cousins regard eating insects as a delicacy or even a game? Explain your answer.

2. Think about the experiment Harris describes in paragraph 2. Would you eat fried grasshoppers, chocolate-covered ants, or the pupae of a small fly if they were offered to you? Explain why you would or would not eat such food.

3. Reread some of the graphic descriptions of the kinds of insects people have been known to eat and the ways in which they eat them. Why do you think Harris included so many detailed examples in his essay?

4. Is there any other kind of food that you would not eat but that other people seem to enjoy? What, exactly, do you find distasteful about this food?
5. Are there particular foods that you like to eat that other people avoid?
6. What do you think has had the most influence on the sort of food you eat—childhood habits, peer influence, advertisements, nutritional awareness? Describe instances in which one or more of these has influenced what you ate.
7. What other reading have you done that discusses unusual food? Have you seen or heard about people eating food that seemed strange to you?

WRITING A RESPONSE PAPER

In college writing, you will probably be asked not only to summarize the main ideas of an article or chapter you have read but also to respond to those ideas in some way. Writing a response paper gives you practice reading a text and writing about it critically. The response essay may include a brief summary of the writer's ideas as well as a detailed response. This reader-response approach to the text has an added benefit. In general, students who interact with a text and are engaged in the material assigned to them are likely to stay interested in the subject they are studying and do well in their courses.

FINDING MAIN POINTS

Response papers aren't difficult to write if you take the process in stages. First select main points that you think are key to understanding the writer's meaning. It is a good idea to check your selection of main ideas with other readers to be sure that your list includes all the writer's central points and excludes lesser points. After reading "Small Things" carefully, students in one class listed the following as key ideas they might use in the summary portion of their response paper.

- Europeans and Americans won't eat insects because they reject the idea and not because of anything intrinsically true about the animal itself.
- Human evolution and studies in anthropology support the argument that it is "natural" for us to eat insects.
- Chimpanzees and other primates consume insects regularly, and Harris thinks that "insectivory" helped develop the keen eyesight, sense of smell, coordination, and observant mind that account for the uniqueness of the genus *Homo*.
- Many indigenous groups as well as people living in advanced civilizations (and that includes ancient European populations as well) included insects in their diets.
- These groups found nutritional as well as practical reasons for eating insects.
- The indigestibility of chitin, the substance that protects most insects, poses a slight problem from the standpoint of human consumption.
- Americans and Europeans also argue that insects carry diseases, but that concern is easily taken care of simply by cooking the insects.

- The truth is, Europeans and Americans are simply disgusted by the idea of eating the useless vermin that have the audacity to bore into their houses and attack them at night.

RESPONDING TO THE TEXT

Once you have a listing of main ideas in the text, write out your responses. These responses draw on your experience, observations, cultural background, education, or assumptions about life—in short, they represent the collection of ideas you have been given as well as those you have formed for yourself.

A response paper may include one or more of the following:

- An explanation of what was effective or lacking in the text. This might involve evaluating the ideas presented; exploring the strength, uniqueness, or weakness of the author's approach to the subject; examining his or her tone or style of writing; commenting on the arrangement of ideas; examining what was convincing or engaging; or evaluating the use of examples and explanations.
- An analysis of the reader's experiences, observations, or assumptions as they complement or contradict the text.
- A comparison with ideas in other texts.

As in all responses for this or any other subject, writers must include a thesis—the larger point that holds together the general ideas and specific support in the paper. The more convincing responses explain *why* writers responded as they did. These papers also offer relevant supporting ideas, examples, details, and explanations.

SAMPLE RESPONSE PAPER

```
                                               Suarez 1
    Gloria Suarez

    English 101

    Professor Rudolph

    12 March 1999

             Response Paper for "Small Things"

       In "Small Things," a chapter in Marvin Harris's

    Good to Eat, the author examines the revulsion

    Europeans and Americans express at the idea of

    eating insects. Such revulsion is cultural rather

    than "natural" says Harris, and in the absence of
```

nutritional need, we are not likely to change our minds. What I find most effective about "Small Things" is Harris's strategy of building his historical argument. His examples and analysis are convincing up to a point. I think his attitude toward the reader is, however, suspect.

Harris initially examines primate behavior in order to argue that eating insects is the "natural" thing for apes to do and, by extension, for humans to do as well. I can verify chimpanzees' love of insects from my occasional trips to the local zoo with my daughter. Termite posts are part of the chimps' habitat, and occasionally we have watched them stick bamboo shoots into the termites' nests, pull out dozens of the surprised insects, and promptly eat them as a midday snack. Harris effectively begins the chapter with examples of such primate behavior, works his way through a discussion of insectivores, mammals who subsist on insects, and offers the enlightening view that our own "stereoscopic vision," manual dexterity, and brain capacity may be partly attributed to the insect-eating habits developed by our ancient predecessors. A discussion of precedents from biblical times and references to indigenous populations follows, but Harris is not through. He points out that in more recent times, the Chinese and Southeast Asian peoples have included insects in their diets. He ends this detailed anthropological discussion with the crowning example: Europeans themselves, including their philosophical star, Aristotle, ate insects with relish. In this way Harris organizes his discussion so that it ends with the provocative suggestion that the consumption of insects might be claimed as a European birthright.

 His research, impressive throughout the piece, is again in good form as Harris uncovers only one instance since medieval times when Europeans were willing to eat insects. He discovered other occasions when the French government tried in vain to get its subjects to eat insects in order to reduce the population of vermin, and English citizens were told they should regard insects as a good source of "cheap meat" for lower economic classes.

 The association Harris makes between shellfish and insects also works well. The comparison he offers between the chitin-formed shells of lobsters and shrimp and the chitin that protects the bodies and legs of insects goes a long way toward making the consumption of insects sound just as reasonable as eating mussels or clams.

 There are times, however, when Harris's analysis comes close to being an attack on the reader. His

> Suarez 4
>
> insistence on offering example after example of insect food consumed by primate and human groups, combined with extensive descriptions of food preparation and the consumption of insects, seems designed to disgust the reader at least as much as it enlightens him or her. The anecdote about the glee Harris felt when his students showed disgust at the idea of eating the grasshoppers he passed around his classroom is the reader's first clue that here is an author who enjoys teasing, if not assaulting, his audience. It may even reveal a sadistic side to his nature. At times Harris seems ready to bludgeon his readers with their own silly attitude toward insects, all the while realizing that we will not be willing, or perhaps even able, to change our minds about wanting to chew up and swallow these creepy, crawly creatures we think of as pests.
>
> Marvin Harris's "Small Things" can teach us tolerance for peoples who follow their anthropoid history and eat insects without thinking much about it. It is a bit much, though, to revel in the practice and occasionally belittle Westerners for not following suit.

Ideas for Writing

Read "Parents and Children," page 86, or "Children and Ritual in Bali," page 102. Use the guidelines you have just read to write a response paper to one of these essays.

CHAPTER 3
MAKING COMPARISONS

First Thoughts

ПЕРВЫЙ ВЗГЛЯД

Pierwsze wrażevia

In this terrible agitation of mind I could not forbear thinking of Lilliput, whose inhabitants looked upon me as the greatest prodigy that ever appeared in the world: where I was able to draw an imperial fleet in my hand, and perform those other actions which will be recorded for ever in the chronicles of that empire, while posterity shall hardly believe them, although attested by millions. I reflected what a mortification it must prove to me to appear as inconsiderable in this nation as one single Lilliputian would be among us. But this I conceived was to be the least of my misfortunes: for, as human creatures are observed to be more savage and cruel in proportion to their bulk, what could I expect but to be a morsel in the mouth of the first among these enormous barbarians who should happen to seize me? Undoubtedly philosophers are in the right when they tell us that nothing is great or little otherwise than by comparison.

Jonathan Swift
Lemuel Gulliver in Brobdingnag
Gulliver's Travels

Jonathan Swift wrote one of the earliest spoofs about the folly of thinking that we can accurately interpret the behavior of beings whose assumptions about the world and each other are radically different from ours. Lemuel Gulliver, Swift's congenial and gullible voyager, used pseudo-empirical observations to minimize even the most fantastic of customs. In the passage from *Gulliver's Travels* that opens this chapter, Gulliver was wrong about his association between enormity and savagery (the Brobdingnagians proved to be ethical giants). However, his conclusion about the importance of making comparisons is quite sound. With regard to textual analysis, comparisons can reveal the relative merits of a piece and the success or failure of a text.

PERSPECTIVES ON CULTURE

This chapter continues the discussion of ways to analyze texts and cultures. With the help of background information and questions for writing and discussion, you will examine two additional readings about culture and study a sample essay that compares ideas and writing strategies present in two texts. In addition to offering prompts in the usual sections ("Writing before Reading," "Reading for Meaning," and "Ideas for Writing"), this chapter introduces yet another category of activities for discussion and writing that appear under the title, "Comparing Texts." This category follows the "Reading for Meaning" sections in this chapter and accompanies reading selections in the remaining chapters of this book. These prompts encourage you to use techniques for comparing texts introduced in this chapter.

The selections here, "The Land of Meaningless Courtesy" and "Looking to the West," form the basis of our discussion about comparing texts. Be sure to read the author's biography and background information on the writer's native country. This information will give you a sense of the text before you begin reading. In general, "The Land of Meaningless Courtesy," written for Russian businessmen, critiques the American way of doing business. In "Looking to the West," taken from a chapter in *The Captive Mind,* Czeslaw Milosz describes the cultural assumptions that inform the Eastern Europeans' distrust of the West in general and the United States in particular.

Writing before Reading

1. Based on what you have observed in the business world, write about your opinion of people who work in businesses. Would you characterize them as courteous, rude, indifferent, thorough, shoddy, honest, untrustworthy, highly skilled, or does some other quality come to mind? Are any of these traits typical of Americans in general?

2. Drawing on your experiences with businesspeople, compose a summary of the behavior you have come to expect from people in the business world. Do most people you know have these expectations?

THE LAND OF MEANINGLESS COURTESY

Nikita Pokrovsky

Nikita Pokrovsky's article first appeared in the Moscow publication Nezavisimaya Gazeta. *The article was reprinted in the May 1994 issue of the* World Press Review. *In his essay, Pokrovsky analyzes American business practices and advises Russians about what to expect when dealing with American businessmen.*

Facts about Russia

Russia is the largest country in the world with an area roughly double that of the United States. Modern Russia traces its origins to the medieval Slavic principalities of Kievan Rus', a loose federation that occupied most of what is now the Ukraine, Belarus, and European Russia. The Mongol invasions that swept across Asia and eastern Europe destroyed Kievan Rus' in the 13th century. Nearly two centuries later, the autocratic state of Moscovy emerged with Moscow rather than Kiev as its center. By the sixteenth century, the Muscovite state extended from European Russia into Siberia and formed the basis for the later Russian Empire, which was ruled by the Romanov dynasty from 1613 to 1917. The Russian revolution of 1917 ended monarchical rule in Russia and began the era of Communist government. From 1922 to 1991, Russia was the political and cultural center of the Union of Soviet Socialist Republics. Under the dictatorship of Joseph Stalin, the USSR experienced rapid industrialization and fought a devastating war with Nazi Germany. During World War II, approximately 12 million Soviets, civilian and military alike, lost their lives. Immediately following the Second World War, the Cold War began—a political and strategic battle between the Soviet Union and its allies, and the Western powers, principally the United States. The struggle lasted until Mikhail Gorbachev came to power forty years later (1985) and introduced *perestroika*—reforms aimed at moving the USSR away from the Stalinist-style central government and toward democratization. His successor, Russian president Boris Yeltsin, presided over the collapse of the Soviet Union in 1991. Yeltsin has emphasized the privatization of businesses and the establishment of a market-based economy. Since 1995, the unpopular invasion of the rebellious republic of Chechnya as well as a chronic heart condition have threatened Yeltsin's presidency. Clashes between free-market advocates and defenders of Communism also plague the Yeltsin government. In October 1998, Yeltsin's failing health required him to transfer his powers to Yevgeny Primakov.

1   Not every Russian who comes to America dreams of staying in this country for good (contrary to what Americans themselves think). I am one of those who don't nurture such dreams, so I would like to share some

thoughts about how one can build relationships with Americans—while keeping in mind a plan to return home.

2   I have always doubted such judgments as, "Russians and Americans have an astonishing amount in common," or "Our national characters almost coincide." These beautiful thoughts are for noisy conferences of "people's diplomats," Christmas stories, and television shows with Phil Donahue and his partner Vladimir Pozner.[1]

3   My entire experience and that of my fellow Americanologists teach one simple truth: Russians and Americans have no more in common than Russians and Chinese or, say, Russians and Polynesians. The American national character, way of thinking, and reference points in everyday life differ greatly from what we are used to in Russia. But realizing differences stirs a sense of mutual interest.

4   Let's begin with outward—but by no means superficial—displays of the American character. Take the well-known propensity of Americans to demonstrate immediately how friendly they are: to laugh loudly, smile broadly, slap you on the shoulder, and show you every conceivable sign of warmth and fondness. Russians are not accustomed to anything of the kind. Decades of dominance by an aggressively bureaucratic system have instilled in us a great caution toward contacts, a reserved demeanor, and restraint in gestures and in other ways of revealing our egos. To us, the American style of behavior seems at first to be like a fairy tale in which everybody loves one another and no one says anything rude.

5   Rudeness and bad manners are much rarer in America than they are in Russia. In the business environment, they do not occur at all. But external politeness merely conceals an inner toughness, a highly demanding nature. America's business world is much tougher than ours. Contacts in it are determined only by a person's real value, which your partner calculates by one method or another. What value am I speaking of? Let's try to define it in practical American terms.

- Your actual capital at the given moment (in dollar terms, of course).
- Your accomplishments in a certain field, as corroborated by the authoritative opinion of experts and by international prizes, publications, exhibitions, and mentions in the *New York Times*.
- Your prestigious relatives in Russia: a high position in the Soviet Union prior to Mikhail Gorbachev or in Gorbachev's Russia, especially any spot involving access to behind-the-scenes manipulations in the "corridors of power."

---

[1] In 1991 Vladimir Pozner, a Russian television star and spokesperson for Mikhail Gorbachev' *Perestroyka,* joined Phil Donahue on a weekly talk show entitled *Pozner and Donahue.*

- Your social standing at home. High marks are given for membership in Parliament and close ties to President Boris Yeltsin and his ministers or any government leaders and existing official structures.
- Frequent TV appearances in Russia (it is downright marvelous if you host some program and can invite an American guest to appear on it) or your picture on the cover of an illustrated magazine.
- Your connections with large U.S. firms, publishers, and universities.
- Finally, your physical features—particularly a relatively young age (under 35). Americans believe, somewhat idealistically but selflessly, that "young" Russians can be remade, never doubting the premise that all Russians must be remolded and refashioned.

6   A few words now about what Americans don't like about Russians. From my observations, the following behavior can make a bad impression on American partners:

- When speaking about Russia, you constantly complain about the country's disastrous situation, you complicate everything, you sketch the state of your affairs in somber tones and deviate rather obviously from the line of the *New York Times*. You imply that Russia's future is unclear and fail to totally back the country's current leadership.
- You speak English suspiciously well. This contradicts the common image of a Russian.
- You ask difficult questions concerning the domestic situation in the U.S. In so doing, you suggest that the future of the U.S. is not altogether cloudless.
- You tell time in terms of the 24-hour clock rather than the 12-hour clock. The former is used only by the U.S. military so you will immediately be exposed as a "spy."

7   Strange as it may seem, some Russian peculiarities are actually a benefit. Somewhat unrefined manners, a poorly tailored suit, a shot of vodka swallowed in a single gulp, an unrestrained rendition at the dinner table of "Coachman, Don't Drive Those Horses"—all this, on occasion, can leave your American partner with fond memories.

8   Let us set aside America's white-toothed smiles, as well as open invitations to visit homes, sail on a yacht, or pass an evening at a luxurious restaurant. It may be wonderful and fascinating, but you should not confuse these signs of favor with any business interest in you.

9   For an American, spending some loud leisure time with a foreigner from Russia is absolutely natural. But don't be surprised and dismayed if, a couple of days later, you call your host who was so hospitable and find that he cannot remember who you are or what you do. He may not show the slightest interest in meeting you again, but he will treat you politely.

10   This kind of distancing occurs all the time. If it happens to you, it is not worth getting too upset. Instead, without any hard feelings, adjust your relationship with the now less-interested American partner. Make occasional phone calls, mail him newspaper clippings that might illustrate the subject of your last conversation, convey holiday wishes. It may well happen that, as soon as your partner's (or your own) situation changes and a new state of affairs requires your participation, he will remember you and take a new liking to you.

11   For all of the reasons discussed, it is extremely difficult to transform what we might call "having a good time with an entertaining businessman from Russia" into "real business with a Russian." The best indication that somebody is beginning to treat you seriously is having them include you in a business project and, especially, having them pay you. Anything else is nothing more than a semblance of business ties. Under no circumstances will any American "promote" you on the basis that you are a "good and talented" person. No one will help you simply because you might be a friend—or because you have interesting ideas and business-like proposals.

12   So, forget about dependency and rely only on your own resources during your stay in the U.S. Your success in America and with Americans depends largely on you—on your intelligence, your acumen, and your ability to understand people and to learn as you go along. If you get a business started with Americans, and it is an interesting and expanding business, then you know that you are the master of your domain. You can be proud of your Russian smarts and talent.

Reading for Meaning

1. In "The Land of Meaningless Courtesy" Pokrovsky advises his Russian audience about how to establish business relations with people whose "national character, way of thinking, and reference points" are altogether different from the Russian's way of doing things. Underline phrases in his article that indicate his advice was meant for Russian eyes only.

2. At the end of Pokrovsky's first paragraph he promises to show his Russian audience "how one can build relationships with Americans—while keeping in mind a plan to return home." What might have prompted Pokrovsky to add this last phrase? How does his opening paragraph clarify the writer's tone or attitude toward his subject?

3. In what ways might America become the "Land of Meaningless Courtesy" for the Russian businessman? Is the experience Pekrovsky describes limited to Russians, or might Americans also experience a "meaningless courtesy" in their business dealings?

4. Summarize in a few sentences what Pokrovsky thinks Americans mean by "real value." Do you agree with his estimation?

5. What stereotypes do American businessmen use to evaluate Russians' behavior, according to Pokrovsky? Is Pokrovsky's discussion of stereotypes convincing?

6. Given what you know about American character as an "insider," do any of Pokrovsky's seven points about what American businessmen value offer an accurate estimation of what Americans in general seem to value? Are there points that you find completely incorrect? Support your evaluation by offering specific examples of people's behavior.

Comparing Texts

According to Pokrovsky, if your accomplishments have been mentioned in the *New York Times,* you are likely to receive approval from your American contacts. Conversely, if your opinions about Russia don't square with the received ideas published in the *Times,* American businessmen are not likely to have a good opinion of you. Consult the microfiche in your school or local library, or log onto the Internet to retrieve a few articles about the political or economic situation in Russia as discussed in the *New York Times* during February 1994, the month Pokrovsky's article was published in the *World Press Review.* What seems to be the "line," as Pokrovsky calls it, or the assumptions writers for the *New York Times* make about Russia's political situation or the future of that country? How accurate is Pokrovsky's description of the *Times'* theories about Russia?

Ideas for Writing

Write a response paper for this article. Use your journal to help you gather information and organize your essay.

Writing before Reading

1. Based on news reports, discussions you have heard, people you have known, or your own personal experience, what do you know or remember about central or eastern Europeans, the majority of whom live in countries once dominated by the Soviet Union?

2. How would you define "Communism"? What experiences, readings, or other sources contributed to your definition?

LOOKING TO THE WEST[2]

Czeslaw Milosz

Born in Vilnius, Lithuania, in 1911, Czeslaw Milosz fought against the Nazis in the Warsaw resistance. He served briefly in the postwar

---

[2] Translated by Jane Zielonko.

government in Poland, then immigrated to the United States in 1960. In 1980 he won the Nobel Prize for literature.

His works include The Seizure of Power *(1955) and* Land of Ulro *(1977), a selection of his essays on literature. More recently, Milosz published a collection of his poetry (1988), a collection of essays,* Beginning with My Streets *(1992), and* Provinces *(1992), an autobiography. "Looking to the West" appeared in* The Captive Mind *(1953), a collection of essays on the Eastern European's intellectual adaptation to Communism.*

Facts about Poland

From the fourteenth to the seventeenth century, Poland was a major power in Eastern Europe. Invaded in turn by Cossacks, Tartars, Turks, Russians, and Swedes during the 1600s, Poland was eventually partitioned by Russia, Prussia, and Austria in 1795. Poland had ceased to exist until it was reconstituted in 1918 at the end of World War I. In September 1939, Poland was attacked from the east by Stalin's army and from the west by Hitler's considerable forces. Within six weeks, Polish resistance was crushed, and the country was absorbed once more, this time by Russia and Germany. By the end of World War II, the Nazis had killed 3 million ethnic Poles and exterminated virtually all Polish Jews. The Stalinist regime was responsible for the deaths of another 2 million Poles. By 1948 Poland had come under Communist rule and been absorbed by the former Soviet Union. Three years after Czeslaw Milosz published *The Captive Mind* in 1953, the "Polish October" brought Wladyslaw Gomulka to power and with him the promise of political pluralism and greater religious freedom. His subsequent crackdown on churches and political dissidents, however, dashed such hopes. The Solidarity labor movement began in 1980 with workers' strikes at the Gdansk shipyards. Communist leader Wojciech Jaruzelski imposed martial law, forcing the movement to go underground, but a deteriorating economy and wide-spread unrest forced him to negotiate with leaders of the labor movement in 1989. Solidarity leader Lech Walesa was elected president in 1990. A period of economic hardship followed until, with the help of foreign investments, the country's economy began to grow. By 1995 Poland's unemployment rate and currency had stabilized. In the fall of 1997, a conservative coalition headed by members of Solidarity took control of parliament. The new prime minister, Jerzy Buzek, was backed by a center-right alliance.

1 "Are Americans *really* stupid?" I was asked in Warsaw. In the voice of the man who posed the question, there was despair, as well as the hope that I would contradict him. This question reveals the attitude of the average person in the people's democracies toward the West: it is despair mixed with a residue of hope.

2   During the last few years, the West has given these people a number of reasons to despair politically. In the case of the intellectual, other, more complicated reasons come into play. Before the countries of Central and Eastern Europe entered the sphere of the Imperium,[3] they lived through the Second World War. That war was much more devastating there than in the countries of Western Europe. It destroyed not only their economies, but also a great many values which had seemed till then unshakeable.

3   Man tends to regard the order he lives in as *natural*. The houses he passes on his way to work seem more like rocks rising out of the earth than like products of human hands. He considers the work he does in his office or factory as essential to the harmonious functioning of the world. The clothes he wears are exactly what they should be, and he laughs at the idea that he might equally well be wearing a Roman toga or medieval armor. He respects and envies a minister of state or a bank director, and regards the possession of a considerable amount of money as the main guarantee of peace and security. He cannot believe that one day a rider may appear on a street he knows well, where cats sleep and children play, and start catching passers-by with his lasso. He is accustomed to satisfying those of his physiological needs which are considered private as discreetly as possible, without realizing that such a pattern of behavior is not common to all human societies. In a word, he behaves a little like a Charlie Chaplin in *The Gold Rush,* bustling about in a shack poised precariously on the edge of a cliff.

4   His first stroll along a street littered with glass from bomb-shattered windows shakes his faith in the "naturalness" of his world. The wind scatters papers from hastily evacuated offices, papers labeled "Confidential" or "Top Secret" that evoke visions of safes, keys, conferences, couriers, and secretaries. Now the wind blows them through the street for anyone to read; yet no one does, for each man is more urgently concerned with finding a loaf of bread. Strangely enough, the world goes on even though the offices and secret files have lost all meaning. Farther down the street, he stops before a house split in half by a bomb, the privacy of people's homes—the family smells, the warmth of the beehive life, the furniture preserving the memory of loves and hatreds—cut open to public view. The house itself, no longer a rock, but a scaffolding of plaster, concrete, and brick; and on the third floor, a solitary white bathtub, rain-rinsed of all recollection of those who once bathed in it. Its formerly influential and respected owners, now destitute, walk the fields in search of stray potatoes. Thus overnight money loses its value and becomes a meaningless mass of printed

---

[3] A reference to the former Soviet Union.

paper. His walk takes him past a little boy poking a stick into a heap of smoking ruins and whistling a song about the great leader who will preserve the nation against all enemies. The song remains, but the leader of yesterday is already part of an extinct past.

5   He finds he acquires new habits quickly. Once, had he stumbled upon a corpse on the street, he would have called the police. A crowd would have gathered, and much talk and comment would have ensued. Now he knows he must avoid the dark body lying in the gutter, and refrain from asking unnecessary questions. The man who fired the gun must have had his reasons; he might well have been executing an Underground sentence.

6   Nor is the average European accustomed to thinking of his native city as divided into segregated living areas, but a single decree can force him to this new pattern of life and thought. Quarter A may suddenly be designated for one race; B, for a second; C, for a third. As the resettlement deadline approaches, the streets become filled with long lines of wagons, carts, wheelbarrows, and people carrying bundles, beds, chests, cauldrons, and bird cages. When all the moves are effected, 2,000 people may find themselves in a building that once housed 200, but each man is at last in the proper area. Then high walls are erected around quarter C, and daily a given lot of men, women, and children are loaded into wagons that take them off to specially constructed factories where they are scientifically slaughtered and their bodies burned.

7   And even the rider with the lasso appears, in the form of a military van waiting at the corner of a street. A man passing that corner meets a leveled rifle, raises his hands, is pushed into the van, and from that moment is lost to his family and friends. He may be sent to a concentration camp, or he may face a firing squad, his lips sealed with plaster lest he cry out against the state; but, in any case, he serves as a warning to his fellow-men. Perhaps one might escape such a fate by remaining at home. But the father of a family must go out in order to provide bread and soup for his wife and children; and every night they worry about whether or not he will return. Since these conditions last for years, everyone gradually comes to look upon the city as a jungle, and upon the fate of twentieth-century man as identical with that of a cave man living in the midst of powerful monsters.

8   It was once thought obvious that a man bears the same name and surname throughout his entire life; now it proves wiser for many reasons to change them and to memorize a new and fabricated biography. As a result, the records of the civilian state become completely confused. Everyone ceases to care about formalities, so that marriage, for example, comes to mean little more than living together.

9   Respectable citizens used to regard banditry as a crime. Today, bank robbers are heroes because the money they steal is destined for the

Underground. Usually they are young boys, mothers' boys, but their appearance is deceiving. The killing of a man presents no great moral problem to them.

10   The nearness of death destroys shame. Men and women change as soon as they know that the date of their execution has been fixed by a fat little man with shiny boots and a riding crop. They copulate in public, on the small bit of ground surrounded by barbed wire—their last home on earth. Boys and girls in their teens, about to go off to the barricades to fight against tanks with pistols and bottles of gasoline, want to enjoy their youth and lose their respect for standards of decency.

11   Which world is "natural"? That which existed before, or the world of war? Both are natural, if both are within the realm of one's experience. All the concepts men live by are a product of the historic formation in which they find themselves. Fluidity and constant change are the characteristics of phenomena. And man is so plastic a being that one can even conceive of the day when a thoroughly self-respecting citizen will crawl about on all fours, sporting a tail of brightly colored feathers as a sign of conformity to the order he lives in.

12   The man of the East cannot take Americans seriously because they have never undergone the experiences that teach men how relative their judgments and thinking habits are. Their resultant lack of imagination is appalling. Because they were born and raised in a given social order and in a given system of values, they believe that any other order must be "unnatural," and that it cannot last because it is incompatible with human nature. But even they may one day know fire, hunger, and the sword. In all probability this is what will occur; for it is hard to believe that when one half of the world is living through terrible disasters, the other half can continue a nineteenth-century mode of life, learning about the distress of its distant fellow-men only from movies and newspapers. Recent examples teach us that this cannot be. An inhabitant of Warsaw or Budapest once looked at newsreels of bombed Spain or burning Shanghai, but in the end he learned how these and many other catastrophes appear in actuality. He read gloomy tales of the N.K.V.D.,[4] until one day he found he himself had to deal with it. *If something exists in one place, it will exist everywhere.* This is the conclusion he draws from his observations, and so he has no particular faith in the momentary prosperity of America. He suspects that the years 1933–45 in Europe pre-figure what will occur elsewhere. A hard school, where ignorance was punished not by bad marks but by death, has taught him to think sociologically and historically. But it has not freed him from irrational feelings. He is apt to believe in theories that foresee violent changes in the countries of the West, for he finds it unjust that they should escape the hardships he had to undergo.

---

[4] Ministry of Internal Affairs of the Soviet Union, The Soviet Secret Police.

13   The only system of thought that is accessible to him is dialectical materialism, and it attracts him because it speaks a language that is understandable in the light of his experience. The illusory "natural" order of the Western countries is doomed, according to dialectical materialism (in the Stalinist version), to crash as a result of a crisis. Wherever there is a crisis, the ruling classes take refuge in fascism as a safeguard against the revolution of the proletariat. Fascism means war, gas chambers, and crematoria. True, the crisis in America predicted for the moment of demobilization did not occur; true, England introduced social security and socialized medicine to a hitherto unknown degree; and it is true, as well, that anti-Communist hysteria in the United States, whatever else may have inspired it, was largely motivated by fear of an armed and hostile power. Still these are merely modifications of a formula that is being proved in other respects. If the world is divided between Fascism and Communism, obviously Fascism must lose since it is the last, desperate refuge of the bourgeoisie. The bourgeoisie rules through demagoguery, which in practice means that prominent positions are filled by irresponsible people who commit follies in moments of decision. Just such follies were Hitler's ruthless policy toward the Eastern peoples, or Mussolini's involvement of Italy in the war.

14   A man need not be a Stalinist to reason thus. On the contrary, knowing how doubtful are any benefits from the system evolved in the Center, he would be overjoyed to see a gigantic meteor wipe that cause of his misery off the face of the earth. He is, however, only a man. He weighs his chances and concludes it is unwise to align himself with the side that has been damned by the Being which has taken the place of God in this century, i.e. History. The propaganda to which he is subjected tries by every means to prove that Nazism and Americanism are identical in that they are products of the same economic conditions. He believes this propaganda only slightly less than the average American believes the journalists who assure him that Hitlerism and Stalinism are one and the same.

15   Even if he stands on a higher rung of the hierarchy and so has access to information about the West, he is still unable to weigh the relative strength and weakness of that half of the world. The optical instrument he sees through is so constructed that it encompasses only pre-determined fields of vision. Looking through it, he beholds only what he expected to see. For example, accustomed to living in a society in which law exists exclusively as a Party tool, and in which the sole criterion of human action is its effectiveness, he finds it hard to imagine a system in which every citizen feels himself bound by the sanctions of the law. These sanctions may have been introduced in order to protect the interests of privileged groups, but they remain even after the interests change; and it is not easy to supplant old laws with new. Every citizen is entangled in a network of statutes whose origin lies in some remote past. As a result, the mechanism of collective life is so unwieldy that anyone who tries to be truly active struggles helplessly to free himself of its restrictions.

16   The inhabitant of Central or Eastern Europe is incapable of understanding delays, absurd decisions, political campaigns, mutual recriminations, public opinion polls, and demagoguery, which he considers to be characteristic of the West. But at the same time, these encumbrances assure the private citizen a certain security. To seize a man on the street and deport him to a concentration camp is obviously an excellent means of dealing with an individual who displeases the administration; but such means are difficult to establish in countries where the only criminal is the man who has committed an act clearly defined as punishable in a specific paragraph of the law. Nazi and Communist criminal codes are alike in that they efface the frontier between penal and non-penal deeds—the first, by defining crime as any act directed against the interests of the German nation; the second, as any act directed against the interests of the dictatorship of the proletariat. What the man of the East calls the "lifeless formalism of the bourgeoisie" does, on the other hand, afford some guarantee that the father of a family will return home for supper instead of taking a trip to a region where polar bears thrive but human beings do not.

17   Nor is it easy in legally minded countries to adopt the use of scientific torture under which every man confesses with equal fervor whether he be innocent or guilty. Propaganda tries to convince the citizens of the people's democracies that law in the West is no more than a fiction subservient to the interests of the ruling classes. Perhaps it is a fiction, but it is not too subservient to the wishes of the rulers. If they want to condemn a man, they must sweat to prove him guilty in fact; his defense lawyers hide behind all the technicalities of the law; the case drags on through various appeals, etc. Obviously, crimes are committed under its cover, but so far Western law serves to bind the hands of the rulers as well as of the ruled which, depending on one's beliefs, may be a source of either strength or weakness.

18   Americans, aware of the nature of their law, compare democracy to an awkward raft on which everyone paddles in a different direction. There is much hubbub and mutual abuse, and it is difficult to get everyone to pull together. In comparison with such a raft, the trireme of the totalitarian state, speeding ahead with outspread oars, appears indomitable. But on occasion, the totalitarian ship crashes on rocks an awkward raft can sail over.

19   New developments in the West are not easily ascertained in the people's democracies. In certain Western countries, above all in the United States, something has occurred which is without analogy in the preceding centuries: a new civilization has arisen which is popular, vulgar, perhaps in some respects distasteful to more "refined" people, but which assures its masses a share in the output of its machine production. It is true that what these masses rejoice in is frequently tawdry and superficial, and that they purchase it with hard labor. Yet a girl working in a factory, who buys cheap mass-production models of a dress worn by a movie star, rides in an old but nevertheless private

automobile, looks at cowboy films, and has a refrigerator at home, lives on a certain level of civilization that she has in *common* with others. Whereas a woman on a collective farm near Leningrad cannot foresee the day when even her great-granddaughter will live on a level that approaches such an average.

20   What he refers to as the "stupidity" of the American masses, who are satisfied by the purely material advantages of this new civilization, is exceptionally irritating to the Eastern intellectual. Raised in a country where there was a definite distinction between the "intelligentsia" and the "people," he looks, above all, for ideas created by the "intelligentsia," the traditional fermenting element in revolutionary changes. When he meets with a society in which the "intelligentsia," as it was known in Central or Eastern Europe, does not exist, he has great difficulty in translating his observations into conceptual terms. The ideas he finds are clearly obsolete and far outdistanced by economic and technical developments. The purely pragmatic and empirical resolution of problems and the inability to swallow even a small dose of abstraction (whereas the German bourgeoisie, for example, had this ability in abundance) introduce unknowns into his calculations. If one regards these characteristics as signs of "backwardness" in comparison with Europe, then one must acknowledge that the "stupidity" which produced a technology immeasurably superior to that of Europe is not entirely a source of weakness.

21   In fact, if the impetus to perfect and use new discoveries has lost none of its drive, the credit lies with the West. The effort Japan made to overtake the West ended unsuccessfully; and Japan was beaten by the peace-minded and internally disunited United States of Roosevelt's day. Russia, copying Western models of automobiles, airplanes, jet engines, television sets, atom bombs and submarines, and such things as radar and penicillin, has now entered the race. The youngest generation in Eastern Europe, raised in the worship of Russia, is beginning to believe that she is taking the foremost place in the realm of science and technology. The older people consider such a belief absurd; but, given her untapped natural resources, a planned economy and the subsequent ability to allocate unlimited sums of money to scientific research and experimentation, they feel she may be well on the way toward supremacy.

22   This supposition seems to be refuted by the purely practical aims of contemporary Russian science for, as we know, the greatest discoveries are perfected in the course of long, disinterested work on the part of many scientists and often bear no immediate concrete results. It seems to be refuted, as well, by the insistence with which propaganda attributes most discoveries to the Russians even while they copy American construction, from bridges to motors, in the minutest detail. Such propaganda, pushed often to the point of the ridiculous, does not indicate a high degree of self-confidence. And such occurrences as the sale of Swedish machinery to the people's democracies under the stamp of Russian manufacture disproves its boastful claims. Nevertheless, this

propaganda effort to destroy the Russian inferiority complex and to raise "technological morale" is proof of the importance the Center places upon this scientific race. Who knows to what results such a concentration of will may lead? Perhaps all that Russia needs is time.

23   Let us admit—and the Eastern or Central European will do so—that *at this moment* the superiority of the West in potential production, technology, and replacement of human hands by machines (which means the gradual effacing of the distinction between physical and mental work) is unquestionable. But, the Eastern intellectual asks, what goes on in the heads of the Western masses? Aren't their souls asleep, and when the awakening comes, won't it take the form of Stalinism? Isn't Christianity dying out in the West, and aren't its people bereft of all faith? Isn't there a void in their heads? Don't they fill that void with chauvinism, detective stories, and artistically worthless movies? Well then, what can the West offer us? Freedom *from something* is a great deal, yet not enough. It is much less than freedom *for something*.

24   While such questions are posed, actually they can be countered with others. American Communists (mostly the intellectually minded sons of middle-class or lower middle-classes families) complain about the spiritual poverty of the masses. They do not realize, however, that the Imperium they pine for is a combination of material poverty and lack of technology, plus Stalinism. Nor do they realize how fascinating it might be to try to imagine a combination of prosperity and technology, plus Stalinism. The new man of the Imperium is being remolded under the slogan of the struggle against poverty (which is simultaneously induced and conquered), and the advancement of technology (which is simultaneously demolished and rebuilt). If these two powerful motives were absent, what would happen? One suspects that the wheels of that gigantic machine would then turn in a vacuum. The stage of fully realized Communism is the "holy of holies." It is Heaven. One dare not direct one's eyes toward it. Yet if one dared to visualize that Paradise, he would find it not unlike the United States in periods of full employment. He would find (granting the alleviation of fear, which is improbable) the masses living physiologically, profiting from the material achievements of their civilization. But their spiritual development would meet an insuperable obstacle in a doctrine which considers its aim to be the liberation of man from material cares towards something which it, itself, defines as sheer nonsense.

25   These are utopian considerations which Western Communists may avoid, but their Eastern brothers do not. I remember one who said, "I do not want to live to see Communism realized, it will probably be so boring." When the great re-educational task is accomplished and the hated "metaphysical being" in man is utterly crushed, what will remain? It is doubtful whether Party imitations of Christian liturgy, and mass-like rites performed before portraits of the leaders will give the people perfect satisfaction.

26   More than the West imagines, the intellectuals of the East look to the West for *something*. Nor do they seek it in Western propaganda. The *something* they look for is a great new writer, a new social philosophy, an artistic movement, a scientific discovery, new principles of painting or music. They rarely find this *something*. The people of the East have already become accustomed to thinking of art and society on an organizational and mass scale. The only forms of culture in the West which attain such a scale are movies, best sellers, and illustrated magazines. No thinking person in the West takes most of these means of mass recreation seriously; whereas, in the East, where everything has a mass character, they take on the dignity of being the sole representatives of the "decadent culture of the West." It is easy to sneer at most films, novels, or articles (to say nothing of the fact that one is well-paid for such criticism and that it releases one from the more painful obligation of writing enthusiastically about the Center). Hence it is the pet activity of most Eastern journalists, and the influence that this sort of criticism has on its public is considerable.

27   The real cultural life of the West is very different. But even there the Eastern intellectual stumbles upon treacherous appearances, for he finds both imitation and innovation, decadence and vigor, advertised mediocrity and imperfectly recognized greatness. The social and intellectual currents, which he knows from his pre-war trips to the West, continue to exist and arouse his impatience as products of a stage he has left behind. Still these are the aspects that attract his attention, and not the new creative forces sending up shoots amid a forest of dead trees.

28   The gravest reproach leveled against Western culture is that it is exclusive and inaccessible to the masses. This reproach is largely valid. Poetry, painting, and even music, shutting themselves up in ivory towers, become susceptible to numerous stylistic maladies. At the same time, however, their link with the everyday life of the people is considerably stronger than it seems to be at first glance. For example, avant-garde painting which is so "difficult" and "obscure" reaches a tremendous number of people through its influence on advertising, dress design, stage sets, interior decoration, and most important of all, perhaps, on the shape of universally used machines. In comparison with this, the "Soviet Empire" style, which is based on the painting on huge canvases of groups of dignitaries standing about in various positions and poses, is completely severed from everyday life. By destroying all experimentation in art, the Center confined its applied art (if one can speak of its existence at all) to a clumsy imitation of Western applied art which, however, is constantly renewed under the influence of experimental easel painting. When the cult of ugliness reigns in painting or sculpture and any daring passes as formalism, then applied art, cut off from its roots, is bound to prove sterile.

29   The multi-colored setting of Western life is subject to the law of osmosis. The average citizen of the West has no idea that a painter in a

garret, a little-known musician, or a writer of "unintelligible" verse is a magician who shapes all those things in life which he prizes. Government officials give little thought to such matters for they consider them a waste of time. Since it is not a planned economy, the Western state cannot come to the aid of people working in the various arts. They go on, each pursuing his own chimera, sometimes dying of hunger; while nearby, wealthy men, not knowing what to do with their money, spend it on the latest whims of their benighted souls.

30   This order of things revolts a person from the East. In his country, anyone who displays any talent is used. In the West, the same man would have very little chance of success. Western economy squanders talent to an incredible degree; and the few who do succeed owe their success as often to pure luck as to native ability. In the countries of the New Faith,[5] the counterpart to this waste lies in the fact that the capacity to follow the political line is a selective criterion by which the most mediocre often attain the greatest renown. Nevertheless, the artist or scholar in the East earns his living more easily than his colleague in the West. Even though the pressure of the Method is burdensome, its material compensations are not to be scorned. Many musicians, painters, and writers who had the opportunity to flee to the West did not do so because they felt it was better to compose, paint, or write somehow or other, rather than to teach or work in a factory, with no time or energy left in which to perfect their true craft. Many of those who were abroad returned to their own countries chiefly for this reason.

31   Fear of the indifference with which the economic system of the West treats its artists and scholars is widespread among Eastern intellectuals. They say it is better to deal with an intelligent devil than with a good-natured idiot. An intelligent devil understands their mutual interests and lets them live by a pen, a chisel, or a brush, caring for his clients and making his demands. A good-hearted idiot does not understand these interests, gives nothing and asks nothing—which in practice amounts to polite cruelty.

32   To the people of the East it is axiomatic that the basic means of production should belong to the State, that they should be regulated according to a planned economy, and that their proceeds should be used for hygienic, cultural, scientific, and artistic ends. It is naïve to seek partisans of capitalism in their midst. The *something* these people look for in the West is certainly not warmed-over watchwords of the French Revolution or the American War of Independence. They laugh at the argument that factories and mines should belong to private individuals. Their search for *something* springs from a more or less clear understanding of the fact that the New Faith is incapable of satisfying the spiritual needs of mankind, for its efforts in that direction have with inexorable regularity

---

[5] The belief in a Communist utopia which replaced the "old" Christian faith.

turned into caricature. If they were forced to formulate what they seek, they would undoubtedly reply that they want a system with a socialist economy, but one in which man need not struggle desperately in the snake-like embrace of the Method. So they seek some sign indicating that real cultural values can arise outside the scope of the Method. But they must be lasting values, geared to the future, and therefore not products of obsolete concepts. Anything less would serve merely to confirm the Method. The people in the countries of the New Faith know that *only* in the West can there appear works that will bear the seeds of hope for the future. Perhaps discoveries no less important than those of Marx or Darwin have already been perfected in the workrooms of isolated philosophers. But how does one find them?

33   The Eastern intellectual is a severe critic of everything that penetrates to him from the West. He has been deceived so often that he does not want cheap consolation which will eventually prove all the more depressing. The War left him suspicious and highly skilled in unmasking sham and pretense. He has rejected a great many books that he liked before the War, as well as a great many trends in painting or music, because they have not stood the test of experience. The work of human thought *should* withstand the test of brutal, naked reality. If it cannot, it is worthless. Probably only those things are worth while which can preserve their validity in the eyes of a man threatened with instant death.

34   A man is lying under machine-gun fire on a street in an embattled city. He looks at the pavement and sees a very amusing sight: the cobblestones are standing upright like the quills of a porcupine. The bullets hitting against their edges displace and tilt them. Such moments in the consciousness of a man *judge* all poets and philosophers. Let us suppose, too, that a certain poet was the hero of the literary cafés, and wherever he went was regarded with curiosity and awe. Yet his poems, recalled in such a moment, suddenly seem diseased and highbrow. The vision of the cobblestones is unquestionably real, and poetry based on an equally *naked* experience could survive triumphantly that judgment day of man's illusions. In the intellectuals who lived through the atrocities of war in Eastern Europe there took place what one might call the *elimination of emotional luxuries*. Psychoanalytic novels incite them to laughter. They consider the literature of erotic complications, still popular in the West, as trash. Imitation abstract painting bores them. They are hungry—but they want bread, not hors d'oeuvres.

Reading for Meaning

1. What knowledge about human behavior do Europeans have that Americas don't? What assumption about Americans do Europeans make because of this difference?

2. One of the more disheartening conclusions that Milosz draws is that the human is "so plastic a being that . . . a thoroughly self-respecting citizen will crawl about on all fours sporting a

tail of brightly colored feathers as a sign of conformity to the order he lives in." What are possible consequences of such plasticity? First consider the negative effects of absolute conformity; then analyze this characteristic as a method of survival.

3. The Eastern European believes that *"If something exists in one place, it will exist everywhere."* Write a brief explanation of what this statement means. What irrational feeling does Milosz think underlies this assumption? Might there be some truth to this belief?

4. In paragraphs 13 and 16, Milosz introduces his reader to the fundamentals of Communist-Stalinist thinking espoused by the Soviet government. Consult a dictionary or encyclopedia to find definitions for words like "dialectical materialism," "the bourgeoisie," and "the proletariat," which may not be familiar to you. Then summarize the most important assumptions that Milosz's Eastern European makes.

5. What does Milosz mean when he refers to the United States as a "vulgar" civilization? What "refinements" might be missing, according to Milosz and many Eastern Europeans, and how might this lack of intellectual sophistication have become an asset?

6. What do Eastern Europeans, who have been deprived of it for so long, think freedom is for? What do they seem to want from the West?

7. An American songwriter once wrote: "Freedom's just another word for nothin' left to lose." What do you think freedom means for yourself, for people you know, and, perhaps, for Americans in general? How well do we use our freedom?

8. Explain Milosz's analysis of the ways that "legitimate" art in the United States has both excluded common people and become part of their everyday lives.

Comparing Texts

1. In paragraphs 3 and 10 in "Looking to the West," Czeslaw Milosz describes the behavior adopted by Eastern Europeans that helped them survive the atrocities of World War II and an oppressive Communist dictatorship. Although hardships for people in the United States are not comparable to what Europeans suffered during that war, we have learned to adapt to threats and dangers in our lives as well. Write a paper in which you explain a few strategies for survival in the United States. You might discuss techniques for survival in the workplace, in school, or on the street.

2. Milosz describes how the assumptions about life changed for the average person in Central and Eastern Europe who lived under the Nazis. If these Europeans have a sense of despair, he adds, it is because they saw their economies and values destroyed during World War II. Milosz drew his portrait of Eastern Europeans shortly after the Second World War. Find one or two sources that offer a recent assessment of life in parts of the former Soviet Union. Use the details you find about people's everyday lives to write a reassessment of what it is currently like to live in Eastern Europe.

Ideas for Writing

1. Today Milosz is a renowned Polish-American writer. Read a few chapters from one or more of his books (see the list of his works in the background paragraph that precedes "Looking to the West") and write an assessment of his work. You might discuss one of the

following: themes that recur in Milosz's writing, perspectives he offers on his subjects, unique strategies or arrangements of ideas, or the overall importance of his work.

2. Milosz criticizes Soviet art for being "completely severed from everyday life." Search computer databases or look for resources in your college or local libraries to find explanations of what art is like in one or two Eastern European countries now that the Soviet Union has collapsed. You might look at the subjects artists are choosing, whether they are free to produce their work, and whether their art is appreciated by "the masses" of common people.

WRITING TO COMPARE

Writing comparatively involves a process, as does any kind of writing and responding to a text. Before you think about comparing texts, it is a good idea to understand the main points and features of each text separately. To help you do this, make notations in the margins of each text, noting main points and other important characteristics of the text. You might also use a journal to write out fuller notations and to record your responses to the texts. Once you have fully understood the ideas and intentions of each text, review them to make connections between ideas, themes, approaches to the subjects, purpose, audience, writing strategies, effectiveness, validity of the arguments, style, or tone. Record your comparisons in the margins of your journal using a different-colored ink. Another strategy for making connections between texts is to use a double-entry journal to record separate entries for each text. Finally, try sectioning your journal paper into three columns, two for ideas from your texts, and a third for your responses. This three-column approach is illustrated in the sample journal entry below that makes comparisons between Pokrovsky's "The Land of Meaningless Courtesy" and Milosz's "Looking to the West."

```
            Making Comparisons: Pokrovsky and Milosz
    "The Land . . ."      "Looking . . ."        Comparisons
    Audience: Rus-        Audience: West-        Pokrovsky writes
    sians who want        erners, espe-          a guide to help
    to "build rela-       cially Americans,      Russians inter-
    tionships" but        who need help          pret American
    who plan to re-       understanding how      behavior.
    turn to Russia.       Eastern Europeans      Milosz, on the
```

"The Land . . ."	"Looking . . ."	Comparisons
—Stresses differences between Russians and Americans in terms of "national character," value system, and "reference points" or touchstones in their everyday lives. —Gives examples of boisterous friendliness, belly laughs, broad smiles, slaps on the back. Contrasts to Russian reserve and sense of restraint. —A person's "real value," according to Pokrovsky, is	think about the West and what they hope the West can give them. —Looks at the history that formed the Eastern European's worldview. —Adds the personal anecdote of a man who lives in what he considers to be a "natural world" but who is forced to "walk" through a world in ruins where the social fabric and identity itself has unraveled, and life has taken on the aspect of the jungle.	other hand, is more interested in having the West understand the complexities of the Eastern Europeans' experience and what has shaped their views of the West. Pokrovsky examines the personal style of Americans in order to advise Russian businessmen how to work with them. Milosz, on the other hand, looks at broader historical, psychological, and institutional differences between Americans and Eastern Europeans.

"The Land..."	"Looking..."	Comparisons
not measured by talent or the fact that others like you. Instead, it is based on seven features: capital, acknowledged accomplishments, well-positioned relatives, social standing in Russia, media importance, connections in the United States, and looks.	—His experience has taught the Eastern European that "judgments and thinking habits" are relative, a lesson they are sure Americans have not learned.	The style of writing is very different as well. Pokrovsky offers straightforward advice and lists of Americans' characteristics and appropriate ways to respond to Americans. Milosz is more lyrical in his approach; his piece begins and ends with anecdotes that personalize the European's experience and illustrate why they have so little tolerance for the "emotional luxuries" expressed in Western art.

After taking notes on the texts to find elements that you might compare, your next step is to arrange ideas by locating possible points you want to discuss in each paragraph or group of paragraphs. At this point you can write a tentative thesis, the main point your essay will convey. Keep in mind that the thesis should clarify the purpose of the comparison. In other words, it should be clear to your reader what point you want the comparison to make.

SAMPLE COMPARATIVE ESSAY

The following essay compares audience, purpose, tone, and depth of thinking in "The Land of Meaningless Courtesy" and "Looking to the West."

Nadine Patel

English 1A

Dr. Linda Greene

25 October 1999

Examining the West: A Comparison of
"The Land of Meaningless Courtesy"
and "Looking to the West"

In the two texts about American character and behavior, one by a Russian, the other by a Polish émigré living in the United States, we find differences in the tone and degree of seriousness each author assumes toward his subject. Nikita Pokrovsky writes a guide for Russian businessmen, who might otherwise find American behavior baffling. Milosz examines shortcomings in the American system, but he also explains what produced the attitudes of Eastern Europeans toward America and the West. He hopes to enlighten the West about the forces that have shaped Eastern European thinking and to clarify what the East expects of the West. Milosz's arguments are more complicated because he wants to explain the complex views that Eastern Europeans have of the West. Pokrovsky, on the other hand, sets down some straightforward rules about how Russians can do business with Americans.

    Because Nikita Pokrovsky's main concern is to give advice about how to work with American businessmen, he focuses on what Russians can expect when they meet Americans. He examines Americans' personal style, values, and revered authorities. For example, he advises his Russian readers that the American style of boisterous, friendly exchanges, loud laughs, broad smiles, and slaps on the shoulder appear to be the picture of happiness reminiscent of fairy tales, but they are actually meaningless displays of conviviality. Moreover, Americans will measure a foreign business acquaintance not by his or her talent or on the merit of the businessperson's ideas or proposals. Instead, Americans look for certain indicators of status. These include how much money you have, your published accomplishments, influential relatives, social standing in Russia, media importance, business and academic connections in the United States, and your looks and age. Finally, Pokrovsky advises Russians who want to do business in the United States not to contradict opinions about

Russia's hopeful future under Boris Yeltsin, opinions that Pokrovsky thinks Americans pick up from the *New York Times*.

    Milosz's broader audience and more in-depth look at both the flaws and triumphs of Western institutions as well as the cultural blind spots of their Eastern European critics necessitate writing a very different kind of essay. Unlike Pokrovsky, Milosz is not concerned with individual style when discussing American character. Instead, Milosz undertakes a serious examination of Eastern European skepticism of the West in general, and of the United States in particular, and looks at the broader historical, psychological, and institutional assumptions that produced this skepticism. Historically, Milosz argues, Eastern Europe was devastated in the Second World War, a war in which the average citizen watched while the social fabric and individual identity itself unraveled. Life became savage, and the cave and the jungle replaced the old laws of civilization. These experiences taught Eastern Europeans that "judgments and thinking habits" are relative. Hence, they cannot take seriously North Americans who think their system is inviolate, who judge their way of life as "natural" and any other social order "unnatural." The Eastern European judges American laws as cumbersome and unworkable, whereas in East Bloc countries, laws are efficient tools of the Communist party. Milosz points out that party propaganda, which declares that Western laws serve the interests of the ruling class and not the people, shaped the Eastern view of those laws. Here Milosz adds the kind of insight missing in Pokrovsky's article not only by explaining why Eastern Europeans are critical of the United States but also by looking at what they have missed in their evaluation—the fact that as cumbersome as it may seem, laws in Western democracies ensure the private citizen a measure of protection against whimsical arrests that is unknown in countries like Poland and Lithuania.

Both writers examine things superficial in American thinking. Pokrovsky looks at superficial assessments of Russians and their country that he thinks are typical of businessmen in the United States. In Pokrovsky's view, Americans are unwilling to entertain gloomy predictions about their own future or the future of Russia under Boris Yeltsin. Moreover, they have not arrived at this view on their own but rather have accepted the arguments offered by what Pokrovsky considers the American businessman's sole source of information about the international scene—the *New York Times.* Americans have other shortcomings as well in Pokrovsky's estimation. Although he doesn't identify them as such, he describes stereotypes of Russians so that Russians can either use or avoid them. Acting tipsy and unrefined will fit American expectations of Russians and, perhaps, help advance an important business connection in the United States. Speaking perfect English and using a twenty-four-hour clock, however, are likely to end a budding business relationship.

    Characteristically, Milosz takes a much broader view of the superficiality of American culture. He does not dispute the Eastern view that materialism accounts for the lack of refinement and the vulgarity endemic to the United States. Nor does he question the Easterner's evaluation of the Western mind as "purely pragmatic and empirical" and unable to grasp "abstractions." In a way, Pokrovsky also looks at Western materialism when he lists what has "real value" in American eyes. Most of the seven characteristics he lists have something to do with money and influence, traits akin to the superficial satisfactions Milosz's Eastern Europeans find in the American's "purely material" lifestyle.

    Unlike Pokrovsky, however, Milosz insists on adding truths that he thinks critics of Western capitalism have missed. In fact, Milosz asserts, the West's materialistic and conceptual "stupidities" have produced an economy in which the average worker enjoys a larger share in its production than the Eastern European can ever hope to attain. Moreover, this unsophisticated culture enjoys the fruits of a highly superior technology; therefore, Milosz argues, such "stupidity" cannot be "entirely a source of weakness." Again, Milosz's argument cuts both ways: he acknowledges certain shortcomings of capitalist democracies while pointing out the shortsightedness of the East Bloc critics whose own biases and rigid economic notions can blind them to the benefits workers experience in the West.

    American and Western indifference is also a subject both Pokrovsky and Milosz have in common. The kind of indifference Pokrovsky discusses is, again, in keeping with his focus on how to do business in the United States, and the indifference he speaks of amounts to a personal slight. He discusses the American tendency to enjoy "loud leisure time" with business contacts without intending to meet them again. He offers suggestions for getting these distracted businessmen to notice how sincere the Russians are and how capable they are of doing business. The indifference Milosz speaks about has to do with the capitalist's indifference toward the artist. Because his intention differs from Pokrovsky's, Milosz does not offer anecdotes to illustrate this indifference. Instead, he explains that despite their doubts about the West, Easterners expect that the greatest cultural productions will come from the West, not from the East. This argument also connects to his earlier discussion of vital art produced in the West, as opposed to mass-produced art that the West exports and Eastern Europeans take as representative of Western culture. The truly developed arts in Western countries, he argues, have important links to the "everyday life of the people." Indifference, then, is only part of the story. In reality, Milosz asserts, Western art permeates and renews the life of the average citizen. In contrast, East Bloc governments have destroyed experimentation in the arts and have left their citizens with deadened, lifeless formalism.

> Patel 8
>
> Purpose and audience account for internal consistencies in "The Land of Meaningless Courtesy" and "Looking to the West." Nikita Pokrovsky does not venture beyond his promise to explore the superficiality of the American character and how knowledge of those shortcomings should shape the behavior of Russians who wish to have successful business ventures in the United States. Czeslaw Milosz, on the other hand, never wavers from his complex analysis of both the Easterners' perception of the West and the validity and shortsightedness of that perspective. Although his argument is sometimes difficult to follow, and he expects his readers to have knowledge of his subjects that they may not always possess, his is the more engaging of the two texts, and he offers the most penetrating view of his subject.

ORGANIZING COMPARATIVE ESSAYS

Papers that make comparisons follow one of two patterns and sometimes combine these patterns. Writers may discuss one subject of their comparison first, then devote a paragraph or two to the second subject. Paragraphs two and three in the comparison between "The Land of Meaningless Courtesy" and "Looking to the West" illustrate this subject-by-subject arrangement. The second paragraph analyzes the purpose and audience for Nikita Pokrovsky's article, whereas paragraph three examines the broader audience and more complex purpose of Czeslaw Milosz's "Looking to the West." Whole essays may use this alternating pattern and discuss one subject completely, then devote the last section of the essay to the second subject. In "An Anthropologist Looks at the Hopi," a selection from chapter 9, Dorothy Lee first describes the uniform approach to group tasks she found in her children's classrooms. The second section of her essay explains how the Hopi balance the needs of the group with those of the individual. The contrast between the two ways of weighing the individual against the group—one in a midwestern school, the other on a Hopi Reservation—illustrate the shortcomings of the first approach.

The second organizational strategy used in writing papers that compare is the point-by-point comparison. For this method the writer discusses both subjects in the same paragraph or section of the essay according to a particular point. Paragraph six of the sample comparative essay explains how each author regards indifference as part of the American character but each examines that trait in an entirely different way. Pokrovsky is concerned with the personal indifference Russians are likely to face; Milosz analyzes the indifference toward the arts that Eastern Europeans find so threatening. The two patterns for comparing—subject-by-subject and point-by-point—can easily be combined when writing an essay.

CHAPTER 4
EXPLORING IDEAS FROM SEVERAL CULTURES

First Thoughts

Primeras impresiones

Premières impressions

Each age, each society reinvents or rediscovers childhood within its own sociohistorical framework. The nature of childhood is fluid, anchored as it is in the prevailing world views supporting societies and created by societies. . . . What constitutes parenting is as much a cultural invention as what constitutes childhood and, in this century, adolescence. As a socially defined phenomenon, the requisites and boundaries of parenting will differ by historical period, culture, class, and ethnicity or race.

Anne-Marie Ambert
"An International Perspective on Parenting:
Social Change and Social Constructs"
Journal of Marriage and the Family

One of the more interesting ways to extend your study of cultural analysis is to read several articles on a general subject and write about how people from different parts of the world or from cultures within a single country offer unique expressions of that subject. For example, you might wish to write an essay about the dating and mating practices in several cultures. Your work might lead you to examine arranged marriages in India, the chaperoned dating process in some Latin American countries, and the more free-form dating practices in the United States. Your investigation would produce an essay that examines dating and mating practices using information from several texts. The work you completed for assignments in chapter 3 gave you practice working with more than one text. Now you can build on this knowledge by completing activities in this chapter, which include investigating a particular subject and writing an information paper.

THE INVESTIGATION OR INFORMATION PAPER

One of the more complex responses to readings about culture, the investigation paper, examines a subject using ideas from several texts. This chapter offers a sample investigation of various roles assigned to parents and children in several cultures. First you will become familiar with the three texts used in the sample investigation—Barbara Kingsolver's "Somebody's Baby," Raymonde Carroll's "Parents and Children," and Margaret Mead's "Children and Ritual in Bali." After studying background information on each of the cultures in question and reading a short biographical note on each author, you can then read the articles and respond to the readings with the help of questions for discussion and writing. A sample investigation paper at the end of the chapter illustrates ways to incorporate information from several texts into your paper. This sample paper also serves as an introduction to the format for writing a research paper that was developed by the Modern Language Association. This format is the standard for writing research papers in English and foreign language classes.

Writing before Reading

How are children usually treated in your family or community? Do you think they are appreciated enough, or are they dismissed or even abused? How do you account for the treatment of children you have seen?

SOMEBODY'S BABY
Barbara Kingsolver

Barbara Kingsolver (b. 1955) is a novelist, essayist, journalist, and poet. She grew up in Nicholas County, Kentucky. In 1979 she moved to Tucson, Arizona, two years after completing her B.A. in biology from DePauw University in Greencastle, Indiana. She published her first novel, The Bean Trees, *a largely autobiographical work, in 1988. A supporter of populist and feminist causes, Kingsolver wrote* Holding the Line: Women in the Great Arizona Mine Strike of 1983 *(1989), an oral history of the women who organized an eighteen-month walkout despite harassment and financial hardships. This work of nonfiction was followed by several fictional works.* Homeland and Other Stories *appeared in 1989. Her second novel,* Animal Dreams *(1990), won the Edward Abbey Award for Ecofiction and the PEN West Fiction Award. Kingsolver published a book of poems in English and Spanish titled* Another America/Otra America *(1991). Her latest novel,* Pigs in Heaven *(1993), won several literary awards.* High Tide in Tucson *(1995) is a collection of essays that includes the selection, "Somebody's Baby."*

Facts about Spain

Spain, and its smaller neighbor Portugal, occupy the Iberian Peninsula in southwestern Europe. The Canary Islands, located off the African coast, Ceuta and Melilla, cities on the north coast of Morocco, and the Balearic Islands in the Mediterranean Sea are also part of Spain. Ferdinand and Isabella united Spain in the fifteenth century, and in 1492 the Muslims, who had once conquered most of Spain, lost it in a final defeat at Granada. In the same year, the Catholic king and queen expelled the Jews. Queen Isabella is famous not only for financing the voyages of Christopher Columbus but also for supporting the Spanish Inquisition. The people of modern Spain are predominantly Roman Catholic, with a few enclaves of Protestants, Jews, and Muslims in metropolitan areas. Two-thirds of the people live in cities. Education is free to Spanish children and is compulsory after age six.

1. As I walked out the street entrance to my newly rented apartment, a guy in maroon high-tops and a skateboard haircut approached, making kissing noises and saying, "Hi, gorgeous." Three weeks earlier, I would have assessed the degree of malice and made ready to run or tell him to bug off, depending. But now, instead, I smiled, and so did my four-year-old daughter, because after dozens of similar encounters I understood he didn't mean me but *her*.
2. This was not the United States.
3. For most of the year my daughter was four we lived in Spain, in the warm southern province of the Canary Islands. I struggled with dinner at midnight and the subjunctive tense, but my only genuine culture shock reverberated from this earthquake of a fact: people there like kids. They don't just say so, they *do*. Widows in black, buttoned-down CEOs, purple-sneakered teenagers, the butcher, the baker, all would stop on the street to have little chats with my daughter. Routinely, taxi drivers leaned out the window to shout *"Hola, guapa!"* My daughter, who must have felt my conditioned flinch, would look up at me wide-eyed and explain patiently, "I *like* it that people think I'm pretty." With a mother's keen myopia I would tell you, absolutely, my daughter is beautiful enough to stop traffic. But in the city of Santa Cruz, I have to confess, so was every other person under the height of one meter. Not just those who conceded to be seen and not heard. Whenever Camille grew cranky in a restaurant (and really, what do you expect at midnight?) the waiters flirted and brought her little presents, and nearby diners looked on with that sweet, wistful

gleam of eye that I'd thought diners reserved for the dessert tray. What I discovered in Spain was a culture that held children to be its meringues and éclairs. My own culture, it seemed to me in retrospect, tended to regard children as a sort of toxic-waste product: a necessary evil, maybe, but if it's not our own we don't want to see it or hear it or, God help us, smell it.

4   If you don't have children, you think I'm exaggerating. But if you've changed a diaper in the last decade you know exactly the toxic-waste glare I mean. In the United States I have been told in restaurants: "We come here to get *away* from kids." (This for no infraction on my daughter's part that I could discern, other than being visible.) On an airplane I heard a man tell a beleaguered woman whose infant was bawling (as I would, to clear my aching ears, if I couldn't manage chewing gum): "If you can't keep that thing quiet, you should keep it at home."

5   Air travel, like natural disasters, throws strangers together in unnaturally intimate circumstances. (Think how well you can get to know the bald spot of the guy reclining in front of you.) Consequently, airplanes can be a splendid cultural magnifying glass. On my family's voyage from New York to Madrid we weren't assigned seats together. I shamelessly begged my neighbor—a forty-something New Yorker traveling alone—if she would take my husband's aisle seat in another row so our air-weary and plainly miserable daughter could stretch out across her parents' laps. My fellow traveler snapped, "No, I have to have the window seat, just like you *had* to have that baby."

6   As simply as that, a child with needs (and ears) became an inconvenient *thing*, for which I was entirely to blame. The remark left me stunned and, as always happens when someone speaks rudely to me, momentarily guilty: yes, she must be right, conceiving this child was a rash, lunatic moment of selfishness, and now I had better be prepared to pay the price.

7   In the U.S.A., where it's said that anyone can grow up to be President, we parents are left pretty much on our own when it comes to the Presidents-in-training. Our social programs for children are the hands-down worst in the industrialized world, but apparently that is just what we want as a nation. It took a move to another country to make me realize how thoroughly I had accepted my nation's creed of every family for itself. Whenever my daughter crash-landed in the playground, I was startled at first to see a sanguine, Spanish-speaking stranger pick her up and dust her off. And if a shrieking bundle landed at *my* feet, I'd furtively look around for the next of kin. But I quickly came to see this detachment as perverse when applied to children, and am wondering how it ever caught on in the first place.

8   My grandfathers on both sides lived in households that were called upon, after tragedy struck close to home, to take in orphaned children and raise them without a thought. In an era of shortage, this was

commonplace. But one generation later that kind of semipermeable household had vanished, at least among the white middle class. It's a horrifying thought, but predictable enough, that the worth of children in America is tied to their dollar value. Children used to be field hands, household help, even miners and factory workers—extensions of a family's productive potential and so, in a sense, the property of an extended family. But *precious* property, valued and coveted. Since the advent of child-labor laws, children have come to hold an increasingly negative position in the economy. They're spoken of as a responsibility, a legal liability, an encumbrance—or, if their unwed mothers are on welfare, a mistake that should not be rewarded. The political shuffle seems to be about making sure they cost us as little as possible, and that their own parents foot the bill. Virtually every program that benefits children in this country, from *Sesame Street* to free school lunches, has been cut back in the last decade—in many cases, cut to nothing. If it takes a village to raise a child, our kids are knocking on a lot of doors where nobody seems to be home.

9   Taking parental responsibility to extremes, some policymakers in the United States have seriously debated the possibility of requiring a license for parenting. I'm dismayed by the notion of licensing an individual adult to raise an individual child, because it implies parenting is a private enterprise, like selling liquor or driving a cab (though less lucrative). I'm also dismayed by what it suggests about innate fitness or nonfitness to rear children. Who would devise such a test? And how could it harbor anything but deep class biases? Like driving, parenting is a skill you learn by doing. You keep an eye out for oncoming disasters, and know when to stop and ask for directions. The skills you have going into it are hardly the point.

10   The first time I tried for my driver's license, I flunked. I was sixteen and rigid with panic. I rolled backward precariously while starting on a hill; I misidentified in writing the shape of a railroad crossing sign; as a final disqualifying indignity, my VW beetle—borrowed from my brother and apparently as appalled as I—went blind in the left blinker and mute in the horn. But nowadays, when it's time for a renewal, I breeze through the driver's test without thinking, usually on my way to some other errand. That test I failed twenty years ago was no prediction of my ultimate competence as a driver, anymore than my doll-care practices (I liked tying them to the back of my bike, by the hair) were predictive of my parenting skills (heavens be praised). Who really understands what it takes to raise kids? That is, until after the diaper changes, the sibling rivalries, the stitches, the tantrums, the first day of school, the overpriced-sneakers standoff, the first date, the safe-sex lecture, and the senior prom have all been negotiated and put away in the scrapbook?

11   While there are better and worse circumstances from which to launch offspring onto the planet, it's impossible to anticipate just who

will fail. One of the most committed, creative parents I know plunged into her role through the trapdoor of teen pregnancy; she has made her son the center of her life, constructed a large impromptu family of reliable friends and neighbors, and absorbed knowledge like a plant taking sun. Conversely, some of the most strained, inattentive parents I know are well-heeled professionals, self-sufficient but chronically pressed for time. Life takes surprising turns. The one sure thing is that no parent, ever, has turned out to be perfectly wise and exhaustively provident, 1,440 minutes a day, for 18 years. It takes help. Children are not commodities but an incipient world. They thrive best when their upbringing is the collective joy and responsibility of families, neighborhoods, communities, and nations.

12   It's not hard to figure out what's good for kids, but amid the noise of an increasingly antichild political climate, it can be hard to remember just to go ahead and do it: for example, to vote to raise your school district's budget, even though you'll pay higher taxes. (If you're earning enough to pay taxes at all, I promise, the school needs those few bucks more than you do.) To support legislators who care more about afterschool programs, affordable health care, and libraries than about military budgets and the Dow Jones industrial average. To volunteer time and skills at your neighborhood school and also the school across town. To decide to notice, rather than ignore it, when a neighbor is losing it with her kids, and offer to baby-sit twice a week. This is not interference. Getting between a ball player and a ball is interference. The ball is inanimate.

13   Presuming children to be their parents' sole property and responsibility is, among other things, a handy way of declaring problem children to be someone else's problem, or fault, or failure. It's a dangerous remedy; it doesn't change the fact that somebody else's kids will ultimately be in your face demanding *now* with interest what they didn't get when they were smaller and had simpler needs. Maybe in-your-face means breaking and entering, or maybe it means a Savings and Loan scam. Children deprived—of love, money, attention, or moral guidance—grow up to have large and powerful needs.

14   Always there will be babies made in some quarters whose parents can't quite take care of them. Reproduction is the most invincible of all human goals; like every other species, we're only here because our ancestors spent millions of years refining their act as efficient, dedicated breeders. If we hope for only sane, thoughtful people to have children, we can wish while we're at it for an end to cavities and mildew. But unlike many other species we are social, insightful, and capable of anticipating our future. We can see, if we care to look, that the way we treat children— *all* of them, not just our own, and especially those in great need—defines the shape of the world we'll wake up in tomorrow. The most remarkable feature of human culture is its capacity to reach beyond the self and encompass the collective good.

15   It's an inspiring thought. But in mortal fact, here in the United States we are blazing a bold downhill path from the high ground of "human collective," toward the tight little den of "self." The last time we voted on a school-budget override in Tucson, the newspaper printed scores of letters from readers incensed by the very possibility: "I don't have kids," a typical letter writer declared, "so why should I have to pay to educate other people's offspring?" The budget increase was voted down, the school district progressed from deficient to desperate, and I longed to ask that miserly nonfather just *whose* offspring he expects to doctor the maladies of his old age.

16   If we intend to cleave like stubborn barnacles to our great American ethic of every nuclear family for itself, then each of us had better raise and educate offspring enough to give us each day, in our old age, our daily bread. If we don't wish to live by bread alone, we'll need not only a farmer and a cook in the family but also a home repair specialist, an auto mechanic, an accountant, an import-export broker, a forest ranger, a therapist, an engineer, a musician, a poet, a tailor, a doctor, and at least three shifts of nurses. If that seems impractical, then we can accept other people's kids into our lives, starting now.

17   It's not so difficult. Most of the rest of the world has got this in hand. Just about any country you can name spends a larger percentage of its assets on its kids than we do. Virtually all industrialized nations have better schools and child-care policies. And while the United States grabs headlines by saving the occasional baby with heroic medical experiments, world health reports (from UNESCO, USAID, and other sources) show that a great many other parts of the world have lower infant mortality rates than we do—not just the conspicuously prosperous nations like Japan and Germany, but others, like Greece, Cuba, Portugal, Slovenia—simply because they attend better to all their mothers and children. Cuba, running on a budget that would hardly keep New York City's lights on, has better immunization programs and a higher literacy rate. During the long, grim haul of a thirty-year economic blockade, during which the United States has managed to starve Cuba to a ghost of its hopes, that island's child-first priorities have never altered.

18   Here in the land of plenty a child dies from poverty every fifty-three minutes, and TV talk shows exhibit teenagers who pierce their flesh with safety pins and rip off their parents every way they know how. All these punks started out as somebody's baby. How on earth, we'd like to know, did they learn to be so isolated and selfish?

19   My second afternoon in Spain, standing in a crowded bus, as we ricocheted around a corner and my daughter reached starfish-wise for stability, a man in a black beret stood up and gently helped her into his seat. In his weightless bearing I caught sight of the decades-old child, treasured

by the manifold mothers of his neighborhood, growing up the way leavened dough rises surely to the kindness of bread.

20   I thought then of the woman on the airplane, who was obviously within her rights to put her own comfort first, but whose withheld generosity gave my daughter what amounted to a sleepless, kicking, squirming, miserable journey. As always happens two days after someone has spoken to me rudely, I knew exactly what I should have said: Be careful what you give children, for sooner or later you are sure to get it back.

Reading for Meaning

1. What reactions to children does Barbara Kingsolver find typical of people in the United States? Based on your experience, how accurate is her depiction of attitudes toward children in this country?

2. How did Kingsolver's experiences in Spain make her reexamine her own ideas about the obligation of the larger community toward children?

3. Why does Kingsolver discuss the history of child labor in the United States in paragraph 8? How does it contribute to her discussion of current attitudes toward children in this country?

4. Why does Kingsolver think requiring a license for parenting is a bad idea? Do you agree? What other problems might arise from instituting such a requirement?

5. On what grounds does Kingsolver defend a collective, community approach to child rearing?

Comparing Texts

Barbara Kingsolver decries the idea that indifference, if not downright hostility, toward children is responsible for a woefully low literacy rate and high infant mortality in the United States. In what ways does David Elkind's analysis of families in the United States in "WAAAH!!: Why Kids Have a Lot to Cry About," page 168, complement or extend Kingsolver's argument?

Ideas for Writing

1. Write an essay in which you respond in some way to ideas Kingsolver presents in "Somebody's Baby."

2. Check a library or bookstore for Barbara Kingsolver's collection of essays, *High Tide in Tucson,* which includes "Somebody's Baby." Read three or four of the essays in this collection; then write a paper discussing several characteristics of the style, tone, themes, or ideas of Kingsolver's writing.

3. If you know someone who has traveled to Spain or who emigrated from that country, ask him or her if children are treated as differently in Spain and the United States as Kingsolver claims.

4. Find a chatroom on the Internet that discusses issues related to Spain or start one yourself. Summarize a few of Kingsolver's descriptions of the attitude toward children she witnessed in Spain, and ask chatroom respondents how their observations compare to hers.

Writing before Reading

Ideally, what should parents provide for their children? Do children have certain obligations toward their parents? After answering these questions, analyze your responses carefully to determine the assumptions about parents and children that help explain your position.

PARENTS AND CHILDREN

Raymonde Carroll

"Parents and Children" is a chapter from Raymonde Carroll's book *Cultural Misunderstandings,* a series of essays in which Carroll examines the cultural contexts that produce different values and behavior in France and in the United States. For a biography of Raymonde Carroll, see page 8.

Facts about France

France is one of the oldest and most important countries in Europe. It has played a prominent role in world politics since the time of Charlemagne in the early Middle Ages. France became part of the Roman Empire when Julius Ceasar completed his conquest of the country in 50 B.C.E. Germanic tribes invaded France after the fall of Rome, but the country was reunified under Charlemagne in the ninth century. In more recent times, France became the model of the peasants' revolt against the old medieval hierarchy when the Bastille prison fell on July 14, 1789, an event that marked the beginning of the French Revolution. Four years later Louis XVI, the first European king to lose his head in a popular revolution, was executed. In the years that followed, hundreds of French aristocrats were beheaded. What is more, the centuries-old notion of the king's rule by divine right, along with the idea that the entire aristocratic hierarchy was sanctioned by the Christian God, died with these noblemen. Napoleon Bonaparte established an aristocracy of sorts when he declared himself emperor of France in 1804, but his empire fell when he was defeated by Lord Wellington at the battle of Waterloo. In the twentieth century, France was occupied by Germany during World War II, and in the years following the war France suffered significant defeats in Indochina and Algeria. The French colonies in Indochina and North Africa gained their independence in the 1950s and 1960s. France remains a key player in these and other areas of the world.

The French have a strong national identity and are composed of several cultural groups. Descendants of the Gauls, Celtic tribes that began migrating from the Rhine Valley more than a thousand years ago, form the largest cultural group in France. Other groups include the Basque people, Germanic peoples, and, more recently, southeast Asians and African émigrés from France's former colonies and protectorates.

1   "While I was living in France," an American academic told me, "I often saw the following scene: a child does something which his parents don't like, or one of his parents doesn't like. The parent tells him to stop. The child continues. Nothing happens, the parents don't say anything and don't do anything. The child continues to do what he was doing. The parents repeat, 'Will you stop that?' and it continues. What good does it do to tell children to stop doing something, if nothing happens when they don't?"

2   An American student who had just spent the year in France after having made several shorter visits told me, still horrified, about her experience in a Parisian student dorm, which she summarized in these indignant terms: "They treated us like children." What had deeply shocked her was that during one residents' meeting, the director of the dormitory announced that she had gone into the students' rooms while they were away, "because you can learn a lot about people by seeing how they keep their rooms." This particular student shared her room with a French woman and unflinchingly accepted the comings and goings of the maid. It was therefore the fact that the director had entered without permission that seemed an intolerable assault on her private life. In addition, she was surprised that the French students, who were in the majority, did not seem to find this intrusion upsetting or even surprising. Similarly, the nightwatchman treated her "like a little girl" the first time she arrived a quarter of an hour after the curfew at 11 p.m. Not knowing where else to go hardly a month after her arrival in Paris, she insistently banged on the door of the dormitory. The night watchman "lectured her" and "yelled at her." She added this remark which I found surprising: "And he didn't even ask me where I had been; he would have found out that I was coming from the other side of Paris where I had seen a play for a class, and that I had a good reason for being late." The last straw (which convinced her to leave the dormitory) was when the director's assistant ("hardly older than I was") reprimanded her for having forgotten to sign the register upon leaving by making a gesture as if to slap her, while she was "in the presence of an American friend who was in France for the first time" (and who therefore could only interpret the scene from an American perspective).

3   Americans and the French seem to be in complete agreement on only one point: they do not understand (which means they do not approve

of) the way in which the children of "the other culture" are raised. Thus, many "American" situations can be displeasing to a French person. Here are a few, such as they were recounted to me:

4 —I am engaged in an interesting conversation with X, an American. Just as he is about to answer my question, or else at the most important point in my discourse, his child comes in and interrupts our conversation in what I consider to be an intrusive manner. Instead of teaching him manners, X turns and listens to him. He may even get up, apologize for the interruption by saying that he must give or show something to the little one and that he will return "in a few minutes." X comes back, a smile on his lips, asking, "Where were we?" and resumes the conversation. The worst of it is that if the little child comes back because he didn't find what he was looking for or because something is not working or because he is proud of having finished what he was doing and wants to tell X, he won't hesitate to do so. And X will not hesitate to respond. No doubt about it, these Americans have no manners.

5 —We're at the dinner table. Y, an American, is sitting next to her three-year-old daughter, who has demanded a setting identical to that of the grown-ups (and received it from the hostess, since the mother seemed to think it was only normal) and is "acting cute." She asks for soup, then refuses to eat it. Her mother is trying to persuade her, saying, "You'll see, it's very good." The little girl finally takes a spoonful, then exclaims, "I hate it, it's yucky." The mother says, "You're going to make Z (the hostess) feel bad," or "No, it's very good," or else (are you ready for this?) "Z's cooking doesn't seem to be a hit with the little one." Slaps, that's what they deserve, these kids! And the parents too, while we're at it! You should see them in restaurants. The kids get up, mosey about, sometimes they even come up to your table to make conversation; they eat like pigs, talk loudly, do whatever they please, as if they were at home; they think they can do anything.

6 —I'm riding in my car, on the main street of a residential neighborhood. It is not a small, out-of-the-way street that is isolated and quiet, and it certainly is not a dead end. It is a major, busy street. I have to slow down. Right in the middle of the street, on the road, children, yes, children are playing baseball, or with frisbees. They stop, "allow me" to go by with big smiles, sometimes even a little tap on my car. Can't they play elsewhere? This isn't a ghetto—there are big parks nearby, huge lawns surrounding their houses. No, they must have the street, and so they take it, that's all there is to it. They are nice enough to let me go by, why should I complain? You should see how they're dressed, barefoot, right in the middle of the street. These Americans are impossible. . . .

7 The preceding examples represent just a partial collage of comments that I have heard repeatedly concerning American children. And I am sure we (French) can all provide examples, which we have either seen or heard about, concerning their "lack of manners." Spoiled,

ill-bred, undisciplined; with no manners, no reserve; egotistical, impolite, constantly moving, running all over, touching everything, making noise ... Everyone has his favorite story, and not only in France. Many French parents who have been living in the United States for a long time, whose children have been raised in the American style "despite" them, complained about American schools during interviews conducted by my students. "No discipline," "they let them do what they want," "not enough homework," "no general education ... even I, with the little education I have, know the capital of every country in the world. ... Go find an American who can tell you that." "No respect," "spoiled rotten," are comments I have often heard and recorded myself. "Here, Madame, it is not the parents who raise their children, it is the children who raise their parents. ... I'm proud to have remained French. ... But don't get me wrong, I'm also proud of being an American."

8. Similarly, Americans have much to say about French children, or rather, perhaps, about French parents. Here is an example told to me by an American, who had obviously been mystified by the scene: "We were having a drink at the house of some friends. She's French (like my wife), and he's an American (like me). Our children are having fun together, running in and out of the room, absorbed in chasing each other. The adults' conversation is suddenly interrupted by G., the French lady of the house, who loudly scolds the kids, all the kids, hers and ours, 'because they're making too much noise and preventing us from speaking calmly.' This threatening and screaming happens again—with increasing stridency—each time the children forget G.'s command in the heat of their chasing. When we get home, I mention to my wife that G. was the one who had made any conversation nearly impossible with her loud interruptions." He adds, with a look of amusement, that G. is always complaining about the "rudeness" of Americans, and about the "atrocious" manner in which they bring up their children ("and in addition she annoys me because she always says to her husband and me each time she criticizes Americans, 'not you two, of course, you're the exception, we've found the only two tolerable Americans' ... but I'm also an American"). ...

9. The opinion of my students on this subject is the same as that of many Americans. Indeed, more than one American has expressed surprise, in my presence, at how French children can remain quiet *(sage)* for hours. Even the expression *être sage,* or *rester sage* makes them smile. It is an expression which is (literally) untranslatable into English (in this case, one would use *well-behaved* which is closer to *qui se conduit bien*). For an American, a child who remains quiet for long periods of times is either sick or, in a sense, oppressed by his parents—parents who restrain his movements, his space, his words, and his freedom. An American would say that he is not a child but a small grown-up.

10 A scene on the platform at the train station in Rambouillet would seem to confirm the American interpretation. A mother says to her daughter (two or three years old) who is squatting, "Come on, get up. . . . I'll help you walk! . . . Just you wait and see." Then, a few seconds later, "I told you not to mess around like that. . . . Now look how dirty you are. . . . Come on, let me wipe off your hand . . . and then you go and put it in your mouth!" And, as if to prevent her daughter from getting her hands dirty again by touching the ground, she picks her up.

11 A young American who had spent a year in South of France, told me how she had been reprimanded by a little three- or four-year-old French girl in the park. A "teeny-weeny girl" who was passing by, a few steps behind her father, stopped and lectured her on her bare feet, adding that a big girl like her should know better. The father didn't reprimand his daughter. For the American in question, French people "learn to be arrogant" from day one.

12 And then there are scenes, like the ones described at the beginning of this essay, which evoke the incomprehension or the surprise of the foreigner faced with an unfamiliar situation, a question mark rather than a judgment. Thus the comments of students who have spent some time in French families. One au pair girl said, "When guests were coming for dinner, the parents repeated the rules to the children before the meal." Another one, who took care of a little two-year-old boy in an upper-middle-class family (in a house so large that the children had a separate apartment from their parents, with a remote monitor video camera in their room), said, "I was not supposed to let B. cry, because his father didn't like the noise when they had guests." "When French children are young, the father doesn't pay much attention to them; the children must remain quiet and well-behaved in his presence." "French children do not often sit down just to chat with their parents. One evening, after dinner, I stayed with the parents to talk and watch television. The next morning, their daughter asked me why I had done that." "Madame N. had two sons, a three-year-old and an eight-year-old. The boys always played together, and it was rare to see them with other children. One Sunday, we had a big meal with the entire family. The two boys remained completely still for hours. They didn't say a word at the table. . . . The French demand that a child, even if he is very young, know how to behave himself." "Obedience is very important in French families, the child must respect his parents' wishes and, above all, must not question things. The children are very well-behaved, especially when the father is present. In contrast, when an American child is told to do something by his parents, he often asks "why?" and very often the parents explain why. In the French family, the father is always right." "In the family I lived with, the mother accompanied her daughter to her piano lessons and stayed there during the lessons. She monitored her daughter's progress, even if she had already heard her

play a thousand times at home. American children go by themselves to their music or dance lessons, and even if their mothers go with them, they usually don't stay. In the same way, American parents let their children go to school all alone, or else, very often, with friends. In France, I had to bring the children to school and pick them up every day, even if they lived only two minutes away. There was also a crowd of parents who came to pick up their children. They too lived very close to the school." "Parents protect their children in several ways. Outside, their physical movements are restricted: 'Don't run,' 'calm down,' 'slowly,' 'not so loud,' 'don't yell.' In the bookstore, the mother helps her daughter to choose her books. The mother is really the one who chooses them. American children choose their own books." "French children can play all by themselves. . . . When I brought the little girl to the park, she played with her doll all alone, unless her brother was there, in which case, before going to play with her brother, she liked to say to her doll 'don't get dirty, you hear' in imitation of her mother." "My friend's children were five, ten, and thirteen, but they had no problem in playing together. American children, on the other hand, don't like playing with their little brothers or sisters." "It is not uncommon to see a parent slap his child in public. . . . American parents wait to get home to punish their children, because it is very important that the child not be ridiculed in front of his friends."

13   This final sentence explains why the American who had told me of her experience in a student dormitory was so annoyed at having been reprimanded, even gently, in front of her American friend who was in France for the first time. She considered herself to be an adult and was treated like a child, and in the cruelest fashion to boot: ridiculed in front of a friend.

14   I cannot go into all the cases that I collected. But if there were any doubts as to the differences between the French and the Americans in the realm of parent-child relationships, I think that the preceding pages will have sufficed to eliminate them. The analysis of these firsthand reports, of my interviews and observations, helped me become aware of the distance separating the cultural premises informing these relationships.

15   A French woman told me, to show her joy and approval on the day of her daughter's second marriage; "For me, it's the first time she's marrying," thereby erasing, in one fell swoop, the seven years of her daughter's life which had been dedicated to her first marriage and the first husband, whom—as she was aware—I knew well. Only the second marriage counted for her (as she told all the guests) not only, I think, because she liked and approved of the second husband very much, but also, and especially, I believe, because her daughter, who until then had refused maternity, was expecting a baby and was radiant with joy. In her eyes, her daughter had finally reached maturity. During the intimate reception which followed the ceremony, the mother expressed concern more than

Chapter 4 Exploring Ideas from Several Cultures 91

once about her daughter's health, insisting that she sit down and rest. The other members of her family, and of her husband's family, were doing the same. My young friend's nice round belly no longer seemed to belong to her. She had suddenly become the repository of a being over whom both families had rights.

16 Getting married or living together is already a social act, of course, inasmuch as it consists of presenting oneself, if only to one's closest friends and family, as someone's partner in a permanent association (even if it later turns out to be temporary). But neither the family nor society acquires rights over the partner in question. As soon as two people become parents, however, they are expected to become "good parents," under the surveillance of many vigilant eyes. To bring a child into the world is therefore an eminently social act in France. It is easier to understand, in this context, why many French feminists sang the praises of childbirth as self-discovery, as physical joy, as intimately personal, as egotistical. What seems to be a contradiction to American feminists (a feminist expressing joy at being a mother) becomes easily understandable once we see that these women are reclaiming the experience of childbirth for themselves, which goes against the implicit definition of childbirth as a social act.

17 Indeed, as soon as I become a parent in France, I must answer to society for my behavior toward the child. As a parent, my role is to transform this "malleable, innocent, impressionable, and irresponsible" creature into a social being, a responsible member of the society, which is prepared to integrate him or her in exchange for a pledge of allegiance. This means that on becoming a parent, it is first and foremost to the society that I incur an obligation, a debt, rather than to my child, who comes second. If I give priority to my child, I isolate myself from this society.

18 A child is therefore a link between his parents and society—others, people in general, whoever is outside of the father-mother-child triangle; and even within this triangle, whoever, at any moment is outside of the relationship between one parent (mother or father) and the child. In other words, my behavior with respect to my child is constantly subject to the judgment of others, which explains why I am always tempted to justify myself when my child's conduct does not correspond, or might not correspond, to what a third party, even someone totally unknown to me, might expect. If my child "behaves badly," therefore, I am immediately placed in a conflictful situation: I must show others that I know the rules and that I am wearing myself out trying to teach them to my child; at the same time, I must show my child that I love him or her anyway, that the bond between us cannot be destroyed so easily, since it is precisely because of this given of parental love that the child will attempt to change, to improve the conduct that displeases me so because it displeases others. This could even lead me, as a parent, to create a perfect double-bind: "You are not my daughter any more" or "You are not my son any more." As

a matter of fact, this threat, which is quite common, can have meaning and thereby bring about results only insofar as it contains its own negation. Indeed, if by saying "You are not my child any more" I were confirming a real rupture, as when I say "You are not my friend any more" or "You are no longer my lover," my child would have no reason to behave differently in order to please me. It is because I, and (French) society, have established my love as noncontingent and the ties that bind us as indestructible, even if we no longer want them, that my threat can have an effect. My child and I know, implicitly, that what I am saying is: "You are behaving yourself in a way that shames me, that makes me feel bad, that hurts me. You are not behaving like the perfect child worthy of my love. Other people's disapproval of your conduct is a reflection on me."

19   From this perspective, it becomes apparent that the constant commands at the table ("Don't put your elbows on the table," "Sit up straight," "Don't talk with your mouth full," etc.), the scolding in cafés, the "bawling out" in the street, the quick spanking or slap just about anywhere, the lecture, or even, simply, the reproving gesture or look, all fall into a single category. It is less a matter of showing my anger, which would be impolite since I must remain in control of myself in public (hence the "wait till we get home . . ."), than it is of showing others the efforts I am making to bring up my child correctly. In other words, by scolding, slapping, and repeating "Are you going to stop that?" I am justifying myself in the eyes of others. If my child behaves poorly, it is not my fault, I've done everything I could to make things different. I am a "good parent," but I have to fight against the nature of children ("You know how kids are") or, even worse, against "bad influences." The older my child gets, the more the "bad influences" will be responsible for his deviant behavior, and certainly for all criminal conduct. (Question: Are there parents who prevent their children from having a bad influence on their friends?)

20   The pressure must be very strong for it to maintain such a hold over parents. It is. We are all familiar with the reproving glances that converge upon parents who "don't know how to control their child." If these glances have no effect, bystanders turn to each other with gestures of disapproval for the "guilty parents" and finally resort to making comments indirectly addressed to the parents. In an extreme case, if the parents remain oblivious to even the most clearly expressed reprobation, it is not unusual to see others intervene directly, as often happens at the beach ("It isn't nice to throw sand on people," "If I catch you . . ."). Moreover, in the absence of parents—in the neighborhood, in the street, and so on—neighbors feel invested with parental responsibility with respect to all the children they know and even those they don't ("If your mother (father) could see you . . ."). A little scene, which I very recently witnessed in Paris, illustrates this perfectly. A waiting room, filled with various families. It is a long wait, people are getting impatient, children are running around, but in what is still a "tolerable" fashion. One little

boy has obviously gone too far, as a grandmother, who is part of our group, tells me: "There was a little boy who was kicking his grandmother, so I caught him and told him, 'You're tired, aren't you, I'm sure you didn't mean to kick your grandmother, but you're very tired. Now be a good little boy and go ask your grandmother to forgive you.' Really, I wouldn't want to be his grandmother." The woman who told me this seemed satisfied and rather proud of her action (she told me about it several times), of having put the little boy on the right track. I think she would have been scandalized if I had told her even in a polite manner that "she should mind her own business" or that she had assumed rights that in no way were hers, which would probably have been the American interpretation of the scene.

21   This assumption of responsibility works both ways. A child by himself (or with other children) who is crying will be consoled, protected, helped, and reassured by a passing adult. Thus, on the whole, all adults are responsible for all children, and, within this group, certain adults have the exclusive care of certain children, their own, but on condition that they "pass the test" to which they are constantly subjected by any member of the group.

22   To understand the American situation, one need only in a sense reverse all the signs. Of course, in this case too, the parents take responsibility for the education of their children. But the essential difference is that this responsibility is theirs alone. When I (an American) become a parent, I incur an obligation to my children rather than to society, which comes second. My obligation is not to teach my children the rules and practices of society, but above all to give them every possible chance to discover and develop their "natural qualities," to exploit their gifts, and to blossom.

23   Thus, when I raise my child in the French style, in a sense what I am doing is clearing a patch of ground, pulling out the weeds, cutting, planting, and so on, in order to make a beautiful garden which will be in perfect harmony with the other gardens. This means that I have in mind a clear idea of the results I want to obtain, and of what I must do to obtain them. My only difficulty will lie in the nature of the soil, given that I apply myself regularly to the task, that is. But when I raise my child American-style, it is almost as if I were planting a seed in the ground without knowing for sure what type of seed it was. I must devote myself to giving it food, air, space, light, a supporting stake if necessary, care, water—in short, all that the seed needs to develop as best it can. And then I wait, I follow the developments closely, I attend to any needs what may arise, and I try to guess what type of plant it will be. I can hope for the best, of course. But if I try to give shape to my dreams, to transform my tomato seed into a potato, for example, I am not a "good parent." To be a good parent, I must therefore give my children every chance, every "opportunity" possible, and then "let nature take its course." If I teach them good

manners and social practices, it is to give them an additional chance, knowing that they will need these things to "succeed" in life, to fulfill themselves—that music, dance, and sports lessons, books, toys and all types of gadgets, will favor their development. Once I have assured them a "higher education," that is to say, four years of study at the universities of their choice, I will have done everything possible to give them the best means to realize all their dreams, to choose who and what they want to be.

24   In other words, it is the French parents who are put to the test; their role as spokespersons for society and their performance as teachers are evaluated. But it is the American children who are put to the test; it is up to them to show their parents what they can do with the chances that have been given them; up to them to prove that they haven't wasted these chances but made maximum use of them; up to them to satisfy the hopes their parents have blindly placed in them.

25   From this perspective, it becomes clear that French childhood is an apprenticeship, during which one learns the rules and acquires "good habits"; it is a time of discipline, of imitation of models, of preparation for the role of adult. As one French informant told me, "we had a lot of homework to do and little time to play." American childhood is, on the contrary, a period of great freedom, of games, of experimentation and exploration, during which restrictions are only imposed when there is a serious threat of danger.

26   In the same vein, American parents avoid as much as possible criticizing their children, making fun of their tastes, or telling them constantly "how to do things." French parents, on the other hand, train their children to "defend themselves well," verbally that is. Thus, by ordering the child "not to speak if he has nothing to say," "not to act cute," or "not to say silly things," I force her or him to discover the best ways of retaining my attention. According to an American informant, "In France, if the child has something to say, others listen to him. But the child can't take too much time and still retain his audience; if he delays, the family finishes his sentences for him. This gets him in the habit of formulating his ideas better before he speaks. Children learn to speak quickly, and to be interesting." To be amusing as well. This is to say, the child is encouraged to imitate adults but not to copy them "like a parrot." The implicit message is "do like me, but differently." While teaching my child the rules by criticizing or making fun of him or her ("you're really going out like that?"; "you look ridiculous in those clothes"; "Come on, you're joking; you couldn't be going out dressed like that"; "A green shirt and red shorts? Sure . . . going to the circus?"; I force him or her at the same time to break free of me by affirming very definite tastes and well-formed opinions.

27   An American parent will try to do exactly the opposite. As an "ideal" parent, I will patiently listen to all that my child wants to tell me without

interrupting. I will compliment him or her for having dressed without assistance (in the beginning), with no comment on the strange assortment he or she has chosen. Later, I will allow my child to buy the clothes he or she chooses, even if they make my hair stand on end, if my suggestions ("don't you think that . . .") have been rejected. The most important thing here, as in all the games we play together, is to give children plenty of room to make their own mistakes and to find their own solutions.

28   When a child reaches adolescence (the exact age is unimportant, let's just say that it represents the period between childhood and adulthood), the situation seems to reverse itself. For French children, the prize for this long apprenticeship, for these years of obedience and good conduct, is the freedom to do what they want, that is, to stay out late, to "have a good time," maybe to get drunk, to have sexual experiences, to travel, and so on. Even if their parents continue their roles as educators and critics, deep down they recognize the adolescents' rights to "do exactly as they please," or at least they resign themselves to this ("youth must have its fling"). The fact that the adolescent continues to be fed, housed, and clothed by his or her parents in no way affects his or her "independence": I am independent if I know what I want and do what I want no matter how things look from the outside. It is therefore possible for my parents to continue to remonstrate with me, to "give me orders," or to advise me; I may grow impatient with this, but it is essentially unimportant, since I can always let them "say what they want," let them play their roles, without it producing any greater change in my behavior than a nominal acquiescence. Thus, in the student dormitory described by the American earlier, it is likely that the French students weren't bothered by the director's inspection of their rooms, the assistant's remonstrances, or the night watchman's yelling and lecturing because all that corresponded to the quasi-parental roles that these people in charge were supposed to assume, and all one had to do was let them play their roles in order to be "left in peace." On the other hand, it seems to me that a French student would have found any questions from the night watchman concerning her arrival at the dormitory after the curfew out of place (and would have refused to answer them), whereas the American student regretted the fact that he had accused her without giving her the opportunity to explain her lateness and justify it.

29   American adolescents insist more on the exterior signs of independence. The first sign will be economic: very early on, they will show that they can earn money and "take care of themselves," that is, pay for everything they would consider it "childish" to expect parents to pay for (records, a stereo, sporting equipment, a motor bike, etc.). This is often interpreted by French people as indisputable proof of the "well-known American materialism." In fact, what young Americans are doing, is, on the contrary, proving that they are capable of taking care of themselves,

showing that they are capable of putting to good use the chances their parents made every effort (to the point of sacrifice) to give them. The second exterior sign of independence is affective: it is important to "leave home," even if one gets along marvelously with one's parents, if only to reassure them. American parents worry if their children hesitate to "stand on their own two feet," if they give what parents interpret as signs of "dependency," of "insecurity," of an "unhealthy" need for protection, or if they "act like children." This means that even if, deep down, I (an American) think that my child is still immature, it is important that the outward signs I give to the child show the opposite, not because I am a hypocrite but because I am convinced that it will help him or her to reach maturity. And it is even more important that I do this in the presence of others—in the presence of my child's friends as well as in the presence of mine.

30   In exchange, all my children's "successes" belong to them alone. I can go to all their tennis matches, or anxiously attend their concerts, but I would indignantly reject the slightest suggestion that they owe their success to me in any way. I only gave them the chance.

31   Since Americans "do what they want," in a sense, from childhood, it is much less important for them to "know" what they want very early on. Parents accept, if they do not encourage, having their children "experience different lifestyles," hesitate between careers—in short, not "settle down too soon," which could reduce their chances and restrict their potential (which explains why most programs of university study, including law and medicine, include four preliminary years of college). The weight of these maximum opportunities given to young Americans puts very strong pressure on them, early on, to "prove themselves," to show their parents (and the world) what they are capable of. But since the expectations have never been clearly defined, and ideally cannot be so, logically there can be no moment when the goal is reached. The implicit parental injunction is to always seize every opportunity, to climb farther and higher, without rest, to always be "on the go." Not to do so is to condemn oneself to mediocrity, to wasted chances, to the ultimate failure which consists of not exploiting one's human potential to the fullest.

32   One of the consequences of all of the above is that the majority of French people interviewed have better memories of their adolescence ("it was sheer madness") than of their childhood, happy as it may have been. Childhood is full of restrictions: adolescence is, or is reconstructed in retrospect to be, a burst of freedom, memorable experiences with friends, a kind of happy interlude. One can let loose and kid around, have an attack of the giggles, or play "practical jokes," which Americans of the same age have trouble understanding, because for them these are the hallmarks of childish behavior.

33   In contrast, when Americans reach adolescence, they are suddenly confronted with all sorts of expectations, real or imagined; they are

expected to take on responsibilities and to perform. It is time for them to take their places on a stage from which they will no longer step down without a profound sense of failure. Hence the nervousness, the panic which often seizes American adolescents when they must say goodbye to the total freedom, the games and carefree attitude of their childhood world. For the majority of Americans, childhood becomes a paradise lost. Whether or not I had a happy childhood is irrelevant; if I hadn't, it means that I was cheated twice: cheated of my right to "opportunities" and cheated of my right to a few years of paradise, to that blessed time when I neither had to be an adult nor pretend to be one.

34   Thus, whereas young Americans do not understand why young French people often "act like children," young French people in the United States often remark that young Americans are "too serious," that they "don't know how to have fun," that they "give boring parties," in short, that they "act like adults."

35   These differences between young American and French people, this systematic inversion of the signs, so to speak, between the two systems, are also found in the relationships between children and adults in the two cultures.

36   While French parents educate their children, they cannot, at the same time, be their playmates, save in exceptional circumstances when the rules are, so to speak, suspended. And in this case, the parent plays at being a child, thus putting him- or herself on the same level as the child. Whenever he or she wants to play, the French child turns to the other children in the family, no matter what their ages, and is heartily encouraged by his or her parents to do so. He or she is also encouraged to serve as a replacement for the parents when with the younger children, at school and in the street. Parents reinforce this solidarity between the children by refusing to intervene in case of a dispute. In the words of one informant, "When I went to my mother, I got an extra smack . . . so it didn't take me long to learn." It is therefore up to the children to "work things out among themselves." And never, never should they come and "tell"; this is definitely not a way of getting on the parents' good side, but quite the contrary. Little by little, this sytem teaches children to stick together against parental authority. And this relationship is reproduced at school. At the same time, within the family structure, each parent establishes an independent relationship with each child, and each child does the same with his or her brothers and sisters. Each family member is therefore engaged in a network of independent relationships and is witness to (or judge of) the relationships between each family member and the others. In the case of an argument between two family members, this allows a third, who is uninvolved in the dispute, to play the role of the go-between, to interpret one's behavior for the other ("You know, you have to understand your father"; "You know, your mother is very tired these days"; "Don't get angry, he's studying for finals and is very nervous"). The

child therefore gets used to a multitude of simultaneous relationships and to the presence of intermediaries, of go-betweens.

37   The role played by the intermediary in "arranging the situation" explains why a parent's intervention at school and, as we shall see, at the university is accepted or at least tolerated by French children, whereas it would be unacceptable if not unbearable to American children. Thus, a French couple, in France, asked me to explain the higher education system in the United States because their son wanted to go there. Both of them were educated and "modern." I explained. Armed with my experience of frequent cultural misunderstandings, I was preparing to discuss what I consider to be most important, that is to say, the expectations to which French people would not be accustomed. To illustrate this, I began to tell a story that some (French) friends had just told me, about how they had furiously intervened at the *grande école* (a unique French institution) because their son, it seems, had been slighted by the "incompetence" of some of its staff. I was about to say that this type of thing could not happen in the United States or would be considered very inappropriate (by the son himself, who would feel he was being taken charge of "like a child") when, fortunately for the relationship between the couple and myself, I was interrupted by the mother who said, "Oh, yes, it's like Alain," and told me, indignantly, about all of her protests at the medical school in which her son was enrolled concerning the "stupid" aggravation they had given him. I immediately stopped talking, experiencing the dizzy sensation one feels at the edge of a cliff.

38   American children are encouraged very early on to play with other children their own age (and therefore outside the family), to "make friends," to learn to establish relationships with strangers, to "become popular" among their peers. At home, they seek the approval or encouragement (and, hopefully, some day, admiration) of their parents; it is therefore only logical that they feel in competition with their brothers and sisters. The same thing happens at school: they must both make friends among their classmates and compete with them for the attention and approval of teachers, and later on of professors, for whom they will "do the best they can." This competition is not meant to be destructive; rather it aims to stimulate children, to extract or elicit the best possible performance from each one, and "may the best one win." And like the parent, the teacher will not allow him- or herself to criticize a student's work in public, but will give the student the means to find and develop the area he or she can excel in. A teacher who makes curt, scornful, or even joking comments about each paper he or she returns, as would be possible in the French system, might be considered sick or deranged—in any case, Inept at teaching. The class would simply be deserted, as I've seen happen in an American university to a young instructor right off the boat from France. The American student, accustomed since childhood to explanations rather than to pronouncements or encouragements to emulate, does not

hesitate to ask questions, to discuss, to disagree, to question—behavior which always surprises French students visiting the United States. What surprises them even more is that the professor does not take the question as a sign of hostility, a challenge to his or her authority, but treats it as a sign of intellectual independence, or a sincere desire to better understand the question or to participate in the discussion of a subject that interests her or him—an attitude which a "good" professor will seek to encourage. We should note here that American students spontaneously turn to the professor rather than to their classmates, thereby recreating the relationship they have established with their parents. The relationship is of concern only to two people. No one has the right to intervene, to "interfere" in this relationship, not even, in the family, the other parent.

39 For the young French person, then, reaching maturity consists of assuming the role for which my parents and other educators have prepared me, that of being an "educator" (in the broadest sense) in turn, of taking my place and taking on my responsibilities in society, and beginning the cycle all over again. Whatever my age, though, my conduct will always be a reflection on my parents, who share my successes as well as my disappointments. At this time, I will also begin to attend to my parents' well-being and will tacitly commit myself to taking care of them in their old age, to reversing the roles. I will, in turn, be judged, by whoever feels it is his right, on the way in which I treat my parents.

40 For an American, maturity is a much more fluid concept which varies from person to person. I can, therefore, be a responsible adult (I have a permanent job, a house, a family, I pay my bills and taxes) and still be considered immature by certain people, whereas others will envy the fact that I have retained a certain "childlike" side (a taste for taking risks, a capacity for wonderment and amazement, a refusal to accept the impossible, etc.). In the end, I alone decide if I have reached maturity or not. And just as my parents always went out of their way to allow me to be responsible for myself, often at the price of a strict control on their desires to do otherwise, so I will not treat my old parents as children by inflicting on them the "indignity" of taking care of them (at my home) but will make certain of the security and comfort of their environment and of the possibility of their having a "social life" with people whose company they appreciate, that is to say, people their own age. My family and I will visit them, but they have earned the right to have a quiet or fast-paced life, as they choose, in any case a life free of the demands and tears of small children. For a French person, however, this means that Americans "abandon" their aged parents.

41 Faced with such profound cultural differences at practically each stage in the life cycle, we can only marvel, not at the number of sources for misunderstandings, but rather at the possibilities for—and the existence of—any understandings at all.

Reading for Meaning

1. Raymonde Carroll shows that having a child "is . . . an eminently social act in France." Reread her examples of parenting in France and explain what she might mean by this statement.

2. What does it mean to be a "good parent" in America? How does this definition differ from the expectations of parents in France?

3. Carroll describes adolescence in France as a relatively carefree time following a well-disciplined childhood. The American adolescence, in contrast, is the time when the child is expected to take responsibility for his or her own life and make use of the advantages his or her parents have provided. How would you describe your teen years and the adolescence of people you know or have observed?

4. To what extent do parental expectations influence young people's lives in your experience?

Comparing Texts

1. In "Somebody's Baby," published initially in the *New York Times Magazine,* Barbara Kingsolver finds that Americans are not sympathetic with children's irrational public displays. She reports: "In the United States, I have been told in restaurants: 'We come here to get *away* from kids.' (This for no infraction on my daughter's part that I could discern, other than being visible.) On an airplane, I hear a man tell a beleaguered woman whose infant was bawling . . . 'If you can't keep that thing quiet, you should keep it at home.'" Kingsolver concludes that in the United States "we think of child rearing as an individual job, not a collective responsibility." How do the French express their disapproval of children's undisciplined behavior? Do they also regard child rearing as "an individual job" rather than a "collective responsibility," or does the community seem to play some role in training the child?

2. Barbara Kingsolver remarks in "Somebody's Baby" that Spaniards genuinely appreciate children, in marked contrast to attitudes toward kids in the United States. She describes the culture shock she experienced while living in Spain when she realized that "people there like kids."

> They don't just say so, they *do*. Widows in black, buttoned down C.E.Os, purple-sneakered teen-agers, the butcher, the baker, all would stop on the street to have little chats with my daughter. . . . Whenever Camille grew cranky in a restaurant . . . the waiters flirted and brought her little presents, and nearby diners looked on with that sweet, wistful gleam of eye I'd thought diners reserved for the dessert tray. What I discovered in Spain was a culture that held children to be its meringues and eclairs. My own culture, it seemed to me in retrospect, tended to regard children as a sort of toxic-waste product.

How does Raymonde Carroll's description of the way children are treated in the United States compare to Kingsolver's experiences? In your own experience, are children appreciated in the United States? How does this culture show its appreciation or disregard for children?

Ideas for Writing

1. Interview several people you know who have been to other countries or who do not necessarily identify with middle class culture in the United States. Ask them to describe the kinds of behavior they have observed as common and acceptable for children in public places. Also ask them to comment on the extent to which children are appreciated, tolerated, or frowned upon. Write a paper in which you discuss your findings.

2. Write a paper in which you examine whether freedom or discipline were most characteristic of the child rearing experienced by people in your age group, by family members, or by fellow students. Interview your subjects to discover how their parents or other adults taught them social skills and how they were expected to behave in supermarkets, restaurants, and other public settings.

3. Choose a few situations that Raymonde Carroll describes in "Parents and Children." Write a paper in which you imagine how you or adults you know would react in similar situations. Then describe what motivations or assumptions about children and the role of parents might explain those reactions.

Writing before Reading

To what extent were music, singing, dance, or drama available to you when you were growing up? What values did these activities or similar pastimes have for you and other members of your family?

CHILDREN AND RITUAL IN BALI
Margaret Mead

Margaret Mead (1901–1978) is known for her studies in cultural anthropology. As a graduate student at Columbia University, she wrote Coming of Age in Samoa (1928), *a published dissertation that established her reputation. In 1938 she wrote* Sex and Temperament in Three Primitive Societies. *In this book Mead discusses sex roles and aggression among native populations in New Guinea, Bali, and Samoa, cultures she had studied extensively. In 1972 she published her autobiography,* Blackberry Winter: My Earlier Years. *Because of her insistence that culture determines personality, Mead's methods and the results of her research have been challenged in the past few decades. Her defenders point out that her work is most valuable for its implied comparisons with cultural practices in the United States.*

Facts about Bali

Bali is located on one of the islands that form part of Indonesia. Dutch traders opened Bali to the West in 1597. For more than two hundred years, the Dutch and Indonesians were major trading partners. In 1816 the Dutch established colonial rule over Bali and the rest of Indonesia. The country gained its independence in 1949. The people of Bali are mostly farmers and ranchers. Unlike the rest of Islamic Indonesia, the people of Bali practice Hinduism: the Balinese favor the ceremonial and dramatic elements in the religion.

1. In Bali, children are called "small human beings," and the conception of the nature and place of the child is different from that of the West. The whole of life is seen as a circular stage on which human beings, born small, as they grow taller, heavier, and more skilled, play predetermined roles, unchanging in their main outlines, endlessly various and subject to improvisation in detail.

2. The world of the dead is one part of the circle, from which human souls return, born again into the same family every fourth generation, to stay too briefly—dying before they have shared rice—or for a long time, or even for too long, for it is inappropriate for great-grandparents to be alive at the same time as their great-grandchildren. Such lingerers have to pay a penny to their great-grandchildren, chance-met on the street. The newborn child and the aged great-grandparent are both too close to the other world for easy entrance into the temple. The baby cannot enter until after a special feast at three and a half or seven months, and the very aged enter though a special side gate.

3. The newborn are treated as celestial creatures entering a more humdrum existence and, at the moment of birth, are addressed with high-sounding honorific phrases reserved for gods, the souls of ancestors, princes, and people of a higher caste. Human beings do not increase in stature and importance, as is so often the case in societies where men have only one life to live; rather, they round a half-circle in which middle age, being farthest from the other world, is the most secular. There is little acceptance of any task being difficult or inappropriate for a child, except that an infant at birth is, of course, expected to do nothing for itself. Words are put into the mouth of the infant, spoken on its behalf by an adult; the hands of the seven-month-old baby are cupped to receive holy water, folded in prayer, opened to waft the incense offered to it as a god,

and when the ceremony is over the child sits, dreamily repeating the gestures which its hands have momentarily experienced.¹

4   The Balinese may comment with amusement but without surprise if the leading metallophone player in a noted orchestra is so small that he has to have a stool in order to reach the keys; the same mild amusement may be expressed if someone takes up a different art after his hands have a tremor of age to confuse their precision. But in a continuum within which the distinction between the most gifted and the least gifted is muted by the fact that everyone participates, the distinction between child and adult—as performer, as actor, as musician—is lost except in those cases where the distinction is ritual, as where a special dance form requires a little girl who has not reached puberty.

5   This treatment of human history as an unending series of rebirths is matched in the treatment of the calendar. The Balinese have a whole series of weeks, of three, four, five, six, up to ten days, which turn on each other, like wheels of different sizes, and there are important occasions when two or three weeks recurrently coincide. These have special names and may be an occasion for festival—like Galungan, a New Year's feast associated with the souls of the dead, and a post-festival season of special theatricals. But, although there is a way of noting the year in a continuous irreversible sequence, it is seldom used. A man who has labored long to recopy a sacred text on pages of *lontar* palm will simply note, when his task of intricate elaboration of a beautiful archaic script is over, that this was finished on the such-and-such, a recurrent combination of days—as we might say, on Friday the thirteenth of September. The principal calendrical unit, the ceremonial year, is two hundred and ten days long. The lunar calendar simply marks the pattern of planting and harvest.

6   Children, then, are smaller and more fragile than adults, as well as closer to the other world. Their essential personality characteristics—gaiety and seriousness, gentleness or harshness—are recognized early, and those around each child combine to set its formal character in an expected mold. The baby of six months with silver bracelets welded on its tiny wrists, waves and bangs its arms; if someone is hurt in the process, there comes the exclamation, "Isamă is harsh." It takes only a few such acts to stereotype the judgment which will be echoed and re-echoed through its life, setting and defining its ways, but quite forgotten after death as other events—day of birth, experience in other incarnations—combine to give new personality. So, while the people take ritual pains over a corpse—that the individual may be born again fleeter of foot or more beautiful of face—they cannot describe the character or the looks of someone who died two years ago. Personality characteristics are accidents, held gently constant through any given incarnation, that dissolve

---

¹ See *Karba's First Years* (film); Gregory Bateson and Margaret Mead, *Balinese Character: A Photographic Analysis* (New York, New York Academy of Sciences, 1942), Pl. 100, Figs. 1 and 2.

at death. But the baby who is identified as "gay and mischievous" has a way of life plotted out for it, which again is independent of age. Old men who have been "gay" all their lives still know who sleeps with whom in the fields at night in the brief, wordless first encounters which for the Balinese represent the height of passion; and men and women labeled "serious" may bear many children, but people will comment instead on their industriousness in the rice fields or their faithfulness at the temple.

7   The child is made conscious of its sex very early. People pat the little girl's vulva, repeating an adjective for feminine beauty, and applaud the little boy's phallus with the word for "handsome male." The child is fitted into words appropriate to its caste, gestures appropriate to each ceremony, and, before the child can walk, it is taught to dance with its hands. Before he can stand, the little boy, who has sat on his father's knees while his father played the *gamelan,* begins to play himself. Peeking over a house wall, one may see diminutive girls of three, sitting all alone, practicing hand gestures. The child learns to walk around a single walking rail,[2] learning that it is safe as long as it holds to this central support, in danger of falling when it loosens its hold and strays out into the unknown. When it learns to walk, its ventures away from support and parents are controlled by the mother or child nurse mimicking terror and calling it back with threats that are random in content—"Tiger!" "Policeman!" "Snake!" "Feces!"—but constant in theatrical affect, until the child learns that undefined outer space may at any moment be filled with unknown terrors.[3]

8   In the village, in familiar territory, the child learns the directions—*kajă,* the center of the island, where the high mountain of the gods stands; *kĕlod,* toward the sea, the point of least sanctity; and *kangin,* to the right, *kauh,* to the left, when one faces *kajă*. Every act is likely to be expressed in these terms as babies are bidden to come a little *kajă* or to brush a speck off the *kĕlod* side of their face, and little boys of different caste play together happily but learn that the boy of higher caste must get into bed first or sit on the *kajă* side of the food tray.

9   Children learn the vertical hierarchies of life—that the head, even of a casteless peasant child, is something sacred, that a flower which has fallen to the ground from an offering carried on the head may not be replaced in the offering, that those of highest caste or sanctity must be given the highest seats. As they learn to speak, they learn that the words addressed to them by their elders and superiors are never the words in which they may answer, although sometimes the lesson is imperfectly learned, and a low-caste boy will marvel at the fact that "they say Brahmană parents are very polite to their children, that they say *tiang* to

---

[2] See Bateson and Mead, *Balinese Character,* Pl. 17, Figs. 1 and 2; Margaret Mead and Frances Cooke Macgregor, *Growth and Culture: A Photographic Study of Balinese Childhood* (New York, Putnam, 1951), Pl. XXVI, Fig. 7, and Pl. LII, Fig. 3.

[3] See *Karba's First Years* (film); Bateson and Mead, *Balinese Character,* pp. 30–32 and Pl. 46.

them," not knowing that the children must reply with an exaggeratedly more polite term, *titiang,* in which the pronoun "I" is made more self-deprecating by a stylized stutter.

10   From birth until long after they can walk, children live most of their waking hours in human arms, carried in a sling or on the hip, even sleeping suspended about the neck of an adult or a child nurse.[4] They learn a plastic adaptation, to take cognizance of the other's movement in limp relaxation, neither resisting nor wholly following the pounding of the rice or the game the child nurse is playing. When there is teaching to be done, the teacher uses this flaccid adaptivity and, holding the hands and body of the learner with vigorous, precise intent, twists and turns them into place or pattern.[5] Verbal directions are meager; children learn from the feel of other people's bodies and from watching, although this watching itself has a kinesthetic quality. An artist who attempts to draw a group of men will draw himself over and over again, feeling the image.

11   The children are everywhere. Very little babies cannot enter the temple, but the toddler is present in the midst of the most solemn ceremonial, attached to parent or grandparent, watching the blessing of a trance dancer, the throw of coins of the diviner, the killing of the fowl as exorcism. Women attending a theatrical performance carry their babies in their arms, and the front row of every performance is given over to the very small children, who watch and doze and are hastily rescued when the play threatens to break the bounds of the audience square and to involve the crowd in the plot. At the shadow play the children sit in front, and the puppet master increases the number of battles in the plot in proportion to the number of children. As the women kneel in the temple, placing the petals of a flower between their praying fingers, a flower is placed in the hands of the child who is with them. For the temple feast, small children, who at other times may run about stark naked, will appear elaborately dressed, boys in headdress and kris.

12   They look like dolls, and they are treated like playthings, playthings which are more exciting than fighting cocks—over which the men spend many fascinated hours—or the kites and crickets which amuse little boys. Everyone joins in the mild titillating teasing of little babies, flipping their fingers, their toes, their genitals, threatening them, playfully disregarding the sanctity of their heads, and, when the children respond by heightened excitement and mounting tension, the teaser turns away, breaks the thread of interplay, allows no climax.[6] Children learn not to respond, to resist provocation, to skirt the group of elders who would

---

[4] See Bateson and Mead, *Balinese Character,* Pl. 79; Mead and Macgregor, *Growth and Culture,* Pl. XVII.

[5] See *Karba's First Years* (film); Bateson and Mead, *Balinese Character,* Pl. 16.

[6] See *Karba's First Years* (film); Bateson and Mead, *Balinese Character,* p. 32 and Pls. 47–49.

touch or snatch, to refuse the gambit when their mothers borrow babies to make them jealous. They develop an unresponsiveness to the provocative intent of others at the same time that they remain plastic to music and pattern. It is a childhood training which, if followed here, would seem dangerously certain to bring out schizoid trends in the growing child's character.

13   But there is one great difference between Bali and the changing Western world as we know it. In the Western world children are traumatized in childhood in ways which are new and strange, for which no ritual healing, no artistic form, exists in the culture. Those who are very gifted may become prophets, or artists, or revolutionaries, using their hurt, their made deviancy, or their innate deviancy exaggerated by adult treatment as the basis for a new religion or a new art form. Those who are not so gifted or who are less fortunate in finding a medium for their gifts go mad or dwindle away, using little even of what they have. We are beginning to recognize how damaging a trauma can be—administered by a parent who is ignorant of the world the child lives in and lived out by the child in a still different world later. The present emphasis in America is on the application of psychiatric techniques—in childhood itself—to undo the damage, take out the false stitches, relearn the abandoned stance. Our conception of life is a sequential, changing, and climactic one. So a trauma in childhood is seen as producing mental damage or intolerable yearning, which must then be solved in later life—and solved alone by the traumatized individuals.[7]

14   Old Bali is a striking example of a quite different solution, in which the child each day meets rituals accurately matched to the intensities and the insatiabilities which are being developed by the interplay between itself and others. Little children are not permitted to quarrel, they are not allowed to struggle over toys, or to pull and claw at each other—there are always elders there to separate them, gently, impersonally, and inexorably, and so completely that, in over two years of living in Balinese villages, I never saw two children or adolescents fight. When conflict arises, the elder child is continually told to give in to the younger; the younger, responding to the invitation of the older, is jealous of every favor and demanding of anything the elder has.

15   But day after day, as the child is prevented from fighting, he sees magnificent battles on the stage, and the children are part of the crowd that streams down to the river bank to duck some character in the play. He sees the elder brother—who must always be deferred to in real life—insulted, tricked, defeated, in the theater. When his mother teases him in the eerie, disassociated manner of a witch, the child can also watch the witch in the play—the masked witch wearing the accentuated symbols of both sexes, with long protruding tongue, pendulous breasts, covered

---

[7] See Mead, "The Arts in Bali," *Traditional Balinese Culture,* p. 551.

with repulsive hair—watch her recurrent battle with the dragon, who in his warmer and puppy-like behavior resembles his father. He can see the followers of the dragon attack the witch and fall down in a trance, as if killed, only to be brought back to life again by the magic healing power of the dragon.[8] These followers of the dragon, like the younger brother, go further than he will ever dare to go in showing hostility to his mother, in open resentment of her laughter. He sees his possible destructive wish lived out before his eyes, but in the end no one is slain, no one is destroyed, no one is hurt. The trancers, who have fallen into convulsions when they attack the witch, are revived by holy water and prayers, the play ends, the masks are taken off, the actors lay aside their golden garments for stained workday clothes; the young men who lay twitching in convulsions half an hour ago go off singing gaily for a bath. Over and over again, as babies in their mothers' arms, as toddlers being lifted out of the path of a pair of dancing warriors, as members of the solemn row of children who line the audience square, they see it happen—the play begins, mounts to intensity, ends in ritual safety. And in the villages, when theatrical troupes under the protection of the dragon mask, patron of the theater and enemy of death, parade about a village in which they have just arrived, people buy a little of the dragon's hair as bracelets for their children to protect them from evil dreams.[9]

16   In this absence of change, the experience of the parent is repeated in that of the child, and the child, a full participant in ritual and art, is presented with the last elaborations almost with its first breath. The people themselves treat time as a circular process rather than a progressive one, with the future ever behind one, unrolling beneath one's feet, an already exposed but undeveloped film. Here we find a perfect expression of the historical nature of culture, in which any separation between cause and effect, any attempt to turn either childhood experience or adult ritual into the cause, one of the other, is seen to be a hopeless endeavor. The two recur together, at every stage; the teased baby of the witchlike human mother watches the witch on the stage, and the teasing mother, even as she teases her baby, also sees the witch, attacked, apparently destroying, but in the end doing no harm. The effect on child and mother must both be reckoned in a round of simultaneous events, repeating and repeating until the child in arms again becomes a parent.

17   And yet, in spite of their conception of life as a circle, we may, if we wish, break the circle—as they are unwilling to do—and, for purposes of a type of scientific analysis born of our Western conceptions of time, space, and casuality, ask the question: What happens as babies born to

---

[8] See *Trance and Dance in Bali* (film); Bateson and Mead, *Balinese Character*, pp. 34–35 and Pls. 55–58.

[9] See Margaret Mead, "The Strolling Players in the Mountains of Bali," *Traditional Balinese Culture*, p. 157.

Balinese parents, equipped at birth with the same potentialities as other human babies, learn to be Balinese? How do they make the ritual of Balinese life part of themselves and so become as able to dance the intricate dances, carve or play or weave or go into trance, as did their parents or their grandparents? How do they learn to be Balinese and so perpetuate Balinese culture? This is no question which treats Balinese culture as a mere projection from childhood experience. The themes enacted in the Balinese theater have a long history.[10] On the shadow-play screen there appear the heroes and heroines of the *Ramayana,* the great Indian epic. The witch *rangdă* is also the Javanese Chalonarang, and she is also Durgă, the destroyer. The dragon is found around the world—in Japan, in the streets of New York for Chinese New Year, where he blesses the local merchants whose restaurants may contain a juke box or a cigarette-vending machine. It is only in the particular details of the plots that one can find the distinctive mark of Balinese culture—in the refusal to let the witch die, in the permission to show a violence on the stage which is not permitted in real life, and in the way in which artist, actor, and priest participate in everyday life.

18   But children in Bali, like human children everywhere, are born helpless, dependent, and cultureless and must be bathed and fed and protected, taught to balance and to walk, to touch and to refrain from touching, to relate themselves to other people, to talk, to work, to become sure members of their own sex, and finally to marry and produce and rear children. We cannot find that which is distinctively Balinese in the mere presence of the witch and the dragon, who recur in many forms throughout the world. It is necessary to look at fine details of difference. For example, the Balinese witch has got hold of a dragon's fiery tongue—and the Balinese dragon has no tongue at all. This can be seen as a part of the way in which the witch combines all the gross overaccentuated aspects of secondary sex characters. In the Balinese ideal physical type, both men and women are slender; male breasts are more pronounced than among us; women's breasts are high and small; hips of both sexes are closer in dimensions. Men are almost beardless, and the muscles of their arms are not developed. The witch's hairy legs and long pendulous breasts accentuate the frightening aspects of highly developed sex differences, and we find, counterpointing her, protecting the people from the illness and death she brings, and presiding with her over the theater, the dragon, a mythical creature, wearing lovely fluffy, feather-like "hair" or crow feathers sent especially by the gods. Only as the Balinese witch is contrasted with her historical predecessors and as the Balinese dragon is seen in a world perspective of other dragons, it is possible to say what is distinctively Balinese. In the same way, by placing Balinese childhood

---

[10] See Jane Belo, *Bali: Rangda and Barong* (New York, J. J. Augustin, 1949).

experience in a context of our knowledge of child development, we can see in what particular ways Balinese children, while repeating universal human experiences, also have special ones.

19   The Balinese infant has preserved a kind of neonatal flexibility, which in the children who have been studied in Western culture tends to disappear very early, so that both the way a baby relaxes in its mother's arms and the way the mother holds it are sharply contrasting to our patterns.[11] The disallowance of infancy, as adults speak in behalf of the child or press its compliant learning hands into ritual gestures, is again distinctive; and the way in which the child is constantly discouraged from walking, taught to use its right hand rather than the left, which is exposed by the carrying posture, left free to drink from its mother's breast when it chooses, as it is carried high above her high breast, but fed in a helpless prone position as a mound of prechewed food is piled on its mouth—all these details go to build the kind of Balinese personality which will be receptive to rituals danced and acted by others who have been treated in the same way. The constant provocative teasing and threatening which never reaches any but a theatrical climax, the denial of all violence and expressed hostility toward siblings, the serial experience of being the pampered baby, the displaced knee baby, and the child nurse, who, as guardian of the baby, stays to see the usurper dethroned in turn, all these form a background for the plots of ritual and theater to which the child is exposed.[12]

20   But there is something more here than the correspondence between childhood experience and dramatic plot, something different from the sort of cultural situation discussed by Róheim when a terrifying infantile experience—of a male child sleeping beneath the mother—is abreacted by initiation rites in adolescence.[13] In Bali the absence of sequence even in the life-span of the individual and the absence of discontinuity between ritual role and everyday role seem crucial. The artist, the dancer, the priest, is also a husbandman who tills his rice fields. Occasionally an artist becomes so famous that he lets his fingernails grow as he does no other work, and, say the Balinese, he begins to grow fat and careless and lazy, and his artistic skills decrease. The priest may stand robed in white during a ceremony, officiating at the long ritual of inviting the gods down to earth, dressing them, feeding them, bathing them, presenting them with dance and theater, and then sending them back

---

[11] See Mead and Macgregor, *Growth and Culture*.

[12] See Margaret Mead, "Age Patterning in Personality Development," *American Journal of Orthopsychiatry,* XVII, No. 2, (1947), 231–40.

[13] Geza Róheim, *The Riddle of the Sphinx* (London, Hogarth Press and Institute of Psychoanalysis, 1934).

again for another two hundred and ten days in heaven.¹⁴ But the day after the ceremony he is a simple citizen of the village, only owing the land which he cultivates to his work on feast days as guardian of the temple.

21   Nor is there any gap between professional and amateur. These are virtually no amateurs in Bali, no folk dancing in which people do traditional things without responsibility to an artistic canon.¹⁵ There are enormous differences in skill and grace and beauty of performance, but prince and peasant, very gifted and slightly gifted, all do what they do seriously and become, in turn, critical spectators, laughing with untender laughter at the technical failures of others. Between the audience that gathers to watch the play and the players there is always the bond of professional interest, as the audience criticizes the way the actor or actress who plays the princess postures or sings, rather than identifying with her fate—however lost she may be in some dense theatrical forest.

22   Nor is there any gap between rehearsal and performance. From the moment an orchestra begins to practice an old piece of music, there is a ring of spectators, aspiring players, substitute players, small boys, and old men, all equally engrossed in the ever fresh creation of a new way of playing an old piece of music.¹⁶ Where in Java the shadow-play screen divided men from women, the women seeing only the faint shadow on the screen, the men the brightly painted figures, in Bali people can sit on either side, in front to watch the finished play, behind—and this is where little boys prefer to sit—to watch the individual designs on the figures and the deft hands of the puppet master. When a village club decides to learn a new play—a play in which the main serious parts are traditional and the parts of clowns, servants, and incidental characters are all improvised, never set, even in consecutive performances—half the village attends the rehearsals, enjoys the discussions of costume, the sharp words of the visiting virtuoso come to teach a dance step, the discovery of some new talent among the actors. In the rectangular piece of ground which becomes a four-sided stage as the audience gathers around it, isolated pairs of curtains borrowed from a theater with a quite different style of handling surprise may be set up near each end. The actors, their crowns a little askew, sit in almost full view dozing behind these curtains or among the audience, and then, as they make their appearance, part the curtain for a prolonged stylized "entrance," from which they later return to their full visibility offstage.¹⁷ People advance from the audience to pin up a

---

[14] See Jane Belo, *Bali: Temple Festival* (Locust Valley, NY, J. J. Augustin, 1953).

[15] See Margaret Mead, "Community Drama, Bali and America." Colin McPhee, "Dance in Bali," *Traditional Balinese Culture,* p. 290.

[16] See Colin McPhee, *A House in Bali* (New York, John Day, 1946).

[17] See Margaret Mead, "The Strolling Players in the Mountains of Bali," *Traditional Balinese Culture,* p. 157.

dancer's fallen scarf, and dramatic scenes of chase and conquest will be pursued into the midst of the audience.

23   Thus in Bali the ritual world of art and theater and temple is not a world of fantasy, an endless recurrent daydream, or a new set of daydreams woven from the desperations of the gifted of each generation. It is rather a real world of skill and application—a world in which members of a dance club scheme to get money for the gold of a new headdress or to buy new instruments for the orchestra; where long hours are spent in the basic work of learning to dance; where disciplined hands and wrists and eyes that click to one side in perfect time to the music, are all the result of continuous, although relaxed, rather dreamy, work. And the temple feasts, where many of these activities combine to make a great spectacle, are called appropriately "the work of the gods."

24   Children have not only the precocious postural participation in prayer and offering, dance and music, but also a whole series of parallel participations. A little boy will be given bamboo clappers with which to imitate the clapping of the dragon's tongueless jaws and, covered by his mother's cloth shawl—the same shawl with which the witch will dance in the play and which she will carry in her arms as if it were a baby—goes about clapping in imitation of the dragon. In the nonceremonial seasons, when life is a little less crowded, secular dance clubs go about with a tinkly orchestra, which has a hurdy-gurdy quality, and a little girl dancer, who dances with the young men of the village and, in between, dances as the witch, combining the beautiful ballet of the witch's disciples with being the witch herself and placing her foot firmly on the neck of a doll, enacting her role of bringing death.[18]

25   Children stay in a deep resistant sleep during a childbirth in their houses, a sleep from which it is necessary to shake them awake, lest they see the witches which may come to kill the child. But the same children participate with delight in the play in which the witch child, after stealing a doll, born of a man and dressed as a woman, is chased up a tree or into a nearby stream. Children make puppets of banana leaf and parody the puppet master, especially the puppet master who performs with puppets in the daytime, whose screen has shrunk to a single line of thread. They draw in the sand with twigs while master artists work at little shallow wooden tables. And children may form clubs of their own, make their own dragon and witch, and progress about the village, collecting pennies for further finery for the masks.[19]

26   If one follows these activities carefully, notes the expressions on the children's faces at different kinds of ceremonies, follows the same child on different occasions, and watches the play in which the children think they are reproducing the full theatricals, one begins to get clues to the

---

[18] See Bateson and Mead, *Balinese Character*, Pls. 60–62.
[19] See Colin McPhee, *A Club of Small Men* (New York, John Day, 1947).

dynamic mechanisms by which the children, born human like all other human children, become such very different people from other people—as Balinese. The mother who teases her child—who borrows a baby to provoke its jealousy, although preventing any expression of jealousy of a real sibling; who borrows a baby to set on its head, although at the same time protecting its head from real insult—has learned that all this is a safe game. When she watches the witch dance and watches the men and women who have gone into trance and are slow in coming out, she watches with the same relaxed enjoyment or ready criticism for some ritual or technical defect with which she watches the trance dance in which children dance as goddesses. But the child, teased into a violent temper, screaming and clawing to get the borrowed baby away from his mother's breast, has not yet learned that all this is safe. In his intensity and grief, in his fervent acceptance of his mother's theatrical amends for a real hurt, he still shows a capacity for hurt which will not be manifest later. Even as he withdraws from the recurrently disappointing sequences which have no climax, he learns to trust the arts, and he learns to avoid hurting responsiveness to human stimulation.[20]

27 The faces of the children who watch the trance dance in which little girls replace dancing wooden puppets—and child dancers are indulged by their parents and wilful in their demands—are as relaxed as their parents' faces. But during the witch dance the children's faces are strained and anxious.[21] When the witch dances or when some woman worshiper in the temple is possessed by the witch, the fingers are flexed backward in a gesture of fear, spoken of as *kapar*—the gesture made by a baby falling or a man falling from a tree—for the witch is both frightening and afraid, the picture of Fear itself.[22] But when children play the witch, especially when they play her without benefit of costume or music or any of the elements which accompany the finished ritual, their hands are bent like claws, and they threaten an attack in witchlike gestures which can be found in many parts of the world. When the young men, who, as followers of the dragon, fall down before the witch's magic, thrust their daggers against their breasts, they thrust them in response to an intolerable itching feeling in their breasts—a possible reciprocal to the mother's breast during the period when they were so teased, provoked, and given only theatrical climaxes.

28 When Balinese children are frightened of strangers or strange situations, their elders shout at them, "Don't show fear!" and they learn not to run but to stand stock still, often with their hands pressed over their

---

[20] See Bateson and Mead, *Balinese Character*.

[21] See *Trance and Dance in Bali* (film).

[22] See *Trance and Dance in Bali* (film); Bateson and Mead, *Balinese Character*, Pl. 62.

eyes.[23] In situations of danger or uncertainty—during childbirth in a tiny one-room house, after an accident for which one may be blamed—children and older people also fall into a deep sleep from which it is hard to rouse them.

29   The Balinese move easily in a group. A whole village may make a pilgrimage of two or three days to make offerings at the seaside or in the high mountains. A troupe of Balinese went to the Paris Exposition in 1931, and a troupe visited New York in 1952. But one Balinese, isolated from those he knows and taken to a strange place, wilts and sickens; people say it is because he is *paling*—disoriented—the word used for trance, insanity, for being drunk, confused, or lost. And the Balinese are mortally afraid of drunkenness, where the clues to the directions, the calendar, the caste system, the framework of life—which gives safety as the walking rail gave it to the little child who learned how dangerous it was to venture away from it—are lost or blurred.

30   Following the children as they grow up reveals that, even within the simultaneity of ritual satisfaction and individual fear, the capacity to enjoy such rituals, to dance the lovely dances and fill the air with music, has been—in the case of the Balinese—developed at certain costs. The culture contains—or did contain until the recent upheavals about which we know little—ritual solutions for the instabilities it created, and the people, on their little island, were safe. But it was the safety of a tightrope dancer, beautiful and precarious.

References

Originally published in Margaret Mead and Martha Wolfenstein, eds., *Childhood in Contemporary Cultures* (Chicago. University of Chicago Press, 1955), pp. 40–51.

Author's note: "Based on field work done in Bali, in 1936–39, by Gregory Bateson, Colin McPhee, Katharane Mershon, and myself. Bali is now part of modern Indonesia, and many parts of this description would no longer hold. I am using a historical present for the description of old, that is, pre–World War II, Bali." Cf. Margaret Mead, "Researches in Bali, 1936–1939; on the Concept of Plot in Culture," *Transactions of the New York Academy of Sciences,* Ser. II, Vol. II, No. 1 (November, 1939), pp. 1–4.

Reading for Meaning

1. Margaret Mead says that in Bali, "Human beings do not increase in stature and importance, as is so often the case in societies where men [and women] have only one life to live." What does she mean when she says people maintain the same "stature and importance" in the culture? Discuss ways a person's status might change for the better in the United States.

---

[23] See Bateson and Mead, *Balinese Character,* Pl. 67.

2. What about their beliefs explains the Balinese tendency to characterize infants according to their behavior (harsh, gentle, happy, etc.) and to rely on this identifying characteristic throughout the child's life?

3. Why do the Balinese have such trouble remembering how their dead acted or what they looked like? Do you think this loss of memory is unique to people in Bali or is it fairly common in human experience?

4. How do children and adults interact in Balinese culture? What purpose does this interaction seem to serve? Mead says that similar exchanges between adults and children in Western cultures would probably "bring out schizoid trends in the growing child's character." Is Mead correct in her estimate of the effects that the stimulation-neglect cycle in Bali might have on children in this culture? What prevents such trends from occurring in Balinese children?

5. Explain how concepts of "art" and "life" differ in Bali from the way we think of them.

6. Margaret Mead finds that the Balinese have developed an elaborate interplay among individuals, family group, and the larger community, but these connections exact "certain costs." What are these "costs" according to Mead?

7. How does Mead organize her discussion of what makes a child Balinese? Is there a way in which the sequence of ideas in her essay imitates the concept of circularity and return in Balinese life?

Comparing Texts

1. In Bali, the tensions of childhood find release in the safety of community rituals. Read Susan Orlean's "Debuting: Phoenix, Arizona" on page 180 and discuss the purpose ritual serves in the Chicano community that author describes.

2. In "An Anthropologist Learns from the Hopi," page 386, Dorothy Lee offers a brief description of what it is like to grow up Hopi. What similarities and differences do you see between the way children are brought into the Hopi culture and the way Balinese children become Balinese?

3. How do adults make Balinese children part of the cycle of life in Bali? Compare their attempts to integrate children into Balinese culture with the grandfather's role in Malidoma Patrice Somé's "Slowly Becoming," page 537.

Ideas for Writing

1. Write a short essay summarizing main points in Mead's essay on Bali.

2. Write a response paper in which you discuss what you find strange or admirable in the way the Balinese raise their children.

3. Write an essay in which you explain how the behavior of adults or children in Bali compares to the way children and their parents act in a culture with which you are familiar.

4. Find several sources whose authors either defend Mead's interpretations of "primitive" cultures or criticize her methods. Use ideas in these articles to write an interpretation of "Children and Ritual in Bali."

INVESTIGATING: USING INFORMATION FROM SEVERAL TEXTS

In additional to possibilities for comparison, cultural and textual analyses offer opportunities for research. You may still wish to write a paper that primarily compares points or writing strategies in several texts, or you can develop a position of your own on a particular issue and use information from sources either as supporting evidence for your own points or as opposing arguments that you can refute, perhaps with the help of other sources. Another kind of research paper uses secondary sources to investigate a subject. The sample research paper in this chapter presents the results of such an investigation.

Evaluating the ideas of other writers and formulating responses to them in an organized paper is a writing process required in many college courses. In spite of its importance, the idea of gathering ideas from sources and arranging those ideas in an intelligible, reasonable, interesting way can seem frightening, even to a writer who has developed some measure of confidence. One note of reassurance is that writing a research paper follows a process not unlike other strategies for writing essays we have examined in this book. Specifically, techniques for writing a research paper are similar to strategies you might use in writing a reader-response paper or a paper that compares texts. Reading your sources thoroughly and offering your own thoughtful responses to them are important steps to take when preparing to write a research paper.

There are a few differences between a research paper and other writing assignments, however. For one thing, support for general points in a research paper comes primarily from information gathered from sources rather than the author's own personal experiences and observations. The writer must also give credit to the sources that provided this information. Regardless of whether ideas are quoted directly or paraphrased, the writer must identify the source of any borrowed ideas. Most disciplines have their own style of documentation. For this discussion, we use the format for citing sources recommended by the Modern Language Association. Under the MLA guidelines, credit for borrowed ideas appears in two places in the paper: in the body of the paper following quoted or paraphrased information from sources and on the Works Cited page at the end of the essay. References in the text appear in parentheses. For the Modern Language Association's style of documentation, the author and page of the source—(Jackson 114)—are most often the items included in the parentheses. For additional ways of using in-text citations and for a thorough list of bibliographical arrangements to use in your list of works cited, including sources from various computer databases, see the *Modern Language Association's Handbook for Writers of Research Papers*.

INVESTIGATING: SAMPLE RESEARCH PAPER

The following sample paper discusses parenting styles in several countries. The assignment was to write an essay that draws conclusions about adult expectations of children in at least three cultures. The sources used in this research paper—"Somebody's Baby," "Parents and Children," and "Children and Ritual in Bali"—appear earlier in this chapter. This paper compiles research on the topic and evaluates adults' assumptions about the role of children in the family and in the larger culture in Spain, France, Bali, and the United States.

Cherí Jones

English 1A

Mr. Knight

10 April 1999

Bringing up Baby:

Growing up in Spain, France,

the United States, and Bali

The way we behave with our parents and their responses to us are so familiar that it is difficult to imagine any changes in the pattern of this relationship. In truth, the roles of children, parents, and other adults internationally can be surprisingly different. In Spain, for example, strangers might look on lovingly while a child throws a tantrum in a restaurant (Kingsolver 100). An elderly woman in France might correct a child whom she feels is not behaving properly (Carroll 49). Neighbors in Bali will tease a child mercilessly, then suddenly turn and walk away if the game becomes too confrontational (Mead 202). A hostess in America might smile politely as a guest's child remarks that she hates the soup she has been served, whereas a Frenchwoman would be horrified that the parent didn't slap the offending child (Carroll 41). A child's behavior and adult responses to it are determined by the culture's view of the parents' role in shaping a child, expectations adults have of how children should behave, and the role the community plays in child rearing.

    Adults in various countries make certain assumptions about a parent's role in that culture. In France, for example, the parents' job is to rear obedient children. This means disciplining children who interrupt adults, talk out of turn, or assert themselves in any way against adult authority. Ultimately, the French parent is supposed to "transform" a basically uncivilized creature into "a social being, a responsible member of the society" (Carroll 47). As a result, parents prove they are doing their job by making public displays of discipline. A French parent will slap a child, yell at him or her for small infractions, and might be heard saying, "You are not my daughter [or son] anymore," as a warning to a disobedient child. Such public displays of parental authority put French parents in what Carroll considers a double-bind. Although they might feel compelled to chastise a child in public, their children quickly learn that parental love is actually unconditional. Their parents are really telling them that their behavior is embarrassing and is exposing their mother and father to ridicule for being bad parents who are unable to control their children (Carroll 48). Because they are accountable for their children's behavior, French parents are likely to be very

Jones 3

protective of their children and may intervene in all facets of their children's lives. They monitor piano lessons, transport them to and from school, and walk with their children if the family lives close to school (Carroll 45).

In the United States, parents do not have the same degree of accountability for their children's acts nor the involvement in decision making and oversight that we see in French households. French parents see themselves as responsible for producing an obedient, socially acceptable "French" child. In contrast, American parents are more interested in fostering independence, protecting their child from public ridicule, and offering their child the opportunity to realize his or her own potential in life (Carroll 46, 50). Consequently, their children's behavior is not hammered into a particular social mold as it is in France. The American style of parenting is not without its public reprobation, however. Barbara Kingsolver cites several instances when parents have been held responsible for a child's distracting behavior. For example, a mother on an airplane was chastised for not being able to keep her infant quiet (100). Hence, in the United States, as in France, people may feel strongly that parents should control their children and prevent them from becoming nuisances, but American parents, unlike their French

Jones 4

counterparts, show respect for their children and work with them to correct a problem.

Not only are the roles parents play quite different from one culture to another, expectations for their children can be vastly different as well. Children in Bali, for example, are regarded as recent arrivals from a sacred place. They are addressed in terms reserved for royalty, for honored ancestors, and for gods. Even infants enter instantly into the ritual life of the culture as "small adults" whose elders speak for them, uttering words appropriate to their part in the ceremony. For the first few years of life, everything is done for them, and they are carried in the arms of adults or transported in slings for the first few years of their lives, even after they are able to walk. Their physical closeness to adults helps them learn the rhythms of the body, and adults aid them in this effort by manipulating their limbs according to patterns of movement they are to learn (Mead 201).

Although American children don't enjoy quite the privileges afforded their sacred counterparts in Bali, relatively few demands are placed on them during childhood, the time when they are expected to explore "'their natural qualities' to exploit their gifts and to blossom" (Carroll 49). Parents respect their children's needs and may interrupt a conversation with another adult in order to tend to their child. Unlike the physical attachment a Balinese child has to adults, contacts between adults and children in America and France are more verbal than physical. American children are likely to hear words of encouragement and support, and perhaps a suggestion to behave differently or to make a different choice. In France, parental communication is likely to take the form of commands. Children are lectured and harangued into obedience. In the French view, children are learning the discipline and "good habits" that will prepare them for adulthood (Carroll 50).

    Perhaps the most important issue in child rearing around the world is the degree to which the larger community participates in the process. The Balinese child is the darling of the culture, carried and protected not just by the parents but by nurses and other adults in the community. The entire community conveys the central cultural point that the Balinese must remain passive in the face of everyday disappointments. At the same time, the ritualized art that forms the parallel life of the community provides the forum for symbolic solutions to frustrations with parents, siblings, and other authorities who thwart the child's will (Mead 209). Adults practice the same means of quelling conflicts. They gently separate children if they start to fight. The rather aggressive playing allowed among Balinese children is meant to teach them not to act out their frustrations on the secular stage but to fold them into the shadow-plays, the ritual dramas that mirror their domestic lives. The community provides such a solid framework for the Balinese that as adults, if they become separated from that community, they enter a trancelike state and remain disoriented until returned to the community (Mead 211).

    The people of Spain show public appreciation and approval of their children. When she was living in Spain, Barbara Kingsolver was amazed that strangers would come up to her daughter and remark how cute she was or look on lovingly while she fussed at a restaurant (100). Kingsolver found such signs of appreciation of anyone "under the height of one meter" typical of Spanish adults in public places. Spaniards support the efforts of parents by wholeheartedly approving of their children, much like doting aunts and uncles, regardless of what they are doing. A French child also understands that he or she will be comforted or assisted by strangers if for some reason his parents are unable to help (Carroll 49). But because childhood in France is a time when children must learn conformity to strict social rules, the more important role of the public in France is to put pressure on French parents to make their child conform to the accepted standards of behavior. For this reason, when parents correct their children in public, they are aware that other adults will observe that they are doing all they can to control their children (Carroll 48).

    Americans have the least sense of community when it comes to raising children. Americans' attitude toward children, as Kingsolver observed, is that parents choose to have their children, and those choices make children entirely their parents' responsibility. Above all, she found, childless adults think that parents should not let their children destroy other adults' peace of mind. Moreover, this attitude appears widespread, judging from the unpopularity of proposals to increase funding for schools. Kingsolver can only conclude that parents are on their own in the United States (101). Raymonde Carroll explains this attitude from a slightly different perspective. American parents, she argues, feel very differently about their responsibility to the community than do French parents. Since their first obligation is to the child, not to other adults, American parents are less likely to correct or help other people's children (49). Their interventions, unlike those of French adults, merely announce their disapproval and have nothing to do with judging the worth of a parent or attempting to correct a wayward child. Adults outside the family are interested only in creating some space for themselves, as Kingsolver's examples show, and any effect their words might have on a child are purely coincidental and unintentional.

   The behavior of adults and children, as "natural" as it may seem to us, is not a foregone conclusion. We are inextricably bound to the culture that has given us our freedom to develop our potential or has taught us how to "fit in." The phrase "It takes a whole village to raise a child" has some validity. But the community's expectations of both parents and children and whether that community is willing to participate in the rearing of other people's children can vary radically from one culture to another.

                                                      Jones 9
                        Works Cited

Carroll, Raymonde. "Parents and Children." <u>Cultural

   Misunderstandings: The French-American

   Experience.</u> Trans. Carol Volk. Chicago:

   University of Chicago Press, 1988. 40–57.

Kingsolver, Barbara. "Somebody's Baby." <u>High Tide in

   Tucson.</u> New York: Harper Collins, 1995. 99–107.

Mead, Margaret. "Children and Ritual in Bali."

   <u>Traditional Balinese Culture.</u> Ed. Jane Belo. New

   York: Columbia University Press, 1970. 198–211.

PART 2
READINGS FOR CULTURAL ANALYSIS AND COMPARISON

CHAPTER 5
The Family

CHAPTER 6
Rites of Passage

CHAPTER 7
Working

CHAPTER 8
Custom and Gender Roles

CHAPTER 9
The Individual and the Group

CHAPTER 10
Immigrants and Exiles

CHAPTER 11
The Artist in Society

CHAPTER 12
The Spiritual Life

CHAPTER 5
THE FAMILY

First Thoughts

最初的印象

Primeras impresiones

Marriage is a lifelong covenant between one man and one woman. . . . A husband has the God-given responsibility to provide for, to protect, and to lead his family. . . . A wife is to submit graciously to the servant leadership of her husband even as the church submits to the headship of Christ.

Baptist Faith and Message
Southern Baptist leadership statement, June, 1998

The use of the blanket term "family" to indicate groups which are specifically defined by residence and descent as well as those defined by the existence of the marriage bond may be adequate for Euro-American systems in which there is considerable overlap, but it can be highly confusing in terms of other societies.

Jack Goody
The Developmental Cycle in Domestic Groups

These, Sadie, are the things I know, scraps of memory I've retrieved from my past, stumbled upon by accident but retold purposely carefully so that we never again forget.

Connie May Fowler
River of Hidden Dreams

The family is the basic unit of human society. Despite the universality of the idea of family, the way families are structured can differ dramatically from one country to another, from one culture to another, and from one social group to another. A "family" may consist of two parents and their children; one parent and one or more children; a single adult; a patriarchal head of household and his wives, concubines, and children; joint families with several adults living in common with their children; an extended family whose members may live together or in close proximity; or kinship networks that may extend around the world. In addition, these family groupings may be heterosexual, homosexual, bisexual, celibate, polygamous, or monogamous. Whatever the arrangement, the family serves to protect, nurture, educate, and socialize the children of cultural groups the world over. Making distinctions among these family arrangements can be challenging and, at times, a politically sensitive activity. There are, however, many rewards. Studying the family history and personal experiences of other people—as well as looking at the points of view of the social scientist, anthropologist, and psychologist—provides us with material for reflection and comparison that can lead to insights and perhaps a new understanding of our own conception and experience of the family.

Readings in this chapter explore a variety of family structures and points of view on the family. Li Zhai writes about the changing family dynamic in households in the expanding cities in China. When searching for her family history, Connie May Fowler discovered a larger story in her Cherokee ancestors' battle with American history to retain their Native American identity. In "The Water-Faucet Vision," Gish Jen tells the story of an imaginative child who believes that she can use miracles to correct what goes wrong in her family. The last two readings analyze the meaning of the family from several points of view. Nancie Solien Gonzalez writes "Household and Family in the Caribbean: Some Definitions and Concepts" to correct what she thinks are Eurocentric misinterpretations of the family structure typical of African families in the Americas, particularly in Caribbean countries. The fluidity of family arrangements in the United States and its costs and benefits to children and to the larger culture are David Elkind's concerns in "WAAAH!!: Why Kids Have a Lot to Cry About."

In this and the remaining chapters in this book, excerpts from longer readings sometimes appear in the "Comparing Texts" section that follows each of the main readings. These texts provide you with additional points of view and offer suggestions for making comparisons. In this chapter, for example, Connie May Fowler's essay, "No Snapshots in the Attic: A Granddaughter's Search for a Cherokee Past," explores some of the more dehumanizing ideas about native peoples that European Americans once had. In the "Comparing Texts" section for Fowler's reading, selections by two of the first settlers in North America, William Wood and Thomas Morton, give you an idea of just how much Europeans' impressions of "Indians" varied.

Writing before Reading

1. What associations do you have with the ideas of "mother" and of "father"? What distinctions do you make between them? Do these words have different emotional meanings for you?

2. What in your experience has shaped your feelings about the terms "father" and "mother"? Do you know people for whom these words might have different associations? Are your feelings about these ideas fairly common among people you know?

ROLE REVERSAL: THE KIND FATHER AND STERN MOTHER

Li Zhai

In "Role Reversal," an article published in the Beijing Review *for January 1994, Li Zhai examines the changing roles of men and women in Chinese families. As people have migrated from agrarian collectives to the burgeoning cities of China (echoing an international pattern), Chinese women have started working outside the home, some as professionals, and, according to Li Zhai, they and their families are witnessing some startling changes in behavior.*

Facts about China

The People's Republic of China is the third largest country in the world, behind Russia and Canada, and with just under 1.3 billion people it has the world's largest population. More than one-fifth of the people in the world are Chinese, and that does not include the number of ethnic Chinese living outside the People's Republic. China is an ancient civilization with more than 4,000 years of recorded history. The discovery of Yuanmou man, an ancestor of modern man, revealed that China was inhabited by early humans 1.7 million years ago. Fossils of the more famous Beijing (Peking) man are 460,000 years old. Fully advanced humans were in China 30,000 years ago, roughly the time the first inhabitants of North America were crossing the Bering Land Bridge. Until recently, China has evolved culturally in relative isolation, with the exception of the spread of Buddhism from India to China in the first century A.C.E. A series of cultural and military invasions from the mid-nineteenth century and well into the twentieth century devastated China. The country secured its borders once again after the Communists assumed power in 1949. Deng Xiaoping is credited with bringing economic modernization to China beginning in 1978. Declaring a new economic era, Deng affirmed, "To get rich is glorious." Hu Yabang became general secretary of National People's Congress in 1982. Massive student demonstrations caused Hu to resign in 1987. Deng Xiaoping remained China's principal leader and in June 1989 following several months of pro-democracy demonstrations, Deng ordered the army to suppress the students' protest. In October 1992, Jiang Zemin became the new party general secretary. The Party Congress initiated economic reforms but remained adamantly opposed to political dissent. In 1997 Deng Xiaoping died and the British government returned Hong Kong to China. In March 1998, Zhu Rongji was named premier of China and Communist Party leader Jiang Zemin began a program to sell or close approximately 30,000 companies owned by the Chinese military.

1. The stern father and kind mother has always been the traditional image of parents in a Chinese family. But now, to many children, parents are playing different roles. The mother is strict and the father is kind and tolerant.

2. The writer once asked six children aged four to six whom they liked best, mother or father. Four of them said they preferred their father. "Mom is the worst," said one boy, stamping his foot. Another said that both parents were equally kind. When asked why they liked their fathers better than their mothers, they said that their fathers always hug them, take them to parks and buy toys and candies for them. Fathers smile when they talk. Unlike mothers, fathers never spank them. "Mom spanks me so hard, and she always gets angry with me," one of them said.

3. Zhi Yan, a 23-year-old kindergarten teacher said she believes what the children said. Working in a kindergarten attached to the Ministry of Public Health, Zhi said she could see that mothers are generally stricter than fathers. It is mothers who force their children to take up various classes to study musical instruments, dancing, painting and foreign languages, whether their children like it or not. Some children complain to their teachers or fathers, but they have to continue to study since their mothers are so determined. Mothers accompany their children to study in evening classes, sacrificing their own interests. In her kindergarten, Zhi said, many kids are overjoyed to see their fathers, not mothers, coming to take them home in the evening. Unlike mothers who forever ask them to behave and study, fathers often listen to their children, praising them for their cleverness and discussing plans for the weekend with them.

4. After visiting several families, the author found that "the kind father and strict mother" is really a common family phenomenon. Zhang Qin, a 28-year-old factory worker, admits that her son likes his father better. "It's unfair," she said. "I'm much more tired after a day's work than his father. All day I work hard and then come home to cook and do all the housework. I'm so exhausted that I have no patience to answer all the questions from

my 4-year-old son, let alone tell him stories. I often feel inadequate because I have only a limited education and earn a low salary. I hope my son will have a good future. I often ask him to recite poems, and I'm so strict that I don't allow him to make mistakes. His father is an engineer at a design institute and his job is more flexible. He often takes the child out playing while I'm cooking. Sometimes he buys candies or small toys on their way home. Of course our son likes his father."

5   Which parent a child prefers depends on the particular situation of each family, according to a man whose wife is a manager of a hotel. "I'm not willing to be loaded down with housework and to look after the child. But I have no choice. Both her social status and income are higher than mine. And she is too busy. By the time my wife has gotten home at night the child has fallen asleep and is still sleeping when she goes to work the next morning. Even though she sometimes stays at home during the day, she is busy with her work and has no time to spend with the child. The child cannot receive love and warmth from her mother, so it is understandable she is closer to me."

6   To further support his point, the man said women in the old days were seen as kinder because the mother's duty was to look after her children and husband and do housework. Since they had no social or economic status, they had time to devote themselves wholly to the care of the family. It was natural that mothers were seen as kind.

7   While analyzing this family phenomenon, Professor Zhu Laoshi of the People's University of China said it is natural for parents to love their children and both are willing to spend more time with the kids. As mothers, women had been at the bottom of the social ladder for thousands of years, and they had a low position in their families, too. Although women's present social status is higher, the feudal concept that men are superior to women still exists. Some women unconsciously behave as "strong-willed woman" both at work and at home so as to gain a mental balance. Men, who are used to being in a superior position in society, often appear to be tolerant with children. Furthermore, most men are careless about family income and expenditure, so they will buy without hesitation whatever their children want.

8   Zhu added that in many families, fathers have received better educations than mothers and are more experienced in social interactions. Nowadays children are eager to lean things that their mothers find it hard to teach. It is natural that they admire their fathers who can given them satisfactory answers to their many questions. Zhu said the fact that many mothers are willing to let fathers spend more time with the children also contributes to the lack of mutual understanding between mothers and their children.

9   Moreover, many mothers still try to live up to the traditional expectations of children. They fail to adjust their thinking to a changing time during which family education should also be brought up to date.

Fathers can generally keep a clear mind on how to educate children in these modern times. Meanwhile, they try to relieve the pressures on their children without offending their wives and keep the family going smoothly. It is no wonder that children like their fathers better.

Reading for Meaning

1. To what does Li Zhai attribute the traditional roles of the "stern father" and "kind mother" in the Chinese household?

2. How does Zhai explain the reversal in the traditional roles of Chinese parents?

3. What is gained and what is lost in the role reversal that Zhai examines in his article?

4. Zhi Yan, a kindergarten teacher that Li Zhai interviewed, says that in China, mothers "force their children to take up various classes to study musical instruments, dancing, painting, and foreign languages, whether their children like it or not." To what extent should parents force their children to participate in educational activities?

5. How might China's patriarchal assumptions about women's inferiority explain women's aggressiveness and men's more easygoing approach?

6. Zhai suggests that parents play a variety of roles: the wage earner, housekeeper, nurturing parent, disciplinarian, and educator. What roles do the mother, father, or guardian play in your family or in families with which you are familiar? How do these roles compare with the duties that Zhai ascribes to parents in China?

Comparing Texts

1. Despite the recent changes in the family, Li Zhai assumes that the Chinese household maintains a nuclear family structure. How does Zhai's definition of the family compare to definitions Nancie Solien Gonzalez offers of the Caribbean household in "Household and Family in the Caribbean: Some Definitions and Concepts," page 159?

2. In *Pink Samurai*, a study of the family in Japan, Nicholas Bornoff describes the lives of Kimiko and Shigeru Yamashita as follows.

1   Women account for over 40 percent of today's work force [in Japan], out of which over two-thirds of them are married. When their youngest son, Shoji, at eighteen entered junior high school some eight years ago, Shigeru's wife Kimiko began her current job with an accounting firm—at first on a part-time basis. Like most local womenfolk, she used to devote some of her free afternoons to various community activities before she began working again, and also attended classes in flower arrangement, playing a traditional instrument such as the *koto* and versing herself in the ritualized art of the tea ceremony.... Each morning Kimiko is the first to rise to prepare breakfast and the second to last to take the evening bath, coming in between her mother-in-law and her daughter. The latter two frequently help with household chores and preparing meals. Owing to their various professional and scholastic schedules, however, family

members often dine at different times. The male contingent expect meals whenever they ask for them; on days when they get home before Kimiko, Obaasan will oblige. Whenever Shigeru asks for tea, Kimiko will drop whatever she is doing to make it. Even when they dine alone, male family members stack dishes in the sink; they would never wash up so much as a glass themselves. Forever returning late from work, men are said to function at home according to a mono-syllabic routine ironically referred to as *Meshi-Furo-Neru*—Food! Bath! Bed! Mild-mannered Shigeru would never use such terse wording and nor would he have to— his wife's ministrations are automatic.

2   The home, on the other hand, is always the wife's domain. Her husband hands over his monthly pay either in an envelope or has it credited to a joint bank account. She manages every side of running the home, including purchasing clothes for the menfolk, the children's schooling and any expenses incurred through repairs, new household appliances and even new houses. Her book-keeping commonly goes as far as handling stocks and shares. Every month she gives her husband his *kozukai,* or pocket money. On average this is 15 percent of his salary, and it has to cover fares, petrol, meals and the minimum incidental expenses. . . .

3   If Japanese society opens few doors to the career woman, the degree of power the housewife enjoys around the home is something almost inconceivable to her western counterparts. Superficially apparent, the traditions of female compliance, subservience and delilcatesse are often belied, not least by the prevalence of the hen-pecked husband as a stock-in-trade in popular culture, as typified from the seventies by TV's *Hisatsu* samurai drama series focusing on the exploits of a middle-aged swordsman. In between bouts of daring-do, he spends most of his time at home cringing before a shrill wife and a nagging mother-in-law. For many unemployed housewives, domestic power, a great deal of leisure time, and a steady cash flow provide few reasons to challenge the status quo.

How does the focus on family life in Nicholas Bornoff's discussion compare to themes Li Zhai selects for his article on the family in China? Is one of these descriptions closer to the division of roles you are used to, or does your family have yet another configuration?

Ideas for Writing

1. Write a response paper in which you examine a few of the benefits or drawbacks of the parental arrangements that Li Zhai describes as "a common family phenomenon" in China.

2. Li Zhai discusses the roles assumed by mothers and fathers in both the traditional and modern Chinese families. Write an essay in which you discuss how any of these roles compare to those that parents or guardians play in your family or in families you have observed. Try to explain why people you know have taken on these roles.

3. One father whom Li Zhai interviewed asserts that the "parents a child prefers depends on the particular situation of each family." In other words, who works, how much they work,

and who has the more physically or mentally taxing job are factors that help determine the amount of time and energy each parent has to devote to their children. Write an essay in which you explain which parent you or your siblings preferred when you were growing up. In your essay identify the "particular situation" as well as emotional characteristics that explain such preferences.

4. Write a paper in which you explore a few of the reasons why people's feelings about a parent or guardian may change from childhood to adulthood. In preparation for this paper, interview five or six people to determine which parent or guardian they feel close to now. Ask your interviewees why they have such feelings and whether or not these feelings have changed since they were children. Use your paper to examine the situations that can cause feelings about a parent to change.

Writing before Reading

What information have you gathered about your family's past? What stories have you heard about unique characters or situations in your family? How do these stories help explain the behavior of certain people in your family or events in your family history? Are there stories that give you an idea of who you are and where you have come from?

NO SNAPSHOTS IN THE ATTIC: A GRANDDAUGHTER'S SEARCH FOR A CHEROKEE PAST

Connie May Fowler

Connie May Fowler is a novelist who currently lives in Florida, the state where she was born. She is the author of Sugar Cage *(1991) and* River of Hidden Dreams, *(1994) a book about the grandmother she discusses in the following essay. She has also written articles for the* New York Times Book Review, Allure, *and* Southern Living. *"Snapshots in the Attic: A Granddaughter's Search for a Cherokee Past" was originally published in the* New York Times Book Review *in May 1994. It is included as an appendix to* River of Hidden Dreams, *published in the same year. In her essay, Connie May Fowler writes about her quest for any stories, myths, and facts she could find about her family's history. Fowler is mainly concerned about her grandmother, a Cherokee by birth.*

Facts about the Cherokee People

The history of the Cherokee people is both rich and tragic. Originally, the Cherokee inhabited the Great Lakes region of the United States but migrated south when defeated by the Iroquois and Delaware peoples. Before the Europeans arrived, the Cherokee, like their Creek neighbors in the southeast, lived in a confederation of "red" and "white" villages designated as "war" and "peace" villages, respectively. War ceremonies took place in the red villages, while the white towns were reserved as sanctuaries. During the Revolutionary War, the Cherokee sided with the British against the American colonists. In the eighteenth century, a series of wars and treaties resulted in millions of tribal acres being taken from the Cherokee people. Sequoyah[1] developed a written language in 1821, and most Cherokees attained literacy shortly afterward. They lost the last land they held in Georgia in the Treaty of Echota in 1835 and were evicted in 1838 under the Indian Removal Act. The Trail of Tears, a forced march from Georgia to what is now northeastern Oklahoma, claimed the lives of 4,000 of the 15,000 Cherokee people who began the trip. Approximately 47,000 of their descendants live in eastern Oklahoma and another 3,000 lives in western North Carolina.

1   For as long as anyone can remember, poverty has crawled all over the hearts of my family, contributing to a long tradition of premature deaths and a lifetime of stories stymied behind the mute lips of the dead. The survivors have been left without any tangible signs that evoke the past: no photographs or diaries, no wedding bands or wooden nickels.

2   This absence of a record seems remarkable to me since our bloodline is diverse: Cherokee, Irish, German, French; you would think that at least a few people would have had the impulse to offer future generations a few concrete clues as to who they were. But no; our attics are empty. Up among the cobwebs and dormer-filtered light you will find not a single homemade quilt, not one musty packet of love letters.

3   Lack of hard evidence of a familial past seems unnatural to me, but I have developed a theory. I believe that my relatives, Indians and Europeans alike, couldn't waste free time on preserving a baby's first bootee. There were simply too many tales to tell about each other, living and dead, for them to be bothered by objects that would only clutter our homes and our minds.

4   The first time I noticed this compulsion to rid ourselves of handed-down possessions was in the summer of my eighth year when my mother decided to fix the front screen door, which was coming off its hinges. As she rummaged through a junk drawer for a screwdriver, she

---

[1] Sequoyah (1760–1843), also known by the name George Guess, was a Cherokee warrior who fought against intrusions by the United States into Cherokee lands. He developed a syllabic system of 86 characters by adapting letters of the English alphabet to represent sounds in the Cherokee language.

came upon a dog-eared photograph of her father. He stood in front of a shack, staring into the camera as though he could see through the lens and into the eyes of the photographer. "Oh, that old picture," my mother said disdainfully. "Nothing but a dust catcher." She tossed the photo in the trash, pulled up a chair, lit a cigarette and told me about how her Appalachian-born daddy could charm wild animals out of the woods by standing on his front porch and singing to them.

5   The idea that my family had time only for survival and storytelling takes on special significance when I think of my grandmother, my father's mother, Oneida Hunter May, a Cherokee who married a white man. Hers was a life cloaked in irony and sadness, yet 30 years after she died her personal history continues to suggest that spinning tales is a particularly honest and noble activity.

6   Throughout her adult life, the only time Oneida Hunter May felt free enough to claim her own heritage was in the stories she told her children. At all other times, publicly and privately, she declared herself white. As both a writer and a granddaughter, I have been haunted by her decision to excise her Indian heart and I have struggled to understand it. Of course, her story would work its way into my fiction, but how it did and what I would learn about the truth of cultural and familial rumors when they contradict the truth of our official histories would change the way I see the world, the way I write, and how and whom I trust.

7   Until I became an adult this is what I accepted as true about my grandmother: She was a Cherokee Indian who married a South Carolinian named John May. Early in the marriage they moved to St. Augustine, Fla. They had three children, two boys and a girl. Shortly after moving to Florida, John May abandoned his wife and children. The family believed he joined the circus. (When I was a child my family's yearly pilgrimage to the Greatest Show on Earth took on special significance as I imagined that my grandfather was the lion tamer or the high-wire artist.) Grandmama May was short and round. While she was straightforward with the family about her Indian ancestry, she avoided instilling in us a shred of Native American culture or custom. Through the use of pale powder and rouge, she lightened her skin. Her cracker-box house on the wrong side of the tracks was filled with colorful miniature glass animals and hats and boots, all stolen from tourist shops downtown. According to my father, she was "run out of town on a rail" more than once because of the stealing, and she even spent time in the city jail. Her laughter was raucous. She tended to pick me up by putting her hands under my armpits, which hurt, and it seemed as if every time I saw her she pinched my cheeks, which also hurt. My grandmother mispronounced words and her syntax was jumbled. I've since realized that her strange grammar patterns and elocution were the results of having no formal education and of speaking in a language that was not her native tongue.

8   For me, growing up was marked not only by a gradual loss of innocence but by the loss of the storytellers in my life: grandparents, aunts

and uncles, parents. With them went my ability to believe and know simple truths, to accept the face value of things without needless wrestling. As the cynicism of adulthood took hold, I began to doubt the family stories about my grandmother and I even decided my recollections were warped by time and the fuzzy judgment of childhood, and that the stories were based on oral tradition rooted in hearsay. What is this ephemeral recitation of our lives anyway? A hodgepodge of alleged fact, myth and legend made all the more unreliable because it goes unchecked by impartial inquiry. After all, don't scholars dismiss oral histories as anecdotal evidence?

9   I told myself I was far too smart to put much stock in my family's Homeric impulses. In choosing to use my grandmother's life as a stepping-off point for a new novel, I decided that everything I knew as a child was probably exaggerated at best and false at worst. I craved empirical evidence, irrefutable facts; I turned to governmental archives.

10   I began my inquiry by obtaining a copy of my grandmother's death certificate. I hoped it would provide me with details that would lead to a trail back to her early life and even to her birth. The document contained the following data: Oneida Marie Hunter May was born Aug. 14, 1901, in Dillon, S.C. She died June 8, 1963, of diabetes. But from there her history was reduced to no comment. Line 13, father's name: five black dashes. Line 14, mother's maiden name: five dashes. Line 16, Social Security number: none. The most chilling, however, because it was a lie, was line 6, color or race: white.

11   Her son, my uncle J. W., was listed as the "informant." Perhaps he thought he was honoring her by perpetuating her longstanding public falsehood. Perhaps, despite what he knew, he considered himself white—and therefore so was she. Perhaps in this small Southern town he was embarrassed or frightened to admit his true bloodline. Did he really not know his grandparents' names? Or did he fear the names would suggest his Indian lineage? Whether his answers were prompted by lack of knowledge or a desire to be evasive, the result was that the "facts" of the death certificate were suspect. The information recorded for posterity amounted to a whitewash. The son gave answers he could live with, which is what his mother had done, answers that satisfied a xenophobic society.

12   Thinking that perhaps I had started at the wrong end of the quest, I went in search of her birth certificate. I contacted the proper office in South Carolina and gave the clerk what meager information I had. I realized that without a Social Security number, my chances of locating such a document were slim, but I thought that in its thirst for data the government might have tracked Indian births. "No, I'm sorry," I was told over the phone by the clerk who had been kind enough to try an alphabetical search. "South Carolina didn't keep detailed files on Indians back then. You could try the Cherokees, but I don't think it will help. In those days they weren't keeping good records either."

13 I was beginning to understand how thoroughly a person can vanish and how—without memory and folklore—one can be doomed to oblivion. But I pursued history, and I changed my focus to Florida. I began reading accounts of St. Augustine's Indian population in the last century, hoping to gain insight into my grandmother's experience. There is not a great amount of documentation, and most of what does exist was written by long-dead Roman Catholic missionaries and Army generals, sources whose objectivity was compromised by their theological and military mandates. Nevertheless, I stumbled on an 1877 report by Harriet Beecher Stowe about the incarceration of Plains Indians at Castillo de San Marcos (then called Fort Marion) at the mouth of the St. Augustine harbor.

14 During their imprisonment, which lasted from 1875 to 1878, the Indians were forced to abandon their homes, religions, languages, their dress and all other cultural elements that white society deemed "savage"—a term used with alarming frequency in writings of the time. Calling the Indians in their pre-Christian state "untamable," "wild," and "more like grim goblins than human beings," Stowe apparently approved of what they became in the fort: Scripture-citing, broken-spirited Indians dressed like their tormentors, United States soldiers. She writes, "Might not the money now constantly spent on armies, forts and frontiers be better invested in educating young men who shall return and teach their people to live like civilized beings?"

15 The written record, I was discovering, was fabulous in its distortion, and helpful in its unabashedness. It reflected not so much truth or historical accuracy as the attitudes of the writers.

16 The most obvious evidence of the unreliable nature of history is the cultural litany set down in tourist brochures and abstracted onto brass plaques in parks and on roadsides across America. My family has lived for three generations in St. Augustine, "The Oldest Continuously Inhabited City in America. Founded in 1565." What this proclamation leaves out is everything that preceded the town's European founding. Like my uncle's carefully edited account of my grandmother's life, St. Augustine's official version amounts to historical genocide because it wipes away all traces of the activities and contributions of a specific race. For hundreds of years this spit of land between two rivers and the sea was the thriving village of Seloy, home to the Timucuan Indians. But while still aboard a ship, before ever stepping onto the white and coral-colored shores of the "New World," Pedro Menéndez renamed Seloy in honor of the patron saint of his birthplace. Then he claimed this new St. Augustine and all of "La Florida" to be the property of Spain; the Timucuans and their culture had been obliterated by a man at sea gazing at their land.

17 These distinctions between European facts and Indian facts are not trivial. The manipulation of our past is an attempt, unconscious or not, to stomp out evidence of the success and value of other cultures. My grandmother's decision to deny her heritage was fueled by the fear of what

would happen to her if she admitted to being an Indian and by the belief that there was something inherently inferior about her people. And the falsehoods and omissions she lived by affected not just her; her descendants face a personal and historical incompleteness.

18   But when the official chronicles are composed of dashes and distortions and you still hunger for the truth, what do you do? For me, the answer was to let my writer's instincts take over. I slipped inside my grandmother's skin and tried to sort out her motives and her pain. I imagined her birth and what her mother and father might have looked like. I gave them names, Nightwater and Billy. I called the character inspired by my grandmother Sparrow Hunter. She would bear a daughter, Oneida. And it would be Oneida's offspring, Sadie Hunter, who would uncover the stories that revealed the truth.

19   But I needed to know how a young Indian woman with three babies to feed survives after she's been abandoned in a 1920's tourist town that promoted as its main attraction an ancient and massive fort that had served as a prison for Comanches, Kiowas, Seminoles, Apaches, Cheyennes, Arapaho, Caddos and others. The writer-granddaughter listened to her blood-born voices and heard the answers. Her grandmother made up a birthplace and tried to forget her native tongue. She stayed out of the sun because she tanned easily, and she bought the palest foundations and powders available. She re-created herself. For her children and grandchildren never to be called "Injun" or "savage" must have been one of her most persistent hopes. And what bitter irony it must have been that her children obeyed and took on the heritage of the man who had deserted them. I was discovering that my novel would be far better served if I stopped digging for dates and numbers and instead strove to understand my grandmother's pain.

20   My research had another effect, one far more important than causing me to question our written record. It pushed me forward along the circle, inching me back to where I had started: the oral history. My family has relentlessly nurtured its oral tradition as though instinctively each of us knew that our attics would be empty for generations but our memory-fed imaginations could be filled to overbrimming with our tales of each other. And certainly, while the stories are grandiose and often tall, I decided they are no more slanted than what is fed to us in textbooks.

21   I have come to view my family's oral history as beautifully double-edged, for in fiction—oral or written—there is a desire to reveal the truth, and that desire betrays my grandmother's public lie. It is in the stories shared on our beloved windy porches and at our wide-planked pine tables, under the glare of naked moth-swept light bulbs, that the truth and the betrayal reside. Had my grandmother not felt compelled to remember her life before John May stepped into it and to relate to little Henry and J. W. and Mary Alice what times were like in South Carolina in the

early 1900's for a dirt-poor Indian girl, then a precious link to her past and ours would have been lost forever. And while she raised her children to think of themselves as solely white, she couldn't keep secret who she really was.

22   Those must have been wondrous moments when she tossed aside the mask of the liar to take up the cloak of the storyteller. It was a transformation rooted in our deepest past, for she transcended her ordinary state and for a brief time became a shaman, a holy person who through reflection, confession and interpretation offered to her children an opportunity to become members of the family of humankind, the family that traces its history not through DNA and documents but through the follies and triumphs, the struggles and desires of one another. So I turn to where the greatest measure of truth exists: the stories shared between mother and child, sister and brother, passed around the table like a platter of hot biscuits and gravy and consumed with hungry fervor.

23   My attempt to write about my grandmother's life was slow and often agonizing. But turning a tangle of information and inspiration into a novel and into a facet of the truth that would shine was the process of becoming a child again, of rediscovering the innocence of faith, of accepting as true what I have always known. I had to believe in the storyteller and her stories again.

24   The novel my grandmother inspired is fiction, for sure, but it reinforces the paradox that most writers, editors and readers know: fiction is often truer than nonfiction. A society knows itself most clearly not through the allegedly neutral news media or government propaganda or historical records but through the biased eyes of the artist, the writer. When that vision is tempered by heaven and hell, by an honesty of the intellect and gut, it allows the reader and viewer to safely enter worlds of brutal truth, confrontation and redemption. It allows the public as both voyeur and safely distanced participant to say, "Aha! I know that man. I know that woman. Their struggles, their temptations, their betrayals, their triumphs are mine."

25   One of my favorite relatives was Aunt Emily, J. W.'s wife. I saw her the night of my father's death in 1966 and—because my aunt and uncle divorced and because my father's death was a catastrophic event that blew my family apart—I did not see her again until 1992. She was first in line for the hometown book signing of my debut novel, *Sugar Cage*. We had a tearful and happy reunion, and before she left she said, "I remember the day you were born and how happy I was that you were named for your Grandmother Oneida."

26   I looked at her stupidly for a moment, not understanding what she was saying. Then it dawned on me that she misunderstood my middle name because we pronounced Oneida as though it rhymed with Anita. "Oh no," I told her. "My name is Connie Anita." Aunt Emily smiled and said, "Sweetheart, the nurse wrote it down wrong on your birth certificate. All

of us except for your grandmother got a big laugh out of the mistake. But believe me, it's what your parents said: you're Connie Oneida."

27   I loved that moment, for it was a confirmation of the integrity of our oral histories and the frailties of our official ones. As I go forward with a writing life, I accept that my creative umbilical cord is attached to my ancestors. And to their stories. I've decided to allow their reflective revelations to define me in some measure. And I have decided not to bemoan my family's bare attics and photo albums, because as long as we can find the time to sit on our porches or in front of our word processors and continue the tradition of handing down stories, I believe we will flourish as Indians, high-wire artists, animal charmers and writers all. And the truth will survive. It may be obscured occasionally by the overblown or sublime, but at least it will still be there, giving form to our words and fueling our compulsion to tell the tale.

Reading for Meaning

1. What are some of the reasons why Connie May Fowler is unable to find "photographs . . . diaries, . . . wedding bands or wooden nickels"—of her family's past? Discuss the value or limitations of taking family photographs or videos.

2. What purpose does storytelling serve for Fowler's grandmother? Why are those stories important to the author?

3. How do you explain Fowler's fascination with her grandmother? What does she seem to represent for her granddaughter?

4. Fowler says that "fiction is often truer than nonfiction" (paragraph 24). What does she mean by that? What circumstances can you think of in which her statement might be true?

5. Fowler maintains that Harriet Beecher Stowe's comments on Native Americans (paragraphs 13 and 14) and historical records in general reflect "not so much truth or historical accuracy as the attitudes of the writers." Examine Stowe's comments closely, describe her attitude toward native Americans, and examine the assumptions behind her conclusions about Native peoples.

Comparing Texts

1. Summarize the facts Connie May Fowler is able to gather about the attitude of whites toward Native Americans in general and her family in particular. How does this conflict compare with the tension between European Americans in the United States and Japanese Americans described in David Mura's essay "Fictive Fragments of a Father and Son," page 436?

2. What follows are two descriptions of Native Americans written in the seventeenth century. The first, by William Wood, is the eighth chapter of his book, *New England's Prospect*, published in 1634; the second passage, published in Amsterdam three years later, appears in chapter 20 of Thomas Morton's *New English Canaan*. As you read these texts, identify the attitudes toward Native peoples that the writers reveal through their choice of language, details, and subjects.

CHAPTER 8
OF THEIR HARDINESS

1. For their hardiness it may procure admiration, no ordinary pains making them so much as alter their countenance. Beat them, whip them, pinch them, punch them, if they resolve not to winch for it, they will not. Whether it be their benumbed insensibleness of smart, or their hardy resolutions, I cannot tell. It might be [that] a Perillus his bull[1] or the disjointing rack might force a roar from them, but a Turkish drubbing would not much molest them. And although they be naturally much afraid of death, yet the unexpected approach of a mortal wound by a bullet, arrow, or sword strikes no more terror, causes no more exclamation, no more complaint or winching than if it had been a shot into the body of a tree.

2. Such wounds as would be sudden death to an Englishman would be nothing to them: some of them having been shot in at the mouth and out under the ear; some shot in the breast, some run through the flanks with darts, and other many desperate wounds which either by their rare skill in the use of vegetatives or diabolical charms they cure in short time.[2]

3. Although their hardiness bear them out in such things wherein they are sure death will not ensue, yet can it not dispel the fear of death; the very name and thoughts of it is so hideous to them, or anything that presents it or threatens it so terrible, insomuch that a hundred of them will run from two or three guns though they know they can but dispatch two or three at a discharge. Yet every man, fearing it may be his lot to meet with his last, will not come near that in good earnest which he dare play withal in jest. To make this good by a passage of experience: three men having occasion of trade amongst the western Indians went up with some such commodities as they thought most fit for trade. To secure their person they took a carbine, two pistols, and a sword, which in outward show was not great resistance to a hundred well-skilled bowmen. The Indians hearing their guns making a thundering noise desired to finger one of them and see it discharged into a tree, wondering much at the percussion of the bullet. But they abiding two or three days, the guns were forgotten and they began to look at the odds (being a hundred to three), whereupon they were animated to work treason against the lives of these men and to take away their goods from them by force. But one of the English, understanding their language, smelt out their treachery, and being more fully informed of their intent by the Indian women, who had more pity, he steps to their king and hailing him by the long hair

---

[1] The hollow bronze bull of the tyrant Phalaris, in which criminals were roasted to death. Built by Perillus (ca. 550 B.C.) who became its first victim.

[2] On Indian remedies for wounds and diseases see Williams, *Key into the Language,* ch. 31; and Virgil J. Vogel, *American Indian Medicine* (Norman, OK, 1970).

from the rest of his council commanded him either to go before him and guide him home or else he would there kill him. The sagamore seeing him so rough had not the courage to resist him, but went with him two miles. But being exasperated by his men who followed him along to resist and go no further, in the end he would not, either for the fair promises nor fierce threatenings, so that they were constrained there to kill him, which struck such an amazement and daunting into the rest of that naked crew, with the sight of the guns, that though they might easily have killed them, yet had they not the power to shoot an arrow, but followed them, yelling and howling for the death of their king, forty miles. His goods being left among them, he sent word by other Indians that unless they sent him his goods again, which he there left, he would serve them as he served their king, whereupon they returned him his commodities with entreaty of peace and promises of fairer trade if he came again.

4   If these heartless Indians were so cowed with so slender an onset on their own dunghill, when there were scarce six families of ours in the country, what need we now fear them, being grown into thousands and having knowledge of martial discipline? In the night they need not to be feared for they will not budge from their own dwellings for fear of their Abamacho (the Devil) whom they much fear, especially in evil enterprises. They will rather lie by an English fire than go a quarter of a mile in the dark to their own dwellings. But they are well freed from this scarecrow since the coming of the English and less care for his delusions. And whereas it hath been reported that there are such horrible apparitions, fearful roarings, thundering and lightning raised by the Devil to discourage the English in their settling, I for mine own part never saw or heard of any of these things in the country. Nor have I heard of any Indians that have lately been put in fear, saving two or three, and they worse scared than hurt, who seeing a blackamore in the top of a tree, looking out for his way which he had lost, surmised he was Abamacho or the Devil (deeming all devils that are blacker than themselves) and being near to the plantation they posted to the English and entreated their aide to conjure this devil to his own place, who finding him to be a poor wandering blackamore, conducted him to his master.

Chapter 20
That the Salvages Live a Contended Life[1]

1   Gentleman and a traveller, that had bin in the parts of New England for a time, when hee retorned againe, in his difcourfe of the Country,

---

[1] Because Morton's essay is an authentic copy of the original text, it retains the seventeenth century style of lettering, which means the letter "s" looks like an "f" whenever it appears in the text.

wondered, (as hee faid,) that the natives of the land lived fo poorely in fo rich a Country, like to our Beggers in England. Surely that Gentleman had not time or leafure whiles hee was there truely to informe himfelfe of the ftate of that Country, and the happy life the Salvages would leade weare they once brought to Chriftianity.

2   I muft confeffe they want the ufe and benefit of Navigation, (which is the very finnus of a flourifhing Commonwealth,) yet are they fupplied with all manner of needefull things for the maintenance of life and lifelyhood. Foode and rayment are the cheife of all that we make true ufe of; and of thefe they finde no want, but have, and may have, them in a moft plentifull manner.[2]

3   If our beggers of England fhould, with fo much eafe as they, furnifh themfelves with foode at all feafons, there would not be fo many ftarved in the ftreets, neither would fo many gaoles be ftuffed, or galloufes furnifhed with poore wretches, as I have feene them.

4   But they of this fort of our owne nation, that are fitt to goe to this Canaan, are not able to tranfport themfelves; and moft of them unwilling to goe from the good ale tap, which is the very loadftone of the lande by which our Englifh beggers fteere theire Courfe; it is the Northpole to which the flowre-de-luce of their compaffe points. The more is the pitty that the Commonalty of oure Land are of fuch leaden capacities as to neglect fo brave a Country, that doth fo plentifully feede maine lufty and a brave, able men, women and children, that have not the meanes that a Civilized Nation hath to purchafe foode and rayment; which that Country with a little induftry will yeeld a man in a very comfortable meafure, without overmuch carking....

5   Now fince it is but foode and rayment that men that live needeth, (though not all alike,) why fhould not the Natives of New England be fayd to live richly, having no want of either? Cloaths are the badge of finne; and the more variety of fafhions is but the greater abufe of the Creature: the beafts of the forreft there doe ferve to furnifh them at any time when they pleafe: fifh and flefh they have in greate abundance, which they both roaft and boyle.

---

[2] "They live in a country where *we* now have all the conveniences of human life: but as for *them,* their *houfing* is nothing but a few *mats* tyed about *poles* faftened in the earth, where a good *fire* is their *bed-clothes* in the coldeft feafons; their *clothing* is but a fkin of a beaft, covering their *hind-parts,* their *fore-parts* having but a little apron, where nature calls for fecrecy; their *diet* has not a greater dainty than their *Nokehick,* that is a fpoonful of their *parched meal,* with a fpoonful of *water,* which will ftrengthen them to travel a day together; except we fhould mention the flefh of *deers, bears, mofe, rackoons,* and the like, which they have when they can *catch* them; as alfo a little *fifh,* which, if they would preferve, it was by *drying,* not by *falting;* for they had not a grain of *falt* in the world, I think, till we beftowed it on them." *Magnalia,* B. III. part iii. In his *Letters and Notes on the North American Indians (Letter No. 17)* Catlin comments on the failure of the Indians to make ufe of falt, even in localities where it abounds.

6   They are indeed not ferved in difhes of plate with variety of Sauces to procure appetite; that needs not there. The rarity of the aire, begot by the medicinable quality of the fweete herbes of the Country, always procures good ftomakes to the inhabitants.

7   I muft needs commend them in this particular, that, though they buy many commodities of our Nation, yet they keepe but fewe, and thofe of fpeciall ufe.

8   They love not to bee cumbered with many utenfilles, and although every proprietor knowes his owne, yet all things, (fo long as they will laft), are ufed in common amongft them: a bifket cake given to one, that one breakes it equally into fo many parts as there be perfons in his company, and diftributes it. Platoes Commonwealth is fo much practifed by thefe people.

9   According to humane reafon, guided onely by the light of nature, thefe people leades the more happy and freer life, being voyde of care, which torments the mindes of fo many Chriftians: They are not delighted in baubles, but in ufefull things.

10   Their naturall drinke is of the Criftall fountaine, and this they take up in their hands, by joyning them clofe together. They take up a great quantity at a time, and drinke at the wrifts. It was the fight of fuch a feate which made Diogenes hurle away his difhe, and, like one that would have this principall confirmed, *Natura paucis contentat,* ufed a difh no more.

11   I have obferved that they will not be troubled with fuperfluous commodities. Such things as they finde they are taught by neceffity to make ufe of, they will make choife of, and feeke to purchafe with induftry. So that, in refpect that their life is fo voyd of care, and they are fo loving alfo that they make ufe of thofe things they enjoy, (the wife onely excepted,) as common goods, and are therein fo compaffionate that, rather than one fhould ftarve through want, they would ftarve all. Thus doe they paffe away the time merrily, not regarding our pompe, (which they fee dayly before their faces,) but are better content with their owne, which fome men efteeme fo meanely of.

12   They may be rather accompted to live richly, wanting nothing that is needefull; and to be commended for leading a contented life, the younger being ruled by the Elder, and the Elder ruled by the Powahs, and the Powahs are ruled by the Devill;[3] and then you may imagin what good rule is like to be amongft them.

---

[3] The relations fuppofed to exift between the Indians and the devil have been referred to in a pervious note. It is, however, a fomewhat curious fact that the aboriginal hierarchy, fuggefted in the text, had a few years before found its exact political counterpart in the talk of the Englifh people. "'Who governs the land?' it was afked. 'Why, the King?' 'And who governs the King?' 'Why, the Duke of Buckingham.' 'And who governs the Duke?' 'Why, the Devil.'" (Ewald's *Stories from the State Papers,* vol. ii. p. 117.) (Editor's note to the 1883 edition.)

Ideas for Writing

1. Write an oral history about one or two important periods in the life of a person in your family. As an alternative, write about someone you know whose life seems interesting to you. Interview your subject first, and develop questions that will help your interviewee focus on an important historical or personal period in his or her life. Record factual details and emotional situations that define the importance of that period for the person you are interviewing.

2. Briefly explain the value of storytelling for Connie May Fowler's family. Then describe the role that this kind of storytelling has in your family or explain what your family uses in its place.

3. In the search for facts about her grandmother's life, Fowler discovers that what she once thought were "irrefutable facts" of history have less to do with "historical accuracy" than with "the attitudes of the writers." Write a short essay in which you discuss other events in U.S. history in which the biases of historians or other authorities may have distorted the truth.

4. In the beginning of her essay, Fowler discounts her family's stories because they embellish the truth and lack "empirical evidence." Write an essay explaining why such stories are valuable. Use examples from Fowler's account and your own experiences and observations to support your position.

5. If it is available to you, view the film *Aguirre, Wrath of God*, directed by Werner Herzog. Analyze Herzog's attitude toward the conquistadors in the film. Be sure to specify how he conveys this attitude through the characters' behavior, their interaction with native cultures, and their ideals and obsessions.

6. The following selections are from *River of Hidden Dreams*, Fowler's novel based on her fictional re-creation of her grandmother's life. In the novel, Sadie Hunter, a fictional double for Connie May Fowler, writes about her grandmother's forced removal from her Native American family. Sadie speculates that Alice Motherwell, a widow who had just lost her only child, adopted Sadie's grandmother out of a "mixture of self-righteous charity and soul-spoiling revenge." Sadie describes Miss Motherwell's attempts

   > to lighten my grandmama's hair with lemon juice as she told her that for the rest of her days she would be known not by an Indian name but called Susannah and as she taught her Southern manners and dressed her in lovely clothes picked out of mail-order catalogues, she must have been giddy with all the bloodletting, just absolutely satiated by the belief that she was destroying the Indian part of my grandmama . . . as she resurrected in Sparrow-now-Susannah the image of her dead daughter.

   In passages included here, Fowler recreates the abduction of Sadie's grandmother in the grandmother's voice. After you have read the following excerpt carefully, write a paper in which you explain how well Fowler seems to "understand [her] grandmother's pain," a goal she set herself in "No Snapshots in the Attic," and whether she is able to convey that pain to the reader.

Chapter 5 The Family **149**

1. Listen to me, Sadie, that is what I was like as a budding young woman: beautiful and obedient and wild. Sometimes I managed to be all three at once—an ability firmly rooted in youth.

2. I remember the day Miss Alice took me away from my captors and family and brought me to her house, which was just across the street from the fort and had a fragrant garden of white roses. The rose beds were thick and well kept and were edged in seashells. But I didn't know that yet. The only thing I knew about up to that day was the fort, its dankness, its stale smell of death.

3. The day of my departure, I was standing on the fort terreplein with my parents. My father was looking out to sea and my mother was fitfully stringing a necklace of shells, and I had my hand on her skirt but she wasn't looking at me. She hadn't looked at me in two days, not since it was decided I would not return west with them. I had become, you see, enraptured with the idea of living in the looming house that faced the bay, with its gingerbread scrollwork and its rooms filled with treasures and its owner, Miss Alice, who would care for and nurture me as if I was a worthy Christian child and had never been a "savage." I hated that term, and my new self held great disdain for anyone who was a "savage." I thought I could leave my mother and father because I wasn't like them anymore. But then, as the act of leaving became more than just a fanciful idea and progressed to the point that the matter had, as the captain announced, "been settled," my resolve weakened and I found myself wishing that my mother and father could move with me into that grand house. But it was too late. The die had been cast.

4. A slack-jawed soldier walked up the narrow steps and past a cannon and over to me and muttered, "Let's go." I didn't fully understand what was happening, I didn't recognize the finality of the unfolding events. I tried to put my arms around my mother's neck. She pulled away and said, "Go, now." And then she touched my hair, but her gaze never met mine. I looked to my father, who still had his back to me. He said something softly and in a language I no longer wanted to understand. I turned to the soldier to see if he'd heard that forbidden tongue. If he did he chose to ignore it, pushing me toward the stairs and warning, "Don't give me any trouble."

5. He held on to my arm as he led me to the captain's office. But the captain wasn't there. No one was. The soldier told me to wait inside and to not touch anything. I didn't. I tried to do what I was told. But I was alone and fearful: Maybe Miss Alice wasn't coming for me. Maybe they were going to send me to yet another strange and awful place. I had to bite back my tears. I listened to the captain's mantel clock tick tick tick tick. The sound echoed off the thick coquina walls like water dripping into an empty pail. I wanted to spin the big hand around to see if time would tick by faster. I may have even reached toward the clock. But then I heard the door open and I jumped back and Miss Alice was standing in the doorway, dressed in

a proper charcoal skirt and bustle and white silk blouse. She said, "Susannah, dear, I'm so glad to see you. I've come to take you home!"

6 She walked over to me and put her hands on my shoulders. She knelt down—her skirts rustling like crumpled paper—so that we were eye to eye. I knew that she was a powerful person, maybe even capable of sorcery, for surely anyone marked by God with eyes of brown and blue knew and saw things beyond this world.

7 "Susannah, child," she said, "when you leave this fort you will begin a new life. The past for you doesn't exist. You are my child now. The savage in you is dead." She squeezed my fingers and prayerfully shut her eyes as she said, "And a God-fearing white child is born." Then she looked at me intently, as if my answer mattered, and said, "Do you understand?"

8 I responded the way a good child should: "Yes, ma'am." Then, with one hand on my back, she guided me out of the captain's office and away from the ticking clock, past three soldiers, through the courtyard and out the massive door, over the moat, and we started down the fort's rolling green. But I thought I heard wailing. My mother wailing.

9 I looked over my shoulder, toward the sound. Suddenly I wanted to run back to my mother, crawl into her lap, and tell her everything was fine. I didn't want her to be sad.

10 But I couldn't stop. Miss Alice grabbed my arm and we walked swiftly. I couldn't keep up. Each time I stumbled she pulled me so that even though I wasn't exactly walking I was always headed in forward motion, propelled by her iron grip until we were across the street and standing among her roses.

11 It was strange to me then and is strange to me now, but as soon as Miss Alice opened her front door, the wailing stopped. I never heard it again. Except sometimes in the early morning, upon waking, I would look out my bedroom window with its view of the bay and the fort and I was almost positive that I'd listened to it all night long in my dreams. But I could never be sure.

Writing before Reading

1. Have you suffered a loss that at the time felt devastating? How did you come to terms with that loss? What kinds of things did you do to keep yourself going?

2. In your experience, how do children cope with the pain and disappointment that follows a divorce, a conflict in the family, or the loss of a loved one? Do some methods of coping seem to work better than others?

THE WATER-FAUCET VISION

Gish Jen

Gish Jen is a novelist and short story writer who currently lives in Cambridge, Massachusetts. Jen was born in New York in 1955. She attended Harvard University, and has a master's of fine arts from the University of Iowa. She has taught in China as well as at Tufts and the University of Massachusetts. She has received grants and awards from the James Michener/Copernicus Society and the Bunting Institute. Her novel, Typical American, *was a nominee for the National Book Critics' Circle Award. Her short story, "The Water-Faucet Vision," which takes place in the United States, depicts a little girl's belief in the power of miracles to correct things that have gone wrong in her life.*

The characters in Gish Jen's short story are ethnic Chinese living in the United States. For information about China, see page 131.

1 To protect my sister Mona and me from the pains—or, as they pronounced it, the "pins"—of life, my parents did their fighting in Shanghai dialect, which we didn't understand; and when my father one day pitched a brass vase through the kitchen window, my mother told us he had done it by accident.

2 "By accident?" said Mona.

3 My mother chopped the foot off a mushroom.

4 "By accident?" said Mona. "By *accident?*"

5 Later I tried to explain to her that she shouldn't have persisted like that, but it was hopeless.

6 "What's the matter with throwing things," she shrugged. "He was *mad.*"

7 That was the difference between Mona and me: Fighting was just fighting to her. If she worried about anything, it was only that she might turn out too short to become a ballerina, in which case she was going to be a piano player.

8 I, on the other hand, was going to be a martyr. I was in fifth grade then, and the hyperimaginative sort—the kind of girl who grows morbid in Catholic school, who longs to be chopped or frozen to death but then has nightmares about it from which she wakes up screaming and clutching a stuffed bear. It was not a bear that I clutched, though, but a string of three malachite beads that I had found in the marsh by the old aqueduct one day. Apparently once part of a necklace, they were each wonderfully striated and swirled, and slightly humped toward the center, like a jellyfish; so that if I squeezed one, it would slip smoothly away, with a grace that altogether enthralled and—on those dream-harrowed nights—soothed me, soothed me as nothing had before or has since. Not that I've lacked occasion for soothing: Though it's been four months since my

mother died, there are still nights when sleep stands away from me, stiff as a well-paid sentry. But that is another story. Back then I had my malachite beads, and if I worried them long and patiently enough, I was sure to start feeling better, more awake, even a little special—imagining, as I liked to, that my nightmares were communications from the Almighty Himself, preparation for my painful destiny. Discussing them with Patty Creamer, who had also promised her life to God, I called them "almost visions"; and Patty, her mouth wadded with the three or four sticks of doublemint she always seemed to have going at once, said, "I bet you'll be doin' miracleth by seventh grade."

9   Miracles. Today Patty laughs to think she ever spent good time stewing on such matters, her attention having long turned to rugs, and artwork, and antique Japanese bureaus—things she believes in.

10   "A good bureau's more than just a bureau," she explained last time we had lunch. "It's a hedge against life. I tell you, if there's one thing I believe, it's that cheap stuff's just money out the window. Nice stuff, on the other hand—now that you can always cash out, if life gets rough. *That you can count on.*"

11   In fifth grade, though, she counted on different things.

12   "You'll be doing miracles too," I told her, but she shook her shaggy head and looked doleful.

13   "Na' me," she chomped. "Buzzit's okay. The kin' things I like, prayers work okay on."

14   "Like?"

15   "Like you 'member that dreth I liked?"

16   She meant the yellow one, with the criss-cross straps.

17   "Well gueth what."

18   "Your mom got it for you."

19   She smiled. "And I only jutht prayed for it for a week," she said.

20   As for myself, though, I definitely wanted to be able to perform a wonder or two. Miracle-working! It was the carrot of carrots: It kept me doing my homework, taking the sacraments; it kept me mournfully on key in music hour, while my classmates hiccuped and squealed their carefree hearts away. Yet I couldn't have said what I wanted such powers *for,* exactly. That is, I thought of them the way one might think of, say, an ornamental sword—as a kind of collectible, which also happened to be a means of defense.

21   But then Patty's father walked out on her mother, and for the first time, there was a miracle I wanted to do. I wanted it so much I could see it: Mr. Creamer made into a spitball; Mr. Creamer shot through a straw into the sky; Mr. Creamer unrolled and re-plumped, plop back on Patty's doorstep. I would've cleaned out his mind and given him a shave en route. I would've given him a box of peanut fudge, tied up with a ribbon, to present to Patty with a kiss.

22	But instead all I could do was try to tell her he'd come back.
23	"He will not, he will not!" she sobbed. "He went on a boat to Rio Deniro. To Rio Deniro!"
24	I tried to offer her a stick of gum, but she wouldn't take it.
25	"He said he would rather look at water than at my mom's fat face. He said he would rather look at water than at me." Now she was really wailing, and holding her ribs so tightly that she almost seemed to be hurting herself—so tightly that just looking at her arms wound around her like snakes made my heart feel squeezed.
26	I patted her on the arm. A one-winged pigeon waddled by.
27	"He said I wasn't even his kid, he said I came from Uncle Johnny. He said I was garbage, just like my mom and Uncle Johnny. He said I wasn't even his kid, he said I wasn't his Patty, he said I came from Uncle Johnny!"
28	"From your Uncle Johnny?" I said stupidly.
29	"From Uncle Johnny," she cried. "From Uncle Johnny!"
30	"He said that?" I said. Then, wanting to go on, to say *something*, I said, "Oh Patty, don't cry."
31	She kept crying.
32	I tried again. "Oh Patty, don't cry," I said. Then I said, "Your dad was a jerk anyway."
33	The pigeon produced a large runny dropping.
34	It was a good twenty minutes before Patty was calm enough for me just to run to the girls' room to get her some toilet paper; and by the time I came back she was sobbing again, saying "To Rio Deniro, to Rio Deniro" over and over again, as though the words had stuck in her and couldn't be gotten out. As we had missed the regular bus home and the late bus too, I had to leave her a second time to go call my mother, who was only mad until she heard what had happened. Then she came and picked us up, and bought us each a fudgsicle.
35	Some days later, Patty and I started a program to work on getting her father home. It was a serious business. We said extra prayers, and lit votive candles; I tied my malachite beads to my uniform belt, fondling them as though they were a rosary, I a nun. We even took to walking about the school halls with our hands folded—a sight so ludicrous that our wheeze of a principal personally took us aside one day.
36	"I must tell you," she said, using her nose as a speaking tube, "that there is really no need for such peee-ity."
37	But we persisted, promising to marry God and praying to every saint we could think of. We gave up gum, then gum and slim jims both, then gum and slim jims and ice cream—and when even that didn't work, we started on more innovative things. The first was looking at flowers. We held our hands beside our eyes like blinders as we hurried by the violets by the flagpole, the window box full of tulips outside the nurse's office. Next it was looking at boys: Patty gave up angel-eyed Jamie Halloran and I, gymnastic

Anthony Rossi. It was hard, but in the end our efforts paid off. Mr. Creamer came back a month later, and though he brought with him nothing but dysentery, he was at least too sick to have all that much to say.

38   Then, in the course of a fight with my father, my mother somehow fell out of their bedroom window.

39   Recently—thinking a mountain vacation might cheer me—I sublet my apartment to a handsome but somber newlywed couple, who turned out to be every bit as responsible as I'd hoped. They cleaned out even the eggshell chips I'd sprinkled around the base of my plants as fertilizer, leaving behind only a shiny silverplate cake server and a list of their hopes and goals for the summer. The list, tacked precariously to the back of the kitchen door, began with a fervent appeal to God to help them get their wedding thank-yous written in three weeks or less. (You could see they had originally written "two weeks" but scratched it out—no miracles being demanded here.) It went on:

40   *Please help us, Almighty Father in Heaven Above, to get Ann a teaching job within a half-hour drive of here in a nice neighborhood.*

41   *Please help us, Almighty Father in Heaven Above, to get John a job doing anything where he won't strain his back and that is within a half-hour drive of here.*

42   *Please help us, Almighty Father in Heaven Above, to get us a car.*

43   *Please help us, A. F. in H. A., to learn French.*

44   *Please help us, A. F. in H. A., to find seven dinner recipes that cost less than 60 cents a serving and can be made in a half-hour. And that don't have tomatoes, since You in Your Heavenly Wisdom made John allergic.*

45   *Please help us, A. F. in H. A., to avoid books in this apartment such as You in Your Heavenly Wisdom allowed John, for Your Heavenly Reasons, to find three nights ago (June 2nd).*

46   Et cetera. In the left hand margin they kept score of how they had fared with their requests, and it was heartening to see that nearly all of them were marked "Yes! Praise the Lord" (sometimes shortened to PTL), with the sole exception of learning French, which was mysteriously marked "No! PTL to the Highest."

47   That note touched me. Strange and familiar both, it seemed like it had been written by some cousin of mine—some cousin who had stayed home to grow up, say, while I went abroad and learned what I had to, though the learning was painful. This, of course, is just a manner of speaking; in fact I did my growing up at home, like anybody else.

48   But the learning *was* painful: I never knew exactly how it happened that my mother went hurdling through the air that night years ago, only that the wind had been chopping at the house, and that the argument had started about the state of the roof. Someone had been up to fix it the year before, but it wasn't a roofer, it was some man my father had insisted

could do just as good a job for a quarter of the price. And maybe he could have, had he not somehow managed to step through a knot in the wood under the shingles and break his uninsured ankle. Now the shingles were coming loose again, and the attic insulation was mildewing besides, and my father was wanting to sell the house altogether, which he said my mother had wanted to buy so she could send pictures of it home to her family in China.

49   "The Americans have a saying," he said. "They saying, 'You have to keep up with Jones family.' I'm saying if Jones family in Shanghai, you can send any picture you want, *an-y* picture. Go take picture of those rich guys' house. You want to act like rich guys, right? Go take picture of those rich guys' house."

50   At that point my mother sent Mona and me to wash up, and started speaking Shanghaiese. They argued for some time in the kitchen, while we listened from the top of the stairs, our faces wedged between the bumpy Spanish scrolls of the wrought iron railing. First my mother ranted, then my father, then they both ranted at once until finally there was a thump, followed by a long quiet.

51   "Do you think they're kissing now?" said Mona. "I bet they're kissing, like this." She pursed her lips like a fish and was about to put them to the railing when we heard my mother locking the back door. We hightailed it into bed; my parents creaked up the stairs. Everything at that point seemed fine. Once in their bedroom, though, they started up again, first softly, then louder and louder, until my mother turned on a radio to try to disguise the noise. A door slammed; they began shouting at one another; another door slammed; a shoe or something banged the wall behind Mona's bed.

52   "How're we supposed to *sleep?*" said Mona, sitting up.

53   There was another thud, more yelling in Shanghaiese, and then my mother's voice pierced the wall, in English. "So what you want I should do? Go to work like Theresa Lee?"

54   My father rumbled something back.

55   "You think you're big shot because you have job, right? You're big shot, but you never get promotion, you never get raise. All I do is spend money, right? So what do you do, you tell me. So what do you do!"

56   Something hit the floor so hard that our room shook.

57   "So kill me," screamed my mother. "You know what you are? You are failure. Failure! You are failure!"

58   Then there was a sudden, terrific, bursting crash—and after it, as if on a bungled cue, the serene blare of an a cappella soprano, picking her way down a scale.

59   By the time Mona and I knew to look out the window, a neighbor's pet beagle was already on the scene, sniffing and barking at my mother's body, his tail crazy with excitement; then he was barking at my stunned and trembling father, at the shrieking ambulance, the police, at crying

Mona in her bunny-footed pajamas, and at me, barefoot in the cold grass, squeezing her shoulder with one hand and clutching my malachite beads with the other.

60 My mother wasn't dead, only unconscious, the paramedics figured that out right away, but there was blood everywhere, and though they were reassuring about her head wounds as they strapped her to the stretcher, commenting also on how small she was, how delicate, how light, my father kept saying, "I killed her, I killed her" as the ambulance screeched and screeched headlong, forever, to the hospital. I was afraid to touch her, and glad of the metal rail between us, even though its sturdiness made her seem even frailer than she was; I wished she was bigger, somehow, and noticed, with a pang, that the new red slippers we had given her for Mother's Day had been lost somewhere along the way. How much she seemed to be leaving behind, as we careened along—still not there, still not there—Mona and Dad and the medic and I taking up the whole ambulance, all the room, so there was no room for anything else; no room even for my mother's real self, the one who should have been pinching the color back to my father's grey face, the one who should have been calming Mona's cowlick—the one who should have been bending over us, to help us to be strong, to help us get through, even as we bent over her.

61 Then suddenly we were there, the glowing square of the emergency room entrance opening like the gates of heaven; and immediately the talk of miracles began. Alive, a miracle. No bones broken, a miracle. A miracle that the hemlocks cushioned her fall, a miracle that they hadn't been trimmed in a year and a half. It was a miracle that all that blood, the blood that had seemed that night to be everywhere, was from one shard of glass, a single shard, can you imagine, and as for the gash in her head, the scar would be covered by hair. The next day my mother cheerfully described just how she would part it so that nothing would show at all.

62 "You're a lucky duck-duck," agreed Mona, helping herself, with a little *pirouette,* to the cherry atop my mother's chocolate pudding.

63 That wasn't enough for me, though. I was relieved, yes, but what I wanted by then was a real miracle, not for her simply to have survived but for the whole thing never to have happened—for my mother's head never to had to have been shaved and bandaged like that, for her high, proud forehead to never have been swollen down over her eyes, for her face and neck and hands never to have been painted so many shades of blue-black, and violet, and chartreuse. I still want those things—for my parents not to have had to live with this affair like a prickle-bush between them, for my father to have been able to look my mother in her swollen eyes and curse the madman, the monster that could have dared done this to the woman he loved. I wanted to be able to touch my mother without shuddering, to be able to console my father, to be able to get that crash

out of my head, the sound of that soprano—so many things that I didn't know how to pray for them, that I wouldn't have known where to start even if I had the power to work miracles, right there, right then.

64 A week later, when my mother was home, and her head beginning to bristle with new hairs, I lost my malachite beads. I had been carrying them in a white cloth pouch that Patty had given me, and was swinging the pouch on my pinky on my way home from school, when I swung just a bit too hard, and it went sailing in a long arc through the air, whooshing like a perfectly thrown basketball through one of the holes of a nearby sewer. There was no chance of fishing it out: I looked and looked, crouching on the sticky pavement until the asphalt had grazed the skin of my hands and knees, but all I could discern was an evil-smelling musk, glassy and smug and impenetrable.

65 My loss didn't quite hit me until I was home, but then it produced an agony all out of proportion to my string of pretty beads. I hadn't cried at all during my mother's accident, and now I was crying all afternoon, all through dinner, and then after dinner too, crying past the point where I knew what I was crying for, wishing dimly that I had my beads to hold, wishing dimly that I could pray but refusing, refusing, I didn't know why, until I finally fell into an exhausted sleep on the couch, where my parents left me for the night—glad, no doubt, that one of the more tedious of my childhood crises seemed to be finally winding off the reel of life, onto the reel of memory. They covered me, and somehow grew a pillow under my head, and, with uncharacteristic disregard for the living-room rug, left some milk and pecan sandies on the coffee table, in case I woke up hungry. Their thoughtfulness was prescient: I did wake up in the early part of the night; and it was then, amid the unfamiliar sounds and shadows of the living room, that I had what I was sure was a true vision.

66 Even now what I saw retains an odd clarity: the requisite strange light flooding the room, first orange, and then a bright yellow-green, then a crackling bright burst like a Roman candle going off near the piano. There was a distinct smell of coffee, and a long silence. The room seemed to be getting colder. Nothing. A creak; the light starting to wane, then waxing again, brilliant pink now. Still nothing. Then, as the pink started to go a little purple, a perfectly normal middle-aged man's voice, speaking something very like pig latin, told me quietly not to despair, not to despair, my beads would be returned to me.

67 That was all. I sat a moment in the dark, then turned on the light, gobbled down the cookies—and in a happy flash understood I was so good, really, so near to being a saint that my malachite beads would come back through the town water system. All I had to do was turn on all the faucets in the house, which I did, one by one, stealing quietly into the bathroom and kitchen and basement. The old spigot by the washing machine was too gunked up to be coaxed very far open, but that didn't matter. The water didn't have to be full blast, I understood that. Then I

gathered together my pillow and blanket and trundled up to my bed to sleep.

68   By the time I woke up in the morning I knew that my beads hadn't shown up, but when I knew it for certain, I was still disappointed; and as if that weren't enough, I had to face my parents and sister, who were all abuzz with the mystery of the faucets. Not knowing what else to do, I, like a puddlebrain, told them the truth. The results were predictably painful.

69   "Callie had a *vision*," Mona told everyone at the bus stop. "A vision with lights, and sinks in it!"

70   Sinks, visions. I got it all day, from my parents, from my classmates, even some sixth and seventh graders. Someone drew a cartoon of me with a halo over my head in one of the girls' room stalls; Anthony Rossi made gurgling noises as he walked on his hands at recess. Only Patty tried not to laugh, though even she was something less than unalloyed understanding.

71   "I don't think miracles are thupposed to happen in *thewers*," she said.

72   Such was the end of my saintly ambitions. It wasn't the end of all holiness; the ideas of purity and goodness still tippled my brain, and over the years I came slowly to grasp of what grit true faith was made. Last night, though, when my father called to say that he couldn't go on living in our old house, that he was going to move to a smaller place, another place, maybe a condo—he didn't know how, or where—I found myself still wistful for the time religion seemed all I wanted it to be. Back then the world was a place that could be set right: One had only to direct the hand of the Almighty and say, just here, Lord, we hurt here—and here, and here, and here.

Reading for Meaning

1. How does "faith" work for Callie in "The Water-Faucet Vision"?

2. What significance do the malachite beads have for Callie? Why does her loss of those beads produce "an agony all out of proportion" to the loss?

3. What does the list left by the tenants who sublet Callie's apartment reveal about them? How do you explain Callie's feelings of kinship toward them?

4. Several times in the story, Callie mentions events that happened recently—subletting her apartment, her mother's death. Why does she include these particular events from her adult life in a story that is principally about events in her childhood?

5. Identify sources of humor in "The Water-Faucet Vision."

Comparing Texts

1. Read "Slowly Becoming" by Malidoma Patrice Somé, page 537. In what ways are the connections to a supernatural power similar to or different from those expressed in "The Water-Faucet Vision"?

2. Read "Razia Begum in London," page 445, and examine the story for its use of point of view. How do Gish Jen, in "The Water-Faucet Vision," and Ruxana Meer, in "Razia Begum in London," employ the child's point of view in their stories? Does the perspective of the adult writer figure into either story? If so, how is it used?

Ideas for Writing

1. Write an essay in which you describe how you or people you know have used superstition to explain circumstances that appeared hopeless or beyond ordinary human power to control.

2. Analyze the techniques that Gish Jen uses to develop her character Callie.

3. Initially, Callie relied on miracles to correct things in her life and in the lives of her family and friends that were too painful to accept. Do some investigating and write a paper in which you discuss the function(s) that religion seems to have for individuals or groups of people. To gather information for your paper, interview several people you know, post questions on an electronic bulletin board, or consult a few works by social scientists and psychologists who have written on the subject. Consider reading *Civilization and Its Discontents,* which contains Sigmund Freud's analysis of the purpose of religion.

Writing before Reading

1. In recent years, politicians and social scientists have tried to define what constitutes a legitimate, viable family. Summarize a few of these arguments. What are your views on these issues?

2. How do you think the family should be defined? What has contributed to your feelings about the meaning of "family"?

HOUSEHOLD AND FAMILY IN THE CARIBBEAN: SOME DEFINITIONS AND CONCEPTS

Nancie Solien Gonzalez

Born in Illinois, Nancie Solien Gonzalez holds a doctorate in anthropology from the University of Michigan. Her research has taken her to Guatemala (where she worked with Native and Ladino populations), the Dominican Republic, and New Mexico. Her interest in Afro-Caribbean populations began in 1956. Gonzalez has taught at several universities in the United States, including the University of California at Berkeley, the University of New Mexico, and Boston University. At the time she wrote "Household and Family in the Caribbean" she was a vice chancellor and professor of anthropology at the University of Maryland. This article first appeared in Social and Economic Studies *in 1960 and was reprinted in* The Black Woman Cross-Culturally *(1981), a collection of articles about the concerns of Black women internationally.*

Facts about the Caribbean

The tropical islands of the Caribbean lie between North and South America. The region is named for the formidable Carib Indians, once thought to be cannibals, whom Christopher Columbus met during his second voyage to the New World. The Carib traveled among the islands in large canoes and were expert navigators. Waves of French, Dutch, English, and Danish colonists who settled the islands in the seventeenth century killed most of the Carib people, just as the Spanish massacred the Arawak Indians who inhabited the Greater Antilles (today's Cuba, Jamaica, Hispaniola, and Puerto Rico) in the early sixteenth century. Today most Caribbean people are descendants of Europeans and of Africans who were brought to the region as slaves; the two populations have intermarried extensively, and as a result that the population is largely mestizo.[2] Other cultural groups include the descendants of laborers brought from China, Portugal, Spain, India, and what is now Pakistan. The United States acquired Cuba and Puerto Rico from Spain at the end of the nineteenth century and the Virgin Islands from Denmark in 1917. With the exception of Puerto Rico, Caribbean countries gained independence in the 1960s and 1970s.

1   In recent years much attention has been directed toward the family system observed in Afro-American communities. Typical features of this system include the high percentage of "non-legal" or "irregular" conjugal unions, legal marriage being typical only of the upper classes and well-to-do. The separation rate is high and children almost invariably remain with the mother. Women occupy a prominent position in this system; some writers even describe certain household groups, as being "matrifocal" (15), "mother-headed" (4), "matriarchal" (8), "maternal" (8), etc. Such designations have served to emphasize the fact that many domestic groups in these societies include no male in the role of husband-father. In spite of minor differences, especially in regard to quantitative data on the types of families found in any given community, it is apparent that the situation is fundamentally the same in such widespread areas as Jamaica,

---

[2] A person of mixed heritage, usually of both European and Native American ancestry.

Trinidad, British Guiana, Haiti, Brazil, the southern United States, and the Caribbean coast of Central America.

2   The specific object of investigation in many of these societies has been the family (1, 7, 11, 14, 15). There has been a tendency to identify the family with the household, a procedure which, as we shall see, has some precedent in anthropological usage. However, the situation in these societies differs so much from those described in other parts of the world, that great difficulty often arises when one tries to apply the classical concepts of "family" and "household" in Afro-America. Unfortunately, too often the writer merely glosses over the conceptual difficulty, using the terms interchangeably without defining them, and as a result there is much confusion in the literature.

3   It is the purpose of this paper to examine various definitions and usages of the terms "family" and "household" in order to determine their usefulness in analyzing Afro-American society.

4   Few writers have distinguished between family and household on either a theoretical or a descriptive level. Empirically the two are quite often identical, especially when one is dealing with the nuclear family. There is general agreement in the literature that within a household one finds a family of one type or another. Thus, Murdock includes common residence, along with economic co-operation and reproduction, as defining characteristics of the family (12, p. 1).

5   Radcliffe-Brown, after defining his term, "the elementary family," as a father, a mother, and their children, says that this unit "usually provides the basis for the formation of domestic groups of persons living together in intimate daily life" (13, p. 5). He goes on to give several examples of such domestic groups, each of which could be classified as an extended family.

6   Lowie defines the family as "the association" that corresponds to the institution of marriage, recognizing that the character of the interpersonal relations among the members is of more importance than the actual membership. He notes that a household may include persons unrelated by kinship ties who are excluded from the family, yet presumably to him too the family forms the core of the household (10, pp. 215–16).

7   Linton distinguishes between what he calls "conjugal" and "consanguine" families. His definition of each implies common residence of spouses and their offspring, the primary difference between the two types being that in the consanguine family the inmarrying spouses are relatively unimportant (9, pp. 159–63).

8   It is apparent that most anthropologists think of a family as a coresidential group within which there is at least one conjugal pair plus at least some of the offspring of this pair. Various extensions of this unit may occur typically in different societies, such extensions being based upon kinship ties (consanguineal and/or affinal) between other persons and one member of the original conjugal pair. Conversely, the household

generally refers to a group of persons who live together and co-operate in at least some if not all domestic affairs. A family unit of some type is generally assumed to be the nucleus of the household, though there may also be present some unrelated persons.

9   Outside of the Afro-American area there have been a few other societies described in which the above concepts do not prove useful. Notable examples include the Nayars in South Malabar and Cochin in which the household unit traditionally contained as regular members only matri-lineal kin. Gough states that "the simplest traditional dwelling-group is therefore a sibling group, together with the children and maternal grandchildren of the women" (6, p. 85).

10 The Ashanti also exhibit a pattern of duo-locality, in which husbands and wives, especially during the early years of marriage, do not reside together. Fortes describes three types of domestic unit: (a) households grouped around a husband and wife; (b) households grouped around an effective minimal matrilineage, or part of it; and (c) households made up of combinations of the two previous types (2, p. 69). Type (b), containing no conjugal pair, would not be equivalent to a family.

11 Henriques says in regard to Jamaica, "... the best method of classifying family groupings appears to be the adoption of the term domestic group as the unit of family structure in the island" (7). Yet he also notes, "In Jamaica the domestic group is the residential unit which constitutes a household. The domestic group may, but does not always, consist of the elementary biological family." On the other hand, he says, "Family groupings can be divided into those with a conjugal and those with a consanguineous basis" (p. 105).

12 R. T. Smith (16, p. 67), states that "... most writers are agreed that the main functioning family unit in the Caribbean is a household group." He then defines the household as "... a group of people occupying a single dwelling and sharing a common food supply." His data, as well as those of many other writers show that very often the household group contains no conjugal pair. He does not further define the family, but instead uses the term interchangeably with household group.

13 Obviously, these usages do not correspond to the definitions ordinarily used by anthropologists. As we have seen, in spite of minor differences in phraseology, most writers insist upon some form of marriage as the basis of the family. A household, on the other hand, is primarily a residential unit, and although it *may* and usually does include some sort of family as its core, the definition does not insist upon this as a criterion.

14 Goody (5, p. 56) takes this view when he says "... the use of the blanket term 'family' to indicate groups which are specifically defined by residence and descent as well as those defined by the existence of the marriage bond may be adequate for Euro-American systems in which there is considerable overlap, but it can be highly confusing in terms of other societies."

15   Fortes too, has pointed out that in many cases it is useful to distinguish analytically between the elementary family and the domestic group. He notes that the actual composition of the two may be identical, but that the reproductive functions of the group may be separated from the householding and housekeeping functions. He differentiates the two units on the basis of the types of bonds obtaining among the members. An elementary family is constituted solely by the bonds of marriage, filiation, and siblingship, while the household or domestic group may include persons bound together by various kinds of jural and affective bonds other than these (3).

16   One aspect of the problem in the Caribbean has been well phrased by Clarke, who says:

17   The anthropologist in search of the family *sees* [italics hers] first the house... Within that house, be it hut or cottage, is contained, for some part of the day or night, part of the group which he is about to study.

18   But what part of it? Will he find the majority of these households to contain parents and their children, or mothers only with their daughters and their daughters' children; or a man and woman with some only of their offspring? Or, instead, will he find a heterogeneous collection of kin, brought together by some new pattern of association, based on a system of relationships fundamentally different from that found in other societies elsewhere? (1, p. 28).

19   In fact, all of these situations may be found within most Caribbean communities today. Clarke suggests a typology in which she distinguishes between "family" households and "consanguineous" households. The latter may be one of three types: (a) denuded family households in which there is only one parent, plus children, grandchildren, or other lineal relatives of the parent; (b) sibling households in which adult brothers and sisters live under one roof; and (c) single person households (common only in towns on which people travel to obtain wage-labour during part of the year) (1).

20   It is my view that some distinction between family and household such as that made by Clarke is not only useful but necessary in dealing with Caribbean society. It seems to me that the fact that some households contain no family as ordinarily defined by anthropologists is one of the most important characteristics of Caribbean society. Elsewhere I have stressed the consanguineal nature of these households as a key to their understanding (17).

21   It is, of course, perfectly legitimate to view the society in terms of household units as long as the investigator distinguishes these from families. Presumably, the universe may be completely divided with a classification like Clarke's, for all persons would belong to one or another type of household. Does this mean then, that some persons are members of families and others are not? Undoubtedly, this is sometimes the case, but I suggest that in order fully to understand Afro-American society it is

necessary to view it in terms of household units on the one hand, and family units on the other. I would maintain that many, if not most, individuals belong to both a family and to a household. At times the two units coincide, but quite often they do not.

22 In order to illustrate this point I shall draw upon my fieldwork of a year's duration among the Black Carib of Livingston, Guatemala—a group of people whose culture is similar enough to other Afro-American groups to warrant classifying them together (18). The nuclear family unit among the Carib may be scattered in several different households. For example, the husband-father may be living with his own mother, one or more children may be with their maternal relatives or with non-Caribs, while the mother may be working and "living in" as a maid in one of the port towns. Some may then assert that under such circumstances this no longer constitutes a family unit. However, if the nature of the personal interrelationships among the group members is considered, it may be seen that there exists a pattern of affective and economic solidarity among them. It is true that many such groups are extremely brittle and unstable, but they do exist for varying lengths of time. And for their duration the members think of themselves as a unit; when questioned as to their family connections they will immediately name and locate their primary relatives. Furthermore, there is some economic co-operation among them, the man generally contributing a part of his wages (or money from sale of cash crops) to the woman and the children. The woman too, if working, may give money to the man, and certainly sends clothing and money to the household(s) in which her children are living.

23 Another common arrangement is that in which the husband maintains a single-person household in one town, leaving his wife and children living together in another. The latter would appear to be Clarke's denuded family household. However, I think it is important to recognize that within this type of household one may find either of two fundamentally different relationship patterns. The man, though living elsewhere, may make frequent trips to visit his wife and children, contributing a large part of his wages toward their support. They consider that he "lives" with them, though he may not actually have resided there for a number of years. The man will return to his family immediately in times of crisis, or when important decisions must be made. He also returns whenever possible to assist the woman in clearing fields, to make repairs on the house, etc. He remains a highly important influence in the socialization of his children. I would call this group a non-localized family.

24 On the other hand, the single parent (most often the mother, although occasionally one finds a father alone with his children) may be completely unattached to any individual who might be called a spouse. She may receive a small amount of economic assistance from the father or fathers of her children, but for the most part she is dependent upon herself and her consanguineal relatives in maintaining and socializing her children. This situation, which on the surface appears identical to that

described above, is obviously entirely different. Although Clarke's term, the "denuded family," is somewhat descriptive of the situation, it is nevertheless ambiguous since it may refer to either set of relationships described above. I would not call this unit a family at all; consisting only of a mother and her children, it is on a lower level of organization than a family which must include a conjugal relationship and what Fortes would call patri-filiation (3).

25   Another interesting and pertinent example is that of the Israeli *kibbutz*. Here we find a situation in which married couples co-reside, but their children live elsewhere. Although Spiro (19), following Murdock's definition of marriage (12), states that the relationship between these couples does not constitute marriage, it seems clear from his data that the society itself recognizes the relationship as such. He points out that these couples are eventually united in accordance with the marriage laws of the state. Furthermore, he goes on to state that the family does not exist within the *kibbutz* system, unless one wishes to consider the *kibbutz* itself as a large extended family. Again, Spiro has followed Murdock's definition of the family in arriving at this conclusion.

26   However, Spiro makes it clear that within the *kibbutz* there does exist a group which could, by another definition, be termed a nuclear family. He says: "The social group in the *kibbutz* that includes adults of both sexes and their children, although characterized by reproduction, is not characterized by common residence or by economic co-operation" (19, p. 840). He goes on to show that this group is characterized by psychological intimacy, affection, and joint recreational activities. Although the children's physical and mental development for the most part is supervised by persons outside this family unit, Spiro notes that, "Parents are of crucial importance in the *psychological* development of the child" (italics his). "They serve as the objects of his most important identifications, and they provide him with a certain security and love that he obtains from no one else" (19, p. 844). In view of the strength of the affective bonds among this group, which includes their own recognition of themselves as a separate, cohesive, and enduring unit, I suggest that the family as an institution *does* exist within the *kibbutz*. If one wishes to liken the entire *kibbutz* to an extended family, then why not consider these smaller units of mother, father, and children as nuclear families?

27   In conclusion, I propose that the family be defined as a group of people bound together by that complex set of relationships known as kinship ties, between at least two of whom there exists a conjugal relationship. The conjugal pair, plus their offspring, forms the nuclear family. Other types of family may be defined as extensions of the nuclear type, each being identified by the nature of the relationship between the conjugal pair (or one member of that pair) and other members.

28   The household, on the other hand, implies common residence, economic co-operation, and socialization of children. Although the members of the household may be bound by kinship relationships, no

particular type of tie is necessarily characteristic. In any given society a particular family may or may not form a household. Conversely, a household may or may not contain a family. Although it is probably useful to make an analytical distinction between the two concepts in all cases, the investigator must be particularly careful to examine the structure and functioning of both types of units in those societies in which their membership does not coincide.

REFERENCES

1. Clarke, Edith. 1957 *My Mother Who Fathered Me.* London.
2. Fortes, Meyer. 1949 "Time and Social Structure: An Ashanti Case Study," in *Social Structure: Studies Presented to A. R. Radcliffe-Brown,* Meyer Fortes, ed. Oxford.
3. Fortes, Meyer. 1945 Introduction to *The Development Cycle in Domestic Groups,* Jack Goody, ed. Cambridge Papers in Social Anthropology, No. 1.
4. Frazier, E. Franklin. 1939 *The Negro Family in the United States.* Chicago.
5. Goody, Jack. 1958 "The Fission of Domestic Groups among the Lodagaba," in *The Developmental Cycle in Domestic Groups,* Jack Goody, ed. Cambridge Papers in Social Anthropology, No. 1.
6. Gough, E. Kathleen. 1952 "A Comparison of Incest Prohibitions and the Rules of Exogamy in Three Matrilineal Groups of the Malabar Coast," *International Archives of Ethnography,* XLVI, No. 1, pp. 82–105.
7. Henriques, Fernando M. 1953 *Family and Colour in Jamaica.* London.
8. Herskovits, Melville J. 1958 *The Myth of the Negro Past.* Beacon Edition, Boston.
9. Linton, Ralph. 1936 *The Study of Man.* New York.
10. Lowie, Robert H. 1950 *Social Organization.* London.
11. Matthews, Dom Basil. 1953 "Crisis of the West Indian Family," *Caribbean Affairs,* Vol. 9. University College of the West Indies.
12. Murdock, George P. 1949 *Social Structure* New York.
13. Radcliffe-Brown, A. R. 1950 Introduction to *African Systems of Kinship and Marriage,* A. R. Radcliffe-Brown and Daryll Forde, eds. London.
14. Simey, T. S. 1946 *Welfare and Planning in the West Indies.* Oxford.
15. Smith, Raymond T. 1956 *The Negro Family in British Guiana.* London.
16. Smith, Raymond T. 1957 "The Family in the Caribbean," in *Caribbean Studies: A Symposium,* Vera Rubin, ed. University College of the West Indies, Jamaica.
17. Solien, Nancie L. 1958 "The Consanguineal Household Among the Black Carib of Central America." PhD dissertation, University of Michigan.
18. Solien, Nancie L. 1959 "West Indian Characteristics of the Black Carib," *Southwestern Journal of Anthropology,* Vol. 15, No. 3, pp. 300–7.

19. Spiro, Melford E. 1954 "Is the Family Universal?", *American Anthropologist,* Vol. 56, No. 5, pp. 839–46.

Reading for Meaning

1. What are some of the definitions of "family" that anthropologists have used in examining family groups in Caribbean and Afro-American cultures? What are Nancie Solien Gonzalez's concerns about these definitions?

2. What approach to examining family systems in the Caribbean does Gonzalez favor? What advantages does she see in this perspective?

3. Under what circumstances might members of a biological family and a household be different? Use examples from Gonzalez's article and from your own experience to answer this question.

4. Gonzalez begins her study by noting that household groups in Afro-American communities in the Caribbean, the Southern United States, and in parts of Central and South America differ from those in other areas of the world. Which examples of family and household groups in Gonzalez's article best describe the arrangement you and people you know experienced when growing up?

Comparing Texts

1. William Tucker writes in "Monogamy and Its Discontents" that "Family values are basically the belief that monogamy is the most peaceful and progressive way of organizing a human society." This view of the family sees the social order represented by the monogamous, nuclear family threatened by "easy divorce, widespread pornography, legalized prostitution, out-of-wedlock child bearing, blatant homosexuality." A version of this "threatened" view of the family appears in the quotation from the Southern Baptists' "Faith and Message," the first epigraph for this chapter. How might those and like-minded defenders of the Anglo-American idea of family evaluate the diverse arrangements that Gonzalez describes in her article about Caribbean households? What objections might Gonzalez raise to these observations about the family? What problems might this more conservative view cause for people who have different assumptions about what constitutes a household?

2. Read "The *Bilal's* Fourth Wife," a short story by Sembene Ousmane, page 316. What assumptions about the family do characters in that story make? What comment does Ousmane offer on the family structure depicted in his story?

Ideas for Writing

1. Interview several friends, relatives, or classmates to determine how their households are organized. Keep in mind the varieties of household structure described in Gonzalez's article, "Household and Family in the Caribbean." As you conduct your interviews, try to find out why the households are arranged the way they are and the purpose such an arrangement might serve. Write your own analysis of how families of the people you interviewed are arranged and how well each arrangement seems to work.

2. Do some research on the nuclear family to find out what supporters and detractors have to say about it. Write a paper in which you explore the benefits or limitations that living in a nuclear family might present for its members.

Writing before Reading

In your experience, are children who grow up in the United States allowed to enjoy the pleasures of childhood, or are they pressured into growing up too fast? What do you think might influence a child's rate of maturity?

WAAAH!! WHY KIDS HAVE A LOT TO CRY ABOUT

David Elkind

David Elkind (b. 1931) is a professor of child studies at Tufts University in Massachusetts. He has written seventeen books and numerous essays about the family. He is the author of All Grown Up and No Place to Go: Teenagers in Crisis *(1984), and* The Hurried Child: Growing Up Too Fast Too Soon *(1988). His latest book,* The Ties That Stress: The New Family Imbalance, *was published in 1994.* Psychology Today *published the following article by Elkind in its May–June 1992 issue.*

1 "Mommy," the five-year-old girl asked her mother, "why don't you get divorced again?" Her thrice-married mother was taken aback and said in return, "Honey, why in the world should I do that?" To which her daughter replied, "Well, I haven't seen you in love for such a long time."

2 This young girl perceives family life and the adult world in a very different way than did her counterpart less than half a century ago. Likewise, the mother perceives her daughter quite differently than did a mother raising a child in the 1940s. Although this mother was surprised at her daughter's question, she was not surprised at her understanding of divorce, nor at her familiarity with the symptoms of romance.

3 As this anecdote suggests, there has been a remarkable transformation over the last 50 years in our children's perceptions of us, and in our perceptions of our children. These altered perceptions are a very small part of a much larger tectonic shift in our society in general and in our

families in particular. This shift is nothing less than a transformation of the basic framework, or paradigm, within which we think about and thus perceive our world. To understand the changes in the family, the perceptions of family members, and of parenting that have been brought about, we first have to look at this broader "paradigm shift" and what is has meant for family sentiments, values, and perceptions.

FROM MODERN TO POSTMODERN

4   Without fully realizing it perhaps, we have been transported into the postmodern era. Although this era has been called "postindustrial" and, alternatively, "information age," neither of these phrases is broad enough to encompass the breadth and depth of the changes that have occurred. The terms modern and postmodern, in contrast, encompass all aspects of society and speak to the changes in science, philosophy, architecture, literature, and the arts—as well as in industry and technology—that have marked our society since mid-century.

THE MODERN AND THE NUCLEAR FAMILY

5   The modern era, which began with the Renaissance and spanned the Industrial Revolution, was based upon three related assumptions. One was the idea of *human progress*—the notion that the natural direction of human and societal development is toward a more equitable, peaceful, and harmonious world in which every individual would be entitled to life, liberty, and the pursuit of happiness. A second assumption is *universality*. There were, it was taken as given, universal laws of nature of art, science, economics, and so on that transcended time and culture. The third basic assumption was that of *regularity*—the belief that the world is an orderly place, that animals and plants, geological layers and chemical elements could be classified in an orderly hierarchy. As Einstein put it, "God does not play dice with the universe!"

6   These assumptions gave a unique character and distinctiveness to modern life. Modern science, literature, architecture, philosophy, and industry all embodied these premises. And they were enshrined in the Modern Family as well. The modern nuclear family, for example, was seen as the end result of a progressive evolution of family forms. Two parents, two or three children, one parent working and one staying home to rear the children and maintain the home was thought to be the ideal family form toward which all prior, "primitive" forms were merely preliminary stages.

SENTIMENTS OF THE NUCLEAR FAMILY

7   The Modern Family was shaped by three sentiments that also reflected the underlying assumptions of modernity. One of these was Romantic Love. In premodern times, couples married by familial and community

dictates. Considerations of property and social position were paramount. This community influence declined in the modern era, and couples increasingly came to choose one another on the basis of mutual attraction. This attraction became idealized into the notion that "Some enchanted evening, you will meet a stranger" for whom you and only you were destined ("You were meant for me, I was meant for you"), and that couples would stay together for the rest of their lives, happily "foreveraftering."

8   A second sentiment of the Modern Family was that of Maternal Love—the idea that women have a maternal "instinct" and a need to care for children, particularly when they are small. The idea of a maternal instinct was a thoroughly modern invention that emerged only after modern medicine and nutrition reduced infant mortality. In premodern times, infant mortality was so high that the young were not even named until they were two years old and stood a good chance of surviving. It was also not uncommon for urban parents to have their infants "wet-nursed" in the country. Often these infants died because the wet-nurse fed her own child before she fed the stranger, and there was little nourishment left. Such practices could hardly be engaged in by a mother with a "maternal instinct."

9   The third sentiment of the Modern Family was Domesticity, a belief that relationships within the family are always more powerful and binding than are those outside it. The family was, as Christopher Lasch wrote, "a haven in a heartless world." As a haven, the nuclear family shielded and protected its members from the evils and temptations of the outside world. This sentiment also extended to the family's religious, ethnic, and social-class affiliations. Those individuals who shared these affiliations were to be preferred, as friends and spouses, over those with different affiliations.

PARENTING THE INNOCENT

10   The modern perceptions of parenting, children, and teenagers grew out of these family sentiments. Modern parents, for example, were seen as intuitively or instinctively knowledgeable about child-rearing. Professional help was needed only to encourage parents to do "what comes naturally." In keeping with this view of parenting was the perception of children as innocent and in need of parental nurturance and protection. Teenagers, in turn, were seen as immature and requiring adult guidance and direction. Adolescence, regarded as the age of preparation for adulthood, brought with it the inevitable "storm and stress," as young people broke from the tight nuclear family bonds and became socially and financially independent.

11   These modern perceptions of parenting and of children and youth were reinforced by the social mirror of the media, the law and the health professions. Motion pictures such as the Andy Hardy series (starring

Mickey Rooney) depicted a teenage boy getting into youthful scrapes at school and with friends from which he was extricated by his guardian the judge, played by Harlan Stone. Fiction similarly portrayed teenagers as immature young people struggling to find themselves. Mark Twain's Huck Finn was an early version of the modern immature adolescent, while J. D. Salinger's Holden Caulfield is a modern version.

12   Modern laws, such as the child-labor laws and compulsory-education statutes were enacted to protect both children and adolescents. And the health professions attributed the mental-health problems of children and youth to conflicts arising from the tight emotional bonds of the nuclear family.

POSTMODERNITY AND THE POSTMODERN FAMILY

13   The postmodern view has largely grown out of the failure of modern assumptions about progress, universality, and regularity. Many of the events of this century have made the idea of progress difficult to maintain. Germany, one of the most educationally, scientifically, and culturally advanced countries of the world, engaged in the most heinous genocide. Modern science gave birth to the atomic bomb that was dropped on Hiroshima and Nagasaki. Environmental degradation, pollution, population explosions, and widespread famine can hardly be reconciled with the notion of progress.

14   Secondly, the belief in universal principles has been challenged as the "grand" theories of the modern era—such as those of Marx, Darwin, and Freud—are now recognized as limited by the social and historical contexts in which they were elaborated. Modern theorists believed that they could transcend social-historical boundaries; the postmodern worker recognizes that he or she is constrained by the particular discourse of narrative in play at the time. Likewise, the search for abiding ethical, moral, and religious universals is giving way to a recognition that there are many different ethics, moralities, and religions, each of which has a claim to legitimacy.

15   Finally, the belief in regularity has given way to a recognition of the importance of irregularity, indeterminancy, chaos, and fuzzy logic. There is much in nature, such as the weather, that remains unpredictable—not because it is perverse, but only because the weather is affected by non-regular events. Sure regularity appears, but irregularity is now seen as a genuine phenomenon in its own right. It is no longer seen, as it was in the modern era, as the result of some failure to discover an underlying regularity.

16   In place of these modern assumptions, a new, postmodern paradigm with its own basic premises has been invented. The assumption of progress, to illustrate, has given way to the presumption of *difference*. There are many different forms and types of progress, and not all progressions are necessarily for the better. Likewise, the belief in universals has moved

aside for the belief in *particulars*. Different phenomena may have different rules and principles that are not necessarily generalizable. For example, a particular family or a particular class of children is a non-replicable event that can never be exactly duplicated and to which universal principles do not apply. Finally, the assumption of regularity moved aside to make room for the principle of *irregularity*. The world is not as orderly and as logically organized as we had imagined.

17 As the societal paradigm has shifted, so has the structure of the family. The ideal nuclear family, thought to be the product of progressive social evolution, has given way to what might be called the *Permeable Family* of the postmodern era. The Permeable Family encompasses many different family forms: traditional or nuclear, two-parent working, single-parent, blended, adopted child, test-tube, surrogate mother, and co-parent families. Each of these is valuable and a potentially successful family form.

18 The family is permeable in other ways as well. It is no longer isolated from the larger community. Thanks to personal computers, fax and answering machines, the workplace has moved into the homeplace. The homeplace, in turn, thanks to childcare facilities in office buildings and factories, has moved into the workplace. The home is also permeated by television, which brings the outside world into the living room and bedrooms. And an ever-expanding number of TV shows *(Oprah, Donahue, Geraldo,* and *Sally Jessy Raphael),* all detailing the variety of family problems, brings the living room and the bedroom into the outside world.

19 Quite different sentiments animate the postmodern Permeable Family than animated the modern nuclear family. The transformation of family sentiments came about in a variety of ways, from the civil-rights movement, the women's movement, changes in media, and laws that were part of the postmodern revolution. Because there is a constant interaction between the family and the larger society, it is impossible to say whether changes in the family were brought about by changes in society or vice versa. Things moved in both directions.

20 For a number of reasons, the Modern Family sentiment of Romantic Love has been transformed in the Postmodern era into the sentiment of *Consensual Love*. In contrast to the idealism and perfectionism of Romantic Love, consensual love is realistic and practical. It recognizes the legitimacy of premarital relations and is not premised on long-term commitment. Consensual Love is an agreement or contract between the partners; as an agreement it can be broken. The difference between Romantic Love and Consensual Love is summed up in the prenuptial agreement, which acknowledges the possible rupture of a marriage—before the marriage actually occurs. The current emphasis upon safe sex is likewise a symptom of consensual, not romantic, love.

21 The Modern Family sentiment of maternal love has yielded to other changes. Today, more than 50 percent of women are in the workforce,

and some 60 percent of these women have children under the age of six. These figures make it clear that non-maternal and non-parental figures are now playing a major role in child-rearing. As part of this revision of child-rearing responsibilities, a new sentiment has emerged that might be called *shared parenting*. What this sentiment entails is the understanding that not only mothers, but fathers and professional caregivers are a necessary part of the child-rearing process. Child-rearing and childcare are no longer looked upon as the sole or primary responsibility of the mother.

22   The permeability of the Postmodern Family has also largely done away with the Modern Family sentiment of domesticity. The family can no longer protect individuals from the pressures of the outside world. Indeed, the impulse of the Permeable Family is to move in the other direction. Permeable Families tend to thrust children and teenagers forward to deal with realities of the outside world at ever earlier ages. This has resulted in what I have called the "hurrying" of children to grow up fast. Much of the hurrying of children and youth is a well-intentioned effort on the part of parents to help prepare children and youth for the onrush of information, challenges, and temptations coming at them through the now-permeable boundaries of family life.

Postmodern Parents of Kids without Innocence

23   These new, postmodern sentiments have given rise to new perceptions of parenting, of children, and of adolescents. Now that parenting is an activity shared with non-parental figures, we no longer regard it as an instinct that emerges once we have become parents; it is now regarded as a matter of learned *technique*.

24   Postmodern parents understand that doing "what comes naturally" may not be good for children. There are ways to say things to children that are less stressful than others. There are ways of disciplining that do not damage the child's sense of self esteem. The problem for parents today is to choose from the hundreds of books and other media sources bombarding them with advice on child-rearing. As one mother said to me, "I've read your books and they sound okay, but what if you're wrong?"

25   With respect to children, the perception of childhood innocence has given way to the perception of childhood competence. Now that children are living in Permeable Families with—thanks to television—a steady diet of overt violence, sexuality, substance abuse, and environmental degradation, we can no longer assume they are innocent. Rather, perhaps to cover our own inability to control what our children are seeing, we perceive them as competent to deal with all of this material. Indeed, we get so caught up in this perception of competence that we teach four- and five-year-olds about AIDS and child abuse and provide

"toys" that simulate pregnancy or the dismemberment that accidents can cause unbuckled-up occupants. And the media reinforce this competence perception with films such as *Look Who's Talking* and *Home Alone*.

26 If children are seen as competent, teenagers can no longer be seen as immature. Rather they are now seen as sophisticated in the ways of the world, knowledgeable about sex, drugs, crime, and much more. This is a convenient fiction for parents suffering a time-famine. Such parents can take the perception of teenage sophistication as a rationale to abrogate their responsibility to provide young people with limits, guidance, and supervision. Increasingly, teenagers are on their own. Even junior and senior high schools no longer provide the social programs and clubs they once did.

27 This new perception of teenagers is also reflected in the social mirror of media, school and law. Postmodern films like *Risky Business* (in which teenager runs a bordello in the parents' home) and *Angel* (demure high school student by day, avenging hooker by night) are a far cry from the Andy Hardy films. Postmodern TV sitcoms such as *Married with Children* and *Roseanne* present images of teenage sophistication hardly reconcilable with the teenagers portrayed in modern TV shows such as *My Three Sons* or *Ozzie and Harriet*. Postmodern legal thinking is concerned with protecting the *rights* of children and teenagers, rather than protecting children themselves. Children and teenagers can now sue their parents for divorce, visitation rights, and for remaining in the United States when the family travels overseas.

REALITY IS HERE TO STAY

28 The postmodern perceptions of children as competent and of teenagers as sophisticated did not grow out of any injustices nor harm visited upon children and youth. Rather they grew out of a golden era for young people that lasted from the end of the last century to the middle of this one. Society as a whole was geared to regard children as innocent and teenagers as immature, and sought to protect children and gradually inculcate teenagers into the ways of the world.

29 In contrast, the perceptions of childhood competence and teenage sophistication have had detrimental effects upon children and youth. Indeed, these perceptions have placed children and teenagers under inordinate stress. And it shows. On every measure that we have, children and adolescents are doing less well today than they did a quarter century ago, when the new postmodern perceptions were coming into play. While it would be unwise to attribute all of these negative effects to changed perceptions alone—economics and government policy clearly played a role—it is also true that government policy and economics are affected by the way young people are perceived.

30   The statistics speak for themselves. There has been a 50-percent increase in obesity in children and youth over the past two decades. We lose some ten thousand teenagers a year in substance-related accidents, not including injured and maimed. One in four teenagers drinks to excess every two weeks, and we have two million alcoholic teenagers.

31   Teenage girls in America get pregnant at the rate of one million per year, twice the rate of the next Western country, England. Suicide has tripled among teenagers in the last 20 years, and between five and six thousand teenagers take their own lives each year. It is estimated that one out of four teenage girls manifests at least one symptom of an eating disorder, most commonly severe dieting. The 14- to 19-year-old age group has the second-highest homicide rate of any age group.

32   These are frightening statistics. Yet they are not necessarily an indictment of the postmodern world, nor of our changed perceptions of children and youth. We have gone through enormous social changes in a very brief period of time. No other society on Earth changes, or can change, as rapidly as we do. That is both our strength and our weakness. It has made us, and will keep us, the leading industrial nation in the world because we are more flexible than any other society, including Japan.

33   But rapid social change is a catastrophe for children and youth, who require stability and security for healthy growth and development. Fortunately, we are now moving toward a more stable society. A whole generation of parents was caught in the transition between Modern and Postmodern Family sentiments; among them, divorce, open marriage, and remarriage became at least as commonplace as the permanent nuclear family. The current generation of parents have, however, grown up with the new family sentiments and are not as conflicted as their own parents were.

34   As a result, we are slowly moving back to a more realistic perception of both children and teenagers, as well as toward a family structure that is supportive of all family members. We are moving towards what might be called the *Vital Family*. In the Vital Family, the modern value of togetherness is given equal weight with the Postmodern Family value of autonomy. Children are seen as *growing into competence* and as still needing the help and support of parents. Likewise, teenagers are increasingly seen as *maturing into sophistication,* and able to benefit from adult guidance, limits, and direction.

35   These new perceptions pop up in the media. Increasingly, newspapers and magazines feature articles on the negative effects pressures for early achievement have upon children. We are also beginning to see articles about the negative effects the demands for sophistication place upon teenagers. A number of recent TV shows (such as *Beverly Hills 90210)* have begun to portray children and youth as sophisticated, but also as responsible and accepting of adult guidance and supervision. There is still much too much gratuitous sex and violence, but at least

there are signs of greater responsibility and recognition that children and adolescents may not really be prepared for everything we would like to throw at them.

36 After 10 years off traveling and lecturing all over the country, I have an impression is that the American family is alive and well. It has changed dramatically, and we are still accommodating to the changes. And, as always happens, children and youths are more harmed by change than are adults. But our basic value system remains intact. We do have a strong Judeo-Christian heritage; we believe in hard work, democracy, and autonomy. But our sense of social and parental responsibility, however, was temporarily deadened by the pace of social change. Now that we are getting comfortable in our new Permeable Family sentiments and perceptions, we are once again becoming concerned with those who are young and those who are less fortunate.

37 As human beings we all have a need to become the best that we can be. But we also have a need to love and to be loved, to care and to be cared for. The Modern Family spoke to our need to belong at the expense, particularly for women, of the need to become.

38 The Permeable Family, in contrast, celebrates the need to become at the expense of the need to belong, and this has been particularly hard on children and youth. Now we are moving towards a Vital Family that ensures both our need to become and our need to belong. We are not there yet, but the good news is, we are on our way.

Reading for Meaning

1. According to David Elkind, how has the paradigm of the modern family changed in the postmodern era? Does his analysis seem accurate to you?

2. Elkind says that "Consensus Love" has replaced "Romantic Love," the concept on which the modern family was based. How do these two kinds of love differ? What might be the advantages and drawbacks of each from the point of view of the lovers involved? In your experience, does "Romantic Love" survive?

3. What does Elkind mean by the "sentiment of domesticity," a feeling that he says once informed the modern family? What opinion does he have of the attitude that has replaced it? What evidence does he offer in support of his position? Do you agree with his argument?

4. What hope does Elkind see for the future of American children?

Comparing Texts

1. Compare the strains on the American household David Elkind describes to the pressures on the child growing up in Bali discussed in Margaret Mead's essay in chapter 4, page 102.

2. Read Martin King Whyte's essay, "Choosing Mates—The American Way," chapter 6, page 199. In what ways might the changes in the way Americans find partners correspond to changes in the family structure described in David Elkind's article?

Ideas for Writing

1. In his discussion of the postmodern concept of the teenager, David Elkind gives examples of how movies and television have reinforced the image of the sophisticated teen. In your experience, what is the current image of the adolescent presented by the media?

2. Examine half a dozen families you know to see whether Elkind's assumptions about the structure of the American household, which in his view has lost its "sentiment of domesticity," hold true. Write an essay about your findings.

CHAPTER 6
RITES OF PASSAGE

First Thoughts

第一印象

الانطباع الأول

The nice clothes were for me: they hennaed my hands and feet one morning and dressed me in one of the dresses that same afternoon. They took me to my father's house where Jauhar and Najeeya and my father's fourth wife were waiting. . . . My mother and my aunt were there to accompany me, and I suddenly wondered if this could be my own wedding. The neighbour's daughter once told me that she'd known about her father's second marriage because there had been so many baskets and metal containers around, full of cooked rice and meat, and here I was confronted with bags and boxes of provisions, and my mother tasting a bit of rice and saying, "They're obviously mean. God help us! You can count the cardamon pods and cumin seeds with the naked eye. God help my precious Tamr!" Then I heard drumming and women trilling. "Mother, mother!" I cried. "Are you marrying me off? I'm not even a woman yet! . . . Are you marrying me off when you know it's wrong?" I asked again. "It doesn't make any difference whether it's to a boy or a grown man." Hush, Tamr," replied my aunt. "Don't be ungrateful. A man is an adornment, a crown for your head, a staff to strengthen your heart." I wept, without knowing why.

Hanan al-Shaykh
Women of Sand & Myrrh[1]

Thomas Fleming, editor of *Chronicles,* a magazine about North American culture published in Rockford, Illinois, points out that in ancient Greece, parents helped teens find their place in society by passing them through rigorous rites of initiation. "Teens would be sent

---

[1] Translated by Catherine Cobham.

on a kind of permanent camp-out in the woods for upwards of five years, under the supervision of an elder. They would live like savages and be taught the rules of society. . . . "

Girls also took part in special ceremonies in Athens, although the discipline wasn't as harsh because they weren't as restless as boys. At Sparta, adolescent girls sang the "Maiden Song" at a festival as one of their rites of initiation. Some religious rites also required them to live outside the home for a period before marriage and make sacrifices to Athena. . . .

Some modern cultures also put young males and females through painful and physically difficult rituals. The Masai people of Kenya require young warriors to kill a lion before they are regarded as men. In some African countries and parts of Asia, female circumcision is a common rite of passage, usually performed around the time of first menstruation. . . .

The protracted period of adolescence in modern Western society is considered by some to be a leading cause of rebellion among teens. Current culture has no universal rite of passage from childhood to adulthood; instead, it focuses on adolescence as a period of transition of undefined length and debatable purpose.

Peter Verberg
"How Other Cultures Have Solved the Teen Dilemma"

Ceremonies and rituals mark an individual's passing from one stage of life to another. For some cultures, like the traditional Balinese culture, ritual is a continual and dramatic part of life. Most cultures provide formalized rituals to acknowledge important events such as birth, puberty, marriage, death, and other turning points in a person's life. In some non-Western cultures, initiation ceremonies involve leaving the family group, often in the company of elders. Ceremonies worldwide are designed to take the young person into the larger communal group as an equal, as a man or woman in his or her own right.

Heightened self-consciousness often accompanies these and other important transitions in our lives, and the results can be quite positive. Rites of passage can encourage emotional growth and an awareness of our place in a larger world. Along with this development comes a sense of duty to communal rules and assumptions of responsibility that can signal maturity but may also cause anxiety. Readings in this chapter recognize the complex feelings roused by community celebrations and other milestones in people's lives. Susan Orlean's article, "Debuting," describes a *quinceañera,* or coming-of-age party in one Latino community in Phoenix, Arizona. In

"Body Ritual among the Nacirema," anthropologist Horace Miner offers a parody of cultural studies in this spoof on a few of the "magical beliefs and practices" of the Nacirema (American spelled backwards). Various ways of finding mates and of arranging marriages are explored in "Choosing Mates—The American Way" and "The Marriage-Go-Round." In "Choosing Mates—The American Way," Martin King Whyte analyzes the history of dating in the United States and concludes that the custom of couples living together outside of marriage does not necessarily lead to a long-term commitment and eventually to marriage. Instead, living together may well be a method of avoiding marriage altogether. Nicholas Bornoff, author of "The Marriage-Go-Round" adopts an outsider's view of arranged marriages in Japan and writes a critique of the custom that gives parents virtual control over the choice of their children's spouse. Nahid Toubia offers a serious argument against Islamic practices that endanger women's health, if not their lives, in "Women and Health in Sudan."

Writing before Reading

Describe any coming-of-age ceremonies with which you are familiar. What seems to be the purpose of these ceremonies? What changes once the teenager has taken part in this ritual?

DEBUTING: PHOENIX, ARIZONA

Susan Orlean

Susan Orlean is a staff writer for The New Yorker. *She has also written articles for* Rolling Stone Magazine *and has been on the staff of* Willamette Week, *a newspaper in Portland, Oregon, and two Boston newspapers, the* Phoenix *and the* Globe. *Her articles cover a variety of subjects, including sports celebrities, beauty pageants, orchid-poaching, and a guide to buying necklaces. Orlean's first collection of articles, titled* Red Sox and Bluefish: Meditations on What Makes New England New England, *was published in 1987. Three years later her collected observations of ways Americans spend their weekends was published under the title* Saturday Night. *The article "Debuting: Phoenix, Arizona" is taken from this collection. This article was also printed in the February 12, 1990 issue of* The New Yorker.

1 Azteca Plaza, the biggest formal wear shopping center in the world, is on a skinny strip of sandy, cactus-studded Arizona real estate, a few miles east of downtown Phoenix, in a neighborhood that does not yet illustrate the vitality of the Sunbelt economy. There used to be nice small houses in the area, but in the last few decades they became unfashionable and then funky and finally abandoned. Azteca Plaza, in the meantime, did nothing but grow. When it opened in 1962, the plaza was just one shop with an inventory of three wedding gowns and five bridesmaid outfits. It is now a complex of forty thousand square feet with a florist, an invitation shop, a tuxedo annex, a bridesmaid wing, a veil wing, parking for two hundred, and a wedding-gown center the size of a suburban roller rink, with dozens of dress racks and yards of satin, netting, and peau de soie billowing all over the floor. Azteca Plaza has the corner on the greater metropolitan Phoenix prom-dress trade. It also does a brisk business in the fancy ball gowns Hispanic girls wear at their *quinceañeras,* the ceremony that takes place when they are fifteen years old—*quince años*—to celebrate their passage into womanhood, commitment to Catholicism, and debut into society. In the last decade, the number of Hispanics in Phoenix has grown by 125 percent. The *quinceañera* business at Azteca Plaza has enjoyed a corresponding upswing.

2 Azteca Plaza is just a few blocks away from Immaculate Heart Church, a boxy stucco-colored structure that serves as a central parish for the Hispanic community in the Phoenix diocese. Immaculate Heart was built in 1928, fourteen years after it was revealed that the priests at the main basilica in Phoenix, St. Mary's, had been obliging their Mexican parishioners to hold their masses and weddings and *quinceañeras* in the basement rather than on the main floor of the church. It used to be common for certain churches to serve an ethnic group rather than a geographical area—in most American cities, there would be French, Hispanic, Polish, Irish, and German Catholic churches. The practice is rare these days, and Immaculate Heart is one of the few such ethnic parishes left in the entire country. Someone in Phoenix, recounting for me the history of Hispanic mistreatment at St. Mary's, credited the continued existence of a national parish in Phoenix to the dry Arizona desert air, which, he claimed, had preserved the unpleasant memory of bargain-basement weddings at the basilica in many Hispanics' minds. Hispanics in Phoenix now regularly attend the churches in their immediate neighborhoods, but for sentimental and historical reasons they continue to think of Immaculate Heart as the mother ship. Not coincidentally, Immaculate Heart was for years the site of most of Phoenix's many *quinceañeras*— that is, the site of the mass when the girl is blessed and is asked to affirm her dedication to the Church. The party in which she is introduced to society and celebrates her birthday is held after the mass at a hotel or hall. For a while, there were so many *quinceañeras* at Immaculate Heart that they outnumbered weddings. For that matter, there were so many

quinceañera masses and parties that they were a standard Saturday-night social occasion in town.

3   In early summer I was invited to a large *quinceañera* in Phoenix at which sixteen girls were to be presented. The event was being sponsored by the girls' parents and the Vesta Club, a social organization of Hispanic college graduates. In the Southwest, constituents of this subset are sometimes known as "Chubbies"—Chicano urban professionals. Chubbies give Azteca Plaza a lot of business. The girls' fathers and the sixteen young men who were going to be escorts at the *quinceañera* had rented their tuxedos from Azteca Plaza and would be picking them up on Saturday morning. The girls, of course, had gotten their gowns months before.

4   The traditional Mexican *quinceañera* gown is white or pink, floor length but trainless, snug on top and wide at the bottom, with a skirt shaped like a wedding bell. But like most traditions that migrate a few hundred miles from their point of origin and make it through a couple of generations in this country, *quinceañeras* have yielded somewhat to interpretation, and the gowns that the Vesta Club girls were going to wear demonstrated the effects of Americanization on taste as well as a certain American-style expansiveness in price. All of the gowns were white and full-length but otherwise they were freestyle—an array of high necks, fluted necklines, sweetheart necklines, leg-o'-mutton sleeves, cap sleeves, cascade collars, gathered bodices, beaded bodices, bustles, and sequins; one had a train and one had a flouncy peplum and a skirt that was narrow from the hip to the floor. Further Americanization has taken place with regards to scheduling. In Mexico, *quinceañeras* traditionally take place on the day the girl actually turns fifteen. In the United States, *quinceañeras*—like many important ceremonies in American life—take place on Saturday nights.

5   When I first mentioned to a woman I know in Phoenix that I wanted to attend a *quinceañera,* that I thought they seemed like interesting ceremonies and great displays of community feeling and a good example of how ethnic tradition fits into American Saturday nights, she clucked sympathetically and said she was very sentimental about her own *quinceañera* but had become convinced that they were now going the way of many other ethnic ceremonies in this country—changed beyond recognition, marketed like theme parks, at the very least irrelevant to assimilated youngsters who would rather spend Saturday nights at keg parties than reenacting an old-world ceremony. An inevitable pattern transforms such things: immigrants gather in their leisure time so that they can bolster one another and share their imported traditions, their children tolerate the gatherings occasionally because they have a likeable familiar ring, and then the children of *those* children deplore them because they seem corny and pointless, and finally there is a lot of discussion about how sad it is that the community doesn't get together anymore.

6 That is partly what has become of *quinceañeras* in Phoenix, but the real problem, ironically, is that they have been too popular for their own good. A few years ago, the bishop of Phoenix, a slight, freckle-faced man from Indiana named Thomas O'Brien, started hearing complaints from some priests about *quinceañeras*. According to the bishop, the chief complaint was that *quinceañera* masses were beginning to dominate church schedules. This would surprise no one with an eye on the city's demographics: three-quarters of the Hispanics in Phoenix are under thirty-five years old and a significant number of them are girls—all potential subjects of a *quinceañera* mass and party. The priests complained that some girls came to their *quinceañera* mass without the faintest idea of its religious significance, never came to church otherwise, demanded a mass even if they were pregnant or using drugs or in some other way drifting outside the categories usually in good stead with the religious community, and badgered their families—some Chubbies, but many not—into giving them opulent post-mass parties. Some *quinceañera* parties in Phoenix were running into the high four figures and beyond. Many families could hardly afford this. In response to these concerns, Father Antonio Sotelo, the bishop's vicar for Hispanic affairs, surveyed the diocese's priests and then wrote a guidebook for *quinceañeras* similar to ones circulated recently in a few other American parishes with large Hispanic populations, advising that girls take five classes on Bible study, Hispanic history, *quinceañera* history, and modern morals, and go on a church-sponsored retreat with their parents before the event. He also recommended that *quinceañeras* be held for groups of girls rather than for individuals, in order to offset the queen-for-a-day quality that many of them had taken on, and so that the cost could be spread around.

7 One morning before the Vesta Club *quinceañera*, I stopped by Father Sotelo's office at Immaculate Heart. Besides being vicar for Hispanic affairs, Father Sotelo is the pastor of Immaculate Heart. His small office in the back of the church is decorated with pictures of his parishioners and dominated by a whale of a desk. Father Sotelo is short and wiry, and has rumpled graying hair, an impish face, and a melodious voice. His manner of address is direct. He is known for holding and broadcasting the opinion that anyone who wears shorts and a T-shirt to church should be escorted out the door, and that the men in his congregation who walk with a sloppy, swinging, barrio-tough gait look like gorillas. Father Sotelo grew up in San Diego. His heritage is Mexican and American Indian. He says that he considered the *quinceañera* issue a simple matter of facing reality, and he doesn't mind that the requirements have discouraged many girls from having *quinceañeras*. "We knew perfectly well that most girls were only thinking about the party," he said. "It was a big dream for them. Everyone wants a fancy *quinceañera* party. Unlike an American debutante ball, *quinceañeras* are not limited to the upper class. Any girl can celebrate it. But there are spoiled brats in every class. Many of these girls

were demanding that their parents spend thousands of dollars on them whether they could afford it or not. People at the lower end of the economic scale cling to tradition most fervently, so they were most determined to have a traditional *quinceañera,* and their daughters would have the most expensive dresses and parties. And when these girls would walk down the aisle with their parents at the mass, you could tell that quite often the girls and their parents couldn't stand one another. It was an empty ceremony. For what they were getting out of the church part of the *quinceañera,* they could have gone out and done the whole thing in the desert and had someone sprinkle magic pollen on their heads."

8   After the guidelines were circulated around the diocese, a few churches, including Immaculate Heart, set up the *quinceañera* classes and retreats. But to the enormous displeasure of parishioners who enjoyed spending Saturday nights at their friends' daughters' *quinceañeras,* and who imagined that on some Saturday night in the future their own daughters would be feted at a mass and nice reception of their own, many priests in Phoenix announced that they agreed with Father Sotelo but they lacked the time and facilities to run classes and retreats. Therefore, they declared, they would no longer perform *quinceañera* masses at all.

9   The one priest who took exception was Frank Peacock, the pastor of a poor church in a scruffy South Phoenix neighborhood. Father Peacock made it known that he thought the guidelines were too strict, and that they inhibited the exercise of a tradition that rightfully belonged to the people, and that as far as he was concerned, anyone in any condition or situation who wanted a *quinceañera* could come to him. "We get calls here all the time from people asking very meekly for Father Peacock's number," Father Sotelo said to me, looking exasperated. "They're not fooling anyone. I know exactly what they want."

10 A few weeks before I got to Phoenix, a small yucca plant on the corner of Twelfth and Van Buren, about a half mile down the street from Immaculate Heart, sprouted a stem that then shriveled up into an unusual shape and was subsequently noticed by a passerby who thought it bore a striking resemblance to Our Lady of Guadeloupe. The yucca stem was never certified as a genuine miracle by church hierarchy, but for several weeks, until someone shot at it with a small-caliber handgun and then two artists took it upon themselves to cut it down with a chainsaw as the climax of a performance piece, it attracted large crowds of people who came to marvel at it and pray.

11 Our Lady of Guadeloupe, the vision who appeared to the Mexican Indian Juan Diego on December 9, 1531, and who was so awe-inspiring a sight that she more or less nailed down the entire country of Mexico for the Catholic Church, has appeared in other places as unlikely as the corner of Twelfth and Van Buren. For instance, Our Lady of Guadeloupe also happens to be spray painted on the trunk of at least one souped-up low-rider

car in Phoenix, which I noticed bouncing down the street one afternoon when I was in town. Father Peacock had seen this same car and says he finds it remarkable. The day before the Vesta Club Ball, he and I had gotten together so he could show me videotapes of some of the outlaw *quinceañera* masses he had presided over at Our Lady of Fatima. Before we started the tapes, I said that Father Sotelo had pointed out that people were perfectly entitled to have *quinceañeras* that cost ten thousand dollars and celebrated fifteen-year-olds with heavy marijuana habits, but that the Church shouldn't necessarily endorse them or hold celebration masses for them. "People have a right to enjoy things that the Church doesn't endorse," Father Peacock said. "We don't endorse low-riders, do we?" He interrupted himself. "Actually, I endorse low-riders. I love them. Have you ever seen one? Oh, they can be gorgeous, really beautiful. Did you ever see the one painted with Our Lady of Guadeloupe?"

12 Of Father Peacock, Thomas O'Brien, the Bishop of Phoenix, says, "My druthers are that he conform. I haven't come down on him because I think he's well intentioned." Of Bishop O'Brien, Father Peacock says, "Oh, he's a good guy. I was a priest back when he was just a young novitiate, so I've seen him come through the ranks. We have a playful relationship, really a nice rapport. I kid him around. If he asked me to stop what I'm doing, I'd swear backwards and forwards that I would stop, and then I'd run right out and keep doing it. He knows that, and he lets me keep things in my little parish my way." Although there is a gulf between their positions on how lenient the Church should be with its supplicants, there is genuine goodwill between Father Sotelo and Father Peacock. Father Sotelo told me several times that he feels quite fond of old Frank. Father Peacock, that afternoon, said he is very fond of old Tony. Both of them mentioned that the other is the only other priest they ever see at political rallies and marches for the United Farm Workers or nuclear disarmament. Father Peacock, who is in his mid-sixties and is balding and tall, with a long oval head, high yankee coloring, a beaked nose, and a jittery, nerve racking way of walking, sitting, and talking, did remark that he thought Father Sotelo was most unfortunately under the impression that *quinceañera* masses were followed by wild beer parties and sexual escapades. "There definitely is *beer*," Father Peacock said. "Things are pretty lively. They are good parties. That's part of the tradition. Sometimes there are fistfights and so forth, but that's the way good parties are, isn't it? But I honestly think Father Sotelo thinks that these *quinceañeras* are orgies or some such thing. You know, if I were a married man and someone suggested that about my daughter's *quinceañera*, I'd sue him for libel." He chuckled and then said, "We have a good time at Our Lady of Fatima. We're just a little more savage than at the other churches. We're . . . noisier. We're more natural."

13 Some of the people who come to Father Peacock for a *quinceañera* are poor, or are recent immigrants who are still attached to the traditional

Mexican style of the ceremony and resist what they could well consider pointless time-consuming requirements or irritating Americanizations. Quite often, Father Peacock is approached by affluent Hispanics as well, who tell him they want their daughters to have their own celebrations, not *quinceañeras* with a group of other girls, and that they want to go all out with the six-tiered *quinceañera* cake and the rhinestone crown and the catered sit-down dinner for three hundred and the mariachi band and the lavish gifts from the godparents and the fifteen boy escorts and fifteen girl attendants in matching outfits who traditionally accompany the *quinceañera* girl. Father Peacock says he has given *quinceañera* masses for daughters of state senators as well as for girls whose parents are illiterate. Most of the time, he begins his address at the mass by asking for forgiveness for his failures and then says, "You have asked us to take care of a fifteenth birthday celebration and we say no—this is one of our failures." Sometimes the people at the altar look bored or are wearing dark sunglasses and conspicuous amounts of jewelry and can't even remember the words to the Lord's Prayer when Father Peacock recites it. "That is one of my motivations," he says. "This might be the only chance I have to get that sort of person into church and try to reach them." Some of the families have experienced child abuse, sexual abuse, divorce, separation, or a combination of all four, and Father Peacock says he loves seeing such families together at the occasional happy affair like a *quinceañera*. Some of them take out loans to pay for their daughter's gowns. Father Peacock usually urges the poorer families to hold their parties at South Mountain Park, a city facility with a hall that can be used for free, but he says he can understand if they prefer a fancier place. On this point, he always says something in the homily like, "Through self-sacrifice we get our pleasure," and has said many times that he would rather that people go into hock for a traditional, ethnic, religious occasion—no matter how marginally religious it might turn out to be—than for something like a car or a boat. "A *quinceañera* costs a lot of money," he says. "But it's worth a lot of money. Anyway, I don't try to change people. I like to meet them in their own way."

14   In 1987, Father Peacock performed 10 percent of all the baptisms in the Phoenix diocese. There are sixty-one churches in the diocese, so that is an extraordinary percentage. Unlike other priests, Father Peacock will baptize the babies of unwed mothers or unreligious mothers—essentially, anyone who asks and who might get a lecture and no baptism elsewhere—so he is in high demand. He seems to be amazing himself when he mentions his baptism statistics. "Ten percent," he says. "Oh my! Ten percent of the whole diocese. That's a *lot*." His explanation is that he wants people in the church, and sometimes baptizing a baby with muddled origins is the only way to do it. His *quinceañera* schedule is also busy: usually at least two for every Saturday night in the year. Once, he did seven *quinceañera* masses on a single Saturday night.

15   "Father Peacock will do anything," a young woman named Alice Coronado-Hernandez, this year's chairman of the Vesta Club *Quinceañera* Ball, said to me one afternoon. "Everyone knows that about Father Peacock, so everyone calls him." At the time, I was having lunch at a bad Mexican restaurant in a good part of Phoenix with Alice, her mother, Caroline, and Mary Jo Franco-French, a physician who helped found the Vesta *quinceañera* fifteen years ago. When she was organizing that first *quinceañera*, Mary Jo had just finished medical school and was pregnant with her daughter Laura. This year, Laura was going to be one of the girls up on the stage.

16   The Vesta Club is not going to be calling on Father Peacock anytime soon. "We're really happy with doing our *quinceañera* the way Father Sotelo has suggested," Caroline said. "We felt the classes and the retreat were really good for the girls. We saw what was going on with the *quinceañeras*—we saw the problem out there. Even if we could afford it, we knew it wasn't good to continue the old way."

17   Alice said, "It was crazy what people were spending. When I was that age, the girls were really competitive about their *quinceañeras* and about how nice they would be." Caroline nodded. My *quinceañera* was at the first Vesta Club Ball," Alice went on. "That year, I must have been invited to *quinceañeras* for friends of mine just about every weekend, so it was a pretty regular Saturday-night activity for me. But even then I could see how some people got very extravagant about it."

18   "They were hocking their souls for the fancy private *quinceañera*," Caroline added. "The diocese could see that it was becoming detrimental to the economy of their parishioners."

19   The three of them spent some time talking about last-minute details of the Vesta *quinceañera*. After a mass at Immaculate Heart, there was going to be dinner for the four hundred and fifty guests at Camelback Inn, an elegant resort north of the city, and a short ceremony in which each girl would be presented by her father. Then the girls and their escorts would perform a *quinceañera* waltz—a complicated dance to the "Blue Danube" which the kids had practiced once a week for the last three months. "The waltz is such a beautiful tradition," Mary Jo said. "It's what we have that makes the event really special. That, and having them learn about their Hispanic heritage. The kids have worked so hard at that waltz. They've really practiced, and they've really gotten good at it."

20   They *have* gotten good at it, haven't they?" Caroline said, nodding. "It's hard to believe that some of them had never danced a step before they started to learn."

21   The Fifteenth Annual Vesta Club *quinceañera* Mass began at five o'clock with a procession of the sixteen girls up the center aisle of Immaculate Heart. I sat on the left side of the church, a row behind Mary Jo Franco-French and her husband, Alfred, an eye surgeon of Gallic extraction who

has a large practice in Phoenix. Beside me were four cousins of Mary Jo's who had flown in from Juarez, Mexico, for the event. The day had been dry-roasting hot, and at five, the long, dusty southwestern dusk was just beginning and the light was hitting the city at a flat angle and giving everything a yellowy glow. The *quinceañera* girls in their white dresses had been standing on the sidewalk outside the church when I walked in, and each time a car drove down the street in front of the church, the updraft would blow their big skirts around. Immaculate Heart is a bulky, unadorned building with dark wooden pews, a vaulted ceiling, some stained glass, a wide altar with simple lines, and a pail hanging just outside the side door into which parishioners are advised to deposit their chewing gum. After I sat down, I noticed Father Sotelo and Bishop O'Brien seated together at the altar. The Vesta Club *quinceañera* is the only one in Phoenix at which the bishop celebrates the mass. He told me that it is the only one he attends because he liked the seriousness with which the club approached the spiritual content of the ceremony, and also because no one else having a *quinceañera* had ever invited him.

22   Father Peacock had mentioned that he was going to try to make it to Immaculate Heart for the Vesta Club *quinceañera* because he likes to go to as many *quinceañeras* as he can, but that he might not make it because he was supposed to celebrate a *quinceañera* mass at his own church for a girl from a poor family. The family didn't have a phone, and as of Friday, he hadn't heard from anyone, so he wasn't sure if they were still planning to come. He mentioned that he didn't know any of the particulars of the event except that the party was going to be at a social hall in South Phoenix and that the family had hired a video crew to film the whole thing. *Quinceañera* videos, with title sequences and soundtracks and sometimes introductions showing the girl's baby pictures, are getting to be big business in Phoenix. I glanced around the church and saw about two hundred people. Everyone was wearing tuxedos or formal gowns. I didn't see Father Peacock. I believe that even in such a big crowd he would have stood out. On the occasions I spent with him, he wore a priest's black shirt and white collar; baggy, faded black jeans; and scuffed-up Birkenstock sandals. In all the photographs he showed me of himself standing with girls he had just blessed at the *quinceañera* mass, he was wearing a rough version of a priest's cope that he had made by cutting up a Mexican blanket. "Some of the people at my church don't like when I wear it because they think it's too ratty-looking, but oh, gosh, it was such a beautiful blanket," he had said, gazing at the photographs. Then he stroked his chin and looked contemplative. "Actually," he said, "maybe it was a tablecloth."

23   After a few minutes, the organist hit a chord and the procession began. The Vesta Club girls walked in, trailing satin and netting. The gowns were a spectacle: each one was bright white, with different

structural embellishments and complicated effects. I noticed the girl wearing the dress with the little train and the one with the narrow skirt. "Wow," whispered Carmen Gonzalez, one of Mary Jo Franco-French's cousins, who had celebrated her own *quinceañera* a few years ago at a country club in Juarez. "Pretty nice dresses. These girls look so *grown-up.*"

24 "The third one down is my niece Maria," the woman behind us said. "Fifteen already, but I still think of her as a baby. I think her mother's praying that Maria keeps her figure so she can wear the dress again when she gets married."

25 The procession took several minutes. Then the girls sat down in two rows of chairs at the altar, and the bishop made his greetings and began the mass. After a few prayers, he announced that it was time for the parents to bless their daughters individually. He turned and nodded at the dark-haired girl at the end of the row. She stood up cautiously, walked to the center of the apse and down the three steps, turned around and knelt down, partially disappearing in the folds of her dress. Her parents stood up in their pew and walked over to her, leaned down and made the sign of the cross on her forehead, kissed her, whispered something in her ear, and then returned to their seats. The girl rose up and walked back to the altar. Someone in a pew behind me sobbed lightly and then blew loudly into a handkerchief. A faulty key in the church organ stuck and started to squeal. The next girl stood up, smoothed her huge skirt, stepped down, knelt, was blessed by her parents, and returned to her seat. Laura Josefina Franco-French, a tall and elegant-looking fifteen-year-old with long dark hair and a serene expression, came forward and was blessed by Alfred and Mary Jo. Then the girl who was wearing the tight skirt stood up. We all sat forward. She walked in tiny steps across the apse, eased herself down the stairs, turned around, and then, with the agility of a high-school cheerleader at the season's big game, she folded her legs beneath her and knelt without straining a seam.

26 There were still some golfers on the greens at Camelback Inn when the Vesta Club partygoers arrived. The ballroom wasn't ready for us to be seated, so everyone milled around the pool having drinks and talking. I wondered if the golfers were curious about what we were doing—four hundred well-dressed people, most adult, and sixteen girls in formal white gowns. It might have looked like a wedding, except there were too many young women in white, and it might have looked like a prom, except no one has parents at her prom. It felt mostly like a community reunion. "It's a big group, but it's a small world," said a woman in a beaded lilac gown standing beside me at the bar.

27 "Relatives or friends?" I asked.

28 "Both," she said. "About half of these people were at my daughter's *quinceañera* last year." I must have looked surprised, because she started

to laugh, and then said, "Some of these families even knew each other in Mexico. You could say that we're just keeping the chain or circle or what have you, intact. I had my *quinceañera* longer ago than I'm happy to say. It's an old-fashioned event but I love it." She took her drink and joined a group of people nearby who were talking about an expensive shopping center just opening in Scottsdale. One of the men in the group kept sweeping his hands out and saying "Boom!" and the woman beside him would then slap his shoulder playfully and say "For godsakes, come on, Adolfo!" Alfred Franco-French III, who was escorting his sister Laura, walked past the bar and muttered that he hoped he would remember the waltz when it came time to waltz. The patio got noisier and noisier. No one was speaking Spanish. One of the girls' fathers started a conversation with me by saying, "There are plenty of bums in the world out there, sad to say," but then he got distracted by someone he hadn't seen in a while and walked away. I had driven out to Camelback with one of Laura Franco-French's school friends, and after a few minutes we ran into each other. She said she was impressed with the *quinceañera* so far. She talked about how there was usually never anything to do on Saturday nights in Phoenix, and then she talked about how favorably Laura's involvement in a formal event, in particular one that required the purchase of a really nice fancy dress, was regarded by other students at their largely non-Hispanic private school. It happened that this girl was not Hispanic and had never been to a *quinceañera* before and had also never before considered what advantages ethnicity might include. She looked across the pool where the debutantes were standing in a cluster and said, "I never thought about it one way or another. But now that I'm at one of these *quinceañeras,* I'm thinking that being Hispanic might be really cool." I walked to the far side of the pool, where I had a long view of all the people at the party, in their fresh tuxes and filmy formals; with their good haircuts and the handsome, relaxed posture common to people whose businesses are doing well and to whom life has been generous; who were standing around the glimmery pool and against the dark, lumpy outline of Camelback Mountain, holding up light-colored drinks in little crystal glasses so that they happened to catch the last bit of daylight. It was a pretty gorgeous sight.

29 Finally, Alice Coronado-Hernandez and Caroline Coronado sent word that the ballroom was ready. The doors of the Saguaro Room were propped open. The patio emptied as the crowd moved inside. At one end of the ballroom, a mariachi band was ready to play. Around the dance floor were fifty tables set with bunchy flower arrangements and good china. I had been seated with Alice Coronado-Hernandez and her family. At the tables, each place was set with a program printed on stiff, creamy paper; it listed the Vesta Club officers, last year's *quinceañera* debs and escorts, and this year's debs and escorts, and had formal portraits of each of the girls. This was similar in style to the program for the St. Luke's Hospital

Visitors' Society Cotillion—Phoenix's premier society event—at which the girls being presented are far more likely to have names like Bickerstaff and Collins than Esparza and Alvarez. I had seen the 1988 St. Luke's program when I had dinner one night with the Franco-Frenches. Laura had been studying the program so energetically that some of the pages were fingerprinted and the binding was broken. In the time since Mexicans in Phoenix were forced to hold their masses in the basement of St. Mary's, a certain amount of social amalgamation has come to pass: Laura Franco-French, half-Mexican in heritage and at least that much in consciousness, will also be presented at St. Luke's in a few years. Similarly, there was a Whitman and a Thornton among the debutantes at the Vesta ball.

30 I was reading the Vesta program when Father Sotelo came over to the table. "It's a wonderful event, isn't it?" he said, breaking into a huge smile. He gave Alice a bountiful look. She gave him one back and then got up and hustled off in the direction of the kitchen. The tables around us were soon filled and the conversations bubbling. "It's such a happy occasion for all the families," Father Sotelo said. He ran his finger around his collar. "This is a wonderful, wonderful thing. It's one of my favorite events. These girls are going to remember this forever. If you just do it the old way, with no effort to have it mean anything, it's just like giving candy to a baby. You're just trying to please people. This way, it's something that has significance." Laura Franco-French drifted past our table. Father Sotelo stopped her and told her she looked wonderful. She gave him a dreamy smile and then drifted on toward her family's table. Father Sotelo nodded after her and then crossed the room to his table.

31 After a moment, Alice came back and dropped into her seat. "They don't have enough prime rib, so some people will have to have steak," she said.

32 Her husband, Joe, shrugged, sighed, and picked up the program. "Anything but rubber chicken," he said. "You get a big group of people together like this and it starts to look *political,* you know?"

33 "When do they announce debutante of the year?" Alice's stepdaughter asked her. Alice drummed her fingers on the table and said, "Later." Just then, the master of ceremonies coughed into the microphone and the room got quiet. The girls lined up around the edge of the dance floor with their fathers. The mothers were stationed near them in chairs, so that they would be readily available for the father–mother waltz, which comes after the father–daughter waltz and after the special *quinceañera* waltz—a complex piece of choreography, in which the girls spin around their escorts and then weave through their arms, form little circles and then big circles and finally waltz in time around the dance floor. After all these waltzes, the mariachi band was going to play—although I had heard that for the sake of the teenagers, who appreciated their heritage but who were, after all, American kids with tastes of their

own, the Mexican music was going to be alternated throughout the evening with current selections of rock and roll.

34   The announcer cleared his throat again and said, *"Buenos noches, damas y caballeros."* He had a sonorous, rumbling voice that thundered through the ballroom. *"Buenos noches.* We present to you this year's Vesta Club debutantes."

Reading for Meaning

1. What point of view does Susan Orlean adopt in her essay on the *quinceañera* in Phoenix, Arizona? How does her perspective affect the story she tells?

2. What is the literal meaning of a *quinceañera*? What does the ceremony mean to the girl's parents and to the girl herself?

3. How has the ceremony been "Americanized"? What other evidence of cultural assimilation can you find in Orlean's descriptions?

4. Does Orlean agree with the woman who explained to her that the ceremony is passing out of the Latino culture in this country? What evidence does Orlean offer to counter this skeptical view?

5. What might the *quinceañera* ceremony be like in Father Sotelo's church? How would the ceremony differ in Father Peacock's congregation? What philosophical differences do these two versions of the ceremony represent? What personal differences between the two priests do Orlean's descriptions capture?

Comparing Texts

1. Compare the rites of passage Margaret Mead mentions in her 1926 article on Bali (page 102) to the ceremonial coming of age described in Susan Orlean's story of the *quinceañera*.

2. Read Malidoma Patrice Somé's "Slowly Becoming" in chapter 12. How does the point of view taken by Somé differ from that of Susan Orlean? How well does each perspective complement the writer's approach to his or her subject?

Ideas for Writing

1. Think of an important ceremony in which you participated or that you witnessed. Describe the event in some detail and explain what each part of the ritual meant and what purpose it served.

2. What informal rituals do teenagers and young adults use to set themselves apart from people in other age groups? What assumptions about adults or adult opinions do these rites suggest?

3. Do some research on a ceremony or rite of passage that you would like to know more about. Write an information paper in which you explain what you have learned. (See the discussion of the information paper on page 116.)

Writing before Reading

Imagine you have just met a group of travelers who have lived their entire lives on a remote island in the South Pacific. Pretend that they ask you about values and beliefs common to people living in the United States. Which habits would you discuss? Why might these habits appear strange to someone unfamiliar with them?

BODY RITUAL AMONG THE NACIREMA

Horace Miner

Horace Miner was a professor of anthropology at the University of Michigan and one of the founders of the "Chicago School" of anthropology, a small group of researchers who studied rural communities as representative of other cultural groups of this type. Miner published his observations on Francophone, Canada, with Everett C. Hughes in the 1950s. Despite his importance to the development of investigative theories, Miner is best known for his essay titled "Body Ritual among the Nacirema," which was published in American Anthropologist *in 1956. This pseudo study of the "Nacirema," is a parody of field research in general and cultural habits in the United States in particular.*

1   The anthropologist has become so familiar with the diversity of ways in which different peoples behave in similar situations that he is not apt to be surprised by even the most exotic customs. In fact, if all of the logically possible combinations of behavior have not been found somewhere in the world, he is apt to suspect that they must be present in some yet undescribed tribe. This point has, in fact, been expressed with respect to clan organization by Murdock (1949: 71). In this light, the magical beliefs and practices of the Nacirema present such unusual aspects that it seems desirable to describe them as an example of the extremes to which human behavior can go.

2   Professor Linton first brought the ritual of the Nacirema to the attention of anthropologists twenty years ago (1936: 326), but the culture of this people is still very poorly understood. They are a North American group living in the territory between the Canadian Cree, the Yaqui and Tarahumare of Mexico, and the Carib and Arawak of the Antilles. Little is

known of their origin, although tradition states that they came from the east. According to Nacirema mythology, their nation was originated by a culture hero, Notgnihsaw, who is otherwise known for two great feats of strength—the throwing of a piece of wampum across the river Pa-To-Mac and the chopping down of a cherry tree in which the Spirit of Truth resided.

3   Nacirema culture is characterized by a highly developed market economy which has evolved in a rich natural habitat. While much of the people's time is devoted to economic pursuits, a large part of the fruits of these labors and a considerable portion of the day are spent in ritual activity. The focus of this activity is the human body, the appearance and health of which loom as a dominant concern in the ethos of the people. While such a concern is certainly not unusual, its ceremonial aspects and associated philosophy are unique.

4   The fundamental belief underlying the whole system appears to be that the human body is ugly and that its natural tendency is to debility and disease. Incarcerated in such a body, man's only hope is to avert these characteristics through the use of the powerful influences of ritual and ceremony. Every household has one or more shrines devoted to this purpose. The more powerful individuals in the society have several shrines in their houses, and, in fact, the opulence of a house is often referred to in terms of the number of such ritual centers it possesses. Most houses are of wattle and daub construction, but the shrine rooms of the more wealthy are walled with stone. Poorer families imitate the rich by applying pottery plaques to their shrine walls.

5   While each family has at least one such shrine, the rituals associated with it are not family ceremonies but are private and secret. The rites are normally only discussed with children, and then only during the period when they are being initiated into these mysteries. I was able, however, to establish sufficient rapport with the natives to examine these shrines and to have the rituals described to me.

6   The focal point of the shrine is a box or chest which is built into the wall. In this chest are kept the many charms and magical potions without which no native believes he could live. These preparations are secured from a variety of specialized practitioners. The most powerful of these are the medicine men, whose assistance must be rewarded with substantial gifts. However, the medicine men do not provide the curative potions for their clients, but decide what the ingredients should be and then write them down in an ancient and secret language. This writing is understood only by the medicine men and by the herbalists who, for another gift, provide the required charm.

7   The charm is not disposed of after it has served its purpose, but is placed in the charm box of the household shrine. As these magical materials are specific for certain ills, and the real or imagined maladies of the people are many, the charm box is usually full to overflowing. The magical

packets are so numerous that people forget what their purposes were and fear to use them again. While the natives are very vague on this point, we can only assume that the idea in retaining all the old magical materials is that their presence in the charm box, before which the body rituals are conducted, will in some way protect the worshipper.

8   Beneath the charm box is a small font. Each day every member of the family, in succession, enters the shrine room, bows his head before the charm box, mingles different sorts of holy water in the font, and proceeds with a brief rite of ablution. The holy waters are secured from the Water Temple of the community, where the priests conduct elaborate ceremonies to make the liquid ritually pure.

9   In the hierarchy of magical practitioners, and below the medicine men in prestige, are specialists whose designation is best translated "holy-mouthmen." The Nacirema have an almost pathological horror of and fascination with the mouth, the condition of which is believed to have a supernatural influence on all social relationships. Were it not for the rituals of the mouth, they believe that their teeth would fall out, their gums bleed, their jaws shrink, their friends desert them, and their lovers reject them. They also believe that a strong relationship exists between oral and moral characteristics. For example, there is a ritual ablution of the mouth for children which is supposed to improve their moral fiber.

10   The daily body ritual performed by everyone includes a mouth-rite. Despite the fact that these people are so punctilious about the care of the mouth, this rite involves a practice which strikes the uninitiated stranger as revolting. It was reported to me that the ritual consists of inserting a small bundle of hog hairs into the mouth, along with certain magical powders, and then moving the bundle in a highly formalized series of gestures.

11   In addition to the private mouth rite, the people seek out a holy-mouth man once or twice a year. These practitioners have an impressive set of paraphernalia, consisting of a variety of augers, awls, probes, and prods. The use of these objects in the exorcism of the evils of the mouth involves almost unbelievable ritual torture of the client. The holy-mouth man opens the client's mouth and, using the above mentioned tools, enlarges any holes which decay may have created in the teeth. Magical materials are put into these holes. If there are no naturally occurring holes in the teeth, large sections of one or more teeth are gouged out so that the supernatural substance can be applied. In the client's view, the purpose of these ministrations is to arrest decay and to draw friends. The extremely sacred and traditional character of the rite is evident in the fact that the natives return to the holy-mouth man year after year, despite the fact that their teeth continue to decay.

12   It is to be hoped that, when a thorough study of the Nacirema is made, there will be careful inquiry into the personality structure of these people. One has but to watch the gleam in the eye of a holy-mouth man,

as he jabs an awl into an exposed nerve, to suspect that a certain amount of sadism is involved. If this can be established, a very interesting pattern emerges, for most of the population shows definite masochistic tendencies. It was to these that Professor Linton referred in discussing a distinctive part of the daily body ritual which is performed only by men. This part of the rite involves scraping and lacerating the surface of the face with a sharp instrument. Special women's rites are performed only four times during each lunar month, but what they lack in frequency is made up in barbarity. As part of this ceremony, women bake their heads in small ovens for about an hour. The theoretically interesting point is that what seems to be a preponderantly masochistic people have developed sadistic specialists.

13   The medicine men have an imposing temple, or *latipso,* in every community of any size. The more elaborate ceremonies required to treat very sick patients can only be performed at this temple. These ceremonies involve not only the thaumaturge but a permanent group of vestal maidens who move sedately about the temple chambers in distinctive costume and headdress.

14   The *latipso* ceremonies are so harsh that it is phenomenal that a fair proportion of the really sick natives who enter the temple ever recover. Small children whose indoctrination is still incomplete have been known to resist attempts to take them to the temple because "that is where you go to die." Despite this fact, sick adults are not only willing but eager to undergo the protracted ritual purification, if they can afford to do so. No matter how ill the supplicant or how grave the emergency, the guardians of many temples will not admit a client if he cannot give a rich gift to the custodian. Even after one has gained admission and survived the ceremonies, the guardians will not permit the neophyte to leave until he makes still another gift.

15   The supplicant entering the temple is first stripped of all his or her clothes. In everyday life the Nacirema avoids exposure of his body and its natural functions. Bathing and excretory acts are performed only in the secrecy of the household shrine, where they are ritualized as part of the body rites. Psychological shock results from the fact that body secrecy is suddenly lost upon entry into the *latipso.* A man, whose own wife has never seen him in an excretory act, suddenly finds himself naked and assisted by a vestal maiden while he performs his natural functions into a sacred vessel. This sort of ceremonial treatment is necessitated by the fact that the excreta are used by a diviner to ascertain the course and nature of the client's sickness. Female clients, on the other hand, find their naked bodies are subjected to the scrutiny, manipulation, and prodding of the medicine men.

16   Few supplicants in the temple are well enough to do anything but lie on their hard beds. The daily ceremonies, like the rites of the holy-mouth men, involve discomfort and torture. With ritual precision, the

vestals awaken their miserable charges each dawn and roll them about on their beds of pain while performing ablutions, in the formal movements of which the maidens are highly trained. At other times they insert magic wands in the supplicant's mouth or force him to eat substances which are supposed to be healing. From time to time the medicine men come to their clients and jab magically treated needles into their flesh. The fact that these temple ceremonies may not cure, and may even kill the neophyte, in no way decreases the people's faith in the medicine men.

17 There remains one other kind of practitioner, known as "listener." This witch doctor has the power to exorcise the devils that lodge in the heads of people who have been bewitched. The Nacirema believe that parents bewitch their own children. Mothers are particularly suspected of putting a curse on children while teaching them the secret body rituals. The counter-magic of the witch doctor is unusual in its lack of ritual. The patient simply tells the "listener" all his troubles and fears, beginning with the earliest difficulties he can remember. The memory displayed by the Nacirema in these exorcism sessions is truly remarkable. It is not uncommon for the patient to bemoan the rejection he felt upon being weaned as a babe, and a few individuals even see their troubles going back to the traumatic effects of their own birth.

18 In conclusion, mention must be made of certain practices which have their base in native esthetics but which depend upon the pervasive aversion to the natural body and its functions. There are ritual fasts to make fat people thin and ceremonial feasts to make thin people fat. Still other rites are used to make women's breasts larger if they are small, and smaller if they are large. General dissatisfaction with breast shape is symbolized in the fact that the ideal form is virtually outside the range of human variation. A few women afflicted with almost inhuman hyper-mammary development are so idolized that they make a handsome living by simply going from village to village and permitting the natives to stare at them for a fee.

19 Reference has already been made to the fact that excretory functions are ritualized, routinized, and relegated to secrecy. Natural reproductive functions are similarly distorted. Intercourse is taboo as a topic and scheduled as an act. Efforts are made to avoid pregnancy by the use of magical materials or by limiting intercourse to certain phases of the moon. Conception is actually very infrequent. When pregnant, women dress so as to hide their condition. Parturition takes place in secret, without friends or relatives to assist, and the majority of women do not nurse their infants.

20 Our review of the ritual life of the Nacirema has certainly shown them to be a magic-ridden people. It is hard to understand how they have managed to exist so long under the burdens which they have imposed upon themselves. But even such exotic customs as these take on

real meanings when they are viewed with the insight provided by Malinowski when he wrote (1948: 70):

21   Looking from far and above, from our high places of safety in the developed civilization, it is easy to see all the crudity and irrelevance of magic. But without its power and guidance early man could not have mastered his practical difficulties as he has done, nor could man have advanced to the higher stages of civilization.

References

Linton, Ralph. 1936. *The Study of Man.* New York: D. Appleton-Century Co.
Malinowski, Bronislaw. 1948. *Magic, Science, and Religion.* Glencoe: The Free Press.
Murdock, George P. 1949. *Social Structure.* New York: The Macmillan Co.

Reading for Meaning

1. Examine the vocabulary that Miner uses to describe the Nacirema. What effect does he achieve by describing American habits using this language?

2. What objects and cultural practices is Miner describing in the various sections of his essay? In what ways did his assumed naive view affect your perception of the routines he describes? Have any of the "rituals" that he mentions changed in some way or passed out of the American culture altogether since he wrote the article in 1956?

3. Why do you think Miner adds the last insight from Malinowski's book on magic, science, and religion?

4. What does Miner's choice of "magical practices" and his slant on those subjects reveal about him?

Comparing Texts

Review Margaret Mead's study of Balinese culture in chapter 4, page 102. How does choice of language fit the tone and purpose of Mead's article on Bali and Horace Miner's satire on American cultural practices?

Ideas for Writing

1. Horace Miner's mock study of Americans was published more than forty years ago. Write an update of his study in which you add a few of your own descriptions of curious "rituals"—routines that most of us perform without thinking much about them.

2. Interview several people who are from a different country or section of the United States. Find out which behaviors they consider odd in their new culture and why those practices or rituals appear strange to them. Try writing a paper from as objective a stance as you can discussing their views on cultural practices in the United States.

Writing before Reading

In your experience, how do people date and mate in the United States? How do the rituals for meeting and getting involved with one another differ from one age group to another?

CHOOSING MATES— THE AMERICAN WAY
Martin King Whyte

Martin Whyte teaches sociology at George Washington University. He also taught at the University of Michigan where he was professor of sociology and faculty associate in the Center for Chinese Studies. He has written extensively about social organizations in contemporary China. His books include Urban Life in Contemporary China *(1984) and* Dating, Mating, and Marriage *(1990). He is currently studying methods of choosing mates and marital relations in the United States and China.*

1   As America's divorce rate has been soaring, popular anxieties about marriage have multiplied. Is it still possible to "live happily ever after," and if so, how can this be accomplished? How can you tell whether a partner who leaves you breathless with yearning will, as your spouse, drive you to distraction? Does "living together" prior to marriage provide a realistic assessment of how compatible you and your partner might be as husband and wife? Questions such as these suggest a need to examine our American way of mate choice. How do we go about selecting the person we marry, and is there something wrong with the entire process?

2   For most twentieth-century Americans choosing a mate is the culmination of a process of dating. Examination of how we go about selecting mates thus requires us to consider the American dating culture. Dating is a curious institution. By definition it is an activity that is supposed to be separate from selecting a spouse. Yet, dating is expected to provide valuable experience that will help in making a "wise" choice of a marital partner. Does this combination work?

3   How well dating "works" may be considered in a number of senses of this term. It is easy or difficult to find somebody to go out with? Do dates mostly lead to enjoyable or painful evenings? However, these are not the aspects of dating I wish to consider. The issue here is whether dating

works in the sense of providing useful experience that helps pave the way for a successful marriage.

4   Dating is a relatively new institution. The term, and the various practices associated with it, first emerged around the turn of the century. By the 1920s dating had more or less completely displaced earlier patterns of relations among unmarried Americans. Contrary to popular assumptions, even in colonial times marriages were not arranged in America. Parents were expected to give their approval to their children's nuptial plans, a practice captured in our image of a suitor asking his beloved's father for her hand in marriage. Parental approval, especially among merchants and other prosperous classes, put some constraint on the marriages of the young. For example, through the eighteenth century, children in such families tended to marry in birth order and marriage to cousins was not uncommon. (Both practices had declined sharply by the nineteenth century.) However, parents rarely directly arranged the marriages of their children. America has always exhibited "youth-driven" patterns of courtship. Eligible males and females took the initiative to get to know each other, and the decision to marry was made by them, even if that decision was to some degree contingent on parental approval. (Of course, substantial proportions of later immigrant groups from Southern and Eastern Europe, Asia, and elsewhere brought with them arranged marriage traditions, and contention for control over marriage decisions was often a great source of tension in such families.)

5   How did young people get to know one another well enough to decide to marry in the era before dating? A set of customs, dominant for the two centuries, preceded the rise of the dating culture. These activities came to be referred to as "calling" and "keeping company." Young people might meet in a variety of ways—through community and church socials, informally in shops or on the street, on boat and train trips, or through introductions from friends or relatives. (America never developed a system of chaperoning young women in public, and foreign observers often commented on the freedom unmarried women had to travel and mix socially on their own.) Usually young people would go to church fairs, local dances, and other such activities with family, siblings, or friends, rather than paired off with a partner. Most activities would involve a substantial degree of adult and community supervision. Nonetheless, these gatherings did encourage some pairing off and led to hand holding, moonlit walks home, and other romantic exploration.

6   As relationships developed beyond the platonic level, the suitor would pay visits to the home of the young woman. By the latter part of the nineteenth century, particularly among the middle and upper classes, this activity assumed a formal pattern referred to as "calling." Males would be invited to call on the female at her home, and they were expected to do so only if invited. (A bold male could, however, request an invitation to call.) Invitations might be extended by the mother of a very young woman, but eventually they would come from the young woman

herself. Often a woman would designate certain days on which she would receive callers. She might have several suitors at one time, and thus a number of men might be paying such calls. A man might be told that the woman was not at home to receive him, and he would then be expected to leave his calling card. If this happened repeatedly, he was expected to get the message that his visits were no longer welcome.

7   Initiative and control in regard to calling were in the hands of women (the eligible female and her mother). Although some variety in suitors was possible, even in initial stages the role of calling in examining potential marriage partners was very clear to all involved. The relatively constrained and supervised nature of calling make it certain that enjoyment cannot have been a primary goal of this activity. (During the initial visits the mother was expected to remain present; in later visits she often hovered in an adjacent room.) If dating is defined as recreational and romantic pairing off between a man and a woman, away from parental supervision and without immediate consideration of marriage, then calling was definitely not dating.

8   The supervised and controlled nature of calling should not, however, lead us to suppose that propriety and chastity were always maintained until marriage. If the relationship had deepened sufficiently, the couple might progress from calling to "keeping company," a precursor of the twentieth-century custom of "going steady." At this stage, the primary activity would still consist of visits by the suitor of the woman's home. However, now she would only welcome calls from one man, and he would visit her home on a regular basis. Visits late into the evening would increasingly replace afternoon calls. As the relationship became more serious, parents would often leave the couple alone. Nineteenth-century accounts mention parents going off to bed and leaving the young couple on the couch or by the fireplace, there to wrestle with, and not infrequently give in to, sexual temptation.

9   Even though some women who headed to the altar toward the end of the nineteenth century had lost their virginity prior to marriage, premarital intimacy was less common than during the dating era. (The double standard of the Victorian era made it possible for many more grooms to be nonvirgins at marriage than brides. Perhaps 50 percent or more of men had lost their virginity prior to marriage, as opposed to 15 to 20 percent of women, with prostitutes and "fallen women" helping to explain the differential.) What is less often realized is that the formalization of the calling pattern toward the end of the nineteenth century contributed to a decline in premarital sexual intimacy compared to earlier times. America experienced not one but two sexual revolutions—one toward the end of the eighteenth century, at the time of the American Revolution, and the other in the latter part of the twentieth century.

10   The causes of the first sexual revolution are subject to some debate. An influx of settlers to America who did not share the evangelical puritanism of many early colonists, the expansion of the population into the

unsettled (and "unchurched") frontier, the growth of towns, and the individualistic and freedom-loving spirit of the American revolution may have contributed to a retreat from the fairly strict emphasis on premarital chastity of the early colonial period. Historians debate the extent to which the archetypal custom of this first sexual revolution, bundling (which allowed an unmarried couple to sleep together, although theoretically fully clothed and separated by a "bundling board") was widespread or largely mythical. Whatever the case, other evidence is found in studies of communities, such as those by Daniel Scott Smith and Michael Hindus, which found that the percentage of married couples whose first births were conceived premaritally increased from about 11 percent before 1700 to over 33 percent in the last decades of the eighteenth century.

11   This first sexual revolution was reversed in the nineteenth century. The reasons for its demise are also not clear. The closing of the frontier, the rise of the middle class, the defensive reactions of that new middle class to new waves of immigrants, the growth of Christian revivalism and reform movements, and the spread of models of propriety from Victorian England (which were in turn influenced by fear of the chaos of the French Revolution)—all these have been suggested as having contributed to a new sexual puritanism in the nineteenth century. According to Smith and Hindus, premarital conceptions decreased once again to about 15 percent of first births between 1841 and 1880.

12   It was in the latter time period that the customs of calling and keeping company reached their most formal elaboration—calling, in less ritualized forms, can be traced back to the earliest colonial period. Not long after reaching the formal patterns described, calling largely disappeared. In little more than a generation, dating replaced calling as the dominant custom.

13   Dating involved pairing off of couples in activities not supervised by parents, with pleasure rather than marriage as the primary goal. The rules governing dating were defined by peers rather than by adults. The initiative, and much of the control, shifted from the female to the male. The man asked the woman out, rather than waiting for her invitation to call. The finances and transportation for the date were also his responsibility. The woman was expected to provide, in turn, the pleasure of her company and perhaps some degree of romantic and physical intimacy. By giving or withholding her affection and access to her body, she exercised considerable control over the man and the date as an event. Nonetheless, the absence of parental oversight and the pressure to respond to a man's initiatives placed a woman in a weaker position than she was in the era of calling.

14   The man might pick up the woman at her home, but parents who tried to dictate whom their daughters dated and what they did on dates generally found such efforts rejected and evaded. Parents of a son might not even know where junior was going or whom he was dating. Dates

were conducted mostly in the public arena, and in some cases—such as at sporting events or school dances—adults might be present. But dates often involved activities and venues where no adults were present or where young people predominated—as at private parties or at local dance halls. Or in other cases the presence of adults would have little inhibiting effect, as in the darkened balconies of movie theaters. American youths also developed substantial ingenuity in finding secluded "lovers' lanes" where they would escape the supervision of even peers. (Localities varied in the places used for this purpose and how they were referred to. In locales near bodies of water young people spoke of "watching submarine races;" in the rural area of upstate New York where I grew up the phrase was "exploring tractor roads.") Community dances and gatherings for all generations and ages practically disappeared in the dating era.

15 Greater privacy and autonomy of youths promoted romantic and physical experimentation. Not only kissing but petting was increasingly accepted and widespread. Going beyond petting to sexual intercourse, however, involved substantial risks, especially for the female. This was not simply the risk of pregnancy in the pre-pill era. Dating perpetuated the sexual double standard. Men were expected to be the sexual aggressors and to try to achieve as much intimacy as their dates would allow. But women who "went too far" risked harming their reputations and their ability to keep desirable men interested in them for long. Women were expected to set the limits, and they had to walk a careful line between being too unfriendly (and not having males wanting to date them at all) and being too friendly (and being dated for the "wrong reasons").

16 During the initial decades of the dating era, premarital intimacy increased in comparison with the age of calling, but still a majority of women entered marriage as virgins. In a survey in the greater Detroit metropolitan area, I found that of the oldest women interviewed (those who dated and married prior to 1945), about one in four had lost her virginity prior to marriage. (By the 1980s, according to my survey, the figure was closer to 90 percent.) Escape from parental supervision provided by dating weakened, but did not immediately destroy, the restraints on premarital intimacy.

17 When Americans began dating, they were primarily concerned with enjoyment, rather than with choosing a spouse. Indeed, "playing the field" was the ideal pursued by many. Dates were not suitors or prospects. Seeing different people on successive nights in a hectic round of dating activity earned one popularity among peers. One of the early students and critics of the dating culture, Willard Waller, coined the term "rating and dating complex" to refer to this pattern. After observing dating among students at Pennsylvania State University in the 1930s, Waller charged the concern for impressing friends and gaining status on campus led to superficial thrill-seeking and competition for popularity, and eliminated genuine romance or sincere communication. However, Waller

has been accused of both stereotyping and exaggerating the influence of this pattern. Dating was not always so exploitative and superficial as he charged.

18 Dating was never viewed as an endless stage or an alternative to courtship. Even if dates were initially seen as quite separate from mate selection, they were always viewed as only the first step in a progression that would lead to marriage. By the 1930s, the stage of "going steady" was clearly recognized, entailing a commitment by both partners to date each other exclusively, if only for the moment. A variety of ritual markers emerged to symbolize the increased commitment of this stage and of further steps toward engagement and marriage, such as wearing the partner's high school ring, being lavaliered, and getting pinned.

19 Going steady was a way-station between casual dating and engagement. Steadies pledged not to date others, and they were likely to become more deeply involved romantically and physically then casual daters. They were not expected explicitly to contemplate marriage, and the majority of women in our Detroit survey had several steady boyfriends before the relationships that led to their marriages. If a couple was of a "suitable age," though, and if the steady relationship lasted more than a few months, the likelihood increased of explicit talk about marriage. Couples would then symbolize their escalated commitment by getting engaged. Dating arose first among middle and upper middle class students in urban areas, and roughly simultaneously at the college and high school levels. The practice then spread to other groups—rural young people, working class youths, to the upper class, and to employed young people. But what triggered the rapid demise of calling and the rise of dating?

20 One important trend was prolonged school attendance, particularly in public, co-educational high schools and colleges. Schools provided an arena in which females and males could get to know one another informally over many years. Schools also organized athletic, social, and other activities in which adult supervision was minimal. College compuses generally allowed a more total escape from parental supervision than high schools.

21 Another important influence was growing affluence in America. More and more young people were freed from a need to contribute to the family economy and had more leisure time in which to date. Fewer young people worked under parental supervision, and more and more fathers worked far from home, leaving mothers as the primary monitors of their children's daily activities. These trends also coincided with a rise in part-time and after-school employment for students, employment that provided pocket money that did not have to be turned over to parents and could be spent on clothing, makeup, movie tickets, and other requirements of the dating culture. Rising affluences also fueled the growth of entire new industries designed to entertain and fill leisure

time—movies, popular music recording, ice cream parlors, amusement parks, and so on. Increasingly, young people who wanted to escape from supervision of their parents found a range of venues, many of them catering primarily to youth and to dating activities.

22   Technology also played a role, and some analysts suggest that one particular invention, the automobile, deserves a lion's share of the credit. Automobiles were not only a means to escape the home and reach a wider range of recreation spots. They also provided a semi-private space with abundant romantic and sexual possibilities. New institutions, such as the drive-in movie theater, arose to take advantage of those possibilities. As decades passed and affluence increased, the borrowed family car was more and more replaced by cars owned by young people, advancing youth autonomy still further.

23   All this was part of a larger trend: the transformation of America into a mass consumption society. As this happened, people shifted their attention partially from thinking about how to work and earn to pondering how to spend and consume. Marketplace thinking became more and more influential. The image of the individual as *homo economicus* and of modern life typified by the rational application of scientific knowledge to all decisions became pervasive. The new ideological framework undermined previous customs and moral standards and extended to the dating culture.

24   Dating had several goals. Most obviously and explicitly, dates were expected to lead to pleasure and possibly to romance. It was also important, as Waller and others have observed, in competition for popularity. But a central purpose of dating was to gain valuable learning experience that would be useful later in selecting a spouse. Through dating young people would learn who to relate to the opposite sex. Dating would increase awareness of one's own feelings and understanding of which type of partner was appealing and which not. Through crushes and disappointments, one would learn to judge the character of people. And by dating a variety of partners and by increasingly intimate involvement with some of them, one would learn what sort of person one would be happy with as a marital partner. When it came time to marry one would be in a good position to select "Mr. Right" or "Miss Right." Calling, which limited the possibilities of romantic experimentation, often to only one partner, did not provide an adequate basis for such an informed choice.

25   What emerged was a "marketplace learning viewpoint." Selecting a spouse is not quite the same as buying a car or breakfast cereal, but the process was seen as analogous. The assumptions involved in shopping around and test driving various cars or buying and tasting Wheaties, Cheerios, and Fruit Loops were transferred to popular thinking about how to select a spouse.

26   According to this marketplace learning viewpoint, getting married very young and without having acquired much dating experience was

risky, in terms of marital happiness. Similarly, marrying your first and only sweetheart was not a good idea. Neither was meeting someone, falling head over heels in love, and marrying, all within the course of a month. While Americans recognized that in some cases such beginnings could lead to good marriages, the rationale of our dating culture was that having had a variety of dating partners and then getting to know one or more serious prospects over a longer period time and on fairly intimate terms were experiences more likely to lead to marital success.

27 Eventually, this marketplace psychology helped to undermine America's premarital puritanism, and with it the sexual double standard. The way was paved for acceptance of new customs, and particularly for premarital cohabitation. Parents and other moral guardians found it increasingly difficult to argue against the premise that, if sexual enjoyment and compatibility were central to marital happiness, it was important to test that compatibility before marrying. Similarly, if marriage involved not just hearts and flowers, but also dirty laundry and keeping a budget, did it not make sense for a couple to live together prior to marriage to see how they got along on a day-to-day basis? Such arguments on behalf of premarital sex and cohabitation have swept into popular consciousness in the United States, and it is obvious that they are logical corollaries of the marketplace learning viewpoint.

28 Our dating culture thus is based upon the premise that dating provides valuable experience that will help individuals select mates and achieve happy marriages. But is this premise correct? Does dating really work? What evidence shows that individuals with longer dating experience, dates with more partners, or longer and more intimate acquaintances with the individuals then intend to marry end up with happier marriages? Surprisingly, social scientists have never systematically addressed this question. Perhaps this is one of those cherished beliefs people would prefer not to examine too closely. When I could find little evidence on the connection between dating and other premarital experiences and marital success in previous studies, I decided to conduct my own inquiry.

29 My desire to know whether dating experiences affected marriages was the basis for my 1984 survey in the Detroit area. A representative sample of 459 women was interviewed in three counties in the Detroit metropolitan area (a diverse, multi-racial and multi-ethnic area of city and suburbs containing about 4 million people in 1980). The women ranged in ages from 18 to 75, and all had been married at least once. (I was unable to interview their husbands, so unfortunately marriages in this study are viewed only through the eyes of women.) The interviewees had first married over a sixty year span of time, between 1925 and 1984. They were asked to recall a variety of things about their dating and premarital experiences. They were also asked a range of questions about their marital histories and (if currently married) about the positive and

negative features of their relations with their husbands. The questionnaire enabled us to test whether premarital experiences of various types were related to marital success, a concept which in turn was measured in several different ways. (Measures of divorce and of both positive and negative qualities in intact marriages were used.)

30   The conclusions were a surprise. It appears that dating does not work and that the "marketplace learning viewpoint" is misguided. Marrying very young tended to produce unsuccessful marriages. Premarital pregnancy was associated with problems in marriage. However, once the age of marriage is taken into account, none of the other measures—dating variety, length of dating, length of courtship or engagement, or degree of premarital intimacy with the future husband or others—was clearly related to measures of marital success. A few weak tendencies in the results were contrary to predictions drawn from the marketplace learning viewpoint. Women who had dated more partners or who had engaged in premarital sex or cohabited were slightly less likely to have successful marriages. This might be seen as evidence of quite a different logic.

31   Perhaps there is a "grass is greener" effect. Women who have been led less sheltered and conventional lives prior to marriage may not be as easily satisfied afterward. Several other researchers have found a similar pattern with regard to premarital cohabitation. Individuals who have been living together prior to marriage were significantly less likely to have successful marriages than those who did not.

32   In the Detroit survey, these "grass is greener" patterns were not consistent or statistically significant. It was not that women with more dating experience and greater premarital intimacy had less successful marriages; rather, the amount and type of dating experience did not make a clear difference one way or the other.

33   Women who had married their first sweethearts were just as likely to have enduring and satisfying marriages as women who had married only after considering many alternatives. Similarly, women who had married after only a brief acquaintance were no more (nor less) likely to have a successful marriage than those who knew their husbands-to-be for years. And there was no clear difference between the marriages of women who were virgins at marriage and those who had had a variety of sexual partners and who had lived together with their husbands before the wedding.

34   Dating obviously does not provide useful learning that promotes marital success. Although our dating culture is based upon an analogy with consumer purchases in the marketplace, it is clear that in real life selecting a spouse is quite different from buying a car or a breakfast cereal. You cannot actively consider several prospects at the same time without getting your neck broken and being deserted by all of them. Even if you find Ms. Right or Mr. Right, you may be told to drop dead. By the time you

are ready to marry, this special someone you were involved with earlier may no longer be available, and you may not see anyone on the horizon who comes close to being as desirable. In addition, someone who is well suited at marriage may grow apart from you or find someone else to be with later. Dating experience might facilitate marital success if deciding whom to marry was like deciding what to eat for breakfast (although even in the latter regard tastes change, and toast and black coffee may replace bacon and eggs). But these realms are quite different, and mate selection looks more like a crap-shoot than a rational choice.

35   Is there a better way? Traditionalists in some societies would argue that arranged marriages are preferable. However, in addition to the improbability that America's young people will leave this decision to their parents, there is the problem of evidence. The few studies of this topic, including one I have been collaborating on in China, indicate that women who had arranged marriages were less satisfied than women who made the choice themselves. So having Mom and Dad take charge is not the answer. Turning the matter over to computerized matchmaking also does not seem advisable. Despite the growing sophistication of computers, real intelligence seems preferable to artificial intelligence. As the Tin Woodman in *The Wizard of Oz* discovered, to have a brain but no heart is to be missing something important.

36   Perhaps dating is evolving into new patterns in which premarital experience will contribute to marital success. Critics from Waller onward have claimed that dating promotes artificiality, rather than realistic assessment of compatibility. Some observers suggest that the sort of superficial dating Waller and others wrote about has become less common of late. Dating certainly has changed significantly since the pre-Second World War era. Many of the rigid rules of dating have broken down. The male no longer always takes the initiative; neither does he always pay. The sexual double standard has also weakened substantially, so that increasingly Americans feel that whatever a man can do a woman should be able to do. Some writers even suggest that dating is going out of style, replaced by informal pairing off in larger groups, often without the prearrangement of "asking someone out." Certainly the terminology is changing, with "seeing" and "being with" increasingly preferred to "dating" and "going steady." To many young people the latter terms have the old-fashioned ring that "courting" and "suitor" did when I was young.

37   My daughter and other young adults argue that present styles are more natural and healthier than the ones experienced by my generation and the generation of my parents. Implicit in this argument is the view that with formal rules and the "rating and dating" complex in decline, it should be possible to use dating (or whatever you call it) to realistically assess compatibility and romantic chemistry. These arguments may be plausible, but I see no evidence that bears them out. The

youngest women we interviewed in the Detroit survey should have experienced these more informal styles of romantic exploration. However, for them dating and premarital intimacy were, if anything, less clearly related to marital success than was the case for the older women. The changes in premarital relations did not seem to make experience a better teacher.

38   While these conclusions are for the most part quite negative, my study leads to two more positive observations. First, marital success is not totally unpredictable. A wide range of features of how couples structure their day-to-day marital relations promote success—sharing in power and decision-making, pooling incomes, enjoying similar leisure time activities, having similar values, having mutual friends and an active social life, and other related qualities. Couples are not "doomed" by their past histories, including their dating histories, and they can increase their mutual happiness through the way they structure their marriages.

39   Second, there is something else about premarital experience besides dating history that may promote marital success. We have in America not one, but two widely shared, but quite contradictory, theories about how individuals should select a spouse: one based on the marketplace learning viewpoint and another based on love. One viewpoint sees selecting a spouse as a rational process, perhaps even with lists of criteria by which various prospects can be judged. The other, as song writers tell us, is based on the view that love conquers all and that "all you need is love." Love is a ruler of the heart (perhaps with some help from the hormonal system) and not the head, and love may blossom unpredictably, on short notice or more gradually. Might it not be the case, then, that those couples who are most deeply in love at the time of their weddings will have the most successful marriages? We have centuries of poetry and novels, as well as love songs, that tell us that this is the case.

40   In the Detroit study, we did, in fact, ask women how much they had been in love when they first married. And we did find that those who recalled being "head over heels in love" then, had more successful marriages. However, there is a major problem with this finding. Since we were asking our interviewees to recall their feelings prior to their weddings—in many cases weddings that took place years or even decades earlier—it is quite possible and even likely that their answers are biased. Perhaps whether or not their marriage worked out influenced these "love reports" from earlier times, rather than having the level of romantic love then explain marital success later. Without either a time machine or funds to interview couples prior to marriage and then follow them up years later, it is impossible to be sure that more intense feelings of love lead to more successful marriages. Still, the evidence available does not question the wisdom of poets and songwriters when it comes to love. Mate selection may not be a total crap-shoot after all, and even if dating does not work, love perhaps does.

Reading for Meaning

1. Martin King Whyte's purpose for writing "Choosing Mates—The American Way" is to determine whether dating provides useful experience that "helps pave the way for a successful marriage." Based on his research in Detroit, what does Whyte conclude? Does he reveal any cultural biases in this view?

2. Describe Whyte's views on marriage. What clues does he give about his opinion of the value of marriage? Do you agree with his views? Explain the basis for your answer.

3. Whyte says that the United States has always followed "youth-driven patterns of courtship." What does he mean? What control do adults exert over dating in your experience?

4. Much of "Choosing Mates—The American Way" is a history of dating and methods Americans have used to choose their mates. Why do you think Whyte offers this historical information? How well does it fit his larger argument?

5. To what extent have women controlled dating patterns in the United States? What control do women have over the dating process now?

6. Whyte claims that there were "two sexual revolutions in the United States" (paragraph 9). What were they, what circumstances seem to have caused them, and what were the results of each revolution?

7. How does Whyte define dating? How does it differ from courting (paragraph 13)? Does he seem to have a preference?

8. What is Whyte's overall opinion of dating? Which passages in "Choosing Mates—The American Way" convey his attitude on the subject?

9. What approach to marriage does Whyte prefer to the "marketplace approach? In what ways might his view be culture specific? Do you think his approach is the better choice?

Comparing Texts

1. Use information in "Choosing Mates—The American Way," "The Marriage-Go-Round," and "Growing Up Female in Egypt" (page 325) to discuss the relative control parents in the United States, Japan, and Egypt have over their daughter's marital partner.

2. How does David Elkind's discussion of the changing family in the United States (page 168) complement or contradict Whyte's analysis of the history of dating?

Ideas for Writing

1. Whyte argues that the research he did in Detroit does not support the idea that current dating habits lead to marriage in the long run. Do a survey of your own to determine what the living arrangements are among people you know, such as neighbors or classmates. To what extent is marriage a goal for the people you interviewed? Do they have alternative arrangements in mind?

2. In an article he wrote with Xu Xiaohe for the *Journal of Marriage and the Family,* Whyte points out that when sociologists examine the success of "love" marriages in comparison to arranged marriages, it is important to look at the larger context. Because extended and multigenerational families are more common in China than in Western countries, their relative success with both types of marriage is probably the result of relations with not only the spouse and children but also with "others in the family, including parents-in-law and grandchildren." Discuss factors that in your experience have contributed to successful, committed relationships. Rely on testimony from friends, acquaintances, and classmates for support for this paper.

Writing before Reading

Describe what you know or have heard about arranged marriages. What is your general impression of the way they are set up and their success (or lack of success) in establishing relationships that last? What ideas or experiences have formed your impressions of arranged marriages?

THE MARRIAGE-GO-ROUND
Nicholas Bornoff

Nicholas Bornoff was born in London of English and French parentage. His work as an English language translator took him to Tokyo in 1979, where he lived for the next eleven years. While in Japan he wrote extensively about Japanese culture and business practices. Bornoff and his Japan-born wife currently live in London. The following candid article first appeared in Bornoff's book, Pink Samurai: The Pursuit and Politics of Sex in Japan *(1991).*

Facts about Japan

The Jomon culture, which dates from about 8000 B.C.E., is the earliest culture identified in Japan. The earliest written histories of Japan date from the early eighth century A.C.E. and mention the earliest Japanese emperor, Jimmu, who lived around 660 B.C.E. Japanese culture borrowed extensively from the Chinese and Korean cultures. Japan adopted Chinese script, and Buddhism came into Japan from China and

Korea in the fifth or sixth century. Today, three-quarters of the Japanese are practicing Buddhists. In the twelfth century, private armies of rural warriors—the *Samurai*—emerged. A military government or shogunate gained control of the government at the end of the twelfth century. Military governors *(shoguns)* would rule Japan until 1868.

Japan began industrializing at the beginning of the twentieth century. In the decades since World War II, Japan has developed a formidable economy, second only to the United States. Loss of faith in Asian markets on the part of international investors and political corruption at home have destabilized Japan's economy in recent years. Prior to World War II, the Japanese empire included much of Asia and some islands in the South Pacific. Today Japan consists of four large islands and hundreds of small islands that follow the east Asian coast for 1,800 miles. Roughly 75 percent of the land in Japan is too mountainous for cultivation. The harshness of the land and the scarcity of natural resources help explain Japan's historical tendency to expand beyond its present border. At present Japan imports about half its food supply and most of its raw materials for industrial use. Modern Japan is a constitutional monarchy with a sophisticated technology and a broad industrial base. Since the end of World War II, the monarchy has been a titular head similar to British royalty.

THE HONOURABLE ONCE-OVER

The fact that two families generally lived in widely separated areas and had no knowledge of each other prompted the use of a go-between initiating the marriage. Needless to say, the marriage partners themselves had little or no previous acquaintance with one another until the day of the wedding.

—Harumi Befu, Japan—An Anthropological Introduction *(1971)*

1   The son and heir of the prosperous owner of a large local supermarket, Hiroshi Murakami formally asked his prospective father-in-law for his daughter's hand only days ago. Although he may have lost some sleep over the prospect, there was little chance that Yamashita would refuse him. Such a proposal is nothing more than a ritual involving participants from families who have already agreed on the outcome. Besides, Mayumi had undergone *omiai* (honourable seeing-meetings) or arranged-marriage introductions no less than twenty-three times, so that Shigeru—who likes Hiroshi anyway—was more than relieved at her choice.

2   Obāsan's one and only *omiai* had been for the benefit of her parents and that was that: With her mother and grandmother, it had merely been a pact sealed between families; until fairly recently, that used to set the more educated families apart from the peasants and the poor, who rarely bothered with formal marriage at all. According to ancient custom, too, a family with no sons can "adopt" their daughter's husband. Assuming the role of first son and their family name, he becomes a *yōshi*—a substitute heir assuring the transmission of the patriarchal line. In effect, the formula

has also frequently formed a basis for male *mariages de convenance*, since a husband of lower status can thus take a step up the social ladder or enter a lucrative business partnership.

3   *Omiai* still determines roughly half of all marriages today, although the outcome is generally up to the couple concerned. Rather than choosiness, Mayumi's spurning of scores of bachelors might have had more to do with a former sweetheart. That the Yamashitas and his parents did not see eye to eye eventually prompted her to end the affair, which had been permissible as long as all traces of sexuality were concealed and it showed no signs of becoming serious. Shigeru always prides himself on his open mind and progressive spirit. Mayumi, after all, has been an office employee since she left school. She earns her own income, drives her own car and after office hours her time has largely been her own. There was one point, however, about which both her parents had been quite adamant: Mayumi was to be home by ten. A young lady of twenty-five has no business being out too late after dark—the dire consequences of which are stressed in a great many frightening posters hanging outside the country's plentiful police boxes.

4   That the proliferation of love hotels might allow Mayumi to do what she cannot do at night during the day is neither her nor there to her parents. What really matters is to keep up appearances. Like everyone else in most other contexts too, provided she upholds her own and the family's *tatemae* (front) and keeps her *honne* (true situation) strictly to herself, Mayumi can reasonably do as she pleases. But when it comes to father, he may well remain remote and aloof as a patriarchal figurehead but, when he puts in a word, reverence for filial piety commands obedience.

5   The defiance underlying the passionate and unconventionally feminist verses of the poet Akiko Yosano (1878–1942) was perhaps instigated by her own past. Infuriated that his first-born was not a son, her father dumped her with an aunt, until her brilliance prompted him to take her back home. While she was made to manage the family shop when her mother died, at twenty she was expressly forbidden to walk abroad during the day and locked in her bedroom at night. Yosano's leaving home to marry a noted poet marked the beginning of a career; notwithstanding ostensible servitude to a husband, many women see greater freedom in marriage than in protracted spinsterhood.

6   Even when they have passed *tekireiki*—marriageable age—many single women live at home and their parents' words are law. It is not unusual to see a spinster in her thirties hastening home to honour a curfew before the end of a dinner with friends. I recall a 25-year-old office employee living alone who, faced with opposition over a fiancé, found that a noted Tokyo bank had complied with her father's demand to block her account. A painter of the same age was ordered back to the country by her parents in a bid to end her liaison with a noted avant-garde artist. Since they wanted an adoptive *yōshi* to help out on the farm, in 1988 this

university graduate did as she was bidden as dutifully as a Sicilian peasant daughter of thirty years ago.

7   When Mayumi was still unmarried at the advanced age of twenty-five, however, the family began to share her mounting anxieties. The successive meetings came to nothing, the round of eligible bachelors began to deplete itself; Mayumi lived in such a state of panic that the strain showed on her face, and she soon feared that the *omiai* photographs sent round to prospects were too flattering. *Omiai* portraiture is one of the mainstays of the photographer's studios found in all but the smallest villages. It keeps them especially busy on 15 January during *Seijin no hi* or Adults Day, a national holiday observed by all young people who have turned twenty during the preceding year. Often displayed in their shop windows, the portraits find the young ladies in traditional attire and the gentlemen in business suits, seated in a chair in the Louis XV style or posed rigidly against a cloudy silvan backdrop. Nineteenth-century photography—albeit in colour—is charmingly alive and well in Japan.

8   Relatives or trusted parental friends, who are generally female and can expect a cash contribution for their services, act as *nakodo* (go-between) and present subsequent prints of snapshot size to the prospective family. Informal snapshots are often offered too and, if the girl concerned should have hobbies such as ballet or jazz dancing, skating or aerobics, pictures in accordingly skimpy attire and showing her to her best advantage might work further in her favour. Beach photographs, however, particularly in this age of shrinking swimwear, are out.

9   If expressing interest, the parties will be brought together during an excruciating meeting process, which finds the two families lunching together in a restaurant in a climate of strained conviviality. Both in immaculate tailored suits, the young man and woman in question stare unwaveringly at the tablecloth, hardly daring to exchange a glance—let alone a word. The girl eats practically nothing. The parents talk over their heads. The boy's father reels off his son's academic achievements and his prospects; the girl's father will extol her virtuous nature, schooling, hobbies, housekeeping abilities and fondness of children. At some point, the two will be expected to say something, generally a tremulous and extremely modest version of the already very reticent paternal summary.

10   During the following week, if he doesn't like her, the boy will back out with a range of polite excuses. If he does, he will wipe his sweating palms on the back of his trousers, find his voice and at last grab the telephone to ask her out on a date. If shyness is common among young men in similar circumstances everywhere, its prevalence in Japan is betrayed by the fact that *omiai,* a practice widespread among the rural and the diffident, would otherwise have died out long ago. If mutually impressed, the couple will go out on what might well be a rather painful first date. It may be on a Saturday evening but, where the notion of night holds improper connotations, it might more properly occur on a Sunday

afternoon. The scope of activities is pretty much universal, with movies and perhaps amusement parks high on the list, but the culminating meal or cup of coffee is discernible as an *omiai* date at a glance. Facing each other across the table, they are only nominally more comfortable than with their parents the previous week. Their eyes remain glued to their banana sundaes to avoid contact; they are only animated by the sheer relief of a waiter arriving to break the spell. After about a quarter of an hour of awkward silence, one often sees the boy look up with a sudden flash of inspiration, which culminates in his rather over-loudly blurting out something such as "Do you like tennis?"

11   If the girl stares with blank embarrassment and gently shakes her head, their future as a couple may well be uncertain. If she happens to like tennis and they warm to each other, they will go from date to date, from restaurant to disco and from hotel to the Shinto altar.

12   The pious might opt for the more austere and less popular Buddhist ceremony and, today, the Christian wedding sometimes offers an exotic and romantic alternative to non-Christians. The staggering proliferation of posters throughout Japan's trains and subways present a wide range of wedding alternatives, as do TV commercials and newspaper and magazine advertisements. Some might offer bizarre fantasies such as parading the couple around the wedding hall in a white and gold Venetian gondola on wheels amidst clouds of dry ice and whisking them off to their honeymoon aboard a helicopter. There are underwater weddings for diving enthusiasts and even schemes to have Christian weddings staged in small, mercenary-minded churches in Europe. The underlying message is clear: Thou Shalt Get Married. Being considered as "un-adult" at the very least, detractors are viewed with the gravest suspicion. An eccentric couple of my acquaintance, living in separate cities but regularly meeting at weekends and spending holidays together, felt that their life was fine just as it was. Both being thirty, however, and pressured by their families, they simply staged a grand wedding and carried on exactly as before.

13   With the pull to get married as strong as it is, marriage agencies are a lucrative business. A cheaper alternative for lonely hearts is even to be found in local government offices, in which matchmaking is conducted by civil servants entering the names and particulars of interested parties in ledgers for a nominal fee. Founded in 1967, the Beauty Life Association for one had some 6,000 hopefuls on its books by the mid-seventies, when there were nearly 300 other private agencies catering to all ages and persuasions in Tokyo alone, not a few of which specialize in companions for the widowed and divorced. One might be forgiven for assuming that those who drop out of the *omiai* routine in favour of agencies might be more romantically than practically inclined, but this is far from being the general rule. Well-advertised on posters throughout the Tokyo transport system is an agency aptly called the Magpie Association, which not

untypically targets young ladies with an eye to the main chance: "You can trust us. We arrange introductions only to the élite: doctors, lawyers, dentists."

14 Fully computerized, today's thousands of marriage agencies boast of their ability to match data and preferences to come up with perfect partnerships. Prim middle-aged ladies in business suits aim video cameras at prospects, providing them with what is only just a more animated alternative to the *omiai* photograph. Individuals pay a flat fee of 150,000 yen to join, couples confront each other over a table on the premises and if the romance—or progenitive business partnership—doesn't work out, they shell out 10,000 yen for next time. One Toyko agency calling itself Rodin and unabashedly targeting the élite demands a ten million yen registration fee, degrees and moneyed backgrounds and stages matchmaking procedures including chaste separate-room weekends in plush resorts, culminating with a grand wedding in New York.

15 If some women still throw away their lives by respecting their parents' wishes rather than their own feelings, the majority of people welcome *omiai* as a means of meeting members of the opposite sex—whether the outcome is marriage or not. Nevertheless, a grimly humorous phrase for marriage, especially among women, is *jinsei no hakaba*—the cemetery of life. The alternative to an *omiai* wedding procedure is *renai kekkon*—a love marriage. If the new trend still tends to be more of an urban fantasy concocted by the media than a reality, the fact is that girls and boys are nevertheless going out more together and more freely; the *renai* pattern is becoming more common.

16 When Mayumi Yamashita started to pine away reading weddingwear and honeymoon magazines among the serried ranks of fluffy animals festooning her room, her parents found it difficult to get her out of the house at all. On the rare occasions when she did go out, other than to go to work, she not infrequently drove to Shinto shrines and prayed to the deities more likely to augur a good matrimonial future. Finally, Shigeru resorted to a truly desperate measure: he relaxed the 10 P.M. curfew.

17 So for the few months before Mayumi and Hiroshi were introduced, she went to discos in Nagoya on Saturday nights. She sometimes even came home at two or three in the morning and, in the meantime, she saw a whole lot of boys. But since wherever she went she was invariably with the same three girlfriends, the operative word here is "saw." The four girls would dance together on the dance floor and giggle as they tippled discreetly in the deco-tech interiors of fashionable café-bars, taking turns in being the teetotal and driving fourth. In one disco, a couple of boys sauntered up to ask them to dance, which found them raising their hands in front of their faces and giggling all the more as they shook their heads. Crestfallen and sheepishly grinning, the boys soon went back to join their comrades at another table.

18 Mayumi's aunt Etsuko had acted as the *nakodo* or go-between in the *omiai* process; Hiroshi's aunt was one of her colleagues in the

administrative office of a neighbouring town hall. Before Hiroshi, there had been the son of that Nagoya hotelier whom Mayumi had thought too fat, the young chartered accountant who had talked only of cars and golf in a whiny voice and the boy from the electronics store who suffered from acne. There had been that Yamaguchi boy, too, the one who owned three beauty salons and drove a Porsche. The Yamashitas didn't like him; he had a hairstyle like a gangster and Mayumi's mother pointed out that the signs outside his salons were *purple*. The family hardly needed the sort of fellow who puts up purple signs.

19   In one way or another, everyone agreed. To use purple was presumptuous—for it had once been the colour of the mighty Tokugawa shogunate; mauve is precious for having been the dominant colour of the effete Heian age. Worse still, as a marriage between red and blue, the colour is ambiguous, risqué and thus so very *mizu shobia*.

TYING THE KNOT

Statistics weren't available on those who decided to remarry. Could there really be people out there who would be willing to go through it all again? Irish wakes are much more fun.

—Gail Nakada, The Tokyo Journal *(June 1984)*

20   A legacy of rich merchant ostentatiousness from the late Edo period, weddings are elaborate and expensive. From the exchange of relatively inexpensive symbolic tokens of good luck, the bride's parents have become increasingly saddled with items such as ruinously expensive suites of furniture and a supply of kimonos considered proper (though seldom worn) for the married woman's wardrobe. Wedding expenses thus cover far more than just the ceremony, the cost of which is shared with the groom's parents. In the Nagoya area, ever a bastion of conservatism, the parents of one couple of my acquaintance indulged in a curious and ruinous game of one-upmanship in which the bride's parents, although far less well-off than the groom's, felt obliged to go all-out to contribute as much as they could to the most ostentatious wedding either could afford. That all this is a venerable custom is widely believed, although even a cursory glance at history would prove the notion to be fallacious; the high cost of weddings is upheld by peer pressure buttressed by the sacrosanct commerce sector, in the form of companies specializing only in weddings, furniture stores, clothiers, and the hotel and catering trade.

21   As "tradition" dictates, Mayumi's and Hiroshi's wedding will be a grand affair. The Yamashitas are comfortably off, but far from wealthy; it will take ten million yen out of their savings, even if Hiroshi's parents make substantial contributions. That's life. Besides, all relatives and wedding guests will place a white envelope on a silver tray at the entrance to the wedding hall. Along with their wishes of goodwill, it will contain a minimum of 10,000 yen in cash for a more casual guest, and substantially more for members of the family. In many cases the roster of guests

includes business associates; the cash contributions from those wishing to curry favour with the groom or his father will be commensurate with their involvement or expectations. As with wedding presents, the exact value of each contribution will be carefully totted up afterwards, not through stinginess, but to gauge the effusiveness of subsequent thanks, the degree of favours owed in return and the value of presents marking similar occasions later on.

22   Arriving in a black Nissan limousine of the genus "Cedric" hired for the day, Mayumi will be presented to the groom at a large local Shinto shrine. She will be wearing majestic bridal finery, which is so astronomically expensive today that all but the wealthiest brides hire it. Red and white or plain white and for rent at about 100,000 yen, a wedding kimono is intricately embroidered with floral and bird motifs enhanced with gold and silver thread. On her head, the bride wears a traditional wig made of real human hair spiked with decorative hairpins and combs. A large starched crown in a plant white fabric completes a picture that will have taken a professional dresser almost an hour to prepare. Although she will undoubtedly be lovely, the new wife, with her whitened face and tiny, beestung red lips, will look totally unlike Mayumi Yamashita and very like a standard Japanese bride. Decked out in a black formal kimono and wide *hakama* striped trousers, the groom will meanwhile be processed in only a few minutes.

23   Then there is the Shinto ceremony. As the priest officiates, a *miko* shrine maiden will guide the couple through the proceedings; there is no rehearsal. As a robed *gagaku* ensemble plays instruments imported from China some twelve hundred years ago, the bride and groom ritually exchange cups of sake three times. The groom then reads a document aloud, the gist of which is that he expects his wife to honour and obey. He will complete this by announcing his full name, while his wife announces her forename only, for she has now been adopted by her husband's family.

24   After the ceremony, a photographer freezes the stiffly posing newlyweds in front of their families and principal guests on film for eternity, and then there will be a reception held in one of the capacious wedding halls of a large hotel. Guests will file in over a plush red and yellow carpet in the rococo style beneath a ceiling dripping with shimmering crystal chandeliers. Before entering, Mayumi will have changed into her second kimono (again unlikely to be her own) and enter the room with the groom to the strains of Mendelssohn's Wedding March piped out at deafening volume. Carefully placed around the banqueting hall according to their station, guests sit before round tables impeccably set with flowerpieces and a dazzling array of beautifully presented cold delicacies. The bride and groom preside almost invisibly at one end behind a jungle of flowers. Staring rigidly ahead, they might just exchange a few words together out of the corners of their mouths. In the process of becoming bride and groom, they relinquish their identities.

25   Guests and family members are specially allotted functional roles essential to the event: one or two masters or mistresses of ceremony and a best man, and many will take turns in playing musical instruments and/or singing songs. Nearly all will rise in turn to deliver lengthy speeches, some extolling the background of the bride and others the groom's. We know what schools they went to, what their work and hobbies are and the names of their best friends who, being present, will soon be delivering speeches of their own. Nothing said will come as any kind of surprise, for had everyone not known all there was to know about the newlyweds, they could hardly be assembled here. One also commonly hears someone reading out a farewell letter from the bride to her parents, thanking them poignantly and profusely for her happy childhood years. Some wedding concerns enhance this with a syrupy musical backing and even a retrospective slide-show; either way, there is hardly a dry eye in the hall.

26   Many wedding halls offer all-inclusive package deals. A newly built hotel in Okazaki, Aichi prefecture, for instance, typically owes its vastness less to its room capacity than to the fact that it caters overwhelmingly for weddings. The capacious third and fourth floors are devoted to the entire process, which is conducted with conveyor-belt efficiency. The betrothed are encouraged to make plans months beforehand. Some shops on the third floor deploy selections of appropriate gifts, others offer wedding attire for hire or purchase; another handles all the announcements, invitations and banquet place cards and the honeymoon can be organized in an adjacent travel agency. On the day, the bride can be processed in an all-inclusive beauty parlour providing everything from a sauna, through facials and make-up to dressing; a barber shop offers similar facilities for the groom. On the fourth floor are dressing rooms for each, on either side of an antechamber in which the guests of both families sit facing each other before the ceremony, which is held in a specially consecrated Shinto shrine a few doors down the corridor. Then everyone troops into the elevators to go down to the capacious banquet halls. Coming as part of the package is a professional wedding supervisor, who steers the couple firmly through their duties like a strict nanny. As does the shrine maiden or priestess during the Shinto ceremony, she will instruct them on how and when to move or speak. Under her guidance, they will ritually hammer open a keg of sake, which is ladled out to guests.

27   Then the bride sometimes dons a third wedding dress. These days it would generally be lacy, expensive and of western design. While she is away changing, the speeches drone on as the groom's male friends and relatives might treat him to a quick toast; to avoid offending anyone, he will refuse none of the proffered glasses. Although he might find himself downing quite a formidable amount of sake, beer and whisky, this will be one of the very rare occasions when he will be expected to keep his composure when tipsy.

28   During the course of the reception, the bride will have no time to eat; but the sight of one eating would be untoward anyway. A demure doll,

she might poke daintily at the delicacies before her with her chopsticks, perhaps daring to nibble at a shrimp. She will anyway soon be grabbed by the wedding supervisor and posed alongside the groom to allow guests to take photographs. These days there will be much amusement when he is even entreated to kiss the bride. The entire event is formalized and rigorously timed to last some three hours, not one second of which will be left to spontaneity or allow anyone time to themselves. Where timing could have left a gap, it will be filled with *Candoru Sabisu* (Candle Service), a ritual which finds the room plunged in darkness and the newlyweds passing from table to table, lighting candles with a gas taper and bowing low to each guest to express their thanks. These days, urban couples might throw a more informal party for their friends later on, but the practice is rarer in the country.

29 The couple will finally change into street clothes which, befitting the occasion, should in the bride's case be of a recognizable and expensive designer brand. Guests start wending their way home bearing huge white carrier bags and silk *furoshiki* bundles full of presents offered by the bride's family. These presents are often fantastically expensive: at the recent wedding of a renowned kabuki actor, for instance, some 2,000 guests were each presented with a pair of small gilt silver chalices, each set with a ruby and a diamond in the bottom.

30 Glad that the exalting if agonizing ceremony is over, the exhausted couple will finally sink into the back of the limousine which carries them symbolically off to their conjugal life. Next, they will board a train for the nearest airport and on to their honeymoon, which may well take the form of a five-day package tour shuttling dozens of bewildered newlyweds to overcrowded tourist hotels in Hawaii, Guam and—recently capping the list—Australia. In tune with the more intrepid new breed, however, Hiroshi and Mayumi will be going to Europe. She has always wanted to go to Paris, which has the Champs-Élysées, and to London, which has Harrods. Wherever they go, this will be the first and probably the last trip they will make abroad until future progeny, the first of which should ideally be born within the first year of their marriage, grows up.

31 That the bride's parents wave tearfully at the departing car is virtually a universal phenomenon. A cherished bird has flown from the nest, leaving the progenitors facing their declining years. In Japan, however, the wedding was once far more poignant—a girl given into marriage became the property of her husband and his family. A custom observed from early times allowed a pregnant wife to go back to her parents' home to give birth, but among the spartan samurai she often never saw her family again.

Reading for Meaning

1. What does Nicholas Bornoff think of arranged marriages in Japan? What support does he offer for his argument? How convincing is it?

2. Bornoff describes the duplicity involved in allowing children to do what they want to during the day, including going to "love hotels," as long as they uphold "the family's *tatemae*," or "front." Discuss other circumstances that require a distinction between the public perception of a situation and the true behavior.

3. Bornoff describes the industries that have grown up around arranged marriages and wedding ceremonies. What businesses are supported by important rituals in this country?

Comparing Texts

1. Compare the degree of parental involvement in choosing a partner for a Japanese couple, as discussed in "The Marriage-Go-Round," and in picking mates for young adults in the United States according to Martin Whyte's "Choosing Mates—The American Way."

2. In the last few pages of his essay, Nicholas Bornoff describes an elaborate, costly Japanese wedding. How do the expense, formality, participation of the guests, and purpose of the marriage of Mayumi and Hiroshi compare with the same elements in the quinceañera that Susan Orlean describes (page 180)?

Ideas for Writing

Find Internet, library, and other sources (interviews, videotaped information) on arranged marriages in several cultures. Write an essay in which you explore unique patterns of meeting, dating, and marriage ceremonies in several of these cultures.

Writing before Reading

Summarize what you know about female circumcision. What interviews, books, or articles have given you your information? What assumptions about women or about individual rights might account for particular positions on female circumcision?

WOMEN AND HEALTH IN SUDAN
Nahid Toubia

Nahid Toubia is a practicing physician in Sudan. She graduated from Cairo University with a specialization in surgery from the Royal College of Surgeons in the United Kingdom. Toubia has written numerous essays on women's social status and health problems, especially female circumcision. She is the editor of Women of the Arab World: The Coming Challenge, *a collection of papers given at the Arab Women's Solidarity Association Conference held in Cairo, September 1986.*

Facts about Sudan

Located in northeast Africa, Sudan is Africa's largest country. Sudan's Nile River valley has been inhabited since Neolithic times. The earliest settlements were in Nubia, the ancient kingdom in northeastern Africa known to Egyptians as the Cushite civilization (1750–1500 B.C.E.). Sudan became Christian in the sixth century and converted to Islam in the mid-seventh century. The country was ruled by a joint British–Egyptian government from 1898 until it gained independence on January 1, 1956. Sudan is currently under the fundamentalist Islamic leadership of General Omar Hassan Ahmed al Bashir.

The population of Sudan is divided into two major regional groups: the Nilotic people in the south and the Arab African group in the north. The northern Arabic/African people speak Arabic, the official language of the country, and practice Sunni Islam. Peoples of the southern region speak a variety of African languages and mostly practice animistic religions. English is a major language in the south.

1. Women, as an integral part of society, are affected by those economic factors that have an impact on the health of society as a whole. Adequate food supplies and effective clinical health services on the one hand, and raising health awareness as well as the provision of preventive health measures on the other, are factors that determine the level of health of a society in general.

2. Certain health problems, however, aggravate women's physical and psychological burden, adding to the already heavy load of a complex social heritage. Such problems ensue from the nature of the socio-cultural structure in each society, generating a peculiar set of individual and collective rituals and traditions. Such ritual and tradition have a greater impact on women than on men as the former are bearers of family honour, and are bartered for a price at marriage, hence they should appear before the eyes of society in the most beautiful and perfect state.

3. The way a woman relates to her body and the psychological reflection of this image on her are, in any society, directly related to both the status of women in that society and the reflected ideal of femininity imposed upon them. Such a conditioning process evidently bears both physically and psychologically on women. True, some common features and preliminary indicators regarding the status of women seem to be universal today, yet each community has its unique socio-economic structure affecting women in various ways, which may at times seem parallel but may vary infinitely in details. In Western societies for example,

there are basic social patterns that govern the relations between a man and a woman, between two women and of the woman with herself. The whole social structure is built around the nuclear family unit, with power exercised from within that family unit with no external influence from close or distant relatives. Then comes the economic factor. The individual's income is related to the labour market, and its direct financial transactions. The families of the individuals concerned are not depended upon to provide direct or indirect financial or other forms of support, consequently there are no overt or subtle pressures to pay back such family favours. Services are institutionalized in industrialized societies. State as well as private institutions cater to the individual's needs in the fields of education, employment, social and health insurance, and so on; an individual is not usually compelled to turn to her/his family support network for the fulfillment of such needs. S/he is a productive unit capable of selling her/his labour to buy the quality of life s/he chooses.

4   Psychologically, an individual in Western society is encouraged to develop her/his unique personality. Individuality could be a means of freeing creativity and innovation, but could equally lead to self-centered, self-protective behaviour even to the extent of alienation—the loss of any sense of belonging. This by no means denies that such societies have their own rituals and social traditions nor that there is a social majority that exerts pressures of conformity on the individual's choice, but this psychological factor is much weaker in Western than in Middle Eastern societies, because the final arbitration between individual and collective interests in the West is secular law.

5   Thus, industrialized societies have converted the individual into a consumer of goods and services offered by capital to generate the jobs the consumers need in order to survive and to continue consuming. At this point we should consider a basic difference between Western and Middle Eastern societies on matters concerning women. To pursue their lives, both physically and socially, women in contemporary Western societies have the choice to marry or to remain single. They may support themselves by selling their labour, and there is a social space for them as single women. In Middle Eastern societies the overwhelming majority of women (85 percent in some countries) are illiterate, and work opportunities outside the home are scarce. Women's work is restricted to the home, the family business or land. Survival outside the family is physically impossible. This vital and practical reality should not be overlooked when we assess Arab women's decision-making powers. In cases where a woman owns some property or income generated by inheritance there is still no "social space" to accommodate her if she remains unmarried. Hence, Arab women in general, and Sudanese women in particular, can survive only within the institutions of marriage and the family—they have no other choice.

6 Meantime, however, I shall here look more closely at those health problems of women in Western society created by the socio-economic structure already mentioned. In such highly consumerist societies selling the products remains the prime and ultimate goal of the economic powers controlling the society, that is "capital." It activates the longstanding social norms of heterosexuality and women's seductive role within it. The media is then mobilized as an increasingly more effective way of imposing certain social attitudes and promoting them as the norm to further serve its own purposes. In fact, despite the apparent progress made by women in the West, the media there still promotes the outdated ideas of women as a sex object, on the one hand the seductress, and on the other the passive recipient of male sexual drive. Within these boundaries women are made to see themselves as objects of pleasure and are used as advertising material valued only for their physical appearance with its implicit and explicit appeal for sex.

7 Through these tactics capital endeavours—with a fair degree of success—to sell almost anything to women: cosmetics, fashion clothes, perfume, diet food, sports clothes and much more. By these means women are exhorted to strive constantly to achieve that media model of perfection which is impossible, because it is an illusion and its components are constantly changing according to "fashion." These tactics are intended to permanently chain women to the market and the never-ending cycle of consumption. Also through women's bodies and sexual messages men are encouraged to consume what they do and do not need, from aftershave to computers, to tractors, posing a constant challenge to their manliness (another word for virility) with the implicit promise that maybe one day they will be rewarded with all the promises of a sexy woman. Many women in Western societies are victims of a dependence on and addiction to tranquillizers, sleeping tablets and alcohol as a result of pressures on them because of jobs outside the home or, because as housewives, they have to cope with the disillusion and the sense of worthlessness experienced, particularly after menopause when children leave the home and the women's positive role in life seems to have ended. One of the potentially very serious diseases that has recently become widespread in the West is anorexia nervosa, an illness that results from excessive dieting and takes the form of an obsessive preoccupation with slimness, leading eventually to a semi-permanent loss of appetite. The motive is evidently a keen desire to reach the model of slimness publicized by the media. This disease can eventually lead to severe and incapacitating malnutrition and the progressive deterioration in health may become irreversible and ultimately cause death; it is, of course, almost exclusively a disease of women.

8 Arab societies have many common features: they share the same predominant religion and language, and the basic structural unit of the society, that is, the extended family. Women's lives are, therefore, in many respects similar. Urban lifestyles have checked the propagation of the

pattern of one extended family sharing one household, but the economic and psychological relations to the extended family still prevail. They still constitute the mainstay of the relation between the individual and the group and even between separate individuals. The tribe, the class, the *housh* (extended family residence) and the big family remain the geographical, psychological and economic unit in most rural areas.

9   In Arab society individuals are taught that the group takes precedence, and the importance of belonging to the majority and rejecting individuality is stressed. This psycho-social concept leads to a close and coherent society that provides the individual with a strong sense of protection and security; a friendly atmosphere of familiarity, affection and harmony. It can, however, also lead to fear of change or of developing an individual opinion, and thus inhibit and restrict a person's ability to choose, question and create.

10 To make a comparison or to judge between Western and Middle Eastern social systems, is too extensive an undertaking to be contained within the limits of this chapter, but I would like to focus on the psycho-social concepts that shape Arab societies in general and Sudanese society in particular, with the aim of finding remedies to our illnesses. If we are genuinely and seriously concerned with change for the better and to achieve our goals of cultural excellence we must analyse our societies objectively in a process of open self-criticism. Only with a scientifically guided, compassionate appraisal of our present situation can we confront our mistakes with the courage and determination of a people confident of themselves, their culture and their heritage. We should be able to retain the most valuable qualities in our societies—self-denial and group coherence—without stifling the individual's potential for creativity and choice.

Some Health Problems of Sudanese Women

11 I have chosen the model of Sudanese women partly because I am myself a Sudanese woman and am concerned about women's health. The only means to achieve progress in this area are, as I have already stated, through rigorous self-criticism while searching for and opening up the dark crevices of our societies and often those of our own minds.

12 Some of the practices cited below may at first glance seem inhuman or horrifying, but in essence they differ little from many harmful practices involving women in other societies, even though these may be more subtle in their effect because of social and cultural guise.

Female Circumcision

13 Over the last decade the issue of female circumcision has received wide exposure by Western media and international organizations as well as national bodies. The West has acted as though they have suddenly discovered a dangerous epidemic which they then sensationalized in

international women's forums creating a backlash of over-sensitivity in the concerned communities. They have portrayed it as irrefutable evidence of the barbarism and vulgarity of underdeveloped countries, a point of view they have always promoted. It became a conclusive validation to the view of the primitiveness of Arabs, Muslims, and Africans all in one blow.[1]

14 Nevertheless, female circumcision is an important and serious problem that both Arab and African women must approach and tackle. Its serious consequences arise from its deep influence on women both physically and psychologically and from the fact that it has withstood all aspects of change in the societies where it is prevalent. Pharonic circumcision or infibulation is still practised on over 85 percent of all Sudanese women with the exception of women of the three southern regions, the remote areas of Western Sudan and the Nuba mountains.[2] In fact, the most recent statistics revealed that 98 percent of females in the northern regions are circumcised, regardless of their level of education (or rather the level of the parents' education) social class or degree of health awareness,[3] including the daughters of doctors, university professors, educationalists, and social workers, for example.

15 In the majority of cases pharonic circumcision (excision of the clitoris, labia minora and labia majora with stitching of the raw edges over the urethral meatus) or intermediate circumcision (excision of labia minora and clitoris with stitching) are performed. Admittedly there are some indications that over the last three years there is a shift towards excision of clitoris only (sunna circumcision). The social implications of the continuity of the practice and its sexual and psychological effects are, however, still the same, regardless of the degree of surgical cutting. The objective is, therefore, that a girl must have a *tihara* (purification) and is socially and psychologically unacceptable in an uncircumcised *ghalaja* state; one of the most important reasons for circumcising a girl is to ensure that she will not lose her chance to marry; as I have already explained this would mean that she loses her chance for a respectable life. Loss of a woman's genitalia is not, therefore, too high a price to pay in order to secure her chances in life through marriage. This is the social significance of female circumcision and its real value. To argue against this practice on the grounds of its physical damage and to attempt to eradicate it through health awareness and education are futile. It is essentially a social phenomenon reflecting the position of women and not a medical problem.

16 Throughout their recent history, Sudanese women have been circumcised, and they know of no other state to be. They cannot therefore develop their conscience from within to demand their right to keep their genitals intact. For a Sudanese woman to be without external genitals is the normal state of female anatomy and all her accumulated experience on sexuality and her normal body responses have been inherited from

generations of circumcised women. How can she possibly penetrate the thick walls of accumulated misconceptions amongst women and overcome the conspiracy of silence that society has woven over the issue?

17 Let us also question how a Sudanese mother (herself circumcised at the age of 4–8 years) can choose not to circumcise her daughter? She will alienate her from her peer group and from the other women in the family, for they are all circumcised. Even if the parents are convinced that they do not want to mutilate their daughter, how can they possibly antagonize the grandmothers, the aunts and the whole family? It is necessary to think of ways to change the beliefs of the extended family and the group, and not restrict our arguments to individualistic conviction for that is too weak against group pressure. The individual in our societies cannot stand alone against the pressure exerted by the group. Our efforts must be geared towards finding a language that will communicate to society as a whole. We have to convince the group that the benefits of this action (in this case stopping circumcision) will be for the society as a whole and not only the individual. This does not, of course, preclude our appeal to the vanguard of intellectuals who can lead this process of change. It is most essential that we find satisfactory answers to the questions a woman will face when she is debating a stand against the practice. She may ask herself: How can I possibly choose a course of action different from my mother's, my aunts' and my friends'? How can I live if I break away from established tradition and choose a path of newly acquired knowledge and unfamiliar practices? How can I possibly risk the only chance for a life for my daughter (marriage) by not circumcising her?

18 These are a few among many questions that must be satisfactorily answered if we really want to eradicate the practice....

PSYCHO-NEUROSES AND DEPRESSION

19 Psycho-neuroses and depression are more common amongst women than officially recognized in medical statistics. Very few professionals understand them as a group phenomenon or analyse them as such. Instead they are seen as individual cases and as an expression of maladjustment with society or as a woman's failure to face up to her marital responsibilities as a wife and a mother. They are considered as pathological illnesses divorced from their causes which may be found in the woman's position in the family and in society. Among the manifestations of these conditions are compulsive eating, excessive introversion or extroversion with accompanied endless chattering.

20 Psychosomatic disease is also widespread among women and this explains the disproportionate numbers of women in doctors' surgeries and clinics. It is often an unconscious cry for help and a plea for a sympathetic ear for their complaints which they are unable to express openly.[4] All these are some of the physical and psychological manifestations of social problems.

21   How does society perpetuate its values and thus manage to withstand the factors of change such as women's education and increasing cultural, social and political awareness amongst them? Why are modern Sudanese women unable to break away from all these negative social phenomena despite their education and increasing participation in public life?

THE NEED TO BELONG TO THE GROUP

22   As I have mentioned earlier, Sudanese society is strongly ethnocentric with a heightened feeling of an individual's need to affiliate to the group. This is compounded by a tribally biased African heritage and an Arab heritage that stresses the importance of strong family lineages. Over the last 20 years, due to harsh economic and political conditions, many families have been dispersed and the individual dislocated from his/her group. This forced separation often strengthens the feelings of belonging and gives rise to the need to jealously guard and protect the manifestations of group identity. Immigrants, for example, may preserve custom and ritual more vigorously, even irrationally, than people in the homeland. In such alienated individuals the need to relate to the roots drives them to hold on even to the brink.

23   The same process seems to apply to the effects of the social disintegration that has taken place over the last two decades. Not only have people clung to their traditional customs and rituals but have reverted to some previously obsolete practices and reaffirmed them in the face of changes in education, in cultural mixing, and unprecedented extremes of wealth and poverty.

24   Another very important cause of slow or imperceptible change is the emphasis on compliance and conformity in the indoctrination of children, and the determined rejection of any deviation at all from the prevailing norm. The material and moral losses incurred by loss of identity could not be compensated for by any individual gains, even if these were more progressive. This inherent fear of social isolation, one of the greatest barriers to change in Arab societies, needs to be examined and analysed in order to find out how it should be tackled so as to retain its positive aspects before these are destroyed by the pressures of Western style modernization, leaving selfish individuality to prevail and Arab social identity lost.

THE INEVITABILITY OF MARRIAGE FOR WOMEN

25   In Middle Eastern societies marriage is still a social act in which the involvement of the two individuals concerned is lesser or greater depending on where and when it takes place. In Sudan, marriage is still primarily concerned with a relationship between two families rather than two individuals, and the personal choices of the couple are still of secondary

importance. Again, marriage for a woman has an existential absolutism that is inescapable; it does not involve a choice of simple human companionship over solitude, nor is it a response to mutual affection. For a Sudanese woman marriage is a non-choice during which it is difficult to be rational or calm, two prerequisites for taking such a major step as binding oneself to another being. No mental space is left to choose or reject the rituals and customs that accompany this step. Marriage in Sudan is, therefore, still burdened with rituals and practices to be performed by the two families, starting from the initial negotiations and ending in the actual festivities which, to this day, continue for three to seven days among all social groups. Society's insistence upon holding on to its values is manifested by these customs and rituals. The marrying couple neither has the right to object nor the right to choose.

26 The man is never consulted about whether or not he wants as his bride a circumcised woman, the bride is not asked whether she would like to be saved all the weeks of tedious, exhausting preparations she has to undergo until the day of the wedding. These preparations are mainly aimed at transforming her into a desirable sexual commodity at the expense of extreme physical and psychological stress. Society dictates and individuals must comply as a piece in a chess board moves where it is directed. Women are the most subordinate in the decision-making hierarchy particularly when young and uncrowned by social consent: marriage. Unmarried women remain unrecognized and considered immature regardless of their educational level or degree of personal or intellectual excellence.

27 How does this tight and complex trap affect the Sudanese woman and formulate her character?

STAGES OF PSYCHOLOGICAL DEVELOPMENT OF WOMEN IN SUDAN

28 **Stage of Alluring.** Alluring in early childhood takes two distinct forms. One is the motivation through the rewards gained from acceptance. For example, circumcision is accompanied by a big celebratory feast, with the slaughtering of a sheep, singing, dancing, new clothes, distribution of sweets and receipt of gifts and money. Every girl and boy must dream of the opportunity to become queen or king, the centre of attention and the cause of all this celebration, even for one day.

29 On the other hand, undergoing such rites of passage means that the child is attaining a new social status in which s/he is considered more mature and deserving of adults' respect. The child must aspire to achieve this status with or without his/her knowledge of the accompanying physical suffering to be endured. This all devolves from the emphasis on the importance of conformity and belonging that is indoctrinated very early in life.

30 Another motivation, one common to children in all societies, is peer group jealousy which drives the child to imitate his peers in order to

overcome any possible sense of alienation or isolation among them. This may drive the child to request such social rites as circumcision or ear-piercing. It is, therefore, imperative that when we tackle these harmful practices, delicate handling of any child whose family decides against performing such rites, is essential.

31 **Stage of Intimidation.** With the onset of puberty and teenage, physiological, psychological and intellectual changes begin. The question "why?" takes a deeper meaning and is more frequently present in the youth's mind and s/he starts to question the significance of some of the apparent constants surrounding him/her. All traditional society's forces are mobilized to combat this inquisitive rebellious stage—particularly in the case of women.

32 Subtle intimidation and not direct threatening is the tactic. Sudanese society is a very sentimental and a gentle, family-oriented society; physical violence is unacceptable, as is direct prohibition. In such a peace-loving atmosphere social pressure must accord with the people's gentle character. The most effective form of intimidation is the fear of upsetting the family; remembering the material and moral importance of family support to the individual, the effectiveness of this fear is understandable. In cases when a young woman persists in her rebellion against social custom and starts taking active steps towards more questioning, or chooses a different path, the mother and other women in the family combine to subdue her. Although it is a male-dominated society the family is organized in such a way (within the household there are separate quarters for men and women) that it is the women's responsibility to put a girl on the acceptable family path. Older women in particular are delegated to be the gatekeepers and internal security bodies in the women's section, and men need only to keep a distant overview of the situation, confident that their wishes and instructions are being observed.

33 A common form of pressure is the exploitation of the girl's feelings towards her mother and other women in the family. With the almost complete absence of a paternal relationship, a girl becomes totally dependent on the mother emotionally, while the father remains the distant symbol of power and authority devoid of any human intimacy. A mother knows of her daughter's weakness and emotional needs and plays upon them when she needs a disciplinary weapon to set her back on the correct path previously designed for her. All Sudanese women must remember when our mothers got very sick (or allegedly so) or silently sulked so as to put pressure on us to accept a decision made on our behalf. Many people may consider that these methods of intimidation are part of natural family relations, but this complex web of subtle pressure, comprising emotional and material dependence and interests is not always easy to identify.

34 If a girl cannot clearly see that she is being intimidated she internalizes her rebellion, anger and frustration, and transforms them into guilt

and shame for having hurt her loved ones and causing disruption in the family. The outcome is often absolute resignation and submission to all that is dictated to her, and acceptance in shame and repentance.

35 **Stage of Adoption.** Soon after puberty a young girl reaches the age of marriage with its implications of changes in her social status. Once married, she must forget all her earlier dreams and her rejection of the negative rituals she once thought to rebel against. She has to forego all her individual aspirations and commit herself whole-heartedly to self-denial with the sole purpose of caring for her husband and children, finding herself only in their successes. This process of serial adjustment just pre- and post-marriage entails crossing the threshold of social acceptability—and at the price of numerous psychological and intellectual compromises. A girl must go through a process of "forced feminization" to gain respect. This raises a persistent question in her subconscious: should she perpetuate her suffering and jeopardize her newly-acquired preferential position, attained through marriage, or utilize the new situation to attain total harmony with those around her. Instincts of self-preservation and the desire for an easy way out almost always win the battle in a society that so fiercely resists social change and condemns individuality. Tactically, it is much more beneficial for the woman to totally adopt prevailing social values or even better be seen to perpetuate them and staunchly resist signs of rebellion in the new generations. Thus the vicious circle repeats itself and the pioneers of change remain few. One of the most important factors that create this new "adoption" stance is the fear of facing one's own self. When a woman passes through the experience of totally compromising on her own choices and accepts what was dictated and forced upon her, it is very difficult to maintain her self-respect unless she adopts these values as her own and pretends she has always accepted them. This is a self-protecting mechanism against duality and frustration. Endless examples can be cited of women who once refused arranged marriages, insisted on a woman's right to work; rejected the exhaustive prolonged rituals in marriage, and so on, only to completely reverse their stance later and become staunch advocates of the views previously rejected. This reversal often takes the form of a well-argued, intellectually sound conviction that may fool the outsider who could not see what lies behind it. I hope that this analysis may have answered some of the allegations that women are by nature conservative and that it is women who promote negative social practices by inflicting them on their own kind.

Conclusion

36 While certain harmful concepts and practices that affect women's health are peculiar to Sudan, some are shared with Arab countries. These concepts and practices are closely related to the prevalent moral values, and the distribution of power within the family, which leaves the young

unmarried girl at the bottom of the power hierarchy. She must be guarded and moulded by the older women in the family under the detached supervision of the men in the household and the society at large outside it.

37 It is, therefore, imperative that if change is to be induced we must create the means and methods of circumventing these social structures and not clash with them head on, for they are too powerful and well established. Forceful confrontation with these entrenched structures could either backfire on the women's movement or create irreparable dents and cracks in our social structures. The following points are my contribution towards formulating a tactical approach for change.

38 1. Approach the group as a whole to neutralize their defences or even win them over to the case for change and avoid as much as possible inciting the individual woman against her class or family. We must avoid alienating individual women or pushing them too far or they will retreat from their initial progressive steps.

39 2. Promote individuality as a positive value in its free creative sense and work towards incorporating the concept into school curricula. We must set a clear example of how individuality need not be in contradiction to belonging but on the contrary that individual initiative will enrich the group and add to its assets.

40 3. Discriminate between positive and beautiful customs and harmful and negative ones encouraging the replacement of the latter by the former. This will diffuse the accusations levelled at the women's movement of modernization trends that reject our heritage. Only through compassion can we win people to our point of view.

41 4. Lastly, change for women will not be brought about by changing just one or a group of social practices. We must emphasize our strong belief that effective change will be brought about within a wider change in the economic and social power structures in the society as a whole. This should guarantee equal opportunities in education and work, plus equal rights and responsibilities inside and outside the home. The balance of social power, particularly within the family and in personal relations, has to be redressed. The sharing of decision-making, planning and executing various activities has to become a reality. This can happen if, while working towards abolishing harmful practices, we link them to the importance of overall change in the basic structures in the society. This socio-economic change is the surest way to radically change women's status and give them the economic and psychological power to realize our dreams.

References

1. Seager, J. and Olsen, A., *Women in the World: An International Atlas*, map 4 "Social Surgery," Pan Books, 1986.

2. Toubia, N., "The Social and Political Implications of Female Circumcision: The Case of Sudan" in *Women and the Family in the Middle East*, Elizabeth Fernea (ed.), Texas University Press, 1985.
3. Al Dareer, A., *Woman, Why Do You Weep?" Zed Press, 1983.*
4. *El Saadawi, N.,* Women and Psychoneurosis, *Dar al-Nashr al-Arabi, Beirut, 1978; and Sadig, "Women and Psychological Disease," in* Ros al-Yussif Magazine, *28 July 1986, pp. 41–3.*

Reading for Meaning

1. What fundamental differences between women in Western societies and Arab women of the Middle East does Nahid Toubia discuss? How does this distinction help the reader understand the position of women in Middle Eastern societies, particularly in Islamic countries?

2. What health problem does Toubia identify as typical of women in the West? Do you think her analysis is accurate?

3. Who is Toubia's audience for this essay? What evidence in the text itself helps you identify both her audience and purpose for writing?

4. How does Toubia criticize the Western view of female circumcision as it is practiced in Arab and African countries? What is her own attitude toward the practice? What does she consider to be the real issue facing Sudanese and other Islamic women?

5. How does Toubia explain the difficulties in trying to change the practices of female circumcision? What are the forms of societal conditioning, and the motivations and rewards of conforming to these practices?

6. Although difficult, Toubia believes that changes in women's status are possible in Arab cultures. Summarize the proposals she makes that she feels will lead to change. Do her proposals seem feasible?

Comparing Texts

1. Nahid Toubia offers the following description of the importance of the group in Arab cultures:

> In Arab society individuals are taught that the group takes precedence, and the importance of belonging to the majority and rejecting individuality is stressed. This psycho-social concept leads to a close and coherent society that provides the individual with a strong sense of protection and security; a friendly atmosphere of familiarity, affection and harmony. It can, however, also lead to fear of change or of developing an individual opinion, and thus inhibit and restrict a person's ability to choose, question and create.

Compare this notion of the individual's place within the group to the Japanese concept of the worker and the company in "Culture and the Communal Organization," page 270.

2. Toubia summarizes the condition of women in Middle Eastern societies as follows:

> The overwhelming majority of women (85 percent in some countries) are illiterate, and work opportunities outside the home are scarce. Women's work is restricted to the home, the family business or land. Survival outside the family is physically impossible. This vital and practical reality should not be overlooked when we assess Arab women's decision-making powers. In cases where a woman owns some property or income generated by inheritance there is still no "social space" to accommodate her if she remains unmarried. Hence, Arab women in general, and Sudanese women in particular, can survive only within the institutions of marriage and the family—they have no other choice.

How does Toubia's background information about women in Arab cultures help the reader appreciate the conflict, self-hatred, and ultimate self-assurance that Nawal El Saadawi describes in the excerpt from her book *Memoirs of a Female Physician*, page 325?

Ideas for Writing

1. Nahid Toubia characterizes the social patterns governing the individual's place in Western societies as follows:

> The whole social structure is built around the nuclear family unit, with power exercised from within that family unit with no external influence from close or distant relatives. Then comes the economic factor. The individual's income is related to the labour market, and its direct financial transactions. The families of the individuals concerned are not depended upon to provide direct or indirect financial or other forms of support, consequently there are no overt or subtle pressures to pay back such family favours. Services are institutionalized in industrialized societies. State as well as private institutions cater to the individual's needs in the fields of education, employment, social and health insurance, and so on; an individual is not usually compelled to turn to his/her family support network for the fulfillment of such needs. S/he is a productive unit capable of selling her/his labour to buy the quality of life s/he chooses.
>
> Psychologically, an individual in Western society is encouraged to develop her/his unique personality. Individuality could be a means of freeing creativity and innovation, but could equally lead to self-centred, self-protective behaviour even to the extent of alienation—the loss of any sense of belonging. This by no means denies that such societies have their own rituals and social traditions nor that there is a social majority that exerts pressures of conformity on the individual's choice . . . the final arbitration between individual and collective interests in the West is secular law.

Based on your own experience, observations, and research, is this an accurate portrait of the individual's relation to the larger society in the United States? Add a few observations of your own, or clarify your objections to Toubia's interpretations.

2. Read several of the representations of the lives of Islamic women in this book. In addition to Nahid Toubia's essay, you might select the excerpt from Nawal El Saadawi's "Growing Up Female in Egypt," page 325, "The *Bilal's* Fourth Wife," page 316, or "Marriage in the

Hausa *Tatsuniya* Tradition: A Cultural and Cosmic Balance" (page 513). Write an investigation essay in which you discuss elements that appear to be common in the lives of women who live in Islamic north Africa.

3. In paragraphs 5 through 7 of her essay, "Women and Health in Sudan," Nahid Toubia discusses the health problems of women in Western cultures. Based on your experience or research on women in the United States, discuss the accuracy of her assessment of health problems of Western women. Propose several solutions to health issues that you consider the most serious.

CHAPTER 7
WORKING

First Thoughts

الانطباع الأول

Primeiro impressões

Traditional manufacturing used to offer [the poor] a niche, but today it is dying on its feet, and the death of such talent and hard work is a tragic spectacle throughout the Third World.

Paul Harrison
Inside the Third World: The Anatomy of Poverty

No other technique for the conduct of life attaches the individual so firmly to reality as laying emphasis on work; for his work at least gives [a person] a secure place in a portion of reality, in the human community. . . . And yet, as a path to happiness, work is not highly prized by men [and women]. They do not strive after it as they do after other possibilities of satisfaction. The great majority of people only work under the stress of necessity, and this natural human aversion to work raises most difficult social problems.

Sigmund Freud
Civilization and Its Discontents

Perhaps it is time the "work ethic" was redefined and its idea reclaimed from the banal men who invoke it. In a world of cybernetics, of an almost runaway technology, things are increasingly making things. It is for our species, it would seem, to go on to other matters. Human matters. Freud put it one way. Ralph Helstein puts it another. He is president emeritus of the United Packinghouse Workers of America. "Learning is work. Caring for children is work. Community action is work. Once we accept the concept of work as something meaningful—

enough jobs. There's no excuse for mules any more. Society does not need them. There's no question about our ability to feed and clothe and house everybody. The problem is going to come in finding enough ways for man[kind] to keep occupied, so he's/[she's] in touch with reality."

Studs Terkel
Working

We spend most of our lives planning for, worrying about, and doing some kind of job. The extent to which we enjoy and respect the work we do often determines how we feel about ourselves and whether we are happy with our lives. In large measure, our jobs define us; our very identity is reflected in the work that we do. Whether we are students, cooks, cashiers, house painters, women managing households, research assistants, or phlebotomists, we are likely to introduce ourselves in terms of what we do for a living. In *Civilization and Its Discontents,* Sigmund Freud says that a person's work gives him or her "a secure place in a portion of reality, in the human community." Writing in *Work and Love: The Crucial Balance,* Jay Rohrlich adds, "Work is who we are: Our work is key to our 'belonging' in contemporary society. It's the label by which others quickly identify us and by which we present ourselves to the world." For the most part, we are what we do.

The kind of work we do and our relative involvement with it varies from individual to individual and from country to country. In addition, whether an employee keeps to a rigid schedule—as is commonplace in Japan, Europe, and the United States—or has a more relaxed sense of time—the average Brazilian's approach—is determined by cultural practice. In industrialized countries, most people work for an employer; occasionally an individual may own and manage his or her own or a family-run business. In the United States it is not unusual for the time at a job to seem burdensome and for us to regard work as something we have to do in order to play. For a Japanese worker, demands of the job can be all-consuming. The *salaryman* or white-collar worker is expected to devote his life to his job, sometimes at the expense of his family. In many developing countries, work may mean selling a farmer's produce at the village marketplace, hawking one's services to tourists on a crowded sidewalk in Calcutta, or simply finding enough grain or berries to ensure survival for another day. The participation of women in the workplace varies from culture to culture as well. In most developing countries, women are likely to have low-paying factory jobs, and in Islamic countries, they usually cannot work outside the home without their husband's permission. The Japanese *salaryman* is, by definition, male, and the position is closed to women. In Europe and the United States, women contend that a "glass ceiling" keeps them out of high-level corporate positions and some prestigious professions.

Selections for reading, discussing, and writing in this chapter explore working conditions, the meaning of work, and the pace at which one works in several cultures.

In "Balancing Act," Betsy Jacobson and Beverly Kaye urge workers to think about not only balancing their working and personal lives but also bringing the elements of employment, commitment, personal development, and nourishment into harmony with one another. In "The Barefoot Businessman," Paul Harrison examines the "informal sector" of self-employed vendors and service people in the Third World. The chapters from *Respected Sir,* a novel by Naguib Mahfouz, depict the religious fervor with which Othman Bayyumi approaches his work. Hugh Williamson's "China's Toy Industry Tinderbox" examines the plight of female factory workers in some countries in the Third World. J. E. Thomas's "Culture and Communal Organisation" explains why the concept of employment for life persists in Japan and the effects it has on the workplace. "Social Time: The Heartbeat of Culture," written by Robert Levine with Ellen Wolff, shows how the concept of "social time" determines how Brazilians, students in particular, schedule their lives. Levine observed this more relaxed attitude toward "clock time" in Indonesia and Italy as well, an attitude that he found very different from people's devotion to "clock time" in Japan, England, and the United States.

Writing before Reading

1. How well have you been able to balance the various aspects of your life—work, school, family, recreation? Do you have difficulty achieving harmony among the areas of your life?

2. In general, do you think people in the United States live a relatively balanced life? What seems to determine the balance or lack of it in people's lives?

BALANCING ACT

Betsy Jacobson and Beverly Kaye

"Balancing Act" appeared in the February 1993 issue of Training and Development, *a journal that publishes articles of interest to owners of small businesses, corporate managers, and directors. The authors of this article are management and organizational consultants who advise their clients on effective strategies for building morale and producing dedicated and efficient workers.*

1   At one time or another, most of us see life as a balancing act. We balance demands at work with demands at home. We juggle the needs of others with our own needs. And so it goes.

2   Achieving balance in our personal lives has traditionally been through our own efforts. But the organizations in which we work can play a role. They can support and enhance our efforts to achieve balance and can even form partnerships with us toward that end.

3   Organizational theorists began addressing the issue of balance when they began insisting that workers be recognized not only as workers, but as human beings. Slowly, organizations began to view employees as real people. And they began to recognize that employees' needs can influence their effectiveness at work.

4   The workplace responded by offering formal programs for employee participation and career development. Some employers now have programs to meet employee needs in such areas as physical fitness, time management, and stress reduction. But it's possible for employees to enhance their effectiveness through those programs and still fail to achieve personal and professional balance.

WORK AND IDENTITY

5   Traditional approaches to achieving balance tend to be dichotomous. The general consensus is that people need to establish a balance between two areas—between work life and family life, for example, or between work hours and leisure time. These two-part approaches heighten awareness, but balance is more than an either/or concept. Balance implies an interconnection among many areas of work and life.

6   The model of balance presented here is divided into four areas: employment, commitment, development, and nourishment. If any of those areas is underdeveloped, employees and organizations are likely to suffer. When employees and organizations understand and act on the need for balancing these elements, they're moving together toward a holistic workplace—one that recognizes a range of employee needs, the interconnection among those needs, and the relationship of such needs to achieving organizational goals.

7   **Employment: I Am What I Do.**   During our most vital years, we tend to focus on our work. We spend most of our waking hours doing our jobs, thinking about work, and getting to and from our workplace. When we feel good about our work, we tend to feel good about our lives. When we find our work unsatisfying and unrewarding, we don't feel good.

8   Jay Rohrlich, in his book *Work and Love: The Crucial Balance* (Summit Books, 1980), has this to say about work:

9   "Work is who we are: Our work is key to our 'belonging' in contemporary society. It's the label by which others quickly identify us and by which we present ourselves to the world.

10 "We typically hear comments such as, 'This is my friend, Mary. She's a tax accountant.' Or questions such as, 'And what kind of work do you do?' If we feel good about our work identity, we're likely to feel good about

ourselves. If not, we're frustrated by the inability to be identified through some other means than our work. Anyone who has ever been embarrassed by the type of work he or she does understands this frustration."

11   According to Rohrlich, work gives us order. Work gives us a reason to get up in the morning and a place to go. We find comfort in our jobs and in seeing familiar faces at work. Even when we're about to come apart at the seams, we manage to present a professional image at work. At those times, we recognize that work is what holds us together.

12   Work provides challenges. Most of us like the feeling that comes from having solved a tough problem. Work offers tangible rewards. Our salaries help us define the importance of our work and help determine our willingness to work. Our pay influences our levels of motivation, satisfaction, and self-worth.

13   Work contributes to our psychological well-being. Most work involves meeting goals. And accomplishing even minor objectives can give us a sense of achievement. Work provides a guideline by which we measure success and failure.

14   People whose "employment" area is underdeveloped tend to feel insecure, disappointed, and isolated at work. They don't care about their jobs or how well they do them. Dissatisfied employees may let quality standards slip. They may show a lack of commitment to their organizations by refusing to join committees and task forces or by refusing to engage in other work-related activities. For fear of failing, they may shirk new challenges. They may appear to keep busy, but never complete tasks. They may stop initiating new actions and new ideas.

15   **Commitment: I Am Who I Know.**   Our connections with other people affect all aspects of our lives, including work. Our personal relationships help determine our feelings about ourselves, our work, and our futures. When our relationships are good, they provide a network of valuable support that can enhance our abilities to accomplish goals. When they're bad, our relationships leave us feeling isolated and devastated. We may start to doubt ourselves and everything we do.

16   The most rewarding relationships result from two-way commitments with people who are significant to us. From these relationships, we get a sense of security and connection. We may want "our space" at times, but we want it in the context of knowing that someone out there cares about us. Belonging to a family, a group of colleagues, or an organization helps each of us define our identity.

17   When we feel valued or needed by other people, we feel worthy. This feeling readily translates into a feeling of confidence that enables us to take charge, take initiative, and take risks.

18   Relationships help us solve problems. We have people to turn to for advice or just to be heard. The more connected we are to a network of supportive people, the more resources for information we have. Even when we aren't actively soliciting help, valuable information may sift

19   Often, the busier we are at work, the more we need the support of others. At those times, we use survival skills such as the ones described by Dennis Jaffee and Cynthia Scott in their book, *Self Renewal* (Simon and Schuster, 1984). Survival skills include forging relationships with colleagues and friends, establishing emotional ties with others, and maintaining relationships with people whom we can ask for assistance and advice.

20   People whose "commitment" area is underdeveloped often appear to be loners. At work, they may have trouble asking for and giving help. They may avoid or put off tasks that call for interaction. And they may fail to involve and include others when it's appropriate to do so.

21   **Development: I Am What I Can Be.**   Our visions of the future—whether conscious and calculated or subconscious and subtle—affect our self-identities, our feelings about ourselves and others, and our performances on and off the job.

22   The term "development" implies a bright future and personal and professional well-being. Career development no longer connotes just higher salaries or higher job levels. It has come to mean doing something in the workplace that is personally meaningful.

23   Development can occur when people move laterally or even downward in an organization. It can occur when people take on short-term assignments to learn new tasks. For some, development happens when they transfer to a new job or move to a new organization, even at the same job level.

24   Development isn't a series of promotions; it's the ability to create challenges in one's job and to visualize challenges for the future. Employees whose opportunities for promotion may be waning can still experience development.

25   True development depends on a person's needs and the nature of his or her work. Consequently, it's more important than ever to find the right work. Fernando Bartolome and Paul Evans's concept of job fit may be more appropriate than ever. In their 1980 book *Must Success Cost So Much?* (Basic Books) they describe job fit as the achievement of finding what one does well, what one likes, and what one can truly commit to. The better we understand our own competencies, interests, and values, the more easily we can create opportunities for good job fits.

26   Employees whose "development" area is lacking may feel that their creative juices have dried up. They may spend more time at lunch and engaging in conversations at work that have nothing to do with work. They may no longer seek visibility, and they may show little interest in their organizations beyond their own work units.

27   **Nourishment: I Am What I Feel.**   Nourishment has to do with our physical, emotional, and spiritual well-being.

28   Nourishment occurs outside the workplace. We nourish ourselves when we set aside time to relax, regroup, and recoup. We can accomplish nourishment in various ways. One way is by "tuning out"—reading a novel, taking a nap, or watching television. Another way is by "tuning in"—getting in touch with our spiritual selves by practicing meditation, for example.

29   Another way to nourish ourselves is by venting tensions through such activities as sports and hobbies. This "toning up" is done by physically and mentally exerting ourselves in ways that are different from the activities we engage in at work.

30   We experience further nourishment by trying out new things or by taking time to develop interests other than work. For example, we may take classes or volunteer our time.

31   People don't always realize that overwork can lessen their effectiveness. When they're involved in all-out efforts, they may not see that there's a point beyond which performance starts to fade. People who don't take the time to nourish themselves may show physical and emotional signs of stress. They may unexpectedly blow off steam or avoid showing their feelings. And they may be uncomfortable in situations that call for anything other than intellectual interaction.

PRACTICAL STEPS TOWARD A MORE BALANCED WORKFORCE

Organizations can take various short-term and long-term actions to help employees achieve balance between their work lives and their personal lives. Here are some suggestions for specific steps:

- Support creative scheduling.
- Reduce the number of meetings and conferences that require employees to travel on weekends.
- Include balance issues in diversity training programs.
- Add balance to competency lists for supervisors and managers.
- Add balance to quality agendas.
- Promote peer relationships such as mentoring to encourage networking on the job.
- Discourage workaholism and encourage taking vacations.
- Include child-care and elder-care programs in employee benefits packages.
- Rewrite policy and procedure manuals so that they support employees' needs for balance.
- Broaden organizational visions and values to include and legitimize balance as a core strategy.
- Implement multiple-reward systems so that development is defined more by growth than by promotions.
- Include employees' families in decisions regarding relocation and hiring.

32 **Enjoyment: Armor for the Battle.** Enjoyment is the thread that runs through and connects all aspects of balance. When we enjoy our work, our relationships, and our free time—and feel positive about our futures—we experience true balance. If we don't have enjoyment, then employment, commitment, development, and nourishment seem like so many demands we have to handle—if we could only find the time.

33 Balance isn't better time management; it's better boundary management. We *can* have it all, just not all at once. Balance means making choices and enjoying those choices.

34 As Rohrlich notes, "The vitality of our lives is a function of our capacities to work and to love. Without satisfying work and pleasurable love, life becomes a kind of death."

35 It's far too easy for organizations to relegate balance to the status of a "personal issue." Human resource people may ask whether organizations can be expected to intervene in employees' free time or in their personal relationships. They may contend that it's an employee's responsibility to determine his or her best job fit.

36 Realistically, organizations can't assume responsibility for ensuring that all employees achieve balance. But organizations can acknowledge that balance affects work and workers. And they can assess what they are currently doing to undermine employees in any of the four areas. Organizations that remove those barriers can help their employees to achieve balance in their work and personal lives.

Reading for Meaning

1. Examine internal clues in "Balancing Act" that reveal the writers' purpose and audience.

2. Locate a copy of *Training and Development* and try to determine who is most likely to read this magazine. Look at the advertisements and table of contents, and skim a few articles to determine the purpose of most of the articles and the likely audience for the magazine.

3. Jacobson and Kaye concur with Jay Rohrlich that in the general culture in the United States, the kind of work we do determines our identity. Does your work have this close a connection with who you are?

4. Why do Jacobson and Kaye try to connect what we do for a living to Americans' identity? How does this identification support their argument or purpose for writing?

5. Apart from the work they do, what are other reasons people are important or valuable?

6. What rewards as well as frustrations might the workplace offer? What examples can you think of that illustrate either situation?

7. What recommendations do you have for getting the most enjoyment out of our working and personal lives?

Comparing Texts

1. For his book, *Working*, Studs Terkel interviewed more than 130 workers from unskilled laborers to professionals. As a result of his extensive research, his book includes a wide range

of experiences in the workplace. In one chapter he discusses the uncertainty that haunts most workers in the United States. That uncertainty, he says, has to do with "the planned obsolescence of people that is of a piece with the planned obsolescence of the things they make. Or sell. It is perhaps this fear of no longer being needed in a world of needless things that most clearly spells out the unnaturalness, the surreality of much that is called work today (xxii)." What do you think Jacobson and Kaye might say about the fears these workers expressed?

2. After reading the excerpt from Naguib Mahfouz's *Respected Sir* (page 257), evaluate how well the main character in his novel has been able to keep the various aspects of his life in perspective.

Ideas for Writing

1. Jacobson and Kaye have written a "feel good" article that offers some simple advice about what we need to do to achieve balance in our lives. Write a paper advising your readers about how to lead a balanced, effective life. Consider some of the stresses of urban life and possible ways to minimize the pressures we experience. Feel free to experiment with humor or satire.

2. As management consultants, Jacobson and Kaye advise businesses and corporations about how to improve the lives of their workers and, by extension, improve their employees' performances. Write an investigation paper in which you analyze the extent to which American corporations are using this logic and have been willing to accommodate their workers' needs. In gathering information for your paper, try to locate two or three articles, or interview a few people you know who work for corporations.

3. The authors of "Balancing Act" discuss the importance of arranging our lives so that the needs for "employment, commitment, development, and nourishment" are in harmony. Read "The Barefoot Businessman" and "China's Toy Industry Tinderbox," both located in this chapter. Then write a report identifying the most important elements in the life of a worker in a third world economy.

4. In *Working,* Studs Terkel observed that most workers feared "no longer being needed in a world of needless things." That perception of the profound meaningless of the work itself might be a source of deep anxiety. Discuss the extent to which either of these fears informs your work experience or that of friends, family, or people with whom you work.

Writing before Reading

1. What is your understanding of Harrison's subject from reading his title?

2. List a few "informal" or "marginal" businesses with which you are familiar. What makes it so difficult for these small companies to survive?

THE BAREFOOT BUSINESSMAN: TRADITIONAL AND SMALL-SCALE INDUSTRY

Paul Harrison

Paul Harrison is a freelance writer and journalist who makes his home in London. A world traveler, Harrison has been in twenty-eight countries throughout the developing world. He writes for United Nations' publications as well as for journals such as New Society *and* New Scientist *and has contributed to the* Encyclopedia Britannica. *Harrison has master's degrees from Cambridge and the London School of Economics and is the author of several books, including* The Third World Tomorrow: A Report from the Battlefront in the War against Poverty *(1983) and* The Third Revolution: Environment, Population, and a Sustainable World *(1992). "The Barefoot Businessman" was originally published as a chapter in Harrison's book* Inside the Third World: The Anatomy of Poverty *(1980). The book is based on Harrison's research from 1975 to 1980 during which time he visited eleven countries including Sri Lanka, the Ivory Coast, Kenya, Peru, Indonesia, India, and Bangladesh. The result is a "general survey of the entire field of development problems" in the Third World.*

Facts about the Third World

Originally the term "Third World" meant countries not aligned with the Western, industrialized world (The First World) or included in the Communist bloc (the Second World). Today it is used to refer to about 100 countries in Asia, Africa, and Latin America. Their governments are frequently run by military dictatorships, made unstable by competing forces within the country, or subject to outside influence, including that of a former colonial government. The economies of the Third World tend to be fragile; wage distribution is much less equal than it is in industrialized nations; and individual income, as well as the countries' gross national product, falls well below the per capita income in the West. The middle class is usually quite small, if it exists at all, and the wealth of these countries is concentrated almost entirely at the top. Third World countries often export raw materials. Manufacturing may be limited to handicrafts or simply made goods. Recently, some countries in the Third World have developed profitable industries or have become wealthy because of petroleum exports. A new term, the "Fourth World" is sometimes applied to countries whose economies have remained stagnant.

"A man on foot is automatically suspect."

—Jean Cocteau

1. The Victoria memorial gleams white under the hot sun in Calcutta's Maidan, and the black statue of the imperial queen, squat and scowling as ever, heats up. At her feet, a snake charmer lies in wait for the passing prey of tourists. I look easy game. He stares at me with black-rimmed eyes and fumbles at a flat, round basket. "See snake sir, quick quick." His hands tremble with haste and anxiety that he may miss an opportunity to earn, as they pass by like oases in a long desert day of waiting and hoping. Finally he whips off the top, grasps for his pipe and starts up a slow wailing dirge. The snake lies still, as if dead. He clouts it with the back of his hand, blows his pipe furiously, cheeks distended to bursting, weaving his head from side to side, but still the snake will not budge. He keeps banging it on the head with his pipe until it stirs and half rises and peers at him with a look of irritated boredom.

2. By his side his daughter has a long, furry mongoose with a pointed nose, clinging to her shoulder. The charmer notices my attention wandering: "Okay sir, you want to see mongoose and snake fighting, only thirty rupees." He opens a second basket and roots nervously through half a dozen squashed reptiles, drags one out and straightens it a bit. "No thank you," I reply. "It may kill the snake." "No no, not kill." "I haven't got time." "It will be very very quick." "I'll give you five rupees for what I've seen." "Okay, give me ten rupees and you can see fight."

3. The snake charmer, like the majority of non-agricultural workers, belongs to the informal sector, that great mass of untrained, underpaid toilers who are unfortunate enough to be excluded from the bright new modern sector of industry, government work and western-style services. He may do a bit better than most, provided enough tourists stroll by and other snake charmers keep away. But he shares with all the informal sector the insecurity, the dependence on chance demand and chance encounters, the almost daily exposure to disaster. The land has less and less room for the poor, the modern sector cannot use them. Yet they have to earn a living somehow. Traditional manufacturing used to offer them a niche, but today it is dying on its feet, and the death of such talent and hard work is a tragic spectacle throughout the Third World. So the disinherited are shifting their ground, moving into what one could call spontaneous business—all that multitude of trades half way between tradition and modernity that springs up unbidden among the marginal masses of the cities.

The Death of Tradition

4. Traditional manufacturing and services had many virtues. For the most part, they were decentralized into the villages, evenly spread across the country. They provided much-needed extra employment in rural areas—even today non-farm activities employ between a quarter and a half of

the workforce in rural areas. They offered work for the slack season when there is little to do on the land—in this period of the year, they may make up three quarters of all employment. And they are still an important source of additional family income to supplement the meagre earnings from agricultural work. This is especially important for the landless and the smallest landowners. In five Pakistan villages surveyed in 1968, non-farm work provided one quarter of all the income of farm families, but for the smallest farms it provided two fifths. In north Thailand three quarters of the income of the smallest farmers came from this source.

5   Clearly, any threat to non-farm work in rural areas is a double threat to the incomes of the most vulnerable groups. And threat there is. In one sphere after another, city-based industry has destroyed the livelihoods of village artisans. Nigerian village potters become redundant as cheap plastic bowls and buckets flood the market, and blacksmiths are pauperized as farmers turn to mass-produced hoes and matchets. Families in the Peruvian *altiplano* abandon their handlooms as women buy their woollen skirts at market, ready made, from the factories of the coastal cities.

6   Not all non-farm work in rural areas is in manufacturing, of course. Almost equal amounts may be created by trading and services, and lesser proportions by construction and transport. But these activities can flourish only if agriculture and rural industry are flourishing. All the principal branches of rural manufacturing are threatened. Perhaps a third of its workforce is in textiles, clothing and leather work. Another sixth may be in each of food processing, wood and furniture, and metalwork. All these activities are precisely those in which Third World countries start up their first industries. The growth of modern industry has dealt a heavy blow to the villages.

7   But traditional manufacturing exists in towns too. Indeed, many towns have, in the course of history, become great centres for a particular craft such as brasswork, jewellery, ceramics or carperts. It is not just village enterprise, but the whole of the traditional sector that is dying, leaving its workers to seek work elsewhere, or remain jobless and impoverished. Its central problems are low productivity in relation to the competition from factories; low quality, in the eyes of consumers brainwashed into believing that standardized factory products are superior (and, it is true, in some cases they do last longer or work better); and lack of organization and marketing.

8   Take the crafts of Kashmir. The Moguls retired to this mountain paradise to escape the oppressive heat of the Gangetic plains in early summer. They and their courtiers provided a ready market for Kashmir's specialities: papier-mâché boxes lacquered with flowers and leaves and animals, wood carvings, jewels made from jade, sapphires, rubies from near-by Ladakh. The British colonial rulers continued the tradition of holidaying in the temperate climate of the hill stations. As they were not allowed to buy land here, they had themselves built luxurious houseboats on the reedy banks of lotus-carpeted Dal Lake. They too patronized

9 local crafts—brought to them by traders on *shikara* boats. When the British left, the market dried up, and tourism has not replaced it.

9 Kashmiri carpets are skillfully built up on great vertical frames, each tuft individually hand-knotted. The traditional patterns are inscribed on yellowed parchments, in an esoteric script that the carpet weavers can read fluently, even though they may not read or write their own language. Wages have sunk so low in relation to the cost of living that a family man cannot survive on them. Most of the adult men in the trade have left for other jobs—they can earn double as unskilled road labourers. They have been replaced by their own sons. Young boys aged seven or eight upwards crouch by the looms all day long, their tiny fingers working with unbelievable speed. Using these methods a medium-sized carpet can take anything from one month up to nine months or more for the closest knotted silk. But when factories can turn out passable imitations at much lower prices, who will buy the labour-intensive Kashmiri carpets, however beautiful? The only market now is among tourists and western buyers from upmarket shops. Traditional carpets seem to be in chronic oversupply as so many villages in the Middle East and western Asia are making them. There is no way the trade can continue to employ so many people and go on paying them a living wage.

10 Low productivity and changing tastes threaten another venerable and skilled craft: Java's batik industry. As westernized tastes spread and traditions weaken among the young, women are turning away from hand-made batik sarongs to machine-printed cloths from India or Hongkong. Batik is too labour-intensive to survive the competition of machinery. Each piece of material has first to be washed alternately in alkaline water and coconut oil, left in the sun to bleach to the delicate creamy tint of batik cloth, starched in rice water, then pounded to soften it. After this, the artist sketches the pattern in charcoal on the cloth. Then the women take over. In the batik sweatshops of Jogjakarta's back streets, they kneel or squat gracefully around little stoves, warming pans full of melted wax. They dip in their *tjantings*—bamboo-handled copper cups with a capillary spout—and apply the wax meticulously to both sides of the material. This is then dipped in cold water to harden the wax, and immersed in baths of die, previously brewed up in bubbling stone vats. The wax is removed by washing several times in petrol and hot water, and the white areas thus exposed are dyed again in a second or third colour. One labour-saving innovation has been introduced: most of the cloths for women's sarongs are now waxed by *tjap*—a copper pattern mounted on a wooden block, which is heated, dipped into wax, and printed onto the fabric by hand. Even with this change, batik cannot stave off the challenge from cheaper machine-made prints. Sadly, it may eventually survive only in a truncated form, catering for local ceremonial occasions, western high-fashion tastes and the tourist trade.

11   Because of the low productivity of labour in traditional industries, they can compete with factories only if their wages are extremely low too. But lack of organization is another cause of poverty, especially under the widespread putting-out or homework system. In many cases this is dominated by middlemen who supply the raw materials at excessive prices and buy back the finished work at too low prices, squeezing the poor worker in the middle to the margin of survival. Again and again one is astonished by how little homeworkers—often women and children working in spare moments—earn for considerable amounts of work. The wife of a landless labourer in central Java took two weeks to make a floormat of palm leaves, working an hour or two every day. The selling price: just 300 rupiahs (40p or 80 cts). In north-east Brazil women hand-sew entire tablecloths, or patiently crochet complex lace patterns with half a dozen needles at once, for the equivalent of 5p or 10 cts an hour or less. A study in this area found that the full-time work of six handicraft homeworkers would be needed to get an income equal to the legal minimum wage.

12   Middlemen can force homeworkers' incomes down by their superior organization. They control the sources of raw materials and the market outlets. They act in collusion. The artisans or homeworkers are scattered and unorganized. They have no contacts of their own to buy supplies and sell their produce. They need the money immediately and cannot hold back their goods to push the price up. Indeed, they are often in debt to the middlemen.

13   Agra—famous for the Taj Mahal—is also India's foremost centre for hand-made shoes, with perhaps 80,000 craftsmen involved in the trade. Every day the cobblers bring some 75,000 pairs of shoes to the wholesale market, but the buyers are in a stronger position; there are fewer of them so they have a monopsony—a buyer's monopoly. They have funds behind them and can tide over a while without buying, whereas the cobblers have to sell there and then to get money to buy food to keep alive and more leather to keep working.

14   The death of the traditional sector, and all the disruption and human suffering that involves, is not entirely inevitable. Significant parts of it could be rescued, albeit with a smaller workforce. Governments could help it to compete, pump in funds to help it improve its technology, product quality and marketing, organize producers to freeze out parasitic middlemen.

15   A few governments have pursued imaginative policies of this kind. Most have worked on the theory that the traditional sector will wither away naturally and its workers get absorbed into the modern sector. They are certainly right on the first count, but dangerously wrong on the second. So, instead of building on existing skills and traditions, most governments have pumped all available funds into large-scale modern industry. Instead of gradual organic growth, there have been abrupt discontinuities.

16   The westernized modern sector is killing the traditional sector. The displaced workers of the latter have not, for the most part, found work in the modern sector, but have shifted into the informal sector. Here too they suffer from government neglect, low productivity, low pay, lack of organization. But they move into activities that are not so inevitably doomed by changing tastes. The enterprising village blacksmith will not lie down and die with his fellows, but give up making matchets and start repairing pumps and tractors.

THE BAREFOOT BUSINESSMEN

17   The bustling market of Bouaké, second biggest city in the Ivory Coast, hums with activity. Diviners sit crosslegged on collapsed boxes, waiting to tell your future. Traditional medicine men sell rams' horns, snakes' heads and desiccated chameleons. The tiny glass booth of Watch Doctor Monsieur Emmanuel Ipadé is decorated with childish paintings of giant watch faces, while over a boy tailor dreaming at his treadle sewing machine, a sign proclaims: "Pop fashions here, dress yourself at Mr O Dao's." Meanwhile King Hairdresser invites you in for a crop—take your pick of the exotically named but uninviting convict-style profiles painted on his door: Mirano, 75 style, Afro, Hercules, Casino, Ghana style, Santiago, Cockroach or the two-penny all off, Ordinary. Round the corner they are doing a brisk trade in used cardboard for packing or making houses with, and you can even buy empty bean cans, shampoo jars and White Horse whisky bottles to keep your savings, cooking oil or plastic flowers in.

18   This is the spontaneous business of the informal sector, varied, inventive, booming in numbers if in nothing else. A survey of Bouaké in 1969 found more than 3,100 informal enterprises in the city. Among them were: 513 tailors, 440 weavers, 459 taxis, 425 rickshaw men, 259 masons, 207 prostitutes, 136 car and bike repairers, 131 joiners and carpenters, 112 restaurants and bars, 87 hairdressers, 60 blacksmiths, 54 jewellers, 43 watch repairers, 36 photographers, 15 hair dyers and ten bootblacks. Today the number of businesses will have doubled or trebled.

19   Spontaneous business is growing even faster than the cities themselves: 12 per cent more hopeful entrepreneurs every year join the crowd in Kumasi, seat of the Ashanti kings, 25 per cent more in Freetown, the perpetually rainy capital of Sierra Leone.

20   According to the International Labour Office's definition, an enterprise should be classified as informal if it employs only a handful of workers, on low incomes, using rudimentary equipment, and works outside the framework of laws and regulations. The informal sector covers services—shoeshine boys, cigarette vendors, sweepers, porters, scribes—and manufacturing, anything from palm-leaf roofing panels and twig brushes to religious objects. Jakarta's *makan* sellers, pushing their little

carts with glowing charcoal fires warming soups and fried pancake rolls by the light of storm lamps, are into food processing just as surely as a canning factory—so are the corncob roasters of Africa or the sweet and biscuit bakers of the Middle East.

21 The informal sector employs a large proportion of the urban population. Surveys from Bombay, Nairobi, São Paulo, Abidjan, Jakarta and cities in Peru put its share of city employment at between 40 and 60 per cent. And, as the rural exodus continues, this share is unlikely to decrease. Most migrants start off their working city lives in this sector and, conversely, a majority of informal-sector workers are migrants. Four fifths of Lima's hawkers and nine tenths of Jakarta's come from outside these cities. After a few years in this kind of work, a migrant may have learned enough of the city's ways and made enough contacts to land a steady job in the modern sector. Many migrants will find themselves trapped in a life of poverty and insecurity, although in most cases they are still better off than if they had remained in their rural area of origin, at least in monetary terms.

22 A survey in Lima, Peru, found that three quarters of street vendors were earning less than the government's minimum wage, indeed an unlucky 13 per cent of them were actually making a loss. Most had gone into trading for the simple reason that they could find no other work. After a difficult period, they began to make some kind of living and developed their own style of expertise: knowing which street corners or thoroughfares produced the richest crop of customers at different times of day. Their incomes were low not because they didn't work hard—more than half of them were putting in forty-five hours a week or more—but because there were too many competitors. Productivity was low as they might have to wait an hour or two between each customer. Nearly half of Jakarta's one million workers are in the informal sector. The 70,000 rickshaw drivers buzz around like wasps and earn, on average, less than £50 each ($100) per year. Unknown to them, the city's official plan predicts that by 1980 "the function of the *betjak* rickshaw as a means of transportation would become non-existent." Two thirds of the city's 30,000 hawkers were found to have a daily turnover of less than £6 ($12). A similar proportion were so abysmally poor that virtually 100 per cent of their income was spent on food. Three quarters of them had turned to hawking because there were no other jobs available.

23 Migrants are much more likely to be poor and underemployed than natives of the cities they have come to: in São Paulo 44 per cent of migrants had monthly incomes below 200 cruzeiros in 1970 (about £20 or $40 at the time), against only 29 per cent of non-migrants. Nearly one migrant in three was underemployed, but only one non-migrant in five. Migrants—though more educated than the neighbours they left behind—were less educated than life-long city dwellers, so the latter were more likely to pick up steady, well-paid jobs in the modern sector. A

1970 survey in Peru found that 59 per cent of informal-sector workers earned below $47 a month, compared with only 18 per cent in the formal sector.

24   Their poverty is due to two factors: first, as we shall see, governments have shamefully neglected this sector, leaving it with primitive technology, management and marketing, and low productivity. Second, there are far too many informal-sector workers chasing far too little work. There is not much work because there is not enough spending power among their customers, poor like themselves. And there are too many work-seekers because of the never-ending flow of refugees from rural poverty. Because of this massive growth of people seeking work in the informal sector, and because of lack of investment in it, there is a danger that it will go the way of so much small-holder agriculture, towards what might be called industrial involution: supporting an ever-increasing population with a steadily declining income per head.

The Virtues of Spontaneity

25   In spite of all this, the informal sector has considerable hidden potential.

26   The modern sector is out of bounds for most of the poor. It cannot and often will not give them work. Nor will it provide for many of their needs, as they can afford few of its products and even less of its services. The dualism found on the land is here again in the cities. The modern sector is the economy of the privileged. It employs them, houses them and pays them enough to afford its products. The informal sector is the economy of the poor. Through it they house themselves and employ each other and produce goods and services they can afford. There is precious little contact between the two economies.

27   The greatest advantage of spontaneous business is that it requires an absolute minimum of capital and skills. The barriers to entry are so low that virtually anybody can set up in business. So the informal sector mobilizes the savings of the poor, spares them the indignity of begging others for work and allows them the liberty (with attendant risks) of being self-employed. Two out of five Ivory Coast entrepreneurs had a capital of less than 10,000 francs CFA (about £25 or $50) and only one in five had more than 50,000 francs. Almost all of them had got the money together themselves or borrowed it from relatives and friends. The informal sector requires no diplomas, no degrees or school leaving certificates—bits of paper the poor in any case do not possess. Two thirds of its workers in Freetown, for example, had no schooling at all, along with two fifths of its entrepreneurs. Most of the rest had not completed their primary schooling. Nine out of ten skilled informal-sector workers in Kumasi had picked up what they knew on the job. That does not mean they had no training. Recruits are often taken on as apprentices, becoming almost part of the family, sharing the boss's house and table as well

as his workshop. The sector offers the cheapest and simplest models for improving the skills of the workforce, a precondition for improving their incomes.

28   The sector does provide real and necessary services and products, too. When I was in Nigeria, bush garages were a handy institution whenever the car broke down (which, given the state of the roads at that time, was frequently). The premises: an inspection pit dug in the ground under a bamboo shelter to keep the rain off. The equipment: a few spanners, sandpaper, tape and several old wrecks cannibalized for spare parts. The staff: a ragged, oily crew of teenagers and young men willing to learn. They would rush out eagerly as you chugged to a halt and after half an hour's improvisation and experiment with a few bits of wire could usually get you on the road again.

29   There is, hiding its light under the informal bushel, probably the greatest reservoir of adaptiveness and invention that exists in developing countries. While western consultants and agencies are urging Third World governments to adopt small-scale appropriate technology, the barefoot businessmen are actually putting many of the precepts into practice. The technology they use is of necessity small-scale and labour-intensive, since they have so little capital. They use local materials because they can't afford or get licences for imports. Recycling of waste is a speciality at which they are past masters. In Ouagadougou they make passable flip-flop sandals out of old car tyres and donkey harnesses out of rusty bike chains. In southern Peru I met one old village blacksmith forging bright new kettles, pans and funnels out of polished-up used tin cans. In Calcutta I came upon a tiny workshop cutting up old cooking oil containers and working them into neat round tins for rough local *beedi* cigarettes.

30   Development agencies now recommend the use of secondhand equipment for some industries: it is much cheaper than new, and usually provides more jobs. Calcutta's Daramtolla Road is lined with little engineering shops that have been doing just that for decades, working on small contracts for bigger firms or garages. "Sri Kali Engineering Works, repairers of petrol engines," says one sign over a ten-foot-wide booth. Or the next: "Das Engineering Works, mechanical engineers and labour contractors, specialists in vibrator machine milling and vertical milling jobs and general orders." Most of the proprietors here seem to be men who picked up their skills in a factory, saved up and bought old lathes or drills for the odd two thousand rupees (around £100 or $200), rented a shop-front, hired some likely lads, and trained them up themselves.

31   Most informal-sector business is physically located in the squatter and slum areas. Haransar Para, the Calcutta bustee we looked at earlier, is a hive of industry and trade. Teenage boys nail together tea chests on an empty space where another family graze two muddy-black water buffaloes and sell their milk. A gang of grubby, khaki-clad mechanics

sandpaper an ancient car ready for a paint job. A laundryman pulls the tabs off vests and *dhotis* while a brush vendor calls from house to house.

32 Indeed, spontaneous business is the exact economic parallel to spontaneous settlements. The same forces give rise to both. The urban bias of investment generates higher city incomes, which pull in the marginal rural poor. But that investment, in jobs as in housing, is used up in expensive western-style packages that can only benefit the few. The many are left to house themselves, and to employ themselves. As long as rural incomes are so far below urban, and as long as the obsession with western architecture, tastes and technology continues, the informal sector will go on growing. There is no chance of it fading away for a very long time to come.

33 Logically, governments should face up to the fact and make the most of it. Informal businesses are the ideal place to try out small-scale, intermediate technology approaches. Their machinery can be improved, their owners can be provided with credit and trained in better management, quality control and marketing, their workers' skills upgraded. They could be tied in with the modern sector by encouraging big factories to subcontract work out to them. This whole vast mass of self-improvement could be built on to provide an unprecedented groundswell of manufacturing and services in the city economies of the Third World.

34 In practice, from most governments spontaneous business gets the same treatment as spontaneous housing. It is seen as a transitory, deviant sort of activity; a nuisance that contributes little to the kind of economy political leaders want to build up; and, like the shanties it is housed in, a hazard to public health and political stability.

35 At the best it is ignored and neglected. It enjoys none of the access to official credit, cheap foreign exchange and government assistance that big business can count on. Banks will advance money to the small informal-sector businessman even less readily than to the smallholding farmer. He has no collateral apart from his cranky old machines or tumbledown shack. He keeps no books other than those in his head. All in all, he is a decided credit risk. Only 4 per cent of Kumasi enterprises and 2 per cent of Freetown's had had loans from banks or official credit agencies. Without credit, the small man finds it much harder to improve his business and is usually doomed to stay small.

36 Into the bargain, he may suffer a good deal of government discrimination, restriction and even outright harassment. Official standards of quality or safety are set artifically high, with the modern sector in mind. The informal sector cannot hope to comply, and hence is excluded from many markets. Spontaneous businesses are no better provided with services than are slums: the majority have no roof over their heads or are housed in tents or shacks. Most have no water or electricity—essentials for manufacturing activity. City governments copy western city ways and insist on licences, which are often restricted in number. Few small

businesses apply for them and even fewer obtain them. Hence they are often, strictly speaking, illegal and even more exposed to risk and uncertainty than they need be. They become sitting ducks for the extortions of corrupt officials and policemen. If they will not pay these under-the-counter taxes on their activities, they are liable to be moved on, perhaps even to get what little capital they have broken up. Whenever a slum is demolished, the bulldozers are knocking down not only wood, cardboard and tin, but dozens of businesses with their laboriously built-up good will, and hundreds of jobs.

Reading for Meaning

1. Discuss the anecdote that Harrison uses to open his chapter on the "barefoot businessman." How well does this beginning catch the reader's attention? Is it appropriate to Harrison's subject? Explain your answer.

2. Putting aside the differences in the products they sell, how does the sales pitch of the snake charmer compare to approaches from sales people with whom you are familiar?

3. Harrison offers specific examples of traditional manufacturing that is being replaced by mass-produced goods. From an anthropological point of view, what cultural treasures are being lost as the competition with manufactured goods eliminates the old style of making goods by hand?

4. What strategies does Harrison propose for improving the wages and competitiveness of goods produced in home industries of the Third World? Why does he think it is important that governments intervene on behalf of the impoverished rural laborers?

5. How might a government official in Lagos, Nigeria, or Lima, Peru, defend a Western-style economic development program that favors large-scale manufacturing and mass-produced housing?

6. Harrison identifies two economies in Third World countries and concludes that they have little contact. How does Harrison think the two might interact to the benefit of both?

7. In Harrison's view, how appropriate are Western-style industries and housing in Third World economies? How do the problems and benefits he identifies compare to those they create in Western countries?

Comparing Texts

1. What are Paul Harrison's opinions of governments that are in charge of running the "informal sector" in which many Third World people must work? Compare his position to the perspective on business or government presented in Hugh Williamson's report on "China's Toy Industry Tinderbox" (page 263).

2. Describe the varieties of work discussed in reading selections in this chapter. What social or cultural factors determine the kind of work an individual is able to do?

Ideas for Writing

1. Write an analysis of the *sub rosa* or "informal" sector of the United States' economy. In your inquiry, include, as Harrison does, work that is unregulated, falls outside of licensing, and is unprotected by city or county services. Try to determine the value or detriment to such work in the United States.

2. After examining the kinds of work discussed in readings for this chapter (see question 2 under "Comparing Texts"), compare the concerns that employees in the industrialized West might have about their jobs to problems workers face in the Third World.

3. Paul Harrison generally decries the interventions of central governments in the Third World as favoring the modern sector at the expense of the "informal" sector. Write a defense of what seems to be the "proper" role of the United States government in its domestic workplace.

4. Harrison's analysis of poverty in the Third World, published in 1979, assumes the presence of a central government capable of allocating resources to its overlooked "informal" workers. In "The Coming Anarchy," an article published in *The Atlantic Monthly,* in February, 1994, Robert D. Kaplan takes a much dimmer view of the ability of governments to provide minimal protection for their citizens, much less provide economic assistance. In this article, Kaplan discusses Sierra Leone as a microcosm of what is occurring, albeit in a more tempered and gradual manner, throughout West Africa and much of the underdeveloped world: the withering away of central governments, the rise of tribal and regional domains, the unchecked spread of disease, and the growing pervasiveness of war. West Africa is reverting to the Africa of the Victorian atlas. It consists now of a series of coastal trading posts, such as Freetown and Conakry, and an interior that, owing to violence, volatility, and disease, is again becoming, as Graham Greene once observed, "blank" and "unexplored" (p. 48). Kaplan's *The Ends of the Earth: A Journey at the Dawn of the 21st Century,* published in 1996, extends this argument as follows:

> It was in Sierra Leone that I first considered the possibility that just as states and their governments were meaning less and less, the distinctions between states and armies, armies and civilians, and armies and criminal gangs were also weakening; that the volume and intensity of the savagery permeating third-world conflicts during the Cold War, whether in El Salvador, Afghanistan, Cambodia, Burundi, the border between Iraq and Iran, the Indian subcontinent, and Sri Lanka, and elsewhere, were only in varying degrees connected to the ideological struggle of the superpowers. They were part of something else. These "low-intensity" conflagrations were not merely sideshows of the Cold War; they were harbingers of the post–Cold War world, which would include more of the same in Bosnia, the Caucasus, Somalia, Liberia, Kashmir, Sierra Leone, and so on (p. 45).

Do some research on one of the recent locations of a "'low-intensity' conflagration" that Kaplan mentions. Write an essay in which you test the validity of Kaplan's conclusion that violence in that area, like conflicts throughout the undeveloped world, is fueled by "the withering away of [a] central government [and] the rise of tribal and regional domains." If you discover more compelling reasons for the conflict, write a defense of your position.

Writing before Reading

1. If you or someone you know works for a government entity, describe what it is like to work for such an institution. What kind of work do people do? Is it monotonous or varied? What is the attitude of employees? What accounts for their attitude?

2. What general impression do you have of public employment? Try to determine what has formed your impression.

RESPECTED SIR[1]
Naguib Mahfouz

Naguib Mahfouz gained international recognition in 1988 when he became the first Arab writer to receive the Nobel Prize for literature. He has written forty novels; several have been translated into English. Mahfouz was born in Cairo in December, 1911, and grew up in a stable, middle-class Moslem household. He attended a Quranic school, a school whose teachings were based on laws from the Qu'ran. Ever since his high school days, Mahfouz has frequented coffeehouses in Cairo where he meets friends for relaxing conversations. After graduating from the University of Faud (now Cairo University) in 1934, Mahfouz began reading masterpieces of Western literature. In a 1973 interview, Mahfouz declared Shakespeare a favorite author who "was the son of my own country, not another." He also appreciates Conrad's Heart of Darkness *and works by Marcel Proust and Franz Kafka. He considers* Moby Dick, *Herman Melville's complex, symbolic work, possibly the greatest novel ever written. As a graduate student, Mahfouz worked on a thesis in which he explored the aesthetics of Islamic philosophy. His interest in the beauty of Islamic thought is often reflected in his novels. It is matched with an artist's eye for detailed descriptions of everyday life and a concern for social justice. One of his better-known works is* The Cairo Trilogy *(1982), an epic portrayal of life in Egypt*

---

[1] Translated by Rasheed El-Enany.

between the two world wars. The Children of Gebelawi *(1988) offers an allegorical interpretation of human history, beginning with Genesis. In recent works, Mahfouz returns to themes of classic Arab literature. In* The Nights of "The Thousand and One Nights" *(1995), for example, he uses supernatural elements to examine human behavior. His politics have offended some Islamic readers, and his books have been banned in a few Arab-speaking countries. Nearly as controversial a figure as Muslim writer Salmon Rushdie, Mahfouz survived an attempted assassination by an Islamic fundamentalist in 1994.*

Mahfouz is remarkable for the number of novels he has written, but his achievement is even more impressive when we consider that, like his protagonist in Respected Sir, *he was a civil servant for most of his life. When he published* Respected Sir *in 1975, Mahfouz had been a government employee for nearly forty years (1934-1971). Unlike his character, Othman Bayyumi, who feels that his career is progressing according to a divine plan, Mahfouz wished God would deliver him from his job. Bayyumi, on the other hand, is convinced that the climb to the top of the organization for which he works is part of a sacred journey. He is willing to sacrifice nearly everything else in his life for the sake of this "blessed" mission.*

Facts about Egypt

Naguib Mahfouz's native Egypt has the largest population of any country in the Arab world. Egypt's population is concentrated along the Nile River, where 96 percent of its people live. The majority of Egyptians are Fellahin, descendants of the Arabs who conquered Egypt in the seventh century. Coptic Christians form a small minority in the country. Their culture evolved from the Roman and Byzantine empires, which Islam has largely replaced. Other groups in Egypt include nomadic peoples, Nubians, Armenians, Italians, Jews, and Greeks.

Egypt's recorded history stretches back to 4000 B.C.E. In its more recent history, Egypt was ruled by the Ottoman Turks from 1517 to 1798, then controlled by the British from 1882 to 1922. Colonel Gamal Abdel Nasser became president of an independent Egypt in 1954 and brought about sweeping social reforms. In 1967 Egypt suffered defeat in the six-day war with Israel, a defeat that Naguib Mahfouz found devastating. Mahfouz's later support for Anwar al-Sadat's peace treaty with Israel, signed in 1979, earned him the enmity of many fundamentalist Moslems. Sadat himself was assassinated by Islamic fundamentalists in 1981. Hosni Mubarak, who succeeded Sadat as president, honored Egypt's peace treaty with Israel but criticized the Israeli government's lack of progress on Palestinian issues. Mubarak was reelected in 1987 and 1993. In 1991 Mubarak helped form the anti-Iraq Arab coalition that fought Iraq during the Persian Gulf War. In 1996 he hosted an Arab summit in an attempt to promote the postwar peace process. Following a 1995 assassination attempt, Mubarak has been forced to crack down on Muslim dissidents. In spite of continuing threats from Muslim fundamentalists in Egypt, Mubarak's political party maintained its majority in the 1995 elections.

ONE

1. The door opened to reveal an infinitely spacious room: a whole world of meanings and motivations, not just a limited space buried in a mass of detail. Those who entered it, he believed, were swallowed up, melted down. And as his consciousness caught fire, he was lost in a magical sense of wonder. At first, his concentration wandered. He forgot what his soul yearned to see—the floor, the walls, the ceiling: even the god sitting behind the magnificent desk. An electric shock went through him, setting off in his innermost heart an insane love for the gloriousness of life on the pinnacle of power. At this point the clarion call of power urged him to kneel down and offer himself in sacrifice. But he followed, like the rest, the less extreme path of pious submissiveness, of subservience, of security. Many childlike tears he would have to shed before he could impose his will. Yielding to an irresistible temptation, he cast a furtive glance at the divinity hunched behind the desk and lowered his eyes with all the humility he possessed.

2. Hamza al-Suwayfi, the Director of Administration, led in the procession.

3. "These are the new employees, Your Excellency," he said, addressing the Director General.

4. The Director General's eyes surveyed their faces, including his. He felt he was becoming part of the history of government and that he stood in the divine presence. He thought he heard a strange whispering sound. Perhaps he alone heard it. Perhaps it was the voice of Destiny itself. When His Excellency had completed his examination of their faces, he opened his mouth. He spoke in a quiet and gentle voice, revealing little or nothing of his inner self.

5. "Have they all got the Secondary Education Diploma?" he inquired.

6. "Two of them have the Intermediate Diploma of Commerce," Hamza al-Suwayfi replied.

7. "The world is progressing," said the Director General in an encouraging tone. "Everything is changing. And now here is the Diploma, replacing the Certificate of Primary Education."

8. This was reassuring, but they all sought to conceal their delight under still greater submissiveness.

9. "Live up to what's expected of you," His Excellency went on, "through hard work and honesty."

10. He looked over a list of their names and suddenly asked, "Which of you is Othman Bayyumi?"

11   Othman's heart pounded within him. That His Excellency had uttered his very own name shook him to the core. Without raising his eyes he took a step forward and mumbled, "Me, Your Excellency."

12   "You got an excellent grade in your Diploma. Why didn't you go on to finish your education?"

13   In his confusion he remained silent. The fact that he did not know what to say, even though he knew the answer.

14   The Director of Administration answered for him, apologetically, "Perhaps it was his circumstances, Your Excellency."

15   Again he heard that strange whispering, the voice of Destiny. And for the first time he felt a sensation of blue skies and of a strange but pleasant fragrance pervading the room. The reference to his "circumstances" was no worry to him, now that he had been sanctified by His Excellency's kindly and appreciative notice. He thought to himself that he could take on a whole army and vanquish it all alone. Indeed his spirit soared upward, higher and higher, till his head disappeared into the clouds in a surge of wild intoxication. But His Excellency tapped the edge of the desk and said, by way of ending the interview, "Thank you. Good morning."

16   Othman went out of the room, silently reciting the Throne verse from the Qur'an.

Two

17   I am on fire, O God.

18   Flames were devouring his soul from top to bottom as it soared upward into a world of dreams. In a single moment of revelation he perceived the world as a surge of dazzling light which he pressed to his bosom and held on to like one demented. He had always dreamed and desired and yearned, but this time he was really ablaze, and in the light of this sacred fire he glimpsed the meaning of life.

19   But down on earth it was decided that he should join the Archives Section. It did not matter how he started; life itself evolved from a single cell or perhaps from something even less. He descended to his new abode in the basement of the ministry, his wings still fluttering. He was greeted by gloom and the musty smell of old paper. Outside, through a barred window, he saw that the ground was on the same level as his head. Inside, the huge room spread out in front of him. Rows of filing cabinets stood on either side, and another long row divided the room down the middle. Staff desks were placed in gaps between cabinets. He walked behind one of the employees toward a desk at the front placed crosswise in a recess like a prayer niche. At the desk was seated the Head of the Archives Section. Othman had not yet recovered from the upsurge of divine inspiration. Even his descent into the basement could not wake him up. He walked behind the clerk, perplexed, distracted, and excited.

20   "Man's aspirations are infinite," he said to himself.

21	The clerk introduced him to the Head of Section: "Mr. Othman Bayyumi, the new clerk," he said, and then introduced the Section Head to him: "Our chief, Mr. Sa'fan Basyuni."

22	He recognized something familiar in the man's features, as if he were a native of his own alley. He liked the protruding bones of his face, its dark and taut skin and the white, disheveled hair of his head. He liked even more the kind and friendly look in his eyes which strove in vain to reflect an air of authority. The man smiled, revealing his ugliest feature: black teeth with wide gaps in between them.

23	"Welcome to the Archives Section! Sit down!" he said, and started to shuffle through the documents of his appointment.

24	"Welcome! Welcome! Life," he went on to say, "can be summed up in two words: hello and goodbye." Yet it was infinite, Othman thought. There blew around him a strange mysterious wind, full of all kinds of probabilities.

25	It was infinite, he thought again, and because of that it demanded infinite willpower.

26	The Head of Section pointed to a vacant, neutral-colored desk whose leather top was worn-out and spotted with faded stains of ink.

27	"Your desk," he said. "Examine the chair carefully. The tiniest nail can rip a new suit."

28	"My suit is very old anyway," replied Othman.

29	"And remember," the man carried on with his warning, "to recite a prayer before opening a filing cabinet. On the eve of last Bairam festival a snake, at least three feet long, came out of one of the cabinets." He choked with laughter and continued, "But it wasn't a poisonous one."

30	"How can one tell whether it is poisonous or not?" asked Othman anxiously.

31	"You ask the section messenger. He comes from Abu Rawwash, the city of snakes."

32	Othman took the warning for a joke and let it pass. He chided himself for failing to study meticulously His Excellency the Director General's room and print on his mind's eye a full picture of the man's face and his person, for not trying to unravel the secret of the magic with which he dominated everyone and had them at his beck and call. This was the power to be worshipped. It was the ultimate beauty too. It was one of the secrets of the universe. On earth there existed divine secrets without number for those who had eyes to see and minds to think. The time between hello and goodbye was short. But it was infinite as well. Woe betide anyone who ignored this truth. There were people who never moved, like Mr. Sa'fan Basyuni. Well-meaning but miserable, paying tribute to a wisdom of which he had learned nothing. But not so those whose hearts had been touched by the sacred fire. There was a happy path which began at the eighth grade in the government service and ended at the splendid position of His Excellency the Director General.

This was the highest ideal available to the common people, beyond which they could not aspire. This was the highest heaven where both divine mercy and human pride became manifest. The eighth grade. The seventh. The sixth. The fifth. The fourth. The third. The second. The first. Director General. The miracle could be brought about in thirty-two years. Or perhaps rather more. Those who fell by the wayside were innumerable. Still the celestial order did not necessarily apply to mankind, least of all to government employees. Time nestled in his arms like a gentle child, but one could not prophesy one's future. He was on fire: that was all. And it seemed to him that this fire blazing in his breast was the same as that which lit the stars in their courses. We were creatures of mystery whose secrets were hidden to all but their Creator.

33   "You will first learn to handle the incoming mail," said Mr. Basyuni. "It is easier." He then added, laughing, "An archivist should take off his jacket while working. Or at least have elbow patches sewn on his sleeves to protect them against dust and paper clips." All that was easy. What was really difficult was how to deal with time.

Reading for Meaning

1. Identify the point of view Naguib Mahfouz adopts in the chapters from *Respected Sir*. How does he use this perspective to develop the central character, Othman Bayyumi?

2. What assumptions does Bayyumi make about the ultimate purpose of his working life and the meaning of the system of which he is a part?

3. Find passages in the excerpt from *Respected Sir* where Naguib Mahfouz uses the language of religious ecstasy and those that convey realistic descriptions. How does Mahfouz employ these distinctly different writing styles to comment on his character's dreams about a career in public service?

4. What is the symbolic meaning of having Othman Bayyumi begin his career in the archives section of the bureaucracy for which he works?

5. What is Bayyumi's quarrel with time? What problems might arise for people who are obsessed with achieving a particular goal?

6. What do you anticipate will happen in this novel? Find a copy of this short novel in your local library or bookstore, and read it to see if your predictions are accurate.

Comparing Texts

1. Read "The Religion of Americans and American Religion" by Will Herberg, a selection that appears in chapter 12 of this book. Are there aspects of Othman Bayyumi's secular religion that are similar to the American "faith" that Herberg describes?

2. Compare the assumptions about work and advancement described in "Respected Sir" to the assumptions a Japanese *salaryman* makes about his job according to J. E. Thomas's, "Culture and the Communal Organization," which appears later in this chapter.

Ideas for Writing

1. Write a paper in which you analyze techniques that Naguib Mahfouz employs to develop his main character. Consider his use of style, tone, description, dialogue, and point of view.

2. Read the rest of Naguib Mahfouz' short novel, *Respected Sir,* and write a paper in which you discuss the author's purpose for writing the novel.

Writing before Reading

Briefly summarize any news stories you recall that drew attention to substandard working conditions in third world factories owned by European or United States–based corporations. You might also consult the Internet or a full-text database. What seemed to be the point of view of the reporter? Did you detect any bias in the report?

CHINA'S TOY INDUSTRY TINDERBOX

Hugh Williamson

Hugh Williamson is a freelance journalist who frequently writes about international labor issues. He is the author of Coping with the Miracle: Japan's Unions Explore New International Relations *(1994). He wrote the following article about working conditions in China's toy factories for the* Multinational Monitor *published in September 1994.*

Facts about China

The People's Republic of China has been a Communist state since 1949. The Chinese name for the country means the Middle Country, a reference to the location of China at the center of the world. The word "China," used largely outside the country, may have derived from the Ch'in dynasty, which dates from the third century B.C.E. Most Chinese live in the east and southeast. In the thirty years from 1952 to 1982, China's urban population went from 13.3 percent to 21 percent, due in large part to metropolitan annexation of rural counties. China nationalized its industries after the Communist victory in 1949. Since the 1979 economic reforms, the government has seen an increase in outside investment in China. Textiles, consumer products, handicrafts, and food processing are four of China's most important industries. One-fourth of China's manufactured goods come from its rural areas. The cities of Beijing and Shanghai lie in two of China's most heavily industrialized urban areas. (See also page 131 for more background on China.)

1 If the Workers' Daily says so, it must be true. China's official workers' paper commented recently that "many people say the foreign-invested economy is China's burgeoning new heaven. But sometimes, heaven is only a step away from hell."

2 The statement rings especially true for 84 former colleagues of Tao Chun Lan, a 20-year-old woman from Zhongyuan, a poor village in Sichuan province in central China. Last year, Tao and many village friends migrated to Shenzhen, the "Special Economic Zone," which borders Hong Kong and exemplifies China's rush to open its doors to foreign business.

3 Tao and her friends found work in the Zhili Handicrafts factory, making stuffed toys. They earned poverty wages, about $46 a month. On the night of November 19, 1993, an electrical fault sparked a fire that ripped through Zhili's dual factory-dormitory building. The workers were locked inside—only one of four exits was open. In all, 84 workers were suffocated, burnt or trampled to death. Most of the victims were women, and many were Tao's friends from Zhongyuan village.

4 Tao was lucky. She survived, although she crushed both ankles jumping to safety from a second-floor window. Hospitalized for four months, she received no compensation from the company or the local government. "They don't care if I'm crippled for life," she told the local press.

5 International toy makers and distributors refuse to acknowledge any responsibility for preventing such industrial disasters. When presented with a suggestion to adopt a toy industry code to prevent future fires like the one at Zhili, Dennis Ting, head of the Hong Kong Toy Council, which represents major investors in China, called the idea "ridiculous," and fumed, "someone is out of their minds."

6 Ting and others are eager to maintain business as usual. The $40 billion per year international toy industry is increasingly centered on China. The country houses the world's biggest toy manufacturing industry, which continues to expand. The Southeast China province of Guangdong, where Shenzhen and many other special economic zones are located, is the industry's heartland, where at least one-third of the world's toys are made. Neighboring Hong Kong is China's toy export gateway, shipping toys worth $8 billion in 1993, making it the world's leading toy exporter.

7 Despite the economic promise of this scenario, toy industry boosters are finding it increasingly difficult to use such statistics to hide the plight of Tao and her fellow Chinese workers. A realistic picture of the Chinese toy industry is emerging—highlighted through profiles of several Asian multinational companies' Chinese operations—revealing that many

of the toys that delight children around the world are the product of rock-bottom wages, horrendous working conditions, appalling health and safety risks and a de facto ban on free labor organizing. In opposition to this exploitation, toy workers' demands and protest actions are increasing, supported by international campaigns.

8   The toy industry also opens a window into broader aspects of today's China. What is happening in the toy industry may be repeated in other sectors in the coming years. In the face of its ailing state enterprises, many reformers in China see the foreign-controlled joint ventures that dominate the toy industry as the fastest route to economic development. Yet worker hardship and industrial disasters raise questions about the sustainability of this approach.

9   Further, most of the foreign companies involved are Asian-based, commonly from Hong Kong and Taiwan. The way these corporations operate in China demonstrates how the world's "new" multinationals may approach labor–management relations in the twenty-first century.

THE LABOR BEHIND THE LABELS

10   The toy industry's famous brands—Fisher-Price, Hasbro, Tyco and Mattel from the United States and Europe, Bandai and Tomy from Japan—rarely appear on the name-plates of Chinese factories. These corporate giants rely mainly on original equipment manufacturing agreements with manufacturers, which then have exclusive rights to produce toys according to the specifications set by the brand-name buyers. Some of these local contractors—many of which are also multinationals, with Asia-wide operations—also sell toys under their own brandnames.

11   Offering labor unorganized by free unions (explicitly banned in China) at as little as 12 cents an hour, China has come to dominate major segments of the international toy trade. In Germany, the center of the European toy trade, China is the main source of plastic dolls, doll accessories, toy animals, toy musical instruments, motorized toys and toy guns.

12   Many toys popular in the United States come from China as well. Over 90 percent of three- to eight-year-old boys in the United States have at least one toy Teenage Mutant Ninja Turtle, according to market research in the early 1990s. Hong Kong-based Harbour Ring International Holdings, the world's leading producer of Ninja action-figures, can be held mainly responsible. While the Ninja craze has now faded, it catapulted Harbour Ring into the ranks of Asia's top toy corporations.

13   Harbour Ring, with major investments in southern China, is typical of such Hong Kong-based companies. Combined, these firms employ at least 120,000 workers across the border. Harbour Ring, which made 1993 profits of $30.1 million, started out with factories in Hong Kong, then shifted north in the early 1980s in search of cheaper labor. A family-run business incorporated in Bermuda—for tax purposes and to avoid uncertainty over Hong Kong's handover to China in 1997—its subsidiaries and

contractors operate six factories in Guangdong, employing 10,000 to 18,000 seasonal production workers. They make 300 toy lines, mainly on contract for brand-name toy companies.

14 Harbour Ring itself is now escalating its sales and marketing in China, where it already has 90 sales outlets and is planning more. "The overall improvement is disposable income... creates opportunities for the group's business," says Chairman Luk Chung Lam.

15 His workers, however, will not be customers. Harbour Ring workers earn on average only $46 to $58 a month, and, as migrants, most send part of this back to their villages, keeping only enough for subsistence needs. Rapid economic growth—reaching 30 percent in Shenzhen in 1993, double the nationwide average—has also fueled inflation, pushing up living costs, especially in industrial areas.

16 Working hours are long, overtime and weekend work are common and job security is low. Most of Harbour Ring's Chinese workers are unskilled—they get less than half-a-day's training. In the summer, Harbour Ring works at maximum production and employment levels in order to stock toy store shelves for Christmas. Each winter, it sheds about half its workforce until they need to gear up again the following summer.

17 There are also international factors that make this employment insecure. The issue of China's most favored nation (MFN) status has been resolved in favor of investors in China for the time being, but Harbour Ring made contingency plans to relocate investment if the human rights lobby had won, and the company intends to follow through on those plans despite the U.S. decision to renew China's MFN status. The company retains some production in Hong Kong, and is currently building what it calls the "largest... hard toy factory in Indonesia." It "promises" to pay minimum wages of $1.30 to $1.50 a day. Meanwhile, production of its Macau plant—currently the largest toy factory in that territory—is expected to expand by 50 percent.

18 Yet high-profile plans to build several so-called "toy production cities" show that Harbour Ring's roots remain in China. The first such "city," in Zhongshan, is due to be completed this year, with another planned for Guangdong. With a floor area of around 600,000 square feet, the Guangdong development will be "one of the biggest toy factories in China," according to Chairman Luk.

19 He says the factory will bring economies of scale, but will also "improve the workers' sense of belonging in this labor-intensive business. As many workers are from distant provinces, adequate accommodation and welfare facilities in these cities should help create continuity in the workforce."

ANATOMY OF A DISASTER

20 What such promises will mean in reality is as yet unclear. To date, Harbour Ring's labor practices have attracted little critical attention. Its low wages

are normal for the industry, and higher than those of Chinese school teachers, say industry analysts. Yet Luk's description of the new "city" might ring alarm bells for Tao Chun Lan and her former colleagues in the Zhili factory, since a similar rationale could have been used to justify Zhili's factory design. If so inclined, Harbour Ring and other toy makers could learn much from what happened last November 19, and from the frequent, often fatal safety lapses which continue to occur.

21   The Zhili Handicrafts factory was run by a Hong Kong–Chinese joint venture, on contract to produce the Italian "Chicco" brand of stuffed toys. The plant had 472 employees, but more than one third of these were unrecorded casual laborers, a common state of affairs which led to major identification problems after the fire.

22   Local Shenzhen authorities had warned the factory managers about safety provisions earlier in the year—it had no fire alarm, no sprinklers or fire hoses, and no fire escapes—but no action was taken.

23   The windows were fitted with heavy wire mesh and most exits were locked; the bodies of 50 of the victims were found behind a locked gate. "The factory itself had the now-notorious three-in-one design," says a regular visitor to Shenzhen, Wong Wai Ling, of the Hong Kong-based labor advocacy group Asia Monitor Resource Center (AMRC). "Like many factories, the workshops, warehouse and living and eating quarters were all in one building—a major fire risk, especially when flammable materials are on site," she says.

24   An investigation by China's official, Communist party-controlled trade union, the All-China Federation of Trade Unions [ACFTU], found the fire started in the warehouse, caused by an electrical short circuit. Raw materials and finished products partly blocked the staircase and exit that was open, endangering more lives, the union investigation found. To make matters worse, in an effort to avoid adverse publicity after the fire, the local authority held 50 or so survivors as virtual prisoners for several days in a local hall, banning them from contacting friends or relatives.

25   Relatives of those killed received compensation of between $2,600 and $6,500; those injured received nothing as of June 1994. In mid-January, the factory owner, Lo Chiu Chuen, and three other managers were arrested for violating state safety regulations and two local fire department officers were charged with accepting bribes.

Crisis? What Crisis?

26 Besides bribery, which is already rampant in Guangdong, the Chinese government blames most accidents on "numb minds, lax discipline, chaotic management and unlawful operation and supervision," but it takes little effective preventative action.

27   Official statistics record 28,200 industrial fires in the first 10 months of 1993 in China. These fires killed 1,480 people and injured more than 50,000. There were more than 15,000 officially recorded work-related

deaths in 1992 (the latest year figures were available), and the real figures are much higher, experts say. Fires are by no means the only problem. Poisoning by chemicals and fumes is also common in the toy industry; 81 people were poisoned in three separate toy factories in Guangdon in 1993; three of them later died.

28   One executive from a toy industry multinational with "extensive operations" in Guangdong told the Far Eastern Economic Review in 1993 that "industrial safety is the last thing that anybody worries about in Shenzhen, or anywhere else in the province."

29   In January 1994, the Zhili fire and other disasters finally provoked the provincial government to pass tighter laws on factory safety. The new laws spell out standards on fire prevention, emergency exits and ventilation and ban three-in-one factory buildings. Lee Cheuk Yan, head of the Hong Kong Confederation of Trade Unions (CTU) and a leading campaigner for labor rights in China, welcomed the laws, but was skeptical about whether they would be enforced. "Although the rules exist, if the safety inspectors take bribes, employers will ignore the rules, and we will have to wait for another tragedy," Lee said in January.

30   Sadly, Lee did not have to wait long. On June 4, the workers' dormitory at the Hong Kong-funded Xiecheng Plastics toy factory in Shenzhen collapsed. The factory, which, despite the new laws, retained the three-in-one system, had been illegally built on a crumbling river bed. Eleven workers were killed and 27 were injured.

LIVE AND LET DIE

31 Various international labor movement initiatives aim to support Chinese toy workers in their demands for better working conditions. The International Textile, Garment and Leather Workers' Federation (ITGLWF) and the AFL-CIO's youth support group Frontlash have called for "toycott" campaigns to boycott Chinese toys until labor conditions improve. Neil Kearney, ITGLWF general secretary, says "China has a live and let die approach to its workers. The only way to make China listen is to block off markets for products made in such appalling conditions." Lee Cheuk Yan, of Hong Kong's CTU, favors boycotting "products of factories where clear evidence of poor working conditions exists."

32   In May, trade unions and other groups in Hong Kong launched a long-term campaign to draw up and enforce a set of "Toy Industry Safety Guidelines," to be implemented by multinationals in China and throughout Asia. The draft guidelines cover factory and job safety, a ban on three-in-one buildings and regular monitoring.

33   "Guidelines covering toy safety for consumers already exist in the West," says Tian Chua of AMRC, one of the groups involved. "But shouldn't products be safe for workers too?" he asks.

34   It was this proposal that Dennis Ting of the Hong Kong Toy Council found "ridiculous." The fact that 189 workers, mostly women, died in a

May 1993 fire at the Thai subsidiary of Ting's Kader Industrial Company which produces such items as Bart Simpson dolls and toy trains, sheds some light on his ardent opposition to a workplace safety code.

35   In China, however, the success of Kader's employees in winning improved working conditions show that while these international initiatives are important, it is workers' own actions, probably backed by broader political reforms, which hold the best hope of sparking widespread improvements for toy industry workers.

36   Kader set up a factory in Shekou, Guangdong, in the mid-1980s, maintaining abysmal working conditions. A 1993 ACFTU survey identified Kader as one of the province's harshest employers; daily wages were 52 to 64 cents, less than half the official minimum wage.

37   In mid-May 1993, the Kader workers refused to work overtime, extending this initiative to an all-out strike two weeks later. The strike brought results. Wages now stand at about $1.70 to $2.30 per day, and canteen and living quarters—other major areas of complaint—have been improved. Workers now occupy separate dormitories, rather than their old three-in-one building.

38   Duplicating these results across the toy sector and beyond in China poses an enormous challenge to Chinese workers. Strikes and free union organizing remain illegal, although workers are engaging in both activities with increasing frequency. As many as 800 underground independent labor groups exist in Guangdong, according to newspaper reports in March 1994, and in 1993, China saw 12,358 arbitrated labor disputes, a 50 percent increase from the previous year. Thousands of other disputes did not reach arbitration.

39   China's migrant toy industry workers undoubtedly would like to agree with Harbour Ring's 1994 company motto, "The future will be brilliant for the upcoming years, and the sky is the limit." But it will take an uphill struggle before workers can share this assessment.

Reading for Meaning

1. What is the "three-in-one plan"? How does Williamson feel this plan contributed to the disaster in Zhili?

2. What role did local politics play both before and after the fire swept through the Zhili Handicrafts factories?

3. Describe the various official responses to the tragedy at Zhili Handicrafts. What does Williamson think the government's final response might be? What is his opinion of that response? Do you agree with him?

4. Does Williamson offer any hope that the situation in China's factories might change? Do you think U.S. consumers might have a role in effecting change? Explain your response.

5. What do you think Williamson's purpose was for writing "China's Toy Industry Tinderbox"? For whom is he writing?

6. Identify Williamson's sources for his article. Give examples of how he has used source material to support his position. How effectively has Williamson arranged his data overall?

Comparing Texts

Find out what happened in the famous Triangle Shirtwaist Company's fire in New York in 1911. Compare this New York fire to the one in the Zhili Handicrafts factory in Shenzhen, China, on November 19, 1993. Examine what seems to have caused both fires and the responses of management, government officials, or the workers themselves.

Ideas for Writing

Writing for the *New York Times,* Alan Finder reports that Chinese immigrants are currently working in sweatshops "throughout New York City, in the garment center and Chinatown in Manhattan, in Sunset Park and Williamsburg in Brooklyn, in Long Island City and Corona in Queens, and in the South Bronx." Research the topic of dangerous working conditions in sweatshops in the United States, or in other employment that is notoriously below industry standards, and write your own exposé of the labor practices in this industry.

Writing before Reading

What is your understanding about either working life in Japan or policies of Japanese companies who have branches in the United States? What benefits or problems might an American employee encounter while working for a company based in Japan?

CULTURE AND THE COMMUNAL ORGANIZATION

J. E. Thomas

J. E. Thomas is director of adult education at the University of Nottingham and helps edit the International Journal of Life-long Education. *In addition to his works on adult education, Thomas writes extensively on penal systems. The Japan Society for the Promotion of Science awarded him a fellowship for his work. The following selection first appeared in 1993 in Thomas's book,* Making Japan Work.

Facts about Japan

Modern Japan has a sophisticated technology and a broad industrial base. It is a constitutional monarchy. Since the end of the Second World War, the monarch has been a titular head similar to British royalty. Japan began industrializing at the beginning of the twentieth century. In the decades since World War II, Japan has developed a formidable economy, second only to the United States. In recent years, the Japanese have made considerable advances in the development of new technology. The current crisis in global markets and charges of corruption at home have slowed the Japanese economy. Even in 1995–1996, the year when four successive prime ministers were forced to resign, Japan's trade surplus continued to increase. For additional information on Japan, see page 211.

1 Training and education do not take place in a vacuum, but within the context of a given industrial culture, which in turn provides, especially in Japan, a specific company culture. Both are embraced by the broader social context. This point cannot be stressed enough in discussing Japan, since the generic tendency to assume that education operates in isolation is an especial barrier to understanding the subtleties of the Japanese company. There is one specific factor in this culture which is especially relevant to this discussion. This is the practice of employment for life.... The privilege, if that is what it is, of life-time tenure though by no means universal, is an important custom of company life. It has been noted that:

> ... some 70 per cent of university graduates and some 60 per cent of high school graduates work for a single company ... roughly one-third of the total workforce.[1]

2 Perhaps surprisingly, there is some doubt as to whether this is a part of any ancient Japanese tradition. Morita,* surely a very reliable source, notes that:

> ... lifetime employment ... was actually imposed on us by the labour laws instituted by the Occupation, when a lot of liberal, left-wing economic technicians were sent out from the United States to Japan with the goal of demilitarising the country and making it a democracy.[2]

3 Indeed, employers believed that the enactment of these laws would lead to anarchy in the workplace. Even where this is evidenced in historical times "tenure" did not amount to the rather cosy commodity commonly imagined. What it meant was that the worker was bound in a semi-slave state to an employer who could dismiss him out of hand.[3]

---

* Morita built the Sony company in Japan.

4   Van Wolveren, on the other hand, sees the tenure tradition as having arisen from the activities and policies of the pre-1945 *sangyo hokokukai*—"patriotic industrial associations." These organised the labour force, and central to that organisation was the understanding that workers would not move jobs. This practice persisted, even after the dramatic changes of the post-war period.[4]

5   This, however, as has been shown in respect of women employees and contract companies, is by no means universal. But it is true of salarymen, because, it is often suggested, of the reluctance to undermine group cohesion. The eviction of a member of the group would signal a collective failure and loss of face, and so is to be avoided. As well as such rather esoteric reasons there are more mundane explanations for the tenure system. The most lucid of these is the fact that changing companies is very much discouraged, and would bring with it a loss of income, status, and prospects.

6   The employers find the practice attractive, otherwise they would certainly not allow it. In defending it though, they sometimes come forward with reasons which seem very altruistic. Morita, for example, pronounces as "absurd" the fact that:

> ... every year in the United States hundreds, or maybe thousands, of technicians, researchers, and executives of American high-technology firms are given lay-off notices, are fired, or just quit. When they go to a new company, they take on a new allegiance and they bring with them all the previous company's secrets, or all the ones they are allowed to know.[5]

7   Whatever the origins and reasons for tenure amongst managers, for training in practice, such stability means that investment in employee education is well placed, since the likelihood of movement to another company, with the concomitant loss of that investment is remote. Thus, not only are secrets of technology safe, but the benefits of training are not transferred.

8   The second factor in the industrial milieu which is relevant to training is also to do with manpower, and this is its intensity. At least hitherto, manpower had been recognised as the most important resource. This fact, together with the stability already mentioned, leads inevitably to the conclusion that training is important as a means of maximising the potential of that resource. The next contextual factor is the pliability of the workforce, and the restraints on union activity. . . .

9   It may be noted that this tradition of stability is enabled by two rather odd practices, which make it possible for companies to ensure that permanent staff are always employed. The first of these is the movement of such staff, when necessary from the parent company to an affiliate, and the second is the "usual practice" of the contracting firm positioning

staff in the subcontracting firm, another example of the tyranny inflicted upon the subcontractors in the Japanese configuration.[6] And so the custom of employment for life may not be so much a statement about the generosity of employers as a demonstration of the never failing power of the big company.

10   The development of subsidiaries is a usual way in Japanese business life both of coping with changing markets, and diverting surplus staff who in the West would be declared redundant.[7] As far as it is possible it seems to be the case that major Japanese companies will go to great lengths to ensure continued employment:

> As far as they can, they retrain employees and move them from one division that is not profitable to some other profitable or new division. Some companies create new business. For example, iron and steel mill companies in Japan produce new business like electronic materials and service industries, to which they can move employees from the old operation.[8]

11   In the same speech, Saba, who is the Vice Chairman of Keidanren, expressed the same surprise as Morita, quoted earlier, at the speed and willingness with which Westerners dispose of businesses, and particularly of staff.

12   Normally in the West recession brings redundancy, but in Japan, because of the custom of tenure recession may bring some benefit to the training organisation, since the man-hours that are freed because of a slackening in output are deployed for increased training. While tenure has clear advantages for the employee, it brings considerable benefit to the employer. Such stability can lead to great commitment in general, and the scale of that commitment is described by Saba:

> In Japan . . . one's company is on a par with other important group affiliations and thus represents one of the basic social group situations in which real life is lived . . . all corporate members perceive their fates as being closely linked.[9]

13   This means that investment in training and education is well placed. Saba goes on to point out that:

> . . . the company views them (employees) as a permanent resource and works to increase their value through energetic in-house training programmes for both management and union members.[10]

14   One of the facts, though, of modern company life, and a source of great concern to managers, is what is called "job hopping" from company to company. This seriously undermines all of this. Mobility would reduce the trust, upon which so much of Japanese company life is predicated. But in an increasingly volatile industrial world, even this precious

Japanese tradition is being eroded by the "headhunting" phenomenon. There is evidence of a growth in job hopping, and it has been suggested that in high technology, there may be as much as 25 per cent mobility in those grades which would be traditionally regarded as immobile. And as Dore and Sako point out:

> Increasingly, in recent years, companies have sought to accelerate the process of building up new expertise by mid-career recruitment—bringing in people with specific skills. A twice-monthly *Beruf*, was started in 1982, specifically to provide a channel for technologist and technician job advertisements.[11]
>
> This trend has caused some alarm in the business community. It prompted Keidanren, the Federation of Economic Organisations, to issue a report clarifying that this development should be considered an undesirable trend to be kept within bounds. The administrators in the business world make no secret of their wish that salarymen should remain wholly dependent on their firms, as children are dependent on their parents.[12]

15   Finally, the increasing presence of foreign companies employing Japanese and foreign employees in Japanese companies is bound to lead to changing assumptions about mobility in employment. The most important task which industrial trainers in Japan set themselves is to reawaken in the recruits the importance of loyalty to the group. The relationship of the individual to the group is the most distinctive feature of Japanese social structure. Put simply, the group is more important than the individual, and the latter must submit to the former.

16   In the earlier discussion about the tensions in education we saw how those tensions derive from deeply engrained traditions, and the supremacy of the group is an example. On the one hand there is a call for greater individual development in schools, but, on the other, as Duke points out:

> Every teacher is struggling to develop the cohesiveness of the group. How do you encourage individual initiative when the fundamental object is to develop group loyalty? Individual capabilities interfere with the group.[13]

17   Although the Japanese fully understand the pivotal nature of loyalty to the group, they are also aware that the conflict produced by the need to subordinate gives rise to such terrible tension. In everyday life this can be seen by the number of what Durkheim called "altruistic" suicides, that is those suicides which express an inability to live outside the group, or without its approval. The sad recital on television at the beginning of the school year of the details of suicides by children is an especially poignant example.

18   Buruma points out that the futility of existence outside the group is a dominant theme in the dramatic tradition. It is reflected in every part of that tradition, from the classical Kabuki theatre, to the TV dramas about *ronin* (masterless samurai) or *yakuza* (gangsters).

> Salarymen are often obliged to sacrifice their private lives for the company. They are frequently compelled to see more of their colleagues—often the only people they see—than of their families, whether they want to or not. Human relations on the shop floor are bound by similar restraints or hierarchy to those of the cinema *yakuza*. I was even told by a foreman in a motor-cycle plant that he watches *yakuza* films to learn how to cope with his job.... An individual in Japan is always part of something larger (the few exceptions are considered to be bizarre loners)... one can only really exist in the context of one's group... relationships in these groups are not necessarily based on friendship... as soon as one leaves the fold one ceases to be a member.
>
> For example, a well-known *avant-garde* theatre group recently published a book about its history. There was one peculiar omission: the leading star of the group who had been the major attraction for the last ten years was not mentioned even once. The reason: he had decided to leave the troupe just before the book was written, so he simply did not exist any more. An interesting detail in this story is that the book was edited by one of the country's leading drama critics. He defended the omission by claiming *giri*.[14]

19   In a discussion about the differences between the American hero and the Japanese hero in fiction, Buruma points out that the American believes that the world can be changed, but the Japanese does not:

> Centuries of Buddhist resignation and Tokugawa rule have beaten any illusions of fundamental change out of him long ago.... Social tragedy... Japanese drama revolves around a closed world from which there is no escape.[15]

20   Too much individuality leads to ostracism, the worst possible fate for anybody, but especially for the Japanese. One of the most important figures in society is the *ronin,* literally "waveless man," the most recognisable figure in Japanese cosmology. This is the term used to describe students who are seeking places at university, and some of the most adored figures in Japanese history are the heroes known as the Forty-Seven *Ronin*. In the eighteenth century after avenging their lord, who had been betrayed, they committed suicide, and their shrine is one of the most revered in the country. The ultimate expression of loyalty for the group is willingness to die, as the forty-seven did, and Buruma gives a superb example of this.

21   In 1972, after torturing eleven members of their group to death for alleged lack of loyalty, five members of the Japanese "Red Army," took

refuge in a house, holding a hostage. After a dramatic siege, they surrendered. Their actions were deplored by one of the most eminent papers in the country, but for an unexpected reason, at least to the Western observer. It was expected, the paper pointed out, that they would either die in hand-to-hand fighting, or that they would take their own lives. But their "pampered spirit" led to this expectation being "utterly betrayed." The paper went on to approve the suicide of the father of one of the five:

> But the sad part of it is that the father's death cannot fill the spiritual gap existing between father and son.[16]

22   Such feelings are very much a reality in Japanese life, and it would clearly be impossible to leave them outside the factory gates, especially since the central notion of group loyalty is so happily consonant with industrial harmony.

23   In this, as in so much of Japanese culture, in society and at work, the Japanese are sensitive to criticism from the outside, although ... it is a sensitivity increasingly tinged with anger. In this case of group loyalty, it is not uncommon to hear the expression of a realisation that the exclusivity of a group can lead to a lack of overall social responsibility:

> In Japan, companies represent one community, and human relationships within that community are regarded as extremely important. Little attention, however, is paid to relationships outside that community. Such neglect invites criticism against Japan; we are accused of striving for economic success but contributing nothing to the community. Moreover, in Japan, cultural contributions have not been considered as something companies should naturally make as a social responsibility. I think such a perception gap also tends to stir up criticism in the United States.[17]

24   Although the group is so important, Japanese companies are careful to make a distinction between the cooperative element in the group, and the elimination of individual initiative. Morita in his account of Sony makes clear that without that initiative there can be no progress. So it is not the mindless conformity of the Prussian army which is required, apart from anything else because it does not work. Rather the ideal is the creation of a feeling of family in the Japanese sense and tradition. In his description of Sony, he describes what has come to be a generally held perception of life in a Japanese company:

> We deal with our employees as members of the Sony family ... all of whom wear the same jackets and eat in our one-class cafeteria ... we urged the management staff to sit down with their office people and share the facilities ... every foreman ... looks carefully at the faces of his team members. If someone doesn't look good, the foreman makes it a point to find out if the person is ill, or has some kind of a problem or worry.[18]

25   When it comes to practice, the whole is dominated by a belief that the recruits need to be retrained to respect the two great traditions: loyalty, and obligation to the group. Japanese companies believe that these values have been lost because of schooling and lack of discipline in the home. A primary task of training for the new recruits, therefore, is the re-establishment of these traditional values:

> Rising income levels and the influence of Western societies has led to a weakening of corporate-group identity among young people.[19]

26   What is it that they believe is wrong?

27   The Japanese business community believes that the trouble began with the introduction of an alien educational system in 1945. The consequence is that in 1989 recruits to the companies continue to be seriously disadvantaged by their educational experience. Introduced by the U.S. Occupation Forces in 1945, it is upon the American system that the schools were reformed. It seems to many Japanese that central to this system was too much emphasis on individuality, and too much encouragement to challenge things hallowed. The coarseness of things Western, especially American, has been somehow intertwined with the radicalism of the teachers' unions, with no counterbalance, especially with the removal of "morals" from the curriculum, at least until after the Americans left.

28   The pernicious influence of education and the West is a constant theme in Japanese public life, and perhaps the most eminent and persistent purveyor of this view was the former Prime Minister Nakasone. He was reported in 1984, for example, to have described the system as a "foreign educational system and principles of education prescribed for our country by the Allied Occupation Forces."[20] Such statements have always caused the greatest alarm amongst Japanese liberals, always wary of talk about "traditional" values. The insidious nature of this perceived alien influence, and the effort of business trainers to counteract it is a matter to which we will return.

29   When it comes to university graduates, the same criticism is made. Nor is there any consolation in the supposition that they at least bring advanced skills to the company. The expectation of the latter is that all entrants are novices. This conviction, as one interviewee pointed out, "is not a criticism, it is a fact." The main advantage of the university graduates, even in engineering or science, is that they bring to the company, as well as a grounding, a flexibility which is of infinitely more value in a fast-changing industry than a high degree of practical skill, which may quickly become redundant. Nor is there any doubt that they do want graduates:

> Usually in the case of a big corporation like Toshiba or Sony we have close relations with university or college. We keep in communication

with college to enable us to recruit good students, and also we encourage companies' cooperative research work with universities and colleges which help us to recruit graduates. In the case of small and medium-sized companies there is more difficulty in recruiting the best graduates, but nowadays we have so many universities and colleges that the level of education is getting higher and higher.[21]

30   In the opinion of one engineering company visited during this research, universities lag behind in technological development. There is a widespread feeling that there ought to be more liaison between industry and the universities, a view held very strongly by MITI. To that end there has been set up a Japanese Industrial Education Association, but contact overall remains slight. To the university observer, one comment was not without humour. One respondent stated that in his company the top management might have seminars conducted by university professors. These "are behind the times, but the professors can put the ideas over in a more organised way."

31   At the point of entry into the company, however, whether they are graduates of universities or of vocational schools, whether white- or blue-collar, they have only a limited general knowledge, which does not mean that they are ready for industry in any useful sense. They do have some theoretical knowledge, but that is all.

32   What an individual's academic record indicates to the employer seems to be two things. The first of these is the capacity for hard work, and the second is intelligence. In the strictly élitist education system, a typical result of an extremely large quantity of both produces a graduate from a top-grade university, such as Tokyo, which, it will be remembered, is at the very peak. Companies are anxious to recruit such graduates, partly because they are possessed of these qualities, and partly because the graduates of Tokyo University are in positions of great influence throughout Japanese life and are in a network which can be very useful.

33   Companies believe that defects in knowledge and skill can be remedied in training. But, to return to the other, and more substantial criticism of education, the first task is to change the attitudes which the system has instilled, and which the families have allowed to go unchecked, since the blame is commonly put upon parents who do not bring up their children properly.

34   The point has been made that the focus of the complaint is something about individuality. Young people put their private lives, and more generally their individual concerns, above that of the company and of other "groups." The evidence for this, it is claimed, can be adduced from their bad manners, lack of respect for their elders—especially their parents—and their rejection of those values which are believed to be integral to the maintenance of Japanese society which, it should be remembered, is regarded by its members as superior to all others.

35   One giant company with whom I explored this matter explained that they administered questionnaires to recruits which showed the

following personal and social defects. They were too inclined to "pursue rationalism," saw a clear demarcation between work and leisure, and were hostile to authority. They tended to be interested in building "a framework for individual life." Furthermore, the recruits of 1988 were much more guilty of such behaviour than those of ten years ago, who were, in any case bad enough.

36   The logical conclusion is that training must seek to do nothing less than to demolish this negative experience. One does not have to travel far to hear views from industrial educators like this:

> School makes them self-oriented: they do not understand obligations and duties.

37   This is summed up in a comprehensive account of company education:

> The education of new recruits, including graduates, at this time was aimed at removing the last vestiges of school life, raising their awareness of being adult members of society, and teaching them the company's philosophy embodied in the company's operation since its foundation.[22]

38   Despite such problems the first thing that must strike the visitor is the considerable commitment, notably by bigger companies, to education and training. This commitment and the experience which underlie it, was summed up by Numakura Toshio, General Manager, and Kuma Hisao, Senior Engineer, of the Hitachi Institute of Technology. Speaking at the 1986 World Conference on Continuing Engineering Education held in Florida, they pointed out that the central planks of company policy were Research and Development (R&D), and employee training. They went on to say that these had been recognised as vital, and made the pivot of company policy by the founder, Odaira Namihei:

> He started Hitachi's in-house school system almost at the same time as the foundation of Hitachi Ltd in 1910. It has contributed largely to make Hitachi what it is today.[23]

39   There is plenty of evidence to support this claim about the eminence of training. One investigation points out that:

> The personnel division, the section in charge of educational training in particular, was given strategic importance in the late 1970s as the division controlling human resources, rather than simply conducting recruitment and training.[24]

40   In the course of field research for this account, it was claimed, and demonstrated, that the planning and execution of training takes place at a very senior level, with the active involvement of the most powerful people in the company. There are other measures of the fact that training is seen as important. One is the acceptance of the need for training to take place often. In one of the companies studied, it was pointed out

that it would be impossible for an employee to go for more than a year without being engaged in some training or other. Another measure lies in the fact that training takes place at all levels, which was verified in a survey carried out by the Recruit Co. in 1983 which concluded that:

> ...new recruits and middle management are subject to particularly extensive educational training with all employees being subject to in-house training of some kind or another.[25]

41   The survey went on to show that on a scale of 1 (not very important) to 5 (extremely important) and applied to a range of seniority, the rating of the importance of educational training went from 4.0 to 4.4, except for "top" management. Here no doubt were the last vestiges of an increasingly obsolete belief that people at the top do not need education. But even so, the importance ascribed to it in respect of that group was 3.6.[26]

42   There are some interesting, and rather remarkable, examples of the recognition that the most senior staff need to engage in the kind of reflective activity which training provides. The very top managers of one major automobile company which was studied in the course of this research periodically went out on what was called "town watch." One of the central problems facing an organisation which is, in the nature of things cooped up and isolated from the community, is keeping up with current, and volatile, opinion about design. In an attempt to combat this the senior staff spend about four days standing in one of the most fashionable areas of Tokyo, making notes on what seems to be the latest styles and fashion, in choice of colour for example. Afterwards they analyse and discuss their findings. This is supplemented with discussion about fashion in a number of fields with the top designers in those fields.

43   Nor apparently is this approach unique. Saba reports that:

> Toshiba has established a Lifestyle Research Institute in one of Tokyo's most fashionable districts, Harajuku, which would correspond to Chelsea in London. The centre investigates the tastes and needs of young people, who will determine the nature of future demand trends. Most of the major consumer electronics' companies have established similar organisations....[27]

44   Apart from the rather diffuse, and intangible creation of an "atmosphere" or "culture," companies employ some interesting learning frameworks designed to achieve these aims. Many companies, and all of those visited in the course of this research, state specifically that "education includes training in courtesy and basic skills." Nor is it difficult to find examples. One company in the survey, lists as a prime objective in its initial training for new employees the acquisition "of proper attitudes and manners to use in relation to clients' agents and guests." Another company

administers a self-assessment exercise on etiquette. They then issue a booklet which demonstrates, in words and pictures, the correct way in which to exchange business cards, how to dress for work, how to behave in public (giving up a seat for an old lady for instance), and how to seat people, according to their status, in a car.

45   The rationale for all this is that as well as the desirability of maintaining those courtesies which are vital to Japanese life, people must now begin to realise that they are first and foremost representatives of the company. They are physical representatives of it, and other people will judge the company by their behaviour.

46   Concomitant with such exercises is a carefully studied attempt early in the training programme to reassert the group, and to ensure the subordination of all to it, and its most important form, the company. An important element in this is the instillation of the culture of the company. It should be noted that this means the particular company culture. The success of this effort can be gauged from the observation that:

> ...one can guess the company of a person after he or she has worked there for some time because the person embodies the managerial philosophy and the behaviour patterns of the company.[28]

47   Quite what this means is difficult to gauge in practice. The Japanese company commonly sets out a "Statement of Mission," "Corporate Philosophy" and "Basic Principles." In themselves these do not reveal much. Nissan has, as one of its corporate principles, "to foster the development of an active and vital group of people who are ready and willing at all times to take on the challenge of achieving new goals." One of Honda's principles is rather exotic—"never to part with our dreams or our youthful approach." The advertising agency Dentsu, is more practical: "Manipulate those around you; over the long run the manipulators rise way above the manipulated." Sony, remarkably, has no statement of mission,[29] and no corporate precepts, although Morita of Sony describes how they devised "a kind of prospectus and philosophical statement for the company":

> If it were possible to establish conditions where persons could become united with a firm spirit of teamwork and exercise to their hearts' desire their technological capacity, then such an organisation could bring untold pleasure and untold benefits.[30]

48   The emphasis given the company philosophy and culture has profound effects on the way in which the company operates. Long-term employment (which used to be taken for granted by Western companies) ensures a continuity of philosophy which even survives the most senior of changes. If juniors expect to stay with the company then they will be considering how it should be in 20 years. The long-term view permeates everything, including training:

If top management looks down at middle and lower management and is always pressing them to show profits this year or next, as is common in the West, and fires these managers for not producing profits, it is killing the company. If a middle manager says his plan or programme may not break even now, but will make big profits ten years from now, nobody will listen to him, and he may even be fired.[31]

49 This notion of a company culture is developing in other countries too, including the United Kingdom. In one very successful clothes shop there, the creation and transmission of the desired culture centres around conscious informality, the maximising of contact between exemplary senior staff and newcomers, and a graded system of competence evidenced by a series of badges carrying prestige.

50 The total pattern which emerges is important both for the commitment to industrial education, and the nature of its content. Despite the exclusion of large groups, women, minorities, contract workers, and the self-employed, and even allowing for the seminal beginning of job mobility, for the managers tenure and stability are the most important elements in their professional lives. It is also the case that the group remains the most important social dynamic, even though so much concern is expressed about its allegedly stagnating influence. Put these together with the acceptance that, for whatever reason, companies do not have very lively expectations of the educational benefits of the formal educational system, and the background is complete for the training and educational enterprise. This is aimed at a stable workforce, of demonstrated high intelligence and industry, which has probably been adversely affected by education, and which needs its priorities re-established. These are that the individual must give way to the group, and all must give way to the needs of the company, as expressed in the culture of the company.

References

1. Institute for International Cooperation, Japan International Cooperation Agency (JICA), *Japan's Industrialisation and Human Resources Development: The Role and Characteristics of In-House Training,* published jointly by the International Cooperation Service Centre, and The International Development Journal Co. Ltd, n.d. 1988, p. 5.
2. Morita Akio, with Reingold, E. M. and Shimomura, M., *Made in Japan: Akio Morita and Sony,* Collins, 1987, p. 132.
3. *Ibid.,* p. 152.
4. van Wolferen, Karel, *The Enigma of Japanese Power: People and Politics in a Stateless Nation,* Macmillan, 1989, pp. 66–7.
5. Morita, p. 212.
6. JICA, p. 5.
7. Dore, Ronald P. and Sako, Mari, *How the Japanese Learn to Work,* Routledge, 1989, p. 78.

8. Saba, Shoichi, "The Japanese Style of Doing Business," *The RSA Journal,* October 1989, United Kingdom, p. 721.
9. *Ibid.,* p. 717.
10. *Ibid.*
11. Dore and Sako, p. 78.
12. van Wolferen, pp. 162–3.
13. Benjamin Duke, The *Guardian,* 28 November 1989.
14. Buruma, Ian, *A Japanese Mirror: Heroes and Villains of Japanese Culture,* Penguin Books, 1988, p. 183. By *giri* is meant a sense of honour, duty of debt, in this case to the founder of the theatre.
15. *Ibid.,* p. 185.
16. *Ibid.,* pp. 159–60.
17. Kobayashi, Yotaro, *Look Japan,* November 1989, p. 13.
18. Morita, pp. 143–4.
19. Saba, p. 717.
20. The *Guardian,* 18 April 1984.
21. Saba, p. 721.
22. JICA, p. 7.
23. Numakura Toshio and Kuma Hisao, "The Educational System of the Hitachi Institute of Technology" in the Proceedings of the World Conference of Continuing Engineering Education, ASEE Continuing Professional Development Division, IEEE Education Society, 1986, p. 883.
24. JICA, p. 9.
25. *Ibid.*
26. *Ibid.,* p. 4.
27. Saba, p. 719.
28. *Ibid.,* p. 3.
29. These examples are taken from "The Corporate Creeds of Eleven Successful Companies" in *Japan Echo,* vol. xvii, Special Issue, 1990.
30. Morita, p. 83.
31. *Ibid.,* p. 200.

Reading for Meaning

1. What cultural and business reasons does Thomas give for the policy of lifetime employment generally practiced in Japan?

2. What advantages does the "salaryman" in Japan enjoy? What are possible detriments to being an employee for life?

3. Describe the dynamics between the individual and the group in Japan. How do they compare with the relative importance of the individual and the group in the United States? Consider drawing your examples from education and the workplace.

4. What is Thomas's purpose for writing this essay? What attitude does he express toward his subject?

5. What criticisms do Japanese companies have against education in Japan? What kind of education and training are workers likely to get from their company? Have your employers provided you with training and educational opportunities?

Comparing Texts

1. In the essay "An Anthropologist Learns from the Hopi" (chapter 9) Dorothy Lee describes the relationship between the individual and the larger group in the Hopi culture. Compare the dynamics that she describes to the relationship between the "salaryman" and the corporate "community" that Williamson discusses.

2. Read the description of the corporate culture of International Business Machines (IBM) reprinted here. This excerpt comes from the book by Ross and Kathryn Petras, *Inside Track: How to Get into and Succeed in America's Prestigious Companies.* The book gives information about major U.S. corporations, including a brief history, a description of what it is like to work for that corporation, and the kinds of jobs available for employees, as well as the type of worker the new employee is likely to meet. The book was written to help prospective employees in their job search. Analyze the language in this text to determine the "beliefs" under which this corporation operates. Then compare the "culture"—the assumptions about employees and the corporation—described in this essay to assumptions typical of the corporate culture in Japan, according to J. E. Thomas.

As Seen from the Outside

1 There's no avoiding IBM. And that's something the other computer companies get a little tired of.

2 No wonder. Even its competitors concede that IBM is the undisputed leader in the field. Where "Big Blue" goes, the others follow. Well, of course IBM followed the others into the personal computer market. But now the IBM PC has a one-third share of the total personal computer market, and the other computer companies are forced to come up with IBM clones. It's all in the name.

3 But IBM didn't start out as IBM. It began with three other initials—C-T-R—and Thomas Watson, a former employee of a three-letter competitor, NCR (National Cash Register). The Computing-Tabulating-Recording Co. was formed in 1911 when the Computing Scale Co., the Tabulating Machine Co., and the International Time Recording Co. merged.

4 Three years later, Thomas Watson joined CTR, and in 1924 the company was renamed International Business Machines, or IBM.

5 Under Mr. Watson (always *Mr.* Watson at IBM) the company acquired its distinctive conservative character, and a reputation for good service. It also acquired a motto—"Think!"—which Watson used to exhort his sales force.

6 And it worked wonders. Today, IBM is ranked No. 6 on the Fortune 500. It's the world's largest producer of computers and electric typewriters, doing business in 130 countries. Big Blue is still rolling on, most recently into the telecommunications field. In 1984, it bought the remaining shares

in the ROLM Corporation (a major manufacturer of computerized business communications [PBX] systems), and acquired a 16 percent interest in MCI Communications (the nation's second largest long-distance telephone service).

7   In competition with another three letter competitor, AT&T, IBM is getting into telecommunications. Meanwhile, AT&T is getting into computers. The battle is just beginning . . .

Heard at the Water Cooler—What It's Really Like to Work Here

8   It's tough to hear *anything* at the water cooler—unless you're one of the IBM army. This is a company that firmly believes in Uncle Sam's old saying that "loose lips sink ships."

9   "Once you're accepted and you do your work, you won't be let go," said one employee, "Unless, of course, you start stealing secrets and selling them to the Japanese companies!"

10 Or if you talk to outsiders about the company. IBM has a very strict interview policy, we were told—so we weren't able to get interviews with employees through an open route.

11 But we didn't give up there, and we managed to scout out a few personal contacts working at Big Blue. And, through them, we learned that IBM apparently isn't keeping employees from talking because they're unhappy. On the contrary, IBM isn't hiding anything but trade secrets (something we didn't ask about), and real employee enthusiasm. You just have to get behind the tight security to uncover it.

12 And security there is. Some IBM offices and plants have a double security check, for employees and nonemployees alike. Staffers wear picture ID badges. It's like walking into a fortress. But those inside the fortress walls find the atmosphere less military than parental. It's all part of absorbing and accepting the IBM way.

13 One staffer explained IBM's principles. "There are golden rules here—like respect for the individual. Everybody has to have respect for the next person, whether they're doing the job or not. Respect for the individual is our No. 1 priority."

14 It's even set down in print. IBM puts out a booklet for employees, stating the company's philosophy. Listed as IBM's "enduring principles, the cornerstones of its success" are number one, respect for the individual, two, customer service, and three, excellence.

15 One employee summed up IBM succinctly, "They'll take care of you if you take care of them."

16 And that's what IBM staffers do—very quietly.

17 **People.**   There's the traditional picture of the IBM employee—white shirt, blue suit, serious, loyal, and dedicated. A sort of corporate Boy Scout, if you will.

18 So what's the truth behind the myth? First of all, scrap the uniform—sort of. "It doesn't necessarily have to be a white shirt, blue tie kind of

thing," said one staffer. "I don't think they won't hire you if you wear a *blue* shirt. As a matter of fact, I did wear a blue shirt when I was interviewing."

19   Basically, IBM is big on "professional appearance," like most major corporations, but maybe a little more so. Although an employee pointed out that employees on the production lines are allowed to dress casually, "as long as it's neat." So much for the myth of suited employees from the bottom on up.

20   But, obviously, clothes don't make the employee. What truly seems to distinguish an IBM employee is dedication—both to work and to the company itself. It's actually a two-way street. IBM has a policy called "full employment," meaning no layoffs. "You have their promise," said a staffer. "And it has never been broken. So you do have a lifetime career with IBM."

21   That's why employees repay IBM's loyalty to them with loyalty to the company. As one employee explained, "It's a career here. It's not a question of 'I want a job; I'll work at IBM.'" So IBM staffers, on the whole, do their best not to rock the boat. And who can blame them? All in all, it seems as if they've got a pretty good deal.

22   As long as they believe in what IBM believes in.

23   **Jobs.**   Corporate benevolence doesn't mean that employees don't have to work hard here. One staffer termed the work "demanding," adding "but they do take care of you." Of course.

24   Still, as far as moving ahead goes, it's up to the individual to a great extent. Like many other technical companies, IBM offers different jobs in a variety of departments—from sales and marketing to technical positions in design and development, production, manufacturing, applications programming, and much more.

25   Given the number of different positions, training also varies. In some areas, it's on-the-job training; in others, employees go through formal training programs. But for all the differences, there are similarities from job to job and department to department in IBM.

26   First, there's IBM's "Open Door Policy." Employees who feel they have a problem with their manager can go over his or her head. "It's called 'skip level,'" explained a staffer. "And, actually you can go all the way to the top if you're getting a raw deal. You can go *all* the way—up to the chairman of the board."

27   There's also something called the "Speak Up Program," under which employees with a question, complaint, or comment that they don't want to discuss with their manager may mail in a Speak Up Form. According to a company brochure, "you'll get an answer by the person deemed most qualified to give it. And your anonymity is assured." The answer will be mailed to the employee's house, and only the Speak Up administrator will know his or her identity.

28   In addition, IBM believes strongly in promoting from within—something most employees find very attractive. Especially those who intend to work their way up into management. Said one such staffer,

"Management is all from the ranks. It's nothing like 'here's a guy from GE who just snuck in there.'"

29   As with other high tech firms, there's a dual career ladder for technical staffers. Upon reaching a certain level, staffers who qualify may elect to branch off into the management side or stick with a purely technical career track.

30   "You come in as an engineer and, theoretically, you can get into the management chain, get into higher level management and become president of a division," explained an employee.

31   Promotion and pay are based largely on a merit system. Employees sit down with their managers, discuss job responsibilities, and make out a performance plan based upon them. After that, managers periodically go over the performance plan with the employees. There's no formal time frame established for those meetings. As one staffer described it, "A lot of managers will say, 'Hey, why don't you come into my office one day. Stop in any time and we'll bull.'" When the formal performance evaluation period is up, an employee and his manager discuss how well the employee met the plan and fill out a Performance Planning, Counseling and Evaluation Form, which is then reviewed by the manager's manager.

32   One employee summed up the process: "Basically, if you do well for the company, they'll reward you. If you don't, they won't. It's really as simple as that."

Ideas for Writing

1. In large measure, the group defines the individual in Japan. Being denied approval by the group can lead to "altruistic" suicides according to one researcher. Margaret Mead reports a similar dependence on the group in Balinese culture. The Balinese who find themselves cut off from their people grow sick and are said to be *paling*, literally "disoriented," because they have lost the protective "framework of life." Write a paper in which you explore the individual's dependence on the group in the United States. Consider focusing on a particular age group or activity—work or school, for example.

2. How do the training programs in Japanese companies that J. E. Thomas describes compare to training that U.S. workers are likely to receive? Try to establish how the training reflects the "culture" of the company.

Writing before Reading

How important do you think it is to be punctual? Are there times when you prefer to be late to an appointment or event? What social forces have shaped your attitude toward time?

SOCIAL TIME: THE HEARTBEAT OF CULTURE

Robert Levine with Ellen Wolff

Robert Levine is a professor of psychology at California State University at Fresno. While a visiting professor of psychology at the federal university in Niteroi, Brazil, he observed how the Brazilians' concept of "social time" resulted in a more relaxed, less frantic way of life than he had been used to in the United States. His observations in the classroom prompted him to study other societies' ideas of time. With the help of former student and freelance writer Ellen Wolff, Levine compiled his informal research and observations of cultures that are driven by "clock time" and those that rely more on "social time," as do Brazilians. The article was originally published in Psychology Today *(March 1985).*

Facts about Brazil

The Federative Republic of Brazil, the largest country in South America, occupies nearly half the continent and ranks as the fifth largest country in the world. Its population, however, is less than half that of the United States, which is the world's fourth largest country in area. In 1500 the Spaniard, Vicente Pinzon, became the first European in Brazil. He was followed by Pedro Cabral who claimed the territory for Portugal in the same year. The Portuguese didn't begin settlement of Brazil until 1532. Brazil was given its independence in 1822, but was ruled by descendants of the Portuguese king, John VI, until 1889 when the army, aided by a popular revolt, overthrew the Portuguese emperor. In the 1950s the country's capital moved from Rio de Janeiro to Brasilia in an effort to develop Brazil's interior. Since that time Brazil has alternated between military and civilian leadership.

1 *"If a man does not keep pace with his companions, perhaps it is because he hears a different drummer."* This thought by Thoreau strikes a chord in so many people that it has become part of our language. We use the phrase "the beat of a different drummer" to explain any pace of life unlike our own. Such colorful vagueness reveals how informal our rules of time really are. The world over, children simply "pick up" their society's time concepts as they mature. No dictionary clearly defines the meaning of "early" or "late" for them or for strangers who stumble over the maddening incongruities between the time sense they bring with them and the one they face in a new land.

2 I learned this firsthand, a few years ago, and the resulting culture shock led me halfway around the world to find answers. It seemed clear that time "talks." But what is it telling us?

3   My journey started shortly after I accepted an appointment as visiting professor of psychology at the federal university in Niteroi, Brazil, a midsized city across the bay from Rio de Janeiro. As I left home for my first day of class, I asked someone the time. It was 9:05 a.m., which allowed me time to relax and look around the campus before my 10 o'clock lecture. After what I judged to be half an hour, I glanced at a clock I was passing. It said 10:20! In panic, I broke for the classroom, followed by gentle calls of "Hola, professor" and "Tudo bem, professor?" from unhurried students, many of whom, I later realized, were my own. I arrived breathless to find an empty room.

4   Frantically, I asked a passerby the time. "Nine forty-five" was the answer. No, that couldn't be. I asked someone else. "Nine fifty-five." Another said: "Exactly 9:43." The clock in a nearby office read 3:15. I had learned my first lesson about Brazilians: Their timepieces are consistently inaccurate. And nobody minds.

5   My class was scheduled from 10 until noon. Many students came late, some very late. Several arrived after 10:30. A few showed up closer to 11. Two came after that. All of the latecomers wore the relaxed smiles that I came, later, to enjoy. Each one said hello, and although a few apologized briefly, none seemed terribly concerned about lateness. They assumed that I understood.

6   The idea of Brazilians arriving late was not a great shock. I had heard about "mãnha," the Portuguese equivalent of "mañana" in Spanish. This term, meaning "tomorrow" or "the morning," stereotypes the Brazilian who puts off the business of today until tomorrow. The real surprise came at noon that first day, when the end of class arrived.

7   Back home in California, I never need to look at a clock to know when the class hour is ending. The shuffling of books is accompanied by strained expressions that say plaintively, "I'm starving. . . . I've got to go to the bathroom. . . . I'm going to suffocate if you keep us one more second." (The pain usually becomes unbearable at two minutes to the hour in undergraduate classes and five minutes before the close of graduate classes.)

8   When noon arrived in my first Brazilian class, only a few students left immediately. Others slowly drifted out during the next 15 minutes, and some continued asking me questions long after that. When several remaining students kicked off their shoes at 12:30, I went into my own "starving/bathroom/suffocation" routine.

9   I could not, in all honesty, attribute their lingering to my superb teaching style. I had just spent two hours lecturing on statistics in halting Portuguese. Apparently, for many of my students, staying late was simply of no more importance than arriving late in the first place. As I observed this casual approach in infinite variations during the year, I learned that the "mãnha" stereotype oversimplified the real Anglo/Brazilian differences in conceptions of time. Research revealed a more complex picture.

10   With the assistance of colleagues Laurie West and Harry Reis, I compared the time sense of 91 male and female students in Niteroi with that of 107 similar students at California State University in Fresno. The universities are similar in academic quality and size, and the cities are both secondary metropolitan centers with populations of about 350,000.

11   We asked students about their perceptions of time in several situations, such as what they would consider late or early for a hypothetical lunch appointment with a friend. The average Brazilian student defined lateness for lunch as 33 1/2 minutes after the scheduled time, compared to only 19 minutes for the Fresno students. But Brazilians also allowed an average of about 54 minutes before they'd consider someone early, while the Fresno students drew the line at 24.

12   Are Brazilians simply more flexible in their concepts of time and punctuality? And how does this relate to the stereotype of the apathetic, fatalistic and irresponsible Latin temperament? When we asked students to give typical reasons for lateness, the Brazilians were less likely to attribute it to a lack of caring than the North Americans were. Instead, they pointed to unforeseen circumstances that the person couldn't control. Because they seemed less inclined to feel personally responsible for being late, they also expressed less regret for their own lateness and blamed others less when they were late.

13   We found similar differences in how students from the two countries characterized people who were late for appointments. Unlike their North American counterparts, the Brazilian students believed that a person who is consistently late is probably more successful than one who is consistently on time. They seemed to accept the idea that someone of status is expected to arrive late. Lack of punctuality is a badge of success.

14   Even within our own country, of course, ideas of time and punctuality vary considerably from place to place. Different regions and even cities have their own distinct rhythms and rules. Seemingly simple words like "now," snapped out by an impatient New Yorker, and "later," said by a relaxed Californian, suggest a world of difference. Despite our familiarity with these homegrown differences in tempo, problems with time present a major stumbling block to Americans abroad. Peace Corps volunteers told researchers James Spradley of Macalester College and Mark Phillips of the University of Washington that their greatest difficulties with other people, after language problems, were the general pace of life and the punctuality of others. Formal "clock time" may be a standard on which the world agrees, but "social time," the heartbeat of society, is something else again.

15   How a country paces its social life is a mystery to most outsiders, one that we're just beginning to unravel. Twenty-six years ago, anthropologist Edward Hall noted in *The Silent Language* that informal patterns of time "are seldom, if ever, made explicit. They exist in the air around us. They are either familiar and comfortable, or unfamiliar and wrong."

When we realize we are out of step, we often blame the people around us to make ourselves feel better.

16   Appreciating cultural differences in time sense becomes increasingly important as modern communications put more and more people in daily contact. If we are to avoid misreading issues that involve time perceptions, we need to understand better our own cultural biases and those of others.

17   When people of different cultures interact, the potential for misunderstanding exists on many levels. For example, members of Arab and Latin cultures usually stand much closer when they are speaking to people than we usually do in the United States, a fact we frequently misinterpret as aggression or disrespect. Similarly, we assign personality traits to groups with a pace of life that is markedly faster or slower than our own. We build ideas of national character, for example, around the traditional Swiss and German ability to "make the trains run on time." Westerners like ourselves define punctuality using precise measures of time: 5 minutes, 15 minutes, an hour. But according to Hall, in many Mediterranean Arab cultures there are only three sets of time: no time at all, now (which is of varying duration) and forever (too long). Because of this, Americans often find difficulty in getting Arabs to distinguish between waiting a long time and a very long time.

18   According to historian Will Durant, "No man in a hurry is quite civilized." What do our time judgments say about our attitude toward life? How can a North American, coming from a land of digital precision, relate to a North African who may consider a clock "the devil's mill"?

19   Each language has a vocabulary of time that does not always survive translation. When we translated our questionnaires into Portuguese for my Brazilian students, we found that English distinctions of time were not readily articulated in their language. Several of our questions concerned how long the respondent would wait for someone to arrive, as compared with when they hoped for arrival or actually expected the person would come. In Portuguese, the verbs "to wait for," "to hope for" and "to expect" are all translated as "esperar." We had to add further words of explanation to make the distinction clear to the Brazilian students.

20   To avoid these language problems, my Fresno colleague Kathy Bartlett and I decided to clock the pace of life in other countries by using as little language as possible. We looked directly as three basic indicators of time: the accuracy of a country's bank clocks, the speed at which pedestrians walked and the average time it took a postal clerk to sell us a single stamp. In six countries on three continents, we made observations in both the nation's largest urban area and a medium-sized city: Japan (Tokyo and Sendai), Taiwan (Taipei and Tainan), Indonesia (Jakarta and Solo), Italy (Rome and Florence), England (London and Bristol) and the United States (New York City and Rochester).

21   What we wanted to know was: Can we speak of a unitary concept called "pace of life"? What we've learned suggests that we can. There appears to be a very strong relationship between the accuracy of clock time, walking speed and postal efficiency across the countries we studied.

22   We checked 15 clocks in each city, selecting them at random in downtown banks and comparing the time they showed with that reported by the local telephone company. In Japan, which leads the way in accuracy, the clocks averaged just over half a minute early or late. Indonesian clocks, the least accurate, were more than three minutes off the mark.

23   I will be interested to see how the digital-information age will affect our perceptions of time. In the United States today, we are reminded of the exact hour of the day more than ever, through little symphonies of beeps emanating from people's digital watches. As they become the norm, I fear our sense of precision may take an absurd twist. The other day, when I asked for the time, a student looked at his watch and replied, "Three twelve and eighteen seconds."

24   *"'Will you walk a little faster?' said a whiting to a snail. 'There's a porpoise close behind us, and he's treading on my tail.'"*

25   So goes the rhyme from *Alice in Wonderland*, which also gave us that famous symbol of haste, the White Rabbit. He came to mind often as we measured the walking speeds in our experimental cities. We clocked how long it took pedestrians to walk 100 feet along a main downtown street during business hours on clear days. To eliminate the effects of socializing, we observed only people walking alone, timing at least 100 in each city. We found, once again, that the Japanese led the way, averaging just 20.7 seconds to cover the distance. The English nosed out the Americans for second place—21.6 to 22.5 seconds—and the Indonesians again trailed the pack, sauntering along at 27.2 seconds. As you might guess, speed was greater in the larger city of each nation than in its smaller one.

26   Our final measurement, the average time it took postal clerks to sell one stamp, turned out to be less straightforward than we expected. In each city, including those in the United States, we presented clerks with a note in the native language requesting a common-priced stamp—a 20-center in the United States, for example. They were also handed paper money, the equivalent of a $5 bill. In Indonesia, this procedure led to more than we bargained for.

27   At the large central post office in Jakarta, I asked for the line to buy stamps and was directed to a group of private vendors sitting outside. Each of them hustled for my business: "Hey, good stamps, mister!" "Best stamps here!" In the smaller city of Solo, I found a volleyball game in progress when I arrived at the main post office on Friday afternoon. Business hours, I was told, were over. When I finally did get there during

28   business hours, the clerk was more interested in discussing relatives in America. Would I like to meet his uncle in Cincinnati? Which did I like better: California or the United States? Five people behind me in line waited patiently. Instead of complaining, they began paying attention to our conversation.

28   When it came to efficiency of service, however, the Indonesians were not the slowest, although they did place far behind the Japanese postal clerks, who averaged 25 seconds. That distinction went to the Italians, whose infamous postal service took 47 seconds on the average.

29   *"A man who wastes one hour of time has not discovered the meaning of life. . . . "*

30   That was Charles Darwin's belief, and many share it, perhaps at the cost of their health. My colleagues and I have recently begun studying the relationship between pace of life and well-being. Other researchers have demonstrated that a chronic sense of urgency is a basic component of the Type A, coronary-prone personality. We expect that future research will demonstrate that pace of life is related to rate of heart disease, hypertension, ulcers, suicide, alcoholism, divorce and other indicators of general psychological and physical well-being.

31   As you envision tomorrow's international society, do you wonder who will set the pace? Americans eye Japan carefully, because the Japanese are obviously "ahead of us" in measurable ways. In both countries, speed is frequently confused with progress. Perhaps looking carefully at the different paces of life around the world will help us distinguish more accurately between the two qualities. Clues are everywhere but sometimes hard to distinguish. You have to listen carefully to hear the beat of even your own drummer.

Reading for Meaning

1. How did Robert Levine's concept of time differ from that of his Brazilian students? What assumptions did he make about the students' lateness? Is there any evidence that his original impressions have changed?

2. How did attitudes toward arriving early and being late differ among students attending the federal university in Niteroi, Brazil, and those at California State University, Fresno? What misunderstandings might occur as a result of these differences?

3. In paragraph 18 Robert Levine asks how judgments about time predict our "attitude toward life." How does his study of the accuracy of clocks, the walking pace, and the postal service in six countries answer that question?

4. What did you think of Levine's connection between a society's concern for "clock time" and the pace at which the people live? Did the results of his study surprise you?

5. What attitudes about "clock time" or "social time" are typical of people you know.

Comparing Texts

1. In her "Introduction to *Cultural Misunderstandings*," which appears in chapter 1 of this book, Raymonde Carroll suggests that there are several things we can do that will help us understand behavior that seems very different from what we are used to. Examine her suggestions to determine which ones Robert Levine applied to his inquiry about Brazilians' use of time. Did he take any additional steps?

2. Robert Levine's informal study of the attention various cultures pay to "clock time" shows Japan ranking first for the accuracy of its clocks. In what ways does this Japanese preference for "clock time" over "social time" either correspond to or contradict the behavior of Japanese employees, the *salaryman* in particular, as described in J. E. Thomas's "Culture and the Communal Organisation" (page 270)?

Ideas for Writing

1. Imagine what it might be like to exchange the North American reliance on "clock time" for the Brazilians' preference for "social time." In what ways might this switch transform the world of business, politics, or everyday life?

2. Compare your own reliance on punctuality with a Brazilian student's idea of being "on time." What assumptions about time is each of you making?

CHAPTER 8
CUSTOM AND GENDER ROLES

First Thoughts

Primeras impresiones

Premières impressions

What I'm suggesting, then, is that every modern male has lying at the bottom of his psyche, a large, primitive being covered with hair down to his feet. Making contact with the Wild Man is the step the Eighties male or the Nineties male has yet to take. That bucketing-out process has yet to begin in our contemporary culture. . . .

Going down through water to touch the Wild Man at the bottom of the pond is quite a different matter. The being who stands up is frightening, and seems even more so now, when the corporations do so much work to produce the sanitized, hairless, shallow man. When man welcomes his responsiveness, or what we sometimes call his internal woman, he often feels warmer, more companionable, more alive. But when he approaches what I'll call the "deep male," he feels risk. Welcoming the Hairy Man *is* scary and risky, and it requires a different sort of courage. Contact with Iron John requires a willingness to descend into the male psyche and accept what's dark down there, including the *nourishing* . . . dark.

Robert Bly
Iron John

There is a Persian myth of the creation of the world which precedes the biblical one. In that myth a woman creates the world, and she creates it by the act of natural creativity which is hers and which cannot be duplicated by men. She gives birth to a great number of sons. The sons, greatly puzzled by this act which they cannot duplicate, become frightened. They think, "Who can tell us, that if she can *give* life, she cannot also *take life*." And so, because of their fear of this mysterious ability of woman, and of its reversible possibility, they kill her.

Frieda Fromm-Reichmann
"On the Denial of Woman's Sexual Pleasure"

D. H. Lawrence asserted that the sole purpose of literature is to depict the connections between man and woman because that relationship is "the central clue to human life." In a larger sense, the "central clue" to the makeup of any culture is the relative worth of men and women. That value determines the cultural expectations of each and the roles assigned to them. When we study the links between gender and culture, it is easy to see how the assumptions about gender held by our families, communities, workplaces, schools, and government help shape who we are and whether we feel encouraged in our lives or defeated at every turn.

Readings in this chapter explore the way culture shapes not only a society's expectations of men and women but also the individuals' own self-images and the choices open to them. What individuals do with the choices presented to them makes for character and individual integrity. Gordon Murray, an instructor and psychotherapist, bases "Picking on the Little Guy: In Boyhood and in the Battlefield" on personal experiences of the way boys learn to be bullies, both in childhood and later in the adult years. In "Mexican Masks" Octavio Paz discusses the psychology of the intensely masculine or "macho" culture of his countrymen. Sembene Ousmane writes a humorous debunking of polygyny in "The *Bilal's* Fourth Wife," a story about a *bilal* or caretaker for a village mosque. He is "past middle-age" when he decides to takes a fourth wife, who proves to be intelligent enough to outwit the *bilal* and to work the patriarchal legal system to her advantage. Whereas Ousmane writes about one woman's ability to gain control of her life within the context of a system that would seem to render her powerless, the narrator of Nawal El Saadawi's fictionalized memoir, "Growing Up Female in Egypt," reveals her daily humiliations and intense suffering as a female in a fiercely male-dominated culture. The next major readings, "Front and Rear: The Sexual Division of Labour in the Israeli Army" and "An Officer and a Feminist" examine women's role in the military as a reflection of the woman's position in her culture.

Writing before Reading

Are you the sort of person who tries to "get even" or do you have another approach to wrongdoing? Why do you think you have this attitude?

PICKING ON THE LITTLE GUY: IN BOYHOOD AND IN THE BATTLEFIELDS

Gordon Murray

Gordon Murray, originally from Chicago, Illinois, lives in San Francisco. He is a psychotherapist, consultant, and an instructor at John F. Kennedy University and New College. Murray's essay, "Picking on the Little Guy," was published in Boyhood, Growing Up Male: A Multicultural Anthology *(1993).*

Facts about the Persian Gulf War

The military action against Iraq's annexation of Kuwait has become known as the Persian Gulf War. The war lasted a little over a month—from January 16 to February 28, 1991. An international coalition of armed forces from 31 countries fought against the Iraqi army. In contrast to the protracted ground war that the United States fought in Vietnam, the Persian Gulf War was largely an air war and involved ground troops for only about 100 hours. Advanced military weaponry—such as the Tomahawk antimissile, laser guidance systems, and infrared tracking devices—kept hand-to-hand combat to a minimum. In response to the bombing of Teheran, Saddam Hussein ordered the bombing of Israeli targets in an attempt to draw Israel into the war. Under pressure from the United States, Israel stayed out of the fight. Ironically, the United States and other partners in the coalition had supplied arms to Iraq during that country's war with Iran (1980–1988). Those weapons were then used against Hussein's former allies.

1   During the Gulf War, I found myself in a discussion group organized by the Men's Center for Counseling and Psychotherapy in Berkeley. We'd come together to explore our feelings about the war. I was opposed, vehemently and sincerely. Yet I could feel a deeper, darker place—a mean place, a shadow place I'm uncomfortable acknowledging—where picking on the little guy felt good. And I found myself wondering how much of the war was about oil and democracy, and how much about how good it feels to beat someone up.

2   One of the men in our group, Peter, spoke of Elias Canetti's book *Crowds and Power,* a sort of psychological history, in which he develops the concept of the "sting." When someone more powerful than you makes you do something (a "command") you're left feeling wounded (the "sting") which impels you to pass the command on to another. Here's Canetti describing the process:

3   "Those most beset by commands are children. It is a miracle that they ever survive the pressure and do not collapse under the burden of

the commands laid on them by their parents and teachers. That they in turn, and in an equally cruel form, should give identical commands to their children is as natural as mastication or speech. What is surprising is the way in which commands are retained intact and unaltered from earliest childhood, ready to be used again as soon as the next generation provides victims.... It is as though a man pulled out an arrow which had hit him, fitted that same arrow to his bow and shot it again.

4 "The sting forms during the carrying out of the command. It detaches itself from the command and, as an exact image, imprints itself on the performer.... It remains isolated within the person concerned, a foreign body lodged in his flesh.... It is very difficult to get rid of the sting.... For this to happen there must be an exact repetition of the original command-situation, but in *reverse*. This is what the sting waits for through months, years and decades.... When this moment comes, the sting seizes its opportunity and hastens to fall on its victim."

5 I can remember the sting from my boyhood. One incident in particular illustrates perfectly how I received a sting and then passed it on. Quite often on my way home from school, Reed Lincoln used to threaten to throw me off the bridge onto the railroad tracks. I was, naturally, terrified. The terror lodged deep within me—fifteen years later I still dreamt about the bridge: I cross the bridge on the way home from school with my friend Bob B. We are eating home-made cookies. The bridge is long, deserted, icy. Under it an icy torrent splashes high into the air. I am frightened; we eat cookies as we cross.

6 My parents understood something of my terror. My father took me to a jujitsu school. I remember him taking me on the "L" to downtown Chicago. I remember a large empty cold room with white mats on the floor. I remember throwing the robust instructor backwards over my head. I imagine they meant to reassure me that I could master a force bigger and stronger than myself. I lasted one session. Perhaps it helped a little, yet I still felt small, cold, afraid.

7 A few years after I received the sting from Reed, my mother began getting phone calls from Mrs. McNally. Her son Buddy was complaining of being bullied on his way home from school. The bully? Me.

8 Canetti says the sting wants revenge in a scene much like the original one. Picking on a weak little kid filled the bill for me. To master my own humiliation, I needed to prove to myself I wasn't the little guy anymore, that someone else was. By tormenting Buddy, I was able to fix a little of whatever Reed's terrorism had broken in me. In Canetti's image, I pulled out Reed's arrow that had hit me, fitted that same arrow to *my* bow and shot it again, hitting little Buddy McNally.

9 All this my mother tells me. But all I remember is the sting. I'd banished the uncomfortable memory of myself as tormentor, passing on the sting.

10 As I thought about the sting, I remembered a particularly brutal murder here in San Francisco a while back. In this case, the sting was passed

on quickly, in a matter of days. A gay man in his fifties named Smoot was found murdered in his apartment. Nothing was stolen; the motive must have been something less obvious than need or greed. They found the culprit, a young man. He claimed in his defense that Smoot had made unwelcome sexual advances towards him. As his story unfolded, it turned out that not long before he murdered Smoot, a group of the young man's peers had raped him with a broom handle.

11 Gang-raped with a broom handle. To be physically violated, to be invaded in that most utterly private and taboo place, to suffer powerlessly this public ridicule, and, most likely, to have no one in whom to confide this humiliation. What deep unspeakable shame must have lodged inside him at that time?

12 And so the sting lodged in the young man. The days that passed after the rape may have felt like years. When the chance came to pass on the sting, he took it, ruthlessly, and what is worse, guiltlessly.

13 So the sting is a way we, as boys and later as men, attempt to heal our hurts. We pass them on to others. What outlets do we have, after all, for our hurts? We learn from the culture that we're supposed to appear strong; not let things bother us; not give in to hurt or pain; not cry. So we bury the hurt, the pain, the anger, the shame—the stings of our boyhood. We forget about them. But when we find someone weaker than us, the buried feelings take their long-awaited revenge. It is our desperate attempt to heal ourselves.

14 This is not a new idea. Freud spoke of the repetition compulsion in which we find a somewhat disguised way to re-enact old traumas and thereby heal them. Nor is it unique to boys. Perhaps girls have more emotional outlets as children—girls tend to be socialized to cry more easily, they tend to have more cultural permission to show vulnerability, they talk over their problems more easily with dolls and, later, friends—but no doubt wounded girls grow into wounded women and wounded mothers. No doubt, their stings are passed to their mates, lovers, children.

15 But boys and men put a particular spin on the repetition compulsion. We elevate it to an art form, we institutionalize it, celebrate it. It becomes a ritual of manhood, a rite of passage, a call to war.

16 Back in Berkeley, where we'd come to discuss the war, we wondered if there were such a thing as a collective sting. As I thought about it, several pieces of the Gulf War puzzle came together in a story that sounds suspiciously like boys picking fights after school, but is really the stuff of headlines and death.

17 The day after Lyndon Johnson ordered the first bombing of North Vietnam, he made his famous remark about his enemy's penis: "I didn't just screw Ho Chi Minh, I cut his pecker off." Of a member of his Administration who was becoming doubtful of the war, he said, "Hell, he has to squat to piss." Sure, Johnson was a plain-talking Texan, but these sentiments are buried deep in the American male psyche: losers are like men

who get anally penetrated, men who are eunuchs, men who are like women. That our elected leader can say such things is simply evidence that homophobia and misogyny are pillars of the American male's manhood.

18   Johnson clung tenaciously to his pledge not to be the first American president to lose a war. This unwillingness to back down helped the Vietnam War unfold, like a Greek tragedy, to our inevitable defeat. The sting of that first defeat lodged deep in our collective psyche.

19   George Bush had been accused of being a "wimp" during his campaign for President. He overcame the accusation by becoming ugly, mean-spirited, ruthless. But even after the election, could doubts about his own manhood be very far under the surface of his own bravado, or our public assessment of him? Was trashing Dukakis enough to rid him of this sting?

20   When Iraq invaded Kuwait, George Bush found the perfect opportunity to pass on the personal sting of being called a "wimp," and the collective sting of Vietnam. He made our collective sting an explicit reason for going to war: there would be "no more Vietnams." Vietnam had proven a tougher enemy than we'd thought. Bush and the military built an image of the Iraqi forces as powerful and "elite," and prepared us to pounce.

21   A new generation of eighteen-year-old American boys had been born, come of age, and were ready for initiation into manhood. They were particularly ready to hear Bush's call to war.

22   So we went to war: we massacred uncounted tens of thousands of soldiers and civilians, while losing a few hundred of our own. Under the surface reasons given for the Gulf War were three powerful forces: a generation of boys were becoming men through the ritual of war; Bush was passing on his personal sting; and, most importantly, the sting of Vietnam was removed from the flesh of our collective body politic and hurled, bloody, deep into a Middle Eastern desert people we understood so poorly. Only one outcome of the war is certain: sooner or later this sting, too, will be removed and passed on, with consequences no one can predict.

23   So, I wonder, is there a way out? Are we doomed to bury our stings only to have them reappear later? Or are there ways of exposing and expressing the pain so it needn't be passed on?

24   I tend toward optimism, and see around me many ways men are trying to uncover their wounds and express them in healthy ways rather than live them out through lovers, families, children. Surely, for example, one of the reasons Robert Bly and the new men's movement have been so phenomenally popular is that men find it a safe place to expose personal wounds and experiment with ancient healing techniques: drumming, dancing, storytelling. Easy as it is to make fun of this movement, its wide appeal tells us much about men's need to grieve.

25   My own path has been through psychotherapy. As a therapist, I see men discover and express their buried stings, and know that this can be a powerful and effective path to healing. Here's a story from my practice:

26   Robert came to me for psychotherapy because he found himself flying into fits of rage towards his girlfriend for reasons which seemed disproportionately petty. They usually happened when she had left him: she'd get out of the car to run a short errand, take longer than she'd said she would, and he would become enraged. He cared about this person, this relationship; he was afraid his uncontrolled anger would destroy it.

27   Before long we identified the real objects of his anger: not surprisingly, Mom and Dad. Dad had been a violent alcoholic, falling into unpredictable fits of screaming at home or in public. Mom had fallen ill, helpless and dependent; Robert was assigned the task to take care of her from an early age. Many days he stayed home from school, smoked pot, listened to the Beatles. Whatever fear or anger he had towards his unpredictable father and needy mother he buried. How does a child know what is "normal"? What child can stand to consider his parents less than ideal? Robert grew up thinking his parents were a little wacky but pretty cool because they allowed him his independence at an early age.

28   Decades later, he got to replay the scene with Paula. When Paula would leave him, even for short errands in the course of daily life, the sting of his parents' emotional and physical abandonment stirred. When she returned, the hidden rage erupted, for at last he was in a relationship where he wasn't powerless. Under the rage, we discovered the pain, and through the rage and pain, the healing.

29   Last summer Robert and Paula had a child. Sometimes, when he is holding the baby and she is screaming inconsolably, he feels a flash of the old rage of powerlessness. At these moments, we both understand how child abuse happnes, about the natural tendency to take revenge for old stings, to pass them on from generation to generation. In therapy, Robert had found substitutes—sharing his pain and anger with me, screaming at pillows, punching his punching bag—and so the sting was somewhat vented. And he'd achieved a plateau of self-understanding from which he could watch his rage, recognize the senselessness of passing it on, and simply hold his screaming daughter.

30   I think of Robert when I find myself doubting if therapy works: it *is* possible to transcend the power of the sting.

31   But is it possible to transcend generations of cultural conditioning, of collective stings? I'm less sure. The conditioning goes so deep, it's so unconscious. I wasn't paying much attention when I learned to pick on the little guy, any more than the soldiers in the Gulf War were paying attention when they learned to become men on the battlefield. We learn how to be men when we aren't looking, when we think we're doing something else.

32   Here's a final story from my boyhood, about how I learned some differences between women and men:

33   During World War II, my mother, like so many American women, kept a Victory Garden. After the war, when I was very little, she started a garden on the edge of town. She would take me there and set me under a large poplar tree whose leaves rustled in the breeze, making the sound of rain. I sat under the Rain Tree and watched my mother work the earth, cultivating, seeding, tending, and eventually pulling sweet things from the dirt. With a gentle tug, my mother pulled from the earth a sweet orange carrot. Raw carrots were a staple around our house; I still love raw carrots.

34   During World War II, my father, like so many American men, kept a gun, as they fought island by island towards Japan. After the war, each fall he went hunting with his buddies to the Wisconsin woods. Once he took me along. We moved through woods beautiful with bright leaves, air crisp and clear. I shot a bird, a grouse. It wobbled about before it collapsed; perhaps I had to shoot it again. I felt a certain excitement at aiming right, but mostly I felt squeamish. I never liked eating these birds anyway; they tasted strong, and you had to watch out for buckshot. This was my last hunting trip.

35   Women harvest carrots; men shoot birds. This, I learned, is how the world works. I don't believe it can work that way much longer.

Reading for Meaning

1. Paraphrase Gordon Murray's definitions of "the sting." What evidence have you seen that either supports or challenges his idea about the origin of the bully?

2. According to Murray, "we learn to be men when we aren't looking, when we think we're doing something else." What does he mean?

3. Explain why Murray concludes his essay with the story about what his parents were doing during World War II. How does that story contribute to the larger meaning of his essay?

4. Murray defines men and women's roles symbolically in his final paragraph: "Women harvest carrots; men shoot birds. This, I learned, is how the world works. I don't believe it can work that way much longer." Which of his discussions is most helpful in clarifying why he thinks it is dangerous to maintain such radical separations of the male and female functions?

Comparing Texts

Review the essays in this chapter and discuss possible alternatives to some of the more restrictive gender conditioning described by several of the writers.

Ideas for Writing

1. Gordon Murray mentions Robert Bly as one of the leaders of the "new men's movement," a movement that advocates the practice of ancient healing techniques. Gather

some information about this movement from Internet and library resources. What are important attributes of this movement? How effective might they be in countering "the power of the sting"?

2. Murray says that girls as well as boys may experience the "sting." Although girls have more outlets for their feelings, he adds, "no doubt wounded girls grow into wounded women and wounded mothers. No doubt, their stings are passed to their mates, lovers, children." What is your experience of the female "sting"? Have you, women you know, or those you have observed experienced the "sting" either as victims or as aggressors?

Writing before Reading

How easy is it for you to express your emotions? What might have contributed to your behavior, whether open or closed?

MEXICAN MASKS[1]
Octavio Paz

In October 1990, Octavio Paz became the first Mexican writer and the fifth Latin American author to receive the Nobel Prize for literature. Paz, a brilliant writer of poetry, fiction, and essays, also served his country as a diplomat. He founded an avant-garde literary journal when he was 17, and at the age of 21 Paz left Mexico for Spain, where he fought in the Republican Army against Franco's Phalangist forces. The fall of Republican Spain and the institution of Franco's fascist dictatorship and later disillusionment with Communism under Stalin helped shape Paz politically as well as poetically. Years later he would resign his post as ambassador to India when Mexico's "revolutionary" government massacred leftist students in 1968. After experiencing much political upheaval and many disappointments, Paz came to the conclusion that "Democratic liberalism is a civilized mode of living together... [and] the best of all that political philosophy has conceived." Paz lived in the United States for part of the 1970s and taught at Harvard University and the University of Texas. His poetry was influenced by surrealist André Breton and the English Romantic, William Blake. In 1950

---

[1] Translated by Lysander Kemp.

Paz wrote his most famous work, El laberinto de la soledad (The Labyrinth of Solitude), *a collection of essays on Mexican character that includes our selection, "Mascaras Mejicanas" ("Mexican Masks"). Since writing* El laberinto, *Paz has written both poetry and nonfiction, including the following collections of essays:* Una Tierra: Quatro o Cinco Mundos (One Earth: Four or Five Worlds), *(1985),* Convergences, Essays on Art and Literature *(1987),* La Llana Doble (The Double Flame) *(1995), and* Vislumbres de India (In Light of India), *published in 1996, just two years before his death.*

Facts about Mexico

The United States' neighbor to the south is the largest Spanish-speaking country in the world. The country was named after the Mexica, one of the Nahuatl tribes of Native Americans that live in the central part of Mexico. Numerous pre-Columbian civilizations—Maya, Olmec, Zapotec, Mixtec, Toltec, and Aztec—flourished for 2,700 years before being conquered by the Spanish in the sixteenth century. Mexico was a colony of Spain for the next 300 years until it won independence on October 4, 1824. An oil-rich country, Mexico enjoyed a period of some prosperity, although many of its people remained quite poor. Mexico was close to bankruptcy during the recessions in the 1980s. Recovery from the years of inflation and unemployment has been slow. The growth in manufacturing may be helping the recovery. Besides the industries that produce steel, textiles, and various chemicals and pharmaceuticals, Mexico has begun to rely on the *maquiladora* or "corn-ration" factories (meaning very low paying) that have sprung up along its border with the United States. Currently, Mexico ranks fifth in the world for its exportation of oil. Tourism has become an industry equal to oil production for Mexico. The arts flourish in Mexico, and Octavio Paz and Carlos Fuentes are two of its more famous writers. José Clemente Orozco, Diego Rivera, and David Alfaro Siquieros are three of Mexico's renowned mural artists. Dance, music, and folk art add to the wealth of Mexico's culture.

Impassioned heart, disguise your sorrow . . .

—*Popular song*

1   The Mexican, whether young or old, *criollo* or *mestizo*,* general or laborer or lawyer, seems to me to be a person who shuts himself away to protect himself: his face is a mask and so is his smile. In his harsh solitude, which is both barbed and courteous, everything serves him as a defense: silence and words, politeness and disdain, irony and resignation. He is jealous of

---

* *Criollo:* a person of pure Spanish blood living in the Americas.—*Tr.*
  Mestizo: a person of mixed Spanish and Indian blood.—*Tr.*

his own privacy and that of others, and he is afraid even to glance at his neighbor, because a mere glance can trigger the rage of these electrically charged spirits. He passes through life like a man who has been flayed; everything can hurt him, including words and the very suspicion of words. His language is full of reticences, of metaphors and allusions, of unfinished phrases, while his silence is full of tints, folds, thunderheads, sudden rainbows, indecipherable threats. Even in a quarrel he prefers veiled expressions to outright insults: "A word to the wise is sufficient." He builds a wall of indifference and remoteness between reality and himself, a wall that is no less impenetrable for being invisible. The Mexican is always remote, from the world and from other people. And also from himself.

2   The speech of our people reflects the extent to which we protect ourselves from the outside world: the ideal of manliness is never to "crack," never to back down. Those who "open themselves up" are cowards. Unlike other people, we believe that opening oneself up is a weakness or a betrayal. The Mexican can bend, can bow humbly, can even stoop, but he cannot back down, that is, he cannot allow the outside world to penetrate his privacy. The man who backs down is not to be trusted, is a traitor or a person of doubtful loyalty; he babbles secrets and is incapable of confronting a dangerous situation. Women are inferior beings because, in submitting, they open themselves up. Their inferiority is constitutional and resides in their sex, their submissiveness, which is a wound that never heals.

3   Hermeticism is one of the several recourses of our suspicion and distrust. It shows that we instinctively regard the world around us to be dangerous. This reaction is justifiable if one considers what our history has been and the kind of society we have created. The harshness and hostility of our environment, and the hidden, indefinable threat that is always afloat in the air, oblige us to close ourselves in, like those plants that survive by storing up liquid within their spiny exteriors. But this attitude, legitimate enough in its origins, has become a mechanism that functions automatically. Our response to sympathy and tenderness is reserve, since we cannot tell whether those feelings are genuine or simulated. In addition, our masculine integrity is as much endangered by kindness as it is by hostility. Any opening in our defenses is a lessening of our manliness.

4   Our relationships with other men are always tinged with suspicion. Every time a Mexican confides in a friend or acquaintance, every time he opens himself up, it is an abdication. He dreads that the person in whom he has confided will scorn him. Therefore confidences result in dishonor, and they are as dangerous for the person to whom they are made as they are for the person who makes them. We do not drown ourselves, like Narcissus, in the pool that reflects us; we try to stop it up instead. Our anger is prompted not only by the fear of being used by our confidants—that fear is common to everyone—but also by the shame of having renounced our solitude. To confide in others is to dispossess oneself;

when we have confided in someone who is not worthy of it, we say, "I sold myself to So-and-so." That is, we have "cracked," have let someone into our fortress. The distance between one man and another, which creates mutual respect and mutual security, has disappeared. We are the mercy of the intruder. What is worse, we have actually abdicated.

5   All these expressions reveal that the Mexican views life as combat. This attitude does not make him any different from anyone else in the modern world. For other people, however, the manly ideal consists in an open and aggressive fondness for combat, whereas we emphasize defensiveness, the readiness to repel any attack. The Mexican *macho*—the male—is a hermetic being, closed up in himself, capable of guarding both himself and whatever has been confided to him. Manliness is judged according to one's invulnerability to enemy arms or the impacts of the outside world. Stoicism is the most exalted of our military and political attributes. Our history is full of expressions and incidents that demonstrate the indifference of our heroes toward suffering or danger. We are taught from childhood to accept defeat with dignity, a conception that is certainly not ignoble. And if we are not all good stoics like Juárez and Cuauhtémoc, at least we can be resigned and patient and long-suffering. Resignation is one of our most popular virtues. We admire fortitude in the face of adversity more than the most brilliant triumph.

6   This predominance of the closed over the open manifests itself not only as impassivity and distrust, irony and suspicion, but also as love for Form. Form surrounds and sets bounds to our privacy, limiting its excesses, curbing its explosions, isolating and preserving it. Both our Spanish and Indian heritages have influenced our fondness for ceremony, formulas, and order. A superficial examination of our history might suggest otherwise, but actually the Mexican aspires to create an orderly world regulated by clearly stated principles. The turbulence and rancor of our political struggles prove that juridical ideas play an important role in our public life. The Mexican also strives to be formal in his daily life, and his formalities are very apt to become formulas. This is not difficult to understand. Order—juridical, social, religious or artistic—brings security and stability, and a person has only to adjust to the models and principles that regulate life; he can express himself without resorting to the perpetual inventiveness demanded by a free society. Perhaps our traditionalism, which is one of the constants of our national character, giving coherence to our people and our history, results from our professed love for Form.

7   The ritual complications of our courtesy, the persistence of classical Humanism, our fondness for closed poetic forms (the sonnet and the *décima,* for example), our love for geometry in the decorative arts and for design and composition in painting, the poverty of our Romantic art compared with the excellence of our Baroque art, the formalism of our

political institutions, and, finally, our dangerous inclination toward formalism, whether social, moral or bureaucratic, are further expressions of that tendency in our character. The Mexican not only does not open himself up to the outside world, he also refuses to emerge from himself, to "let himself go."

8   Sometimes Form chokes us. During the past century the liberals tried vainly to force the realities of the country into the strait jacket of the Constitution of 1857. The results were the dictatorship of Porfirio Díaz and the Revolution of 1910. In a certain sense the history of Mexico, like that of every Mexican, is a struggle between the forms and formulas that have been imposed on us and the explosions with which our individuality avenges itself. Form has rarely been an original creation, an equilibrium arrived at through our instincts and desires rather than at their expense. On the contrary, our moral and juridical forms often conflict with our nature, preventing us from expressing ourselves and frustrating our true wishes.

9   Our devotion to Form, even when empty, can be seen throughout the history of Mexican art from pre-Conquest times to the present. Antonio Castro Leal, in his excellent study of Juan Ruiz de Alarcón, shows how our reserved attitude toward Romanticism—which by definition is expansive and open—revealed itself as early as the seventeenth century, that is, before we were even aware of ourselves as a nation. Alarcón's contemporaries were right in accusing him of being an interloper, although they were referring more to his physical characteristics than to the singularity of his work. In effect, the most typical portions of his plays deny the values expressed by his Spanish contemporaries. And his negation contains in brief what Mexico has always opposed to Spain. His plays were an answer to Spanish vitality, which was affirmative and splendid in that epoch, expressing itself in a great Yes! to history and the passions. Lope de Vega exalted love, heroism, the superhuman, the incredible; Alarcón favored other virtues, more subtle and bourgeois: dignity, courtesy, a melancholy stoicism, a smiling modesty. Lope was very little interested in moral problems: he loved action, like all his contemporaries. Later, Calderón showed the same contempt for psychology. Moral conflicts and the hesitations and changes of the human soul were only metaphors in a theological drama whose two personae were Original Sin and Divine Grace. In Alarcón's most representative plays, on the other hand, Heaven counts for little, as little as the passionate wind that sweeps away Lope's characters. The Mexican tells us that human beings are a mixture, that good and evil are subtly blended in their souls. He uses analysis rather than synthesis: the hero becomes a problem. In several of his comedies he takes up the question of lying. To what extent does a liar really lie? Is he really trying to deceive others? Is he not the first victim of his deceit, and the first to be deceived? The liar lies to himself, because he is afraid of himself. By discussing the problem of authenticity, Alarcón anticipated

one of the constant themes of Mexican thinking, later taken up by Rodolfo Usigli in his play *The Gesticulator*.

10 Neither passion nor Grace triumph in Alarcón's world. Everything is subordinated to reason, or to reasonableness, and his archetypes are those of a morality that smiles and forgives. When he replaces the vital, Romantic values of Lope with the abstract values of a universal and reasonable morality, is he not evading us, tricking us? His negation, like that of his homeland, does not affirm our individuality vis-à-vis that of the Spaniards. The values that Alarcón postulates belong to all men and are a Greco-Roman inheritance as well as a prophecy of the bourgeois code. They do not express our nature or resolve our conflicts: they are Forms we have neither created nor suffered, are mere masks. Only in our own day have we been able to answer the Spanish Yes with a Mexican Yes rather than with an intellectual affirmation containing nothing of our individual selves. The Revolution, by discovering popular art, originated modern Mexican painting, and by discovering the Mexican language it created a new poetry.

11 While the Mexican tries to create closed worlds in his politics and in the arts, he wants modesty, prudence, and a ceremonious reserve to rule over his everyday life. Modesty results from shame at one's own or another's nakedness, and with us it is an almost physical reflex. Nothing could be further from this attitude that that fear of the body which is characteristic of North American life. We are not afraid or ashamed of our bodies; we accept them as completely natural and we live physically with considerable gusto. It is the opposite of Puritanism. The body exists, and gives weight and shape to our existence. It causes us pain and it gives us pleasure; it is not a suit of clothes we are in the habit of wearing, not something apart from us: we *are* our bodies. But we are frightened by other people's glances, because the body reveals rather than hides our private selves. Therefore our modesty is a defense, like our courtesy's Great Wall of China or like the fences of organ-pipe cactus that separate the huts of our country people. This explains why prudence is the virtue we most admire in women, just as reserve is in men. Women too should defend their privacy.

12 No doubt an element of masculine vanity, the vanity of the "señor," of the lord or chieftain (it is an inheritance from both our Indian and Spanish ancestors), enters into our conception of feminine modesty. Like almost all other people, the Mexican considers woman to be an instrument, sometimes of masculine desires, sometimes of the ends assigned to her by morality, society and the law. It must be admitted that she has never been asked to consent to these ends and that she participates in their realization only passively, as a "repository" for certain values. Whether as prostitute, goddess, *grande dame* or mistress, woman transmits or preserves—but does not believe in—the values and energies entrusted to her by nature or society. In a world made in man's image,

woman is only a reflection of masculine will and desire. When passive, she becomes a goddess, a beloved one, a being who embodies the ancient, stable elements of the universe: the earth, motherhood, virginity. When active, she is always function and means, a receptacle and a channel. Womanhood, unlike manhood, is never an end in itself.

13   In other countries these functions are realized in public, often with something of a flair. There are countries that revere prostitutes or virgins, and countries that worship mothers; the *grande dame* is praised and respected almost everywhere. In contrast, we prefer these graces and virtues to be hidden. Woman should be secretive. She should confront the world with an impassive smile. She should be "decent" in the face of erotic excitements and "long-suffering" in the face of adversity. In either event her response is neither instinctive nor personal: it conforms to a general model, and it is the defensive and passive aspects of this model, as in the case of the *macho,* that are emphasized, in a gamut ranging from modesty and "decency" to stoicism, resignation and impassivity.

14   Our Spanish-Arabic inheritance is only a partial explanation of this conduct. The Spanish attitude toward women is very simple. It is expressed quite brutally and concisely in these two sayings: "A woman's place is in the home, with a broken leg" and "Between a female saint and a male saint, a wall of mortared stone." Woman is a domesticated wild animal, lecherous and sinful from birth, who must be subdued with a stick and guided by the "reins of religion." Therefore Spaniards consider other women—especially those of a race or religion different from their own—to be easy game. The Mexican considers woman to be a dark, secret and passive being. He does not attribute evil instincts to her; he even pretends that she does not have any. Or, to put it more exactly, her instincts are not her own but those of the species, because she is an incarnation of the life force, which is essentially impersonal. Thus it is impossible for her to have a personal, private life, for if she were to be herself—if she were to be mistress of her own wishes, passions or whims—she would be unfaithful to herself. The Mexican, heir to the great pre-Columbian religions based on nature, is a good deal more pagan than the Spaniard, and does not condemn the natural world. Sexual love is not tinged with grief and horror in Mexico as it is in Spain. Instincts themselves are not dangerous; the danger lies in any personal, individual expression of them. And this brings us back to the idea of passivity: woman is never herself, whether lying stretched out or standing up straight, whether naked or fully clothed. She is an undifferentiated manifestation of life, a channel for the universal appetite. In this sense she has no desires of her own.

15   North Americans also claim that instincts and desires do not exist, but the basis of their pretense is different from ours, even the opposite of it. The North American hides or denies certain part of his body and, more often, of his psyche: they are immoral, ergo they do not exist. By denying them he inhibits his spontaneity. The Mexican woman quite simply has

no will of her own. Her body is asleep and only comes really alive when someone awakens her. She is an answer rather than a question, a vibrant and easily worked material that is shaped by the imagination and sensuality of the male. In other countries women are active, attempting to attract men through the agility of their minds or the seductivity of their bodies, but the Mexican woman has a sort of hieratic calm, a tranquility made up of both hope and contempt. The man circles around her, courts her, sings to her, sets his horse (or his imagination) to performing caracoles for her pleasure. Meanwhile she remains behind the veil of her modesty and immobility. She is an idol, and like all idols she is mistress of magnetic forces whose efficacy increases as their source of transmission becomes more and more passive and secretive. There is a cosmic analogy here: woman does not seek, she attracts, and the center of attraction is her hidden, passive sexuality. It is a secret and immobile sun.

16 The falsity of this conception is obvious enough when one considers the Mexican woman's sensitivity and restlessness, but at least it does not turn her into an object, a mere thing. She is a symbol, like all women, of the stability and continuity of the race. In addition to her cosmic significance she has an important social role, which is to see to it that law and order, piety and tenderness are predominant in everyday life. We will not allow anyone to be disrespectful to women, and although this is doubtless a universal notion, the Mexican carries it to its ultimate consequences. Thanks to woman, many of the asperities of "man-to-man" relationships are softened. Of course we should ask the Mexican woman for her own opinion, because this "respect" is often a hypocritical way of subjecting her and preventing her from expressing herself. Perhaps she would usually prefer to be treated with less "respect" (which anyway is granted to her only in public) and with greater freedom and truthfulness; that is, to be treated as a human being rather than as a symbol or function. But how can we agree to let her express herself when our whole way of life is a mask designed to hide our intimate feelings?

17 Despite her modesty and the vigilance of society, woman is always vulnerable. Her social situation—as the repository of honor, is the Spanish sense—and the misfortune of her "open" anatomy expose her to all kinds of dangers, against which neither personal morality nor masculine protection is sufficient. She is submissive and open by nature. But, through a compensation-mechanism that is easily explained, her natural frailty is made a virtue and the myth of the "long-suffering Mexican woman" is created. The idol—always vulnerable, always in process of transforming itself into a human being—becomes a victim, but a victim hardened and insensible to suffering, bearing her tribulations in silence. (A "long-suffering" person is less sensitive to pain than a person whom adversity has hardly touched.) Through suffering, our women become like our men: invulnerable, impassive, and stoic.

18   It might be said that by turning what ought to be a cause for shame into a virtue, we are only trying to relieve our guilt feelings and cover up a cruel reality. This is true, but it is also true that in attributing to her the same invulnerability that we strive to achieve ourselves, we provide her with a moral immunity to shield her unfortunate anatomical openness. Thanks to suffering and her ability to endure it without protest, she transcends her condition and acquires the same attributes as men.

19   It is interesting to note that the image of the *mala mujer*—the "bad woman"—is almost always accompanied by the idea of aggressive activity. She is not passive like the "self-denying mother," the "waiting sweetheart," the hermetic idol: she comes and goes, she looks for men and then leaves them. Her extreme mobility, through a mechanism similar to that described above, renders her invulnerable. Activity and immodesty unite to petrify her soul. The *mala* is hard and impious and independent like the *macho*. In her own way she also transcends her physiological weakness and closes herself off from the world.

20   It is likewise significant that masculine homosexuality is regarded with a certain indulgence insofar as the active agent is concerned. The passive agent is an abject, degraded being. This ambiguous conception is made very clear in the word games or battles—full of obscene allusions and double meanings—that are so popular in Mexico City. Each of the speakers tries to humiliate his adversary with verbal traps and ingenious linguistic combinations, and the loser is the person who cannot think of a comeback, who has to swallow his opponent's jibes. These jibes are full of aggressive sexual allusions; the loser is possessed, is violated, by the winner, and the spectators laugh and sneer at him. Masculine homosexuality is tolerated, then, on condition that it consists in violating a passive agent. As with heterosexual relationships, the important thing is not to open oneself up and at the same time to break open one's opponent.

21   It seems to me that all of these attitudes, however different their sources, testify to the "closed" nature of our reactions to the world around us or to our fellows. But our mechanisms of defense and self-preservation are not enough, and therefore we make use of dissimulation, which is almost habitual with us. It does not increase our passivity; on the contrary, it demands an active inventiveness and must reshape itself from one moment to another. We tell lies for the mere pleasure of it, like all imaginative peoples, but we also tell lies to hide ourselves and to protect ourselves from intruders. Lying plays a decisive role in our daily lives, our politics, our love-affairs and our friendships, and since we attempt to deceive ourselves as well as others, our lies are brilliant and fertile, not like the gross inventions of other peoples. Lying is a tragic game in which we risk a part of our very selves. Hence it is pointless to denounce it.

22   The dissembler pretends to be someone he is not. His role requires constant improvisation, a steady forward progress across shifting sands.

Every moment he must remake, re-create, modify the personage he is playing, until at last the moment arrives when reality and appearance, the lie and the truth, are one. At first the pretense is only a fabric of inventions intended to baffle our neighbors, but eventually it becomes a superior—because more artistic—form of reality. Our lies reflect both what we lack and what we desire, both what we are not and what we would like to be. Through dissimulation we come closer to our model, and sometimes the gesticulator, as Usigli saw so profoundly, becomes one with his gestures and thus makes them authentic. The death of Professor Rubio changed him into what he wanted to be: General Rubio, a sincere revolutionary and a man capable of giving the stagnating Revolution a fresh impetus and purity. In the Usigli play Professor Rubio invents a new self and becomes a general, and his lie is so truthlike that the corrupt Navarro has no other course than to murder him, as if he were murdering his old commander, General Rubio, all over again. By killing him he kills the truth of the Revolution.

23   If we can arrive at authenticity by means of lies, an excess of sincerity can bring us to refined forms of lying. When we fall in love we open ourselves up and reveal our intimate feelings, because an ancient tradition requires that the man suffering from love display his wounds to the loved one. But is displaying them the lover transforms himself into an image, an object he presents for the loved one's—and his own—contemplation. He asks her to regard him with the same worshipful eyes with which he regards himself. And now the looks of others do not strip him naked; instead, they clothe him in piety. He has offered himself as a spectacle, asking the spectators to see him as he sees himself, and in so doing he has escaped from the game of love, has saved his true self by replacing it with an image.

24   Human relationships run the risk, in all lands and ages, of becoming equivocal. This is especially true of love. Narcissism and masochism are not exclusively Mexican traits, but it is notable how often our popular songs and sayings and our everyday behavior treat love as falsehood and betrayal. We almost always evade the perils of a naked relationship by exaggerating our feelings. At the same time, the combative nature of our eroticism is emphasized and aggravated. Love is an attempt to penetrate another being, but it can only be realized if the surrender is mutual. It is always difficult to give oneself up; few persons anywhere ever succeed in doing so, and even fewer transcend the possessive stage to know love for what it actually is: a perpetual discovery, an immersion in the waters of reality, and an unending re-creation. The Mexican conceives of love as combat and conquest. It is not so much an attempt to penetrate reality by means of the body as it is to violate it. Therefore the image of the fortunate lover—derived, perhaps, from the Spanish Don Juan—is confused with that of the man who deliberately makes use of his feelings, real or invented, to win possession of a woman.

Chapter 8 Custom and Gender Roles **313**

25   Dissimulation is an activity very much like that of actors in the theater, but the true actor surrenders himself to the role he is playing and embodies it fully, even though he sloughs it off again, like a snake its skin, when the final curtain comes down. The dissembler never surrenders or forgets himself, because he would no longer be dissembling if he became one with his image. But this fiction becomes an inseparable—and spurious—part of his nature. He is condemned to play his role throughout life, since the pact between himself and his impersonation cannot be broken except by death or sacrifice. The lie takes command of him and becomes the very foundation of his personality.

26   To simulate is to invent, or rather to counterfeit, and thus to evade our condition. Dissimulation requires greater subtlety: the person who dissimulates is not counterfeiting but attempting to become invisible, to pass unnoticed without renouncing his individuality. The Mexican excels at the dissimulation of his passions and himself. He is afraid of others' looks and therefore he withdraws, contracts, becomes a shadow, a phantasm, an echo. Instead of walking, he glides; instead of stating, he hints; instead of replying, he mumbles; instead of complaining, he smiles. Even when he sings he does so—unless he explodes, ripping open his breast—between clenched teeth and in a lowered voice, dissimulating his song:

> And so great is the tyranny
> of this dissimulation
> that although my heart swells
> with profoundest longing,
> there is challenge in my eyes
> and resignation in my voice.

27   Perhaps our habit of dissimulating originated in colonial times. The Indians and *mestizos* had to sing in a low voice, as in the poem by Alfonso Reyes, because "words of rebellion cannot be heard well from between clenched teeth." The colonial world has disappeared, but not the fear, the mistrust, the suspicion. And now we disguise not only our anger but also our tenderness. When our country people beg one's pardon, they say: "Pretend it never happened, señor." And we pretend. We dissimulate so eagerly that we almost cease to exist.

28   In its most radical forms dissimulation becomes mimicry. The Indian blends into the landscape until he is an indistinguishable part of the white wall against which he leans at twilight, of the dark earth on which he stretches out to rest at midday, of the silence that surrounds him. He disguises his human singularity to such an extent that he finally annihilates it and turns into a stone, a tree, a wall, silence, and space. I am not saying that he communes with the All like a pantheist, or that he sees an individual tree as an archetype of all trees, what I am saying is that he actually blends into specific objects in a concrete and particular way.

29   Roger Caillois has pointed out that mimicry is not always an attempt to foil the enemies that swarm in the outside world. Insects will sometimes "play dead" or imitate various kinds of decomposed material, out of a fascination for death, for the inertia of space. This fascination—I would call it life's gravitational force—is common to all living things, and the fact that it expresses itself in mimicry shows that we must consider it as something more than an instinctive device for escaping from danger or death.

30   Mimicry is a change of appearance rather than of nature, and it is significant that the chosen representation is either of death or of inert space. The act of spreading oneself out, of blending with space, of becoming space, is a way of rejecting appearances, but it is also a way of being nothing except Appearance. The Mexican is horrified by appearances, although his leaders profess to love them, and therefore he disguises himself to the point of blending into the objects that surround him. That is, he becomes mere Appearance because of his fear of appearances. He seems to be something other than what he is, and he even prefers to appear dead or nonexistent rather than to change, to open up his privacy. Dissimulation as mimicry, then, is one of the numerous manifestations of our hermeticism. The gesticulator resorts to a mask, and the rest of us wish to pass unnoticed. In either case we hide our true selves, and sometimes deny them. I remember the afternoon I heard a noise in the room next to mine, and asked loudly: "Who is in there?" I was answered by the voice of a servant who had recently come to us from her village: "No one, señor. I am."

31   We dissimulate in order to deceive ourselves, and turn transparent and phantasmal. But that is not the end of it: we also pretend that our fellow-man does not exist. This is not to say that we deliberately ignore or discount him. Our dissimulation here is a great deal more radical: we change him from somebody into nobody, into nothingness. And this nothingness takes on its own individuality, with a recognizable face and figure, and suddenly becomes Nobody.

32   Don No One, who is Nobody's Spanish father, is able, well fed, well respected; he has a bank account, and speaks in a loud, self-assured voice. Don No One fills the world with his empty, garrulous presence. He is everywhere, and has friends everywhere. He is a banker, an ambassador, a businessman. He can be seen in all the salons, and is honored in Jamaica and Stockholm and London. He either holds office or wields influence, and his manner of not-being is aggressive and conceited. On the other hand, Nobody is quiet, timid, and resigned. He is also intelligent and sensitive. He always smiles. He always waits. When he wants to say something, he meets a wall of silence; when he greets someone, he meets a cold shoulder; when he pleads or weeps or cries out, his gestures and cries are lost in the emptiness created by Don No One's interminable chatter. Nobody is afraid not to exist: he vacillates,

attempting now and then to become Somebody. Finally, in the midst of his useless gestures, he disappears into the limbo from which he emerged.

33   It would be a mistake to believe that others prevent him from existing. They simply dissimulate his existence and behave as if he did not exist. They nullify him, cancel him out, turn him to nothingness. It is futile for Nobody to talk, to publish books, to paint pictures, to stand on his head. Nobody is the blankness in our looks, the pauses in our conversations, the reserve in our silences. He is the name we always and inevitably forget, the eternal absentee, the guest we never invite, the emptiness we can never fill. He is an omission, and yet he is forever present. He is our secret, our crime, and our remorse. Thus the person who creates Nobody, by denying Somebody's existence, is also changed into Nobody. And if we are all Nobody, then none of us exists. The circle is closed and the shadow of Nobody spreads out over our land, choking the Gesticulator and covering everything. Silence—the prehistoric silence, stronger than all the pyramids and sacrifices, all the churches and uprisings and popular songs—comes back to rule over Mexico.

Reading for Meaning

1. What are a few of the assumptions made by the "macho" male in Mexican culture? Have you known men or women who make these assumptions?

2. How well does the title *The Labyrinth of Solitude* fit the ideas in "Mexican Masks"?

3. According to Paz, what are some of the demands placed on Mexican women? What does he mean when he says "woman is never herself, whether lying stretched out or standing up straight"?

4. What are the characteristics of the *mala mujer*? Is there an equivalent "bad woman" in this culture? How does her behavior compare to the *mala* in Mexican culture?

5. What important roles do women play in Mexican culture? Do any of these roles match the function of women in the United States? Explain your answer.

6. Beginning in paragraph 26, Paz discusses dissimulation as a way of life for Mexicans. What problems does such dissimulation cause? Does Paz seem to think there are solutions to this form of lying?

7. Does Paz describe the macho culture of Mexico as an insider or outsider? What phrases and passages gave you that impression?

Comparing Texts

1. Compare the discussion of masculine behavior in Octavio Paz's "Mexican Masks" with Gordon Murray's "Picking on the Little Guy," the first reading in this chapter. What similarities or differences do you find in the ways that boys and men work with their emotions? How do the writers' tones or approaches to the subject compare?

2. Paz characterizes the conflicts in Mexican history as battles between "forms and formulas" and individual expression. Read Dorothy Lee's "An Anthropologist Learns from the Hopi" (page 386) and discuss the ways that the Hopi balance the needs of the individual and those of the group. What might Mexican men learn from the Hopi?

Ideas for Writing

1. Paz says that their Spanish and Indian roots explain the Mexicans' love of formula and predictability. What examples of their love of form stood out for you? How much do you adhere to "form" or set patterns of behavior in your own life?

2. Critics of Octavio Paz's discussion of Mexicans argue that denying one's emotions and victimizing women are typical patterns for most cultures in the world, and that he is being unfair to Mexican men by not discussing other attributes of their character. What do you think of the critics' assessment of Paz's argument?

3. What are characteristics of the *macho* male Paz thinks are common to Mexican men? Think of several movies whose heroes qualify as *macho*. What specific ways do the male characters illustrate the traits that Paz identifies? Do these films offer additional attributes? Are any left out?

Writing before Reading

What have you heard or read about groups in which polygamous relationships are accepted or once were common practice? What problems have you come to associate with polygamous relations?

THE *BILAL'S* FOURTH WIFE[2]

Sembene Ousmane

Sembene Ousmane, a member of the Wolof nation, was born in Senegal in 1923. He has been a soldier and a laborer and has worked as a mason, truck driver, plumber, and stevedore, occupations that may account for his profound interest in the poor, illiterate, and exploited people in his country. He spent most of his life as a writer and filmmaker. Ousmane sees Senegal as a victim of its colonial past, for despite the fact that Senegal won its independ-

---

[2] Translated by Len Ortzen.

ence from France in 1964 and that Dakar, the capital, appears prosperous, Ousmane explained in an interview in 1971 that "the banks, the industries, the wholesale markets are still controlled by the French, who are forgiven their taxes because they supply jobs, and are permitted to take their profits out of the country." In his short story, "The Bilal's Fourth Wife," from the collection Tribal Scars (1974), Ousmane explores a different subject. Here he takes a satirical look at Moslem attitudes toward divorce, and he offers some serious challenges to the assumption of patriarchal rights.

Facts about Senegal

Senegal is a small country on the Atlantic Coast of Africa. Its coastline stretches for more than 300 miles and is the envy of its land-locked neighbors. Mali, Senegal's neighbor to the east, invaded what is now Senegal in the fourteenth century. Subsequently, the Wolof, who account for more than 40 percent of Senegal's population, created their own empire, which lasted for 300 years. Like several of its West African neighbors, Senegal's history is tied to European colonization by both the French and the English. The French colonized Senegal in the seventeenth century. Goree Island was the point of departure of millions of Africans who were being shipped to the New World to become slaves. Today, Senegal is a democracy with an elected president. The internationally known poet Leopold Senghor was president of Senegal for twenty years before resigning in 1980. His successor, Abdou Diouf, was elected president in 1983, 1988, and 1993. The people of Senegal are mostly Muslims; five percent of the population are Christians or tribal people who follow traditional religions.

1   He was past middle-age, but despite his years he still had the vigorous bearing of a healthy man. It could hardly be otherwise, for Suliman was the *bilal* of the mosque. He looked after everything—the cleaning, the repairs and maintenance, and the collections in aid of this holy building. As the mosque was timber-built, he had plenty to occupy him. All the faithful admired him and were inclined in his favour; everyone gave alms willingly. Suliman did not expend much energy, so his body became flabby and his face pleasant to look upon. He stifled his laughter, out of piety, and instead smiled at everyone who spoke to him. To sum up, he was an exemplary person, pious and humble—to all appearances at least. A discreet man, certainly . . .

2   But in private life he was a very different character. He already had three wives, whom he bullied unmercifully because of his vices—and he had quite a few vices, the old humbug! When a young man, Suliman had been in the Sixth Senegalese Rifles, a regiment which served in all the colonial campaigns of the twenties—and everyone knows the reputation of that regiment! Sometimes he made two of his wives share his bed. But he never missed the fleeting Holy Hour. He wished to crown his

later years with a fourth wife, a young one, about the age of his eldest daughter.

3   The door of the mosque faced the public fountain, a meeting-place for all the women and girls. After Suliman had whisked round with his broom, he would go and sit outside on his sheepskin and sum up the women. Some of the girls had holes in their bodice, or the low neck was torn, and certain of their movements caused breasts as firm as unripe fruit to slip into view, the shining flesh streaked with sweat; at which the other women burst out laughing.

4   Suliman was on the look-out for such a treat; he sat there like a sportsman after wild fowl, his eyes reduced to narrow slits and the tip of his tongue protruding between his lips. He would put a hand to his throat, stretch his neck and swallow his saliva. His thoughts ran on the idea of possessing one of these gazelles; and the sight of all this young flesh made him harsher and more intolerant towards his old, worn-out wives. The result of it all was that he made their lives impossible, often beating them.

5   People (the men) said to them: "A man like Suliman! There's no one else so gentle, so calm, so religious as him. You must have done something, for him to beat you."

6   While the wives consoled the one who had been beaten: "It's a woman's lot! We have to be patient. Men are our masters under God. Is there a wife anywhere whose husband has never laid hands on her?"

7   Every evening now, the cries of one or other of them could be heard. But Suliman's taciturn nature acted in his favour.

8   "They've banded together to make his life intolerable," men said between themselves.

9   "It must be that! Such a good man. Never a word too much and never a wrong word. If it weren't for him our mosque would be in ruins."

10 "And you never hear him complain," added another.

11 To all appearances, Suliman was a martyr to polygamy. This only served to make men pity and respect him the more. As for him, he said nothing. But when the women and girls gathered at the fountain, he was in his usual place, sitting on his sheepskin and eyeing them all. In the evening, after the last prayer, he went round visiting people. But it was only a pretext, an opportunity to cast an eye over the girls with their circle of young bloods. In the course of the day he would call one of the girls and ask her to sweep the courtyard of the mosque or to fetch water for the ablutions. When they were alone he would talk a lot of humbug. "What do the young men say to you?" he would ask, fastening his eyes on the girl's bosom. "Be careful of young men . . . my child."

12 Sometimes, while pretending to help them, he fumbled at their clothing and pawed them. The youngsters paid no attention, knowing he was old enough to be their father. At such times, at the height of his perverse pleasure, his mouth fell open, his eyes turned upwards and he

broke into a sweat. Becoming more emboldened, he fell upon one of them . . .

13   The girls dared not complain to anyone. Who would believe them? Such a pious man! And who had three wives . . . The victims had to say nothing or defend themselves. Meanwhile Suliman knocked his wives about for anything and everything. Having whetted his appetite with some of the girls, he began to neglect his duties as *bilal;* all except one—taking the collections. For that, he never missed an opportunity, not a single prayer. But the mosque began to fall into disrepair.

14   In the space of a year, Suliman had become a different man; with increasing age, he was consumed with an insatiable lust. He was like a camel on heat, except that he did not foam at the mouth. But he was still neatly dressed, and was even more polite than usual. There was a lot of talk about him, for the change in him affected all the faithful.

15   "His wives make his life a misery. We must do something about it," said one man.

16   "Ought we to find him a fourth wife?"

17   "That's it. We must find him another wife, one who'll make up for all the beastliness of the others."

18   "Yes, for if it weren't for Suliman, we shouldn't have a mosque at all. The other districts all have fine mosques. A year ago, ours used to be the best kept and the cleanest. Suliman isn't that old—he can still keep a girl satisfied all night."

19   "But where shall we find her? A girl who will show up the other three wives and who doesn't live around here. For they're all of one mind here, the women all stick together."

20   "Then let each of us look around among his acquaintances."

21   The weeks went by. The *bilal* got wind of the elders' deliberations, but made no attempt to limit his indulgences; every morning he sent for a girl and satisfied himself.

22   Eventually they found Yacine N'Doye. She came of a fisherman's family and was not like other girls. She was almost twenty—and what a tongue she had! No man had come to ask for her; she was a tomboy, a hard worker, and joined in the young men's games and competitions, challenging them. And when her father told her that he had found her a husband, she did not quibble, although she would have liked to ask a few questions.

23   One evening Suliman was seen to go into the house. Yacine's father was very flattered. It was a great honour to know that his daughter could please the *bilal.* And Suliman, a prey to his desires, was not niggardly. "If you want the heifer you must take care of the cow." He was generous in helping his future father-in-law; and at the mosque he pretended not to see him at collection time, or else he gave him his coins back when they were alone.

24 One Friday, Yacine was betrothed to him. There was a great feast; a sheep was slaughtered, and all the faithful took part in the festivities. Suliman promised in front of everyone that he would slaughter two bulls for Yacine's virginity.

25 During the months which elapsed between the betrothal and the wedding night, Suliman seemed a new man. Everyone was sure that Yacine was "intact," as pure as spring water. The sole subject of gossip was the coming celebrations. Yacine's father, her mother and all her relations, near and distant, plied her with questions.

26 "But how do you expect me to get on with that old man?" she asked them.

27 "That old man? He's giving you what the young ones haven't got. Honour, rank, esteem—to say nothing of two bulls on your wedding day! Even your mother didn't have that."

28 Then there were the little presents of toiletry, fibre trunks, head-scarves, waist-cloths and bracelets. And despite his age, Suliman decided to build a new hut for Yacine. "Everything must be new for a virgin!" he told the other men.

29 The date for her "induction" was postponed. Suliman controlled his impatience. The hut was not quite ready. "Everything in it is Yacine's. I give it all to her," he said boastfully.

30 "Suliman, there's no one like you," said the men.

31 The day came when Yacine entered into her new home. The following day, a white waist-cloth stained with blood was passed round by the women, from compound to compound, to general rejoicing. This made the bride's parents very proud; their honour was safe. For the whole of that week, everyone ate nothing but meat. Drums beat, and the girls organized dances in the evenings.

32 Everything gradually returned to normal. Yacine was the favoured wife. But at the end of three years, when Yacine was only twenty-three, she had had just one child. She had become a woman, with all a woman's qualities and faults. (In this climate of perpetual spring, passions run deep and fast. A man on the decline cannot hope to satisfy a woman in her prime.) While Yacine's vigour was mounting, Suliman's was diminishing. Night after night, as nothing was forthcoming, Yacine stayed awake. She regretted having had her sensuality aroused. Suliman was still granting three days of his presence to each of his wives. The old ones, broad in the beam and worn out from successive pregnancies, were not particularly interested in "that." Once a month was quite enough for them. But Yacine had only the one child; and she ought to be breeding.

33 One day Yacine went to see her parents. She had this serious problem on her mind.

34 "Father, I want to come back home."

35 "Why?"

36 "Well, I'm afraid I'm not getting on with my husband."

37 "And why not?" he asked again, looking straight at her.

38 Modesty prevented her from entering into explanations. She dropped her eyes and turned to leave again.

39 "Just remember, daughter, that Suliman has spent an enormous amount, and if you leave him for no reason—that is, for no valid reason—I shall have to pay him back... and I can't."

40 Yacine, unable to bear the frustration any longer, took a lover, none other than Suliman's nephew. One morning, having spent three nights with his third wife, Suliman went to Yacine's hut. He found his nephew in bed with her. He said nothing. The lovers had seen him too. "You get sick of what is disagreeable; what is agreeable makes you enterprising."

41 In the days that followed, Suliman said nothing about it to anybody; not did Yacine or the nephew. It was a secret between them. "If you repudiate your wife, you lose the dowry. And for such a reason, witnesses are necessary." Keeping the secret was even worse! It poisoned his thoughts. The mere knowledge that another man had taken his place was enough to age Suliman; and in the space of six weeks he lost his fine bearing and became consumed with jealousy.

42 "Are you ill, *balil?*" the faithful asked him, seeing his wasting away.

43 "What, me? Good heavens, no! Nothing serious, it'll soon go."

44 In Suliman's house a tragi-comedy was being enacted by three silent players, with no spectators but themselves. Yacine could not quit Suliman without refunding all the expense he had gone to on her account. Her father was in no position to return the money if she were declared the guilty party in a divorce. Both husband and wife stuck to their respective positions. Suliman thought "If she returns to her father's house, I shall get my money back and be able to keep my son." While Yacine said to herself "If I go back home, I shall have to return everything to him." Then she thought "But why should I? I didn't ask him for anything. If I leave him, it's because he isn't a man any more."

45 Yacine, meanwhile, had no embarrassment over spending her time pleasantly with her lover. While Suliman, ailing from a disorder that was undermining his prestige and his dignity, quarrelled with his other wives. Once again the men said, "Poor fellow, he's venting his wrath on dead donkeys."

46 Another year went by, and Yacine was pregnant again. When the baby was born, the elders, acting through loyalty and hypocrisy, made preparations to baptize the child. But Suliman, with a final spark of honesty, objected.

47 "I'm not going to baptize a child which isn't mine," he said.

48 "Well, we know that. It is the will of God. This child is yours because Yacine is your wife."

49 "What will of God? God has nothing to do with it."

50 Yacine had not waited for the outcome; she had returned to her parents' taking everything with her, even the broom. She had just appropriated everything Suliman had ever given her. (It must be remembered

that in a case like this, the wife in fact has to return everything.) The *bilal* was to some extent pleased by Yacine's action, for he thought that he could start divorce proceedings and get all his property back. In fact he was very cheerful about it. But he made no move to see his parents-in-law. On the contrary, it was Yacine's father who approached the *bilal* at the mosque, after prayers, hoping that the latter would raise the matter. But the cunning Suliman diverted the conversation to religious subjects.

51 The couple apparently had no intention of taking their case for dispute before the elders. However, people gossiped, and eventually there was a meeting to discuss it. Suliman finally made up his mind to plead his case before the gathering of elders.

52 "I will grant her the divorce, but first she must pay back all my expenses and return my child to me."

53 (He had right on his side, by local law and custom.)

54 "There are two children," was the reply. "Both are yours. Besides, you haven't told us why she left you."

55 "Oh, she can tell you that."

56 "Well, that's very true. She was the one who went away. She must have her reasons, which you may know nothing about."

57 They questioned Yacine's father. "So she wants to divorce him?"

58 "She says not."

59 The elders were astonished. "She says not?"

60 This confused the whole affair beyond comprehension. When the dust had blown away, they would see more clearly, said the elders philosophically. That evening they sent for Yacine.

61 "Yacine, you must go back to your husband."

62 "I tell you I will not."

63 "Very well, so you are bringing a suit for divorce. The sole fact that you are no longer happy with your husband means that you will be granted a divorce. Then you will have to pay back—"

64 "In the first place," retorted Yacine, "I am not asking for a divorce. In the second place, I just can't go on living with him. Thirdly, I've nothing to give back—and the child is not his."

65 The elders, wise men though they were, had to admit that they were baffled by this. Suliman was evidently right; the matter could not be settled among themselves. It was taken to the Cadi.

66 The most learned men from all around were called in. A delegation was even sent to ask the great Froh-Toll to attend, the man whose truths smarted like a squirt of lemon-juice in the eye. The court-house could hold only fifty people, so it was decided that the case should be heard in the open air. Many idlers took up places on the village square the day before the case was due to start. The marabouts consulted the Holy Book of Koranic laws and reviewed the *Farata* and the *Sounna*, the rules and customs governing the union and separation of man and wife.

67 The time came, the case was opened by the *Hali,* the judge, who called upon "anyone who can throw light on this matter" to do so. Then he addressed the contestants.

68 "Suliman, will you agree to take back your wife and your children? And you, Yacine, are you prepared to go back to your husband with his children? We will hear what you have to say."

69 "Yacine left me," replied Suliman. "I want her to pay back all my expenses and give me my child."

70 "So you don't want your wife, Suliman?" said the Hali.

71 "If a wife leaves her husband's house and takes everything with her, it means that she has no intention of returning."

72 "To all appearances, that is true," put in Froh-Toll. "What do you say to that, Yacine?"

73 "I say that I have not divorced Suliman. He was my husband, but later he was no longer capable of being my husband. That is why I left him."

74 "That is what you say. But only Suliman can set you free," said the Hali.

75 "It is not the same thing as leaving her husband's home," commented Froh-Toll.

76 "She left me and she must pay me back," said Suliman.

77 "I have nothing to pay back," retorted Yacine.

78 "Yacine, according to the rules and customs which united the two of you, you must give back the dowry."

79 "Very well, if you think that's fair. But I will only agree on condition that Suliman gives me back my virginity."

80 That was not written in the rules and customs, but it aroused much controversy. Some, especially the young ones, supported Yacine. But the elders failed to see the logic of it and took a different view of her case. Realizing that here was a moot point, the Hali called for silence and went on to consider the question of the children.

81 "There are two children, and as Yacine has broken the marriage contract, as we now know, the custody of the children devolves on their father, Suliman."

82 "I should like to add . . . or rather clear up a small matter. The second child is not mine," Suliman stated for all to hear.

83 "I shan't give him or anything up," retorted Yacine.

84 Until then, most of those present had supported Yacine, but they did not agree with her about the custody of the child. Everyone recognized the father's sacred right to have possession of his offspring—everyone except Froh-Toll.

85 "I should like to put a few questions to you, the wise men," began Froh-Toll. "It appears that the child should be returned to the father. But are we sure that a child should be returned to its father by right of birth?"

86 "Oh yes. It says so in the Holy Book."

87   Froh-Toll was thoughtful for a few moments, then he said composedly: "I myself, here before you, I lost my father when I had been in my mother's womb for only two months. The death of my father did not prevent me from coming into the world..."

88   "The death of a husband will never prevent his pregnant wife from giving birth," stated the Hali.

89   "But now consider that the contrary had happened, that my mother had died when two months' pregnant. Should I be alive now?"

90   "No, no," shouted the crowd.

91   "So by what right does Suliman demand the custody of the child? There can always be doubt as to who is the father of a child. But never as to who is the mother."

Reading for Meaning

1. Discuss the ways in which Sembene Ousmane's short story explores the themes of appearance and reality.

2. Ousmane indulges in authorial intrusions that are less typical of writing in the United States and Europe. Examine a few instances when the author interrupts his story to comment on his characters' behavior. What effect do these intrusions have on the story? What relationship do they establish between the reader and writer?

3. What writing strategies does Ousmane use to satirize the customs of betrothal and marriage in his culture?

4. What role does Ousmane assign to the community in his story? What do the communal conversations reveal about the town's attitudes toward men, women, and marriage?

5. What might be the meaning of the aphorism "You get sick of what is disagreeable; what is agreeable makes you enterprising"? How is it appropriate for Ousmane's story?

6. How does Yacine, with the help of Froh-Toll, challenge Islamic customs?

Comparing Texts

Read "The Miller's Tale" or "The Merchant's Tale" from Chaucer's *Canterbury Tales*. Compare the treatment this medieval English writer gives the "January-May" relationship in one of these stories to Ousmane's handling of a similar mismatch. (See Appendix B for internet access to "The Miller's Tale.")

Ideas for Writing

1. What is Sembene Ousmane's purpose for writing "The *Bilal's* Fourth Wife"? How does he use plot, character, narrative point of view, or theme to achieve his purpose?

2. Read one or two other short stories by Sembene Ousmane and write an essay in which you discuss the range of subjects, styles, or tones that you identify in his writing.

Writing before Reading

Are boys and girls or men and women treated differently in your family? If they are, discuss the assumptions about the value of the two sexes that could explain this treatment. If they are treated equally, explain why your family favors equal treatment.

GROWING UP FEMALE IN EGYPT[3]
Nawal El Saadawi

Nawal El Saadawi received her medical degree in 1955 and is a practicing physician in Egypt. She is also the author of short stories, novels, and feminist studies. Saadawi is best known in Western countries for her outspoken critique of female circumcision and other practices in Islamic cultures. The publication of Woman and Sex *in 1972 resulted in her dismissal by then-president Anwar Sadat from her post as Egypt's director of public health. Her books on feminist topics were routinely censored by Egyptian authorities, and she has also been imprisoned for her writing. Other countries besides Egypt, including Saudi Arabia and Libya, have banned her books as well. Her quasi-fictional account, "Growing Up Female in Egypt," appears in* Memoirs of a Female Physician *(1965). Although not strictly autobiographical, the narrator's memoir parallels the writer's life as the record of her childhood and young adult years up to the age of thirty.*

Facts about Egypt

Egypt is largely a Muslim country, with over 90 percent of the population adhering to the Sunni faith. Clashes with Moslem fundamentalists have helped destabilize the government of Hosni Mubarak. Recently, women in Egypt have been allowed to participate more fully in the economic and professional life of the country, but as we see in Nawal El Saadawi's "Growing Up Female in Egypt," those battles have been hard won. (For more background information on Egypt, see page 258.)

1   The struggle between me and my femininity began very early ... before my femininity sprouted and before I knew anything about myself, my

---
[3] Translated by Fedwa Malti-Douglas.

2. sex, or my origin . . . indeed, before I knew what hollow had enclosed me before I was tossed out into this wide world.

2. All that I knew at that time was that I was a girl, as I heard from my mother. A girl!

3. And there was only one meaning for the word "girl" in my mind . . . that I was not a boy . . . I was not like my brother . . .

4. My brother cuts his hair and leaves it free, he does not comb it, but as for me, my hair grows longer and longer. My mother combs it twice a day, chains it in braids, and imprisons its ends in ribbons . . .

5. My brother wakes up and leaves his bed as it is, but I, I have to make my bed and his as well.

6. My brother goes out in the street to play, without permission from my mother or my father, and returns at any time . . . but I, I do not go out without permission.

7. My brother takes a bigger piece of meat than mine, eats quickly, and drinks the soup with an audible sound, yet my mother does not say anything to him . . .

8. As for me . . . ! I am a girl! I must watch my every movement . . . I must hide my desire for food and so I eat slowly and drink soup without a sound . . .

9. My brother plays . . . jumps . . . turns somersaults . . . but I, whenever I sit and the dress rides up a centimeter on my thighs, my mother throws a sharp, wounding glance at me, and I hide my shame and impurity . . .

10. Shame and impurity!

11. Everything in me is shame and impurity, though I am a child of nine years!

12. I felt sorry for myself.

13. I closed the door of my room on myself and sat crying alone . . .

14. The first tears of my life were not shed because I failed in school or because I broke something expensive . . . but because I was a girl!

15. I cried over my femininity before I knew it . . .

16. I opened my eyes on the world with enmity between myself and my nature.

17. I bounded down the steps three at a time to get to the street before I finished counting to ten . . .

18. My brother and his friends, sons and daughters of the neighbors, are waiting for me to play cops and robbers . . . I have received permission from my mother to go out . . . I love to play! I love to run as fast as I can . . . I feel an overflowing happiness whenever I move my head, my arms, or my legs in the air . . . and I run in great bounds, hindered only by the weight of my body, which the earth draws to itself . . .

19. Why did God not make me a bird so I could fly like a dove, but instead made me a girl? It seemed to me that God preferred birds to girls . . .

20. But my brother does not fly . . .

21 This fact comforted me a bit . . . I felt that boys, despite their wide freedom, were incapable, like me, of flying . . . and I began to always search for the areas of weakness in men to console me for the weakness that my femininity imposed on me.

22 I do not know what happened to me while I was jumping . . . I felt a violent shiver running through my body and a dizziness in my head . . . Then I saw something red!
23 "What is this?"
24 I was extremely alarmed, I stopped playing, mounted the stairs to my house, and locked myself in the bathroom to search secretly for the explanation of this grave event . . .
25 But I did not understand anything . . . And I thought that this might be a sudden illness that had stricken me . . . So I went in terror to ask my mother . . .
26 I saw my mother laughing happily . . . I was amazed that my mother could confront this hideous sickness with such a broad smile . . .
27 My mother saw my surprise and confusion and took me by the hand to my room, where she told me women's bloody story . . .
28 I stayed in my room for four days in a row, not having the courage to face my brother, or my father, or even the servant boy.
29 They have all certainly become aware of my shame and impurity . . . My mother has undoubtedly betrayed my new secret . . . I closed the door on myself to explain this strange phenomenon to myself . . . Was there no other way for girls to mature, other than this unclean way? Is it possible for a person to live for days under the control of his tyrannical, involuntary muscles? God undoubtedly hates girls, so he tarnished them all with this shame . . .
30 I felt that God had sided with boys in everything . . .
31 I got up from my bed, dragging my oppressive existence, and looked in the mirror . . . What is this?
32 Two small protrusions had grown on my chest!
33 Oh! If only I could die!
34 What is this strange body that surprises me every day with a new shame that increases my weakness and my withdrawal into myself?!
35 I wonder what else will grow on my body tomorrow? Or, I wonder through what other new symptom my tyrannical femininity will erupt!

36 I hated my femininity . . .
37 I felt that it was chains . . . chains of my own blood that bind me to the bed so that I am unable to run and jump . . . chains from within my own body . . . that shackle me in fetters of shame and disgrace so that I withdraw within myself, hiding my dejected existence . . .
38 I no longer ran . . . And I no longer played . . .

39 These two protrusions on my chest are getting bigger and they quiver whenever I walk . . .

40 I stood sadly with my tall, slender frame, hiding my chest with my arms, and watched, with sorrow, my brother and his companions playing . . .

41 I grew . . . I outgrew my brother, though he was older than I . . . I outgrew the other children, so I withdrew from them and sat by myself thinking . . .

42 My childhood came to an end . . . a short, breathlessly fast childhood . . . No sooner did I experience it then it slipped away and left me a mature woman's body carrying within it a ten-year-old child . . .

43 I saw the eyes and teeth of the doorkeeper shining in the middle of his coal-black face . . . He approached me while I was sitting by myself on his wooden bench, following my brother and his friends with my eyes, while they ran and jumped . . .

44 I felt the rough edge of his *galabeyya** touching my leg and I smelled the strange odor of his garments, so I moved away with disgust; but he drew near me again and I tried to hide my fear from him by watching my brother and his companions playing, but I felt his rough, coarse fingers groping around my thighs and ascending under my clothing! . . .

45 I got up in terror and quickly ran away from him . . .

46 This repulsive black man is also staring at my femininity?!

47 And I ran until I entered the house . . . My mother asked me the reason for my alarm . . . But I could not say anything to her . . . Perhaps I was afraid or ashamed, or both . . . Or perhaps I thought that she would reprimand me and that there would not be between us that affection that would make me tell her my secrets . . .

48 I no longer went out in the street . . . And I no longer sat on the wooden bench . . .

49 I fled from those strange, rough-voiced and mustached beings that they call men . . . and I created a special world for myself designed by my imagination . . . and I made myself the god of this world, and I made men into weak, ignorant creatures charged with serving me . . .

50 I sat in my world on my high throne arranging the dolls on the chairs and placing the boys on the ground, and I would tell stories to myself . . .

51 No one disturbed my life alone with my imagination and my dolls except my mother . . . with her many orders that never ended . . . the house and kitchen chores . . . the ugly, limited world of women, from which emanated the odor of garlic and onion.

---

* Galabeyya, overdress or robe.—*Tr.*

52 No sooner would I escape to my small world than my mother would drag me to the kitchen, saying, "Your future lies in marriage . . . You have to learn to cook . . . Your future lies in marriage . . . Marriage! Marriage!"

53 That loathsome word that my mother repeated every day until I hated it . . . And I never heard it without imagining in front of me a man with a big belly inside of which was a table of food . . .

54 In my mind, I connected the smell of the kitchen with the smell of a husband . . .

55 And I hated the word "husband" and I hated the smell of food.

56 My old grandmother remained silent amidst the chatter and looked at my chest . . . I saw her worn eyes contemplating the two new protruding buds and weighing them . . . Then I saw her whispering something to my mother . . .

57 I heard my mother say to me: "Wear the light-blue dress so that you can come in and greet the guest who is with your father in the salon . . ."

58 I smelled the odor of conspiracy in the air . . .

59 I used to greet most of my father's friends and serve them coffee . . . And sometimes I would sit with them and listen to my father while he told them about my success in school, and I would feel happy and sense that my father, by recognizing my intelligence, was freeing me from the gloomy world of women, from which emanated the odor of onion and marriage . . .

60 But why the light-blue dress? That new dress that I hate . . . On the front of it was a strange pleat that rested on my breasts and increased their prominence . . .

61 My mother looked at me searchingly . . . She said, "Where is the light-blue dress?"

62 I answered angrily: "I will never wear it!" . . . She saw the stirrings of rebellion in my eyes, looked at me sadly, and said, "Then smooth over your eyebrows . . ."

63 But I did not look at her . . . And before opening the salon door to enter, I ran my fingers through my eyebrows, mussing them up . . .

64 I greeted my father's friend and sat down . . . I saw a strange, frightful face with a relentless, scrutinizing gaze that resembled that of my grandmother . . .

65 My father said, "She is first in her class this year in junior high school . . ."

66 I did not see any expression of admiration in the man's eyes at these words . . . . But I saw his scrutinizing glances hover around my body and settle finally on my chest. So I stood up in terror and left the room, running as though a demon were chasing me . . .

67 My mother and my grandmother met me at the door with a passionate anxiety and said in one breath, "My God! . . . What have you done?"

68 I uttered a single shriek in their faces, ran to my room, and locked myself in... Then I went to the mirror to look at my chest...

69 I hated them! Those two protrusions! Those two small pieces of flesh that circumscribed my future! I wished that I could tear them from my chest with a sharp knife!

70 But I could not... I could only hide them... compress them with a thick corset to flatten them...

71 This long, heavy hair... that I carry on top of my head everywhere... It hampers me every morning, burdens me in the bath, and burns my neck in the summer...

72 Why is it not short, free, like my brother's hair? He does not carry it on top of his head, nor does it hamper him or burden him.

73 But my mother rules over my life, my future, and my body, even down to the locks of my hair...

74 Why...?

75 Because she gave birth to me? But what is her merit in having given birth to me? She pursued her normal life like any other woman, and then I came along without any act of will on her part in one of her moments of happiness... I came without her knowing me... without her choosing me... and without my choosing her...

76 I was imposed on her as a daughter and she was imposed on me as a mother...

77 Is it possible for someone to love a being who has been imposed on her? And, if my mother loved me despite herself, instinctively, then what virtue is there in this love? And is she thus superior to the cat who, at times, loves her kittens, but, at other times, devours them?

78 Is not my mother's harsh treatment more painful to me than if she were to devour me?!

79 And if my mother loved me with a true love whose aim was my happiness and not hers, then why are all her orders and desires in contradiction with my comfort and happiness?!

80 Can she love me while putting chains every day on my feet, on my hands, and around my neck?

81 For the first time in my life, I went out of the house without asking permission from my mother...

82 I walked in the street, and the challenge had given me a kind of power, but my heart was beating from fear...

83 I saw a sign that said "Ladies' Hairdresser"...

84 I hesitated for an instant and then went in...

85 I watched the locks of my hair twisting between the blades of the sharp scissors and then falling to the ground...

86 Are these the locks that my mother spoke of as woman's crown and throne? Does woman's crown fall to the ground like this, in a single moment of decisiveness? I felt great contempt for women... I saw with my

own eyes that they believed in worthless things of no value... And this contempt for them gave me a new strength that permitted me to go home with a firm step, and I was able to stand up before my mother with my short hair.

87. My mother uttered one loud scream and gave me a sharp slap on the face... Then more and more slaps followed... while I remained standing...

88. As though I had become frozen... as though the challenge had made of me a force that nothing could shake... as though my victory over my mother had made of me a hard substance that did not feel the slaps...

89. My mother's hand would crash against my face and then fall back from it, as though it had crashed into granite...

90. How is that I did not cry? I was the one who would be made to cry by a single shout or a light slap.

91. But my tears did not fall... My eyes were wide open, looking into my mother's eyes boldly and strongly...

92. My mother continued to slap me... then she collapsed on the couch, sitting, repeating in a daze: "She has gone crazy!"

93. I pitied her when I saw her face sink in defeat and weakness. I felt a strong desire to hug her, kiss her, and cry between her arms... to say to her: "Reason does not lie in my always obeying you..."

94. But I pulled my eyes away from hers so that she would not be aware that I had witnessed her defeat, and I ran to my room...

95. I looked in the mirror and smiled over my short hair and the flash of victory in my eyes...

96. I knew for the first time in my life what victory was like... Fear leads only to defeat... and victory can only be won through courage.

97. The fear that I used to feel toward my mother left me... That great halo that made me dread her fell from her... I felt that she was an ordinary woman... And her slaps, which were the strongest things she possessed, I no longer feared... because they no longer hurt me...

98. I hated the house except for my study... I loved school except for the home economics class... I loved the days of the week except for Friday...

99. I participated in all the school activities... I joined the acting club, the speech club, the athletics club, the music club, and the drawing club... But this was not enough for me; instead, I got together with some of my girlfriends and I created a club called the Friendship Club... Why did I choose the word "friendship"? I did not know... but I felt that deep within me was a great longing for friendship... for a great big friendship that nothing could satisfy... for vast groups of people who would keep me company, speak to me, listen to me, and go off with me to heaven...

100. I did not believe that any achievement would suffice me... it would not extinguish the fire burning in my soul... I hated the repeated,

monotonous lessons... I used to read the material once... once only... I felt that repetition would suffocate me... kill me... I wanted something new... new... always...

101. I was not aware of him when he entered my room and when he stood beside me while I sat reading my book until he said, "Wouldn't you like to relax a little?"

102. I had been reading for a long time and felt tired. So I smiled and said, "I would like to take a walk outside."

103. "Put on your coat and let's go."

104. I put on my coat quickly and ran to him... I was on the point of putting my hand in his so we could run together, as we used to do when we were children, but my eyes fastened on his and I suddenly remembered the long years I had not played and during which my feet had forgotten how to run and had grown accustomed to walking slowly like adults... So I put my hands in my coat and set out slowly beside him...

105. I hear him say, "You have grown."

106. "And you also."

107. "Do you remember the days when we used to play together?"

108. "You always used to beat me at running."

109. "And you always used to win at marbles."

110. We laughed a long time... A lot of air entered my chest and it invigorated me, making me feel that I was recovering some of my lost childhood...

111. He said, "I want to run a race with you."

112. I said confidently, "I will beat you."

113. He said, "Let's see...!"

114. We drew line of the ground... and stood next to each other... He yelled out: "One... two... three..." And we took off running the course.

115. I was about to reach the finish line before him, but he grabbed me by my clothing from behind so I stumbled and fell to the ground, and he fell next to me... I lifted my eyes to him, breathless, and I saw him gazing at me with a strange look that made the blood rise to my face... Then I saw his arm reach for my waist... and he whispered in my ear with a rough voice, "I will kiss you."

116. My whole being shook with a violent, strange shudder and I wished for an instant—it flashed through my senses like lightning—that his arm would reach further and embrace me strongly... strongly... But my strange secret desire, emerging from my hidden depths, changed into an intense anger...

117. But my anger increased his persistence, and he grabbed me with an iron hand... I do not know where the strength came from that made me push his arm far away from me, and lift up my hand and then let it fall on his face in one violent slap...

118   I tossed around my bed confused... Strange feelings flood my being... and many phantoms pass before me... But one vision lingers before my eyes...

119   My cousin lying on the ground next to me with his arms almost wrapped around my waist and his strange glances piercing my head...

120   I closed my eyes to float with my specter, who began to move his arm until it wound strongly around my waist... and he moved his lips until they touched mine and pressed upon them with force...

121   I hid my head under the covers...

122   Am I sincere?! This hand of mine that rose and slapped him is the very same hand that trembles in his imaginary hand?!

123   I wrapped the covers tightly around my head to shut out this strange illusion, but it slipped under the covers to me... So I put the pillow on my head and I pressed it with all my strength to smother that stubborn specter... and I kept pressing on my head until sleep smothered me...

124   I opened my eyes in the morning, when the sunlight had dispersed the darkness with all the ghosts that lurked in it...

125   I opened the window... The invigorating air entered my chest and it destroyed the remnants clinging to my vision from the delusions of the night...

126   I smiled scornfully at my inner self, this cowardly self that shakes out of fear of me when I am awake and then sneaks into my bed in the dark and fills the bed, surrounding me with specters and illusions!

127   I finished my secondary studies and I was first in my class... Then I sat thinking: What course do I follow?

128   What course can I follow since I hate my femininity, detest my nature, and disown my body?!

129   None but denial... challenge... resistance!

130   I will deny my femininity... I will challenge my nature... I will resist all the desires of my body...

131   I will prove to my mother and grandmother that I am not a woman like them... I will never spend my life in the kitchen peeling onions and garlic... I will never devote my life to a husband who eats and eats...

132   I will prove to my mother that I am smarter than my brother, than man, than all men... and that I am capable of doing all that my father does, and still more...

Reading for Meaning

1. What images from childhood does the narrator use to convey the differences between her and her brother? How was she made to feel about herself because of this difference? What situations have you experienced, observed, or read about that favor males or females?

2. In what ways does the character express her alienation from herself and from the world? What is her response to this increasing withdrawal from the physical world?

3. What importance does her hair have in the narrator's life and in the larger culture?

4. Based on what you can infer from the text, what control do mothers exercise over their daughters' behavior in Islamic Egypt? What might be their reasons for maintaining such control? What motivations does the narrator imagine are behind her mother's fierce control over her life?

5. In your experience, how do parents control their children's behavior? How is this control designed to help them join the larger culture?

Comparing Texts

1. The *Encyclopedia Britannica's* entry on "Family and Kinship" quotes Talcott Parsons, an American sociologist, who defines one of the important functions of the modern family as "the primary socialization of children." Parsons asserts that parents teach their children not only the "more mundane aspects of behavior," like language acquisition and how to get along with others, but "children are also implicitly encouraged to develop the values of the parents and of the society in which they live. In American society, . . . these values include independence, motivation for achievement, and competition." What "values" do parents in "Growing Up Female in Egypt" wish to inculcate in their daughters? Which of those "values" have the strongest impact on the narrator's life? What methods does she use to avoid being controlled by the values that she rejects?

2. Compare the perspectives on arranged marriages presented by Sembene Ousmane in "The Bilal's Fourth Wife," Nicholas Bornoff in "The Marriage-Go-Round," and Nawal El Saadawi in "Growing Up Female in Egypt." What assumptions do these writers make about this and other cultural practices they describe? How do you explain each writer's attitude toward male and female behavior?

3. In "The Political Challenges Facing Arab Women at the End of the 20th Century" (1982), Nawal El Saadawi discusses the role that religious fundamentalism has played in eroding women's rights. She dubs this movement the "new imperialism":

> The religious weapon has become much more dangerous with the ascendancy of the conservative religious forces as new political forces vying with each other for rule in Arab countries, including Egypt, Sudan, Algeria, Tunisia, and Syria. This phenomenon is not limited to Arab countries, or to Islam, but is, rather a global phenomenon which includes other religions and many countries of the world. The new imperialists—like their predecessors, the old colonialists—find in religion a weapon to divide peoples; sectarian rifts are mounted and exploitation based on the global economic order is masked. . . . Concealed beneath the surface are international struggles over petrol and Arab wealth, Israel's occupation of Palestine, the employment of petrol revenue against the interests of the Arab peoples, spurious development projects and greater dependency, more external debt, more unemployment, rising prices, and inflation.

Saadawi concludes that the burden of change falls entirely on women:

> It is women who must reveal these facts, must demonstrate that the particular Islamic *sharia*[4] which the conservative movements have circulated is mostly based on distorted interpretations of Islam and other philosophies that emphasize the inevitability of fate. It is women who must demonstrate that there exist philosophies and interpretations more sophisticated, just, and humane.
>
> The Arab woman must study religion, and interpret it with her own powers of rational intelligence, rather than seeing it through the minds of others. She must link religious concepts and texts to their historical and social contexts, and develop a highly critical outlook in which rationality gets the better of tradition and imitation, and the doctrine of utility replaces a blind adherence to the literalness of the text.

Read the first chapter of Mary Wollstonecroft's *Vindication of the Rights of Women*, "The Rights and Involved Duties of Mankind Considered" (reprinted in Appendix A). Wollstonecroft wrote her *Vindication* in 1792, shortly after the French Revolution of 1789 and following the publication of Thomas Paine's *Vindication of the Rights of Man*. Compare the use Wollstonecroft makes of religion in her defense of women to Nawal El Saadawi's discussion of religion in the passages you have just read.

Ideas for Writing

1. Nawal El Saadawi has written books, articles, and speeches that underscore the plight of Arab women. Her article, "The Political Challenges Facing Arab Women at the End of the 20th Century," mentioned earlier, appeared in a collection of articles, *The Hidden Face of Eve: Women of the Arab World,* published in 1982. In this article she argues that "The public, political challenges and the private, individual challenges in the life of an Arab woman cannot be separated, and she cannot confront one without facing the other as well." In much of the Arab world, she notes:

   > Women may practice their rights by making personal decisions to be active in public life—thereby sacrificing their married lives. Or they may prefer the security of marriage to public activity in the political and cultural spheres. A man may divorce his wife if she goes against his orders; even if he does not divorce her, the spectre of divorce hovers, a sword of Damocles, over her head. . . . In some Arab countries, the law stipulates explicitly that a man has the right to prevent a woman from going outside the home without his permission. In other cases, while there is no explicit statement to this effect, a man is given the right to prevent a woman from going out to work if this conflicts with the welfare of the family; and it is the man who defines what is the welfare of the family.

---

[4] The laws of Islam that govern the rights and behavior of a woman in her private life. These laws ensure that hers is a subordinate role in the household and that "her ancient obligation towards the family" defines her.

Do some research on the personal or political freedom that women enjoy in a country of your choice. Write a paper in which you evaluate the degree to which women in that country enjoy freedom of speech and action equivalent to the men.

2. In her book *Reviving Ophelia,* clinical psychologist Mary Pipher describes adolescence as a time "when individual, developmental and cultural factors combine in ways that shape adulthood. It's a time of marked internal development and massive cultural indoctrination." In Pipher's view, indoctrination in the United States is particularly harmful because just as adolescent girls must turn from their parents and assert their independence, they and their peers must "struggle with countless new pressures. . . . They befriend their peers, who are their fellow inhabitants of the strange country and who share a common language and set of customs. They often embrace the junk values of mass culture" (p. 23). Parents in the 1990s "are not the agents of culture, but rather the enemies of the cultural indoctrination that their daughters face with puberty. They battle to save their daughters' true selves" (p. 65). Write an examination of "messages" that women, particularly adolescents, are given about themselves by the "mass culture" in the United States. You might examine one or two media—a television program, movies, music, or magazines—and interpret what these media teach adolescent girls about themselves, their place in the culture, or what they are supposed to value.

Writing before Reading

1. What impressions do you have of the Israeli armed forces? What has contributed to your ideas about it?

2. What impressions do you have of women in either the Israeli Army or the U.S. Armed Forces? Describe the experiences or observations that formed these impressions.

FRONT AND REAR: THE SEXUAL DIVISION OF LABOUR IN THE ISRAELI ARMY

Nira Yuval-Davis

Nira Yuval-Davis is a lecturer in sociology at the Thames Polytechnic in London. She has written extensively about the Middle East in articles focusing on the Arab-Israeli conflict and the interplay of gender, class, ethnic, and national divisions. A more recent project examines ethnic and gender divisions in southeast London. "Front and Rear" is based on a paper that Nira Yuval-Davis presented at a conference on Women in the Military at the Transnational Institute in Amsterdam and published in Loaded Questions. *The essay was subsequently published in the anthology* Women, State and Ideology: Studies from Africa and Asia *(1987).*

Facts about Israel

On May 14, 1948, the State of Israel was carved out of Palestine following the United Nations' recommendation to create a Jewish and an Arab state out of the former British protectorate. The creation of a Jewish homeland had been the goal of the nineteenth-century Zionists, European Jews who saw a return to the land of Moses and King David as sanctioned by Jewish history and biblical precedent. It also seemed to afford the best insurance against pogroms.[5] The birth of Israel marked the beginning of hostilities between Israel and its neighbors that continue to this day. Arab countries refused to recognize Israel and attacked the new country. When the first Arab-Israeli war ended in January 1949, Israel had acquired new territory in the Galilee and Negev Desert. The Six-Day War in 1967 began with Egyptian and Jordanian preparations to attack Israel. Anticipating an attack, Israel bombed targets in Egypt, Syria, Jordan, and Iraq. Israel once again expanded its territory, this time more than doubling its size with the acquisition of the Sinai Peninsula, the Golan Heights, the West Bank, Gaza, and the Arab quarter in Jerusalem. In an attempt to regain land taken during the October war, Egypt and Syria attacked Israel again in the October War, 1973, also called the *Yom Kippur* War, so named because the assault occurred during the Jewish fast, which is part of *Yom Kippur,* the Day of Atonement. As a result of this war and the peace accord signed on March 26, 1979, Israel gave back the Sinai to Egypt and land in the Golan Heights to Syria. In ensuing years, guerrilla attacks on Israeli settlements precipitated Israel's invasion of southern Lebanon and West Beirut in an attempt to destroy bases held by the Palestine Liberation Organization (PLO). Israel's apparent complicity with the forces of Bashir Gemayel, the assassinated president-elect of Lebanon, in massacring Palestinian refugees became an international outrage. The *Intifada,* "uprising" in Arabic, began in the territories occupied by Israel in late 1987. Yitzhak Rabin signed a historic agreement with Yasir Arafat in September 1993 that made peaceful coexistence seem possible for the first time. The assassination of Rabin on November 4, 1995, by a Jewish fundamentalist and the subsequent election of the Likud Party's leader, Benjamin Netanyahu, cast doubt on Israel's ability to make peace with either the Palestinians or its Arab neighbors. In the late 1990s the peace process has stalled several times. After several failed attempts to negotiate an agreement Arafat and Netanyahu worked out an interim peace accord on October 23, 1998. The agreement called for the withdrawal of Israeli forces from an additional 13

---

[5] An officially sanctioned massacre of a minority group, in particular, the one conducted against Jews in Eastern Europe.

percent of the West Bank and the release of Palestinian political prisoners. In return, Palestinians agreed to arrest political extremists and remove sections in the PLO charter that call for the destruction of Israel. Renewed terrorist attacks on Israelis at home and abroad as well as continued development of Jewish housing in Arab East Jerusalem threatened to overturn this agreement. The election on May 20, 1999 of Labor Party candidate Ehud Barak, the most decorated officer in Israeli history, raises hopes of negotiating a new settlement with the Palestinians.

In spite of its being either close to or in a state of war for much of its existence, Israel has developed much of what was once arid land, in addition to making significant technological advancements. In recent years the population of the state created in 1948, although still about 80 percent Jewish, has changed dramatically with the immigration of Jews from the former Soviet Union, *falashas* from Ethiopia, and other Jewish groups from North Africa and Asia. Populations of Arabs and Druz Moslems account for about 15 percent of the population. Hebrew and Arabic are official languages in Israel; English and Russian are also widely spoken.

1   In recent years the role of women in the military has been widely debated. While some feminists are opposed to women's participation in military activity of any kind, others favour the integration of women into the "mail domain" of the armed forces. The largest feminist organisation in the United States, the National Organization for Women, for example, argues that if men are drafted into military service, women should be as well. In NOW's view, women's equality means an equal share in both the "rights" and the "duties" of society.[1]

2   This issue is generally debated as a moral or philosophical level. This paper explores it more concretely, by examining the historical experience of women in the Israeli army, the first army to recruit women by national law. The Israeli case suggests that the incorporation of women into the military may change the nature of, rather than eliminate, their subordination. Being formally a part of the military does not guarantee equality, either in terms of the actual tasks fulfilled by women or in terms of the power they exercise. On the contrary, in the extremely hierarchical and bureaucratic modern army machinery, gender differentiation can be even more formal and extreme than in the civilian labour market, as the Israeli case illustrates well.

3   Traditionally, the military has been considered an exclusive male domain. This was, however, never absolutely true. For example, in the siege of Jerusalem 2000 years ago, women helped to pour boiling oil on the attacking Romans. Women were also part of the attacking army, accompanying the Roman battalions, not only to fulfil the sexual needs of the soldiers, but also to provide general servicing and maintenance for the army. In a sense, very little has changed since then. However, only since the First World War, and then only in a temporary and marginal way, have women come to constitute a *formal* part of the military. Even today, there

are very few States in which women are conscripted into the armed forces (except in times of emergency) by law.

4   Yet women do constitute an integral part of most armies throughout the world, even if the exact extent of this participation is difficult to determine. For administrative or historical reasons, women performing identical jobs (like clerical work or nursing) in different countries may be considered formally military personnel in one case and strictly civilian employees in another. But if women's work is important in all contemporary armies, in none—be it liberation army, national army, or professional army—are women represented to an extent approaching that of men. In most cases, women constitute no more than 5 to 7 per cent of military personnel, often much less. Furthermore, in no army do women have *de facto*[6] (and almost never *de jure*)[7] equal access to military roles. There are almost always some military professions closed to women and some in which they are heavily concentrated. The allocation of military roles is, then, virtually always sexually ascriptive. This does not necessarily mean that all military professions are exclusively male or female, or that there is no fluctuation in the accessibility of certain jobs to men and women. But it does mean that a vital aspect of each military role is its definition as open to men and/or women.

Front and Rear

5   Front and rear are terms which are used regularly in military discourse. Generally speaking, this dichotomy reflects the actual continuum of geographical and functional areas involved in a military confrontation. The front is where the territory under control of the fighting collectivity ends and the confrontation with the enemy takes place. The rear is where most of the members of the collectivity stay in relative security defended by the fighters, who are prepared to die for the sake of the collectivity—to defend the lives of its members, its territory, or in some cases to expand and glorify it further. The rear, on the other hand, provides for all the needs of the fighters at the front.

6   Rear and front are not static structures. Once the front expands, the rear follows, and certain areas of the former front become part of the new rear. What is crucial though, is that certain functions of the rear, those of service and administration, are always part of the rear, while face-to-face fighting always takes place in the front.

7   Traditionally, the territorial front/rear and combatant/non-combatant dichotomies overlapped considerably. Although there were always people who fulfilled non-combatant roles at the front zone—essential

---

[6] In fact or in actual practice.
[7] By law or legally sanctioned.

medical, communication, and other services—most of the people at the front were engaged in actual fighting. Until relatively recently, no combat roles were actually possible away from the front, although combat-type activities in training and drilling often constituted a significant part of the military rear activities.

8   The development of modern warfare has drastically changed both the ratio of combatant to non-combatant military forces, and the relationship between front and rear positions. It is estimated that approximately twenty non-combatant personnel are needed for every one combat role in a modern army. Many more auxiliary positions are required (in such areas as technology, communications, and administration) in addition to the traditional service and maintenance ones. At the same time, physical proximity is no longer necessary, in a growing number of cases, in order to hit the enemy. The "functional" front, then, does not always overlap, the "territorial" one, nor does the relatively higher safety of being in the rear always exist anymore. The most consistent characteristic of the front which has survived into the era of modern warfare is that it is where the fighting activities considered to be most important for the success of the military operation are located—even if they only involve pressing a button.

9   Men and women are not equally represented at the front and the rear. In most armies, even where women are present, they are formally barred from the front zone and/or combatant roles (the functional front). The sexual division of labour in the military, as in society as a whole, is based on ongoing traditions concerning the "proper" areas of labour for males and females.

10   There is a nearly universal ideological tradition of sexual difference which focuses on the image of men as fighters. In modern patriarchal society this tradition dictates that in the military, even more than in civilian life, men take up the heaviest and most risky jobs. Women, on the other hand, are expected both to reproduce future "man-power" in their capacity as mothers, as well as to serve the men, to raise their morale, and, when front demands expand, to perform the tasks men cannot fulfil, in their capacity as "men's helpmates."

11   The dynamic nature of the front/rear division means that what determines the roles of women in the military is the extent to which the men are needed at the front. In other words, it may not be the specific military task which determines it as a "woman's job" in the army, but rather its relation to the demands on the front and the pressure on "man-power" resources. Women's engagement in occupational roles formerly filled only by men does not necessarily mean, then, a weakening in the sexual division of labour. It often represents simply an expansion of the military and/or economic front with women "filling in" for men—a situation which is easily reversed when the front regresses. As long as non-differential gender roles are a product of emergencies, such as revolution

Chapter 8 Custom and Gender Roles

or war, the sexual division of labour will reassert itself along traditional lines once the crisis has passed.

12 I propose the front/rear model as a convenient framework of description of the shifting sexual division of labour, not only because of its dynamic nature, but also because it focuses attention on how national ideologies and mobilisations, mediated by States or political movements, can affect the sexual division of labour. This is true despite the fact that these national ideologies often focus on the perceived necessary role of men, rather than of women, in the military. I do not contend that even within the military the front/rear dynamic is the only dynamic of the sexual division of labour. Moreover, in each concrete historical situation, there is no unitary category of "women" and "man" in the labour market; ethnicity, class, age or place in the life cycle all affect the specific position of various categories of men and women in the military, as in the civilian labour market. Political and economic forces, from the feminist movement to the multinationals, can affect the front/rear dynamic as well.

13 These issues, however, cannot be discussed only in the abstract. Let us turn now to the case of the Israeli military and explore the dynamics of the sexual division of labour in its pre-State and post-State history.

HISTORICAL BACKGROUND OF THE ISRAELI CASE

14 Cynthia Enloe[2] remarks that the integration of women into the army is usually defined as part of the *national* security policy, while in reality it is an expression of the *State* security policy. This is an important differentiation in every case, but especially in the case of Israel, where women's participation in the military started in the pre-State period, and continued after the State was established. Israel defines itself as a Jewish State, recruiting initially only Jewish people, including women, to its military. Many of its citizens however, and even more so those under its control, are not part of the Jewish national collectivity. The relationship between "the nation" and "the State" is, therefore, of prime importance when examining the sexual division of labour in the Israeli army.

15 The Zionist immigration, which started in 1882 with the first *Aliya* (wave of immigration) from Russia, was the first to conceive of immigration to Palestine as an act of a national movement. Almost from the beginning of the Zionist settlement, the Zionists wanted to establish a Jewish society and State in Palestine. Using socialist ideologies, they wanted to exclude the native Palestinians from the new society they were creating—in other words, to dispossess rather than to exploit them.

16 This strategy had two natural results which affected the involvement of women in the military: almost from the beginning it created confrontations with the Palestinians, who resented the new phenomenon

and, felt more and more threatened. The Palestinians attempted in various ways to struggle against the "invaders." This confrontation started on local levels, and gradually grew to a national movement: on a Palestinian level, it reached its peak in the "rebellion" of 1936–9, and on a national Arab scale, in the war of 1948, with the invasion by Arab armies into Palestine. Thus all through the history of the Zionist settlement and the State of Israel, military occupation had a central place in the life of the settlers. In this sense, Israeli society was from the outset a "war society" needing loyal and trained human power to help with the military effort.

17 The other result of this "socialist strategy" of colonisation was that women were considered (ideologically although not practically) to be equal members of the new society. From the beginning, this enabled women to be potentially part of the human power pool, which would be used in the pursuit of militarisation.

18 Until the establishment of the State only volunteer women (and men) served in the military. There were circles in the *Yishuv* (the pre-State Jewish settlement in Palestine) like the religious sector, from which hardly any women participated at all. Those who did participate, were involved, on the one hand in the military organisation of the *Yishuv* (like the *Hashomer*,[3] *Hagana*,[4] *Palmach*,[5] *Ezel*, and *Lehi*[6]) and on the other hand in the ATS[7] of the British army. The sexual division of labour in the *Yishuv* military organisations, was much less formal than that of the ATS, where women were in separate units and performed very specific "women's" tasks. In the *Yishuv* organisations, the sexual division of labour was dependent to a great extent on the specific state of the conflict. The expansion of the territory controlled by the *Yishuv*, and the growing centralisation of the military organisations made the sexual division of labour more and more distinct, although all along women were a minority in the military forces and even when they were in the front, they fulfilled mainly auxilliary roles of communication and nursing.

19 With the establishment of the State significant changes were brought to the nature of women's participation in the Israeli military. Unlike in the time of the *Yishuv*, the military State policy has had to relate to all sectors of the State population, and not just the volunteers, although not necessarily in the same way.

20 Also, in the pre-State period there was ambivalence, inconsistency and vagueness in relation to the nature of women's participation in the military, and in many cases, it was a result of ad-hoc decisions, rather than a planned policy. In addition there were at least three opposing ideologies (represented most clearly by the *Palmach*, ATS and the religious sectors) concerning the desired nature of women's participation. These ideologies could continue to co-exist as parallel and separate *ideologies* after the establishment of the State, but a coherent, unified (although not necessarily homogeneous) State *policy* had to be crystallised.

Zahal (Israel Defence Army)

21 "*Zahal* is the army of Israel to which the guardianship of its sovereignity and security is commanded. It also fulfils an important role in absorption of immigration, integration of various ethnic groups, education of national consciousness and learning."[8] It was formally established on 31 May 1948, and consists of a small professional core, a large number of conscripts and a reserve army.

22 According to Shif and Haber, its structure and basic strategy is to keep maximum mobility; to transfer the war to the enemy territory and to develop preventive wars. This is based on the assumption that Israel will always be quantitatively inferior, of small strategic importance and surrounded by enemy countries.

Chen (Charm; Women Corps)

23 *Chen* is defined as one of the goal-oriented command units of *Zahal*.[9] Its structure and character emerged from the debate between those who wanted to adopt the model of the British Army and those who wanted to adopt the model of the *Hagana-Palmach*. One of the basic disagreements concerned the extent to which women should be kept in separate corps, as in the British army, or in mixed ones, as in the *Hagana-Palmach*. The solution which was accepted was some kind of compromise. It is not incidental, however, that from the establishment of *Chen* in 1948 until 1970, all the commanding officers were ex-ATS officers. The name of the command unit was also a result of a compromise. It was first suggested that it should be called Auxiliary Women Corps, but the name Women Corps was finally adopted, both because its initials in Hebrew then meant "charm" (a feminine characteristic emphasised in the corps) and because it has more egalitarian connotations.

24 All the women in *Zahal* formally belong to *Chen,* but their membership in the corps is more partial than the membership of the men in their units. This is because most of the women in the army are under the day-to-day authority of male officers from the other units. They are sent to fulfil their various jobs in the army, not as a result of the decision of *Chen,* but as a result of manpower decisions taken by the General Headquarters and the different command units which are all staffed by men. The senior officers of *Chen* only have advisory capacities in the General Headquarters and in the different branches and command units of the army. As Shif and Haber sum up the situation "The synthesis was crystallised (in the 50s) between senior officers (in *Chen*) as consultants, and junior officers as commanders."[10]

25 The commanding power of the junior officers of *Chen* relates to the two areas which are exclusively under *Chen* authority—basic training and juridical authority. Every woman who is recruited to the army undergoes a course of basic training, which usually takes about three

weeks. In this course she is trained in physical fitness and use of personal arms, given lectures on various topics from Zionism to cosmetics, and most of all, is adjusted to military discipline. Exclusive juridical authority over the women soldiers rests with *Chen* officers, who alone can judge women accused of any military offence (although most complaints come from the males under whom they are working). In addition, *Chen* officers in big army bases are usually responsible for the separate living quarters of the women soldiers (women in *Zahal* are not allowed to live in places where separate showers and minimal facilities are not available) and for the guard duties of female soldiers.

26   The length of service of women in *Zahal* has usually been 18–24 months, which is 4–6 shorter than that of the men. They are then obliged to serve in the reserve army until they are pregnant, mothers, or reach the age of 24 (previously 26); in specific desirable professional roles they might be asked to serve in the reserve army until the age of 34. Some women do continue to serve in the professional army, but they constitute less than 10 per cent of its composition and are usually concentrated in the lower ranks.[11] The salaries of female soldiers are identical to those of men at the same rank, as are their welfare benefits (although until a few years ago, there was some discrimination in favour of male soldiers concerning the latter).

THE MILITARY ROLES OF WOMEN IN ZAHAL

27   The aim of the female soldier's service in *Zahal:* Strengthening the fighting force by fulfilling administrative, professional and auxilliary roles, in order to release male soldiers to combat roles; training women to defend themselves and their homes and integrating them in the security effort of Israel, even after the termination of their active military service. The female soldiers also help in the educational activity of *Zahal*—in the educational system as teachers, and in *Zahal* as a whole, in the areas of crystallising the morale of the units and taking care of the soldiers of the units.[12]

Out of 850 military professions recognised by *Zahal* in 1980, women were engaged in only 270.[13] About 50 per cent of the professions open to women were clerical, a percentage more or less identical to the combat roles which were closed to women. According to Ann Bloom, the actual percentage of women soldiers who were engaged in clerical occupations was 65 per cent while the other 35 per cent were engaged in technical, mechanical and operational duties.[14]

28   The exact professions in which women are engaged in the army are not static—they change according to *Zahal*'s manpower needs. The 1952 law concerning the roles of women in regular army gives a list of 25 such roles, but also declares that a woman can fulfil any other military roles if she agrees to it in writing.

29	There are several occupations from which women have been excluded over the years, e.g. hand-grenade throwing, heavy artillery and driving (the latter role was renewed in the 1970s). A significant number of the 35 per cent who are not engaged in clerical work were engaged in welfare and teaching duties for soldiers from lower social strata who need "cultivating." In addition to serving in the army, women are "lent" to fulfil other nationally important teaching and welfare roles outside the army, as well as strengthening the politics, especially the border police, in special units.

30	A major category of women's work in the army, as in the civilian labour market, is that of office work. In that type of work, women are found in positions which are in principle inferior to those of men. As late as February 1981, the military attorney issued a judgement that coffee-making and floor washing cannot be seen as outside the legitimate duties of military secretaries.[15] The power relations between the boss and his clerk is intensified by the added power of the boss's military authority. Although women can be judged only before *Chen* officers—and they can be used as a brake on the boss's power—the complaints about the soldier and her breaking of military discipline come from the boss. Unlike in the civilian market, resignations are not accepted here.

31	Another aspect of the work of women soldiers in the offices of the different units is reflected in the name of the women's corps—"charm."

32	The subject of explicit sexual relations between women and men in the Israeli military is *formally* ignored (except when a soldier becomes pregnant and it becomes known to the military authorities). In this case, her service used to be hastily terminated, but now she is allowed two free abortions first. *Zahal* officially encourages, however, emphasising sexual differences between male and female soldiers. A central demand from the women in the army is that they "raise the morale" of the male soldiers and to make the army "a home away from home." Already, during the basic training of the women, they are coached to emphasise their feminine characteristics and their neat appearance, and they receive cosmetic guidance to help them in this respect. In the words of the *Zahal* spokesman: "*Chen* adds to *Zahal* the grace and charm which makes it also a medium for humanitarian and social activities."[16]

33	The emphasis on the feminine essence of women soldiers puts them in a position of inferiority to that of the male soldiers, that is, as being there for their sake, to make them happier and humanise military service. However, especially when they fulfil jobs in the areas of education and welfare, it also gives them certain powers. Here their femininity is basically an extrapolation of the feminine mother role, and not that of the wife or mistress. This power, however, usually has a class bias. The objects of the work of the women soldiers as teachers and welfare-officers are usually men from lower class origins than that of the women themselves (while in the offices very often the men and women come from the same class background).

34. The pressure on manpower resources in *Zahal* led in 1976 to a conscious policy to widen the range of occupations for women in the army. The new openings have been mainly in two directions: (a) military combat occupations which are fulfilled by women in noncombat conditions (for example, learning to drive tanks in order to become trainers and release experienced men to roles at the front); (b) maintenance and electrical roles which are related to the new technology involved in sophisticated armaments, in the Ammunition and Air Force command units.

35. Such new roles opening to women have created problems concerning the length of service for women in the regular army. This is a "Catch 22" situation: the relatively unskilled character of women's roles enable the army to release them earlier than the men, yet the short length of their service becomes an obstacle in allocating them to professional jobs, which involve a long period of training. The ad-hoc solution found was that women who agree to be involved in these types of occupations have to commit themselves to serve one additional year in the professional army after their regular military service is over. In addition, the army attempted to develop, in co-operation with the Ministry of Labour, pre-army training courses, which would enable the army to use their women graduates in relevant professional jobs and would also enable the women to work in the parallel occupations in the industry after their release. Some of the women involved in the courses have been women whom the army would not otherwise have recruited for "qualitative" educational reasons. However, the new higher status openings for women in the army are only a negligible percentage, in comparison with total number of women in it. Nevertheless, for almost the first time, women are occupying professional jobs in the army and this might affect not only their length of service, but also their dispensability in times of emergency at the front.

36. Over the years, with the acquisition of new kinds of military techniques and changes, there has been a corresponding change in the relative degree of overlap between female and male roles. The crucial factor which determines the sexually ascriptive nature of the military is that each task at each point in time is defined as open either to men and/or women as a vital characteristic of the job description. In spite of the change in the actual roles open to men and women in the army with time, the ascriptive sexual division is not random and is directly related to the division between front and rear.

37. Since the 1948 war, women have not been allowed to remain in the front once an emergency is declared, and the front actually starts to function as such. It was emphatically stressed by the authorities that the three women soldiers who were killed during the 1973 war met their death by staying at the front illegitimately and disobeying explicit orders. Even in

the report of the Government committee on the position of women in Israel, which aspires to egalitarianism, the recommendation is to open all the roles, with the exception of the fighting roles at the front, to women's service.

38   The demand for human resources pressuring the Israeli army during the last few years has opened to women more participation in combat roles, but this has not diminished the basic principle of the front/rear sexual division of labour in the army.

39   The sexual division of labour in the Israeli military bears some similarity to its civilian one. Although the civilian labour market is less rigid than that of the military, 54.8 per cent of women participating in the civilian labour markets are engaged in clerical and administrative jobs, and 52.3 per cent of them are engaged in the areas of public and community service. Similarly, women have started to penetrate into the areas of new mechanical and electronic industry. Because an overwhelmingly major part of the electronic industry is connected to the security and armaments industry, Palestinian men and women are not considered as a suitable "rear" human power source in this context.

40   The exclusion of Palestinians from "security" positions in the civil labour market and from all military positions, raises the question of the relationship between the sexual divisions in the Israeli military and in Israeli society as a whole. We can explore this relationship by finding out not only what positions are filled by women rather than men in the army, but also which *categories* of Israeli women fulfil these roles and which categories of women are excluded, or are not properly represented, in the military.

CATEGORIES OF WOMEN

41   As with many other seemingly universal laws, which in practice are not so, the law of national security service which recruits Israeli men and women to the army is misleading. The law of 1969 states that every Israeli citizen or permanent resident has to enter the regular army; a man between the ages of 18 and 29, and a woman between 18 and 26, unless they are medical doctors or dentists, in which case they can be called up until the age of 38. Nevertheless, in the year 1976–7, only 51.5 per cent of the Jewish women (and none of the non-Jewish women) in that age group were recruited, and it seems that the percentage has been even smaller since, after legal changes in the procedure for releasing religious women from the service were passed by the Begin government. The 48.5 per cent who were not called to serve in the army included: 2 per cent who were released for medical reasons; 0.5 per cent who were released for administrative reasons; 18.5 per cent for religious and conscientious objection; 8 per cent married before recruitment age; 0.5 per cent were dead or otherwise unavailable; 19 per cent were unsuitable for personality reasons or education. It must be noted however, that most non-Jewish

men as well as all non-Jewish women (who constitute about 15 per cent of the female population in Israel proper within the pre-1967 borders) are not called to serve in the army. Within the Jewish population, it is religious-conservative homes and insufficient education which leave about two-fifths of women outside the "universal" recruitment of women to the army.

42   A large category of women who are released from serving in the army are those the army decides are "qualitatively" unsuitable. The qualities required include a knowledge of Hebrew, a minimum level of education and a certain level of performance in psychotechnic tests. Those with a criminal record are also not recruited to the army. The release of soldiers on qualitative grounds is much higher among women than men. One-fifth of those women who are recruited are classified as "officer" quality, in contrast with only one-tenth of male recruits.

43   This differentiation in the class origin of men and women in the Israeli military strengthens a tendency which is found in most labour markets, including Israel, in which the class positions of men in the labour market are much more heterogenous than those of women who are mostly concentrated in the lower-middle class positions.[17] This strengthens my earlier observation that, although in general women are subordinate in the military, their power relations are very different *vis-à-vis* middle-class men (of similar origin to the majority of women who serve in the army) and *vis-à-vis* working class men (who are often their "clients" as pupils or as welfare cases).

44   The second category are women released on religious grounds. In 1977 it was agreed that a "genuine declaration" of "religiosity" would be legitimate grounds for women not to serve in the army. The release of women on these grounds was a concession to the religious parties who had objected initially to any women in the army, for fear of their "moral corruption." Women released from service were originally supposed to work in alternative civil service, but the law was never enforced and only a negligible number volunteer to do so, mainly in hospitals.

45   The third category of women released from regular military service are those who have already started to fulfil their reproductive role: married women, pregnant women, or women with children are released even if they are in the middle of their service, and are not called in to the reserve army. Only women in the small professional army are allowed to serve when they have families.

46   The high percentage of women who are excluded from the military has direct implications for their involvement in the intensive process of social and national integration that takes place in *Zahal*. Constant military confrontation and the relatively small size of the Israeli-Jewish nation created a need for maximum mobility of the people in and out of the army under the slogan of "There is no alternative." This meant creating a strong symbolic identification between the people and the State, with

the army as a major mediating mechanism for solidifying the "national consensus," despite the class and ethnic distinctions reflected within the internal stratification of the army.

47   The exclusion of women from this national integration process, applies to almost *all* Israeli Jewish women; few serve in the army after their early twenties (apart from the few who serve in the professional army). The Israeli men, however, serve in it until they are 50 years old, at least one month a year. Israeli Jewish national cohesiveness is, then, a major product of the patriarchal male bond of the military. Correlatively, the role of the Israeli men as soldiers is their most important national role and has a high symbolic as well as practical significance. (Only in this context can we understand the far-reaching implications that the growing movement of draft resisters in the Israeli army around the Lebanon war has had on the Israeli society.)

48   The most important national role of Israeli Jewish women also relates to the army, namely as reproducers. It used to be common in Israel (before the national mood had changed in the 1980s) to say to a pregnant woman. "Congratulations! I see you are soon going to bring a small soldier into the world!" ... Motherhood—and of boys in particular—is definitely a military role and the most important national role of Israeli Jewish women.

49   As Geula Chohen, an MP and ex-member of the dissenting organisation Lehi, put it:

> The Israeli woman is an organic part of the family of Jewish people and the female constitutes a practical symbol of that. But she is a wife and a mother of Israel, and therefore it is of her nature to be a soldier, a wife of a soldier, a sister of a soldier, a grandmother of a soldier—this is her reserve service. She is continually in military service.[18]

Likewise, David Ben-Gurion expressed the hegemonic ideology in Israel concerning woman's military role, adding that second factor must be remembered: "The woman is not only a woman, but a personality in her own right in the same way as a man. As such, she should enjoy the same rights and responsibilities as the man, except where motherhood is concerned."[19] Women, therefore, can participate as "honorary" men in the army, until they start (and some strata of women are encouraged, by being excluded from the army, to start even earlier) to be mothers.

50   It is not incidental that the attitude of the State of Israel to widows, parents and orphans of war is very different from that of any other state. Israeli society perceives in their loss an active national contribution on their part, and seeks to reward them through the Ministry of Security, by attempting to replace their dead relative, symbolically and practically. The war widow has a high salary from the State and other privileges which do not bear any relation to the income of her husband before death.[20]

51   During the Lebanon war, however, for the first time, "human sacrifice" was not accepted as a legitimate, if heart-breaking aspect of membership in the Israeli-Jewish national collectivity. One of the reasons, it is rumoured, for Begin's nervous breakdown was the impact of bereaved parents, mainly mothers, who continuously demonstrated in front of his house, accusing him of the death of their sons and refusing to be consoled by paeans to maternal sacrifice.

Conclusion

52   The military cannot be seen as totally separate from other spheres in Israeli society. The sexual division of labour in the Israeli army constitutes both a part and an extension of the sexual division of labour in the civilian labour market. The main difference is that of military uniform and discipline. The only major women's occupations in the civilian sphere which are not represented in the military are those connected with the bearing and rearing of children. This reflects the basic nature of women's participation in the military, which unlike men's, is only a temporary phase in their lives, before marriage and motherhood. It also reflects the fact that the categories of women in Israeli-Jewish society who bear the main responsibility for "child production": that is, Oriental, poor, and religious women—are under-represented in the army population....

53   ... Sex difference is by no means the only relevant signifier in allocating positions within the labour processes. Class, ethnic origin and religious beliefs have been operating all along and have to be considered in order to understand the division of labour, both within the military and outside it. Moreover, to understand women's position in the labour market at a specific historical situation, national ideologies and policies concerning the role of the military in general and men's roles within it in particular, are no less important, and sometimes even more so than understanding the specific ideologies concerning women's position. Therefore, the conventional framework of analysing the labour market has to be expanded and included in it in addition to paid employment, not only domestic labour and voluntary work ... but also the categories of work which constitute "national service," military or civil.

Notes and References

1. A discussion on that question, among others, can be found in C. Enloe's book, *Does Kahaki Become You* (Pluto Press, 1983).
2. C. Enloe, "Women—the Reserve Army of Army Labour," *Review of Radical Political Economics,* 12, 1980.
3. *Hashomer*—the first organisation of full-time guards which was established at the beginning of the century to defend Zionist settlements.
4. *Hagana—The Defence,* the largest national military organisation dominated by the labour Zionist movement.

5. *Palmach*—the commando battalions of the *Hagana* in the pre-State period.
6. *Ezel, Lehi*—the "Dissenting organisations" which had an extreme policy of military confrontation with the Palestinians and the British.
7. ATS—Auxiliary Territorial Service: Women's Corps in the British Army, where women from Palestine served in the Second World War.
8. Z. Shif and E. Haber, *Lexicon of the Security of Israel* (Hebrew) (Tel-Aviv: Zmora Bitan, 1976) p. 439.
9. Ibid., pp. 216–18.
10. Ibid., p. 218.
11. The Government Report of the Committee on the Position of Women. The Prime Minister's Office, *Discussion and Facts* (Jerusalem 1978) p. 103.
12. Ibid., p. 89.
13. Ibid., p. 97.
14. A. R. Bloom, "The Women in Israel's Military Forces," p. 46. She quotes the figure from a high ranking officer in 1980.
15. Report in *Ha'aretz* newspaper, Feb. 1981 (Heb.).
16. "*Chen*"—The Women's Corps', Spokesman, Israel Defence Forces, 30 May 1972.
17. D. Israeli and K. Gaier, "Sex and inter-occupational Wage differences in Israel" in *Sociology of Work and Occupations.* November 1979, pp. 404–29.
18. L. Hazelton, *Israeli Women—the reality behind the myth* (Hebrew) (Idanim, 1978).
19. David Ben-Gurion, *Israel, a personal history* (American Israel Pub., 1972) pp. 323–4.
20. L. Shamgar, *War Widows in Israeli Society,* Ph.D. thesis (Hebrew) Hebrew University, 1979. Since the economic crisis, however, the economic position of many of the widows has severely deteriorated, and lately a protest movement of war widows has arisen which receives a wide popular support for their demands.

Reading for Meaning

1. According to Yuval-Davis, how do traditional ideas of gender roles determine the positioning of men in the "front" and women at the "rear" of the army?

2. What roles are allocated to Israeli women who serve in the army? How do these roles compare with those assigned to women in the U.S. military?

3. What class distinctions operate in the Israeli Army? Do they have equivalents in the armed forces of the United States?

4. In what sense is the Israeli woman regarded as part of the military, whether she is in the army or not? What privileges has she enjoyed as a result of the culture's ideology that women have, by nature, an ersatz "military" role?

Comparing Texts

Do some investigation to find out the current U.S. military's policies governing women in the military. Highlight areas in which women are included as well as excluded. Compare the "national ideology" of the United States as reflected in these policies to the Israeli ideology that Yuval-Davis discusses.

Ideas for Writing

1. Nira Yuval-Davis argues that national ideologies affect the sexual division of labor, and she looks specifically at the situation in the Israeli Army. How does Yuval-Davis make her case, and how convincing are these methods in proving her point?

2 Nira Yuval-Davis mentions draft resistance in the Israeli Army during the Lebanon war in the 1980s. Do some research about the history of draft resistance in the United States. Focus on one particular period (World War II, Vietnam, etc.) and explain something about those efforts. You might, for example, focus on the reasons why individuals resisted being drafted at the time, public response to draft resisters, or legal consequences for resisting induction.

3. Examine U.S. citizens' responses to one of Israel's military operations. For example, you might discuss Israel's actions during the *Yom Kippur* War in 1974 or its responses to the Arab *Intifada*.

Writing before Reading

1. What ideas do the words in James Dubik's title evoke for you?

2. Discuss what you remember, what you have heard, or what you have read about the Persian Gulf War. What news stories have circulated more recently about the war? What is your feeling about the war's place in U.S. history?

AN OFFICER AND A FEMINIST
James M. Dubik

When James Dubik wrote "An Officer and a Feminist" for Newsweek *in 1987, he was a major in the Rangers, an elite military force within the U.S. Army. The intensive training of the Rangers prepares them for jungle warfare and airborne attacks. As a specialized fighting corps, the Rangers played a significant role in the Persian*

Gulf War in 1991. Because they are a combat unit, the Rangers can legally exclude women.

Facts about the Persian Gulf War

The war in the Persian Gulf took place in 1991 and lasted a little over a month—from January 16 to February 28. Saddam Hussein's annexation of Kuwait, the military action that started the war, illicited an international response; 31 countries joined the military coalition that helped defeat Iraq. The war became a showcase for advanced weaponry such as the Tomahawk antimissile, laser guidance systems, and infrared tracking devices that allowed the coalition to spot tanks that Iraqi soldiers had buried. Memories of the protracted and devastating war in Vietnam made the U.S. Congress and private citizens cautious about getting involved in a similar war in the Middle East. In sharp contrast to Vietnam, the war on the ground in the Persian Gulf War lasted only 100 hours. The Iraqis found themselves surrounded by coalition troops, and many deserted. Meanwhile, Saddam Hussein ordered the bombing of Israeli targets in an attempt to draw Israel into the war. Under pressure from the United States, Israel stayed out of the fight. One point of embarrassment for the United States, as it was for several other members of the coalition, was that the United States had supplied arms to Iraq during that country's war with Iran (1980–1988). Saddam Hussein used these weapons against his former allies.

Women were in much greater evidence in the United States' armed forces during the Persian Gulf War than they have ever been. Not only were there many more of them, but they also took greater risks than the military usually allows. Of the 148 Americans who died during the war, 15 were women.

1   I'm a member of a last bastion of male chauvinism. I'm an infantry officer, and there are no women in the infantry. I'm a Ranger and no women go to Ranger School. I'm a member of America's special-operation forces—and there, although women are involved in intelligence, planning and clerical work, only men can be operators, or "shooters." Women can become paratroopers and jump out of airplanes alongside me—yet not many do. All this is as it should be, according to what I learned while growing up.

2   Not many women I knew in high school and college in the '60s and early '70s pushed themselves to their physical or mental limits or had serious career dreams of their own. If they did, few talked about them. So I concluded they were exceptions to the rule. Then two things happened. First, I was assigned to West Point, where I became a philosophy instructor. Second, my two daughters grew up.

3   I arrived at the Academy with a master's degree from Johns Hopkins University in Baltimore and a graduation certificate from the U.S. Army

Command and General Staff College at Fort Leavenworth. I was ready to teach, but instead, I was the one who got an education.

4   The women cadets, in the classroom and out, did not fit my stereotype of female behavior. They took themselves and their futures seriously. They persevered in a very competitive environment. Often they took charge and seized control of a situation. They gave orders; they were punctual and organized. They played sports hard. They survived, even thrived, under real pressure. During field exercises, women cadets were calm and unemotional even when they were dirty, cold, wet, tired and hungry. They didn't fold or give up.

5   Most important, such conduct seemed natural to them. From my perspective all this was extraordinary; to them it was ordinary. While I had read a good bit of "feminist literature" and, intellectually, accepted many of the arguments against stereotyping, this was the first time my real-life experience supported such ideas. And seeing is believing.

6   Enter two daughters: Kerith, 12; Katie, 10.

7   Kerith and Katie read a lot, and they write, too—poems, stories, paragraphs and answers to "thought questions" in school. In what they read and in what they write, I can see their adventurousness, their inquisitiveness and their ambition. They discover clues and solve mysteries. They take risks, brave dangers, fight villains—and prevail. Their schoolwork reveals their pride in themselves. Their taste for reading is boundless; they're interested in everything. "Why?" is forever on their lips. Their eyes are set on personal goals that they, as individuals, aspire to achieve: Olympic gold, owning their own business, public office.

8   Both play sports. I've witnessed a wholesome, aggressive, competitive spirit born in Kerith. She played her first basketball season last year, and when she started, she was too polite to bump anyone, too nice to steal anything, especially if some other girl already had the ball. By the end of the season, however, Kerith was taking bumps and dishing them out. She plays softball with the intensity of a Baltimore Oriole. She rides and jumps her horse in competitive shows. Now she "can't imagine" not playing a sport, especially one that didn't have a little rough play and risk.

9   In Katie's face, I've seen Olympic intensity as she passed a runner in the last 50 yards of a mile relay. Gasping for air, knees shaking, lungs bursting, she dipped into her well of courage and "gutted out" a final kick. Her comment after the race: "I kept thinking I was Mary Decker beating the Russians." For the first time she experienced the thrill of pushing herself to the limit. She rides and jumps, too. And her basketball team was a tournament champion. The joy and excitement and pride that shone in the eyes of each member of the team was equal to that in any NCAA winner's locker room. To each sport Katie bring her dedication to doing her best, her drive to excel and her desire to win.

10   Both girls are learning lessons that, when my wife and I were their age, were encouraged only in boys. Fame, aggressiveness, achieve-

ment, self-confidence—these were territories into which very few women (the exception, not the rule) dared enter. Kerith and Katie, most of their friends, many of their generation and the generations to come are redefining the social game. Their lives contradict the stereotypes with which I grew up. Many of the characteristics I thought were "male" are, in fact, "human." Given a chance, anyone can, and will, acquire them.

11   My daughters and the girls of their generation are lucky. They receive a lot of institutional support not available to women of past generations: from women executives, women athletes, women authors, women politicians, women adventurers, women Olympians. Old categories, old stereotypes and old territories don't fit the current generation of young women; and they won't fit the next generation, either. As Kerith said, "I can't even imagine not being allowed to do something or be something just because I am a girl."

12   All this does not negate what I knew to be true during my own high-school and college years. But what I've learned from both the women cadets at West Point and from my daughters supports a different conclusion about today's women and the women of tomorrow from the beliefs I was raised with. Ultimately we will be compelled to align our social and political institutions with what is already becoming a fact of American life. Or more precisely, whenever biological difference is used to segregate a person from an area of human endeavor, we will be required to demonstrate that biological difference is relevant to the issue at hand.

Reading for Meaning

1. Dubik opens his essay by admitting that he belongs to the "last bastion of male chauvinism." What does he mean by that statement? Why does he call himself a "feminist"?

2. Why is it important that James Dubik identify himself and his occupations in the beginning of his essay? How does this information contribute to his argument?

3. In paragraph 10 Dubik declares, "Many of the characteristics I thought were 'male' are, in fact, 'human.' Given a chance, anyone can, and will, acquire them." What characteristics is he referring to? Do you agree with his conclusion that anyone who has the chance can acquire them?

4. Dubik uses his article to compare generational differences in the way Americans view the capabilities of women. What other differences in people's attitudes or expectations in the last five, ten, or twenty years have you detected?

Comparing Texts

Compare James Dubik's approach to the subject of women in the U.S. armed forces with Nira Yuval-Davis's position in "Front and Rear: The Sexual Division of Labour in the Israeli Army," page 336. What does their purpose for writing seem to be? How well does the writer's tone or attitude reinforce that purpose?

Ideas for Writing

1. James Dubik looks forward to a time when "biological difference" will not automatically exclude women from "an area of human endeavor." To what extent have his expectations been realized?

2. Do some research on the current U.S. policy regarding women's role in combat. Do you agree with this policy or do you think it should be changed? Explain your position as specifically as you can.

3. Consult library and Internet sources to learn more about the role women played in the U.S. military during the Persian Gulf War. How extensive was that role? Were women generally fighting near the "front" or were they kept at the "rear"?

CHAPTER 9
THE INDIVIDUAL AND THE GROUP

First Thoughts

Primeras impresiones

Men [and women] being . . . by nature all free, equal, and independent, no one can be put out of his [or her] estate and subjected to the political power of another without his own consent, which is done by agreeing with other men, to join and unite into a community for their comfortable, safe, and peaceable living, one amongst another, in a secure enjoyment of their properties, and a greater security against any that are not of it.

John Locke
"Of the Beginning of Political Societies"
Two Treatises on Government

Under a government which imprisons any unjustly, the true place for a just man is also a prison. . . . It is there that the fugitive slave, and the Mexican prisoner on parole, and the Indian come to plead the wrongs of his race should find him; on that separate, but more free and honorable ground, where the State places those who are not *with* her, but *against* her—the only house in a slave State in which a free man can abide with honor.

Henry David Thoreau
"Civil Disobedience"

There is . . . in the world at large an increasing inclination to stretch unduly the powers of society over the individual both by the force of opinion and even by that of legislation; and as the tendency of all the changes taking place in the world is to strengthen society and diminish the power of the individual, this encroachment is not one of the evils

> which tend spontaneously to disappear, but, on the contrary, to grow more and more formidable.
>
> John Stuart Mill
> *On Liberty*

In the *Social Contract,* John Locke argues that the only compelling reason why an individual possessed of absolute freedom would put him- or herself under the control of any government is to gain protection and access to goods and services that he or she could not otherwise obtain. In the United States, the Constitution and the Bill of Rights ensure that at least in theory the individual has rights that cannot legally be violated by the state. Over the course of this country's history, guarantees of individual rights and liberties have broadened to include African Americans, women, and other groups that were originally excluded. Yet the battle between forces that would include all and those that would exclude some continues.

It isn't just the government against which individuals must assert themselves. An oppressive leveling and uniform way of thinking and behaving also threatens the integrity of the individual. Urban living can produce what William Wordsworth once called "savage torpor," a kind of primitive, blunted, trancelike state of mind produced when people are so overwhelmed with responsibilities and the demands of work that they become preoccupied with survival rather than with developing or deepening their self-awareness. Supposing this state of affairs to be correct, Wordsworth added that in such an atmosphere, getting attention requires stimulation that is somehow shocking, outrageous, or violent. The results are either people who aren't aware of how they are being manipulated (or if they have a suspicion that they are being manipulated, they simply don't care) or individuals who feel alienated, if not disgusted, by the culture in which they find themselves. In Wordsworth's view, the writer's job, particularly the poet's, is to reaffirm the human connection to nature, a source of eternal, universal truths.

Selections in this chapter treat both the larger political questions about the individual's struggle for autonomy and the smaller, more personal dealings with institutions and with an estrangement from others. Some of these texts explore the balance between individual rights and the rule of law. Henry David Thoreau's advice—repeated more than a hundred years later by Martin Luther King—that individuals must defy laws that imprison them unjustly or protest against a government that protects abominable institutions like slavery is relevant to Aung San Suu Kyi's exhortations against passive acceptance of the unjust rule by the military government of Burma and in Andrea Malin's report on the resistance offered by mothers of prisoners jailed by the totalitarian government in Argentina. But the individual has other institutions to fight and rigid or unscrupulous practices to resist. In "Defending against the Indefensible," Neil Postman describes the ways an individual can be manipulated by language and gives us ways to recognize when someone is using language in order to mislead.

Dorothy D. Lee explains how the culture of the classroom can overwhelm the individual, and she offers an alternative in the Hopi way of balancing the needs of the individual with those of the group. The excerpt from Pablo Neruda's poem *The Heights of Macchu Picchu* explores the individual's need to belong somewhere and to find a connection with a group for whom he or she feels a strong identity. The poet-speaker of *Macchu Picchu* rejects the soullessness of modern life in favor of the more genuine life of the ancient Inca, a people whom his poem strives to resurrect.

Writing before Reading

The military dictatorship that rules Myanmar periodically arrests then releases Aung San Suu Kyi. To discover her current status, you might locate the most recent article written about her that you can find using the Internet or computer database through your school's or local library. Write a short summary of the information you find.

FREEDOM FROM FEAR
Aung San Suu Kyi

Aung San Suu Kyi (pronounced chee) is a leader in the National League for Democracy, a prodemocracy party in Burma. She is also the daughter of Aung San, a Burmese nationalist who fought first the Japanese and then the British forces that between them occupied Burma for more than a century. Her father was assassinated when Suu Kyi was two years old. Suu Kyi was educated in Rangoon, Delhi, and at Oxford University. She married a British doctor, Michael Aris, in 1974 and subsequently settled in Britain. She raised a family in England and, after twenty years, returned to Burma to nurse her dying mother. Shortly after her return to Burma in 1988, she became an important leader in her country's struggle for democracy. In September 1988, General U Saw Maung began arresting protesters of the military dictatorship in Burma. In July 1989, Aung San Suu Kyi was placed under house arrest. Her party won elections in May 1990, but Maung's government insisted that a new constitution be written before relinquishing power. Suu Kyi has been freed and rearrested several times under Maung's regime. While under house arrest in 1991, she was awarded the Nobel Peace Prize. Suu Kyi's husband released her essay "Freedom from

Fear" for publication to honor her receipt of the Sakharov Prize for Freedom of Thought, which the European Parliament awarded Aung San Suu Kyi in 1990. The essay later appeared in Freedom from Fear and other Writings *(1995), edited by Suu Kyi's husband, Michael Aris.*

Facts about Myanmar

Myanmar, formerly Burma, is the westernmost country of Southeast Asia. In 1886 Burma became part of India and fell under British rule. The country was occupied by Japan during World War II and then became a colony of Britain once more after Japan's defeat. Since gaining its independence from the British in 1948, Burma has suffered civil wars, political unrest, and military coups. In 1958 Premier U Nu asked the military to take control of the government to dispel civil unrest. By 1960 Nu was again in power with a civilian government, but in 1962 General U Ne Win took over the government when civil war threatened once more. Political unrest endangered the government again in 1988 until the new leader, General U Saw Maung, took control of the government on September 18, 1988, and suppressed dissent. Under Maung's rule, Burma became Myanmar in June 1989, and Rangoon, the country's capital, was renamed Yangon. On May 27, 1990, the National League for Democracy, with Aung San Suu Kyi as general secretary, won control of the legislature, but the government's National Unity Party refused to relinquish its power. The Burmese military remains in control and periodically cracks down on dissenters. The illegal export of heroin to the United States helps finance the military government. General Than Shwe became head of the military government in 1992. He made several concessions to international human rights groups by lifting martial law and freeing some political prisoners. Aung San Suu Kyi was released from house arrest on July 10, 1995 with the understanding that she not engage in political activity. Seventeen months after her release, Suu Kyi held an antigovernment rally and was again placed under house arrest. On April 22, 1997, President Clinton imposed a ban on U.S. investments in Myanmar. The southeast Asian country is shored up by Chinese, Japanese, and South Korean investments; China is a political ally of the socialist dictatorship in Myanmar.

1   It is not power that corrupts but fear. Fear of losing power corrupts those who wield it and fear of the scourge of power corrupts those who are subject to it. Most Burmese are familiar with the four *a-gati,* the four kinds of corruption. *Chanda-gati,* corruption induced by desire, is deviation from the right path in pursuit of bribes or for the sake of those one loves. *Dosa-gati* is taking the wrong path to spite those against whom one bears ill will, and *moha-gati* is aberration due to ignorance. But perhaps the worst of the four is *bhaya-gati,* for not only does *bhaya,* fear, stifle and slowly destroy all sense of right and wrong, it so often lies at the root of the other three kinds of corruption.

2   Just as *chanda-gati,* when not the result of sheer avarice, can be caused by fear of want or fear of losing the goodwill of those one loves, so fear of being surpassed, humiliated or injured in some way can provide the impetus for ill will. And it would be difficult to dispel ignorance unless there is freedom to pursue the truth unfettered by fear. With so close a relationship between fear and corruption it is little wonder that in any society where fear is rife corruption in all forms becomes deeply entrenched.

3   Public dissatisfaction with economic hardships has been seen as the chief cause of the movement for democracy in Burma, sparked off by the student demonstrations of 1988. It is true that years of incoherent policies, inept official measures, burgeoning inflation and falling real income had turned the country into an economic shambles. But it was more than the difficulties of eking out a barely acceptable standard of living that had eroded the patience of a traditionally good-natured, quiescent people—it was also the humiliation of a way of life disfigured by corruption and fear. The students were protesting not just against the death of their comrades but against the denial of their right to life by a totalitarian regime which deprived the present of meaningfulness and held out no hope for the future. And because the students' protests articulated the frustrations of the people at large, the demonstrations quickly grew into a nationwide movement. Some of its keenest supporters were businessmen who had developed the skills and the contacts necessary not only to survive but to prosper within the system. But their affluence offered them no genuine sense of security or fulfilment, and they could not but see that if they and their fellow citizens, regardless of economic status, were to achieve a worthwhile existence, an accountable administration was at least a necessary if not a sufficient condition. The people of Burma had wearied of a precarious state of passive apprehension where they were "as water in the cupped hands" of the powers that be.

> Emerald cool we may be
> As water in cupped hands
> But oh that we might be
> As splinters of glass
> In cupped hands.

Glass splinters, the smallest with its sharp, glinting power to defend itself against hands that try to crush, could be seen as a vivid symbol of the spark of courage that is an essential attribute of those who would free themselves from the grip of oppression. Bogyoke Aung San regarded himself as a revolutionary and searched tirelessly for answers to the problems that beset Burma during her times of trial. He exhorted the people to develop courage: "Don't just depend on the courage and intrepidity of others. Each and every one of you must make sacrifices to become a hero possessed of courage and intrepidity. Then only shall we all be able to enjoy true freedom."

4   The effort necessary to remain uncorrupted in an environment where fear is an integral part of everyday existence is not immediately apparent to those fortunate enough to live in states governed by the rule of law. Just laws do not merely prevent corruption by meting out impartial punishment to offenders. They also help to create a society in which people can fulfil the basic requirements necessary for the preservation of human dignity without recourse to corrupt practices. Where there are no such laws, the burden of upholding the principles of justice and common decency falls on the ordinary people. It is the cumulative effect of their sustained effort and steady endurance which will change a nation where reason and conscience are warped by fear into one where legal rules exist to promote man's desire for harmony and justice while restraining the less desirable destructive traits in his nature.

5   In an age when immense technological advances have created lethal weapons which could be, and are, used by the powerful and the unprincipled to dominate the weak and the helpless, there is a compelling need for a closer relationship between politics and ethics at both the national and international levels. The Universal Declaration of Human Rights of the United Nations proclaims that "every individual and every organ of society" should strive to promote the basic rights and freedoms to which all human beings regardless of race, nationality or religion are entitled. But as long as there are governments whose authority is founded on coercion rather than on the mandate of the people, and interest groups which place short-term profits above long-term peace and prosperity, concerted international action to protect and promote human rights will remain at best a partially realized ideal. There will continue to be arenas of struggle where victims of oppression have to draw on their own inner resources to defend their inalienable rights as members of the human family.

6   The quintessential revolution is that of the spirit, born of an intellectual conviction of the need for change in those mental attitudes and values which shape the course of a nation's development. A revolution which aims merely at changing official policies and institutions with a view to an improvement in material conditions has little chance of genuine success. Without a revolution of the spirit, the forces which produced the iniquities of the old order would continue to be operative, posing a constant threat to the process of reform and regeneration. It is not enough merely to call for freedom, democracy and human rights. There has to be a united determination to persevere in the struggle, to make sacrifices in the name of enduring truths, to resist the corrupting influences of desire, ill will, ignorance and fear.

7   Saints, it has been said, are the sinners who go on trying. So free men are the oppressed who go on trying and who in the process make

themselves fit to bear the responsibilities and to uphold the disciplines which will maintain a free society. Among the basic freedoms to which men aspire that their lives might be full and uncramped, freedom from fear stands out as both a means and an end. A people who would build a nation in which strong, democratic institutions are firmly established as a guarantee against state-induced power must first learn to liberate their own minds from apathy and fear.

8   Always one to practise what he preached, Aung San himself constantly demonstrated courage—not just the physical sort but the kind that enabled him to speak the truth, to stand by his word, to accept criticism, to admit his faults, to correct his mistakes, to respect the opposition, to parley with the enemy and to let people be the judge of his worthiness as a leader. It is for such moral courage that he will always be loved and respected in Burma—not merely as a warrior hero but as the inspiration and conscience of the nation. The words used by Jawaharlal Nehru to describe Mahatma Gandhi could well be applied to Aung San: "The essence of his teaching was fearlessness and truth, and action allied to these, always keeping the welfare of the masses in view."

9   Gandhi, that great apostle of non-violence, and Aung San, the founder of a national army, were very different personalities, but as there is an inevitable sameness about the challenges of authoritarian rule anywhere at any time, so there is a similarity in the intrinsic qualities of those who rise up to meet the challenge. Nehru, who considered the instillation of courage in the people of India one of Gandhi's greatest achievements, was a political modernist, but as he assessed the needs for a twentieth-century movement for independence, he found himself looking back to the philosophy of ancient India: "The greatest gift for an individual or a nation... was *abhaya,* fearlessness, not merely bodily courage but absence of fear from the mind."

10   Fearlessness may be a gift but perhaps more precious is the courage acquired through endeavour, courage that comes from cultivating the habit of refusing to let fear dictate one's actions, courage that could be described as "grace under pressure"—grace which is renewed repeatedly in the face of harsh, unremitting pressure.

11   Within a system which denies the existence of basic human rights, fear tends to be the order of the day. Fear of imprisonment, fear of torture, fear of death, fear of losing friends, family, property or means of livelihood, fear of poverty, fear of isolation, fear of failure. A most insidious form of fear is that which masquerades as common sense or even wisdom, condemning as foolish, reckless, insignificant or futile the small, daily acts of courage which help to preserve man's self-respect and inherent human dignity. It is not easy for a people conditioned by the iron rule of the principle that might is right to free themselves from the enervating miasma of fear. Yet even under the most crushing state machinery courage rises up again and again, for fear is not the natural state of civilized man.

12   The wellspring of courage and endurance in the face of unbridled power is generally a firm belief in the sanctity of ethical principles combined with a historical sense that despite all setbacks the condition of man is set on an ultimate course for both spiritual and material advancement. It is his capacity for self-improvement and self-redemption which most distinguishes man from the mere brute. At the root of human responsibility is the concept of perfection, the urge to achieve it, the intelligence to find a path towards it, and the will to follow the path if not to the end at least the distance needed to rise above individual limitations and environmental impediments. It is man's vision of a world fit for rational, civilized humanity which leads him to dare and to suffer to build societies free from want and fear. Concepts such as truth, justice and compassion cannot be dismissed as trite when these are often the only bulwarks which stand against ruthless power.

Reading for Meaning

1. What audience does Aung San Suu Kyi address in "Freedom from Fear"? What evidence in the essay suggests this audience?

2. What connections does Aung San Suu Kyi make between fear and dictatorship? What specific fears must people of Myanmar face (paragraph 11)?

3. Why did Suu Kyi include the poem about water in cupped hands in her essay? What might the poem mean to Suu Kyi and her supporters? Can you think of other situations that the poem might fit?

4. According to Aung San Suu Kyi, what role must the ordinary citizen play in a repressive dictatorship? Are there times when you or people you have observed asserted their beliefs in defiance of a stronger authority? Describe the results of those actions.

5. What kind of revolution does Suu Kyi call for? How does it differ from rebellion that involves "strictly political takeover"?

6. How does Suu Kyi define "free people" (paragraph 8)? What is the effect of her religious comparison between the free man (or woman) and the saint?

7. Why does Suu Kyi mention her father, Aung San, Mahatma Gandhi, and Nehru?[1] How does the mention of these figures contribute to her argument?

8. Discuss two or three characteristics of Aung San Suu Kyi's writing style. Try to find a few examples of each trait that you identify.

Comparing Texts

1. Compare one or two aspects of Aung San Suu Kyi's writing—tone, organization, support for ideas—to the style used by Andrea Malin in "Mother Who Won't Disappear" page 365.

---

[1] Jawaharlal Nehru (1889–1964) was a follower of Mahatma Gandhi. He became the first prime minister of independent India.

2. How do the responsibilities Aung San Suu Kyi assigned to the private citizen compare to the duties of the artist-insect according to South African writer André Brink in "The Artist as Insect" (page 482)?

Ideas for Writing

1. Write a critique in which you discuss what you appreciate about Aung San Suu Kyi's essay or what might be done to make her argument more effective. In your discussion, consider the audience for which she writes and the occasion for writing.

2. Research instances of rebellion in the United States or another country. Then analyze the circumstances that contribute to the success of a revolt. You might study the revolt of the British colonies in North America, slave revolts in the New World, the liberation of any of the former African or Latin American colonies from European rule, or the defeat of the monarchies in the French (1789) or Russian (1917) revolutions.

Writing before Reading

1. What ideas does Andrea Malin convey in her title? Does the title reveal a particular bias?

2. What is your personal opinion of the fairly recent entry of women into politics? What benefits do you see coming from the increased political activity of women in the United States? Do you perceive any problems associated with the greater participation of women in government? What do you think might have shaped your views of women in politics?

MOTHER WHO WON'T DISAPPEAR
Andrea Malin

Andrea Malin has worked as a journalist and as a producer and writer of public television documentaries. She helped write and produce the PBS series, "The Pacific Century," a documentary on Asia's Pacific Rim. She has also developed programs for National Geographic and for "The Wall Street Journal Report." Malin published her study "Mother Who Won't Disappear" seventeen years after mothers and grandmothers in Argentina began protesting the disappearance of young Argentineans at the hands of the military police. The article was originally published in the Human Rights Quarterly *in February 1994.*

Facts about Argentina

Argentina is the second largest country in South America. Spanish is the official language, and Catholicism is the established religion. Presently, Argentina has a 90 percent literacy rate. The population of Argentina consists of several important groups. Most people are descendants of Europeans who settled the area first in the sixteenth century and again at the end of the nineteenth and beginning of the twentieth centuries. The native peoples and the Africans, who were originally brought into the country as slaves, have blended with the larger population. Both peoples have virtually disappeared as a separate racial group. One-third of all Argentineans live in metropolitan Buenos Aires. Buenos Aires was originally founded and settled by Europeans in the 1530s. Fierce attacks by native peoples forced the Spaniards to abandon their capital. The Spanish resettled Buenos Aires in 1580. The British occupied Buenos Aires during the Napoleonic Wars. Argentina proclaimed its independence in 1816 but fought a long civil war until Juan Manuel de Rosas, federalist governor of Buenos Aires, declared himself ruler of the country. Argentina's most famous ruler, Juan Peron, began as an elected president but gradually formed an absolute dictatorship. Peron was ousted by the military in 1955, but was returned to power in 1973. His third wife, Isabel Peron, succeeded him in 1974. She was ousted by the military in March 1976. What followed was the military government's ruthless slaughter of anyone suspected of being a leftist guerrilla. This so-called Dirty War resulted in thousands of civilian deaths and is the setting of Andrea Malin's study, "Mother Who Won't Disappear." The loss of the war with Great Britain over possession of the Falkland Islands in 1982 helped return a civilian government to power in Argentina. When Raul Alfonsín became president in 1983, inflation was running between 500 and 1,000 percent annually. Carlos Saul Menem, the Peronist Party's candidate, was elected president in May 1989. He launched a program of economic austerity, and by 1993, inflation, foreign debt, and the economy had stabilized. Menem was reelected in 1995.

I. Vanishing Children

> *The dead and the disappeared in Argentina are the price which had to be paid so that Argentineans could live in peace, dignity and liberty. We are proud to have destroyed the forces of evil.*
>
> General Videla, Argentina[1]

1   "To disappear is to vanish, to cease to be, to be lost"; it suggests the unexplained and universal loss of knowledge about something or someone.[2]

---

[1] Jennifer Schirmer, "Those Who Die for Life Cannot be Called Dead," in *The Harvard Human Rights Yearbook 1* (1988):51, quoting General Videla from J. Bousquet, *Las Locas De Plaza de Mayo*, (Fundacion para la Democracia, 1980), 178.

[2] Amnesty International, *Disappearances: A Workbook*, (New York: Amnesty International USA, 1981), 1.

Governments have used the practice of "disappearing" people as a means of repression. Where this repression existed, particularly where large numbers of young adults have been targets, mothers' movements have arisen.

2   Before disappearances were considered a human rights phenomenon, abductions were routine in Nazi Germany. Hitler ordered that everyone arrested for suspicion of "endangering German security" be transferred under the "cover of night."[3] Known as the "Night and Fog Decree," prisoners were to "vanish without leaving a trace" and "no information [was to] be given about their whereabouts or their fate."[4] Death sentences created martyrs, according to Hitler; the German High Command decided the only way to successfully intimidate was to make sure that the relatives of the "criminal" and the population-at-large would not know his fate.

3   Latin America and Sri Lanka provide sweeping examples of the modern day "Night and Fog Decree" in action. The human rights term "disappearances" originated from the Spanish word, *desaparecidos*. It was first used to describe the government tactic practiced on a massive scale in Guatemala in the mid-1960s. In the 1970s, disappearances soared under the military dictatorships of countries like Brazil, Uruguay, and Chile, reaching a climax in Argentina at the end of the 1970s. In the early 1980s the governments of El Salvador, Guatemala and Peru encouraged massive numbers of disappearances and killings, culminating in some 90,000 disappearances in Latin America since 1964.[5] Over the past few years, there have been an estimated 40,000 disappearances in Sri Lanka.[6]

4   Disappearances became a form of state-sponsored terrorism, firmly rooted in the political and economic structures of these countries.[7] This subterranean rule was routine and bureaucratic: teams of men dressed in civilian clothes would usually arrive, heavily armed, in unmarked Ford Falcons. They would enter the homes or places of work and seize their victims. Their weapons and systematic approach indicated that the kidnappers were not terrorists from the hinterlands; they were in the military or police force. What often began as counterinsurgency programs

---

[3] Ibid., 2.

[4] Ibid., quoting Field Marshal Wilhelm Keitel, Chief of German High Command from William L. Shirer, *The Rise and Fall of the Third Reich* (New York: Simon and Schuster, 1960), 958.

[5] Howard Kleinman, "Disappearances in Latin America: A Human Rights Perspective," *New York University Journal of International Law and Politics* 19 (1987): 1040–41, referencing Dieterich, "Enforced Disappearances and Corruption in Latin America," *Crime and Social Justice* 25 (1986): 40, 45, 51.

[6] Christopher Morris, "Mothers Seek Action on the Disappeared," *The Guardian*, 20 Feb. 1991, 11.

[7] Kleinman, note 5 above, 1034.

against protest movements and guerilla groups became, in many countries, a massive campaign to wipe out anyone remotely thought to be terrorists or subversives.

5   In general, the governments defined those terms broadly. Indeed, General Videla, the leader of the military coup that overtook Argentina in 1976, said, "A terrorist is not just someone with a gun or a bomb, but also someone who spreads ideas that are contrary to Western and Christian civilization.[8]

6   Of the some 30,000 who eventually disappeared in Argentina, only a few hundred were actually terrorists. According to Tex Harris, the first secretary at the US embassy given the task of monitoring the human rights violations in Argentina, the great majority of the disappeared were "wine and coffee subversives—kids who sat in cafes talking about socialist ideals and how the country ought to be changed. They were easy meat," he said, "if they'd sent a hundred of them postcards asking them to come and surrender, ninety-five of them would have shown up."[9]

7   Indeed the vast majority of those who disappeared were young, between the ages of twenty and thirty-five; they were usually educated, politically aware, and idealistic. Expressing the tragedy of this practice, Renee Epelbaum said of her disappeared daughter Lila, "It is normal to be idealistic when you're young. If you're not, then you're already old."[10]

8   Harris shared another side to the disappearing practice:

> There was even a guy from Army Intelligence who told me in person that the real tragedy of their operations was that half the people eliminated were innocent even by their own criteria. But it was easier to kill them because it was less risky and less compromising than going through the legal procedures.[11]

9   In Sri Lanka, the state-sponsored terrorism began when a revolutionary movement known as the People's Liberation Front, the JVP, became increasingly determined to overthrow the Sri Lankan government, using terrorist tactics modeled after Pol Pot's Khmer Rouge. The government decided to fight back, sending policemen whose wives and children had been killed by the JVP to avenge their deaths and "do whatever was necessary."[12] As in Latin America, soon anyone thought to harbor

---

[8] Amnesty Int'l, note 2 above, 10.

[9] John Simpson and Jana Bennett, *The Disappeared and the Mothers of the Plaza* (New York: St. Martin's Press, 1985), 25.

[10] "Las Madres de Plaza de Mayo," a film by Susana Munoz and Lourdes Portillo, 1985.

[11] Simpson & Bennett, note 9 above, 25.

[12] Steve Coll, "The Mothers Who Won't Disappear." *The Washington Post,* 3 March 1991, sec. F, 1, col. 1.

antigovernment sentiments, or come into even remote connection with the JVP would "disappear."

10   In all cases, when relatives tried to find out what happened, they hit a blank wall. They approached police stations, jails, and government offices, but they received no information. Authorities denied holding their relatives or knowing anything about their fate. Writs of habeas corpus produced no results. Like their counterparts in Latin America, the relatives found themselves in a "Kafkaesque situation": they had to prove their sons and daughters had been kidnapped to authorities who denied that abductions even occurred in the first place. The kidnappers could not be identified, the courts were under military control, the military censored the press, and the police, like the armed forces, did not admit the counterinsurgency task forces existed.[13]

11   The denial of accountability by authorities, and the uncertainty of the victims' fate placed a disappearance in a unique status among human rights violations and made it particularly difficult for the victims' relatives.[14] As some identifiable bodies of the disappeared were discovered in mass graves in Chile and Argentina, and as a few survivors reappeared to tell their tales, the human rights community started piecing together what "disappearing" meant: torture, ill-treatment and murder.[15] But most of the bodies are not recovered; most victims do not reappear. From a human rights perspective, it became evident that the "disappeared" were not the only victims; families suffered immeasurably, and in many cases were the real targets of the government repression.[16]

12   Many experts acknowledge that relatives suffer in a particular way when their loved ones disappear because that loss is aggravated by uncertainty. Helmet Frenz, while with Amnesty International of Germany, said, "When a loved one disappears, the family is not only left with his

---

[13] Marysa Navarro, "The Personal is Political," in *Power and Popular Protest: Latin American Social Movements,* ed. Susan Eckstein (Berkeley: University of California Press, 1989), 247.

[14] Because the fate of the person who has disappeared is by definition unknown it is difficult to classify a disappearance as a specific violation of international human rights. The United Nations, however, does consider disappearances to violate several internationally recognized human rights in the Universal Declaration of Human Rights: A person's guarantee to life, liberty and security of person (Article 3); the right to an effective remedy by a competent national tribunal for acts violating the fundamental rights granted by the constitution or law (Article 8); and the right to be free from arbitrary arrest and detention (Article 9).

[15] Amnesty Int'l, note 2 above, 76.

[16] Ibid., 82. It may be argued that prisoners' relatives are subject to violations of the right to be free from torture, cruel, inhuman or degrading treatment, as provided in Article 5 of the Universal Declaration of Human Rights.

absence to put up with, but with a constant anguish which grows deeper as the days go by, bringing no sign of the missing person.[17]

13 The psychological impact of denying a relative knowledge of the death of a loved one and, by extension, the final act of bereavement, can be debilitating and tortuous. "It is the crushing reality of loss coupled with the unreality of death that afflicts the families of those who have disappeared. The result is a form of mental torture, brought about by either suspension of bereavement or the feeling of hopelessness."[18] According to psychological experts, grief plays a crucial role in healing and helping the mourner to adapt to the loss. In a dehumanizing way, the mothers of the disappeared are denied their bereavement, such that "their sorrow is unspent, the grief of their wounds is untold, their guilt unexpiated...."[19]

II. Transformation

> I am overwhelmed, o my son
> I am overwhelmed by love
> And I cannot endure
> That I should be in the chamber
> And you on the wood of the cross
> I in the house
> And you in the tomb.[20]

14 The image of the Latin American woman is almost indistinguishable from the *mater dolorosa,* the classic religious figure who tearfully mourns for her lost son.[21] For the mothers whose children disappeared, life was

---

[17] "Human Rights and the Phenomenon of Disappearances," *Hearings before the Subcommittee on International Organizations of the Committee of Foreign Affairs, House of Representatives, Ninety-sixth Congress,* 20, 25 Sept. & 18 Oct. 1979, 4, 186.

[18] Amnesty Int'l, note 2 above, 109.

[19] Ibid., quoting Dr. Robert Kavanaugh in *A Psychology of Death and Dying,* 40:

> The process of mourning or grieving is essential for personal adaptation to loss.... Through mourning one learns to adjust to the changes that must occur following a loss. If the process is unsatisfactory (if one has not completed this process), then the chances of healthy adjustment to loss are not as great.

Also, Chaim Shatan noted in "Genocide and Bereavement," that Freud "elucidated the essential role of grief in helping the mourner let go a missing part of life and acknowledging that it continues to exist only in memory." Also supports notion that prohibitions of bereavement rituals are dehumanizing—"impacted grief." Ibid.

[20] Marina Warner, *Alone of All of Her Sex: The Myth and Cult of the Virgin Mary* (New York: Vintage Books, 1976), 209, quoting Giuseppe Cammelli, ed. Romano il Melode: Inni ([Firenze] Edizioni "Testi Cristiani" 1930), 336–61.

[21] Evelyn P. Stevens, "Marianismo: The Other Face of Machismo," in *Female and Male in Latin America,* ed. Ann Pescatello, (Pittsburg: University of Pittsburgh Press, 1973), 96, citing Edwin Oliver James, *The Cult of the Mother Goddess* (London: Thames and Hudson, 1959)

immediately divided into two drastically different realities: before and after. Nothing would ever be as it was; they would never be the same. They were not content simply to mourn.

15   Middle class housewives, working class, single mothers, the wealthy, and the poor, Catholic, Protestant, and Jewish—mostly those who used to accept authority and the rules of society without question, joined in a struggle to find out what happened to their children, and defend their children's right to life in the face of a regime that was trying to deny their very existence. . . .

16   In addition to Argentina's Mothers who formed their movement in 1977, mothers formed human rights movements in Chile in 1974, and around the same time, they emerged in Brazil, Uruguay, Guatemala, and Honduras. In 1981, a group appeared in El Salvador, and in 1990 they mobilized in Sri Lanka. . . .

17   As the seat of government in Argentina since the eighteenth century, the Plaza de Mayo as the chosen place to demonstrate was charged and significant. Similarly, women in other countries chose symbolic public places. In Chile, the women chained themselves to the railings of the closed national legislature; in El Salvador the mothers staged sit-ins at the National Cathedral.[22] Sri Lankan mothers have also held national conventions and public rallies.

18   The Mothers from Argentina first ventured into the Plaza de Mayo on 30 April 1977. In the beginning, they were a group of fourteen women, who were not sure what to do. Renee Epelbaum explained: "When we would first meet in the Plaza, we were a powerless group. People laughed at us. When it rained, we looked like a bunch of heads smothered by enormous white kerchiefs." . . . [23]

19   By June, the Mothers of the Plaza de Mayo were marching every Thursday at 3:30 p.m.—a practice they continue to this day. By 1982, they claimed to have a membership of 2,500 mothers. Marching gave them strength; it transformed them. They were no longer entirely alone with their pain and grief. They discovered a new side of themselves. "They became 'Las Madres'—women committed to demonstrating every week for however long it took for their children to reappear, and ready to do whatever else was necessary to attain their objective."[24]

---

and Erich Neumann, *The Great Mother: An Analysis of the Archetype* (New York: Pantheon Books, 1955).

[22] Francesca Miller, *Latin American Women and the Search for Social Justice* (Hanover: University Press of New England, 1991), 8, quoting Jean Franco, "Gender, Death and Resistance," in *Plotting Women: Gender and Representation in Mexico* (New York: Columbia University Press, 1989).

[23] Marjorie Agosin, *The Mothers of the Plaza de Mayo: The Story of Renee Epelbaum 1976–1985* (Stratford, Ontario: Williams and Wallace, 1989), 34.

[24] Navarro, note 13 above, 251.

20   The tactics of the Mothers of the Plaza de Mayo reflected a new style eventually adopted by other groups around the world. They used a variety of symbols to bring their children to life. At first, they used Catholic symbols, such as a carpenter's nail in their backs, in memory of Christ's sacrifice.

21   Mostly, their methods involved trying to reverse the effect of the disappearance by proving the existence of their children, countering the state's efforts to obliterate them. They wore their children's photos on their breasts, sometimes hanging the pictures around their necks like medallions, or carrying them on large placards. In a symbol of nonviolence, they wore white handkerchiefs on their heads, with the names of their children embroidered on them. The Sri Lankan mothers wore white saris, and carried the battered photographs of their missing sons. In Argentina, many of the mothers laid on the floor, on a sheet of paper or on the sidewalk and had their contours drawn. These empty silhouettes, thirty thousand of them, appeared throughout Buenos Aires, bearing the name, age and date of a person's disappearance. These "persistent ghosts," as one writer called them in 1984, "have become a form of street art that fulfills the noblest function of art: that of restoring memory."[25]

III. ON BEING A MOTHER—THE WEAPON AND THE SHIELD...

22   In the Plaza, the mothers invoked traditional images of the woman: the lone *mater dolorsa* mourning for her child. Walking peacefully, holding tightly to their children's photographs, they fulfilled conservative expectations; they appealed to the values of family and motherhood.

23   When policemen began attacking some of the Mothers in the Plaza de Mayo, they lashed out indignantly: "Aren't you embarrassed to attack undefended mothers?... Don't you have children? Wouldn't you do what we are doing if you had a disappeared child?"[26] For the most part, the mothers successfully used their traditional mother status to their advantage, as a defense.

24   Women from several mothers groups in different countries seemed to view motherhood similarly as a strategic advantage to them in their human rights struggle and as a motivating factor.... Amalia Gonzalez,... from Uruguay, raised perhaps the most fundamental reason for the mothers' effectiveness as human rights activists: "I believe as mothers we have more strength and courage—because it is our own children we are fighting for."[27]

---

[25] Valenza, "Making Love Visible," *Vogue,* May 1984, 345.

[26] Schirmer, note 1 above, 68 quoting Jean-Pierre Bousquet, *Las Locas de Plaza de Mayo* (3d ed., 1983), 48.

[27] Interview with Amalia Gonzalez, Uruguay, 22 Oct. 1992, trans. by Nelda Meir.

25   Vivian Stromberg, executive director of Madre, a New York agency that addresses the problems of mothers in developing countries suggests a reason why mothers have such universal acceptance: "It is very gripping to hear the plea of a mother. Since everybody has or has had a mother . . . something inside of you sees her when you see another mother. There's a universality to it."[28]

26   The governments distinguished the mother groups from subversive groups. The mothers had no ideological constraints, or political experience to taint them. Based on the cultural and ideological conceptions of motherhood, being a mother offered a sense of security. . . .

27   These women were willing to risk everything because many believed they had nothing to lose. The story of Hebe de Bonafini, a founder and current leader of one division of the Mothers of the Plaza de Mayo, illustrates this particular kind of courage. After her two sons and a daughter-in-law disappeared in 1976, she pursued every avenue to find them to no avail. During repeated visits to the Argentine Ministry of the Interior, she met other mothers looking for their children, and joined them in their Thursday marches. . . . Hebe de Bonafini lost her fear early on. She was not afraid "when the police kicked us [the mothers] out of the Plaza with loaded machine guns . . . [O]ne policeman shouted 'Ready?' and we shouted back 'Shoot!'"[29] She was not afraid when one of the founders of the Mothers disappeared, nor when a Ford Falcon followed her one night as she walked home. "[O]ur desire to find our sons was stronger than our fright," she said, because "[when we are] thinking about our children, we don't think about our sufferings."[30]

28   The courage the mothers exhibited in their movements dramatically changed the traditional, masculine image of courage, associated with machismo. This was a feminine courage, a maternal courage, based on defending their own children and the right to life.[31]

29   Ironically, despite their peaceful tactics and maternal demeanor, the Mothers turned into the ultimate subversives. Refusing to acquiesce to the loss of their children, they were tireless in their struggle. Trying to recapture their families, they confronted the state with the values of motherhood and family which the state claimed to protect.

---

[28] Interview with Vivian Stromberg, Executive Director, Madres, 15 Oct. 1992.
[29] Navarro, note 13 above, 253, quoting Hebe Bonafini from *Humor*, Oct. 1982.
[30] Ibid.
[31] Scott Mainwaring and Eduardo Viola, "New Social Movements, Political Culture and Democracy: Brazil and Argentina," *Working Paper #33*, The Helen Kellogg Institute for International Studies, Dec. 1984, 42.

As the military junta continued ridding the nation of its perceived opponents, it simultaneously created new opponents, formidable opponents in the mothers' movements. In essence, the state created its worst opponent, because it was an enemy that would never rest.

Reading for Meaning

1. What is Andrea Malin's purpose for writing her essay on the women's protest movement in Argentina in 1977?

2. What is the historical background for the use of "disappearance" to stifle criticism of the government? How does this background information help us understand the situation in Argentina?

3. How did the women use their status and roles as mothers and grandmothers in their attempt to make political changes in Argentina? How does knowing the cultural meaning of the mothers' actions help us understand the significance of what they did?

4. What other strategies did the women use to ensure that their protests were heard?

5. How does Malin account for the mothers' determination to stand up to a military regime?

6. Why does Malin mention similar struggles between women and repressive governments in Chile, Sri Lanka, Brazil, Guatemala, and other countries?

Comparing Texts

1. What similarities or differences do you find between Andrea Malin's essay about the mothers' protests and Aung San Suu Kyi's essay "Freedom from Fear"? You might discuss purpose, style of writing, organization, or ideas in the essays.

2. In André Brink's "The Artist as Insect," the author discusses the role the artist should play in emerging democracies in the Third World. How might the mothers of Argentina be considered examples of Brink's "composite insect" (page 485)?

Ideas for Writing

1. Explore both overt and subtle ways that women effect change in the artistic or political life of a country. You might consider using several of the following essays in this book as sources for your information: "Mother Who Won't Disappear," "The Transformation of Silence into Language and Action" page 487, "Marriage in the Hausa *Tatsuniya* Tradition: A Cultural and Cosmic Balance" page 513, or "The Bible and Self-Defense . . ." page 557.

2. Do some research on women's political movements in Chile, Brazil, Guatemala, Kenya, or Sri Lanka. What is similar about these movements? Are some characteristics unique to one or two movements?

3. Write a study of women's political action in the United States. You might focus on a major movement such as women's suffrage or examine the role women played in the Civil Rights movement.

Writing before Reading

Based on your reading of the title and preface to his essay, what assumptions does Postman make? Does your experience support or contradict these ideas?

DEFENDING AGAINST THE INDEFENSIBLE
Neil Postman

Neil Postman is chair of the Department of Culture and Communications at New York University. He is widely recognized as an important critic and communications theorist. Postman has written eighteen books including Teaching as a Subversive Activity *(1969),* Amusing Ourselves to Death *(1985),* The Disappearance of Childhood *(1982),* Technopoly: The Surrender of Culture to Technology *(1992), and* The End of Education *(1995). From 1977 to 1986 he was editor of* Et Cetera, *a journal of semantics. The essay "Defending against the Indefensible" was published in his collection of essays titled* Conscientious Objections: Stirring Up Trouble about Language, Technology, and Education *(1988). Postman attached the following preface to his essay when it appeared in* Conscientious Objections:

> *This essay originated as a lecture I gave in The Hague, Holland, to an audience of people who teach in English-language independent schools throughout Europe. I should stress that they were not primarily teachers of English, whom I have for the most part stopped addressing, since I came to the conclusion several years ago that they are the educators least likely to depart in any significant way from their pedagogical traditions. I do not know why this is so, but it is a serious deficiency, since English teachers are better positioned than any others to cultivate intelligence.*

1 I am sure that many of you will recognize that my title derives from a phrase in George Orwell's famous essay "Politics and the English Language." In that essay, Orwell speaks of the dangerously degraded condition of modern political thought, and proceeds to characterize its language as mainly committed to "defending the indefensible."

2   In the thirty-five years or so since Orwell wrote his essay, it has become even more obvious that the principal purpose of most political language is to justify or, if possible, to make glorious the malignant ambitions of nation states. Perhaps it has always been so—at least since the seventeenth century—and I don't suppose many of us expect it to be different in the future. With the exception of the much misunderstood Machiavelli, no one ever said politics is a pretty profession, and if Orwell thought it could be otherwise, he was an optimist.

3   I, too, am an optimist. But not because I look for any improvement in the purposes of political discourse. I am an optimist because I think it might just be possible for people to learn how to recognize empty, false, self-serving, or inhumane language, and therefore to protect themselves from at least some of its spiritually debasing consequences. My optimism places me in the camp of H. G. Wells, who said that civilization is in a race between education and disaster, and that although education is far behind, it is not yet out of the running. In other words, while I do not think we can count on any relaxation in the defense of the indefensible, I believe we may mount a practical counteroffensive by better preparing the minds of those for whom such language is intended.

4   Thus our attention inevitably turns to the subject of schools and to the possibility of their actually doing something that would help our youth acquire the semantic sophistication that we associate with minds unburdened by prejudice and provinciality. Of course, I am well aware that in most of the world, school is the last place you would expect such an education to be seriously conducted; in most places, school is conceived of as a form of indoctrination, the continuation of politics by gentle means.

5   The idea that schooling should make the young compliant and easily accessible to the prejudices of their society is an old and venerable tradition. This function of education was clearly advocated by our two earliest and greatest curriculum specialists, Confucius and Plato. Their writings created the tradition that requires educators to condition the young to believe what they are told, in the way they are told it.

6   But the matter does not rest there. We are fortunate to have available an alternative tradition that gives us the authority to educate our students to *disbelieve* or at least to be skeptical of the prejudices of their elders. We can locate the origins of this tradition in some fragments from Cicero, who remarked that the purpose of education is to free the student from the tyranny of the present. We find elaborations of this point of view in Descartes, Bacon, Vico, Goethe, and Jefferson. And we find its modern resonances in John Dewey, Freud, and Bertrand Russell.

7   It is in the spirit of this tradition—that is, education as a defense *against* culture—that I wish to speak. I will not address the important issue of how such an education in disbelief can be made palatable to those who pay for our schools. I know next to nothing about that, and

what I know seems to be wrong. Rather, my remarks are aimed at those who would be interested to know how one might proceed if one had the authority and the desire to do so.

8   The method I have chosen for this purpose is to provide you with seven concepts, all of which have to do with language. I will not presume to call these concepts the Seven Pillars of Wisdom, but I believe that, if taken seriously, they have the potential to clear away some of the obtuseness that makes minds vulnerable to indefensible discourse. Before setting them out, I must stress that the education I speak of is *not* confined to helping students immunize themselves against the *politically* indefensible. Such an education would be in itself indefensible, and, fortunately, there is no need for it. We can assume that if we find a way to promote critical intelligence through language education, such intelligence can defend itself against almost anything that is indefensible—from Newspeak to commercial hucksterism to bureaucratese to that most debilitating of all forms of nonsense that afflict the young, school textbooks. The assumption that critical intelligence has wide applicability is, I believe, what the medieval Schoolmen had in mind in creating the Trivium, which in their version consisted of grammar, logic, and rhetoric. These arts of language were assumed to be what may be called "meta-subjects," subjects about subjects. Their rules, guidelines, principles, and insights were thought to be useful in thinking about *anything.* Our ancestors understood well something we seem to have forgotten, namely, that all subjects are forms of discourse—indeed, forms of literature—and therefore that almost all education is language education. Knowledge of a subject mostly means knowledge of the language of that subject. Biology, after all, is not plants and animals; it is language about plants and animals. History is not events that once occurred; it is language describing and interpreting events. And astronomy is not planets and stars but a special way of talking about planets and stars.

9   And so a student must know the language of a subject, but that is only the beginning. For it is not sufficient to know the definition of a noun, or a gene, or a molecule. One must also know what a definition is. It is not sufficient to know the right answers. One must also know the questions that produced them. Indeed, one must know what a question is, for not every sentence that ends with a rising intonation or begins with an interrogative is necessarily a question. There are sentences that look like questions but cannot generate any meaningful answers, and if they linger in our minds, they become obstructions to clear thinking. One must also know what a metaphor is and what is the relationship between words and the things they describe. In short, one must have some knowledge of a meta-language—a language about language. Without such knowledge, a student can be as easily tyrannized by a subject as by a politician. That is to say, the enemy here is not, in the end, indefensible discourse but our ignorance of how to proceed against it.

10   Now, what I want to recommend to you is not so systematic or profound as the Trivium. I do not even propose a new subject—only seven ideas or insights or principles (call them what you will) that are essential to the workings of the critical intelligence and that are in the jurisdiction of every teacher at every level of school.

11   My first principle is about the process of definition. Most people are overcome by a sort of intellectual paralysis when confronted by a definition, whether offered by a politician or by a teacher. They fail to grasp that a definition is not a manifestation of nature but merely and always an instrument for helping us to achieve our purposes. I. A. Richards once remarked, "We want to do something, and a definition is a means of doing it. If we want certain results, then we must use certain definitions. But no definition has any authority apart from a purpose, or any authority to bar us from other purposes." This is one of the most liberating statements I know. But I have, myself, never heard a student ask of a teacher, "Whose definition is that and what purposes are served by it?" It is more than likely that a teacher would be puzzled by such a question, for most of us have been as tyrannized by definitions as have our students. But I do know of one instance where a student refused to accept a definition provided by an entire school. The student applied to Columbia University for admission and was rejected. In response, he sent the following letter to the admissions officer:

> Dear Sir:
> I am in receipt of your rejection of my application. As much as I would like to accommodate you, I find I cannot. I have already received four rejections from other colleges, which is, in fact, my limit. Your rejection puts me over this limit. Therefore, I must reject your rejection, and as much as this might inconvenience you, I expect to appear for classes on September 18....

Columbia would have been well advised to reconsider this student's application, not because it doesn't have a right to define for its own purposes what it means by an adequate student, but because here is a student who understands what some of Columbia's professors probably do not—that there is a measure of arbitrariness in every definition and that in any case an intelligent person is not required to accept another's definition, even if he can't do much about it.

12   What students need to be taught, then, is that definitions are not given to us by God; that we may depart from them without risking our immortal souls; that the authority of a definition rests entirely on its usefulness, not on its correctness (whatever that means); and that it is a form of stupidity to accept without reflection someone else's definition of a word, a problem, or a situation. All of this applies as much to a definition of a verb or a molecule as it does to a definition of art, God, freedom, or democracy. I can think of no better method of helping students to

defend themselves than to provide them with alternative definitions for every important concept and term they must deal with in school. It is essential that they understand that definitions are hypotheses and that embedded in each is a particular philosophical or political or epistemological point of view. It is certainly true that he who holds the power to define is our master, but it is also true that he who holds in mind an alternative definition can never quite be his slave.

13   My second concept is best introduced by a story attributed to the American psychologist Gordon Allport. He tells of two priests who were engaged in a dispute on whether or not it is permissible to pray and smoke at the same time. One believed that it is, the other that it is not, and so each decided to write to the Pope for a definitive answer. After doing so, they met again to share their results and were astonished to discover that the Pope had agreed with both of them. "How did you pose the question?" the first asked. The other replied, "I asked if it is permissible to smoke while praying. His Holiness said that it is not, since praying is a very serious business. And how did you phrase the question?" The first replied, "I asked if it is permissible to pray while smoking, and His Holiness said that it is, since it is always appropriate to pray."

14   The point of this story, of course, is that the form in which we ask our questions will determine the answers we get. To put it more broadly: all the knowledge we ever have is a result of questions. Indeed, it is a commonplace among scientists that they do not see nature as it is, but only through the questions they put to it. I should go further: we do not see *anything* as it is except through the questions we put to it. And there is a larger point even than this: since questions are the most important intellectual tool we have, is it not incredible that the art and science of question-asking is not systematically taught? I would suggest that we correct this deficiency and not only put question-asking on our teaching agenda but place it near the top of the list. After all, in a profound sense, it is meaningless to have answers if we do not know the questions that produced them—whether in biology, grammar, politics, or history. To have an answer without knowing the question, without understanding that you might have been given a different answer if the question had been posed differently, may be more than meaningless; it may be exceedingly dangerous. There are many Americans who carry in their heads such answers as "America should proceed at once with our Star Wars project," or, "We should send Marines to Nicaragua." But if they do not know the question to which these are the answers, their opinions are quite literally thoughtless. And so I suggest two things. First, we should teach our students something about question-asking in general. For example, that a vaguely formed question produces a vaguely formed answer; that every question has a point of view embedded in it; that for any question that is posed, there is almost always an alternative question that will generate an alternative answer; that every action we take is an

answer to a question, even if we are not aware of it; that ineffective actions may be the result of badly formed questions; and most of all, that a question is language, and therefore susceptible to all the errors to which an unsophisticated understanding of language can lead. As Francis Bacon put it more than 350 years ago: "There arises from a bad and unapt formation of words a wonderful obstruction to the mind." This is as good a definition of stupidity as I know: a bad and unapt formation of words. Let us, then, go "back to Bacon," and study the art of question-asking. But we must also focus on the specific details of asking questions in different subjects. What, for example, are the sorts of questions that obstruct the mind, or free it, in the study of history? How are these questions different from those one might ask of a mathematical proof, or a literary work, or a biological theory? The principles and rules of asking questions obviously differ as we move from one system of knowledge to another, and this ought not to be ignored.

15   Which leads me to my third principle: namely, that the most difficult words in any form of discourse are rarely the polysyllabic ones that are hard to spell and which send students to their dictionaries. The troublesome words are those whose meanings appear to be simple, like "true," "false," "fact," "law," "good," and "bad." A word like "participle" or "mutation" or "centrifugal," or, for that matter, "apartheid" or "proletariat," rarely raises serious problems in understanding. The range of situations in which such a word might appear is limited and does not tangle us in ambiguity. But a word like "law" is used in almost every universe of discourse, and with different meanings in each. "The law of supply and demand" is a different "law" from "Grimm's Law" in linguistics or "Newton's Law" in physics or "the law of the survival of the fittest" in biology. What is a "true" statement in mathematics is different from a "true" statement in economics, and when we speak of the "truth" of a literary work, we mean something else again. Moreover, when President Reagan says it is "right" to place cruise missiles in Europe, he does not appeal to the same authority or even logic as when he says it is "right" to reduce the national deficit. And when Karl Marx said it was "right" for the working class to overthrow the bourgeoisie, he meant something different altogether, as does a teacher who proclaims it is "right" to say "he doesn't" instead of "he don't."

16   If we insist on giving our students vocabulary tests, then for God's sake let us find out if they know something about the truly difficult words in the language. I think it would be entirely practical to design a curriculum based on an inquiry into, let us say, fifty hard words, beginning with "good" and "bad" and ending with "true" and "false." Show me a student who knows something about what these words imply, what sources of authority they appeal to, and in what circumstances they are used, and I will show you a student who is an epistemologist—which is to say, a student who knows what textbooks try to conceal. And a student

who knows what textbooks try to conceal will know what advertisers try to conceal, and politicians and preachers, as well.

17   Fourth, I think it would also be practical to design a curriculum based on an inquiry into the use of metaphor. Unless I am sorely mistaken, metaphor is at present rarely approached in school except by English teachers during lessons in poetry. This strikes me as absurd, since I do not see how it is possible for a subject to be understood in the absence of any insight into the metaphors on which it is constructed. All subjects are based on powerful metaphors that direct and organize the way we will do our thinking. In history, economics, physics, biology, and linguistics, metaphors, like questions, are organs of perception. Through our metaphors, we see the world as one thing or another. Is light a wave or a particle? An astrophysicist I know tells me that she and her colleagues don't know, and so at the moment they settle for the word "wavicle." Are molecules like billiard balls or force fields? Is language like a tree (some say it has roots) or a river (some say it has tributaries) or a building (some say it has foundations)? Is history unfolding according to some instructions of nature or according to a divine plan? Are our genes like information codes? Is a literary work like an architect's blueprint or is it a mystery the reader must solve? Questions like these preoccupy scholars in every field because they are what is basic to the field itself. Nowhere is this more so than in education. Rousseau begins his great treatise on education, *Emile,* with the following words: "Plants are improved by cultivation, and men by education." And his entire philosophy is made to rest upon this comparison of plants and children.

18   There is no test, textbook, syllabus, or lesson plan that any of us creates that does not reflect our preference for some metaphor of the mind, or of knowledge, or of the process of learning. Do you believe a student's mind to be a muscle that must be exercised? Or a garden that must be cultivated? Or a dark cavern that must be illuminated? Or an empty vessel that must be filled to overflowing? Whichever you favor, your metaphor will control—often without your being aware of it—how you will proceed as a teacher. This is as true of politicians as it is of academics. No political practitioner has ever spoken three consecutive sentences without invoking some metaphorical authority for his actions. And this is especially true of powerful political theorists. Rousseau begins *The Social Contract* with a powerful metaphor that Marx was to use later, and many times: "Man is born free but is everywhere in chains." Marx himself begins *The Communist Manifesto* with an ominous and ghostly metaphor—the famous "A specter haunts Europe …" Abraham Lincoln, in his celebrated Gettysburg Address, compares America's forefathers to God when he says they "brought forth a new nation," just as God brought forth the heavens and the earth. And Adolf Hitler concludes *Mein Kampf* with this: "A state which in this age of racial poisoning dedicates itself to the care of its best racial elements must someday become the lord of the earth." All

forms of discourse are metaphor-laden, and unless our students are aware of how metaphors shape arguments, organize perceptions, and control feelings, their understanding is severely limited.

19   Which gets me to my fifth concept, what is called reification. Reification means confusing words with things. It is a thinking error with multiple manifestations, some merely amusing, others extermely dangerous. This past summer in the sweltering New York heat, a student of mine looked at a thermometer in our classroom. "It's ninety-six degrees," he said. "No wonder it's so hot!" He had it the wrong way around, of course, as many peole do who have never learned or cannot remember these three simple notions: that there are things in the world and then there are our names of them; that there is no such thing as a real name; and that a name may or may not suggest the nature of the thing named—as, for example, when the United States government called its South Pacific hydrogen-bomb experiments Operation Sunshine. What I am trying to say here is what Shakespeare said more eloquently in his line "A rose by any other name would smell as sweet." But Shakespeare was only half right, in that for many people a rose would *not* smell as sweet if it were called a "stinkweed." And because this is so, because people confuse names with things, advertising is among the most consistently successful enterprises in the world today. Advertisers know that no matter how excellent an automobile may be, it will not sell if it is called the "Lumbering Elephant." More important, they know that no matter how rotten a car may be, you *can* sell it if it is called a "Vista Cruiser" or a "Phoenix" or a "Grand Prix." Politicians know this as well, and, sad to say, so do scholars, who far too often obscure the emptiness of what they are talking and writing about by affixing alluring names to what is not there. I suggest, therefore, that reification be given a prominent place in our studies, so that our students will know how it both works and works them over.

20   Sixth, some attention must be given to the style and tone of language. Each universe of discourse has its own special way of addressing its subject matter and its audience. Each subject in a curriculum is a special manner of speaking and writing, with its own rhetoric of knowledge, a characteristic way in which arguments, proofs, speculations, experiments, polemics, even humor, are expressed. Speaking and writing are, after all, performing arts, and each subject requires a somewhat different kind of performance. Historians, for example, do not speak or write history in the same way biologists speak or write biology. The differences have to do with the degree of precision their generalizations permit, the types of facts they marshal, the traditions of their subject, and the nature of their training. It is worth remembering that many scholars have exerted influence as much through their manner as their matter—one thinks of Veblen in sociology, Freud in psychology, Galbraith in economics. The point is that knowledge is a form of literature, and the various styles of knowledge ought to be studied and discussed, all the more

because the language found in typical school textbooks tends to obscure this. Textbook language, which is apt to be the same from subject to subject, creates the false impression that systematic knowledge is always expressed in a dull, uninspired monotone. I have read recipes on the back of cereal boxes that were written with more style and conviction than textbook descriptions of the causes of the American Revolution. Of the language of grammar books I will not even speak, for, to borrow from Shakespeare, it is unfit for a Christian ear to endure. But the problem is not insurmountable. Teachers who are willing to take the time can find materials that convey ideas in a form characteristic of their discipline. And while they are at it, they can help their students to see that what we call a prayer, a political speech, and an advertisement differ from each other not only in their content but in their style and tone; one might say *mostly* in their style and tone and manner of address.

21   Which brings me to the seventh and final concept—what I shall call the principle of the non-neutrality of media. I mean by this what Marshall McLuhan meant to suggest when he said, "The medium is the message": that the form in which information is coded has, itself, an inescapable bias. In a certain sense, this is an entirely familiar idea. We recognize, for example, that the world is somewhat different when we speak about it in English and when we speak about it in German. We might even say that the grammar of a language is an organ of perception and accounts for the variances in world view that we find among different peoples. But we have been slow to acknowledge that every extension of speech—from painting to hieroglyphics to the alphabet to the printing press to television—also generates unique ways of apprehending the world, amplifying or obscuring different features of reality. Each medium, like language itself, classifies the world for us, sequences it, frames it, enlarges it, reduces it, argues a case for what the world is like. In the United States, for example, it is no longer possible for a fat person to be elected to high political office—not because our Constitution forbids it but because television forbids it, since television exalts the attractive visual image and has little patience with or love for the subtle or logical word.

22   Our students must understand two essential points about all this. Just as language itself creates culture in its own image, each new medium of communication re-creates or modifies culture in *its* image; and it is extreme naïveté to believe that a medium of communication or, indeed, any technology is merely a tool, a way of doing. Each is also a way of *seeing*. To a man with a hammer, everything looks like a nail. To a man with a pencil, everything looks like a sentence; to a man with a television camera, everything looks like a picture; and to a man with a computer, the whole world looks like data. To put it another way, and to paraphrase the philosopher Wittgenstein, a medium of communication may be a vehicle of thought but we must not forget that it is also the driver. A consideration of how the printing press or the telegraph or

television or the computer does its driving and where it takes us must be included in our students' education or else they will be disarmed and extremely vulnerable.

23 There is one more principle about language that is probably occurring to many of you right about now: namely, that one ought not to put up with any lecturer who takes more of your time than he has been allotted. And so I will conclude with three points. First, I trust you understand that the suggestions I have made are not directed exclusively or even primarily at language teachers, English or otherwise. This is a task for everyone. Second, I want to reiterate that to provide our students with a defense against the indefensible, it is neither necessary nor desirable to focus exclusively on political language. Whenever this is attempted, it is apt to be shallow and limited. The best defense is one with a wider reach, which has implications for all language transactions. And finally, I do not claim that my proposals will solve all our problems, or even provide full protection from indefensible discourse. They are only a reasonable beginning, and there is much more to be done. But we have to start somewhere and, as Ray Bradbury once wrote, somewhere lies between the right ear and the left.

Reading for Meaning

1. Neil Postman asserts that education is usually designed as "indoctrination" and serves as "the continuation of politics by gentle means." Could your education or the education of people you know be described as "indoctrination"? What was the indoctrination about, and what purpose might it have served?

2. What is "meta-language" and why does Postman think it is important to know what it is and how "to proceed against it"?

3. Why does Postman think it is important for teachers to supply their students with alternative definitions for the concepts they learn about in school? Do you agree?

4. What use does Postman see in knowing the questions to which answers are posited, particularly those statements involving political policy? Give a few examples of affirmative statements of policy (the United States should . . .) and pose the questions that lie behind them. What better questions might have been asked?

5. Study the metaphors for learning that Postman offers in paragraphs 17 and 18. Discuss the teaching methods that each suggests. Try to identify the methods that a few of your instructors used.

6. What does Postman mean by the "non-neutrality of media"? (paragraph 21)

7. How might computer technology or television involve a "way of seeing"? How does each medium frame experience? What perception of the world or human behavior do they offer?

Comparing Texts

1. The following passage is an excerpt from George Orwell's essay, "Politics and the English Language (1946)," which provided the idea for Postman's title. After reading the passage from Orwell, find ideas that Postman has expanded or changed in some way.

> In our time, political speech and writing are largely the defense of the indefensible. Things like the continuance of British rule in India, the Russian purges and deportations, the dropping of the atom bombs on Japan, can indeed be defended, but only by arguments which are too brutal for most people to face, and which do not square with the professed aims of political parties. Thus political language has to consist largely of euphemism, question-begging and sheer cloudy vagueness. Defenseless villages are bombarded from the air, the inhabitants driven out into the countryside, the cattle machine-gunned, the huts set on fire with incendiary bullets: this is called *pacification*. Millions of peasants are robbed of their farms and sent trudging along the roads with no more than they can carry: this is called *transfer of population or rectification of frontiers*. People are imprisoned for years without trial, or shot in the back of the neck or sent to die of scurvy in Arctic lumbercamps: this is called elimination of unreliable elements. Such phraseology is needed if one wants to name things without calling up mental pictures of them. Consider for instance some comfortable English professor defending Russian totalitarianism. He cannot say outright, "I believe in killing off your opponents when you can get good results by doing so." Probably, therefore, he will say something like this:
>
>> While freely conceding that the Soviet régime exhibits certain features which the humanitarian may be inclined to deplore, we must, I think, agree that a certain curtailment of the right to political opposition is an unavoidable concomitant of transitional periods, and that the rigors which the Russian people have been called upon to undergo have been amply justified in the sphere of concrete achievement.
>
> The inflated style is itself a kind of euphemism. A mass of Latin words falls upon the facts like soft snow, blurring the outlines and covering up all the details. The great enemy of clear language is insincerity. When there is a gap between one's real and one's declared aims, one turns as it were instinctively to long words and exhausted idioms, like a cuttlefish squirting out ink. In our age there is no such thing as "keeping out of politics." All issues are political issues, and politics itself is a mass of lies, evasions, folly, hatred and schizophrenia.

Ideas for Writing

1. Neil Postman argues that education should provide students with a "defense against culture." Write an essay in which you discuss whether or not he makes a convincing case for his argument. Be sure to examine arguments you think are strong as well as any that seem weak to you.

2. Read the analyects of Confucious or the chapter on education in Plato's *Republic*. Apply Neil Postman's premise that these texts assume education "should make the young compliant and easily accessible to the prejudices of their society" (paragraph 5). Discuss any references to obedience or compliance or examine the biases reflected in one of those works.

3. Study half a dozen advertisements either in magazines or on television for their use of words such as "good" or "true" or "value." Discuss what these words imply given the context of the advertisement and the assumptions about "authority" on which they are based.

4. Watch commercial television for an hour or so some evening and note the names of products in the advertisements you have seen. Explain how the product has been confused with the "thing" it names. (Consult Postman's discussion of reification in paragraph 19.)

Writing before Reading

In your experience, when might a person's individuality be enhanced by a larger group, and when might it be stifled?

AN ANTHROPOLOGIST LEARNS FROM THE HOPI

Dorothy D. Lee

Dorothy D. Lee's essay compares the group's usurpation of individual expression and the Hopi way of respecting the individual. The essay appeared in a collection of published lectures titled Integrity and Compromise: Problems of Public and Private Conscience *(1957).*

Facts about the Hopi

The Hopi, whose name means peaceful, are Pueblo Indians living in the southwestern United States. They are descended from the ancient Anasazi people who built the cliff dwellings in what are now Arizona and New Mexico. The Hopi managed to avoid contact with Europeans until late in the conquest of North America. They destroyed missions built by the Spaniards at Oraibi and fled from further contact with the Spaniards by moving their villages to perches located in sandstone cliffs. The Navajo people began encroaching on Hopi land in the 1820s. The land disputes were further complicated by the U.S. government's relocation policies. The Hopi culture is one of the best-preserved native cultures in North America. The Hopi's relative isolation from Europeans and their observance of numerous ceremonies have helped them survive alien invasions. Traditional rituals are part of the rhythm of life in the Hopi community. The best known of these observances are the snake dance and Kachina pageants.

1. When I began considering my experiences in order to find dilemmas for the subject of this paper, every dilemma I found turned out, after I looked at it carefully, not to have been an actual dilemma at all. In every case, when I looked at the situation, I saw very clearly that there was one way that I simply could not go, and another way which was the only way I could go. So that each time I searched for my dilemmas, they turned out to be problematic situations, for which I did not have to compromise but which I could proceed to solve.

2. Eventually I decided to choose such a situation and present it to you, in order to show what made it problematic, what alternatives it posed, what were the basic principles which were involved and what kind of thinking I had to do to solve the situation.

3. I am of Greek origin. I came to this country as a foreign student, eventually married an American and I am now bringing up four children who, of course, are not only American citizens but are potentially all Presidents of the United States—a tremendous responsibility for a mother. I mention this autobiographical item, because it was to some extent responsible for getting me into the situation which I want to discuss. I am constantly aware of the fact that the only upbringing I have experienced immediately is Greek, whereas I am bringing up four American citizens who must feel American, think American, and relate themselves in an American way, not a Greek way.

4. My husband and I raised our children according to principles which we shared. One of these was that the self should never be conceived as an isolate, nor as the focus of the universe, but rather that it should be defined as a social self. We valued society. We believed that only through society could the self grow, be enriched, find strength. We believed to a large extent in what MacIver calls "community"—in the *"Gemeinschaft."* However, we became increasingly aware of the fact that our children were very much individuals, that they liked to make their own choices and decisions. They did not like to conform to the standards of a group, and in fact they did not enjoy groups. They did not seek out gangs of children of their own age. They did not classify according to age; they liked "people," and were given to referring to other children as "people." They enjoyed groups only when these were based on individual friendships binding person to person. They preferred to choose one or two friends, and develop a deep and growing relationship.

5. The one group which they completely enjoyed, in which they were completely involved, was the family. But that was not a group to them;

that just happened to them; it was not a group they went out to join, but one that just grew. They had taken no steps to create such a group. Within the family they did not seem to seek individual independent behavior or choice which went counter to the ends of the family. But when it came to joining organizations such as the Scouts, they all turned away. And this reluctance to see meaning in organized groups with organization and a purpose seemed completely unAmerican.

6   I did not worry about all this while my husband, who came from generations of Americans, was with me to carry the burden of making the children into good Americans. But when I was left to bring up the children alone, I felt the need to go against the family-centered upbringing of the culture of my birth, so as to "socialize" my children in the American way. I was afraid that, falling between two stools, my children would grow into isolated individuals, cut off from all social nourishment. And I believed in society, as a person and as an anthropologist. Among the primitive societies I studied, I found people who were rich in human quality, poised, strong, true, unique, people who grew from birth until death; and these were people who had social selves, who lived in societies where individual ends and social ends coincided.

7   It was while I was considering this problem that I was offered an opportunity to move to the Middle West, to a city where there was much concern over group development and group participation; where group awareness and participation was being implemented at all levels in the schools. It seemed to offer the solution I was looking for. We moved. The children were unhappy at school, but I tried to help them to acquiesce to the new system, to understand its principles, to adjust to a groupcentered environment. But, since my working hours coincided with school hours, I had no direct experience of what went on until the Parents' Open Night before Thanksgiving.

8   I went first of all to my son's room, the seventh grade. The teacher showed me a mural, covering all the walls, depicting the life of the ancient Egyptians. It was a group project; and the teacher pointed out the part for which my son was responsible. The painting depicted a war scene: some pinkish, sleek, placid, fat, lifeless horses. These were nothing like my son's skinny, elongated beasts, full of straining movement and savage life. I protested that this could not be my son's doing. The teacher explained that my son had not been allowed to paint his own unique horses; they were too different. Since this was a group project, uniformity was essential, so the children had all copied illustrations from a history textbook. As I turned away, appalled and only half-convinced, I spotted the tiny figure of a bird, of no known genus, scraggy, leering, menacing, and I knew that my son's uniqueness had not been entirely mowed down in the drive for uniformity; it had burst through, however irrelevantly and illicitly. It reminded me of the mushrooms which push up a cement pavement, cracking and disrupting its even surface; I was happy to see it.

9   Disturbed at this interpretation of the concept of the group, I went to the classroom of my daughter who was in the fourth grade. The teacher pointed to a frieze of Pilgrims and Indians in profile that ran around the wall of the room, and obviously waited for my admiring response. All the Pilgrims were alike, all the Indians alike without deviation; alike in size and shape and color. I did not know what I was expected to admire, and finally asked whether the children had pasted up the frieze. The teacher explained that they not only had pasted it, they had actually made it, as a group project. "It was hard to make all the heads alike," she said. "When the children first painted the pictures they all looked different, so we had to throw them away. And then I made an Indian profile and a Pilgrim profile; I wrote directions for coloring each part, and the children traced them and cut out their own. And now they make *one* frieze."

10   I had another daughter in the tenth grade in high school; and soon after this sad night, her grade decided to have a bake sale to help raise money for the trip they were to take to Washington in their senior year. This did seem like good group participation. The trip was to be a truly cooperative venture, since all the students in the class were working toward it, though not all would manage to go eventually. This time each student was asked to bring cake or cookies for the sale. My daughter took this seriously, and was using it as a learning opportunity. She stayed up late making four batches of cookies for which I contributed the ingredients. She found out the cost of the ingredients, and priced the cookies, adding an appropriate amount for her skilled labor. When she took them to school, she discovered that this was not what had been expected of her. Half the children had asked their mothers to bake for them, and most of the rest had bought baked goods at the corner bakery. Mary's cookies were priced below the cost of the raw materials, as were all the other goods, to make sure that they would sell; yet the students were congratulated on raising all this money for their trip through their own exertions. Mary, concerned over what seemed hypocrisy, decided that the work of the students in selling the cookies would represent their involvement, their share in the raising of funds. But when the time came to sell, the homeroom teacher was there to sell. The teenagers could not be trusted to make change. True, they were studying geometry, but they might make a mistake in subtraction; and besides they might yield to temptation. The group—through its representative, the homeroom teacher—could not expose itself to the fallibility of its members; it could not take a chance on the integrity or the ability of its constituent members. In the interest of insuring good results for the group project, all the strivings of the individual self had to be suppressed.

11   This is what I found in my children's schools. Was this the end of my search for true group experience? Was this the meaning of the self in society? I saw here not nourishment and enrichment, but impoverishment and diminution of the self. The group here demanded the sacrifice of the

very generative force of the self, the vitality, the vagary, the spontaneity. It was superimposed upon the self as an external standard, and could be sustained only through a Procrustean conformity. In these schools the children were not people, not individual persons with integrity peculiar to each. Their being did not call forth respect. What was demanded of them was to form a class based on undeviating similarity; and to achieve this, the striving of the self had to be throttled. Only through destruction of the self could the group thrive.

12 I was not convinced that this was necessary to the creation of a group. In my study of other people, I had come across societies where the group was far more permeating in the life of the individual, where even the private thoughts and feelings of individuals affected the group. I had studied the Hopi where each person had unique significance, where the people were spontaneous, vital, free, strong. So I went back to a consideration of the Hopi, to find out what there was about their culture which made it possible for an individual to maintain uniqueness and significance within the group structure.

13 Whatever I say here about the Hopi refers to them as they have been until recently. Change has been going on, and particularly since the past war, when many Hopi went out, either with the armed forces, or to factories, and became more and more exposed to our ways of arranging things, to our way of life. If I use what seems to be the present tense, I use it in its reference to the timeless; and what I say about the Hopi refers to their timeless philosophy of life, to what they call the Hopi way—the good, the right path; only when I give specific examples, do I speak of the actual events of time and space.

14 The Hopi are Pueblo Indians, living in Arizona. They reckon descent through the mother, and houses belong to the women of the lineage, where their husbands come to join them. In the older villages, the closely related women—sister, mothers and daughters, aunts and cousins—with their families, occupied one or more adjacent households, where the work of living goes on cooperatively. The men herd, farm, hunt, collect fuel, perhaps spin and weave; the women cooperate in preparing food for the group, caring for young children and for the house, hauling water, making pottery and baskets. And when I say men and women I include boys and girls, who from an early age have the right to work alongside the adults, doing work important to the welfare of the group.

15 The group, starting from the unit of the immediate family of birth, but expanding through systematic introduction into wider areas until it includes eventually the entire universe, is the focus to which the behavior and feeling and entire being of an individual is oriented. Much, if not all, of what a person thinks and does, has a reference to the group. For example, if I go visiting a new mother in my society, I shall probably smile with the joy of seeing her again, with congratulations for her new baby. The Hopi visitor will smile, also, but here the smile has a significance beyond this, as the happiness it expresses helps the baby to thrive and the new

16   mother to recover her strength; and, conversely, a face expressing worry would bring harm at this time.

16   A person enters this unit by birth, and all of an individual's behavior is geared to this social unit which he has joined through no choice of his own. His loyalties are to this group; they are not person-to-person loyalties. And parents have been known deliberately to try to shift a child's affection from concentration upon one family member, to diffusion among the group. The area of an individual's work, of responsible participation, is therefore not one he has chosen, but is a given also, as it is coextensive with the group. Every individual, young and old, is charged with responsibility for the welfare of the social unit; and this they apparently accept voluntarily, considering it good.

17   Richard Brandt, a philosopher making a study of Hopi ethics, found that his informants considered that one of the main things which make a man ashamed was that of not having any children alive. This "shows sin"; that is, it shows that a man's behavior, his thoughts, his willing, his emotions were not social enough to keep his children alive. People were expected to be ashamed of not helping in cooperative undertakings, not giving, not participating in ceremonials for the welfare of the unit—in this last case the entire universe. No, said the informants, a man need not be ashamed of being poor, or of being dumb, so long as he was good to others.[1] Brandt made arrangements to see informants in absolute secrecy, to protect them against possible criticism; but he found that the informant might not be ready to talk even so until he had made sure that no harm would come to the group from his disclosures.

18   Related to this is the Hopi reluctance to stand out—to be singled out from the group. Teachers in Hopi schools have reported discomfort and even tears as a reaction to praise in public. It appears that what is in fact disturbing is the comparative evaluation that results in singling out and praising. Hopi do not compare their achievement, nor the importance of their work, and "a highly skilled stone-cutter is perfectly content to accept the same wages as an unskilled day laborer."[2] Children cannot be persuaded to compete in school—in classwork or in playing games. One school reported that the children learned to play basketball easily, and delight in the game; but they cannot be taught to keep score. They play by the hour, without knowing who is winning. The structure of the game, with everyone doing his utmost within his established role, is in a simplified way, similar to the kind of structure we find in the Hopi group.

19   As I have indicated already, it is not only the physical act, or overt behavior, which is effective, according to the Hopi view. Thought and will

---

[1] Richard B. Brandt, *Hopi Ethics: A Theoretical Analysis,* University of Chicago Press, Chicago, 1954, pp. 42, 71.

[2] Laura Thompson, *Culture in Crisis: A Study of the Hopi Indians,* Harper & Brothers, New York, 1950, p. 94.

and intent are at least as effective; so that it is not enough for the individual to act peacefully; he must also feel nonaggressive, think harmonious thoughts, and be imbued with a singleness of purpose. It is his duty to be happy, for the sake of the group—a mind in conflict and full of anxiety brings disruption, ill-being, to the social unit, and, at a time of prayer and ceremonial, to the entire universe.

20   Brandt[3] found that one of the personal traits highly valued was that of being "happy in his heart." One informant told him, "This is like a flower or a cornfield: when in bloom it beautifies the whole earth. . . . It is a kind of gratitude. . . . When you go into the fields you should sing to the corn." Another informant praised a man who, even when upset, made "himself happy while talking" with others. Superficially, this is similar to valued behavior in our own society, too; but with the Hopi, it is an aspect of working for the group.

21   Human society is a part of a larger structured whole, so an individual cooperates with even more than the members of his human group. Every aspect of nature, plants and rocks and animals, colors and cardinal directions and numbers and sex distinctions, the dead and the living, all have a cooperative share in the maintenance of the universal order. Eventually, the effort of each individual, human or not, goes into this huge whole. And here, too, it is every aspect of a person which counts. The entire being of the Hopi individual affects the balance of nature; and as each individual develops his inner potential, as he enhances his participation, so does the entire universe become invigorated. Not his behavior alone, not his achievement, but his entire unique being is significant.

22   Much of the time and energy of the Hopi goes into working at ceremonials. These are highly organized and form part of an established ceremonial cycle. Each ceremony "belongs to" a secret society, usually a man's society and only members of this society have the privilege and the responsibility to carry out the ceremony. Each main ceremony involves an exceedingly complex order of detailed acts: preparatory rites, acts of purification, gathering of materials, preparation of masks, sand paintings, and medicine water; composition of new songs, rehearsal of dances. The women prepare food to be exchanged reciprocally. The ceremonials themselves last nine or seventeen days. Though only one secret society is charged with the responsibility of a specific ceremony, the entire group of "spectators"—all the villagers and visitors from other pueblos who come to the public performances—eventually participate, through keeping a "good heart," through their wholehearted involvement in what they watch, through laughing at the burlesque and pranks afforded by the clowns.

23   Each main ceremony has reference to a phase of the agricultural cycle, helping the universal order to become actual. There is an established course for the sun, for example, within the cosmic order; but the

---

[3] Brandt, *op. cit.*, p. 128.

winter solstice ceremony is necessary to actualize this order into the here and now, so that the sun can actually follow the prescribed course, and so turn northward. The growing of the corn also has its established order; the stages of growth are given in the order of nature; but the corn cannot move through them, from germination to fruition, without the cooperative effort of man, who must transform, by means of his ceremonials, potentiality into actuality. So, in the end, when a field of corn is ready to harvest, it is a result of the cooperative effort of every member of the group, in addition to the man who has dug and hoed and planted and weeded.

24 Though each ceremonial has specific reference within the agricultural cycle, each main ceremony also has reference to the whole of life, to the entire cosmic system. The aim is the well-being of the universal whole, not of the individual. If the individual profits by the ceremonial, it is because he is an integral part of this whole which has become invigorated. The individual maintains harmony with the universe for the sake of the universal order, not for his own sake, except derivatively. Eventually, through the maintenance of this harmony, the human group thrives, the sun moves along its established course from solstice to solstice, the thunderclouds gather and release their rain, the corn sprouts and roots and fills and ripens.

25 In all this, the individual is working along given lines, for given ends, for a group which he did not create of his own choice. This seems the denial of all freedom and initiative.

26 In addition, the geographic location of the Hopi seems to make for determinism, and an absence of individual freedom. They live and practice agriculture in country where it would seem, offhand, to be impossible to depend on the land for a living. The rain may not come at all, or may fall in torrents and wash away the crops; high winds may blow away the seed. The growing cycle of corn, their main crop, is almost coincidental with the growing season, which is cut short at both ends by killing frosts. As Laura Thompson says: "The arid north Arizona plateau posed unyielding imperatives which had to be met habitually and unerringly if the tribe were to survive and reproduce itself...."[4] This means that the environment imposes rigid limits to behavior and choice. How can man have personal freedom, if these circumstances, to will, to act, to be, when the very environment dictates behavior, and where there is so little margin for human fallibility? Where can there be room for personal initiative? Who can be proud of his stand of corn when even the laughter of a child has gone to grow it? How can there be motivation for work, when the responsibility, and the results and the work itself are all shared,to a greater or less extent? Does not this mean that personal effort is lost in the undifferentiated immensity, that the individual is submerged and lost in the group and the universe?

---

[4] Thompson, *op. cit.*, pp. 173–174.

27   Strange to say, the genius of the Hopi culture has made it possible to find spontaneity, significance and freedom, motivation and personal integrity, within this structured universe, within the given society, and the difficult environment. It is true that there is probably no joy of independent achievement, but this does not mean that there is no motivation, no personal initiative.

28   Certainly, there is no such thing as individualism, in our sense of the term. There is no private enterprise, no joy of personal success; and there is avoidance of outstandingness. There is no undertaking which an individual initiates and brings to a conclusion alone, with the pride of success. When a farmer is harvesting a "successful" corn crop, who had "succeeded"? Throughout the year, the members of his pueblo, in different organizations, have performed successive ceremonies, to bring about this harvest. The children have played organized ball games for days with the children from another pueblo, and thus helped the corn to grow. Men have refrained from intercourse with their wives, and sweethearts; eaglets have been captured at considerable risk, women and children have laughed heartily at the antics of ceremonial clowns, priests have gone into retirement and meditation, and much more has been done and wished and thought, to bring about this good harvest. The farmer's achievement in all this may be seen as insignificant; yet it may also be seen as superbly significant.

29   For the immensity of effort is not undifferentiated; the individual effort is not like a grain of sand, lost in the universal whole. Every individual within the system has his unique role, and each role is different and indispensable. The structured whole of the universe, or of the human group, contains a precise position for each and every member. No one is expendable. "Every individual in the group, male and female, young or old, has his proper place and role in the organization of the community, with corresponding duties and privileges ... with duties and rights commensurate with their age and status."[5] And, in the universal whole, every part of nature has its unique and indispensable role. Man supplies the moving principle in this order through his ability to will, and through his ceremonials.

30   So man, each individual person, through the uniqueness of his role, and the indispensability of his own specific effort, has great significance. Group effort and community of ends, does not mean totalitarianism and the loss of individual uniqueness. In fact, the group can prosper only in so far as this uniqueness is fully actualized. Only in so far as each member of each *kiva* carries out his own unique responsibility, fulfils his role in putting on and performing the ceremony which is the responsibility of this particular ceremonial association, will the ceremony help the corn to

---

[5] *Ibid.,* p. 65.

move into the next stage of growth. In this each individual member has an indispensable and precise function.

31   The clarity of role, the preciseness of structure and of place in the structure is such that the individual knows what is open to him to do; and, as it is apparently satisfying to work in terms of the social unit, the individual can and does work autonomously within his role. O'Kane writes, "A Hopi household is a self-directing group, the members of which seem to achieve automatic coordination of their activities. No one tells the others what they should do, or when, or how. No one exercises authority. The various members seem to fall naturally into a pattern in which the abilities of the individual and the needs of the household are satisfactorily served..."[6]

32   Thus an individual can decide to what extent he will fill the responsibility which is his privilege. For example, O'Kane tells how three fellow clansmen decided to get turtles to supply themselves with shell for the leg rattles used in ceremonial dancing. This was done at their own initiative, but within an established framework—i.e., the rattles were to be attached to a specified part of the leg, they were to be of specified shell, worn at specified times in specified roles, etc. The individual decision brought more shell rattles, or newer rattles to the *kivas* involved; it enriched the group. The decision involved much and arduous work, including a return journey of some six hundred miles. Each of the three contributed of what he had to offer—one his car, another gas, the third his knowledge and skill. There was no attempt at uniformity, nor at equalization; there was no suppression of individuality; rather through the variety of individual contribution, the whole could be achieved.

33   The individual is free to choose ways in which to actualize his responsibility; as, for example, when three children asked to stay after school because their grandmother was dying in their home, as they were afraid that they could not avoid anxious thoughts if they went back to the pueblo. Responsible group participation is felt as a happy occasion, as projective tests given to Hopi children show. And a marked correlation exists between the presence of spontaneity in the personality, as revealed in the tests, and degree of participation in the communal life of the pueblo.

34   It is clear that the welfare of the group and of the entire universe eventually depends on the individual; yet the individual is not tethered, nor monitored, nor shackled, nor coerced, to insure his safe carrying out of his responsibilities. When Brandt was asking questions involving ethical principles, he found that there was no adherence to group morals as categorical. "It is up to him to decide" what is right or wrong, was stated

---

[6] Walter Collins O'Kane, *The Hopis: Portrait of a Desert People*, University of Oklahoma, Norman, 1953, p. 8.

35   repeatedly, as well as the desirability of consent: "I don't believe in forcing anybody to do anything.... If he gives his consent, it is all right."⁷

It is evident, then, that a tremendous respect and trust is accorded to the individual since no provision is made for man's failure, neglect, error. The entire group and the entire universe is vulnerable, exposed to the fallibility of the individual. Even a child, allowing himself to have anxious thoughts, can bring ill to the pueblo. This means a great responsibility, and can be seen as a frightening and overwhelming burden. Yet, instead of blocking the individual with its immensity, this responsibility seems to function as a motivating factor, affording a channel for spontaneity. Instead of cutting off the protruding variations, the peculiar differentiating qualities of the individual; instead of submerging the self within a uniform mass, the group encourages individual quality, and enriches itself through it. The significant place given to each unique person and the full trust accorded to each, means that the group can thrive through the full exercise of the individual self.

36   This is what I had missed in the school situation of my children; I had missed significance and respect for unique being. There was no trust in the potentiality of each child. The homeroom protected itself against its members; it would not take a chance on the honesty or mathematical ability or industry of its members. The individual had no significance; and, in fact, all effort was made to make the members of the group interchangeable, until the artistic expression of one could not be distinguished from that of another. There was no appreciation of individual quality; it was treated as disruptive and threatening of group welfare, and, being cast into the outer darkness, it did, in fact, disrupt. If my son could have drawn the Egyptian war scene in his own peculiar lines, he would have had no occasion to introduce his minute discordant bird in the corner. Some growth of the self did occur, because of its tremendous impetus; but it met with discouragement. I found here that the group existed at the expense of the individual; and this was totalitarianism.

37   At this point my problem was clear and I solved it. What did I do? I decided that I needed a school where the group was conceived according to democratic principles: where the individual was given a significant place within the structured group; where the group was considered to prosper only through the optimum growth of each and every member—not through stunting them; where uniqueness was valued; where individual and group could grow and thrive only together. I found such a school and moved to the town where it was, forty miles away. I solved my problem. My children are growing up in true American democracy.

---

⁷ Brandt, *op. cit.,* pp. 190, 191, 203, 221, 224, 225, 229.

REFERENCES

(References have been made only to those items from which direct quotations were given)

Richard B. Brandt, *Hopi Ethics: A Theoretical Analysis,* University of Chicago Press, Chicago, 1954.

Walter Collins O'Kane, *The Hopis: Portrait of a Desert People,* University of Oklahoma, Norman, 1953.

Leo W. Simmons, *Sun Chief: The Autobiography of a Hopi Indian,* Yale University Press, New Haven, 1942.

Alexander M. Stephen, *Hopi Journal,* edited by Elsie Clews Parsons, Columbia University Press, New York, 1936.

Laura Thompson, *Culture in Crisis: A Study of the Hopi Indians,* Harper & Brothers, New York, 1950.

Laura Thompson and Alice Joseph, *The Hopi Way,* University of Chicago Press, Chicago, 1944.

Reading for Meaning

1. What point of view does Dorothy D. Lee use in her essay? Why do you think she chose this perspective? How effective is this point of view in exploring her topic?

2. Lee's essay on the Hopi was written for a collection of essays titled *Integrity and Compromise: Problems of Public and Private Conscience*. In what ways does Lee's essay fit into a book on this subject?

3. Because of her own concern that her children have a sense that they are part of a larger society or community, Lee moved to a city in the Midwest that emphasized "group development and group participation" in the community and in the schools. What ideas about "group effort" did the teachers in her children's school seem to have? What did Lee think of those efforts? Do you agree with her?

4. How is Lee's description of the Hopi way of life (beginning in paragraph 12) relevant to her discussion of her children's struggles at school?

5. In the Hopi culture, Lee tells us, people are so certain that individuals will do all they can to fulfill their responsibilities that there is no anticipation of "failure, neglect, [or] error." In contrast, what attitude toward group effort and participation might Americans have if they are educated in the classrooms like the ones Lee describes in paragraphs 8 through 10.

6. Select a passage (a paragraph or group of paragraphs) from Dorothy Lee's essay that you thought especially interesting or informative. Discuss how well the ideas in this passage are supported or how well the passage fits into the essay as a whole.

7. How does Dorothy Lee structure her essay? How effective is that structure? To help you answer this question, find the two main sections of the article and discuss what she accomplishes by dividing the essay this way.

Comparing Texts

1. How do the teachings of the Hopi compare to the lessons Pablo Neruda learns from the Incas of Macchu Picchu? (page 398).

2. Compare the Hopi idea of individuality to the demands that Aung San Suu Kyi (page 359) or the mothers of Argentina (page 365) make of the individual.

3. In "Culture and the Communal Organisation" (page 270), J. E. Thomas discusses the relationship between the *salaryman* in Japan and the company for which he works. Are there similarities between the place of the *salaryman* within the corporation and the role of the individual in the Hopi culture? What differences do you see?

Ideas for Writing

1. Dorothy D. Lee describes classrooms in which individual expression is sacrificed to conformity. Based on your own experiences in elementary school or what you have read about classrooms in the United States, how accurate are Lee's observations?

2. Analyze the makeup, beliefs, or significance of the community in the lives of the Hopi, the Balinese ("Children and Ritual in Bali," page 101), immigrants who live in the United States ("Immigrants and Family Values," page 450), or European Americans ("The Religion of Americans and American Religion," page 580).

3. Choose one of the questions Dorothy D. Lee asks about the individual's relationship to the community in paragraph 26. Do some research to discover how other cultural groups that emphasize the community rather than the individual address this question. Discuss your findings.

Writing before Reading

1. Do you feel more at home in a rural or an urban setting? What do you think has contributed to these feelings?

2. What connections do you feel to your ancestors? Are there branches of the family tree that you find inspiring or that you prefer not to acknowledge? What do you hope to add to your family or community?

FROM *THE HEIGHTS OF MACCHU PICCHU*

Pablo Neruda

Pablo Neruda was born in Paralle in the south of Chile in 1904. His father worked for the Chilean railway. Born Ricardo Eliezer Neftali

Reyes y Basoalto, Neruda changed his name while still in high school to Pablo Neruda after the Czech poet Jan Neruda. He was awarded the Nobel Prize for literature in 1971, the third Latin American to receive the award. His extensive and varied poetic works include Twenty Love Poems and a Song of Despair *(1924)*, Residence on Earth *(1933)*, Tercera Residencia *(1947), and* Canto General *(1950)*. His early poetic achievements won him consular positions in southern Asia (1927–1932), Latin America, and Europe. He was seated as a member of the Chilean Senate (1945–1948) representing the Communist Party then was forced into exile for four years (1948–1952). He died September 23, 1973, a few days after the death of his friend, President Salvador Allende, who was killed during a military coup led by Augusto Pinochet Ugarte that in all likelihood was supported by the United States' Central Intelligence Agency.

Pablo Neruda's long poem The Heights of Macchu Picchu was inspired by his trip to the site of an ancient Incan city. At the time of the Spanish invasion, the Incas controlled a vast empire. The Incas built a system of fortresses in the Andes mountains, one of which sits between two peaks—Macchu Picchu and Huayna Picchu (the Old and New Picchu). The fortress, Macchu Picchu, named after one of these peaks, was apparently abandoned by its inhabitants. On the heights of Macchu Picchu, Neruda finds evidence of "the old and unremembered human heart" whose presence in the poem becomes the touchstone from which other experience can be understood.

Facts about Chile

Chile stretches along the western coast of South America from Peru in the north to Cape Horn, the southernmost tip of the continent. It averages less than 200 miles across. It features the Andes mountains, a central valley, and steep cliffs along the coast. The people of Chile are of mixed European and Native American ancestry, and about 80 percent are Roman Catholics. Spanish explorers established settlements in Chile in the 1550s, and although they controlled the country until its independence in 1818, the native Araucanians offered fierce resistance to Spanish domination. Macchu Picchu, built high in the Andes Mountains, is the site of a major settlement of Incas. Recently, the country has had serious economic problems caused by periods of rampant inflation, the inequitable distribution of land and wealth, and its dependence on copper mining. The volatile price of copper is set by the U.S. corporations that own several of the richest mines. In 1970 Salvador Allende, backed by a coalition of Socialists, Communists, and Radicals, won the presidential election. In the three years he served as president, Allende nationalized banks and private corporations—including the powerful U.S. copper companies—and instituted a series of land reforms. A military junta supported by the U.S. Central Intelligence Agency overthrew Allende in

1973 and established the repressive government of General Augusto Pinochet Ugarte. Pinochet did not relax martial law until 1988. In October of that year opposition leader Patricio Aylwin was elected president, but was unable to curb Pinochet's power. In 1998–1999 the government of Spain sought Pinochet's extradition from England, where he was receiving medical treatment. Spain intended to put the aging dictator on trial for the deaths of Spanish citizens who were murdered in Chile by military forces under Pinochet's leadership.

II

How many times in wintry city streets, or in
a bus, a boat at dusk, or in the denser solitude
of festive nights, drenched in the sound
of bells and shadows, in the very lair of human pleasure,
have I wanted to pause and look for the eternal, unfathomable
truth's filament I'd fingered once in stone, or in the flash a kiss released.

(That which is wheat like yellow history
of small, full breasts repeats a calculus
ceaselessly tender in the burgeoning
and which, always the same way, husks to ivory—
that which is ghost of home in the translucent water
belling from the lone snows down to these waves of blood.)

I could only grasp a cluster of faces or masks
thrown down like rings of hollow gold,
like scarecrow clothes, daughters of rabid autumn
shaking the stunted tree of the frightened races.

I had no place in which my hand could rest—
no place running like harnessed water,
firm as a nugget of anthracite or crystal—
responding, hot or cold, to my open hand.

What was man? In what layer of his humdrum conversation,
among his shops and sirens—in which of his metallic movements
lived on imperishably the quality of life? . . .

VI

Then up the ladder of the earth I climbed
through the barbed jungle's thickets
until I reached you Macchu Picchu.

Tall city of stepped stone,
home at long last of whatever earth
had never hidden in her sleeping clothes.
In you two lineages that had run parallel
met where the cradle both of man and light
rocked in a wind of thorns.

Mother of stone and sperm of condors.

High reef of the human dawn.

Spade buried in primordial sand.

This was the habitation, this is the site:
here the fat grains of maize grew high
to fall again like red hail.

The fleece of the vicuña[1] was carded here
to clothe men's loves in gold, their tombs and mothers,
the king, the prayers, the warriors.
Up here men's feet found rest at night
near eagles' talons in the high
meat-stuffed eyries. And in the dawn
with thunder steps they trod the thinning mists,
touching the earth and stones that they might recognize
that touch come night, come death....

XI

Through a confusion of splendor,
through a night made stone let me plunge my hand
and move to beat in me a bird held for a thousand years,
the old and unremembered human heart!
Today let me forget this happiness, wider than all the sea,
because man is wider than all the sea and her necklace of islands
and we must fall into him as down a well to clamber back with
branches of secret water, recondite truths.
Allow me to forget, circumference of stone, the powerful proportions,
the transcendental span, the honeycomb's foundations,
and from the set-square allow my hand to slide
down a hypotenuse of hairshirt and salt blood.
When, like a horseshoe of rusting wing-cases, the furious condor
batters my temples in the order of flight
and his tornado of carnivorous feathers sweeps the dark dust
down slanting stairways, I do not see the rush of the bird,
nor the blind sickle of his talons—
I see the ancient being, the slave, the sleeping one,
blanket his fields—a body, a thousand bodies, a man, a thousand
women swept by the sable whirlwind, charred with rain and night,
stoned with a leaden weight of statuary:
Juan Splitstones, son of Wiracocha,
Juan Coldbelly, heir of the green star,
Juan Barefoot, grandson to the turquoise,
rising to birth with me, as my own brother....

---

[1] A llama-like animal valuable for its wool.

XII

Arise to birth with me, my brother.

Give me your hand out of the depths
sown by your sorrows.
You will not return from these stone fastnesses.
You will not emerge from subterranean time.
Your rasping voice will not come back,
nor your pierced eyes rise from their sockets.
Look at me from the depths of the earth,
tiller of fields, weaver, reticent shepherd,
groom of totemic guanacos,[2]
mason high on your treacherous scaffolding,
iceman of Andean tears,
jeweler with crushed fingers,
farmer anxious among his seedlings,
potter wasted among his clays—
bring to the cup of this new life
your ancient buried sorrows.
Show me your blood and your furrow;
say to me: here I was scourged
because a gem was dull or because the earth
failed to give up in time its tithe of corn or stone.
Point out to me the rock on which you stumbled,
the wood they used to crucify your body.
Strike the old flints
to kindle ancient lamps, light up the whips
glued to your wounds throughout the centuries
and light the axes gleaming with your blood.

I come to speak for your dead mouths.

Throughout the earth
let dead lips congregate,
out of the depths spin this long night to me
as if I rode at anchor here with you.
And tell me everything, tell chain by chain,
and link by link, and step by step;
sharpen the knives you kept hidden away,
thrust them into my breast, into my hands,
like a torrent of sunbursts,
an Amazon of buried jaguars,
and leave me cry: hours, days and years,
blind ages, stellar centuries.

And give me silence, give me water, hope.

---

[2] A Chilean term for an animal similar to an alpaca or llama.

Chapter 9   The Individual and the Group   **403**

Give me the struggle, the iron, the volcanoes.

Let bodies cling like magnets to my body.

Come quickly to my veins and to my mouth.

Speak through my speech, and through my blood.

Reading for Meaning

1. How does Pablo Neruda feel about modern urban life? Which lines in his poem convey his feelings?
2. How does Neruda imagine life in the ancient city of Macchu Picchu?
3. How does his imagined connection to humankind change once he reaches the Incan city?
4. What does the poet-speaker expect to find in Macchu Picchu? Are his expectations fulfilled?
5. Locate passages in which the speaker-poet describes his own actions. What does Neruda see as the purpose of the poet?
6. How does Neruda use images of nature in this poem? What does nature seem to stand for? How does it suggest what might be missing from the urban death-in-life that he describes?
7. How does his experience on Macchu Picchu help the poet answer the question "What was man" and where in human activity can be found the imperishable "quality of life"? (section ii).

Comparing Texts

1. In *Modern Man in Search of a Soul*, Carl Jung characterizes people whose consciousness is truly "modern" as cut off from the past and from the sense of human community. Study Jung's ideas in the following passage and compare his assessment to Pablo Neruda's portrait of his contemporaries. What differences do you see in the way these two writers look at modern life? Do you find similarities in the two descriptions? What solution does Neruda pose for the problem of modern alienation?

   Only the man[1] who is modern in our meaning of the term really lives in the present; he alone has a present-day consciousness, and he alone finds that the ways of life which correspond to earlier levels pall upon him. The values and strivings of those past worlds no longer interest him save from the historical standpoint. Thus he has become "unhistorical" in the deepest sense and has estranged himself from the mass of men who live entirely within the bounds of tradition. Indeed,

---

[1] Jung adheres to the old standard of referring to humankind as "man" and by using male pronouns exclusively. To avoid such gender bias, the current convention is to use the term "humankind" and the double pronouns "she or he."

he is completely modern only when he has come to the very edge of the world, leaving behind him all that has been discarded and outgrown, and acknowledging that he stands before a void out of which all things may grow.

2. In his preface to the *Lyrical Ballads,* William Wordsworth wrote that the poet should "endeavour to produce or enlarge" the human mind and help readers appreciate the "beauty and dignity" of the human mind. For Wordsworth, forces were at work to dull human perception:

> For a multitude of causes, unknown to former times, are now acting with a combined force to blunt the discriminating power of the mind, and, unfitting it for all voluntary exertion, to reduce it to a state of savage torpor. . . . Reflecting upon the magnitude of the general evil, I should be oppressed with no dishonorable melancholy, had I not a deep impression of certain inherent and indestructible qualities of the human mind, and likewise of certain powers in the great and permanent objects that act upon it which are equally inherent and indestructive.

How do Wordsworth's description of the blunted nature of human perception and his faith that it can be revived compare to ideas in Neruda's poem?

Ideas for Writing

1. Discuss *The Heights of Macchu Picchu* as an archeological quest for an unchanging truth or identity. Examine what the poet wishes to discover and how successful he is in finding what he seeks.

2. Do some research on ancient Troy, Mycaenae, Beijing (beginning with the eighth century B.C.E.), Jerusalem, Jerico, Chichen Itza (a Maya city in Mexico's Yucatan), or another city whose history survives from ancient times. Provide information about the people, social organization, arts, or scientific or mathematical achievements of that city or its civilization.

CHAPTER 10
IMMIGRANTS AND EXILES

First Thoughts

eeste indruk

Cry, the beloved country, for the unborn child that is the inheritor of our fear. Let him not love the earth too deeply.

I am sometimes astonished that these words were written in 1946 and that it took many of the white people of South Africa thirty years to acknowledge their truth, when black schoolchildren started rioting in the great black city of Soweto on June 16, 1976, on the day after which of all the hundred thousand days of our written history, nothing would be the same again.

Alan Paton
1982

When the Nazis spoke of the necessity of a highly ritualized and symbolized life, I could hear Bigger Thomas on Chicago's South Side saying: "Man, what we need is a leader like Marcus Garvey. We need a nation, a flag, an army of our own. We colored folks ought to organize into groups and have generals, captains, lieutenants, and so forth. We ought to take Africa and have a national home." I'd know, while listening to these childish words, that a white man would smile derisively at them. But I could not smile, for I knew the truth of those simple words from the facts of my own life. The deep hunger in those childish ideas was like a flash of lightning illuminating the whole dark inner landscape of Bigger's mind. Those words told me that the civilization which had given birth to Bigger contained no spiritual sustenance, had created no culture which could hold and claim his allegiance and faith, had sensitized him and had left him stranded, a free agent to roam the streets of our cities, a hot and whirling vortex of undisciplined and unchannelized impulses. The results of these observations made me feel more than ever estranged from the civilization in which I lived, and more than ever resolved toward the task of creating with words a scheme of images and symbols whose direction could enlist the sympathies, loyalties, and yearnings of the millions of Bigger Thomases in every land and race.

Introduction to *Native Son* and its character Bigger Thomas Richard Wright
March 7, 1940

How many overseas Chinese who have lived and prospered in foreign lands all their adult lives say that when the time comes for them to leave this earth, they pray for enough warning to return to the mainland to live out their last days and be buried in the city, town or village where they drew their first breath? How many others toil at ironing boards, restaurant sinks or sewing machines not for themselves but for family members across the seas whom they know only by name? How many eminent Chinese, having won fame and fortune in the west, prefer to contribute their services and treasure not to the countries that nurtured their talents but to China, where their talents, had they remained, would never have flourished?

Bette Bao Lord
Legacies: A Chinese Mosaic

Immigrants are people who move from one country to another with the intention of settling in the new country. Although the definition of immigrants is simple enough, few major movements of people have occurred without complex emotional and political repercussions. Many immigrants intend to return to their homelands, but few actually do. Conditions in the homeland often cause them to leave and then prevent them from returning. In most cases, poverty, political unrest, or persecution cause people to relocate. In the case of migration for economic reasons, one group of emigrants may be replaced by immigrants from other countries. For example, in the 1970s while Italians became temporary workers in central and northern Europe, immigrants from Turkey and north Africa went to Italy looking for jobs.

The exile is a special kind of immigrant whose departure from the home country occurs for personal and political reasons. Exiles may leave a country voluntarily as a protest against existing conditions, as did many artists and musicians from the United States in the 1920s, or they may be forced out of their home country for political reasons, as was Salman Rushdie in 1989. Unlike exiles, immigrants may come to a new land because they were sent for. Beginning in the seventeenth century, officials in the colonies and territories in the New World (Argentina, Brazil, Canada, and the United States) and Australia recruited first farmers and later factory workers to expand their populations and to make up the settlers and workers needed to develop the new land.

Whether they come on their own or are lured by the promise of land or jobs, immigrants sometimes find that the new land is not as hospitable as they had hoped. Industrialized countries have passed various laws over the past hundred years to regulate the flow of legal immigrants across their borders. Some of these laws, like the Chinese Exclusion Acts passed in 1882 and 1917, excluded or limited the number of immigrants from a particular country or part of the world because of the racial biases of the time.

Problems of assimilation and identity face all immigrants and people who have been exiled from their home country. The readings in this chapter present some of the struggles of immigrants and their children as well as the unique problems that confront the individual who, by virtue of his or her culture, is pronounced "foreign" or "alien." Salman Rushdie writes in "Imaginary Homelands" about the dilemma of the exile who can only imagine the country he left because even if he were to return, he would discover that the country he remembers no longer exists. Jenefer Shute, a South African writer, returns to her home country after the dismantling of apartheid only to find that the needed, fundamental changes have not taken place. In "Fictive Fragments of Father and Son," David Mura examines his father's history and his own feelings about his father's choice to assimilate into the larger Anglo-European culture. The short story, "Razia Begum in London," by Ruxana Meer, explores the misunderstandings and the fascination that the descendants of immigrants have with elders from the home country. As you can tell from the title of his article, Francis Fukuyama wrote "Immigrants and Family Values" in order to portray immigrants as upholders of the values that many Americans claim they are eroding. Gloria Anzaldúa's essay, "La Conciencia de la Mestiza: Towards a New Consciousness," celebrates the *"mestiza"* (literally, the woman of "mixed" ancestry) as a rich New World blend of Native American, Spanish, and African heritage.

Writing before Reading

Describe a particular place that you remember with some fondness. What memories have attached themselves to this place? In what ways are you still the same person you were then? In what ways have you changed?

IMAGINARY HOMELANDS

Salman Rushdie

Salman Rushdie was born of Islamic parents in Bombay, India, in June 1947, two months prior to the creation of the Islamic state of Pakistan. His best-known works are Midnight's Children *(1981), which was awarded the prestigious Booker Prize, and* The Satanic Verses *(1989), whose publication prompted the Islamic ruler of Iran, Ayatollah Khomeini, to impose a* fatwa *or death sentence on the writer with a reward of several million dollars. In spite of continued threats against his life and the assassination of his publisher in Japan, Rushdie continues to write, although forced to live a sequestered life somewhere in England. He emerges from time to time to give an interview, deliver a lecture, or appear on television. President Mohammed Khatami, the current leader of Iran, has attempted to distance the country from the* fatwa. *Fundamentalist groups in Iran have responded by raising the bounty on Rushdie's life. Since his exile, Rushdie has written a series of children's tales published as* Haroun and the Sea of Stories *(1991). Rushdie says that he wrote his latest novel,* The Moors Last Sigh *(1995), set in Spain in 1492, to mourn the lost age of democratic pluralism in India. In the following selection, which appeared as a chapter in his collection of essays,* Imaginary Homelands *(1991), Rushdie contemplates the exile's dilemma: the country he left exists only in his imagination, and if he returned, he would find a land that is just as strange to him as is the alien country where he sought refuge.*

Facts about Pakistan

Pakistan was originally part of the ancient Indus civilization, which lasted a thousand years, from roughly 2700 to 1700 B.C.E. Islam was introduced in the eighth century, and the region that is now Pakistan came under Islamic rule in the eleventh century. The Muslim dynasty of Moguls (Mongols in English), lead by a descendant of Genghis Khan, ruled most of the Indian subcontinent until the British extended their empire in the 1750s. Eventually, Britain imposed its rule in 1858. The British partitioned India on August 14, 1947, and made Pakistan an independent country. The result was widespread rioting, war with India over disputed territories, the migration of 8 million Hindus and Sikhs from the new nation of Pakistan to India, and the transfer of 6 million Muslims from India to Pakistan. Bangladesh, formerly East Pakistan, declared its independence from West Pakistan (now Pakistan) in 1971. Since independence, Pakistan has alternated between a dictatorship and a constitutional democracy. During times of civil unrest, the military, particularly under General Zia ul-Haq in the 1970s and 1980s, has taken over the government and imposed martial law. Benazir Bhutto, daughter of former president Zulfikar Ali Bhutto, became prime minister on October 19, 1993, and Farooq Leghari was chosen to be president by local and national legislators. Farooq Leghari dismissed Prime Minister Bhutto in November 1996 following a power struggle between Bhutto and her mother and brother. As a result of the popular election held in February 1997, Nawaz Sharif, head of the conservative party backed by the army, became prime minister.

Pakistan's population is a mixture of the diverse groups of Dravidians, Aryans, Greeks, Persians, Arabs, Afghans, Greeks, Turks, and Mongols who settled there. The majority of the people are Punjabis. With the in-migration of Muslims from India and the out-migration of Hindus and Sikhs following independence, Pakistan is about 97 percent Muslim; most belong to the Sunni sect of Islam. Urdu is the official language of Pakistan, but English remains the language of government and commerce.

1   An old photograph in a cheap frame hangs on a wall of the room where I work. It's a picture dating from 1946 of a house into which, at the time of its taking, I had not yet been born. The house is rather peculiar—a three-storeyed gabled affair with tiled roofs and round towers in two corners, each wearing a pointy tiled hat. "The past is a foreign country," goes the famous opening sentence of L. P. Hartley's novel *The Go-Between*, "they do things differently there." But the photograph tells me to invert this idea; it reminds me that it's my present that is foreign, and that the past is home, albeit a lost home in a lost city in the mists of lost time.

2   A few years ago I revisited Bombay, which is my lost city, after an absence of something like half my life. Shortly after arriving, acting on an impulse, I opened the telephone directory and looked for my father's name. And, amazingly, there it was; his name, our old address, the unchanged telephone number, as if we had never gone away to the unmentionable country across the border. It was an eerie discovery. I felt as if I were being claimed, or informed that the facts of my faraway life were illusions, and that this continuity was the reality. Then I went to visit the house in the photograph and stood outside it, neither daring nor wishing to announce myself to its new owners. (I didn't want to see how they'd ruined the interior.) I was overwhelmed. The photograph had naturally been taken in black and white; and my memory, feeding on such images as this, had begun to see my childhood in the same way, monochromatically. The colours of my history had seeped out of my mind's eye; now my other two eyes were assaulted by colours, by the vividness of the red tiles, the yellow-edged green of cactus-leaves, the brilliance of bougainvillaea creeper. It is probably not too romantic to say that that was when my novel *Midnight's Children* was really born; when I realized how much I wanted to restore the past to myself, not in the faded greys of old family-album snapshots, but whole, in CinemaScope and glorious Technicolor.

3   Bombay is a city built by foreigners upon reclaimed land; I, who had been away so long that I almost qualified for the title, was gripped by the conviction that I, too, had a city and a history to reclaim.

4   It may be that writers in my position, exiles or emigrants or expatriates, are haunted by some sense of loss, some urge to reclaim, to look back, even at the risk of being mutated into pillars of salt. But if we do look back, we must also do so in the knowledge—which gives rise to profound uncertainties—that our physical alienation from India almost inevitably means that we will not be capable of reclaiming precisely the thing that was lost; that we will, in short, create fictions, not actual cities or villages, but invisible ones, imaginary homelands, Indias of the mind.

5   Writing my book in North London, looking out through my window on to a city scene totally unlike the ones I was imagining on to paper, I was constantly plagued by this problem, until I felt obliged to face it in the text, to make clear that (in spite of my original and I suppose somewhat Proustian ambition to unlock the gates of lost time so that the past reappeared as it actually had been, unaffected by the distortions of memory) what I was actually doing was a novel of memory and about memory, so that my India was just that: "my" India, a version and no more than one version of all the hundreds of millions of possible versions. I tried to make it as imaginatively true as I could, but imaginative truth is simultaneously honourable and suspect, and I knew that my India may only have been one to which I (who am no longer what I was, and who by quitting Bombay never became what perhaps I was meant to be) was, let us say, willing to admit I belonged.

6   This is why I made my narrator, Saleem, suspect in his narration; his mistakes are the mistakes of a fallible memory compounded by quirks of character and of circumstance, and his vision is fragmentary. It may be that when the Indian writer who writes from outside India tries to reflect that world, he is obliged to deal in broken mirrors, some of whose fragments have been irretrievably lost.

7   But there is a paradox here. The broken mirror may actually be as valuable as the one which is supposedly unflawed. Let me again try and explain this from my own experience. Before beginning *Midnight's Children*, I spent many months trying simply to recall as much of the Bombay of the 1950s and 1960s as I could; and not only Bombay—Kashmir, too, and Delhi and Aligarh, which, in my book, I've moved to Agra to heighten a certain joke about the Taj Mahal. I was genuinely amazed by how much came back to me. I found myself remembering what clothes people had worn on certain days, and school scenes, and whole passages of Bombay dialogue verbatim, or so it seemed; I even remembered advertisements, film-posters, the neon Jeep sign on Marine Drive, toothpaste ads for Binaca and for Kolynos, and a footbridge over the local railway line which bore, on one side, the legend "Esso puts a tiger in your tank" and, on the

other, the curiously contradictory admonition: "Drive like Hell and you will get there." Old songs came back to me from nowhere: a street entertainer's version of "Good Night, Ladies," and, from the film *Mr 420* (a very appropriate source for my narrator to have used), the hit number "Mera Joota Hai Japani,"[1] which could almost be Saleem's theme song.

8   I knew that I had tapped a rich seam; but the point I want to make is that of course I'm not gifted with total recall, and it was precisely the partial nature of these memories, their fragmentation, that made them so evocative for me. The shards of memory acquired greater status, greater resonance, because they were *remains;* fragmentation made trivial things seem like symbols, and the mundane acquired numinous qualities. There is an obvious parallel here with archaeology. The broken pots of antiquity, from which the past can sometimes, but always provisionally, be reconstructed, are exciting to discover, even if they are pieces of the most quotidian objects.

9   It may be argued that the past is a country from which we have all emigrated, that its loss is part of our common humanity. Which seems to me self-evidently true; but I suggest that the writer who is out-of-country and even out-of-language may experience this loss in an intensified form. It is made more concrete for him by the physical fact of discontinuity, of his present being in a different place from his past, of his being "elsewhere." This may enable him to speak properly and concretely on a subject of universal significance and appeal.

10   But let me go further. The broken glass is not merely a mirror of nostalgia. It is also, I believe, a useful tool with which to work in the present.

11   John Fowles begins *Daniel Martin* with the words: "Whole sight: or all the rest is desolation." But human beings do not perceive things whole; we are not gods but wounded creatures, cracked lenses, capable only of fractured perceptions. Partial beings, in all the senses of that phrase. Meaning is a shaky edifice we build out of scraps, dogmas, childhood injuries, newspaper articles, chance remarks, old films, small victories, people hated, people loved; perhaps it is because our sense of what is the case is constructed from such inadequate materials that we defend it so fiercely, even to the death. The Fowles position seems to me a way of

---

[1] *Mera joota hai Japani*
Yé patloon Inglistani
Sar pé lal topi Rusi—
Phir bhi dil hai Hindustani

—which translates roughly as:

O, my shoes are Japanese
These trousers English, if you please
On my head, red Russian hat—
My heart's Indian for all that.

[This is also the song sung by Gibreel Farishta as he tumbles from the heavens at the beginning of *The Satanic Verses.*]

succumbing to the guru-illusion. Writers are no longer sages, dispensing the wisdom of the centuries. And those of us who have been forced by cultural displacement to accept the provisional nature of all truths, all certainties, have perhaps had modernism forced upon us. We can't lay claim to Olympus, and are thus released to describe our worlds in the way in which all of us, whether writers or not, perceive it from day to day.

12   In *Midnight's Children,* my narrator Saleem uses, at one point, the metaphor of a cinema screen to discuss this business of perception: "Suppose yourself in a large cinema, sitting at first in the back row, and gradually moving up, . . . until your nose is almost pressed against the screen. Gradually the stars' faces dissolve into dancing grain; tiny details assume grotesque proportions; . . . it becomes clear that the illusion itself is reality." The movement towards the cinema screen is a metaphor for the narrative's movement through time towards the present, and the book itself, as it nears contemporary events, quite deliberately loses deep perspective, becomes more "partial." I wasn't trying to write about (for instance) the Emergency in the same way as I wrote about events half a century earlier. I felt it would be dishonest to pretend, when writing about the day before yesterday, that it was possible to see the whole picture. I showed certain blobs and slabs of the scene.

13   I once took part in a conference on modern writing at New College, Oxford. Various novelists, myself included, were talking earnestly of such matters as the need for new ways of describing the world. Then the playwright Howard Brenton suggested that this might be a somewhat limited aim: does literature seek to do no more than to describe? Flustered, all the novelists at once began talking about politics.

14   Let me apply Brenton's question to the specific case of Indian writers, in England, writing about India. Can they do no more than describe, from a distance, the world that they have left? Or does the distance open any other doors?

15   These are of course political questions, and must be answered at least partly in political terms. I must say first of all that description is itself a political act. The black American writer Richard Wright once wrote that black and white Americans were engaged in a war over the nature of reality. Their descriptions were incompatible. So it is clear that redescribing a world is the necessary first step towards changing it. And particularly at times when the State takes reality into its own hands, and sets about distorting it, altering the past to fit its present needs, then the making of the alternative realities of art, including the novel of memory, becomes politicized. "The struggle of man against power," Milan Kundera has written, "is the struggle of memory against forgetting." Writers and politicians are natural rivals. Both groups try to make the world in their own images; they fight for the same territory. And the novel is one way of denying the official, politicians' version of truth.

16   The "State truth" about the war in Bangladesh, for instance, is that no atrocities were committed by the Pakistani army in what was then the East Wing. This version is sanctified by many persons who would describe themselves as intellectuals. And the official version of the Emergency in India was well expressed by Mrs. Gandhi in a recent BBC interview. She said that there were some people around who claimed that bad things had happened during the Emergency, forced sterilizations, things like that; but, she stated, this was all false. Nothing of this type had ever occurred. The interviewer, Mr. Robert Kee, did not probe this statement at all. Instead he told Mrs. Gandhi and the *Panorama* audience that she had proved, many times over, her right to be called a democrat.

17   So literature can, and perhaps must, give the lie to official facts. But is this a proper function of those of us who write from outside India? Or are we just dilettantes in such affairs, because we are not involved in their day-to-day unfolding, because by speaking out we take no risks, because our personal safety is not threatened? What right do we have to speak at all?

18   My answer is very simple. Literature is self-validating. That is to say, a book is not justified by its author's worthiness to write it, but by the quality of what has been written. There are terrible books that arise directly out of experience, and extraordinary imaginative feats dealing with themes which the author has been obliged to approach from the outside.

19   Literature is not in the business of copyrighting certain themes for certain groups. And as for risk: the real risks of any artist are taken in the work, in pushing the work to the limits of what is possible, in the attempt to increase the sum of what it is possible to think. Books become good when they go to this edge and risk falling over it—when they endanger the artist by reason of what he has, or has not, *artistically* dared.

20   So if I am to speak for Indian writers in England I would say this, paraphrasing G. V. Desani's H. Hatterr: The migrations of the fifties and sixties happened. "We are. We are here." And we are not willing to be excluded from any part of our heritage; which heritage includes both a Bradford-born Indian kid's right to be treated as a full member of British society, and also the right of any member of this post-diaspora community to draw on its roots for its art, just as all the world's community of displaced writers has always done. (I'm thinking, for instance, of Grass's Danzig-become-Gdansk, of Joyce's abandoned Dublin, of Isaac Bashevis Singer and Maxine Hong Kingston and Milan Kundera and many others. It's a long list.)

21   Let me override at once the faintly defensive note that has crept into these last few remarks. The Indian writer, looking back at India, does so through guilt-tinted spectacles. (I am of course, once more, talking about myself.) I am speaking now of those of us who emigrated . . . and I suspect that there are times when the move seems wrong to us all, when we seem, to ourselves, post-lapsarian men and women. We are Hindus who

have crossed the black water; we are Muslims who eat pork. And as a result—as my use of the Christian notion of the Fall indicates—we are now partly of the West. Our identity is at once plural and partial. Sometimes we feel that we straddle two cultures; at other times, that we fall between two stools. But however ambiguous and shifting this ground may be, it is not an infertile territory for a writer to occupy. If literature is in part the business of finding new angles at which to enter reality, then once again our distance, our long geographical perspective, may provide us with such angles. Or it may be that that is simply what we must think in order to do our work.

22 *Midnight's Children* enters its subject from the point of view of a secular man. I am a member of that generation of Indians who were sold the secular ideal. One of the things I liked, and still like, about India is that it is based on a non-sectarian philosophy. I was not raised in a narrowly Muslim environment; I do not consider Hindu culture to be either alien from me or more important than the Islamic heritage. I believe this has something to do with the nature of Bombay, a metropolis in which the multiplicity of commingled faiths and cultures curiously creates a remarkably secular ambience. Saleem Sinai makes use, eclectically, of whatever elements from whatever sources he chooses. It may have been easier for his author to do this from outside modern India than inside it.

23 I want to make one last point about the description of India that *Midnight's Children* attempts. It is a point about pessimism. The book has been criticised in India for its allegedly despairing tone. And the despair of the writer-from-outside may indeed look a little easy, a little pat. But I do not see the book as despairing or nihilistic. The point of view of the narrator is not entirely that of the author. What I tried to do was to set up a tension in the text, a paradoxical opposition between the form and content of the narrative. The story of Saleem does indeed lead him to despair. But the story is told in a manner designed to echo, as closely as my abilities allowed, the Indian talent for non-stop self-regeneration. This is why the narrative constantly throws up new stories, why it "teems." The form—multitudinous, hinting at the infinite possibilities of the country—is the optimistic counterweight to Saleem's personal tragedy. I do not think that a book written in such a manner can really be called a despairing work.

24 England's Indian writers are by no means all the same type of animal. Some of us, for instance, are Pakistani. Others Bangladeshi. Others West, or East, or even South African. And V. S. Naipaul, by now, is something else entirely. This word "Indian" is getting to be a pretty scattered concept. Indian writers in England include political exiles, first-generation migrants, affluent expatriates whose residence here is frequently temporary, naturalized Britons, and people born here who may never have laid eyes on the subcontinent. Clearly, nothing that I say can apply across all these categories.

But one of the interesting things about this diverse community is that, as far as Indo-British fiction is concerned, its existence changes the ball game, because that fiction is in future going to come as much from addresses in London, Birmingham and Yorkshire as from Delhi or Bombay.

25 One of the changes has to do with attitudes towards the use of English. Many have referred to the argument about the appropriateness of this language to Indian themes. And I hope all of us share the view that we can't simply use the language in the way the British did; that it needs remaking for our own purposes. Those of us who do use English do so in spite of our ambiguity towards it, or perhaps because of that, perhaps because we can find in that linguistic struggle a reflection of other struggles taking place in the real world, struggles between the cultures within ourselves and the influences at work upon our societies. To conquer English may be to complete the process of making ourselves free.

26 But the British Indian writer simply does not have the option of rejecting English, anyway. His children, her children, will grow up speaking it, probably as a first language; and in the forging of a British Indian identity the English language is of central importance. It must, in spite of everything, be embraced. (The word "translation" comes, etymologically, from the Latin for "bearing cross." Having been borne across the world, we are translated men. It is normally supposed that something always gets lost in translation; I cling, obstinately, to the notion that something can also be gained.)

27 To be an Indian writer in this society is to face, every day, problems of definition. What does it mean to be "Indian" outside India? How can culture be preserved without becoming ossified? How should we discuss the need for change within ourselves and our community without seeming to play into the hands of our racial enemies? What are the consequences, both spiritual and practical, of refusing to make any concessions to Western ideas and practices? What are the consequences of embracing those ideas and practices and turning away from the ones that came here with us? These questions are all a single, existential question: How are we to live in the world?

28 I do not propose to offer, prescriptively, any answers to these questions; only to state that these are some of the issues with which each of us will have to come to terms.

29 To turn my eyes outwards now, and to say a little about the relationship between the Indian writer and the majority white culture in whose midst he lives, and with which his work will sooner or later have to deal:

30 In common with many Bombay-raised middle-class children of my generation, I grew up with an intimate knowledge of, and even sense of friendship with, a certain kind of England: a dream-England composed of Test Matches at Lord's presided over by the voice of John Arlott, at which Freddie Trueman bowled unceasingly and without success at

Polly Umrigar; of Enid Blyton and Billy Bunter, in which we were even prepared to smile indulgently at portraits such as "Hurree Jamset Ram Singh," "the dusky nabob of Bhanipur." I wanted to come to England. I couldn't wait. And to be fair, England has done all right by me; but I find it a little difficult to be properly grateful. I can't escape the view that my relatively easy ride is not the result of the dream-England's famous sense of tolerance and fair play, but of my social class, my freak fair skin and my "English" English accent. Take away any of these, and the story would have been very different. Because of course the dream-England is no more than a dream.

31 Sadly, it's a dream from which too many white Britons refuse to awake. Recently, on a live radio programme, a professional humorist asked me, in all seriousness, why I objected to being called a wog. He said he had always thought it a rather charming word, a term of endearment. "I was at the zoo the other day," he revealed, "and a zoo keeper told me that the wogs were best with the animals; they stuck their fingers in their ears and wiggled them about and the animals felt at home." The ghost of Hurree Jamset Ram Singh walks among us still.

32 As Richard Wright found long ago in America, black and white descriptions of society are no longer compatible. Fantasy, or the mingling of fantasy and naturalism, is one way of dealing with these problems. It offers a way of echoing in the form of our work the issues faced by all of us: how to build a new, "modern" world out of an old, legend-haunted civilization, an old culture which we have brought into the heart of a newer one. But whatever technical solutions we may find, Indian writers in these islands, like others who have migrated into the north from the south, are capable of writing from a kind of double perspective: because they, we, are at one and the same time insiders and outsiders in this society. This stereoscopic vision is perhaps what we can offer in place of "whole sight."

33 There is one last idea that I should like to explore, even though it may, on first hearing, seem to contradict much of what I've so far said. It is this: of all the many elephant traps lying ahead of us, the largest and most dangerous pitfall would be the adoption of a ghetto mentality. To forget that there is a world beyond the community to which we belong, to confine ourselves within narrowly defined cultural frontiers, would be, I believe, to go voluntarily into that form of internal exile which in South Africa is called the "homeland." We must guard against creating, for the most virtuous of reasons, British–Indian literary equivalents of Bophuthatswana or the Transkei.

34 This raises immediately the question of whom one is writing "for." My own, short, answer is that I have never had a reader in mind. I have ideas, people, events, shapes, and I write "for" those things, and hope that the completed work will be of interest to others. But which others? In the

case of *Midnight's Children* I certainly felt that if its subcontinental readers had rejected the work, I should have thought it a failure, no matter what the reaction in the West. So I would say that I write "for" people who feel part of the things I write "about," but also for everyone else whom I can reach. In this I am of the same opinion as the black American writer Ralph Ellison, who, in his collection of essays *Shadow and Act,* says that he finds something precious in being black in America at this time; but that he is also reaching for more than that."I was taken very early," he writes,"with a passion to link together all I loved within the Negro community and all those things I felt in the world which lay beyond."

35   Art is a passion of the mind. And the imagination works best when it is most free. Western writers have always felt free to be eclectic in their selection of theme, setting, form; Western visual artists have, in this century, been happily raiding the visual storehouses of Africa, Asia, the Philippines. I am sure that we must grant ourselves an equal freedom.

36   Let me suggest that Indian writers in England have access to a second tradition, quite apart from their own racial history. It is the culture and political history of the phenomenon of migration, displacement, life in a minority group. We can quite legitimately claim as our ancestors the Huguenots, the Irish, the Jews; the past to which we belong is an English past, the history of immigrant Britain. Swift, Conrad, Marx are as much our literary forebears as Tagore or Ram Mohan Roy. America, a nation of immigrants, has created great literature out of the phenomenon of cultural transplantation, out of examining the ways in which people cope with a new world; it may be that by discovering what we have in common with those who preceded us into this country, we can begin to do the same.

37   I stress this is only one of many possible strategies. But we are inescapably international writers at a time when the novel has never been a more international form (a writer like Borges speaks of the influence of Robert Louis Stevenson on his work; Heinrich Böll acknowledges the influence of Irish literature; cross-pollination is everywhere); and it is perhaps one of the more pleasant freedoms of the literary migrant to be able to choose his parents. My own—selected half consciously, half not— include Gogol, Cervantes, Kafka, Melville, Machado de Assis; a polyglot family tree, against which I measure myself, and to which I would be honoured to belong.

38   There's a beautiful image in Saul Bellow's latest novel, *The Dean's December.* The central character, the Dean, Corde, hears a dog barking wildly somewhere. He imagines that the barking is the dog's protest against the limit of dog experience. "For God's sake," the dog is saying, "open the universe a little more!" And because Bellow is, of course, not really talking about dogs, or not only about dogs, I have the feeling that the dog's rage, and its desire, is also mine, ours, everyone's. "For God's sake, open the universe a little more!"

Reading for Meaning

1. What does Salman Rushdie consider problematic for him as an author writing about India from his exile in a foreign country? What advantages does he see for the writer-in-exile?

2. What does Rushdie mean when he says "It may be argued that the past is a country from which we have all emigrated"? How does this idea apply to your life?

3. How does Salman Rushdie answer the question, "What right do we [who write from outside India] have to speak at all?" Do you agree with his answer?

4. What problems and advantages does Rushdie experience as a bicultural writer?

5. What is the "ghetto mentality" of Indians living in Britain? What problems does Rushdie associate with this way of thinking? How might this description apply to other communities?

6. Why does Salman Rushdie include quotations from African American writers Richard Wright and Ralph Ellison? What does he have in common with them? How do their ideas complement his own?

Comparing Texts

1. In his essay, "The Artist as Insect," South African writer André Brink examines the role of the artist or intellectual in the emerging democracies of the Third World. "In an endangered society, threatened by authoritarian rule," he argues, "the single dissident voice that dares cry out may acquire an inordinate resonance. It can become a rallying point for the oppressed masses. But once the masses have begun to shake off their most visible shackles, once a people as a whole has broken down its walls and fences, has thrown open its prisons and its Gulags and its Robben Islands, what role is left of the individual artist?" Once people gain some measure of freedom," Brink continues, the artist's role changes: "In order to keep alive this faith in something beautiful, something meaningful, in a sordid world; in order constantly to shock the world out of complacency; in order to prod the human mind into that kind of awareness which never takes yes for an answer, the first allegiance of the creator-intellectual-artist is to his or her conscience, not to a party or group, not even to a cause, not even to 'the people.'" He further clarifies that the artist's "conscience [must be] forged in action and in communication with others, with 'the people' in order to have any meaning at all." To what extent do Salman Rushdie's ideas about the writer's purpose and audience correspond to those of André Brink? Are there points or concerns that make their discussions different?

2. The passage that follows is taken from the opening paragraphs of *Native Son* by Richard Wright. Read the excerpt carefully and then decide in what sense Wright is doing what Rushdie calls "redescribing a world" in order to take "the necessary first step towards changing it."

1   Brrrrrriiiiiiiiiiinng!
2   An alarm clock clanged in the dark and silent room. A bed spring creaked. A woman's voice sang out impatiently:
3   "Bigger, shut that thing off!"

4   A surly grunt sounded above the tinny ring of metal. Naked feet swished dryly across the planks in the wooden floor and the clang ceased abruptly.

5   "Turn on the light, Bigger."

6   "Awright," came a sleepy mumble.

7   Light flooded the room and revealed a black boy standing in a narrow space between two iron beds, rubbing his eyes with the backs of his hands. From a bed to his right the woman spoke again:

8   "Buddy, get up from there! I got a big washing on my hands today and I want you-all out of here."

9   Another black boy rolled from bed and stood up. The woman also rose and stood in her nightgown.

10 "Turn your heads so I can dress," she said.

11 The two boys averted their eyes and gazed into a far corner of the room. The woman rushed out of her nightgown and put on a pair of step-ins. She turned to the bed from which she had risen and called:

12 "Vera! Get up from there!"

13 "What time is it, Ma?" asked a muffled, adolescent voice from beneath a quilt.

14 "Get up from there, I say!"

15 "O.K., Ma."

16 A brown-skinned girl in a cotton gown got up and stretched her arms above her head and yawned. Sleepily, she sat on a chair and fumbled with her stockings. The two boys kept their faces averted while their mother and sister put on enough clothes to keep them from feeling ashamed; and the mother and sister did the same while the boys dressed. Abruptly, they all paused, holding their clothes in their hands, their attention caught by a light tapping in the thinly plastered walls of the room. They forgot their conspiracy against shame and their eyes strayed apprehensively over the floor.

17 "There he is again, Bigger!" the woman screamed, and the tiny one-room apartment galvanized into violent action. A chair toppled as the woman, half-dressed and in her stocking feet, scrambled breathlessly upon the bed. Her two sons, barefoot, stood tense and motionless, their eyes searching anxiously under the bed and chairs. The girl ran into a corner, half-stooped and gathered the hem of her slip into both of her hands and held it tightly over her knees. . . .

18 Buddy crouched by the door and held the iron skillet by its handle, his arm flexed and poised. Save for the quick, deep breathing of the four people, the room was quiet. Bigger crept on tiptoe toward the trunk with the skillet clutched stiffly in his hand, his eyes dancing and watching every inch of the wooden floor in front of him. He paused and, without moving an eye or muscle, called:

19 "Buddy!"

20 "Hunh?"

21 "Put that box in front of the hole so he can't get out!"
22 "O.K."
23 Buddy ran to a wooden box and shoved it quickly in front of a gaping hole in the molding and then backed again to the door, holding the skillet ready. Bigger eased to the trunk and peered behind it cautiously. He saw nothing. Carefully, he stuck out his bare foot and pushed the trunk a few inches.
24 "There he is!" the mother screamed again.
25 A huge black rat squealed and leaped at Bigger's trouserleg and snagged it in his teeth, hanging on.
26 "Goddamn!" Bigger whispered fiercely, whirling and kicking out his leg with all the strength of his body. The force of his movement shook the rat loose and it sailed through the air and struck a wall. Instantly, it rolled over and leaped again. Bigger dodged and the rat landed against a table leg. With clenched teeth, Bigger held the skillet; he was afraid to hurl it, fearing that he might miss. The rat squeaked and turned and ran in a narrow circle, looking for a place to hide; it leaped again past Bigger and scurried on dry rasping feet to one side of the box and then to the other, searching for the hole. Then it turned and reared upon its hind legs.
27 "Hit 'im, Bigger!" Buddy shouted.
28 "Kill 'im!" the woman screamed....
29 Bigger swung the skillet; it skidded over the floor, missing the rat, and clattered to a stop against a wall.
30 "Goddamn!"
31 The rat leaped. Bigger sprang to one side. The rat stopped under a chair and let out a furious screak. Bigger moved slowly backward toward the door.
32 "Gimme that skillet, Buddy," he asked quietly, not taking his eyes from the rat.
33 Buddy extended his hand. Bigger caught the skillet and lifted it high in the air. The rat scuttled across the floor and stopped again at the box and searched quickly for the hole; then it reared once more and bared long yellow fangs, piping shrilly, belly quivering.
34 Bigger aimed and let the skillet fly with a heavy grunt. There was a shattering of wood as the box caved in. The woman screamed and hid her face in her hands. Bigger tip-toed forward and peered.
35 "I got 'im," he muttered, his clenched teeth bared in a smile. "By God, I got 'im."
36 He kicked the splintered box out of the way and the flat black body of the rat lay exposed, its two long yellow tusks showing distinctly. Bigger took a shoe and pounded the rat's head, crushing it, cursing hysterically:
37 "You sonofa*bitch!*"

3. The artist and the politician, according to Salman Rushdie, "try to make the world in their own images; they fight for the same territory. And the novel is one way of denying

the official, politicians' version of truth." In his essay, "Defending against the Indefensible," Neil Postman argues that education, if properly construed, would provide students with a defense against the culture's devious uses of language (page 376). Locate passages in Postman's essay where he most clearly denies "the official . . . version[s] of truth." What alternative perspectives does he offer?

Ideas for Writing

1. Salman Rushdie suggests that "the past is a country from which we have all emigrated, that its loss is part of our common humanity." Interview a member of your family or someone you know who is at least fifty years old. Get as much information as you can about this person's history, most vivid memories, and what those memories mean to him or her. Then explain in some detail what the past means to the person you interviewed.

2. In *Imaginary Homelands* Salman Rushdie admits "what I was actually doing was a novel of memory and about memory, so that my India was just that: 'my' India, a version and no more than one version of all the hundreds of millions of possible versions. I tried to make it as imaginatively true as I could, but imaginative truth is simultaneously honourable and suspect." How are these ideas about what Rushdie was doing when he wrote *Midnight's Children* apparent from the opening paragraph of the novel, which is reprinted here?

   > I was born in the city of Bombay . . . once upon a time. No, that won't do, there's no getting away from the date: I was born in Doctor Narlikar's Nursing Home on August 15th, 1947, and the time? The time matters, too. Well then: at night. No, it's important to be more . . . On the stroke of midnight, as a matter of fact. Clock-hands joined palms in respectful greeting as I came. Oh, spell it out, spell it out: at the precise instant of India's arrival at independence, I tumbled forth into the world. There were gasps. And, outside the window, fireworks and crowds. A few seconds later, my father broke his big toe; but his accident was a mere trifle when set beside what had befallen me in the benighted moment, because thanks to the occult tyrannies of those blandly saluting clocks I had been mysteriously handcuffed to history, my destinies indissolubly chained to those of my country. For the next three decades, there was to be no escape. Soothsayers had prophesied me, newspapers celebrated my arrival, politicos ratified my authenticity. I was left entirely without a say in the matter. I, Saleem Sinai, later variously called Snotnose, Stainface, Baldy, Sniffer, Buddha and even Piece-of-the-Moon, had become heavily embroiled in Fate—at the best of times a dangerous sort of involvement. And I couldn't even wipe my own nose at the time.

3. In defending his idea that "description is itself a political act," Rushdie refers to Richard Wright's assertion that "black and white Americans were engaged in a war over the nature of reality. Their descriptions were incompatible." Using sources available to you, work in groups of two or three and gather information about the condition of African Americans during the 1930s and 1940s. Once you have completed your research, work together to write an explanation of the "incompatible" realities that Richard Wright mentions.

Writing before Reading

What facts or images of South Africa do you recall from information learned in school, from news reports, or from reading you have done? How reliable are those sources?

SPORT, AFRICAN CULTURES, VALUE FOR MONEY: A RETURN TO SOUTH AFRICA

Jenefer Shute

Jenefer Shute, an ex-patriot from South Africa, was living and writing in Boston, Massachusetts, at the time she wrote "A Return to South Africa." Shute, who has lived in the United States since 1978, based her essay on a visit to South Africa in the summer of 1991. The essay appeared in the November/December 1992 issue of Tikkun. Shute is also the author of the novels Life-Size *(1992) and* Sex Crimes *(1996).*

Facts about South Africa

The Republic of South Africa occupies the southernmost segment of the African continent. South Africa is the most economically developed country in Africa, but the system of apartheid, instituted in 1948, put the country's wealth in the hands of its white population (13 percent) and kept the black African population (77 percent) and people of Asian or mixed race (10 percent) virtually impoverished. Apartheid means "apartness" in Afrikaans, the language of the seventeenth-century Dutch settlers. The system of enforced racial segregation became the official state policy when the South African National Party gained power in 1948. As a result of apartheid, the government set aside ten "homelands," largely barren, undeveloped areas, which it recognized as separate nations, to be occupied by black South Africans. The government thereby reserved 87 percent of the land for use by whites. This designation of "black" and "white" sections of the country resulted in the massive resettlement of blacks. Some estimates are that between 1960 and 1985 3.5 million blacks were forcefully moved to these "homelands." Moreover, laws similar to the Jim Crow laws passed in the southern United States (in force from 1896 to 1968) mandated segregation in public facilities, including schools, to ensure that blacks and people of mixed race would live apart from whites. Interracial marriage was also outlawed, and blacks working in white townships were required to have a permit in order to remain in white areas for more than 72 hours. Years of violence and demonstrations from 1984 to 1993 led finally to the defeat of apartheid; the lifting of a 30-year ban on the opposition party, the African National Congress; and the release of the ANC party leader, Nelson Mandela, who became the president of South Africa on May 10, 1994. More than 17,000 South Africans were killed in the struggle over apartheid, and thousands more were either injured or held in prison for decades. The laws and regulations established under apartheid were repealed in 1991 under President F. W. de Klerk. However, because reparations were not included in de Klerk's reforms, most blacks could not afford to return to their original residences in what had become "white" South Africa. Wide disparities in health care and education remain. Superior medical facilities and health care programs for whites help explain why, on the average, whites live to age 72 while life expectancy for blacks and people of mixed race is 59. Infant mortality for black South Africans is six times the rate for whites.

1   As the plane begins its descent into Johannesburg, I struggle with the arrival form, finding its blank squares—just so many letters per answer—as good a place as any to pose the problem. **Country of Birth:** South Africa. **Country of Citizenship:** the United Kingdom of Great Britain and Northern Ireland. **Country of Residence:** the United States of America. That about sums it up: citizen (through paternity) of a place I have never lived, nonresident in my native land, and resident where I'm neither native nor citizen.

2   But the question I can't answer comes next. **Main Purpose of Visit?** I hesitate—**Holiday?** well, I hope to enjoy the landscape this time; **Business/Professional?** I carry my laptop like a shield—but then I check **Visiting Friends/Relatives.** It is only half-true. Relatives, yes (my entire immediate family awaits me) but there aren't any friends left, after thirteen years away.

3   **What motivated you most to visit South Africa?** the form then wants to know. **None of Your Business** isn't on the list; neither are **Political Change, Guilt, Nostalgia** (more precisely, the nostalgia for nostalgia), or **Intimations of Mortality.** I waver between **Friends/Family** and **Previous Visits,** then check the latter, though that twenty-two-year previous visit was what drove me to leave.

4   (The other options, by the way, are **Climate, Scenic Beauty, Sport, African Cultures, Value for Money.**)

5   At 7:45 a.m., July 16, 1991, the jet touches down on the African earth. All I can see from the window is the lion-colored winter grass.

6   I thought I would cry but I don't.

7   I try to feel something appropriate to the occasion, but what do you feel when you are about to step back into a reviled and imaginary land? You don't feel anything; you're afraid your ghost-foot will slip through the dream-earth into the past.

8   Two weeks later, on the waterfront in Cape Town, I'm taking a short cut through a parking lot when a man sticks his head out of a van and, in the thick jazzy local accent, shouts "Hallo sweetie, long time no see!" For a moment, I wonder how he knows.

9   My two-year-old nephew, whom I have never seen, toddles out, smiling and trusting, from under the guardrail that cordons off the arrival area, so, crouching instinctively, he is the one I kiss first. Then, so he won't feel neglected, I kiss his shyer four-year-old brother, familiar from photographs that somehow failed to capture the little-old-man quality I sense now. Then my sister, whom I have seen once in these thirteen years, before her incurable illness was diagnosed. Then my mother, then my father, both of whom I saw in London in 1983 and 1987. I suffered the shock of their aging then; are they suffering the shock of mine now?

10 Nobody cries. That is the way we are.

11 As we walk out to the car, Durban's damp subtropical air fingers my face with a remembered feel. It is an hour's drive from the Durban airport to my parents' house in Pietermaritzburg, a sleepy mid-sized Victorian town in the province of Natal. I have never lived there: they moved there after I left home, left Johannesburg for the University of Cape Town (stormed away, more accurately, in seventeen-year-old self-righteousness). Hyperalert, I strain my eyes staring out of the car window. Nothing looks familiar, but nothing looks strange either; I don't recognize anything, but it all seems normal, unremarkable, the way the light and colors of a foreign country never do at first.

12 On the roadside, near a sign for the Lions River Polo Club, Black women are cutting the long dry grass to thatch their huts.

13 I have never seen my parents' house. It could be anyone's: small, neat, anonymous, not in the best of taste. I don't recognize a single thing, which frightens me. Gradually, over the next week or so, I begin to recover odd objects: a battered tea tray, a blue-and-white creamer, a china figurine of two lovers. But they're just objects, old, recognizable, long-lost; they carry no charge of association.

14 What will? I wonder, having hoped for instant epiphany.

15 Weeks later, in Johannesburg, the taxi turns a corner and there before me is a curve of road where, I realize, accidents still happen in my dreams.

16 Dora, my mother's Zulu maid, is washing dishes in the kitchen when my mother introduces me, the legendary daughter from America. I confuse and embarrass her by trying to shake her hand (it is wet, she can't think what to dry it on).

17   The tone my mother uses to speak to her—slow, deliberate, over-enunciating, as if to a child—is painfully familiar, and, when I hear it again, I begin to recall where my politics come from.

18   Dora is raising six children alone on $125 a month. Her grown son, laid off from the mines, works one day a week in the garden.

19   She calls me "Nkosikaan": princess.

20   I ask her not to and merely add to her humiliation as she stumbles, tongue-tied, over my first name, which she cannot quite bring herself to say.

21   There is cake and champagne, flowers, gifts, talk, a daylong effort to impersonate a family rather than the collective hallucination we feel ourselves to be. That night, when I go to bed in the guest room, I hug against me the hot-water bottle that my mother, not knowing how else to offer comfort, has insisted upon.

22   I have never felt lonelier in my life.

23   My parents, the privileged ones, live in a cage. The entire house is barred, with metal grilles on the doors and windows that have to be locked and unlocked every time anyone passes through, even a child going into the garden to play. When we leave for the day or the evening, it takes at least fifteen minutes to close up the house, with an elaborate ritual of shutting windows, securing the metal gates, turning on lights and radios. My mother also locks the drawers against Dora's (alleged) depredations. What she dreads is not, as one might expect, ANC or Inkatha guerrillas rising from her nightmares to claim what is theirs: it is common-or-garden burglary, assault. Her every thought twists back to some threat, some news report of neighbors whose houses have been broken into, who have been bound, raped, shot. The image of her own victimization thrills and obsesses her.

24   There is, in fact, a high rate of violent crime against white suburban householders in Pietermaritzburg, as in South Africa as a whole. The surrounding Black townships have, in fact, been the site of some of the most gruesome clashes between Inkatha and the ANC. But what my mother suffers from, I realize, is paranoia. An empty paper bag on the street is enough to scare her.

25   After a while it begins to infect me too.

26   I have lived alone all over the world, had close calls in strange cities, bolted my own door in Boston. Like other women, I manage most of the time to keep my fear at a subliminal, background-radiation level. But after a week in Pietermaritzburg, returning from dinner one night, I unlock the metal gate and am suddenly too frightened to go in.

27   In the bookstore, *Time* and *Newsweek* sit next to *Mayibuye,* journal of the ANC, which in turn sits next to *Shooting Times*. In the suburbs, houses cower behind high walls adorned with barbed wire, icons of attack dogs, and signs warning that the household is protected by an alarm system

(usually named something macho—*Predator, Power Force*—though there is also the humble and reassuring *Mike's*). At The Workshop, a Durban shopping complex, families can enjoy one-stop shopping: a modest storefront, between Joe's Radioland and The Bead Factory, houses The Arsenal—which is exactly that.

28   A few months after my visit, my parents come out of the house one morning to find both cars propped on bricks, all eight wheels stolen during the night. They're moving.

29   During an afternoon visit to the Durban city centre, my mother is very uncomfortable and, as she puts it, "claustrophobic." She keeps complaining about the crowds, can't wait to leave. At first I assume it is because, as she approaches her sixties and strays less and less often from the suburbs, she finds the urban bustle overwhelming. But later my sister tells me that she complains about the number of Blacks downtown, now that most forms of segregation have been abolished. Although I didn't recognize it at the time, she was experiencing culture shock—disorientation, panic, a sense of her own unreality. (I know the symptoms.)

30   She tells me that since the beaches have been integrated, they're so crowded that "nobody goes there any more."

31   Hamish, age four, on noting the rust-stained bathtub in the maid's bathroom: "Mum, why do Zulu people have brown baths?"

32   At an official function in Pietermaritzburg, where my father is awarded civic honors, the city councilors file in their royal-blue robes and tricorned hats, and I'm astounded to see that about half the faces are of darker pigmentation (Indian and so-called "colored," no Blacks). Later I'm told that they aren't full voting members of the council—just as, in South Africa as a whole, there are separate, powerless "parliaments" for Indians and "coloreds." The person who tells me this is Yvonne Spain, the newest and youngest council member, a small, dark, intense woman of about my age. We recognize each other as similar types: she is a long-time activist now committed to working within the system. She spends most of our short talk trying to convince me that it is time for people like me to come back.

33   I want to leave it all behind me. I want to shed it like a skin.

34   At the end of a week in Pietermaritzburg, spending all my time with my mother and sister in their self-enclosed suburban bubble, the only people of color I have spoken to are:

35   1. My mother's Zulu maid, Dora.

36   2. My sister's Zulu maid, Mavis. (These aren't, of course, their real names. They are the English names, smacking of the mission school, that Black workers use around white people so they won't have to exert themselves by wrapping their tongues around anything foreign—i.e. African.)

37   3. Mrs. Naidoo, an Indian labor organizer I meet briefly at the civic function.

38   4. An Indian woman with a small child, with whom I strike up a conversation in the airport departure lounge.

39   At the South African Airways check-in counter, a large red poster implores me, in English and Afrikaans, to "Look and Save A Life." Beneath the heading "Terrorist Weapons" are arrayed 3-D plastic models of a limpet mine, a mini-limpet mine, a TM 57 Land Mine, an anti-personnel mine, and four types of hand grenades. At the Cape Town post office, a similar display shrieks "The Look of Death!"

40   The first time I hear Afrikaans again is on the plane from London, where the South African Airways stewardesses are chatting in the galley. I can't understand a word they say. But within a week, I'm listening to the news without even noticing whether it is in Afrikaans or English (they alternate). I am, after all, bilingual; I am, after all, a South African.

41   I thought I would be traumatized by how much things had changed. Instead, I'm traumatized by how little they have.

42   The only real difference I notice at first is how drastically my family's standard of living has dropped. Inflation and economic sanctions (which I fought for, a world away) have done their work. My folks are hardly poor, but they're feeling the pinch, and the luxurious way of life I took for granted as a child is gone forever. My sister longs for Lego, lingerie, butterscotch, and bath gel; my parents dread retirement because their savings are worth so little now. I fought for years to achieve this effect, because I believed economic pressure was the only way to force change; I believe it still, but it pains me to see them like this, old and worried before their time—even though I know it is just.

43   On the plane to Cape Town, a middle-aged Black man in a pinstriped suit sits down next to me. Progress, I think—this could never have happened before. His other neighbor, an English-speaking businessman type, strikes up a conversation with him over the white wine and gin-and-tonics. The engine is making too much noise for me to hear what they're saying, but—definitely progress, I think. After a while, my Black seatmate turns to me and we make small talk (I'm from America, I tell him: not exactly a lie). I'm having a little trouble understanding him because of his accent, but we're communicating expansively all the same. Progress, I think, elated.

44   Then I need to go to the bathroom. "Excuse me, please," I say, rising from my seat, indicating that I need to squeeze past him. "Sorry madam!" he stammers, flustered, springing to his feet.

45   At the Market Theatre in Johannesburg, a political balladeer sings of "the year of false hopes and euphoria. The year we thought the struggle had been won." At these words, a profound sadness overcomes me.

46   I used to think that what I felt was guilt. Now I know it is sorrow.

47   Graffiti on a power station wall: *The Human Cause.*

48   Cape Town is one of the most beautiful cities in the world, as moody and intoxicating as a lover. I was afraid that when I went back there I would feel something I have never felt before, a pull on my soul from a piece of the earth. I long for, and dread, a voice that says "you should stay here" when I arrive somewhere: I have drifted around the world listening for it, relieved and bereft because I have never found it.

49   Instead, I spend the first two days shivering and feverish in a darkened hotel room.

50   Then I rent a car and drive down the incomparable coastal route to Cape Point. I stand on the tip of Africa, where the oceans meet—or as close to it as they let you get, anyway—and say to myself, theatrically, without much conviction, "I am an African."

51   My sister buys her gardener a new set of work clothes, a two-piece outfit in heavy blue drill. For some reason this combo is called a "Continental Suit." I wonder which continent the manufacturers have in mind.

52   I revisit the University of Cape Town, nestled on the mountain slopes, and see the first really startling change of my trip. Most of the students strolling from building to building are Black now; in my undergraduate days, you would have had to sit on the steps all day long to glimpse even one. I had precisely one Black classmate, who was later unmasked as a government informer.

53   Wandering around the Rosebank and Rondebosch areas that flank the university, I have the most clichéd experience of all: everything looks smaller, shrunken, a few shabby blocks instead of a whole world. This happens to everyone revisiting the past, I know, but I thought it had something to do with childhood (everything looks smaller because you have grown bigger). But now I see that it has nothing to do with size. It has to do with inhabiting a place fully, living in a saturated world: never seeing it from the outside, never seeing where it ends, that it ends.

54   I keep waiting for an epiphany that doesn't happen. Maybe it is not going to—and that is the epiphany.

55   Roedean hasn't shrunk, it has grown. Roedean is the exclusive British-style private school in Johannesburg where I was schooled in Latin and field hockey and advanced mathematics. We called the teachers "Madame," we wore navy blue pinafores with knee socks and panama hats; I remember it as a prison, site of some of my most spectacular adolescent acting-out. But when I pass through the gates, scarcely able to breathe, I see that it is lush and florescent and green. It looks like a country estate, not a jail.

56   Then I notice the six feet of barbed wire on top of the walls. I find a staircase that still serves (don't ask me why) as a stage set for my anxiety dreams, epics of entrapment. For the first time since setting foot in South Africa, I cry—but not from nostalgia.

57 Graffiti: *Did you vote Nat* (Afrikaaner Nationalist)? *Don't worry, be sorry.*

58 I discover that I still hate white South Africans. I hate the way they think, the way they talk, the way they live. I hate them, and I'm one myself. This causes problems with pronouns, among other things.

59 What hasn't changed, as far as I can see, is the mean-spiritedness of their culture. I find that an Afrikaans word keeps recurring to me: *verkrampte.* Nowadays it is used mainly to mean conservative—as opposed to *verligte,* enlightened—but, in its literal sense of cramped, narrow, pinched, it is the best description of the world white South Africans have created for themselves and of their minds, deformed to fit it.

60 I know this is unfair, a gross generalization, mean-spirited in its own way. I know that, but it doesn't make any difference; my attitudes toward South Africa—Mother country, Fatherland—are frozen in late adolescence. A five-week visit scarcely penetrates the personal mythology I have cultivated, in a vacuum, my whole adult life.

61 Victor Ntoni, a Johannesburg jazz musician, on the subject of revenge: "I don't have time for that, man—there is such a lot of living to do out there."

62 Over cocktails, my mother tells the story, approvingly, of a Pietermartizburg woman who owned an expensive dress shop but refused to allow Black or Indian women to try on the clothes. They could buy but not try. When the local newspaper made an issue of this, rather than change her policy, she emigrated to Australia.

63 There used to be red buses and green buses (red for whites, and green, jam-packed, for Blacks). Now there are only red buses, jam-packed, for everyone.

64 Just when I think this is the only kind of change I'm going to see, I spend ten days in Johannesburg with my brother, who manages the Market Theatre. The Market is an island in the worst part of the city, a small, miraculous world where the future, somehow, has already happened. It is a bubble with enough air for me to breathe: three performance spaces plus an art gallery, a shopping precinct, a restaurant, a jazz club (where Mandela celebrated his seventy-third birthday), and a pub, the Yard of Ale, where, if you hang out long enough, you'll meet everybody in politics and the arts. After two days, I spend most of my time there: the rest of Johannesburg is bleak and violent, and revisiting the suburban wastes of my childhood fills me only with emptiness.

65 My brother has a Black boss, Black staff, Black friends. He treats them all with genuine color blindness (which I would have thought impossible in a white South African raised as we were: at the very least, I'd expect a hint of self-congratulation). He works long hours and smokes a lot; he knows everything that is going down, and is quietly cynical about the current politics of convenience. No one on the Left, he says, knows what is going to happen next.

66   Graffiti: *Mandela Unites, Bad Organizing Divides.*

67   He has been in exile, too; in London for five years, returning to the Market after Mandela's release (the post-February period, people call it, shorthand for a whole cycle of euphoria and letdown). I try to explain to him my confusion, my lack of revelation, my sense of everything being familiar but not meaningful.

68   He understands. "As if you have seen it all before in a movie, right?" He shrugs. Either this is what happens to people who have been away too long, or, being siblings, we have developed the same mechanisms of denial.

69   But now there is something else: cognitive dissonance. The more time I spend talking and listening in the warm, crowded Yard of Ale, the less I can recapture the sour, sealed world my parents inhabit. I can scarcely believe it exists in the same time and place. Yet it does: it is real, too.

70   Which is more real?

71   Which is "South Africa"? (As in, "So, how was South Africa?"—the question I'm supposed to be able to answer when I get back to the States.)

72   I develop a pat answer: Political discourse has changed, I say—you can see Mandela's face on TV—but daily life hasn't. Also, I add, you can read books and see movies that would have been censored before. For instance? *Henry and June.*

73   I go back to Pietermaritzburg, where my mother, a nervous driver, is involved in a near-miss with the car. Shaken, she crawls home at twenty miles an hour and tells us the story again and again over cups of strong tea. She keeps emphasizing that everything happened so quickly she didn't even catch a glimpse of the other driver's face. At first I assume this detail is for dramatic effect, but on the fourth or fifth telling, she rephrases it: "It happened so quickly I couldn't even see if he was Black or white." Then I realize that, without this piece of information, my mother is unable to interpret what happened to her. Without it, she cannot make sense of her experience.

74   John Kani, actor and co-director of the Market Theatre: "Some people are unteachable. That is why we have to pin our hopes on the next generation."

75   My nephews, Hamish and Andrew, watch the English, Afrikaans, and Zulu programs on TV. When I was growing up, there was no television in South Africa. They speak a few sentences of Zulu to Mavis, the maid. I can't say a word in any African language. My sister has taught them to call Blacks "Zulu people." I squeeze hope from that word, people. They call any Black male "the man"—in my childhood, he would have been "the boy," "the kaffir," or "the coon"—but Mavis is still "the girl."

76   Charlotte Bauer, Arts Editor of the *Weekly Mail:* "But tell me, why did we ever think it wouldn't be complicated?"

77   My brother invites me to attend the South African Breweries Mini Arts Festival at the Market Theatre one Sunday afternoon, a celebration of what he calls "corporate guilt-money." In honor of a senior executive's retirement, all the arts groups funded by South African Breweries are showcasing their wares, and, as the program unfolds, I see that the corporation has adopted the American model, spreading its funding neatly across the spectrum, picking out one group per color as if selecting a fistful of M & Ms. There is a Soweto jazz company, a group performing Indian dance, the Transvaal Chinese Association's Harmony Dancers, an all-Black orchestra (with no conductor), and so on, through the rainbow.

78   The audience, consisting of local arts figures, proud parents, and corporate white-hairs, sits politely through a sharp dressing down by a "colored" professor, who attacks private-sector funding as a cosmetic, conscience-easing measure. Then the Black poet Don Mattera, banned for nine years, leaps up to read a passionate indictment of white South Africans. After he has catalogued our collective crimes, we applaud politely. He reads one more poem, dedicating it to his young son beaming shyly in the third row. We applaud again.

79   Next, the arts groups present a gift to the retiring executive. It is a carved wooden figure in traditional African style, about two feet high, outfitted for war and brandishing a large club. As the figure is handed over, its club (called a *knobkerrie*) appears to be aimed right at the recipient's head. A coincidence, I wonder, or a subtle joke?

80   The program ends with a huge massed choir from Soweto, whose motto, they tell us, is "We will sing until justice reigns in our country." They begin with traditional African songs that bring people to their feet, dancing and ululating, and then, without skipping a beat, modulate into western choral music. More cognitive dissonance: the conductor in his African robes drawing forth Mozart from these African throats. Colonialism, carps the cynical part of my brain, but for once I tell it to shut up. In my heart at that moment, I understand something about transcendence: that such sounds should come from Soweto....

81   It takes more courage and generosity of spirit to live in South Africa now—really live there—than I will ever be capable of.

82   On my last day at my parents' house (we're all relieved and exhausted and achingly sad), I say goodbye to Dora and leave her a fairly large tip. When she gets around to counting it, she thinks that I, being unfamiliar with the currency, have miscalculated, and that she will somehow get into trouble for accepting so much cash. So she shows it to my mother and asks her what she should do. My mother is outraged, taking my gesture not only as vulgar ostentation but also as a reproach to her (which it is, in a way); Dora is humiliated (again); and I am unmasked in the act of trying to stanch a yawning, irreparable guilt—a lifetime's worth—with a wad of paper money.

83   My sister tells me that she and her husband have given Mavis R1000 (about $400, a substantial sum in that economy) to build a new mud-brick house, because her family was left homeless in the township violence. But, she adds, "Don't tell Mom."

84   What did I learn from my return to South Africa? I learned that I don't have a well-developed sense of place: that is not how I remember things.

85   I learned that I will never understand South Africa because I don't want to: I just want to reject it.

86   I learned that there are some things in life, in families, that can never be repaired.

87   On the very last night of my visit, my brother, in an ironic gesture, takes me to the Doll House, a classic fifties-style drive-in restaurant where we used to go as children—but rarely, because the whole experience offended my father's sensibilities. He would sit in the driver's seat like a condemned man, radiating finicky distaste, while the car filled with the odor of fried grease, and some accident always befell the upholstery.

88   The garish neon lighting in the parking lot hasn't changed, and neither have the fake doll-house dormers on the restaurant facade. My brother orders a burger and chocolate milkshake, as before; as before, I order a toasted cheese and ginger beer. For realism, we should be squabbling and spilling food in the back seat, but he is a suave thirty-one-year-old now, and time has begun to trace the same fine lines on his English skin as it has on mine.

89   We sit side by side in the pink and cobalt glare, playing at nostalgia, when something that looks like a huge armadillo crawls into the parking lot behind us. A flap opens in the side, disgorging a stream of humanoid creatures in camouflage gear. That, my brother tells me, is a Casspir, an armored vehicle full of police, probably on its way to Alexandria township to quell "disturbances" there. After a while, the armed men wander back, and vast quantities of coffee and burgers begin to appear, served on those little red trays that are supposed to hook on to car windows. But this menacing pachyderm has no windows, and so the flap opens again, and the trays disappear inside, as if the machine itself were ingesting them.

90   I'm leaving in the morning, but there isn't much to say, so we sit side by side in silence: my brother and I at an American-style drive-in somewhere in Africa, pretending to relive a childhood neither of us can recall, sharing the neon intimacy of the parking lot with real families and real children and this obscene machine. The moment is surreal—and that is why, for the first time, it seems to make some kind of sense.

Reading for Meaning

1. What are Jenefer Shute's reasons for returning home? Why do you think she has such difficulty finding a reason for her return?

2. Why doesn't Shute cry when her plane lands in South Africa? How do you explain her parents' similar lack of emotion (paragraphs 6 and 10)?

3. Are there times when Shute does display emotion? What occasions prompt these feelings?

4. What makes it so difficult for Shute to communicate with most whites and blacks in South Africa? Is her dilemma convincing?

5. During her visit with her brother, Shute experiences "cognitive dissonance" (paragraph 69). What does she mean? Why do events at the American-style diner, which she describes at the end of her essay, make more sense to her than most of the rest of her visit?

6. Describe a few characteristics of Shute's writing style. How does it complement the ideas in her essay?

7. Why did Jenefer Shute choose the title "Sport, African Cultures, Value for Money?" How does it clarify the tone of her essay?

8. What organizational pattern does Shute choose for her essay? How effective is that pattern for discussing her return to South Africa?

Comparing Texts

1. Jenefer Shute writes about the difficulty she had going back to South Africa after being away for thirteen years. She asks: "What do you feel when you are about to step back into a reviled and imaginary land? You don't feel anything; you're afraid your ghost-foot will slip through the dream-earth into the past." How do the struggles that Shute describes in this passage and in other sections of her essay compare to the feelings Salman Rushdie expresses about being an artist in exile (page 408)? What differences do you find?

2. Salman Rushdie says that for the writer, "description itself is a political act," and he notes that Richard Wright, an African American novelist, said that "black and white Americans were engaged in a war over the nature of reality. Their descriptions were incompatible" page 412. On her visit to South Africa, Jenefer Shute thinks of the Afrikaans word, *verkrampte,* which means "cramped, narrow, pinched," and finds this word to be "the best description of the world white South Africans have created for themselves and of their minds, deformed to fit it." To what extent does Shute's essay redescribe that world and make, in Rushdie's words, "the necessary first step towards changing it"?

Ideas for Writing

1. Explain the different "realities" in the South Africa that Jenefer Shute describes. In the course of your discussion, clarify Shute's response to each reality.

2. Do some research, either on the Internet or in your local library, to discover the current political and social situation in South Africa. If possible, enter a chatroom on the Net or communicate with a source by e-mail to gather information on your topic. At the end of your search, summarize current conditions in South Africa for your reader.

3. In chapter 9 of *Cry, the Beloved Country,* Alan Paton, a native of Pietermaritzburg, Natal, South Africa, describes the influx of blacks looking for work in Johannesburg at the end of World War II. The blacks' section of Johannesburg, or Shanty Town, as it is called in the novel, would later become part of the segregated city forming the South West Townships

known by the acronym, Soweto. Read the following selection and explain what Paton conveys about the lives of blacks in South Africa in 1946.

1. Shanty Town is up overnight. What a surprise for the people when they wake in the morning. Smoke comes up through the sacks, and one or two have a chimney already. There was a nice chimney-pipe lying there at the Kliptown Police Station, but I was not such a fool as to take it.

2. Shanty Town is up overnight. And the newspapers are full of us. Great big words and pictures. See, that is my husband, standing by the house. Alas, I was too late for the picture. Squatters, they call us. We are the squatters. This great village of sack and plank and iron, with no rent to pay, only a shilling to the Committee.

3. Shanty Town is up overnight. The child coughs badly, and her brow is as hot as fire. I was afraid to move her, but it was the night for the moving. The cold wind comes through the sacks. What shall we do in the rain, in the winter? Quietly my child, your mother is by you. Quietly my child, do not cough any more, your mother is by you.

4. The child coughs badly, her brow is hotter than fire. Quietly my child, your mother is by you. Outside there is laughter and jesting, digging and hammering, and calling in languages that I do not know. Quietly my child, there is a lovely valley where you were born. The water sings over the stones, and the wind cools you. The cattle come down to the river, they stand there under the trees. Quietly my child, oh God make her quiet. God have mercy upon us. Christ have mercy upon us. White man, have mercy upon us.

5. —Mr. Dubula, where is the doctor?
6. —We shall get the doctor in the morning. You need not fear, the Committee will pay for him.
7. —But the child is like to die. Look at the blood.
8. —It is not long till morning.
9. —It is long when the child is dying, when the heart is afraid. Can we not get him now, Mr. Dubula?
10. —I shall try, mother. I shall go now and try.
11. —I am grateful, Mr. Dubula.

12. Outside there is singing, singing round a fire. It is *Nkosi sikelel' iAfrika* that they sing, God Save Africa. God save this piece of Africa that is my own, delivered in travail from my body, fed from my breast, loved by my heart, because that is the nature of women. Oh lie quietly, little one. Doctor, can you not come?

13. —I have sent for the doctor, mother. The Committee has sent a car for the doctor. A black doctor, one of our own.

14   —I am grateful, Mr. Dubula.
15   —Shall I ask them to be quiet, mother?
16   —It does not matter, she does not know.
17   Perhaps a white doctor would have been better, but any doctor if only he come. Does it matter if they are quiet, these sounds of an alien land? I am afraid, my husband. She burns my hand like fire.

18   We do not need the doctor any more. No white doctor, no black doctor, can help her any more. Oh child of my womb and fruit of my desire, it was pleasure to hold the small cheeks in the hands, it was pleasure to feel the tiny clutching of the fingers, it was pleasure to feel the little mouth tugging at the breast. Such is the nature of woman. Such is the lot of women, to carry, to bear, to watch, and to lose.

19   The white men come to Shanty Town. They take photographs of us, and moving photographs for the pictures. They come and wonder what they can do, there are so many of us. What will the poor devils do in the rain? What will the poor devils do in the winter? Men come, and machines come, and they start building rough houses for us. That Dubula is a clever man, this is what he said they would do. And no sooner do they begin to build for us, than there come in the night other black people, from Pimville and Alexandra and Sophiatown, and they too put up their houses of sack and grass and iron and poles. And the white men come again, but this time it is anger, not pity. The police come and drive the people away. And some that they drive away are from Orlando itself. They go back to the houses that they left, but of some the rooms are already taken, and some will not have them any more.

20   You need not be ashamed that you live in Shanty Town. It is in the papers, and that is my husband standing by the house. A man here has a paper from Durban, and my husband is there too, standing by the house. You can give your address as Shanty Town, Shanty Town alone, everyone knows where it is, and give the number that the committee has given you.

Writing before Reading

What disagreements typically crop up between children who have reached their late teens or early twenties and their parents? How might these conflicts compare to problems that arise between older immigrants and their younger offspring?

FICTIVE FRAGMENTS OF A FATHER AND SON

David Mura

David Mura is a third-generation Japanese American. He lives in Minnesota and is working on a book about Asian Americans and race. Mura is also a poet and author of the collection of poems After We Lost Our Way. *Mura's essays on Asian American authors and themes have been published in* New England Review, Mother Jones, Utne, *and the* New York Times. *"Fictive Fragments of a Father and Son" appeared in his award-winning autobiography,* Turning Japanese: Memoirs of a Sansei *(1991).*

Facts about Japanese Internment Camps

The resettlement of 120,000 people of Japanese ancestry during World War II constitutes one of the worst assaults on American civil liberties in the history of the United States. Over half the people who were taken from their homes and placed in internment camps were citizens who had been born in the United States. At the time, federal law did not allow Asians to become naturalized citizens. On February 19, 1942, President Franklin D. Roosevelt issued the presidential order that authorized the creation of "relocation centers" for detaining people of Japanese ancestry, people who had not been charged with any crime and who were never proven guilty of any wrong doing. There were ten such camps in the western United States where people were imprisoned until December 1944. In 1988 Congress passed a reparations act that included an apology for the unjust treatment of Japanese Americans and granted $20,000 to survivors.

> *Someone must have been telling lies about Joseph K., for without having done anything wrong he was arrested one fine morning.*
> —Franz Kafka, The Trial

> *Henry went to the control station to register his family. He came home with twenty tags, all number 10701, tags to be attached to each piece of baggage, and one to hang from our coat lapels. From then on we were known as family #10701.*
> —Monica Sone, A Nisei Daughter

1. When I was in college, I once asked my father what it was like in the camps.

2. "Well, before the war, when I got home from school, I had to work in my father's nursery," he said. "In the camps, after school, I could just go out and play baseball."

3. It's amazing to me how many years I accepted this precis. Or my father's homily, "If you look for prejudice, you'll find it." Or his insistence that

his Horatio Alger rise to upper middle class in the years after the war had been without incidents or insults, without discrimination. All he had to do was work his ass off. (A lesson I never quite seemed to learn.)

4   And then, after I visited Hiroshima last year, during a year long visit to Japan, I started to think of where my father was on the day the war ended. And something changed. There was this story there that hadn't been told. Or many stories. Stories my father would call fictions. Completely untrue.

5 By the last year of the war, my father had been released from the internment camp in Jerome, Arkansas, for more than a year and was going to Western Michigan University in Kalamazoo, living with the family of a professor.

6   Probably my father is both pleased and anxious about this precarious new freedom. Perhaps he has looked through the pages of *Life* or *Time,* has seen the cartoons depicting the Japanese: they are lice, vermin, tiny thoraxes with huge heads attached, a buck tooth smile and squinty eyes behind thick glasses; they are small, slant-eyed rats squirming under a huge boot of a GI giant smashing down with unfathomable power. Perhaps he has seen the way some of his classmates look at him, casting glances sideways in history or English, as he passes in the halls. Perhaps they whisper loud enough for him to hear. Perhaps not. (Is he imagining this? Or am I?) I know he does not date in college. There are no other *Nisei,* none of his kind. Does he admit to himself his desire for the white girls in his classes? Or is the sexual conflict inside him too dangerous to acknowledge?

7   It is the year the war has ended, the summer between his freshman and sophomore year. August, a few days after Hiroshima and Nagasaki. A holiday has been declared, men sweep women up in their arms in the middle of streets and kiss them, and the women, abandoned for a moment, respond; firecrackers, streamers, confetti, all the trappings of a carnival, whirl through intersections and squares throughout the country. People sport the smiles and laughter of peace, as if the muscles, clenched like a fist for so long, have moved on to another task, all brightness, promise and plenty.

8   On August 11, 1945, my father is sitting on the steps of a house in Kalamazoo, Michigan. He hears the swooping sirens of the firetrucks from the center of town, the high school band blaring "Stars and Stripes Forever," the tooting of horns, loudspeakers filling with speeches. He sees in his mind the street filled with banners and flags, the men with faces bright and beet-red from joy and drink, the women yanking their children at the wrist, dabbing their eyes with handkerchiefs. A squirrel comes chittering across the lawn, rears up on its haunches, begging as usual for a handout. My father picks up a stone from the dirt, pulls back his arm, and then drops the stone to his feet. A voice rises inside him, insistent

and restless, a twitch in his muscles, an urge to move, go somewhere, do something. "It won't always be like this," he remembers his teacher in the camps saying. "After the war you will be free again and back in American society. But for your own sakes try and be not one, but two hundred percent American...."

9   I am American he says to himself. I am glad we won. The light through the leaves is bright, blinding. The heat immense, oppressive. The sounds all over town joyous. He repeats his mantra over and over. He learns to believe it.

10 My father never slept with a white women, never, I think, slept with anyone but my mother. Still, I know he must have thought of crossing that line, must have been aware it was there to cross.

11 One fall afternoon in eighth grade, I am home from school with a slight fever. My mother is out shopping. For some reason, I start rummaging in their closet, pushing back the pumps and flats, all lined in a row on the rack, unzipping the garment bags. (What am I looking for? Years later, my therapist will tell me that news travels quickly and silently in families; no one has to speak of it.) From beneath a stack of folded sweaters, I pull a *Playboy* magazine. I start moving through the pages, the ads for albums and liquor, cartoons, the interview with Albert Schweitzer, with photos of the great man in pith helmet and bow tie, his famous walrus mustache. And then the foldout undoes itself, flowing before me with its glossy shine.

12 I've seen a *Playboy* someone brought into the locker room at school. But now I'm alone, in my parents' bedroom. I worry about when my mother is coming back, I forget she is gone. I'm entranced by the woman's breasts, the aureoles seem large as my fists. She is blonde, eighteen, a UCLA coed. She leans against a screen, half her body exposed to the camera.

13 And so, like many other American boys, I discover my sexuality in the presence of a picture. And, like many other American boys, I do not think of the color of the woman's skin. Of course, if she were black or brown or yellow... but she is white, her beauty self-evident. I sense somehow that she must be more beautiful than Asian women, more prestigious. But the forbidden quality of sex overpowers any thought of race. I do not wonder why my father looks at these pictures, these women who are not my mother. The sensations of pleasure, of momentary possession and shame, flood over me quickly, easily, sliding through my body.

14 A few minutes later, I pick up the magazine, slip it back in the garment bag beneath the sweaters.

15 In one of my poems, there's a line about my father, "he worked too hard to be white, he beat his son." Of course, it's more complicated than that.

16 I know that his father, my grandfather, would chase my father around the yard in L.A., brandishing a two by four. Whenever my father referred

to this, his manner was surprisingly casual. The beatings were no different from the long distances he had to walk to school or the work he performed in his father's nursery. They were simply proof that my father's childhood was harsher than mine.

17   Sometimes I try to picture my father running from my grandfather, as he holds his weapon aloft. At a certain moment, the board comes down on flesh, whacks the sweaty, T-shirted back of the young boy, knocking him forward, a flat, dull driving pain, the wind rushing from his lungs, a dizziness of fear, panic, and perhaps relief erupting from his stumbling body. The next blow is harder, more solid; the thought rises in my father that he cannot go on, this can't be happening, each blow softened only by the fact that there is one less to go, it will somehow end.

18   But when I try to imagine my father, squirming in his father's grip, in all likelihood, it is not my father I am seeing, but myself, as my father hovers over me in my room, having read the note from my teacher or having heard from my mother. I've been bad, have talked too much. He grabs my toy whip from the floor, the one modelled after Zorro's. The whip comes down; I do not go limp. I scramble about. The room is small, he catches me and hauls me on his lap. I'm held in this vise. I can't move, can't bear knowing this will happen again and again.

19   Somehow, behind these acts of fathers and sons lies the backdrop of race and relocation.

20   As the war went on, the internees at the Jerome, Arkansas relocation center were given weekend passes. They could travel to Little Rock to eat at a restaurant or watch a movie. My grandfather or grandmother did not go on these trips, only their children. The children spoke English, were enamored of Hollywood's stars.

21   It is summer, 1942. On a dust dry country road, my father waits for the bus with other young *Nisei*. Behind them, like a bad dream, the fences of barbed wire, the rifle towers, the gates, the barracks filled with mothers, fathers, and bawling babies, with aging bachelors, with newlyweds. Down the ridge they can see the shacks of sharecroppers, more ramshackle than any of the barracks, with gaps in the walls and their boards weatherbeaten and cracked. Rougher, looser than his older brother Ken—less Japanese—my father and his friends jostle and joke, talk about the baseball game yesterday, about Carol Hiyama or Judy Endo. These boys frighten some of the *Issei* in camp. They play cards behind the barracks, smoke cigarettes, curse in English.

22   When the bus comes, it is nearly empty. They take their seats in the front, behind an old white woman with a pillbox hat, her purse planted in her lap. Behind them, the anonymous faces of a few Negroes, a couple men in overalls, a mother and her child with pigtails. There's never a question for my father of sitting in the back.

23   It is the same at the lunch counter where they order hamburgers and malts. Perhaps they notice the stares of the whites around them, but

most likely they are too engrossed in their own conversation, in teasing Tosh about his crush on Carol, to notice where the negroes are sitting. Later, these boys will sit below the balcony, below the section for negroes. The faces of Cary Grant and Katharine Hepburn flow off the screen, borne on light, enlarged by glamour and celluloid, becoming part of my father's dreams.

24   Two years later, he's in college, away from the camps, entering the Episcopalian church with Professor Bigelow and his family. It is a sunny fall morning, the leaves, splashes of red and yellow and orange, swirling down to the street, crackling on the walk. The church is white, spired, clean in the sunlight. My father has no suit. He's wearing a white shirt, a tie. It is his first time inside this church.

25   Had my grandfather been a fervent Buddhist, things might have turned out differently. But my grandfather was too much a man of this world. Sharing with most Japanese a passive attitude towards religions, he had grown away from Buddha and the Shinto gods during this time in America. My father is an empty vessel, waiting to be filled.

26   As he ambles along with the Bigelows, he's a little stiff, a bit nervous, not knowing what to do. Inside, he's greeted by streams of light from great stained glass windows: Christ in the garden of Gethsemane, kneeling in prayer with the cross of his destruction in the distance, the disciples gathered around him, questioning, listening; the fish and bread of life laid out in jagged triangles; the haggard bearded man stretched out on the cross, eyes closed, giving up the ghost. What strikes my father more, the beautiful colors or this progression towards suffering? The light or the dark?

27   He sees notices in front of the benches, a little platform that swings down, cushioned green leather. Just as the children enter the pew, they suddenly kneel down, facing straight ahead towards the altar; Mrs. Bigelow and the professor do the same. My father wonders what he should do. Self-conscious, he does the best he can with a half-way gesture, the way seventh-graders in our parish years later used to bow. The professor smiles and tries to reassure him, but my father, watching the altar boy light the candles on the altar, hearing the organ and the voices of the choir, is again wondering what to do. As the service continues and the members in the pews rise up to speak in unison, kneel, rise, kneel, over and over at exactly the right time, my father is disoriented. He feels a slight ache in his back, is thankful at least for the cushioned platform.

28   "This is the body and blood which is shed for you and the New Testament. Take this and drink. Do this often in remembrance of me."

29   Thank God, he thinks, I understand the words. And in all of this there is a music that takes over my father, something beyond sense, beyond God or Christ. What attracts him is a sense of belonging, of crossing some line, a way out of the Buddhist temples and streets of L.A., something he first felt in the radios and comic books, the very language that poured

from his mouth, in the games of mumblety-peg, marbles and baseball, in the pledge he recited in school each morning. Something that wasn't foreign, that did not keep him out.

30   He will convert, he will take up the cross, he will bring us to Church all through my childhood, up until the time we move from our middle class home in Morton Grove to our upper class one in Northbrook, a time when he is finally a vice-president, when religion is no longer needed. By then I will be estranged from the Church, an atheist, wondering what brought him to think a white man must be God.

31   Growing up, I had the usual complaints of most Asian kids about their hard driving parents. There were never enough excellents, enough hundreds on tests, there were always errors I'd made on the field, tackles I missed. When I was seven, my father took me to the sidewalk on Lake Shore drive and pushed me off on my bike, screamed "pedal, pedal," and quickly became disgusted when I fell, yelling I didn't listen to him. Ten years later when I learned to drive, it was the same; sitting beside me in our Buick, he slammed on some imaginary brake in front of him and shook my arm. A terrible teacher, he always ended up screaming and shouting, muttering about my lack of concentration, my refusal to perform.

32   Perhaps the problem was how I took all this. I believed whatever it was that reddened his face, that clenched it so tight, that coiled his fist into a tight ball, must have come from me. I must have created this force, it was what I deserved. I was simply unable to brush it off.

33   Years later, I wonder, where did my father's rage come from?

34   I see my father now as a successful executive, writing speeches for other executives, writing videos, public relations campaigns, giving speeches at conventions and meetings, splicing bits of information with familiar corn-pone jokes. I see him at evening striding down the fairway in back of his house, shading his eyes as his drive soars into the sun, the tiny white ball disappearing in the last blaze of orange light, the first crickets of evening, gnats scribbling their mad circles around his head. His body looks ten years younger, hardened by weights, by Nautilus, though it has begun to stoop, just a touch, to descend towards earth. He is sixty, he is content, the fairway stretches out before him, he wants no other life than this. He has no problems with identity, with the past or race. He has been freed from history.

35   And I am still his son.

36   In the light of Kafka, the story of the camps becomes a parable, a parable whose meaning I must somehow solve.

37   One day, K. steps out of his door to find a notice: he must report to the authorities. Who are the authorities? He does not know, only that he must report to them. When he reports to them, they give him a number, tell him to come back tomorrow. When he comes back the next day, he is

taken by bus to a train and then by train to a place with others who have been given numbers and notices. He realizes he has been imprisoned. He is no longer singular, no longer private. The communal beds, shower stalls and toilets only confirm this, as do the barbed wire and rifle towers with guards. What is his crime? He is K. That is his crime.

38 My father's name was originally Katsuji Uyemura. Then Tom Katsuji Uyeumura. Then Tom Katsuji Mura. Then Tom K. Mura.

39 What is the job of the son of K.? To forgive his crime? To try him again?

Reading for Meaning

1. Describe the point of view David Mura adopts for writing his autobiographical sketch. Why do you think he assumed this particular perspective?

2. What bothers Mura about his father? What does he appreciate about him?

3. How much of his father's life is Mura able to re-create? What isn't he sure about?

4. How does Mura use the concepts of "fact" and "fiction"? Do the ideas sometimes overlap?

5. In general, what is Mura trying to understand about his father and about himself? How successful is he?

6. Does Mura resolve his conflicting feelings about his father and about his own personal history? Explain your answer.

7. How does Mura organize his essay? Why might he have chosen this arrangement?

Comparing Texts

1. Reread Connie May Fowler's essay "No Snapshots in the Attic," page 136. Compare Fowler's and David Mura's use of point of view, purpose, attitude, organization, or theme.

2. Study the following passage from Franz Kafka's *The Trial*. In this novel, K. is accused of a crime, brought to trial, and eventually killed. In this selection, a judge listens halfheartedly to K.'s arguments in his own defense. K. never learns what he is supposed to have done. How does K.'s situation apply to that of Mura's father?

1 The Examining Magistrate kept fidgeting on his chair with embarrassment or impatience. The man behind him to whom he had been talking bent over him again, either to encourage him or to give him some particular counsel. Down below, the people in the audience were talking in low voices but with animation. The two factions who had seemed previously to be irreconcilable, were now drifting together, some individuals were pointing their fingers at K., others at the Examining Magistrate. The fuggy atmosphere in the room was unbearable, it actually prevented one from seeing the people at the other end. It must have been particularly inconvenient for the spectators in the gallery, who were forced to question

the members of the audience in a low voice, with fearful side-glances at the Examining Magistrate, to find out what was happening. The answers were given as furtively, the informant generally putting his hand to his mouth to muffle his words.

2 "I have nearly finished," said K., striking the table with his fist, since there was no bell. At the shock of the impact the heads of the Examining Magistrate and his adviser started away from each other for a moment. "I am quite detached from this affair, I can therefore judge it calmly, and you, that is to say if you take this alleged court of justice at all seriously, will find it to your great advantage to listen to me. But I beg you to postpone until later any comments you may wish to exchange on what I have to say, for I am pressed for time and must leave very soon."

3 At once there was silence, so completely did K. already dominate the meeting. The audience no longer shouted confusedly as at the beginning, They did not even applaud, they seemed already convinced or on the verge of being convinced.

4 "There can be no doubt—" said K., quite softly, for he was elated by the breathless attention of the meeting; in that stillness a subdued hum was audible which was more exciting than the wildest applause—"there can be no doubt that behind all the actions of this court of justice, that is to say in my case, behind my arrest and today's interrogation, there is a great organization at work. An organization which not only employs corrupt warders, oafish Inspectors, and Examining Magistrates of whom the best that can be said is that they recognize their own limitations, but also has at its disposal a judicial hierarchy of high, indeed of the highest rank, with an indispensable and numerous retinue of servants, clerks, police, and other assistants, perhaps even hangmen, I do not shrink from that word. And the significance of this great organization, gentlemen? It consists in this, that innocent persons are accused of guilt, and senseless proceedings are put in motion against them, mostly without effect, it is true, as in my own case...."

5 The first rows of the audience remained quite impassive, no one stirred and no one would let him through. On the contrary, they actually obstructed him, someone's hand—he had no time to turn round—seized him from behind by the collar, old men stretched out their arms to bar his way, ... it seemed to him as if his freedom were being threatened, as if he were being arrested in earnest, and he sprang recklessly down from the platform. Now he stood eye to eye with the crowd. Had he been mistaken in these people? Had he overestimated the effectiveness of his speech? Had they been disguising their real opinions while he spoke, and now that he had come to the conclusion of his speech were they weary at last of pretense? What faces these were around him! Their little black eyes darted furtively from side to side, their beards were stiff and brittle, and to take hold of them would be like clutching bunches of claws rather than beards. But under the beards—and this was K.'s real discovery—

badges of various sizes and colors gleamed on their coat-collars. They all wore these badges, so far as he could see. The were all colleagues, these ostensible parties of the Right and the Left, and as he turned round suddenly he saw the same badges on the coat-collar of the Examining Magistrate, who was sitting quietly watching the scene with his hands on his knees. "So!" cried K., flinging his arms in the air, his sudden enlightenment had to break out, "every man jack of you is an official, I see, you are yourselves the corrupt agents of whom I have been speaking, you've all come rushing here to listen and nose out what you can about me, making a pretense of part divisions, and half of you applauded merely to lead me on, you wanted some practice in fooling an innocent man. Well, much good I hope it's done you, for either you have merely gathered some amusement from the fact that I expected you to defend the innocent, or else—keep off or I'll strike you," cried K. to a trembling old man who had pushed quite close to him—"or else you have really learned a thing or two. And I wish you joy of your trade." He hastily seized his hat, which lay near the edge of the table and amid universal silence, the silence of complete stupefaction, if nothing else, pushed his way to the door. But the Examining Magistrate seemed to have been still quicker than K., for he was waiting at the door. "A moment," he said. K. paused but kept his eyes on the door, not on the Examining Magistrate; his hand was already on the latch. "I merely wanted to point out," said the Examining Magistrate, "that today—you may not yet have become aware of the fact—today you have flung away with your own hand all the advantages which an interrogation invariably confers on an accused man." K. laughed, still looking at the door. "You scoundrels, I'll spare you future interrogations," he shouted, opened the door, and hurried down the stairs. Behind him rose the buzz of animated discussion, the audience had apparently come to life again and were analyzing the situation like expert students.[1]

Ideas for Writing

1. Describe in as much detail as you can the actions, thoughts, and feelings of a family member or guardian to whom you feel close. Make sure your final draft has a thesis or central point.

2. Do some research on the history of one of the internment camps constructed in the United States during World War II. Write an essay in which you supplement David Mura's discussion with a general history of what is now recognized as an unjust act.

---

[1] Translated by E. M. Butler.

Writing before Reading

Think about your relationship to your parents, grandparents, or great-grandparents. How do their ideas, values, or ways of living complement or conflict with your own?

RAZIA BEGUM IN LONDON
Ruxana Meer

Ruxana Meer is a Pakistani American who writes and teaches elementary school in Oakland, California. Her short story, "Razia Begum in London," was published in Charlie Chan Is Dead: An Anthology of Contemporary Asian American Fiction *(1993).*

1   If it didn't stop raining soon, we'd be drowned.

2   If the drops didn't evaporate, steaming up to open our pores like an expensive facial treatment, we'd have to learn to tread water.

3   If the gutters kept sailing trash down our street and the waves kept hitting the sidewalk, sometimes up to our knees, splashing us when speeding cars passed, when we got home we'd be in trouble for getting so wet.

4   If it didn't stop raining soon, umbrella business would go out of business 'cause everyone would know the real value of such a protective device and those who were coming in would pass theirs on to those going out.

5   *We need it* the radio and the bus driver kept saying but if it didn't stop soon, I was going to explode, hearing music outdoors and needing to dance. I would have to wait until I was inside since we need the rain. Under the covers I can hear it's still raining and I don't even try to get up.

6   Razia grandma reminds us *Don't you know better than to go out when it's pouring like this? Here,* she wraps her shawl around me, *good. choke and be dry.* If it didn't stop raining soon, the weeds would take over 'cause grandma's garden will overflow unclipped. If it didn't stop raining, I'd go insane waiting inside, to walk around, over, and above the surfaces outside where if it didn't stop raining soon, some people would drown.

7   It has been raining every single day since we got here and it hasn't stopped once. There are new leaks every day which spring from corners of the disintegrating brick and sometimes it's just the unsure plumbing

in grandma's house that makes it rain. In her vision of modern life, it doesn't matter that these mechanics of technology don't work. As long as there is no powerful hex, she remains in spiritual control of her house, and of us, at least during the summer vacation when it never stopped raining.

8 From the third floor, top of the stairs spiral, I could see her standing at the bottom, talking to us and holding up her cotton shalwar, the wooden spoon directing her words at her side.

9 *Grandma step out of the water please   you're the one getting sick.* I could lie here and just watch the top her covered head, patiently waiting, her hand on the post at the bottom. I stare at the wall and find out where and what the ants go marching in between.

10 *I can wait at the bottom for these children*

11 *Grandma why are you standing still?* now moss had begun to swell, the carpet matching greens and climbing vines, tropical, uncharted and not like the pretty tidepools we saw on our class field trip. Too slippery for Grandma's wood bottom sandals. She might drown if she didn't use her spoon to paddle with.

12 My dreaming, sleepwalking brother had assembled a small fortress of furniture on top of the bed to prevent being found by Grandma because he didn't want to wake up and go downstairs like they do in Pakistan, maybe, before dawn, before time and light is what the clock counts and before dawn is what seeing your breath is.

13 I heard Kaiser, my half-asleep brother asking me *Where are you going don't leave me*

14 I tell him that *I'm hungry. get up. I want to eat something.* I call Grandma up again *come stay on the bed with us get out of the water there's flood.*

15 Kaiser stubbornly refuses to move or let me go *if you're leaving please take me with you*

16 *What are you scared of? There's nowhere to go and we are already here I'm going downstairs*

17 I have my head in between the bannisters, but I turn around and can see into the room where we sleep. Kaiser's face is pained but no sound comes out. The anger does not stop in his sleep because in the cycle of sleep certain conditions must continue as in waking. He is wanting to go back to California where I tell him it is raining too but at least all our friends are there. At least we know something about those people unlike foreign grandma who we are trying to get to.

18 Where we grew up the people shake their heads one way or another depending on who's their president, to divide up the small pie, the world's brown population, slicing the land, the resources, and the heads off mountains filled with red rock. My brother and I imagine that we could dig in our sandbox until we got to the other side of the globe, where everyone would stare at us as we climbed out of the earth patch in

the middle of the market and someone would call the police. We had big dreams about the old country and when we get on the plane at the end of vacation my brother tells me his dreams kept him up at night and asleep in the morning and that's why he could never get up.

19   In my brother's dream, he has just gotten to sleep to find himself running down the city blocks of London in the rain and having his feet freezing through his shoes. In the run for his life, his asthma inhaler and all his change falls out of his pockets and he goes into a sandwich shop where the counters are tall enough to hide behind them. He puts two pastrami sandwiches in his jacket, which he didn't know he was still wearing. He feels invisible except to the woman having a cigarette and trying to talk to him about mayonnaise and her diet. He remembers he has to be home to eat at Grandma's and gives the sandwiches to the woman because she is really hungry. Grandma's voice and his voice are at opposite ends of the house and they are waiting to meet in the morning, hardly light 'cause the sun hasn't risen yet. She can't hear him and he knows she is down there waiting but doesn't know how long she can wait. I am watching his eyelids flicker.

20   I always lie on the floor, resting my stomach. I'm still trying to wake Kaiser though, as I get louder and louder, the harder he ignores me. And then periodically Grandma in a burst of surprising English, asking the same question: *Come downstairs and learn something about yourself.*

21   I relay the message with urgency, *soon we'll be there aye wake up and come downstairs* but my brother crawls deeper into his sheets over the mass of chairs. *Come down before you get in more trouble.*

22   From the bed and chair maze, his voice in the hunchback tractor wailed *Why am I in trouble?*

23   *Because you can't wake up and everyone knows it's because you don't want to have to read Quran   I'm going downstairs so are you coming or not?*

24   *Wait   don't leave without me, rux.*

25   Grandma is still asking the same question in a different way. She has never spoken English so we believe that we aren't sure she's talking to us or getting mad. She says to Ma that we are absent and mythical sort of descendants and it does no good to try to change us radically now. Our tongues are lazy and we cannot speak in the same meanings with which we are spoken to by our elders. We have not been taught in the mind and mouth properly, everyone agrees our resulting behavior is not completely our own fault.

26   We are raised with four place settings, three televisions and only one fireplace. At Grandma's house, even the bathroom has a fire place, plus there is one outhouse. The smells of turmeric, incense, and babies get in your hair, your clothes and your sleep when you stay there. We miss California because the smells there are not so damp. We can leave doors and windows open, the climate is mild and the seasons blur into each other.

27   Grandma is not looking up, reading the Quran and extra prayers in order that we be safe, jet elevated for twelve hours, suctioned in the sky and on our way home. Excited by the peanuts and the stewardesses' colorful manners, my brother and I make siren noises in the baggage check line and distract the security. We behave as world travelers with no manners *as if we just got off the boat.* But we are not scared, not clutching our packages, because we know our contents have insurance.

28   I want to take Grandma with us but that is wishful. She lives in a strangers' country anyway and so why not? In the time which Razia did travel to meet us, she was lost in the San Francisco airport, in the homelessness of the eyes of Indian and Chinese women, in the money exchange, portraitures of men, paying each other off. She discovered the New World too, and she says before America, men thought it was in our homeland, India, now Pakistan. India is hard to get near in America, which calls the Indios, people of god, Indians. My brother and I return from vacation a little clearer on the concept of those who came before us.

29   In the airport, Ma was holding me and I was at least her weight and holding on tighter. I stopped running around and hold my Ma's heart from falling into her lap. *What's wrong* is what I ask because *going home* is all I know. This is when she starts to cry and I tell Kaiser it's his fault because he's losing to the same video game for the fifth time and *we need our change.*

30   Ma tried to pass on whatever Razia said about us while she could still remember. Repeating them in that absence, in the vacuum of a plane made the pilot's head spin and caused the unexpected turbulence.

31   My brother, abandoned in my thoughts, missed the games we had strategized to disrupt the sleeping passengers on the long ride. He wonders what happened to that trip. To him, I never came back, didn't come back the same. I have never heard the shaking of Ma's voice like when she told me the strength of Grandma's words.

32   Ma apologized to Grandma for the unruly fashion of her daughter and hoped I would be grown next time we came to visit. Grandma raising nine children and ten grandchildren said it this way, *I know that the young ladies today must still be faced with fierce hostility from some who believe girls are not good for fighting for themselves, or they are no good once they begin fighting. But I think they may be more willing to persist in who they are and defend their true character, and be able to speak to one another about these times to hopefully grow very strong and energetic.*

33   I need to ask Grandma sometime *where does this energy come from.* Since we came back to these states, all I have are the holes where answers are needed. She would try to tell us what she could when we visited, but we don't wake up that early in the morning. When I think of her, I can't say I know all that she has taught me. The presence of her life in mine is so unmeasured. I can see only the absence so much, then I start to realize the imported way in which I act and talk and sense and the way I am hungry, so American.

Reading for Meaning

1. Describe the point of view that Ruxana Meer uses to write her short story. Explain any difficulties you found in reading the story.

2. What bothers the narrator, Rux, about her grandmother, Razia Begum? Does her attitude change in the course of the story? Explain how you think it changes.

3. What is Razia Begum's attitude toward her grandchildren? What does she want to teach them? What hope does she have for her granddaughter?

4. Why does Meer write some sections of her story in italics? What do those passages seem to signify?

5. What seems to be Meer's purpose for writing "Razia Begum in London"?

6. How does Meer arrange the scenes in her story? What difference(s) do you see between the way she narrates the first scene and the final scene at the airport?

Comparing Texts

1. Compare Ruxana Meer's writing style to that of David Mura in "Fictive Fragments of a Father and Son."

2. Like Ruxana Meer, Connie May Fowler writes about her attempts to understand her grandmother and to learn more about her (page 136). Which of the two authors is most successful? Explain your answer.

Ideas for Writing

1. Describe the fictional techniques that Ruxana Meer uses to recreate Rux's experience in London. How effective is each technique in drawing the reader into the story?

2. Study the elements of "Razia Begum in London" that make it seem like a dream. How does Ruxana Meer use these dreamlike qualities in recording Rux's memories of her visit to grandmother?

Writing before Reading

1. Based on what you have read or what you have seen on television news, what is an important topic of discussion with regard to the immigration and naturalization process? How do you feel about this issue? What has shaped your view?

2. In your experience, what do people usually mean when they mention "family values"? What does the term mean to you?

IMMIGRANTS AND FAMILY VALUES

Francis Fukuyama

Francis Fukuyama is Hirst Professor of public policy at George Mason University. He has also been a research fellow for the Rand Corporation in Washington, D.C. His expertise is in economics, but Fukuyama also writes about politics, history, and culture. He is the author of more than 150 articles and reviews published in Forbes, The Wall Street Journal, Foreign Affairs, U.S. News & World Report, *the* National Review, Esquire, *the* New York Times, *and other publications. While a policy planner for the State Department, Fukuyama wrote an article titled "The End of History" (1989). In this essay he predicted that the twenty-first century would usher in an era of more democratic and less bloody solutions to social conflicts than have been the typical methods of confronting problems in the twentieth century. He developed this theme in his book* The End of History and the Last Man *(1992). His most recent book,* Trust: The Social Virtue and the Creation of Prosperity *(1995), makes a case for the importance of personal trust in the global economy. In the following article, published originally in* Commentary, *May 1993, Fukuyama argues that the fears that newly arrived immigrants threaten the American way of life are unfounded.*

Facts about Immigration to the United States

Since the 1600s more immigrants and refugees have come to the United States than to any other nation in the world. During the colonial period, immigrants came from all over Europe, principally from England. Some had suffered religious persecution, others were looking for adventure, still others came as indentured servants, convicts, or slaves. During the next two hundred years, immigrants arrived from Ireland, France, and Germany. The transport of slaves to the United States was outlawed by Congress in 1808, but not before 375,000 black Africans had been brought to this country as slaves. From 1820 to 1870 over seven million immigrants entered the United States, most from Ireland and Germany. In the mid-1800s Chinese and Canadian immigrants entered the United States as "sojourners," workers who were allowed into the country on a temporary visa. In 1875 during an economic depression, Congress passed the first set of laws restricting immigration and denying entry to convicts and prostitutes. Sentiments against immigrants ran high as well, and in 1882 the Chinese Exclusion Act prevented immigrants from China from entering the United States. From 1880 to 1920 the United States absorbed nearly twenty-four million people, most of whom immigrated from eastern and southern Europe. These new arrivals met with some of the same hostility that had forced many Chinese out of the western United States. In 1921 Congress established a quota system limiting immigrants from any country to three percent of the immigrant population from that country who were living in the United States in 1910. The Immigration Act passed in 1924 limited the numbers of immigrants allowed into the United States to about 154,000 a year and ensured that eighty percent of that number would come from western Europe. After World War II the United States relaxed its immigration laws enough to allow Asians into the country and to grant them citizenship. Since 1965 the number of immigrants allowed into the United States has risen from 290,000 in 1965 to 675,000 beginning in 1995. Quotas now favor relatives of United States citizens and people with special skills.

1   At the Republican convention in Houston August [1992] Patrick J. Buchanan announced the coming of a block-by-block war to "take back our culture." Buchanan is right that a cultural war is upon us, and that this fight will be a central American preoccupation now that the cold war is over. What he understands less well, however, is that the vast majority of the non-European immigrants who have come into this country in the past couple of decades are not the enemy. Indeed, many of them are potentially on his side.

2   Conservatives have for long been sharply divided on the question of immigration. Many employers and proponents of free-market economics, like Julian Simon or the editorial page of the *Wall Street Journal,* are strongly pro-immigration; they argue for open borders because immigrants are a source of cheap labor and ultimately create more wealth than they consume. Buchanan and other traditional right-wing Republicans, by contrast, represent an older nativist position. They dispute the economic benefits of immigration, but more importantly look upon immigrants as bearers of foreign and less desirable cultural values. It is this group of conservatives who forced the inclusion of a plank in the Republican platform last August calling for the creation of "structures" to maintain the integrity of America's southern border.

3   Indeed, hostility to immigration has made for peculiar bedfellows. The Clinton administration's difficulties in finding an attorney general who had not at some point hired an illegal-immigrant babysitter is testimony to the objective dependence of liberal yuppies on immigration to maintain their life-styles, and they by and large would support the *Wall Street Journal*'s open-borders position.

4   On the other hand, several parts of the liberal coalition—blacks and environmentalists—have been increasingly vocal in recent years in opposition to further immigration, particularly from Latin America. The Black Leadership Forum, headed by Coretta Scott King and Congressman Walter Fauntroy, has lobbied to maintain sanctions against employers hiring illegal immigrant labor on the ground that this takes away jobs from blacks and "legal" browns. Jack Miles, a former *Los Angeles Times* book-review editor with impeccable liberal credentials, has in a recent article in the *Atlantic* lined up with the Federation for American

Immigration Reform (FAIR) in calling for a rethinking of open borders, while liberal activist groups like the Southern California Interfaith Task Force on Central America have supported Senator Orrin Hatch's legislation strengthening employer sanctions. Environmental groups like the Sierra Club, for their part, oppose immigration because it necessitates economic growth, use of natural resources, and therefore environmental degradation.

5   But if much of the liberal opposition to immigration has focused on economic issues, the conservative opposition has concentrated on the deeper cultural question; and here the arguments made by the Right are very confused. The symptoms of cultural decay are all around us, but the last people in the world we should be blaming are recent immigrants.

II

6   The most articulate and reasoned recent conservative attack on immigration came last summer in an article in *National Review* by Peter Brimelow. Brimelow, a senior editor at *Forbes* and himself a naturalized American of British and Canadian background, argues that immigration worked in the past in America only because earlier waves of nativist backlash succeeded in limiting it to a level that could be successfully assimilated into the dominant Anglo-Saxon American culture. Brimelow criticizes pro-immigration free-marketeers like Julian Simon for ignoring the issue of the skill levels of the immigrant labor force, and their likely impact on blacks and others at the bottom end of the economic ladder. But his basic complaint is a cultural one. Attacking the *Wall Street Journal*'s Paul Gigot for remarking that a million Zulus would probably work harder than a million Englishmen today, Brimelow notes:

> This comment reveals an utter innocence about the reality of ethnic and cultural differences, let alone little things like tradition and history—in short, the greater part of the conservative vision. Even in its own purblind terms, it is totally false. All the empirical evidence is that immigrants from developed countries assimilate better than those from underdeveloped countries. It is developed countries that teach the skills required for success in the United States ... it should not be necessary to explain that the legacy of [the Zulu kings] Shaka and Cetewayo—overthrown just over a century ago—is not that of Alfred the Great, let alone Elizabeth II or any civilized society.

7   Elsewhere, Brimelow suggests that culture is a key determinant of economic performance, and that people from certain cultures are therefore likely to do less well economically than others. He implies, furthermore, that some immigrants are more prone to random street crime because of their "impulsiveness and present-orientation," while others are responsible for organized crime which is, by his account, ethnically based. Finally, Brimelow argues that the arrival of diverse non-European

cultures fosters the present atmosphere of multiculturalism, and is, to boot, bad for the electoral prospects of the Republican party.

8   A similar line of thought runs through Buchanan's writings and speeches, and leads to a similar anti-immigrant posture. Buchanan has explicitly attacked the notion that democracy represents a particularly positive form of government, and hence would deny that belief in universal democratic principles ought to be at the core of the American national identity.[1] But if one subtracts democracy from American nationality, what is left? Apparently, though Buchanan is somewhat less explicit on this point, a concept of America as a Christian, ethnically European nation with certain core cultural values that are threatened by those coming from other cultures and civilizations.

9   There is an easy, Civics 101-type answer to the Brimelow-Buchanan argument. In contrast to other West European democracies, or Japan, the American national identity has never been directly linked to ethnicity or religion. Nationality has been based instead on universal concepts like freedom and equality that are in theory open to all people. Our Constitution forbids the establishment of religion, and the legal system has traditionally held ethnicity at arm's length. To be an American has meant to be committed to a certain set of ideas, and not to be descended from an original tribe of *ur*-Americans. Those elements of a common American culture visible today—belief in the Constitution and the individualist-egalitarian principles underlying it, plus modern American pop and consumer culture—are universally accessible and appealing, making the United States, in Ben Wattenberg's phrase, the first "universal nation."

10 This argument is correct as far as it goes, but there is a serious counterargument that reaches to the core of last year's debate over "family values." It runs as follows:

11 America began living up to its universalist principles only in the last half of this century. For most of the period from its revolutionary founding to its rise as a great, modern, industrial power, the nation's elites conceived of the country not just as a democracy based on universal principles, but also as a Christian, Anglo-Saxon nation.

12 American democracy—the counterargument continues—is, of course, embodied in the laws and institutions of the country, and will be imbibed by anyone who learns to play by its rules. But virtually every serious theorist of American democracy has noted that its success depended heavily on the presence of certain pre-democratic values or cultural characteristics that were neither officially sanctioned nor embodied

---

[1] See, for example, his article, "America First—and Second, and Third," the *National Interest*, Spring 1990.

in law. If the Declaration of Independence and the Constitution were the basis of America's *Gesellschaft* (society), Christian Anglo-Saxon culture constituted its *Gemeinschaft* (community).

13   Indeed—the counterargument goes on—the civic institutions that Tocqueville observed in the 1830's, whose strength and vitality he saw as a critical manifestation of the Americans' "art of associating," were more often than not of a religious (i.e., Christian) nature, devoted to temperance, moral education of the young, or the abolition of slavery. There is nothing in the Constitution which states that parents should make large sacrifices for their children, that workers should rise early in the morning and labor long hours in order to get ahead, that people should emulate rather than undermine their neighbors' success, that they should be innovative, entrepreneurial, or open to technological change. Yet Americans, formed by a Christian culture, possessed these traits in abundance for much of their history, and the country's economic prosperity and social cohesion arguably rested on them.

14   It is this sort of consideration that underlay the family-values controversy during last year's election. Basic to this line of thought is that, all other things being equal, children are better off when raised in stable, two-parent, heterosexual families. Such family structures and the web of moral obligations they entail are the foundation of educational achievement, economic success, good citizenship, personal character, and a host of other social virtues.

15   The issue of family values was badly mishandled by the Republicans and deliberately misconstrued by the press and the Democrats (often not distinguishable), such that mere mention of the phrase provoked derisive charges of narrow-minded gay-bashing and hostility to single mothers. Yet while many Americans did not sign on to last year's family-values theme, few would deny that the family and community are in deep crisis today. The breakdown of the black family in inner-city neighborhoods around America in the past couple of generations shows in particularly stark form the societal consequences of a loss of certain cultural values. And what has happened among blacks is only an extreme extension of a process that has been preceeding apace among whites as well.

16   The issue, then, is not whether the questions of culture and cultural values are important, or whether it is legitimate to raise them, but whether immigration really threatens those values. For while the values one might deem central either to economic success or to social cohesion may have arisen out of a Christian, Anglo-Saxon culture, it is clear that they are not bound to that particular social group: some groups, like Jews and Asians, might come to possess those values in abundance, while Wasps themselves might lose them and decay. The question thus becomes: which ethnic groups in today's America are threatening, and which groups are promoting, these core cultural values?

III

17 The notion that non-European immigrants are a threat to family values and other core American cultural characteristics is, in a way, quite puzzling. After all, the breakdown of traditional family structures, from extended to nuclear, has long been understood to be a disease of advanced industrial countries and not of nations just emerging from their agricultural pasts.

18 Some conservatives tend to see the third world as a vast, global underclass, teeming with the same social pathologies as Compton in Los Angeles or Bedford-Stuyvesant in Brooklyn. But the sad fact is that the decay of basic social relationships evident in American inner cities, stretching to the most intimate moral bonds linking parents and children, may well be something with few precedents in human history. Economic conditions in most third-world countries simply would not permit a social group suffering so total a collapse of family structure to survive: with absent fathers and no source of income, or mothers addicted to drugs, children would not live to adulthood.

19 But it would also seem *a priori* likely that third-world immigrants should have stronger family values than white, middle-class, suburban Americans, while their work ethic and willingness to defer to traditional sources of authority should be greater as well. Few of the factors that have led to family breakdown of the American middle class over the past couple of generations—rapidly changing economic conditions, with their attendant social disruptions; the rise of feminism and the refusal of women to play traditional social roles; or the legitimization of alternative life-styles and consequent proliferation of rights and entitlements on a retail level—apply in third-world situations. Immigrants coming from traditional developing societies are likely to be poorer, less educated, and in possession of fewer skills than those from Europe, but they are also likely to have stronger family structures and moral inhibitions. Moreover, despite the greater ease of moving to America today than in the last century, immigrants are likely to be a self-selecting group with a much greater than average degree of energy, ambition, toughness, and adaptability.

20 These intuitions are largely borne out by the available empirical data, particularly if one disaggregates the different parts of the immigrant community.

21 The strength of traditional family values is most evident among immigrants from East and South Asia, where mutually supportive family structures have long been credited as the basis for their economic success. According to Census Bureau statistics, 78 percent of Asian and Pacific Islander households in the United States were family households, as opposed to 70 percent for white Americans. The size of these family households is likely to be larger: 74 percent consist of three or more

persons, compared to 57 percent for white families. While Asians are equally likely to be married as whites, they are only half as likely to be divorced.[2] Though dropping off substantially in the second and third generations, concern for elderly parents is high in Chinese, Japanese, and Vietnamese households; for many, the thought of sticking a mother or father out of sight and out of mind in a nursing home continues to be anathema. More importantly, most of the major Asian immigrant groups are intent on rapid assimilation into the American mainstream, and have not been particularly vocal in pressing for particularistic cultural entitlements.

22   While most white Americans are ready to recognize and celebrate the social strengths of Asians, the real fears of cultural invasion surround Latinos. Despite their fast growth, Asians still constitute less than 3 percent of the U.S. population, while the number of Hispanics increased from 14.6 to over 22 million between 1980 and 1990, or 9 percent of the population. But here as well, the evidence suggests that most Latin American immigrants may be a source of strength with regard to family values, and not a liability.

23   Latinos today constitute an extremely diverse group. It is certainly the case that a segment of the Latino community has experienced many of the same social problems as blacks. This is particularly true of the first large Latino community in the United States: Puerto Ricans who came to the mainland in the early postwar period and settled predominantly in New York and other cities of the Northeast. Forty percent of Puerto Rican families are headed by women, compared to 16 percent for the non-Hispanic population; only 57 percent of Puerto Rican households consist of families, while their rate of out-of-wedlock births is almost double the rate for non-Hispanics. In New York, Puerto Ricans have re-exported social pathologies like crack-cocaine use to Puerto Rico over the past generation.

24   Other Latino groups have also brought social problems with them: the Mariel boat lift from Cuba, during which Castro emptied his country's jails and insane asylums, had a measurable impact on crime in the United States. Many war-hardened immigrants from El Salvador and other unstable Central American countries have contributed to crime in the United States, and Chicano gangs in Los Angeles and other Southwestern cities have achieved their own notoriety beside the black Bloods and Crips. Half of those arrested in the Los Angeles riot last year were Latinos.

25   Such facts are highly visible and contribute to the impression among white Americans that Latinos as a whole have joined inner-city blacks to form one vast, threatening underclass. But there are very significant differences among Latino groups. Latinos of Cuban and Mexican origin, for example, who together constitute 65 percent of the Hispanic community,

---

[2] Census Bureau Press Release CB92-89, "Profile of Asians and Pacific Islanders."

have a 50-percent lower rate of female-headed households than do Puerto Ricans—18.9 and 19.6 percent versus 38.9 percent. While the rate of Puerto Rican out-of-wedlock births approaches that of blacks (53.0 vs. 63.1 percent of live births), the rates for Cuban and Mexican-origin Latinos are much lower, 16.1 and 28.9 percent, respectively, though they are still above the white rate of 13.9 percent.[3]

26 When looked at in the aggregate, Latino family structure stands somewhere between that of whites and blacks. For example, the rates of female-headed families with no husband present as a proportion of total families is 13.5 percent for whites, 46.4 percent for blacks, and 24.4 percent for Hispanics. If we adjust these figures for income level, however, Hispanics turn out to be much closer to the white norm.

27 Poverty is hard on families regardless of race; part of the reason for the higher percentage of Latino female-headed households is simply that there are more poor Latino families. If we compare families below the poverty level, the Hispanic rate of female-headed families is very close to that of whites (45.7 vs. 43.6 percent), while the comparable rate for blacks is much higher than either (78.3 percent). Considering the substantially higher rate of family breakdown within the sizable Puerto Rican community, this suggests that the rate of single-parent families for Cuban- and Mexican-origin Latinos is actually lower than that for whites at a comparable income level.

28 Moreover, Latinos as a group are somewhat more likely to be members of families than either whites or blacks.[4] Another study indicates that Mexican Americans have better family demographics than do whites, with higher birth-weight babies even among low-income mothers due to taboos on smoking, drinking, and drug use during pregnancy. Many Latinos remain devout Catholics, and the rate of church attendance is higher in the Mexican community than for the United States as a whole as well. But even if one does not believe that the United States is a "Christian country," the fact that so many immigrants are from Catholic Latin America should make them far easier to assimilate than, say, Muslims in Europe.

29 These statistics are broadly in accord with the observations of anyone who has lived in Los Angeles, San Diego, or any other community in the American Southwest. Virtually every early-morning commuter in Los Angeles knows the street-corners on which Chicano day-laborers gather at 7:00 A.M., looking for work as gardeners, busboys, or on construction sites. Many of them are illegal immigrants with families back in Mexico to whom they send their earnings. While they are poor and unskilled, they

---

[3] Data taken from Linda Chavez. *Out of the Barrio* (Basic Books, 1991), p. 103.
[4] Figures taken from *Poverty in the United States: 1991*. Bureau of the Census, Series P-60, no. 181, pp. 7–9; the percentage of people in families for whites, blacks, and Hispanics is 84.5, 84.8, and 89.0, respectively (pp. 2–3).

have a work ethic and devotion to family comparable to those of the South and East European immigrants who came to the United States at the turn of the century. It is much less common to see African Americans doing this sort of thing.

30   Those who fear third-world immigration as a threat to Anglo-American cultural values do not seem to have noticed what the real sources of cultural breakdown have been. To some extent, they can be traced to broad socioeconomic factors over which none of us has control: the fluid, socially disruptive nature of capitalism; technological change; economic pressures of the contemporary workplace and urban life; and so on. But the ideological assault on traditional family values—the sexual revolution; feminism and the delegitimization of the male-dominated household: the celebration of alternative life-styles; attempts ruthlessly to secularize all aspects of American public life; the acceptance of no-fault divorce and the consequent rise of single-parent households—was not the creation of recently-arrived Chicano agricultural workers or Haitian boat people, much less of Chinese or Korean immigrants. They originated right in the heart of America's well-established white, Anglo-Saxon community. The "Hollywood elite" that created the now celebrated Murphy Brown, much like the establishment "media elite" that Republicans enjoy attacking, does not represent either the values or the interests of most recent third-world immigrants.

31   In short, though the old, traditional culture continues to exist in the United States, it is over-laid today with an elite culture that espouses very different values. The real danger is not that these elites will become corrupted by the habits and practices of third-world immigrants, but rather that the immigrants will become corrupted by them. And that is in fact what tends to happen.

32   While the first generation of immigrants to the United States tends to be deferential to established authority and preoccupied with the economic problems of "making it," their children and grandchildren become aware of their own entitlements and rights, more politicized, and able to exploit the political system to defend and expand those entitlements. While the first generation is willing to work quietly at minimum- or subminimum-wage jobs, the second and third generations have higher expectations as to what their labor is worth. The extension of welfare and other social benefits to noncitizens through a series of court decisions has had the perverse effect of hastening the spread of welfare dependency. Part of the reason that Puerto Ricans do less well than other Latino groups may be that they were never really immigrants at all, but U.S. citizens, and therefore eligible for social benefits at a very early stage.

33   As Julian Simon has shown, neither the absolute nor the relative levels of immigration over the past decade have been inordinately high by historical standards. What *is* different and very troubling about immigration

in the present period is that the ideology that existed at the turn of the century and promoted assimilation into the dominant Anglo-Saxon culture has been replaced by a multicultural one that legitimates and even promotes continuing cultural differentness.

34 The intellectual and social origins of multiculturalism are complex, but one thing is clear: it is both a Western and an American invention. The American Founding was based on certain Enlightenment notions of the universality of human equality and freedom, but such ideas have been under attack within the Western tradition itself for much of the past two centuries. The second half of the late Allan Bloom's *The Closing of the American Mind* (the part that most buyers of the book skipped over) chronicles the way in which the relativist ideas of Nietzsche and Heidegger were transported to American shores at mid-century. Combined with an easygoing American egalitarianism, they led not just to a belief in the need for cultural tolerance, but to a positive assertion of the equal moral validity of all cultures. Today the writings of Michel Foucault, a French epigone of Nietzsche, have become the highbrow source of academic multiculturalism.

35 France may have produced Foucault, but France has not implemented a multicultural educational curriculum to anything like the degree the United States has. The origins of multiculturalism here must therefore be traced to the specific circumstances of American social life. Contrary to the arguments of multiculturalism's promoters, it was not a necessary adjustment to the reality of our pluralistic society. The New York City public-school system in the year 1910 was as diverse as it is today, and yet it never occurred to anyone to celebrate and preserve the native cultures of the city's Italians, Greeks, Poles, Jews, or Chinese.

36 The shift in attitudes toward cultural diversity can be traced to the aftermath of the civil-rights movement, when it became clear that integration was not working for blacks. The failure to assimilate was interpreted as an indictment of the old, traditional mainstream Anglo-Saxon culture: "Wasp" took on a pejorative connotation, and African-Americans began to take pride in the separateness of their own traditions. Ironically, the experience of African Americans became the model for subsequent immigrant groups like Latinos who could have integrated themselves into mainstream society as easily as the Italians or Poles before them.

37 It is true that Hispanic organizations now constitute part of the multiculturalist coalition and have been very vocal in pushing for bilingual/bicultural education. There is increasing evidence, however, that rank-and-file immigrants are much more traditionally assimilationist than some of their more vocal leaders. For example, most Chinese and Russian immigrant parents in New York City deliberately avoid sending their children to the bilingual-education classes offered to them by the

public-school system, believing that a cold plunge into English will be a much more effective means of learning to function in American society.

38   Hispanics generally show more support for bilingual education, but even here a revealing recent study indicates that an overwhelming number of Hispanic parents see bilingualism primarily as a means of learning English, and not of preserving Hispanic culture.[5] This same study indicates that most Hispanics identify strongly with the United States, and show a relatively low level of Spanish maintenance in the home. By contrast, multiculturalism is more strongly supported by many other groups—blacks, feminists, gays, Native Americans, etc.—whose ancestors have been in the country from the start.

39   Brimelow's *National Review* piece suggests that even if immigrants are not responsible for our anti-assimilationist multiculturalism, we need not pour oil on burning waters by letting in more immigrants from non-Western cultures. But this argument can be reversed: even if the rate of new immigration fell to zero tomorrow, and the most recent five million immigrants were sent home, we would still have an enormous problem in this country with the breakdown of a core culture and the infatuation of the school system with trendy multiculturalist educational policies.

40   The real fight, the central fight, then, should not be over keeping newcomers out: this will be a waste of time and energy. The real fight ought to be over the question of assimilation itself: whether we believe that there is enough to our Western, rational, egalitarian, democratic civilization to force those coming to the country to absorb its language and rules, or whether we carry respect for other cultures to the point that Americans no longer have a common voice with which to speak to one another.

41   Apart from the humble habits of work and family values, opponents of immigration ought to consider culture at the high end of the scale. As anyone who has walked around an elite American university recently would know, immigration from Asia is transforming the nature of American education. For a country that has long prided itself on technological superiority, and whose economic future rests in large part on a continuing technical edge, a depressingly small number of white Americans from long-established families choose to go into engineering and science programs in preference to business and, above all, law school. (This is particularly true of the most dynamic and vocal part of the white population, upwardly mobile middle-class women.) The one bright spot in an otherwise uniform horizon of decline in educational test scores has been in math, where large numbers of new Asian test-takers have bumped up

---

[5] See Rodolfo O. de la Garza, Louis DeSipio, et al., *Latino Voices: Mexican, Puerto Rican, and Cuban Perspectives on American Politics* (Westview Press, 1992).

the numbers.[6] In Silicon Valley alone, there are some 12,000 engineers of Chinese descent, while Chinese account for two out of every five engineering and science graduates in the University of California system.

42   Indeed, if one were to opt for "designer immigration" that would open the gates to peoples with the best cultural values, it is not at all clear that certain European countries would end up on top.

43   In the past decade, England's per-capita GNP has fallen behind Italy's, and threatens to displace Portugal and Greece at the bottom of the European Community heap by the end of the decade. Only a fifth of English young people receive any form of higher education, and despite Margaret Thatcher's best efforts, little progress has been made over the past generation in breaking down the stifling social rigidities of the British class system. The English working class is among the least well-educated, most state- and welfare-dependent and immobile of any in the developed world. While the British intelligentsia and upper classes continue to intimidate middle-class Americans, they can do so only on the basis of snobbery and inherited but rapidly dwindling intellectual capital. Paul Gigot may or may not be right that a million Zulus would work harder than a million English, but a million Taiwanese certainly would, and would bring with them much stronger family structures and entrepreneurship to boot.

IV

44 This is not to say that immigration will not be the source of major economic and social problems for the United States in the future. There are at least three areas of particular concern.

45   The first has to do with the effects of immigration on income distribution, particularly at the low end of the scale. The growing inequality of American income distribution over the past decade is not, as the Democrats asserted during the election campaign, the result of Reagan-Bush tax policies or the failure of "trickle-down" economics. Rather, it proceeds from the globalization of the American economy: low-skill labor increasingly has to compete with low-skill labor in Malaysia, Brazil, Mexico, and elsewhere. But it has also had to compete with low-skill immigrant labor coming into the country from the third world, which explains why Hispanics themselves tend to oppose further Hispanic immigration. The country as a whole may be better off economically as a result of this immigration, but those against whom immigrants directly compete have been hurt, just as they will be hurt by the North American Free Trade Agreement (NAFTA), the General Agreement on Tariffs and Trade (GATT), and other trade-liberalizing measures that are good for the country as a

---

[6] This same group of Asians appears also to have lowered verbal scores, though this is something that will presumably be corrected over time.

whole. In a city like Los Angeles, Hispanics with their stronger social ties have displaced blacks out of a variety of menial jobs, adding to the woes of an already troubled black community.

46 The second problem area has to do with the regional concentration of recent Hispanic immigration. As everyone knows, the 25 million Hispanics in the United States are not evenly distributed throughout the country, but are concentrated in the Southwest portion of it, where the problems normally accompanying the assimilation of immigrant communities tend to be magnified. The L.A. public-school system is currently in a state of breakdown, as it tries to educate burgeoning numbers of recent immigrants on a recession-starved budget.

47 The third problem concerns bilingualism and the elite Hispanic groups which promote and exist off of it. As noted earlier, the rank-and-file of the Hispanic community seems reasonably committed to assimilation; the same cannot be said for its leadership. Bilingualism, which initially began as a well-intentioned if misguided bridge toward learning English, has become in the eyes of many of its proponents a means of keeping alive a separate Spanish language and culture. Numerous studies have indicated that students in bilingual programs learn English less well than those without access to them, and that their enrollments are swelled by a large number of Hispanics who can already speak English perfectly well.[7] In cities with large Hispanic populations like New York and Los Angeles, the bilingual bureaucracy has become something of a monster, rigidly tracking students despite the wishes of parents and students. The *New York Times* recently reported the case of a Hispanic-surnamed child, born in the United States and speaking only English, who was forced by New York City officials to enroll in an English as a Second Language Class. Bilingualism is but one symptom of a much broader crisis in American public education, and admittedly makes the problems of assimilation much greater.

48 These problems can be tackled with specific changes in public policy. But the central issue raised by the immigration question is indeed a cultural one, and as such less susceptible of policy manipulation. The problem here is not the foreign culture that immigrants bring with them from the third world, but the contemporary elite culture of Americans—Americans like Kevin Costner, who believes that America began going downhill when the white man set foot here, or another American, Ice-T, whose family has probably been in the country longer than Costner's and who believes that women are bitches and that the chief enemy of his

---

[7] On this point, see Linda Chavez's *Out of the Barrio,* pp. 9–38.

generation is the police. In the upcoming block-by-block cultural war, the enemy will not speak Spanish or have a brown skin. In Pogo's words, "He is us."

Reading for Meaning

1. In his opening paragraph, Francis Fukuyama mentions Patrick Buchanan's idea that people in the United States need to "take back" their culture, which Buchanan feels is being overrun by non-European immigrants. What assumptions about both Europeans and non-Europeans lie behind Buchanan's statement? How does Fukuyama counter Buchanan's argument?

2. What cultural values do Patrick Buchanan and others attribute to Christian, Anglo-Saxon culture? How is this discussion of values relevant to Fukuyama's argument?

3. According to Fukuyama, what fears do conservatives have about Latino immigrants? What defenses does he offer in support of these immigrants? Do you think his evidence would convince his opponents? Why or why not?

4. What, for Fukuyama, caused the "breakdown of cultural values" that critics of immigration decry? Do you agree with Fukuyama's assessment? What cultural assumptions must Fukuyama himself make in order to argue his point?

5. What is Fukuyama's opinion of multiculturalism? How do you explain his position? What does he pose as an alternative to multiculturalism? What do you think of his proposal?

Comparing Cultures

Francis Fukuyama rejects the idea that "the American national identity" can be "linked to ethnicity or religion" (paragraph 9). At the same time he argues that the current focus on multiculturalism has replaced an effective system of assimilation that allowed numerous immigrant groups at the turn of the century to be absorbed by the "dominant Anglo-Saxon culture." Read the following excerpt from the article, "It's Not Just Anglo-Saxon" by Henry Louis Gates, Jr., W. E. B. Du Bois professor of humanities at Harvard University. In his essay, Gates defends a multicultural curriculum, especially at the university level. Select arguments from Gates' essay that respond to Fukuyama's ideas. Which arguments lie closest to your own thinking?

1   The cultural diversity movement arose partly because of the fragmentation of society by ethnicity, class, and gender. To make it the culprit for this fragmentation is to mistake effect for cause. A curriculum that reflects the achievement of the world's great cultures, not merely the West's, is not "politicized"; rather it situates the West as one of a community of civilizations. After all, culture is always a conversation among different voices.

2   To insist that we "master our own culture" before learning others—as Arthur Schlesinger Jr. has proposed—only defers the vexed question: What gets to count as "our" culture? What has passed as "common culture" has been an Anglo-American regional culture, masking itself as universal. Significantly different cultures sought refuge underground.

3   Writing in 1903, W. E. B. Du Bois expressed his dream of a high culture that would transcend the color line: "I sit with Shakespeare and he winces not." But the dream was not open to all. "Is this the life you grudge us," he concluded, "O knightly America?" For him, the humanities were a conduit into a republic of letters enabling escape from racism and ethnic chauvinism. Yet no one played a more crucial role than he in excavating the long buried heritage of Africans and African Americans.

4   The fact of one's ethnicity, for any American of color, is never neutral: One's public treatment, and public behavior, are shaped in large part by one's perceived ethnic identity, just as by one's gender. To demand that Americans shuck their cultural heritages and homogenize themselves into a "universal" WASP culture is to dream of an American in cultural white face, and that just won't do.

5   So it's only when we're free to explore the complexities of our hyphenated culture that we can discover what a genuinely common American culture might actually look like....

6   Our society won't survive without the values of tolerance, and cultural tolerance comes to nothing without cultural understanding. The challenge facing America will be the shaping of a truly common public culture, one responsive to the long-silenced cultures of color. If we relinquish the idea of America as a plural nation, we've abandoned the very experiment America represents. And that is too great a price to pay.

Ideas for Writing

1. Write a summary of the economic and cultural arguments against a more open immigration policy. Then either defend or criticize those arguments based on evidence from your own experience, observations, or reading.

2. What problems does Fukuyama associate with bilingual, bicultural education? Consult a few sources written by both critics and defenders of bilingual education. Evaluate the major defenses as well as criticisms of bilingual education in the United States. Come to you own conclusion based on your research.

3. Fukuyama argues that we have two choices in this country: we "force those coming to the country to absorb its language and rules" or "we carry respect for other cultures to the point that Americans no longer have a common voice with which to speak to one another." Might there be other alternatives to these two views?

4. Evaluate arguments by Patrick Buchanan, Peter Brimelow, and Francis Fukuyama on either the contributions to the culture or the harm done by recent immigrants to the United States. Which argument is the strongest of the three? Defend your choice.

Writing before Reading

Several writers have found phrases to describe the mixing of cultures in the United States, including "the melting pot," "a bouillabaisse," and "a stew." Which of these metaphors do you think is the most accurate in describing the cultural experience in the United States? Can you suggest any of your own?

LA CONCIENCIA DE LA MESTIZA: TOWARDS A NEW CONSCIOUSNESS
Gloria Anzaldúa

Gloria Anzaldúa is a feminist writer and cultural theorist. She is co-editor of This Bridge Called My Back: Writings by Radical Women of Color *(1991), which won the Before Columbus Foundation American Book Award. Anzaldúa is also editor of* Making Face, Making Soul/Haciendo Caras: Creative and Critical Perspective by Feminists of Color *(1990), winner of the Lambda Literary Best Small Book Press Award and has been a contributing editor of the magazine* Sinister Wisdom *since 1984. She has also published two bilingual children's books. Anzaldúa received the 1991 Lesbians Rights Award and the Sappho Award of Distinction in 1992. She has taught creative writing, Chicano Studies, and Feminist Studies at the University of Texas, the University of California at Santa Cruz, and Vermont College of Norwich University. In the following excerpt from her book,* Borderlands/La Frontera: The New Mestiza *(1987), she explores the meaning of her mixed Spanish and Indian heritage. Please note that the author's references appear at the end of the reading. Translations of phrases in Spanish appear at the bottom of the page.*

> *Por la mujer de mi raza hablará el espíritu.*[1a]

1. Jose Vasconcelos, Mexican philosopher, envisaged *una raza mestiza, una mezcla de razas afines, una raza de color—la primera raza síntesis del globo.*[b] He called it a cosmic race, *la raza cósmica,* a fifth race embracing the four major races of the world.[2] Opposite to the theory of the pure

---

[a] "For the woman of my race/ The spirit will speak."

[b] A mixed race, a mixture of related races, a people of color—the first racial synthesis on earth.

Aryan, and to the policy of racial purity that white America practices, his theory is one of inclusivity. At the confluence of two or more genetic streams, with chromosomes constantly "crossing over," this mixture of races, rather than resulting in an inferior being, provides hybrid progeny, a mutable, more malleable species with a rich gene pool. From this racial, ideological, cultural and biological cross-pollinization, an "alien" consciousness is presently in the making—a new *mestiza* consciousness, *una conciencia de mujer.* It is a consciousness of the Borderlands.

UNA LUCHA DE FRONTERAS / A STRUGGLE OF BORDERS

Because I, a *mestiza,*
continually walk out of one culture
and into another,
because I am in all cultures at the same time,
*alma entre dos mundos, tres, cuatro,
me zumba la cabeza con lo contradictorio.
Estoy norteada por todas las voces que me hablan
simultáneamente.*[c]

2   The ambivalence from the clash of voices results in mental and emotional states of perplexity. Internal strife results in insecurity and indecisiveness. The *mestiza's* dual or multiple personality is plagued by psychic restlessness.

3   In a constant state of mental nepantilism, an Aztec word meaning torn between ways, *la mestiza* is a product of the transfer of the cultural and spiritual values of one group to another. Being tricultural, monolingual, bilingual, or multilingual, speaking a patois, and in a state of perpetual transition, the *mestiza* faces the dilemma of the mixed breed: Which collectivity does the daughter of a darkskinned mother listen to?

4   *El choque de un alma atrapado entre el mundo del espíritu y el mundo de la técnica a veces la deja entullada.*[d] Cradled in one culture, sandwiched between two cultures, straddling all three cultures and their value systems, *la mestiza* undergoes a struggle of flesh, a struggle of borders, an inner war. Like all people, we perceive the version of reality that our culture communicates. Like others having or living in more than one culture, we get multiple, often opposing messages. The coming together of two self-consistent but habitually incompatible frames of reference[3] causes *un choque,* a cultural collision.

5   Within us and within *la cultura chicana,*[e] commonly held beliefs of the white culture attack commonly held beliefs of the Mexican culture, and both attack commonly held beliefs of the indigenous culture.

---

[c] Soul between two, three, four worlds, / my head buzzes with contradictions / I am oriented by all the voices that speak to me at once.

[d] The collision of a soul trapped between the world of spirit and the world of technology at times leaves her wounded.

[e] The chicana culture.

Subconsciously, we see an attack on ourselves and our beliefs as a threat and we attempt to block with a counterstance.

6   But it is not enough to stand on the opposite river bank, shouting questions, challenging patriarchal, white conventions. A counterstance locks one into a duel of oppressor and oppressed; locked in mortal combat, like the cop and the criminal, both are reduced to a common denominator of violence. The counterstance refutes the dominant culture's views and beliefs, and, for this, it is proudly defiant. All reaction is limited by, and dependent on, what it is reacting against. Because the counterstance stems from a problem with authority—outer as well as inner—it's a step towards liberation from cultural domination. But it is not a way of life. At some point, on our way to a new consciousness, we will have to leave the opposite bank, the split between the two mortal combatants somehow healed so that we are on both shores at once and, at once, see through serpent and eagle eyes. Or perhaps we will decide to disengage from the dominant culture, write it off altogether as a lost cause, and cross the border into a wholly new and separate territory. Or we might go another route. The possibilities are numerous once we decide to act and not react.

A Tolerance for Ambiguity

7   These numerous possibilities leave *la mestiza* floundering in uncharted seas. In perceiving conflicting information and points of view, she is subjected to a swamping of her psychological borders. She has discovered that she can't hold concepts or ideas in rigid boundaries. The borders and walls that are supposed to keep the undesirable ideas out are entrenched habits and patterns of behavior; these habits and patterns are the enemy within. Rigidity means death. Only by remaining flexible is she able to stretch the psyche horizontally and vertically. *La mestiza* constantly has to shift out of habitual formations; from convergent thinking, analytical reasoning that tends to use rationality to move toward a single goal (a Western mode), to divergent thinking,[4] characterized by movement away from set patterns and goals and toward a more whole perspective, one that includes rather than excludes.

8   The new *mestiza* copes by developing a tolerance for contradictions, a tolerance for ambiguity. She learns to be an Indian in Mexican culture, to be Mexican from an Anglo point of view. She learns to juggle cultures. She has a plural personality, she operates in a pluralistic mode—nothing is thrust out, the good the bad and the ugly, nothing rejected, nothing abandoned. Not only does she sustain contradictions, she turns the ambivalence into something else.

9   She can be jarred out of ambivalence by an intense, and often painful, emotional event which inverts or resolves the ambivalence. I'm not sure exactly how. The work takes place underground—subconsciously. It is work that the soul performs. That focal point or fulcrum, that juncture where the mestiza stands, is where phenomena tend to collide.

It is where the possibility of uniting all that is separate occurs. This assembly is not one where severed or separated pieces merely come together. Nor is it a balancing of opposing powers. In attempting to work out a synthesis, the self has added a third element which is greater then the sum of its severed parts. That third element is a new consciousness—a mestiza consciousness—and though it is a source of intense pain, its energy comes from continual creative motion that keeps breaking down the unitary aspect of each new paradigm.

10   *En unas pocas centurias,*[f] the future will belong to the mestiza. Because the future depends on the breaking down of paradigms, it depends on the straddling of two or more cultures. By creating a new mythos—that is, a change in the way we perceive reality, the way we see ourselves, and the ways we behave—*la mestiza* creates a new consciousness.

11   The work of *mestiza* consciousness is to break down the subject-object duality that keeps her a prisoner and to show in the flesh and through the images in her work how duality is transcended. The answer to the problem between the white race and the colored, between males and females, lies in healing the split that originates in the very foundation of our lives, our culture, our languages, our thoughts. A massive uprooting of dualistic thinking in the individual and collective consciousness is the beginning of a long struggle, but one that could, in our best hopes, bring us to the end of rape, of violence, of war.

La encrucijada / The Crossroads

A chicken is being sacrificed
   at a crossroads, a simple mound of earth
a mud shrine for *Eshu,*
   Yoruba god of indeterminacy,
who blesses her choice of path.
   She begins her journey.

12   *Su cuerpo es una bocacalle.*[g] *La mestiza* has gone from being the sacrificial goat to becoming the officiating priestess at the crossroads.

13   As a *mestiza* I have no country, my homeland cast me out; yet all countries are mine because I am every woman's sister or potential lover. (As a lesbian I have no race, my own people disclaim me; but I am all races because there is the queer of me in all races.) I am cultureless because, as a feminist, I challenge the collective cultural/religious male-derived beliefs of Indo-Hispanics and Anglos; yet I am cultured because I am participating in the creation of yet another culture, a new story to explain the

---

[f] In a few centuries.
[g] Her body is a crossroads.

world and our participation in it, a new value system with images and symbols that connect us to each other and to the planet. *Soy un amasamiento,* I am an act of kneading, of uniting and joining that not only has produced both a creature of darkness and a creature of light, but also a creature that questions the definitions of light and dark and gives them new meanings.

14   We are the people who leap in the dark, we are the people on the knees of the gods. In our very flesh, [r]evolution works out the clash of cultures. It makes us crazy constantly, but if the center holds, we've made some kind of evolutionary step forward. *Nuestra alma el trabajo,*[h] the opus, the great alchemical work; spiritual *mestizaje,* a "morphogenesis,"[5] an inevitable unfolding. We have become the quickening serpent movement.

15   Indigenous like corn, like corn, the *mestiza* is a product of crossbreeding, designed for preservation under a variety of conditions. Like an ear of corn—a female seed-bearing organ—the *mestiza* is tenacious, tightly wrapped in the husks of her culture. Like kernels she clings to the cob; with thick stalks and strong brace roots, she holds tight to the earth—she will survive the crossroads. . . .

El camino de la mestiza / The Mestiza Way

16   Caught between the sudden contraction, the breath sucked in and the endless space, the brown woman stands still, looks at the sky. She decides to go down, digging her way along the roots of trees. Sifting through the bones, she shakes them to see if there is any marrow in them. Then, touching the dirt to her forehead, to her tongue, she takes a few bones, leaves the rest in their burial place.

She goes through her backpack, keeps her journal and address book, throws away the muni-bart metromaps. The coins are heavy and they go next, then the greenbacks flutter through the air. She keeps her knife, can opener and eyebrow pencil. She puts bones, pieces of bark, *hierbas,* eagle feather, snakeskin, tape recorder, the rattle and drum in her pack and she sets out to become the complete *tolteca.*

17   Her first step is to take inventory. *Despojando, desgranando, quitando paja.*[i] Just what did she inherit from her ancestors? This weight on her back—which is the baggage from the Indian mother, which the baggage from the Spanish father, which the baggage from the Anglo?

18   *Pero es difícil* differentiating between *lo heredado, lo adquirido, lo impuesto.*[j] She puts history through a sieve, winnows out the lies, looks at

---

[h] Our soul [is] the work.
[i] Plundering, threshing, separating chaff.
[j] But it is difficult [differentiating between] what is inherited, what acquired, and what imposed.

the forces that we as a race, as women, have been a part of. *Luego bota lo que no vale, los desmientos, los desencuentos, el embrutecimiento. Aguarda el juicio, hondo y enraízado, de la gente antigua.*[k] This step is a conscious rupture with all oppressive traditions of all cultures and religions. She communicates that rupture, documents the struggle. She reinterprets history and, using new symbols, she shapes new myths. She adopts new perspectives toward the darkskinned, women and queers. She strengthens her tolerance (and intolerance) for ambiguity. She is willing to share, to make herself vulnerable to foreign ways of seeing and thinking. She surrenders all notions of safety, of the familiar. Deconstruct, construct. She becomes a *nahual*, able to transform herself into a tree, a coyote, into another person. She learns to transform the small "I" into the total Self. *Se hace moldeadora de su alma. Según la concepción que tiene de sí misma, así será.*[l]

QUE NO SE NOS OLVIDE LOS HOMBRES[m]

"Tú no sirves pa' nada—
you're good for nothing.
Eres pura vieja."

19 "You're nothing but a woman" means you are defective. Its opposite is to be *un macho*. The modern meaning of the word "machismo," as well as the concept, is actually an Anglo invention. For men like my father, being "macho" meant being strong enough to protect and support my mother and us, yet being able to show love. Today's macho has doubts about his ability to feed and protect his family. His "machismo" is an adaptation to oppression and poverty and low self-esteem. It is the result of hierarchical male dominance. The Anglo, feeling inadequate and inferior and powerless, displaces or transfers these feelings to the Chicano by shaming him. In the Gringo world, the Chicano suffers from excessive humility and self-effacement, shame of self and self-deprecation. Around Latinos he suffers from a sense of language inadequacy and its accompanying discomfort; with Native Americans he suffers from a racial amnesia which ignores our common blood, and from guilt because the Spanish part of him took their land and oppressed them. He has an excessive compensatory hubris when around Mexicans from the other side. It overlays a deep sense of racial shame.

20 The loss of a sense of dignity and respect in the macho breeds a false machismo which leads him to put down women and even to brutalize

---

[k] Later she tosses away whatever is worthless, things false, fake, stupifying. She waits for judgment, deep and entwined, of the ancient people.

[l] She has been shaped by her soul. According to the conception she has of herself, so will she be.

[m] Let us not forget men.

them. Coexisting with his sexist behavior is a love for the mother which takes precedence over that of all others. Devoted son, macho pig. To wash down the shame of his acts, of his very being, and to handle the brute in the mirror, he takes to the bottle, the snort, the needle, and the fist.

21 Though we "understand" the root causes of male hatred and fear, and the subsequent wounding of women, we do not excuse, we do not condone, and we will no longer put up with it. From the men of our race, we demand the admission/acknowledgment/disclosure/testimony that they wound us, violate us, are afraid of us and of our power. We need them to say they will begin to eliminate their hurtful put-down ways. But more than the words, we demand acts. We say to them: We will develop equal power with you and those who have shamed us.

22 It is imperative that mestizas support each other in changing the sexist elements in the Mexican Indian culture. As long as woman is put down, the Indian and the Black in all of us is put down. The struggle of the mestiza is above all a feminist one. As long as *los hombres* think they have to *chingar mujeres*[n] and each other to be men, as long as men are taught that they are superior and therefore culturally favored over *la mujer,* as long as to be a *vieja* is a thing of derision, there can be no real healing of our psyches. We're halfway there—we have such love of the Mother, the good mother. The first step is to unlearn the *puta/virgen*[o] dichotomy and to see *Coatlapopeuh-Coatlicue* in the Mother, *Guadalupe.*

23 Tenderness, a sign of vulnerability, is so feared that it is showered on women with verbal abuse and blows. Men, even more than women, are fettered to gender roles. Women at least have had the guts to break out of bondage. Only gay men have had the courage to expose themselves to the woman inside them and to challenge the current masculinity. I've encountered a few scattered and isolated gentle straight men, the beginnings of a new breed, but they are confused, and entangled with sexist behaviors that they have not been able to eradicate. We need a new masculinity and the new man needs a movement.

24 Lumping the males who deviate from the general norm with man, the oppressor, is a gross injustice. *Asombra pensar que nos hemos quedado en ese pozo oscuro donde el mundo encierra a las lesbianas. Asombra pensar que hemos, como feministas y lesbianas, cerrado nuestros corazónes a los hombres, a nuestros hermanos los jotos, desheredados y marginales como nosotros.*[p] Being the supreme crossers of cultures, homosexuals have

---

[n] "Screw" women.

[o] Whore/virgin.

[p] It is frightening to think that we have stayed in this dark pit where the world defines lesbians. It is frightening to think that we have, as feminists and lesbians, closed our hearts to men, to our fellow gays disinherited and marginalized like us.

strong bonds with the queer white, Black, Asian, Native American, Latino, and with the queer in Italy, Australia and the rest of the planet. We come from all colors, all classes, all races, all time periods. Our role is to link people with each other—the Blacks with Jews with Indians with Asians with whites with extraterrestrials. It is to transfer ideas and information from one culture to another. Colored homosexuals have more knowledge of other cultures; have always been at the forefront (although sometimes in the closet) of all liberation struggles in this country; have suffered more injustices and have survived them despite all odds. Chicanos need to acknowledge the political and artistic contributions of their queer. People, listen to what your *jotería*[q] is saying.

25 The mestizo and the queer exist at this time and point on the evolutionary continuum for a purpose. We are a blending that proves that all blood is intricately woven together, and that we are spawned out of similar souls.

Somos una gente

Hay tantísimas fronteras
que dividen a la gente,
pero por cada frontera
existe también un puente.
        —Gina Valdés[6r]

26 **Divided Loyalties.** Many women and men of color do not want to have any dealings with white people. It takes too much time and energy to explain to the downwardly mobile, white middle-class women that it's okay for us to want to own "possessions," never having had any nice furniture on our dirt floors or "luxuries" like washing machines. Many feel that whites should help their own people rid themselves of race hatred and fear first. I, for one, choose to use some of my energy to serve as mediator. I think we need to allow whites to be our allies. Through our literature, art, *corridos*,[s] and folktales we must share our history with them so when they set up committees to help Big Mountain Navajos or the Chicano farmworkers or *los Nicaragüenses*[t] they won't turn people away because of their racial fears and ignorances. They will come to see that they are not helping us but following our lead.

27 Individually, but also as a racial entity, we need to voice our needs. We need to say to white society: We need you to accept the fact that Chi-

---

[q] Gay women.

[r] We are one people.
There are so many borders / that separate people / but for each frontier / a bridge also exists.

[s] Short for bullfights.

[t] Nicaraguans.

canos are different, to acknowledge your rejection and negation of us. We need you to own the fact that you looked upon us as less than human, that you stole our lands, our personhood, our self-respect. We need you to make public restitution: to say that, to compensate for your own sense of defectiveness, you strive for power over us, you erase our history and our experience because it makes you feel guilty—you'd rather forget your brutish acts. To say you've split yourself from minority groups, that you disown us, that your dual consciousness splits off parts of yourself, transferring the "negative" parts onto us. (Where there is persecution of minorities, there is shadow projection. Where there is violence and war, there is repression of shadow.) To say that you are afraid of us, that to put distance between us, you wear the mask of contempt. Admit that Mexico is your double, that she exists in the shadow of this country, that we are irrevocably tied to her. Gringo, accept the doppelganger in your psyche. By taking back your collective shadow the intracultural split will heal. And finally, tell us what you need from us.

BY YOUR TRUE FACES WE WILL KNOW YOU

28   I am visible—see this Indian face—yet I am invisible. I both blind them with my beak nose and am their blind spot. But I exist, we exist. They'd like to think I have melted in the pot. But I haven't, we haven't.

29   The dominant white culture is killing us slowly with its ignorance. By taking away our self-determination, it has made us weak and empty. As a people we have resisted and we have taken expedient positions, but we have never been allowed to develop unencumbered—we have never been allowed to be fully ourselves. The whites in power want us people of color to barricade ourselves behind our separate tribal walls so they can pick us off one at a time with their hidden weapons; so they can whitewash and distort history. Ignorance splits people, creates prejudices. A misinformed people is a subjugated people.

30   Before the Chicano and the undocumented worker and the Mexican from the other side can come together, before the Chicano can have unity with Native Americans and other groups, we need to know the history of their struggle and they need to know ours. Our mothers, our sisters and brothers, the guys who hang out on street corners, the children in the playgrounds, each of us must know our Indian lineage, our afro-*mestisaje*, our history of resistance.

31   To the immigrant *mexicano* and the recent arrivals we must teach our history. The 80 million *mexicanos* and the Latinos from Central and South America must know of our struggles. Each one of us must know basic facts about Nicaragua, Chile and the rest of Latin America. The Latinoist movement (Chicanos, Puerto Ricans, Cubans and other Spanish-speaking people working together to combat racial discrimination in the market place) is good but it is not enough. Other than a common culture

we will have nothing to hold us together. We need to meet on a broader communal ground.

32 The struggle is inner: Chicano, *indio,* American Indian, *mojado, mexicano,* immigrant Latino, Anglo in power, working class Anglo, Black, Asian—our psyches resemble the bordertowns and are populated by the same people. The struggle has always been inner, and is played out in the outer terrains. Awareness of our situation must come before inner changes, which in turn come before changes in society. Nothing happens in the "real" world unless it first happens in the images of our heads.

El día de la Chicana

I will not be shamed again
Nor will I shame myself.

33 I am possessed by a vision: that we Chicanas and Chicanos have taken back or uncovered our true faces, our dignity and self-respect. It's a validation vision.

34 Seeing the Chicana anew in light of her history. I seek an exoneration, a seeing through the fictions of white supremacy, a seeing of ourselves in our true guises and not as the false racial personality that has been given to us and that we have given to ourselves. I seek our woman's face, our true features, the positive and the negative seen clearly, free of the tainted biases of male dominance. I seek new images of identity, new beliefs about ourselves, our humanity and worth no longer in question.

35 *Estamos viviendo en la noche de la Raza, un tiempo cuando el trabajo se hace a lo quieto, en el oscuro. El día cuando aceptamos tal y como somos y para en donde vamos y porque—ese día será el día de la Raza. Yo tengo el conpromiso de expresar mi visión, mi sensibilidad, mi percepción de la revalidación de la gente mexicana, su mérito, estimación, honra, aprecio, y validez.*[u]

36 On December 2nd when my sun goes into my first house, I celebrate *el día de la Chicana y el Chicano.* On that day I clean my altars, light my *Coatlalopeuh* candle, burn sage and copal, take *el baño para espantar basura,*[v] sweep my house. On that day I bare my soul, make myself vulnerable to

---

[u] We are living in the night of the Raza, a time when work takes place in silence, in darkness. The day when we accept what and how we are and where we are going and why—this day will be the day of the Raza. I have promised to express my vision, my sensibility, my perception of the revalidation of the Mexican people, their merit, esteem, honor, and value.

[v] A bath for scaring away trash.

37   On that day I look inside our conflicts and our basic introverted racial temperament. I identify our needs, voice them. I acknowledge that the self and the race have been wounded. I recognize the need to take care of our personhood, of our racial self. On that day I gather the splintered and disowned parts of *la gente mexicana* and hold them in my arms. *Todas las partes de nosotros valen.*[w]

38   On that day I say, "Yes, all you people wound us when you reject us. Rejection strips us of self-worth; our vulnerability exposes us to shame. It is our innate identity you find wanting. We are ashamed that we need your good opinion, that we need your acceptance. We can no longer camouflage our needs, can no longer let defenses and fences sprout around us. We can no longer withdraw. To rage and look upon you with contempt is to rage and be contemptuous of ourselves. We can no longer blame you, nor disown the white parts, the male parts, the pathological parts, the queer parts, the vulnerable parts. Here we are weaponless with open arms, with only our magic. Let's try it our way, the mestiza way, the Chicana way, the woman way.

39   On that day, I search for our essential dignity as a people, a people with a sense of purpose—to belong and contribute to something greater than our *pueblo*. On that day I seek to recover and reshape my spiritual identity. *Anímatei Raza, a celebrar el día de la Chicana.*[x]

El retorno

All movements are accomplished in six stages,
and the seventh brings return.
                                    —I Ching[7]

*Tanto tiempo sin verte casa mía,
mi cuna, mi hondo nido de la huerta.*
                                    —"*Soledad*"[8][y]

40   I stand at the river, watch the curving, twisting serpent, a serpent nailed to the fence where the mouth of the Rio Grande empties into the Gulf.

41   I have come back. *Tanto dolor me costó el alejamiento.*[z] I shade my eyes and look up. The bone beak of a hawk slowly circling over me, checking me out as potential carrion. In its wake a little bird flickering its wings, swimming sporadically like a fish. In the distance the expressway and the

---

[w] Each part of us has value.

[x] Take heart! Raza, and celebrate the day of the Chicana.

[y] So much time without seeing you, my home, / my cradle, my deep garden home. "Solitude."

[z] Leaving caused me such sorrow.

slough of traffic like an irritated sow. The sudden pull in my gut, *la tierra, los aguaceros*. My land, *el viento soplando la arena, el lagartijo debajo de un nopalito. Me acuerdo como era antes. Una región desértica de vasta llanuras, costeras de baja altura, de escasa lluvia, de chaparrales formados por mesquites y huizaches.*[aa] If I look real hard I can almost see the Spanish fathers who were called "the cavalry of Christ" enter this valley riding their burros, see the clash of cultures commence.

42   *Tierra natal.* This is home, the small towns in the Valley, *los pueblitos* with chicken pens and goats picketed to mesquite shrubs. *En las colonias* on the other side of the tracks, junk cars line the front yards of hot pink and lavender-trimmed houses—Chicano architecture we call it, self-consciously. I have missed the TV shows where hosts speak in half and half, and where awards are given in the category of Tex-Mex music. I have missed the Mexican cemeteries blooming with artificial flowers, the fields of aloe vera and red pepper, rows of sugar cane, of corn hanging on the stalks, the cloud of *polvareda* in the dirt roads behind a speeding pickup truck, *el sabor de tamales de rez y venado*. I have missed *la yegua colorada*[bb] gnawing the wooden gate of her stall, the smell of horse flesh from Carito's corrals. *He hecho menos las noches calientes sin aire, noches de linternas y lechuzas*[cc] making holes in the night.

43   I still feel the old despair when I look at the unpainted, dilapidated, scrap lumber houses consisting mostly of corrugated aluminum. Some of the poorest people in the United States live in the Lower Rio Grande Valley, an arid and semi-arid land of irrigated farming, intense sunlight and heat, citrus groves next to chaparral and cactus. I walk through the elementary school I attended so long ago, that remained segregated until recently. I remember how the white teachers used to punish us for being Mexican.

44   How I love this tragic valley of South Texas, as Ricardo Sánchez calls it; this borderland between the Nueces and the Rio Grande. This land has survived possession and ill-use by five countries: Spain, Mexico, the Republic of Texas, the United States, the Confederacy, and the United States again. It has survived Anglo-Mexican blood feuds, lynchings, burnings, rapes, pillage.

45   Today I see the Valley still struggling to survive. Whether it does or not, it will never be as I remember it. The borderlands depression that was

---

[aa] The land, the rains ... the wind blowing sand, the small lizard under the cactus. I remember how it was before. A deserted region of vast plains, low hills, little rain, chaparrals of mesquite and *huizaches*.

[bb] Native land ... the villages ... [cloud of] dust ... the smell of tamales made of rice and venison. [I have missed] the red mare.

[cc] I have missed hot nights without air, nights with lanterns and owls [making holes in the night].

set off by the 1982 peso devaluation in Mexico resulted in the closure of hundreds of Valley businesses. Many people lost their homes, cars, land. Prior to 1982, U.S. store owners thrived on retail sales to Mexicans who came across the border for groceries and clothes and appliances. While goods on the U.S. side have become 10, 100, and 1000 times more expensive for Mexican buyers, goods on the Mexican side have become 10, 100, 1000 times cheaper for Americans. Because the Valley is heavily dependent on agriculture and Mexican retail trade, it has the highest unemployment rates along the entire border region; it is the Valley that has been hardest hit.[9]

46 "It's been a bad year for corn," my brother, Nune, says. As he talks, I remember my father scanning the sky for a rain that would end the drought, looking up into the sky, day after day, while the corn withered on its stalk. My father has been dead for 29 years, having worked himself to death. The life span of a Mexican farm laborer is 56—he lived to be 38. It shocks me that I am older than he. I, too, search the sky for rain. Like the ancients, I worship the rain god and the maize goddess, but unlike my father I have recovered their names. Now for rain (irrigation) one offers not a sacrifice of blood, but of money.

47 "Farming is in a bad way," my brother says. "Two to three thousand small and big farmers went bankrupt in this country last year. Six years ago the price of corn was $8.00 per hundred pounds," he goes on. "This year it is $3.90 per hundred pounds." And, I think to myself, after taking inflation into account, not planting anything puts you ahead.

48 I walk out to the back yard, stare at *los rosales de mamá*. She wants me to help her prune the rose bushes, dig out the carpet grass that is choking them. *Mamagrande Ramona también tenía rosales.*[dd] Here every Mexican grows flowers. If they don't have a piece of dirt, they use car tires, jars, cans, shoe boxes. Roses are the Mexican's favorite flower. I think, how symbolic—thorns and all.

49 Yes, the Chicano and Chicana have always taken care of growing things and the land. Again I see the four of us kids getting off the school bus, changing into our work clothes, walking into the field with Papí and Mamí, all six of us bending to the ground. Below our feet, under the earth lie the watermelon seeds. We cover them with paper plates, putting *terremotes*[ee] on top of the plates to keep them from being blown away by the wind. The paper plates keep the freeze away. Next day or the next, we remove the plates, bare the tiny green shoots to the elements. They survive and grow, give fruit hundreds of times the size of the seed. We water them and hoe them. We harvest them. The vines dry, rot, are plowed

---

[dd] Mama's roses. . . . Big Mama Ramona also has roses.
[ee] Earthquakes.

under. Growth, death, decay, birth. The soil prepared again and again, impregnated, worked on. A constant changing of forms, *renacimientos de la tierra madre.*[ff]

> This land was Mexican once
> was Indian always
> and is.
> And will be again.

REFERENCES

1. This is my own "take off" on Jose Vasconcelos' idea. Jose Vasconcelos, *La Raza Cósmica: Misión de la Raza Ibero-Americana* (México: Aguilar S.A. de Ediciones, 1961).
2. Vasconcelos.
3. Arthur Koestler terms this "bisociation." Albert Rothenberg, *The Creative Process in Art, Science, and Other Fields* (Chicago, IL: University of Chicago Press, 1979), 12.
4. In part, I derive my definitions for "convergent" and "divergent" thinking from Rothenberg, 12–13.
5. To borrow chemist Ilya Prigogine's theory of "dissipative structures." Prigogine discovered that substances interact not in predictable ways as it was taught in science, but in different and fluctuating ways to produce new and more complex structures, a kind of birth he called "morphogenesis," which created unpredictable innovations. Harold Gilliam, "Searching for a New World View," *This World* (January, 1981), 23.
6. Gina Valdés, *Puentes y Fronteras: Coplas Chicanas* (Los Angeles, CA: Castle Lithograph, 1982), 2.
7. Richard Wilhelm, *The I Ching or Book of Changes,* trans. Cary F. Baynes (Princeton, NJ: Princeton University Press, 1950), 98.
8. "Soledad" is sung by the group, Haciendo Punto en Otro Son.
9. Out of the twenty-two border counties in the four border states, Hidalgo County (named for Father Hidalgo who was shot in 1810 after instigating Mexico's revolt against Spanish rule under the banner of *la Virgen de Guadalupe*) is the most poverty-stricken county in the nation as well as the largest home base (along with Imperial in California) for migrant farmworkers. It was here that I was born and raised. I am amazed that both it and I have survived.

Reading for Meaning

1. What are some of the paradoxes that Gloria Anzaldúa mentions as inherent parts of her identity? Are there contradictory things about you?

[ff] Rebirth of mother earth.

2. How does Anzaldúa define the new *mestiza* consciousness? What purpose does she think this consciousness might serve?

3. Anzaldúa calls for moving beyond defiance of the oppressive Anglo-European culture. As cathartic as this combative approach might be, what limitation does it pose in Anzaldúa's view (paragraphs 5 and 6)?

4. What alternatives does Anzaldúa propose for replacing open rage and contempt? How successful do you think they might be?

5. Anzaldúa calls for a new male consciousness as well as a new consciousness for women. Why is it important to create a new sense of what it is to be male? What should this new male be like according to Anzaldúa? Do you agree with her suggestions?

6. Gloria Anzaldúa makes a plea for greater unity and identification among Latino peoples and adds, "We need to meet on a broader communal ground" than that of the coalitions of ethnic peoples who come together for a particular occasion. What, exactly, is she hoping for? What is that "broader communal ground" she envisions?

7. Describe the way Anzaldúa organizes ideas in her essay. How effective is this arrangement?

Comparing Texts

1. In the section of her essay called "*Que no se nos olvide los hombres* (Let us not forget men)," Anzaldúa discusses the macho Chicano male. Compare her discussion of *machismo* males to Octavio Paz's portrait of the Mexican man in "Mexican Masks," page 303.

2. Compare the benefits and drawbacks that Gloria Anzaldúa, Salman Rushdie, or Jenefer Shute find in being a product of several cultures. What do these writers think of the idea that they are outsiders? What alternative views of themselves do they offer?

Ideas for Writing

1. In "The Mestiza Way," one of the sections in "Towards a New Consciousness" Gloria Anzaldúa describes stages in the symbolic journey of the *mestiza* woman. Identify a few of the stages and discuss their importance.

2. Anzaldúa calls for the remaking of male consciousness. Summarize her descriptions of the old male way of thinking that she feels must be changed radically. Then discuss whether the old-style male or the changed male best describes men you know.

3. Identify characteristics of Anzaldúa's writing style or the way she presents her arguments in "*La Conciencia de la Mestiza:* Towards a New Consciousness." How does each characteristic convey her ideas or serve a larger purpose in the essay? What difficulties might her writing pose for a reader?

CHAPTER 11
THE ARTIST IN SOCIETY

First Thoughts

eeste indruk

První dojmy

When power leads man to arrogance, poetry reminds him of his limitations. When power narrows the area of man's concern, poetry reminds him of the richness and diversity of his existence. When power corrupts, poetry cleanses.

President John F. Kennedy
October 26, 1963
Dedication of the Robert Frost Library, Amherst College

(Plato) "We have seen that there are three sorts of bed. The first exists in the ultimate nature of things, and if it was made by anyone it must, I suppose, have been made by God. The second is made by the carpenter, the third by the painter."
(Glaucon) "Yes, that is so. . . . "
(Plato) "Then the artist's representation stands at third remove from reality?"
(Glaucon) "It does."
(Plato) "So the tragic poet, whose art is representation, is third in succession to the throne of truth; and the same is true of all other artists. . . . The artist's representation is a long way removed from truth, and he is able to reproduce everything because he never penetrates beneath the superficial appearance of anything."

Plato
"Theory of Art," *The Republic*
c. 380 B.C.E.

Art has been a valid expression of human concerns and the symbol of the material and aesthetic achievement of civilizations since the time of the pharaohs of ancient Egypt. Ornate vases, elaborate jewelry, and impressive pyramids characterize the more advanced civilizations while the simple beauty of the drawings in the caves at Altamira, Spain, record the human need to depict, in an enduring and aesthetic form, beasts on which we depend as well as supernatural forces that control our lives.

In ancient times, the artist was regarded as a craftsman, and the word *ars,* the Latin derivation of "art," means "skill." The Greek philosopher Plato thought very little of artists and placed them well below craftsmen on the social scale. Given that material objects are imitations of an ideal or transcendent model in the universal mind *(nous),* the artist's work is inferior to that of the craftsman because his work is an imitation of an imitation. Moreover, when Plato defined the role of the artist in his ideal republic, he warned that artists and writers undermine society unless their work is limited to depictions of national heroes and praise of the country's achievements. In more recent times, we have learned to distinguish the craftsman's work from that of the creative artist, whose paintings, sculpture, architecture, photography, and film translate an imagined reality rather than a poor imitation of things in the world. Questions about the value of art, the alienation of the artist, and the experimental nature of most modern art give special complexity to art produced in the twentieth century.

The writers in this chapter offer a variety of views of the artist and the artist's work. André Brink's discussion of "The Artist as Insect" examines the roles that artists can play in cultures that are making the transition from dictatorship to democratic government. Initially, the artist expresses the suffering and grievances of an oppressed people. As the people gain a measure of freedom and self-determination, the artist becomes a "composite insect," an image Brink creates from various fictional sources. For Brink, the artist is most important when he or she shows us new ways to look at ourselves and our lives, and pushes us toward new visions and new meaning. Audre Lorde focuses on the personal struggle of the writer who must write about her experiences regardless of how painful they might be or how greatly she fears being hurt or misjudged. She compares the writer to a warrior who must fight against "the tyrannies of silence." Franz Kafka's "A Hunger Artist" is a fable about an artist who has mastered the art of fasting. The story explores the artist's connection to his art and to the audiences who try in various ways to understand him. In "The Power of Image and Place," Jane M. Young discusses the meaning of art in the Zuni culture. Art has a religious function for the Zuni people, and when rituals are done properly, it is possible to invoke the power of the insects, deer, and other animals depicted in petroglyphic images. Anthropologist Connie Stevens writes about the importance of storytelling as a source of identity and power for Islamic women in the Hausa culture of north Africa.

Writing before Reading

In your experience, what are the things that give life meaning? How might that meaning be expressed?

THE ARTIST AS INSECT
André Brink

André Brink is a South African novelist who writes in English and Afrikaans, the language of the Afrikaner population (formerly called Boers). His novel Looking on Darkness *(1973) was the first work in the Afrikaans language to face the problems of apartheid. It was also the first book banned in that language. He is the author of several other novels, including* A Dry White Season *(1979) and* An Act of Terror *(1991). Brink's books were banned in South Africa from 1970 until the end of apartheid in the early 1990s.* Imaginings of Sand *(1996) was his first novel in twenty years to be published without being censored by South African authorities. In "The Artist as Insect," an essay published in the November 1992 edition of the* UNESCO Courier, *Brink examines the importance of the writer in a country's transition from a totalitarian state to a democracy.*

Facts about South Africa

The Afrikaner people make up roughly 8 percent of the total South African population. Indigenous black Africans comprise 74 percent, people of mixed race account for 9 percent, other whites make up 6 percent, and Asians 3 percent. The Afrikaners are descendants of the Dutch Protestants and French Huguenots who, in the seventeenth century, settled in what is now the Cape Town area of South Africa. They fought native peoples and British colonists in the eighteenth and nineteenth centuries and eventually established two independent countries, the Transvaal (1852) and the Orange Free State (1854). They were defeated by the British at the beginning of the twentieth century and did not return to power until the Afrikaner National Party won national elections in 1948. The party instituted the apartheid system that remained in place for the next forty years. For additional facts about South Africa, see page 422.

1   In this age of violence and strife, terrorism and famine, multinational corporations and global power alliances, we have understandably

abandoned Shelley's romantic faith in poets as the unacknowledged legislators of the world. Yet there is reason to believe that without the poet, the intellectual, the artist, the creator, life might be even worse.

2   If it is always prudent to remind ourselves that no single society in the world dares call itself totally free or totally democratic, I am mainly concerned here with those societies which, having emerged only recently from various forms of absolutism and political oppression, are now groping towards definitions of democracy and freedom of which, as in Czechoslovakia or Germany, they have been deprived for a long time or which, as in the case of South Africa, they have never known.

3   The territory of the intellectual and the creator is culture: it is that territory in which the private and the public interact in order to transform the raw matter of experience into meaning. No wonder that, in a state of oppression, culture should function in particularly intense ways. For decades, *samizdat* in Central Europe has provided a vibrant and electrically charged cultural experience. In Chile, when no other forms of protest were allowed by the Pinochet regime, illiterate washerwomen began to record, in embroidery and weaving and appliqué, the passionate experiences of an entire generation otherwise doomed to oblivion. In a South African dehumanized by apartheid, when successive States of Emergency virtually smothered overt resistance, when children were killed and women maimed and men blown up by parcel bombs, a veritable explosion in the arts—in dance and music, in photography and painting and sculpture, in poetry and the theatre—ensured that the oppressed black masses were activated in solidarity and awareness, and that even the conscience of a white ruling minority was ceaselessly assailed and provoked into a discovery of what was really happening behind the façades of official lies, distortions and half-truths. Even on the basic level of disseminating information, artists were performing an invaluable function.

4   Now comes a transitional stage fraught with difficulties and danger. Much of this derives from a clash between different notions of "culture." And it seems to me that in our attempts to formulate the role of culture in the precarious movement towards freedom and the function of the intellectual creator within that process, much of our effort should be directed towards a redefinition of culture and of the aesthetic which forms an integral part of it.

5   On the one hand there is the Great Tradition of the West, of a Capital-C-Culture for the privileged few. And how can one reject a tradition which has bequeathed to us Sophocles, Dante, Michelangelo, Shakespeare, Rembrandt, Mozart, Tolstoy, Proust, Kafka and Picasso? At the same time this tradition becomes problematic if it is seen, as it so often is, as exclusivist, deriving from a Greek model state which could afford the luxury of distinguishing between manual labour and mental exertion only because the presence of enough slaves made it possible for full citizens to devote their time to "higher pursuits"?

6   In this respect a culture of struggle against oppression brought a valuable corrective, since it activated, not individual artists only, but the masses, the whole of an oppressed people. This grassroots culture has opened, for all societies closed until very recently, new vistas of invaluable opportunities. Yet this culture, too, can be demonstrated to harbour seeds of destruction: directed, through the exigencies of oppression, only towards a struggle for political liberation, the field of focus of such a culture threatens to become extremely narrow and immediate. What is not expedient, what cannot be sloganized or digested immediately, what does not offer itself as a praxis, as "a weapon for liberation," is all too easily discounted or discarded. The problem of this vision of culture, and of the role of the intellectual/creator in it, does not lie in the fact that it summons culture to fulfil a political function, but that it conceives of culture only in function of its political usefulness.

7   A well-known anecdote told by the Spanish poet Federico García Lorca illuminates the problem. A rich farmer and a peasant are walking along a river bank on a particularly beautiful morning. Moved by the scenery, the rich man stops to exclaim, "Isn't it beautiful? Look at those trees... the clouds... the reflections!" But the peasant can only clutch his stomach, groaning, "I am hungry, I am hungry, I am hungry!" This has often been interpreted to suggest that aesthetics are obscene; that our needs are first of all material. But such an interpretation is an insult to our humanity. The poor and the oppressed do indeed require food, and shelter, and comfort. But to suggest that beauty or excellence are attainable only *at the expense of* what are alleged to be more "basic" needs is a denial of what makes us human. The needs of the mind are as essential as those of the body. It is not enough that we live; we also need to ask questions about living: we need to pursue, incessantly, the endless possibilities of meaning in life. And this defines culture as a key dimension of any society's movement towards a fuller experience of freedom and democracy.

8   But what role is to be assigned to the individual intellectual or artist in this process?

9   Our secular world has no room any more for Carlyle's "poet as hero," for the lone thinker or creator as *vates,* as prophet or priest or visionary. In the clamour of a people the *vox clamantis* is all too often drowned, or ignored. It is so easy to fade into irrelevance. In an endangered society, threatened by authoritarian rule, the single dissident voice that dares cry out may acquire an inordinate resonance. It can become a rallying point for the oppressed masses. But once the masses have begun to shake off their most visible shackles, once a people as a whole has broken down its walls and fences, has thrown open its prisons and its Gulags and its Robben Islands, what role is left for the individual artist? Is his or her function not superseded by the collective needs of the people?

10   If the individual persists as a function of an obsolete elitist tradition, then indeed there can be little, if any, justification for him. (And I say "him"

advisedly, as this kind of function is essentially male and chauvinist by nature.) The individual as "free agent" is a figment of the mind, a person without history, ultimately a person without conscience, who denies or ignores his utter involvement in the whole rich fabric of the world. Yet the opposite notion, that of the "commissar," Stalin's "cultural worker," is also suspect: he (again it is essentially a male function) acts primarily as an agent of power and of bureaucracy.

11   For this reason the culturally significant individual should be redefined as a creative and intellectual being with social, historical and moral responsibilities. Such a person can fulfil an indispensable function within the processes that propel a society towards democracy.

12   This function, as I see it, is that of a composite insect.

13   First, it is the function of Gregor Samsa who, one morning, woke up to find himself "transformed in his bed into a gigantic insect." Terrifying his family and acquaintances into a rediscovery of themselves, a redefinition of their own individual and collective roles, he is rejected and "misread" by all. In the end he is starved to death; he becomes forever "the thing next door." He becomes society's Other; he forces society to acknowledge its own alterity. Even if it tries to deny him, it will never be the same again. At the end of the story his sister "sprang to her feet first and stretched her young body": femininity and youth affirm themselves through her; the possibility of rebirth and renewal is admitted to the once stale world of habit and convention.

14   A second insect to bear in mind is the bee in the French novelist Jean Paulhan's essay "L'abeille." If you catch a bee in your hand, says Paulhan, it will sting you before you crush it to death. This may not amount to much; yet had it not been so, there would not have been any bees left in the world.

15   My third insect is very humble indeed. It is the gadfly of Socrates, described by the critic Tzvetan Todorov in his recent essay "Les taons modernes." Superficially the gadfly is nothing but a nuisance, leaving nothing and no-one in peace or at ease, but in the final analysis it is a restless questioning spirit which acts to "reveal and possibly to modify the complex of values which serves as guiding principle to the life of a cultural group."

16   A fourth insect which serves as model to the intellectual/creator is the cricket in Miroslav Krleza's "The Cricket below the Waterfall." This is how the main character in the story describes it:

17   I discovered a cricket in the men's room, my dear fellow; down there in the men's room I discovered a cricket. Underneath the waterfall that splashes over the putrid black-tarred wall, where the citron slices float and the smell of ammonia bites our nostrils as in some laboratory, right down there at the very dregs of the human stench, one night I heard the voice of the cricket. There wasn't even a dog in the pub, the wind roared like a wild beast, and in the stench of the men's room was a voice of the ripe summer, the redolence of August, the breath of meadows

surging like green velvet: the voice of the cricket out of the urine and faeces, the voice of nature that transforms even stinking city toilets into starry sunsets, when the mills are softly humming in the russet horizon, and the first crickets announce themselves as the harbingers of an early autumn. Here, you see, I've brought him some breadcrumbs. Come, let's pay him a visit.

18   In order to keep alive this faith in something beautiful, something meaningful, in a sordid world; in order constantly to shock the world out of complacency; in order to prod the human mind into that kind of awareness which never takes yes for an answer, the first allegiance of the creator-intellectual-artist is to his or her conscience, not to a party or a group, not even to a cause, not even to "the people." But—and this is the crux of the matter—unless that conscience is forged in action and in communion with others, with "the people," and unless the most private of its discoveries is informed by the acknowledgement of a total involvement in the history—the past, the present, the future—of its society, it has no weight and no relevance.

19   Whether the individual creator wills it or not, whatever he or she does, or neglects to do, in a society still groping towards democracy, is allied to one of the two great social dimensions involved in the process: that of the erstwhile power establishment, the haves, the oppressors; or that of the erstwhile victims, the have-nots, the oppressed. The moral choice is obvious. Yet there is no point in simply promoting or advancing a cause, however worthy it may be in itself. And before we can accede to a fuller awareness of the truly democratic, we need to be liberated as much from the mentality of "victim" as from that of "oppressor." This is why our composite insect acquires such vital importance.

20   He or she cannot be circumscribed by, or forced into subservience to, any cause or ideology or programme: yet in his or her freedom lies the assumption of his or her full responsibility as a human being, in the midst of that difficult, dangerous and exhilarating process through which a people numbed by oppression moves tentatively but inexorably towards more democracy and greater freedom.

Reading for Meaning

1. For André Brink, the business of art is "to transform the raw material of experience into meaning." How does the art produced in Chile and South Africa fit this purpose?

2. What are a few of the pitfalls that Brink would have the artist avoid?

3. Why does Brink include the anecdote of the rich farmer and the peasant? How does Brink interpret the story? What meaning might the story have for an artist? For a revolutionary?

4. Summarize Brink's answer to the question "what role is to be assigned to the individual intellectual or artist" in the movement of a culture from dictatorship to democracy?

5. What does Brink mean when he says that the artist should be "a composite insect"?

Comparing Texts

1. How might Pablo Neruda's poem *The Heights of Macchu Picchu* (page 398) illustrate one or more of Brink's ideas about the role of the artist?

2. How do John F. Kennedy's assertions about poetry, which appear at the beginning of this chapter, apply to Brink's concept of the "composite insect"?

3. Brink refers to Gregor Samsa, the insect-narrator of Franz Kafka's *Metamorphosis,* as one of the models for the artist as insect. Study the Kafka short story, "A Hunger Artist," which appears later in this chapter. To what extent does Kafka's story correspond to Brink's expectations of the artist? Does Kafka's fiction include other meanings as well?

Ideas for Writing

1. André Brink claims that art keeps "alive this faith in something beautiful, something meaningful, in a sordid world." Using examples from your own experience or observations, write a response that either supports or challenges Brink's assertion about art.

2. According to Brink, what is the relationship between the artist and "the people"? How close does art come to achieving that connection in your community?

Writing before Reading

Describe a time in your life when you or someone you know showed courage in explaining an important truth about him- or herself or about a difficult situation. How did you feel about the situation?

THE TRANSFORMATION OF SILENCE INTO LANGUAGE AND ACTION

Audre Lorde

Audre Lorde is the author of more than a dozen books of poetry and prose, including The Cancer Journals *(1980),* Zami: A New Spelling of My Name *(1982), and* Our Dead Behind Us *(1986). Lorde died on November 17, 1992, after a fourteen-year bout with cancer. The biographical film* A Litany for Survival: The Life and Work of Audre Lorde *(1978) screened on PBS June 18, 1996. Lorde is a respected author and role model in the gay community and is generally regarded as an accomplished writer with extraordinary lyrical as well as analytical gifts. The following selection is taken from her collection of essays,* Sister Outsider *(1984). Lorde originally wrote "The Transformation of Silence into Language and Action" as a paper, which she presented at a conference sponsored by the Modern Language Association in December 1977.*

1   I have come to believe over and over again that what is most important to me must be spoken, made verbal and shared, even at the risk of having it bruised or misunderstood. That the speaking profits me, beyond any other effect. I am standing here as a Black lesbian poet, and the meaning of all that waits upon the fact that I am still alive, and might not have been. Less than two months ago I was told by two doctors, one female and one male, that I would have to have breast surgery, and that there was a 60 to 80 percent chance that the tumor was malignant. Between that telling and the actual surgery, there was a three-week period of the agony of an involuntary reorganization of my entire life. The surgery was completed, and the growth was benign.

2   But within those two weeks, I was forced to look upon myself and my living with a harsh and urgent clarity that has left me still shaken but much stronger. This is a situation faced by many women, by some of you here today. Some of what I experienced during that time has helped elucidate for me much of what I feel concerning the transformation of silence into language and action.

3   In becoming forcibly and essentially aware of my mortality, of what I wished and wanted for my life, however short it might be, priorities and omissions became strongly etched in a merciless light, and what I most regretted were my silences. Of what had I *ever* been afraid? To question or to speak as I believed could have meant pain, or death. But we all hurt in so many different ways, all the time, and pain will either change or end. Death, on the other hand, is the final silence. And that might be coming quickly, now, without regard for whether I had ever spoken what needed to be said, or had only betrayed myself into small silences, while I planned someday to speak, or waited for someone else's words. And I began to recognize a source of power within myself that comes from the knowledge that while it is most desirable not to be afraid, learning to put fear into a perspective gave me great strength.

4   I was going to die, if not sooner then later, whether or not I had ever spoken myself. My silences had not protected me. Your silence will not protect you. But for every real word spoken, for every attempt I had ever made to speak those truths for which I am still seeking, I had made contact with other women while we examined the words to fit a world in which we all believed, bridging our differences. And it was the concern and caring of all those women which gave me strength and enabled me to scrutinize the essentials of my living.

5   The women who sustained me through that period were Black and white, old and young, lesbian, bisexual, and heterosexual, and we all

shared a war against the tyrannies of silence. They all gave me a strength and concern without which I could not have survived intact. Within those weeks of acute fear came the knowledge—within the war we are all waging with the forces of death, subtle and otherwise, conscious or not—I am not only a casualty, I am also a warrior.

6   What are the words you do not yet have? What do you need to say? What are the tyrannies you swallow day by day and attempt to make your own, until you will sicken and die of them, still in silence? Perhaps for some of you here today, I am the face of one of your fears. Because I am woman, because I am Black, because I am lesbian, because I am myself—a Black woman warrior poet doing my work—come to ask you, are you doing yours?

7   And of course I am afraid, because the transformation of silence into language and action is an act of self-revelation, and that always seems fraught with danger. But my daughter, when I told her of our topic and my difficulty with it, said, "Tell them about how you're never really a whole person if you remain silent, because there's always that one little piece inside you that wants to be spoken out, and if you keep ignoring it, it gets madder and madder and hotter and hotter, and if you don't speak it out one day it will just up and punch you in the mouth from the inside."

8   In the cause of silence, each of us draws the face of her own fear—fear of contempt, of censure, or some judgment, or recognition, of challenge, of annihilation. But most of all, I think, we fear the visibility without which we cannot truly live. Within this country where racial difference creates a constant, if unspoken, distortion of vision, Black women have on one hand always been highly visible, and so, on the other hand, have been rendered invisible through the depersonalization of racism. Even within the women's movement, we have had to fight, and still do, for that very visibility which also renders us most vulnerable, our Blackness. For to survive in the mouth of this dragon we call america, we have had to learn this first and most vital lesson—that we were never meant to survive. Not as human beings. And neither were most of you here today, Black or not. And that visibility which makes us most vulnerable is that which also is the source of our greatest strength. Because the machine will try to grind you into dust anyway, whether or not we speak. We can sit in our corners mute forever while our sisters and our selves are wasted, while our children are distorted and destroyed, while our earth is poisoned; we can sit in our safe corners mute as bottles, and we will still be no less afraid.

9   In my house this year we are celebrating the feast of Kwanza, the African American festival of harvest which begins the day after Christmas and lasts for seven days. There are seven principles of Kwanza, one for each day. The first principle is Umoja, which means unity, the decision to strive for and maintain unity in self and community. The principle for yesterday, the second day, was Kujichagulia—self-determination—the

decision to define ourselves, name ourselves, and speak for ourselves, instead of being defined and spoken for by others. Today is the third day of Kwanza, and the principle for today is Ujima—collective work and responsibility—the decision to build and maintain ourselves and our communities together and to recognize and solve our problems together.

10   Each of us is here now because in one way or another we share a commitment to language and to the power of language, and to the reclaiming of that language which has been made to work against us. In the transformation of silence into language and action, it is vitally necessary for each one of us to establish or examine her function in that transformation and to recognize her role as vital within that transformation.

11   For those of us who write, it is necessary to scrutinize not only the truth of what we speak, but the truth of that language by which we speak it. For others, it is to share and spread also those words that are meaningful to us. But primarily for us all, it is necessary to teach by living and speaking those truths which we believe and know beyond understanding. Because in this way alone we can survive, by taking part in a process of life that is creative and continuing, that is growth.

12   And it is never without fear—of visibility, of the harsh light of scrutiny and perhaps judgment, of pain, of death. But we have lived through all of those already, in silence, except death. And I remind myself at the time now that if I were to have been born mute, or had maintained an oath of silence my whole life long for safety, I would still have suffered, and I would still die. It is very good for establishing perspective.

13   And where the words of women are crying to be heard, we must each of us recognize our responsibility to seek those words out, to read them and share them and examine them in their pertinence to our lives. That we not hide behind the mockeries of separations that have been imposed upon us and which so often we accept as our own. For instance, "I can't possibly teach Black women's writing—their experience is so different from mine." Yet how many years have you spent teaching Plato and Shakespeare and Proust? Or another, "She's a white woman and what could she possibly have to say to me?" Or, "She's a lesbian, what would my husband say, or my chairman?" Or again, "This woman writes of her sons and I have no children." And all the other endless ways in which we rob ourselves of ourselves and each other.

14   We can learn to work and speak when we are afraid in the same way we have learned to work and speak when we are tired. For we have been socialized to respect fear more than our own needs for language and definition, and while we wait in silence for that final luxury of fearlessness, the weight of that silence will choke us.

15   The fact that we are here and that I speak these words is an attempt to break that silence and bridge some of those differences between us, for it is not difference which immobilizes us, but silence. And there are so many silences to be broken.

Reading for Meaning

1. Audre Lorde says that in spite of her fears that she will be hurt or misunderstood, "what is most important to me must be spoken." Based on your reading of her essay, what exactly does she fear? What does she feel she needs to say? In what ways does Lorde "profit" by speaking?

2. Lorde is determined to transform "silence into language and action." What motivated Lorde to break her silence? In what sense might language itself be transformed by her words?

3. During the weeks while she waited for test results, Lorde came to understand "I am not only a casualty, I am also a warrior." In what sense is she both a casualty and a warrior?

4. In paragraph 9 Lorde describes the celebration of Kwanza. Why does she include this discussion in her speech? How does it connect to the rest of her text?

5. Why might Lorde have chosen to make her presentation at the conference of the Modern Language Association? Who is her audience? What message does she bring to them?

Comparing Texts

1. The African American poet bell hooks writes: "for women within oppressed groups . . . coming to voice is an act of resistance." What does hooks mean by this statement? Who might be included in her reference to "oppressed groups" and in what way is speaking out an "act of resistance"? How does hooks's assessment compare to Audre Lorde's argument that Black women must transform silence into "language and action"?

2. Salman Rushdie notes that Richard Wright, a black American writer, said the struggle between whites and blacks in the United States stems from the differences between their descriptions of the nature of reality. Rushdie adds that "redescribing a world is the necessary first step towards changing it" (p. 412). Compare Wright and Rushdie's view on the importance of language in interpreting reality to Audre Lorde's belief in the power of language.

Ideas for Writing

1. Salman Rushdie says that "writers and politicians are natural rivals," and he cites Milan Kundera's observation that "the struggle of man against power is the struggle of memory against forgetting." Write an essay in which you discuss ways that Audre Lorde and other writers in this chapter, such as André Brink and Connie Stephens, depict this conflict between artists and storytellers, and the social or political structure in which they live.

2. Locate a copy of Audre Lorde's *Sister Outsider,* another of her collections, and read three additional essays written by her. After reading these selections carefully, write a response in which you evaluate several aspects of her writing. You might discuss themes, style of writing, her use of point of view, the connection with her audience, or the effectiveness of her arguments.

Writing before Reading

What is your impression of people who call themselves "artists"? What habits or traits do you associate with creative, artistic people? Where have you gotten your ideas about artists?

A HUNGER ARTIST
Franz Kafka

Franz Kafka (1883–1924) was born in Prague, in former Bohemia, now part of the Czech Republic. He grew up in a Jewish household under the critical eye of his domineering father. Kafka earned a law degree in 1906 and eventually went to work for an office specializing in worker's compensation insurance. He wrote at night, after work, and published only a few short stories and none of his novels. After his death, his close friend, Max Brod, defied Kafka's instructions to burn his manuscripts and instead published them, thereby giving the twentieth century its most important writer on modern alienation, guilt, and dogged opposition to an inscrutable, hostile world. At the time of his death, Kafka was assembling A Hunger Artist, *a collection of tales that depict the uneasy relationship between the artist and his audience. The title story, "A Hunger Artist," is taken from this collection.*

Facts about Bohemia

The former kingdom of Bohemia is now a territory in the Czech Republic. During the Roman domination of Europe, Bohemia was inhabited by the Boii, a Celtic people. Slavic peoples migrated to Bohemia in the sixth century. The kingdom became part of the dominion of the Holy Roman Empire in the tenth century. Prague has been an important cultural center in Europe since the fourteenth century when Charles I of Bohemia was crowned Charles IV, Holy Roman Emperor. The Habsburg dynasty ruled Bohemia from 1526 until the mid-seventeenth century when it fell under Austrian rule. After World War I, Bohemia, Moravia, and Slovakia were combined to form Czechoslovakia. In 1938 Hitler laid claim to the Sudetenland, home to a large German-speaking population, and in 1939 most of the rest of Czechoslovakia fell to the Nazis. The country was liberated by the Soviets in 1944. When the Soviet domination of Czechoslovakia ended in 1992, the country split into the Czech Republic, composed of Bohemia and Moravia, and Slovakia.

Chapter 11 The Artist in Society

1   During these last decades the interest in professional fasting has markedly diminished. It used to pay very well to stage such great performances under one's own management, but today that is quite impossible. We live in a different world now. At one time the whole town took a lively interest in the hunger artist; from day to day of his fast the excitement mounted; everybody wanted to see him at least once a day; there were people who bought season tickets for the last few days and sat from morning till night in front of his small barred cage; even in the nighttime there were visiting hours, when the whole effect was heightened by torch flares; on fine days the cage was set out in the open air, and then it was the children's special treat to see the hunger artist; for their elders he was often just a joke that happened to be in fashion, but the children stood open-mouthed, holding each other's hands for greater security, marveling at him as he sat there pallid in black tights, with his ribs sticking out so prominently, not even on a seat but down among straw on the ground, sometimes giving a courteous nod, answering questions with a constrained smile, or perhaps stretching an arm through the bars so that one might feel how thin it was, and then again withdrawing deep into himself, paying no attention to anyone or anything, not even to the all-important striking of the clock that was the only piece of furniture in his cage, but merely staring into vacancy with half shut eyes, now and then taking a sip from a tiny glass of water to moisten his lips.

2   Besides casual onlookers there were also relays of permanent watchers selected by the public, usually butchers, strangely enough, and it was their task to watch the hunger artist day and night, three of them at a time, in case he should have some secret recourse to nourishment. This was nothing but a formality, instituted to reassure the masses, for the initiates knew well enough that during his fast the artist would never in any circumstances, not even under forcible compulsion, swallow the smallest morsel of food; the honor of his profession forbade it. Not every watcher, of course, was capable of understanding this, there were often groups of night watchers who were very lax in carrying out their duties and deliberately huddled together in a retired corner to play cards with great absorption, obviously intending to give the hunger artist the chance of a little refreshment, which they supposed he could draw from some private hoard. Nothing annoyed the artist more than such watchers; they made him miserable; they made his fast seem unendurable; sometimes he mastered his feebleness sufficiently to sing during their watch for as long as he could keep going, to show them how unjust their suspicions were. But that was of little use; they only wondered at his cleverness in being able to fill his mouth even while singing. Much more to his taste were the watchers who sat close up to the bars, who were not content with the dim night lighting of the hall but focused him in the full glare of the electric pocket torch given them by the impresario. The harsh light did not trouble him at all, in any case he could never sleep properly, and he could always drowse a little, whatever the light, at any hour, even

when the hall was thronged with noisy onlookers. He was quite happy at the prospect of spending a sleepless night with such watchers; he was ready to exchange jokes with them, to tell them stories out of his nomadic life, anything at all to keep them awake and demonstrate to them again that he had no eatables in his cage and that he was fasting as not one of them could fast. But his happiest moment was when the morning came and an enormous breakfast was brought them, at his expense, on which they flung themselves with the keen appetite of healthy men after a weary night of wakefulness. Of course there were people who argued that this breakfast was an unfair attempt to bribe the watchers, but that was going rather too far, and when they were invited to take on a night's vigil without a breakfast, merely for the sake of the cause, they made themselves scarce, although they stuck stubbornly to their suspicions.

3   Such suspicions, anyhow, were a necessary accompaniment to the profession of fasting. No one could possibly watch the hunger artist continuously, day and night, and so no one could produce first-hand evidence that the fast had really been rigorous and continuous; only the artist himself could know that, he was therefore bound to be the sole completely satisfied spectator of his own fast. Yet for other reasons he was never satisfied; it was not perhaps mere fasting that had brought him to such skeleton thinness that many people had regretfully to keep away from his exhibitions, because the sight of him was too much for them, perhaps it was dissatisfaction with himself that had worn him down. For he alone knew, what no other initiate knew, how easy it was to fast. It was the easiest thing in the world. He made no secret of this, yet people did not believe him; at the best they set him down as modest, most of them, however, thought he was out for publicity or else was some kind of cheat who found it easy to fast because he had discovered a way of making it easy, and then had the impudence to admit the fact, more or less. He had to put up with all that, and in the course of time had got used to it, but his inner dissatisfaction always rankled, and never yet, after any term of fasting—this must be granted to his credit—had he left the cage of his own free will. The longest period of fasting was fixed by his impresario at forty days, beyond that term he was not allowed to go, not even in great cities, and there was good reason for it, too. Experience had proved that for about forty days the interest of the public could be stimulated by a steadily increasing pressure of advertisement, but after that the town began to lose interest, sympathetic support began notably to fall off; there were of course local variations as between one town and another or one country and another, but as a general rule forty days marked the limit. So on the fortieth day the flower-bedecked cage was opened, enthusiastic spectators filled the hall, a military band played, two doctors entered the cage to measure the results of the fast, which were announced through a megaphone, and finally two young ladies appeared, blissful at having been selected for the honor, to help the hunger

artist down the few steps leading to a small table on which was spread a carefully chosen invalid repast. And at this very moment the artist always turned stubborn. True, he would entrust his bony arms to the outstretched helping hands of the ladies bending over him, but stand up he would not. Why stop fasting at this particular moment, after forty days of it? He had held out for a long time, an illimitably long time; why stop now, when he was in his best fasting form, or rather, not yet quite in his best fasting form? Why should he be cheated of the fame he would get for fasting longer, for being not only the record hunger artist of all time, which presumably he was already, but for beating his own record by a performance beyond human imagination, since he felt that there were no limits to his capacity for fasting? His public pretended to admire him so much, why should it have so little patience with him; if he could endure fasting longer, why shouldn't the public endure it? Besides, he was tired, he was comfortable sitting in the straw, and now he was supposed to lift himself to his full height and go down to a meal the very thought of which gave him a nausea that only the presence of the ladies kept him from betraying, and even that with an effort. And he looked up into the eyes of the ladies who were apparently so friendly and in reality so cruel, and shook his head, which felt too heavy on its strengthless neck. But then there happened yet again what always happened. The impresario came forward, without a word—for the band made speech impossible—lifted his arms in the air above the artist, as if inviting Heaven to look down upon its creature here in the straw, this suffering martyr, which indeed he was, although in quite another sense; grasped him round the emaciated waist, with exaggerated caution, so that the frail condition he was in might be appreciated; and committed him to the care of the blenching ladies, not without secretly giving him a shaking so that his legs and body tottered and swayed. The artist now submitted completely; his head lolled on his breast as if it had landed there by chance; his body was hollowed out; his legs in a spasm of self-preservation clung close to each other at the knees, yet scraped on the ground as if it were not really solid ground, as if they were only trying to find solid ground; and the whole weight of his body, a feather-weight after all, relapsed onto one of the ladies, who, looking round for help and panting a little—this post of honor was not at all what she had expected it to be—first stretched her neck as far as she could to keep her face at least free from contact with the artist, when finding this impossible, and her more fortunate companion not coming to her aid but merely holding extended on her own trembling hand the little bunch of knucklebones that was the artist's, to the great delight of the spectators burst into tears and had to be replaced by an attendant who had long been stationed in readiness. Then came the food, a little of which the impresario managed to get between the artist's lips, while he sat in a kind of half-fainting trance, to the accompaniment of cheerful patter designed to distract the public's attention from the artist's condition; after that, a toast was drunk to the public, supposedly prompted by a whisper from the artist in the impresario's ear; the band confirmed it with a mighty flourish, the spectators melted away, and no one had any cause to be dissatisfied with the proceedings, no one except the hunger artist himself, he only, as always.

4   So he lived for many years, with small regular intervals of recuperation, in visible glory, honored by the world, yet in spite of that troubled in spirit, and all the more troubled because no one would take his trouble seriously. What comfort could he possibly need? What more could he possibly wish for? And if some good-natured person, feeling sorry for him, tried to console him by pointing out that his melancholy was probably caused by fasting, it could happen, especially when he had been fasting for some time, that he reacted with an outburst of fury and to the general alarm began to shake the bars of his cage like a wild animal. Yet the impresario had a way of punishing these outbreaks which he rather enjoyed putting into operation. He would apologize publicly for the artist's behavior, which was only to be excused, he admitted, because of the irritability caused by fasting; a condition hardly to be understood by well-fed people; then by natural transition he went on to mention the artist's equally incomprehensible boast that he could fast for much longer than he was doing; he praised the high ambition, the good will, the great self-denial undoubtedly implicit in such a statement, and then quite simply countered it by bringing out photographs, which were also on sale to the public, showing the artist on the fortieth day of a fast lying in bed almost dead from exhaustion. This perversion of the truth, familiar to the artist though it was, always unnerved him afresh and proved too much for him. What was a consequence of the premature ending of his fast was here presented as the cause of it! To fight against this lack of understanding, against a whole world of nonunderstanding, was impossible. Time and again in good faith he stood by the bars listening to the impresario, but as soon as the photographs appeared he always let go and sank with a groan back on to his straw, and the reassured public could once more come close and gaze at him.

5   A few years later when the witnesses of such scenes called them to mind, they often failed to understand themselves at all. For meanwhile the aforementioned change in public interest had set in; it seemed to happen almost overnight; there may have been profound causes for it, but who was going to bother about that; at any rate the pampered hunger artist suddenly found himself deserted one fine day by the amusement seekers, who went streaming past him to other more favored attractions. For the last time the impresario hurried him over half Europe to discover whether the old interest might still survive here and there; all in vain; everywhere, as if by secret agreement, a positive revulsion from professional fasting was in evidence. Of course it could not really have sprung up so suddenly as all that, and many premonitory

symptoms which had not been sufficiently remarked or suppressed during the rush and glitter of success now came retrospectively to mind, but it was now too late to take any countermeasures. Fasting would surely come into fashion again at some future date, yet that was no comfort for those living in the present. What, then, was the hunger artist to do? He had been applauded by thousands in his time and could hardly come down to showing himself in a street booth at village fairs, and as for adopting another profession, he was not only too old for that but too fanatically devoted to fasting. So he took leave of the impresario, his partner in an unparalleled career, and hired himself to a large circus; in order to spare his own feelings he avoided reading the conditions of his contract.

6   A large circus with its enormous traffic in replacing and recruiting men, animals and apparatus can always find a use for people at any time, even for a hunger artist, provided of course that he does not ask too much, and in this particular case anyhow it was not only the artist who was taken on but his famous and long-known name as well, indeed considering the peculiar nature of his performance, which was not impaired by advancing age, it could not be objected that here was an artist past his prime, no longer at the height of his professional skill, seeking a refuge in some quiet corner of a circus: on the contrary, the hunger artist averred that he could fast as well as ever, which was entirely credible, he even alleged that if he were allowed to fast as he liked, and this was at once promised him without more ado, he could astound the world by establishing a record never yet achieved, a statement which certainly provoked a smile among the other professionals, since it left out of account the change in public opinion, which the hunger artist in his zeal conveniently forgot.

7   He had not, however, actually lost his sense of the real situation and took it as a matter of course that he and his cage should be stationed, not in the middle of the ring as a main attraction, but outside, near the animal cages, on a site that was after all easily accessible. Large and gaily painted placards made a frame for the cage and announced what was to be seen inside it. When the public came thronging out in the intervals to see the animals, they could hardly avoid passing the hunger artist's cage and stopping there for a moment, perhaps they might even have stayed longer had not those pressing behind them in the narrow gangway, who did not understand why they should be held up on their way toward the excitements of the menagerie, made it impossible for anyone to stand gazing quietly for any length of time. And that was the reason why the hunger artist, who had of course been looking forward to these visiting hours as the main achievement of his life, began instead to shrink from them. At first he could hardly wait for the intervals; it was exhilarating to watch the crowds come streaming his way, until only too soon—not even the most obstinate self-deception, clung to almost consciously,

could hold out against the fact—the conviction was borne in upon him that these people, most of them, to judge from their actions, again and again, without exception, were all on their way to the menagerie. And the first sight of them from the distance remained the best. For when they reached his cage he was at once deafened by the storm of shouting and abuse that arose from the two contending factions, which renewed themselves continuously, of those who wanted to stop and stare at him—he soon began to dislike them more than the others—not out of real interest but only out of obstinate self-assertiveness, and those who wanted to go straight on to the animals. When the first great rush was past, the stragglers came along, and these, whom nothing could have prevented from stopping to look at him as long as they had breath, raced past with long strides, hardly even glancing at him, in their haste to get to the menagerie in time. And all too rarely did it happen that he had a stroke of luck, when some father of a family fetched up before him with his children, pointed a finger at the hunger artist and explained at length what the phenomenon meant, telling stories of earlier years when he himself had watched similar but much more thrilling performances, and the children, still rather uncomprehending, since neither inside nor outside school had they been sufficiently prepared for this lesson—what did they care about fasting?—yet showed by the brightness of their intent eyes that new and better times might be coming. Perhaps, said the hunger artist to himself many a time, things would be a little better if his cage were set not quite so near the menagerie. That made it too easy for people to make their choice, to say nothing of what he suffered from the stench of the menagerie, the animals' restlessness by night, the carrying past of raw lumps of flesh for the beasts of prey, the roaring at feeding times, which depressed him continually. But he did not dare to lodge a complaint with the management; after all, he had the animals to thank for the troops of people who passed his cage, among whom there might always be one here and there to take an interest in him, and who could tell where they might seclude him if he called attention to his existence and thereby to the fact that, strictly speaking, he was only an impediment on the way to the menagerie.

8   A small impediment, to be sure, one that grew steadily less. People grew familiar with the strange idea that they could be expected, in times like these, to take an interest in a hunger artist, and with this familiarity the verdict went out against him. He might fast as much as he could, and he did so; but nothing could save him now, people passed him by. Just try to explain to anyone the art of fasting! Anyone who has no feeling for it cannot be made to understand it. The fine placards grew dirty and illegible, they were torn down; the little notice board telling the number of fast days achieved, which at first was changed carefully every day, had long stayed at the same figure, for after the first few weeks even this small task seemed pointless to the staff; and so the artist simply fasted

on and on, as he had once dreamed of doing, and it was no trouble to him, just as he had always foretold, but no one counted the days, no one, not even the artist himself, knew what records he was already breaking, and his heart grew heavy. And when once in a time some leisurely passer-by stopped, made merry over the old figure on the board and spoke of swindling, that was in its way the stupidest lie ever invented by indifference and inborn malice, since it was not the hunger artist who was cheating; he was working honestly, but the world was cheating him of his reward.

9   Many more days went by, however, and that too came to an end. An overseer's eye fell on the cage one day and he asked the attendants why this perfectly good cage should be left standing there unused with dirty straw inside it; nobody knew, until one man, helped out by the notice board, remembered about the hunger artist. They poked into the straw with sticks and found him in it. "Are you still fasting?" asked the overseer. "When on earth do you mean to stop?" "Forgive me, everybody," whispered the hunger artist; only the overseer, who had his ear to the bars, understood him. "Of course," said the overseer, and tapped his forehead with a finger to let the attendants know what state the man was in, "we forgive you." "I always wanted you to admire my fasting," said the hunger artist. "We do admire it," said the overseer, affably. "But you shouldn't admire it," said the hunger artist. "Well, then we don't admire it," said the overseer, "but why shouldn't we admire it?" "Because I have to fast, I can't help it," said the hunger artist. "What a fellow you are," said the overseer, "and why can't you help it?" "Because," said the hunger artist, lifting his head a little and speaking, with his lips pursed, as if for a kiss, right into the overseer's ear, so that no syllable might be lost, "because I couldn't find the food I liked. If I had found it, believe me, I should have made no fuss and stuffed myself like you or anyone else." These were his last words, but in his dimming eyes remained the firm though no longer proud persuasion that he was still continuing to fast.

10   "Well, clear this out now!" said the overseer, and they buried the hunger artist, straw and all. Into the cage they put a young panther. Even the most insensitive felt it refreshing to see this wild creature leaping around the cage that had so long been dreary. The panther was all right. The food he liked was brought him without hesitation by the attendants; he seemed not even to miss his freedom; his noble body, furnished almost to the bursting point with all that it needed, seemed to carry freedom around with it too; somewhere in his jaws it seemed to lurk; and the joy of life streamed with such ardent passion from his throat that for the onlookers it was not easy to stand the shock of it. But they braced themselves, crowded round the cage, and did not want ever to move away.

Reading for Meaning

1. Identify several kinds of audiences who come to watch the hunger artist. What is his relationship to these spectators and how important are they?

2. What role does the impresario play in Kafka's story? Is he a sympathetic character?

3. Several times in "A Hunger Artist," the narrator draws a parallel between the hunger artist and an animal. At one point he is put in a cage, he later loses control and acts like a wild animal, and he is placed near the animal exhibits when he joins the circus. Finally, he is replaced by a panther. Why do you think Kafka insists on making this connection?

4. In an era when his performance has fallen out of favor, the children who pass by the hunger artist's cage suggest "by the brightness of their intent eyes that new and better times might be coming." What does this suggestion imply about the work of the hunger artist or the times in which he lives?

5. Although the artist knows that he has kept his fast faithfully, he remains unsatisfied. Give several explanations of his dissatisfaction. What might Kafka be implying about the artist's relationship to his craft?

6. Discuss the paradoxical attitude toward public fasting that the hunger artist expresses in paragraph 9. How might his attitude help explain why he was never satisfied with his work?

7. The hunger artist asserts that he would have "stuffed" himself "like you or anyone else," but he "couldn't find the food [he] liked." What kind of "food" or nourishment is the artist looking for?

8. Why does Kafka introduce the panther at the end of his story? What does it signify?

Comparing Texts

1. Read the following poem by Lawrence Ferlinghetti and discuss any parallels you find between Ferlinghetti's artist and Kafka's hunger artist. What is different about their views of the artist or his purpose?

> Constantly risking absurdity
> >and death
> whenever he performs
> >above the heads
> >>of his audience
> the poet like an acrobat
> >climbs on rime
> >>to a high wire of his own making
> and balancing on eyebeams
> >above a sea of faces
> paces his way
> >to the other side of day

```
              performing entrechats¹
                                             and slight-of-foot tricks
     and other high theatrics
                                         and all without mistaking
                     any thing
                                          for what it may not be
                 For he's the super realist
                                              who must perforce perceive
                      taut truth
                            before taking of each stance or step
        in his supposed advance
                                toward that still higher perch
     where Beauty stands and waits
                                   with gravity
                                             to start her death-defying leap
     And he
          a little charleychaplin man
                                            who may or may not catch
           her fair eternal form
                        spreadeagled in the empty air
                of existence
```

2. Edmund Wilson devotes a chapter in his book *The Wound and the Bow: Seven Studies in Literature* to his interpretation of Sophocles' story of the Greek archer, Philoctetes, whose reeking wound and unpleasant temperament cause the Greeks to abandon him before reaching Troy. They come back for him when they discover that they cannot defeat the Trojans unless he is with them. For Wilson, Philoctetes symbolizes the paradoxical necessity and discomfort inherent in the relationship between the artist and his community. Read the following excerpt from Edmund Wilson's discussion of *Philoctetes*. Then, based on your understanding of Wilson's analysis, compare the story of Philoctetes to Kafka's tale about the hunger artist.

1   And now let us go back to the *Philoctetes* as a parable of human character. I should interpret the fable as follows. The victim of a malodorous disease which renders him abhorrent to society and periodically degrades him and makes him helpless is also the master of a superhuman art which everybody has to respect and which the normal man finds he needs. A practical man like Odysseus, at the same time coarse-grained and clever, imagines that he can somehow get the bow without having Philoctetes on his hands or that he can kidnap Philoctetes the bowman without regard for Philoctetes the invalid. But the young son of Achilles [Neoptolemus] knows better. It is at the moment when his sympathy for

---

¹ A vertical leap in ballet that requires much foot crossing or heel knocking.

Philoctetes would naturally inhibit his cheating him—so the supernatural influences in Sophocles are often made with infinite delicacy to shade into subjective motivations—it is at this moment of his natural shrinking that it becomes clear to him that the words of the seer had meant that the bow would be useless without Philoctetes himself. It is in the nature of things—of this world where the divine and the human fuse—that they cannot have the irresistible weapon without its loathsome owner, who upsets the processes of normal life by his curses and his cries, and who in any case refuses to work for men who have exiled him from their fellowship.

2   It is quite right that Philoctetes should refuse to come to Troy. Yet it is also decreed that he shall be cured when he shall have been able to forget his grievance and to devote his divine gifts to the service of his own people. It is right that he should refuse to submit to the purposes of Odysseus, whose only idea is to exploit him. How then is the gulf to be got over between the ineffective plight of the bowman and his proper use of his bow, between ignominy and his destined glory? Only by the intervention of one who is guileless enough and human enough to treat him not as a monster, nor yet as a mere magical property which is wanted for accomplishing some end, but simply as another man, whose sufferings elicit his sympathy and whose courage and pride he admires.

Ideas for Writing

1. Readings in this chapter offer several perspectives on the artist's role in society. Form a research team with another student or two in your class, and examine two or three other views of the artist. (You might review ideas about the artist in "The Artist as Insect," page 482, "The Transformation of Silence into Language and Action," page 487, and "Marriage in the Hausa *Tatsuniya* Tradition," page 513.)

2. How does Franz Kafka use the images of the cage and the panther to suggest several levels of meaning for his story?

3. Identify elements in Kafka's short story that you would consider realistic and those that make the story more of a parable or fable. Weigh carefully both aspects of Kafka's story and discuss how they work together.

Writing before Reading

Imagine for a moment that you are a cultural anthropologist. What biases might you need to overcome to study the spiritual teachings of another culture?

THE POWER OF IMAGE AND PLACE
Jane M. Young

Jane M. Young is an anthropologist who has completed extensive recordings of the rock art on and near the Zuni Indian Reservation in western New Mexico. Her study of Zuni art, discussed in Signs from the Ancestors: Zuni Cultural Symbolism and Perceptions of Rock Art *(1988), is well respected in the anthropological community. Her analysis of Zuni art is shaped not only by her own observations but also by numerous interviews with Zuni people. Young concludes that modern-day Zunis do not attempt to understand the exact meaning the ancestors gave their art. Instead, they use these "signs from the ancestors" to interpret activities in their own lives. In this way, the ancient images validate the present in terms of the past.*

Facts about the Zuni

The Zuni are a Native American group of Pueblo Indians. Approximately 8,500 Zuni live in western New Mexico. At the time of the Spanish conquest of what is now the western United States, the Zuni were living in villages later identified with the Spanish myth of the seven golden cities of Cibola. The Zuni are farmers who cultivate corn and wheat and raise sheep. The Zuni religion is a natural part of their everyday life. Ceremonial and religious practices are rooted in ancestor worship and the deification of the forces in nature.

ICONIC POWER: POWER BY SIMILARITY AND ASSOCIATION

1   I... wish to explore the related issues of why rock carvings and paintings are produced and the function of certain rock art sites at Zuni in the present day or the recent past. Underlying both concerns is the concept of power, whether it be the power *evoked* by certain images that recall the time of the beginning or the power *invoked* through the depiction of particular figures. On the one hand, the power inherent in those images ... is frequently related to their ambiguity of both form and meaning. On the other hand, the power inherent in those images that depict beings associated by the Zunis with vital aspects of the physical world is related to their specificity—their ability to "represent" those living beings. The *meaning* of these latter images may at times be metaphorical or ambiguous, but their form rarely is. Furthermore, these more representational images are generally produced in more recent times than those that are evocative of the myth time.

2   One way in which to answer the question of why pictographs and petroglyphs are produced by the Zunis is to see if the same figures are prevalent in other media as well. If so, one would then ask if the production of

such similar figures across various media is motivated by the same factors. Certain categories of efficacious rock art images, such as those depicting Beast Gods and creatures associated with water, do appear in other graphic forms at Zuni. Perhaps this is because the Zunis would most naturally surround themselves with those elements regarded as potentially powerful and capable of bringing benefits to them, whatever the artistic mode. The use of such imagery may be an instance of what Bunzel has called "compulsive magic"; that is, the attempt to attain desired events or outcomes by their ritual depiction, either in the form of graphic illustrations or by means of their dramatic enactment.[1] In semiotic terms, these images may be said to invoke power because of their iconicity, their resemblance or similarity to living beings that are potent in and of themselves or associated with some efficacious aspect of the natural world.[2] Examples include painting water-related creatures on prayer meal bowls so that rain will fall[3] and carrying the fetish of a Beast God while hunting its natural prey.[4] Likewise, Bunzel reports that Zuni potters often painted deer enclosed in a "house" on their pottery so that their husbands would have good luck in hunting.[5]

3   It is quite possible that Zunis created some rock carvings and paintings for similar reasons. For instance, the following descriptions of insect figures in rock art link the carving of the image to beneficial results, such as stinging the enemy with poison or making Zunis invisible to their enemies. The latter power is derived from insects whose protective coloring and shape render them invisible to their predators. As illustrated by the story of the Water Skate finding the Center as well as by the association of ants with the six directions, insects play a major role in Zuni cultural symbolism; like the Beast Gods, they form another category of raw beings whose potency humans can accrue to themselves through ritual activity. Although they did not necessarily associate them with events that occurred in the myth time, Zunis frequently identified insectlike rock art figures as beings with special efficacy, their depictions evoked descriptions of their important position in the Zuni hierarchy of powerful beings.

4   The identification one Zuni woman offered for [one such figure] illustrates the use medicine men make of the special powers of insects:

> I don't know its name,
>   but it is a gray insect.
> It draws its legs next to its body
>   and then looks like a stick.
> Medicine society men who go to war crush up
>   and eat these insects
>   so that they will be invisible to their enemies.

Similarly, according to many Zunis, a panel of insect petroglyphs at the Village of the Great Kivas site was carved there for purposes of warfare. They said the panel depicted poisonous insects that were carved on the rocks by the war chief so that they would sting the enemies of the Zunis. Such belief in the potency and wisdom of insects is echoed by one man who said the following about ants:

> They are so wise,
>   they always remember where their home is.
> They travel great distances,
>   but always find their way back.
> We make offerings to ants for their wisdom,
>   so that we will have the ability
>   to keep the prayers in our memory.

These descriptions and identifications reveal the particular powers Zunis attribute to insects and their belief that, if they perform the proper ritual procedures, they can invoke the help of these creatures.

5   Not only does the portrayal of certain images effect desired outcomes—that is, a result occurs because of the iconic power of the figure—so, too, can such portrayals lead to the prevention of undesired outcomes. A petroglyph identified as "stink bug" evoked the following story from one man who described its role in Zuni beliefs about reincarnation:

> My grandfather told me not to kill stink bugs,
>   because in Zuni belief when you die the first time
>   you go to Kachina Village.
> Then you go through four reincarnations.
> The last one is a stink bug.
> If you kill that there is no more life,
>   that is the end of the cycle.

This man concluded that the rock carving was produced to remind Zunis that they should respect all living beings and, in this case, the stink bug in particular. Other Zunis said that one could become a variety of raw beings after the fourth death, not just stink bugs; nevertheless, this example serves to underscore the prominent place of this particular insect in the Zuni taxonomy of raw beings.

6   Just as powerful insects are carved on the rocks to effect desired outcomes, so are other images depicted because of their association with certain powerful characteristics of the species represented. For instance, according to a number of Zunis, water-related creatures such as frogs, toads, and hump-backed fluteplayers were carved and painted on the rocks in some areas to bring rain to the village, and the depiction of game animals not only recorded a successful hunt but propitiated the spirits of the animals that had been slain, ensuring more such success in the future. Other representations of game animals in rock art, especially the many carved images of mountain sheep struck with spears and deer with arrows projecting from their bodies, may also have been created in the hopes of assuring good luck in the hunt. Although most of the animal

figures in rock art of the Zuni-Cibola region are not so explicitly related to hunting, a number of them may have been produced for this reason. [One] figure for instance, is a pecked figure of a mountain sheep that has been carved with a hole in the center of its body, perhaps indicating the heart that the successful hunter's arrow will strike. In any case, whatever the original motive for their production, such images, once made, might very well have been used in ritual activities aimed at ensuring the success of the hunt. For example, in her major work on Zuni published at the turn of the century, Stevenson states that men sometimes shot rock art depictions of game animals, especially deer, with arrows before they set out to hunt.[6] Some evidence suggests that suitable pictographs and petroglyphs are still used in this way, at least on a limited scale, although the weapons are now guns rather than arrows, spears, or atlatls. Whether shooting at rock art figures is motivated by a belief in the efficacy of ritual activity to ensure a successful hunt or by a simple desire for target practice, the bullet holes and disfigured images are mute testimony to the fact that such shooting occurs.

7   When I initially undertook the project of recording rock art at Zuni, I assumed that bullet holes, like spray-painted, chalked, and carved graffiti, were examples of vandalism. Now I have come to believe that, at least in some cases, the bullet holes are the visible remains of the modern version of the sort of ritual activity described by Stevenson rather than the result of vandalism. The choice of targets, generally game animals such as mountain sheep, bear, buffalo, and deer, supports such a conclusion. My re-examination of two panels of painted masks and animal figures at the site called the Village of the Great Kivas reveals that while none of the other kachina masks had been used as targets, some masks and paintings of game animals had been disfigured by bullet holes.[7] The deer figure ... is riddled with bullet holes, as are the bear (also identified as coyote) and buffalo masks.[8] The only image marked by bullet holes in the other panel of masks is a deer. Overall, at this site only the masks and figures of the buffalo, bear, and deer have been shot at. It would appear, then, that some Zunis are less concerned with the preservation of these pictographs as "art" than with their use toward more practical ends. This is quite in keeping with the numerous accounts in the ethnographic literature describing the purposeful "destruction" by Zunis of pottery, baskets, sand paintings, and kiva murals in rites of cleansing, renewal, and purification.[9] Zunis even place the sacred images of the Twin War Gods in open shrines on mesa tops so that they are slowly eaten away by weathering—a process that, in this case, Zunis regard as desirable. While an outsider might consider the destruction of such material culture items to be a deplorable loss to the scientific community that seeks to preserve and study such things, the Zunis place a high value on newness and do not necessarily value their old things as others do. Barbara Tedlock points out this emphasis on change and newness in her description of kachina

dance songs, many of which are made new for every dance. Although these songs are tape recorded by many Zunis, they are not preserved for posterity but taped over and replaced by newer songs when they have become old.[10] This attitude may change with increased emphasis on the preservation of the "old ways" by many tribal agencies and individuals, but for the present it certainly remains.

8   At the same time many Zunis do value "old" rock art because of its presumed great antiquity, which is related to their perception of it as having been made by "the ancestors." This is a somewhat different situation from that of the rain-dance songs created last week or last year or even pots made fifty to one hundred years ago. Nor are all songs created for particular rain dances and then forgotten. For example, Barbara Tedlock distinguishes between songs that should be new each time and those most sacred prayers and ritual activities that should never be changed but must be learned word for word and carried out in the same manner from year to year.[11] Thus, both the new and the old can be valued for different reasons or in different contexts and one needs to pay attention to such contexts, particularly given the emphasis on preservation that is a contemporary concern, in certain situations, for both Native American and non-Native American peoples.

9   Finally, though some Zunis may shoot at rock art images, others are disturbed by this practice, stating that it is "a shame" and attributing it to "young kids who don't know any better." Whatever the reason for the shooting of the bear mask it is apparent that since the time of the shooting someone has tried to repair the damage. The lines of the mouth have been repainted over the bullet holes.

10   Although I have made use of Bunzel's term "compulsive magic," I dislike the sense of causality and legerdemain it seems to imply. The relationship between the action and the desired result is not conceived of by Zunis as causal in the Western scientific sense of the term. As already noted, Zunis do not believe themselves to be so endowed with power that they can make things happen. Instead, they consider that they are relatively weak beings who must consequently depend on the aid of more efficacious mediators to gain desired ends. In return for this help Zunis make appropriate offerings both to the mediators and to those even more potent beings to whom such mediators convey their prayers. Zuni religious belief is thus based not on a notion of the ability of humans to cause things to happen but on the idea of reciprocity between humans and other more powerful beings who do have the ability to effect change in the physical world.

11   An interesting illustration of the way in which Zunis view religious activity as couched in a framework of reciprocal activity, a dialectic between humans and the gods, is provided by an examination of the structure and texts of Zuni ritual prayers. Frequently the main body of these often lengthy prayers consists of a recitation, in the past tense, of all of

the ritual activities undertaken during the year; special emphasis is given to the places where such activities were carried out, including spring areas and sites marked by rock art depictions. The prayers are concluded with a request section, in the future tense, which could be summed up as meaning: "we've done our part, now you will do yours." The specific Zuni verb used to make this "request," *shema* (translated most often as "ask for"), has more accurately the meaning of "demand." In the context of the prayer, the use of this word does not strike an arrogant chord but instead expresses the Zuni belief that certain actions must inevitably happen upon the completion of others—because A has been accomplished, B surely will follow.[12]

12   Conversely, activities intended to ensure successful hunting, such as painting a deer enclosed in his "house" on a piece of pottery or carving deer with arrows through their bodies on rocks, are not simply magical acts, believed to be sufficient to produce the desired outcome. Rather, the creation of those depictions is only one part of the ritual activity believed necessary to achieve the desired end, albeit the most explicitly communicative of what is being asked for. To be effective, such depictions must be accompanied by the appropriate prayers and offerings, and the entire ritual must be carried out by one who has a "good heart."[13] When those prayers are not answered—if, for example, the dry spell continues despite the rain dances—the Zunis attribute this inefficacy to the involvement in the ceremony of someone who has a "bad heart."[14] Thus, the core of Zuni religion may be said to be a belief not in magic but in the potency of reciprocal relations, the belief that if ritual activities are carried out in the proper manner, with a good heart, the desired result will be obtained. The central issue here, then, is the power of ritual activity and related visual imagery, but only as they exist within this framework of reciprocity....

INDEXICAL POWER: INTERACTION OF IMAGE AND SITE

13   If rock art depictions such as those mentioned earlier (water beings that bring rain, insects that render one invisible or sting the enemy, and game animals and their predators that relate to successful hunting) may be regarded as powerful or capable of invoking power, does this efficacy extend to the places where such figures are found? In other words, is the potency of the imagery an index of the power of the site to which it is integral? Many early anthropologists and archaeologists have suggested that pictographs and petroglyphs were often used to mark shrine areas.[15] But what exactly is a shrine area? Can a clustering of rock art images be sacred in itself? Can it make the place where it is found powerful? It may be impossible to separate in this manner the power of the place and the power of the images found there or to distinguish one or the other as being prior or prime. This is because rock art characteristically

brings together both the power of place and the power of imagery, juxtaposing the natural world with the human creative world. Nevertheless, a discussion of certain places where rock art occurs in the Zuni-Cibola region will be useful at this point.

14   At Zuni, rock art is found beyond the confines of the pueblo proper, beyond the central dwelling place and in potentially dangerous areas less controlled by the people—areas in which raw, powerful beings dwell. Pictograph and petroglyph sites include cliff walls and caves, places where game animals and predators roam, and places where Zunis say even the powerful kachinas sometimes assume animal form and walk about. Perhaps inaccessibility itself may be a power-producing attribute of such sites. Certainly the location of a number of rock carvings and paintings far above the ground on a seemingly sheer cliff wall or high on the ceiling of a cave often led my Zuni colleagues to muse: "How did they get up there?" Although they speculated on the use of devices such as scaffolds, ropes, or arrows dipped in paint, the reasons for employing such methods remained perplexing and intriguing to contemporary Zunis. Nevertheless, images that were produced in recent times, especially those images that relate to the central themes of Zuni religion, are sometimes also located in out-of-the-way places. An obscure or hard-to-reach location is not the only means by which to render rock art inaccessible to the casual observer; diminutive size can be a contributing factor as well. One site contained finely incised and highly detailed depictions of the masks of the Council of the Gods (a group of kachinas who play a central role in the Shalako ceremony); each mask was only five centimeters high and the entire group could be easily overlooked by someone who did not already know they were there.

15   Sometimes the cultural meaning of rock art relates to its particular location. At one site, for example, a spiral and a concentric circle were carved in the rock face at a point that is directly above several connecting pools of water. One Zuni man suggested that this placement was due to the fact that the spiral figure sometimes represents water. On the day we visited this site the sun shining on the water was reflected onto the petroglyphs above, almost in a spiral design; it is possible that the figures were carved to depict this phenomenon, as well as to symbolize water. Significantly, Zuni ceremonialism and mythology link sun and water. According to the Zuni origin myth, the Twin War Gods were born of the union of the sun and a waterfall; hence they represent two of the most important aspects of Zuni ritual: prayers to the Sun Father asking that he allow the crops to thrive and prayers to the ancestors that they may send rain.[16] The connection between the meaning of a rock art depiction and the place where it is located is illustrated further by the comment made by a Zuni man who was very familiar with a number of the rock art sites when we were looking at projected slides. Even though I had not grouped these slides by site and was not asking for any sort of

information concerning location, this man quite accurately accompanied his identifications of images with descriptions of the sites where they occur. Every now and then, however, he encountered a figure he hadn't seen before. His response on one such occasion was: "I don't know what it means because I've never been out there." Thus, for him meaning was tied to specific location and he couldn't be expected to identify an image on a slide that he hadn't seen in reality, situated in its appropriate context. The importance of context was also revealed by those Zunis who came with me to rock art sites. They not only looked closely at the carved and painted figures on rock surfaces, but carefully observed the features of the landscape within which the rock art was located, paying particular attention to varieties of plants, sources of water when available, bird nests, and animal tracks. Sometimes they spent as much time instructing me in the uses of wild plants as they did talking to me about rock art—obviously, they consider all of these aspects of their environment to be significant....

16   Whether or not Zunis regard them as officially sacred, then, they do perceive certain rock art images and sites to be powerful either because they evoke the myth time or because they depict beings that Zunis associate with vital aspects of the physical world; they regard these latter figures as efficacious in achieving various desired ends. Generally, such potent carvings and paintings are highly representational or iconic, they are powerful because of their similarity, both in form and function, to beings associated with the central theme of Zuni life—increase or fertility. Thus, because particular creatures live in or near the water, their depiction on rock surfaces near the village contribute to "making it rain." And, of course, the creatures themselves have this ability by virtue of their association with water; hence, on certain occasions, those who dance for rain carry living turtles in their hands. Sometimes this power derives not from association with life-supporting natural phenomena but from physical characteristics that make these creatures powerful. Certain insects and prey animals, for instance, possess desirable attributes that humans can accrue to themselves through ritual activities; such ritual activities seem sometimes to involve the depiction of these creatures as rock art images. Rock art elements in the Zuni area are thus integral to a complex symbolic system—a system that reflects concepts basic to Zuni life and definition of the world.

REFERENCES

1. Ruth L. Bunzel, "Introduction to Zuñi Ceremonialism," pp. 489–92.
2. For a further discussion of such iconic power, *see* Kay Turner, "The Cultural Semiotics of Religious Icons: La Virgen de San Juan de los Lagos," pp. 317–61.
3. Ruth L. Bunzel, *The Pueblo Potter: A Study of Creative Imagination in Primitive Art,* pp. 23–24, 69–71. Bunzel points out that the water-related

designs are painted not on pottery water jars, but on the bowls that are used to hold sacred cornmeal. This emphasizes the connection between sufficient water and the growth of plants, especially life-giving corn.
4. Frank H. Cushing, "Zuñi Fetiches," pp. 11–12.
5. Bunzel, *The Pueblo Potter,* pp. 94–95.
6. Matilda C. Stevenson, "The Zuñi Indians: Their Mythology, Esoteric Fraternities, and Ceremonies," p. 439.
7. Occupied during the early part of the eleventh century, this area contains the ruins of a large, multiroomed living complex that included two large and several smaller circular kivas. For a discussion of the rock art here, *see* M. Jane Young, "Images of Power, Images of Beauty: Contemporary Zuni Perceptions of Rock Art," p. 66, and the description of site I in the Appendix of this book. Frank H. H. Roberts, Jr., "The Village of the Great Kivas on the Zuñi Reservation, New Mexico," describes the archaeological work conducted at this site.
8. Zunis made these and the following identifications.
9. Bunzel, "Introduction to Zuñi Ceremonialism," p. 506; M. Stevenson, "The Zuñi Indians," pp. 97, 141, 146, 564.
10. Barbara Tedlock, "Kachina Dance Songs in Zuni Society: The Role of Esthetics in Social Integration," pp. 90–92.
11. Ibid.
12. Ruth L. Bunzel, "Zuñi Ritual Poetry," pp. 615–20; M. Jane Young, "Translation and Analysis of Zuni Ritual Poetry."
13. Bunzel, "Introduction to Zuñi Ceremonialism," pp. 492, 505–6, 522; Elsie C. Parsons, "Notes on Zuñi," pp. 238–41; M. Stevenson, "The Zuñi Indians," pp. 166, 252.
14. M. Stevenson, "The Zuñi Indians," p. 166.
15. *See, for example,* J. Walter Fewkes, "A Few Summer Ceremonials at Zuñi Pueblo," pp. 9–10; M. Stevenson, "The Zuñi Indians," pp. 40, 43, 294.
16. Frank H. Cushing, "Outlines of Zuñi Creation Myths," p. 381; Frank H. Cushing, *Zuñi Folk Tales,* pp. 378–79; M. Stevenson, "The Zuñi Indians," p. 24.

Reading for Meaning

1. What powers do the Zunis associate with particular images that appear in their art?
2. Compare the Zunis' attitude toward art with outsiders' ideas about the importance of preserving ancient artifacts. What seems to influence the Zuni's appreciation of the "new" and the "old" art?
3. Young explains that for the Zunis, image and ritual work together to achieve desired results but only "within [a] framework of reciprocity." What does "reciprocity" mean in this context?

4. What characterizes the locations that Zunis, both ancient and modern, select as sites for their artwork? What are possible explanations for these choices?
5. In her analysis of Zuni art, what sources does Jane M. Young use to support her ideas? How convincing are her interpretations?

Comparing Texts

1. Read "The Water-Faucet Vision," page 151, and compare Callie's belief in the power of certain objects to help her get what she wants to the Zuni belief in the efficacy of certain images.
2. In following excerpt from *The Intellectual Adventure of Ancient Man*, H. A. Frankfort describes the "speculative thinking" characteristic of ancient peoples. Identify elements of this kind of thinking that the Zunis seem to have retained, perhaps from their ancestors.

1   If we look for "speculative thought" in the documents of the ancients, we shall be forced to admit that there is very little indeed in our written records which deserves the name of "thought" in the strict sense of that term. There are very few passages which show the discipline, the cogency of reasoning, which we associate with thinking. The thought of the ancient Near East appears wrapped in imagination. We consider it tainted with fantasy. But the ancients would not have admitted that anything could be abstracted from the concrete imaginative forms which they left us....

2   The ancients saw man always as part of society, and society as imbedded in nature and dependent upon cosmic forces. For them nature and man did not stand in opposition and did not, therefore, have to be apprehended by different modes of cognition. Natural phenomena were regularly conceived in terms of human experience and human experience was conceived in terms of cosmic events.... The fundamental difference between the attitudes of modern and ancient man as regards the surrounding world is this: for modern, scientific man the phenomenal world is primarily an "It." For ancient—and also for primitive—man it is a "Thou."

3   Now the knowledge which "I" has of "Thou" hovers between the active judgment and the passive "undergoing of an impression" between the intellectual and the emotional, the articulate and the inarticulate.... "Thou" is a live presence, whose qualities and potentialities can be made somewhat articulate—not as a result of active inquiry but because "thou," as a presence, reveals itself.

Ideas for Writing

1. Several of the Zuni people interviewed by Jane M. Young for her study of Zuni rock art felt that paintings and carvings of game animals like the deer, mountain sheep, bear, and buffalo "not only recorded a successful hunt but [also] propitiated the spirits of the animals that had

been slain, ensuring more such success in the future." Find information on cave paintings from western Europe, especially those in Spanish caves like the ones at Altamira. Use the research material you gathered and information from Young's article on the Zunis to discuss possible meanings of the animals depicted in the paintings and petroglyphs of these cultures.

2. Choose an ancient civilization, such as the ones in Sumaria, China, Egypt, or one of the pre-Columbian cultures of Latin America. Use library and electronic sources to find information about the civilization you have chosen. After recording and arranging the information you have gathered, write an investigation paper that discusses how the art of this ancient culture reflects the people's beliefs or way of life.

Writing before Reading

What folktales or fairy tales do you remember reading? How are women or young girls depicted in those tales?

MARRIAGE IN THE HAUSA *TATSUNIYA* TRADITION: A CULTURAL AND COSMIC BALANCE

Connie Stephens

The following essay appeared in the collection of studies titled Hausa Women in the 20th Century *(1991). In the essay Stephens analyzes elements in the stories* (tatsuniya) *of the Hausa women of northwest Africa that give women some measure of self-worth in the male-dominated Islamic culture in which they live.*

Facts about the Hausa People of West Africa

The Hausa constitute a major linguistic and ethnic group in West Africa. They are an ancient people with a vibrant oral tradition. The first history of the Hausa people appeared in the eleventh century in the Arabic *Kano Chronicle*. Today, Hausa is the most commonly spoken language in West Africa. There are approximately 9 million Hausa people living in North Africa; most live in Nigeria and Niger. They became Muslim in the fourteenth century, but elements of their former tribal religions remain, particularly in the countryside. Most Hausa are farmers, although many are skilled craftspeople and traders.

1 *Ga ta nan, ga ta nanku*—"Here it is, here is a tale for you," the traditional storyteller begins. *Ta zo, mu ji ta,* the children reply—"Let it come, let's hear it." Storytelling is as old as humanity, and so it is among the Hausa, where folktale narrative *(tatsuniya)* is an important form of entertainment among children and adults alike.

2 Folktales are only one of many forms of Hausa oral literature. Other types include: the song poem *(wak'a);* the historical narrative *(labari);* the praise song *(kirari);* drama *(wasan kwaikwayo);* the proverb *(karin magana);* and fiction *(litafin hira)* (Skinner 1980). Many of these latter forms are contained in or overlap with the folktale narrative.

3 It is not surprising that women are the primary storytellers, entertaining the children they tend with didactic tales (M. G. Smith 1969; Skinner 1969; Stephens 1981). Yet it is a function of social circumstance that the earliest published Hausa oral narratives were told by Hausa men for inclusion in collections by European explorers like Frederick Schoen in the nineteenth century and British colonial officers at the turn of the twentieth century. Collecting Hausa tales and histories as language and cultural materials, British colonial officers made significant contributions to the preservation of early Hausa literature (M. G. Smith 1969). The most extensive such collection was made by Frank Edgar in the Sokoto region about 1911. The first of three volumes included materials given to him by Resident Officer, Major John Alder Burdon. It was followed by two other volumes of material that Edgar collected later (Skinner 1969; M. G. Smith 1969). Translations of these materials to English came much later when H. A. S. Johnston published some of Edgar's collection in *A Selection of Hausa Stories* in 1966, and A. Neil Skinner translated the largest portion of Edgar's work for *Hausa Tales and Traditions,* published in several volumes in 1969 and 1977.

4 Although Hausa men still perform *tatsuniyoyi,* probably more so in Niger than in Nigeria, the tales are more often told by women. The steady growth of Islam, with its own narrative and poetic traditions, has encouraged the idea that men should concentrate on more overtly religious themes. Women, who generally spend less time in Qur'anic school and at the mosque, are more likely to perpetuate the pre-Islamic *tatsuniya* tradition. Contemporary folktales do incorporate many Islamic images, but they also reflect roles, rituals, and social relationships with a much longer history in Hausaland. They speak to the culture's dependence on nature—and on Hausa wives and mothers to nurture families in their agricultural milieu.

5 Both Hausa men and women are profoundly shaped by their agricultural subsistence economy. From early childhood girls anticipate a productive domestic role. Women contribute significantly to labor-intensive

food preparation as mothers of numerous children and also as farmers on their husbands' or their own personal plots. Yet within this context, performers of the Hausa *tatsuniya,* a predominantly women's oral narrative tradition, argue in a feminist vein.¹ Their narratives suggest that women in traditional family roles are not dependent and inferior, but rather independent of and even superior to their male counterparts. Recognizing the self-esteem these narratives foster among women is especially significant in light of the recurrent accusation that Muslim societies accord women very low status.

6   Over 90 percent of some 40 million or more Hausa people in West Africa consider themselves to be Muslim; certainly many elements of Hausa Islam suggest a low status for women. Religious scholars teach that a virtuous woman always owes obedience to a man, either her father or her husband. Whereas men pray in public, women pray within the confines of their compounds because it is felt their presence might provoke lustful desires in men, for which women would be responsible. Under Islamic law a woman inherits less of the family property than her brother does; her husband can divorce her by pronouncement, but she must go through a complex legal process to divorce him. Economically, her options for generating income traditionally are far less remunerative than those open to men.

7   Narratives of the *tatsuniya* tradition repeatedly offer a counterpoint to this Islamic ideology. Although the *tatsuniyoyi* predate the mass adoption of Islam in Hausaland, contemporary narratives incorporate many Muslim images. Women are most often portrayed in traditional roles as cook and mother. But far from playing dependent wives, many of these heroines consistently challenge and best their husbands. Moreover, oppositions recur, aligning female antagonists with natural and supernatural powers against husbands who represent worldly, political authority. Conflicts occur between these counterforces and are mediated by women with supernatural abilities to nurture and produce life. If anyone must acknowledge dependency, it is a husband, whose political power is no match for his wife's supernatural power and whose cultural role is sustained by her culinary and reproductive abilities. In these tales women are separate and superior; they are highly esteemed in their traditional domain. Examining four narratives reveals how Hausa performers subtly

---

¹ Especially since the popular assimilation of Islam, men have elected to emphasize Qur'anic studies rather than the folktale tradition as an appropriate pursuit for serious Muslim men. However, especially in Niger, some men of all ages continue to perform *tatsuniyoyi.* In fact, in my own collection I found that these men count among the most outstanding performers. Two factors may contribute: (1) since they are at least somewhat nonconformist, only the most skilled male artists persist in performing the *tatsuniyoyi,* and (2) in general, Hausa men are much more accustomed than women in public speaking of any kind, and community roles may encourage their narrative abilities.

build their argument. Their heroines are associated with other natural and supernatural figures, and they resolve conflicts through their womanly expertise in bearing and nurturing life.

The Narratives

8   One of the simplest Hausa narratives involves a marital competition (Stephens 1981:511–18). The daughter of a Muslim religious scholar *(malam)* desires to marry a prince. Initially her father objects because he prefers that she marry another Qur'anic scholar like himself. Although he capitulates, his hesitation reinforces the tension between the bride's association with her father's supernatural, religious authority and her groom's worldly, political power.

9   The marriage is made, and the *malam*'s daughter becomes a second wife. Immediately the prince launches a contest with his new bride. He offers rice to his first wife and stones to the new spouse, instructing each to make a meal. The *malam*'s daughter returns home, and her father miraculously turns the co-wife's rice to stones and his daughter's stones to rice.

10   This simple contest establishes important patterns. First, the bride, through ties to her supernatural father, is able to defeat her royal husband, despite his supreme political status. Second, the contest she wins is in the traditionally feminine domain of food preparation. She requires a miracle but fulfills her task to nourish her new family.

11   This pattern is varied but repeated in the second, more taxing challenge spelled out by the prince. As he mounts his stallion to ride to another country, he instructs his bride that before he returns, her mare must bear his stallion's colt and she must bear his son. Once again her *malam* father works a miracle, this time by disguising her as a prostitute and transporting her to her husband's lodgings. Her man is smitten, and she bargains for their horses to mate before she accepts him as a lover. Thus when the prince returns, his new bride has had his child and her mare the required colt. The senior wife is cast out and the marriage is at last stabilized.

12   A female contest affiliated with supernatural power has bested her male, political rival a second time. Moreover, her triumph concerns another traditionally female province, the bearing of children. Even the prince is dependent on his wife to produce his heir, and he is incapable of preventing that miracle. Symbolically, their stabilized marriage portrays a viable balance between supernatural, female authority and worldly, male authority, a balance that assures new life. As established in the tale of the *malam*'s daughter, a woman and her supernatural affiliation play an equal, if not a superior, part in that equilibrium.

13   The first two major conflicts in another popular Hausa tale specifically pose the question of whether sons or daughters are more valuable

(Stephens 1981:531–43). The King of the East, father of several sons, is indebted to the King of the West, whose children are all daughters. The debtor refuses to make good his loan until his friend has a son come collect the debt. Sons, as opposed to daughters, thus represent superior wealth; without them the debt cannot be claimed.

14   However, the King of the West has a daughter, 'Yal Baturiya, a bold girl who declares that she is just as suited as a brother would be to collect her father's due. So she disguises herself as a boy and queries her father's stallion, "Kili, horse of my father, if you take me, will you bring me back?" Receiving an affirmative reply, 'Yal Baturiya mounts her steed and sets off.

15   Along the way she politely greets an ant who joins her quest. Once at her destination she announces her mission, and the men at court give her a series of tasks to prove that she is indeed a son, not a daughter. Each trial involves a choice, and each time alternatives are presented, the stallion Kili reveals the appropriate response for a boy. First she chooses correctly between two staple foods. Next, she sorts, rather than mixes, a collection of grain; her new friend, the ant, gives invaluable help. Finally, she must go swimming to expose her private parts. Kili distracts her audience by charging after the king's horse. In an alternate version of the narrative, the horse's supernatural powers enable him to exchange sexual organs with his mistress (Stephens 1981:551). This final test passed, the debtor's nobles conclude they must pay off the disguised princess. As she departs, she taunts them with her proven equality, "I'm 'Yal Baturiya and I came to fetch my father's money. I'm a girl, not a boy" (Stephens 1981:537). They mount a chase, but the heroine, master of nature and magic, throws thickets, water, and fire in their path.

16   The bested King of the East is furious at the deception and seeks revenge by marrying 'Yal Baturiya. Once again he disadvantages her and sends her off to poverty as an outcast leper's wife. She resolutely accepts this fate until a messenger appears from the palace in search of cooking fire. Along with the fire, the messenger takes home tales of 'Yal Baturiya's dazzling gold draftsmen. When the same messenger returns to borrow the draftsmen, their mistress insists first on having a night with the king while the king's wife sleeps with 'Yal Baturiya's leper husband. Disguised, each wife conceives a son who looks like his actual father.

17   Later 'Yal Baturiya takes her son to the palace, where the courtiers immediately recognize him as a prince. They set a trial to identify the king's and the leper's respective offspring; her son reveals his royal origins. 'Yal Baturiya and her prince are promptly installed at the palace, establishing a final equilibrium within both her marriage and the kingdom.

18   This tale argues forthrightly that girls are equal to and as independent as boys. By disguising herself as a son, the heroine effectively portrays both genders simultaneously; her challengers are unable to tell the difference. She matches any brother she might have had in defending her family's fortune, and her deception makes her superior to a large

group of male adversaries. Moreover, she is strongly associated with supernatural powers which are, in turn, related to the life-sustaining female roles identified in the previous tale of the *malam*'s daughter.

19 Through her religious father, the earlier heroine gained supernatural powers to defeat her royal husband. 'Yal Baturiya also performs supernatural feats to defy her male political adversaries, but the sources of her magic are the animals and plants of nature. Her father's stallion becomes her collaborator at the beginning of her quest, and his supernatural powers increase as the tale continues. He magically discerns the responses his mistress must give to preserve her disguise as a son. In the version in which he exchanges sexual organs with her, he can also manipulate the physical world at will. The heroine acquires another ally in the ant, who also displays supernatural abilities when it helps sort her grain. Additionally, when she escapes with her father's money, she fends off her pursuers with her command of nature by hurling thickets, fire, and water to block their path.

20 Like the *malam*'s daughter, 'Yal Baturiya displays supernatural powers in cooking and childbearing, two ways Hausa women traditionally nurture life. With help, she is able to preserve her disguise by choosing the correct staple food and sorting grain for food. Once married, she attracts the attention of her husband's household because she controls the fire they need for cooking. As in the previous *tatsuniya*, her final triumph occurs because, disguised, she can bear her rightful husband's child despite his efforts to the contrary. Motherhood assures harmony in her domestic life and in the cosmic balance between her natural and supernatural affinities and her husband's political world. By dominating traditionally female roles, the heroine resists oppression.

21 'Yal Baturiya's story also juxtaposes sexual oppression with other forms of cosmic disequilibrium and social oppression. As she sets off to prove her sexual equality, she draws a parallel with the equality between man and nature necessary to their mutual harmony. When the ant asks to accompany her, she answers, "A person is going to refuse another person?" (Stephens 1981:533). By granting equal status to even the smallest of nature's creatures, she gains the ant's help to preserve her disguise as a boy. Then following her marriage, the narrative criticizes another social equality. When her husband orders her banished to a life of poverty as a leper's wife, she responds, "So be it. A leper is human" (Stephens 1981:539).[2]

22 Tyranny, she suggests, has not rightful place in Hausa culture. To be humane is to acknowledge the equality and interdependence of diverse

---

[2] In the Hausa practice of Islam, leprosy is viewed as the punishment of those who have committed the heinous sin of swearing falsely on the Qur'an. This belief and the increasingly repulsive appearance of lepers as the disease progresses combine to give them a supremely low social status.

elements of the Hausa milieu: nature and humanity, rich and poor, powerful and weak, male and female. Man and woman may be as distinct as man and animal, king and subject, but each plays an independent role vital to the other.

23   'Yal Baturiya's affiliation with nature and its supernatural potential was strongly suggested through her collaboration with Kili. In other Hausa tales a young bride bridges the human and natural realm even more explicitly. She is a creature of two identities, the first expressing her origin in nature, and the second reflecting the royal human identity she gains by marrying a prince. Moreover, her links to nature permit her to lead her husband to a stable cultural and political identity and full adulthood. The heroes of these *tatsuniyoyi* portray Hausaland's highest authority, the *sarki,* or emir. But in these narratives the *sarki*'s authority depends on his wife's natural and supernatural ties, which are once again associated with women's traditional role of sustaining human life.

24   Laɓo is the heroine of one such narrative (Stephens 1981: 731–58). Her mother is a python impregnated by "a great stud of a man." The daughter they produce is born an exquisite human child. However, her snake mother promptly swallows and regurgitates her as a pitiful urchin with festering sores whom she calls "God's poor slave" (Stephens 1981:731). Then she sends the girl away from the wilderness to beg for a home in God's name, as if she were a Muslim Qur'anic student. Laɓo is thus an ambiguous heroine, simultaneously a child of the human, natural, and supernatural realms. Combined with her natural origins, her supernatural characteristics reflect the beliefs of Islam.[3]

25   An old woman from the royal palace takes the sorry Laɓo home, where Maman, the spoiled prince, threatens to kill her. However, the girl joins the household as a servant and maintains a relationship to her animal mother by visiting her when she fetches wood for the cooking fires.

26   When the prince gives a grand party, Laɓo reveals that she is something special, worthy to be his royal mate. Like the other maidens vying for his attention, she cooks him a tempting sweet. Before she attends the festivities, her mother swallows and regurgitates her in her original stunning human form. Maman is enchanted, and as she leaves he offers her his ring and promises to pursue her.

27   Before her suitor comes to visit, Laɓo's mother retransforms her to an urchin. This time, when she prepares his favorite sweet, she hides his ring inside. Discovering the ring, he realizes that the urchin and her dazzling alter-ego are the same Laɓo. His earlier threat to murder her changes to a marriage proposal. Laɓo's role as nature's bride is reinforced when her python mother attends the wedding accompanied by many

---

[3] As a part of their religious training, Qur'anic students are literally expected to beg for their food. Thus Laɓo at least partially assumes this religious role when she sets off with instructions to beg for both food and shelter.

other wild beasts. Just before the ceremony the snake swallows and spits forth her daughter in a form befitting royal splendor. The marriage of man and woman, culture and nature, and political and supernatural power seems to have been made.

28 Yet the narrative further elaborates the relationship of these spheres. Laɓo must help her prince establish his own relation with nature before their marriage is fully cemented. This process is initiated when Maman's father, the king, plots to usurp Laɓo for himself by sending his son away to be killed in the bush. As Maman leaves, his bride gives him dates and her ring. Far into the wilderness the king orders that his son be buried alive at the bottom of a well.

29 The dates, Laɓo's gift from nature, permit Maman's resurrection. They nourish him, and their seeds produce the tree that he climbs to the top of the well. Maman's rebirth thus symbolizes his passage through nature. He emerges as nature's wild man, unshaven and barely clothed. By dropping Laɓo's ring into her servant's calabash of milk, he signals her that he has returned to life. She rides out to meet him with barbers and royal clothing to transform him permanently into a ruler. When his father appears, Maman deposes him and assumes the royal throne.

30 The repeated images symbolizing the heroine's identification with the natural and the supernatural have been noted in the narrative summary and need be only briefly listed here: Laɓo's mother is a snake whom she visits regularly when she collects firewood in the wilderness; a variety of wild beasts attends her wedding; her animal mother is also magically able to transform her into God's poor beggar, the Muslim guise in which she joins the royal household; the dates that she offers her husband represent the food man reaps from nature; supernaturally, they save his life by sprouting a tree he climbs to new life.

31 Laɓo's portrayal fuses both the religious elements of the *malam*'s daughter and the aspects of nature manifested in 'Yal Baturiya. And like her narrative counterparts, Laɓo relates these affiliations to women's culinary skills. However, she varies their pattern of producing new offspring. Instead, she orchestrates another life-giving miracle, the rebirth of her prince and husband.

32 She repeatedly helps nourish her household. Initially she is responsible for fetching the wood to feed the cooking fires. When Maman is still threatening to murder her, she twice signals her exquisite second self by preparing his favorite sweet, first when she attends his party and then when he returns to visit her. The second time he discovers his ring inside the cake, and their marriage is sealed. Later she sends him off to certain death with dates to nourish him and bring about his rebirth. Moreover, the servant who discovers the resurrected prince and returns with his ring has been sent to fetch a foodstuff, milk, from the palace herds.

33 Laɓo's image as a female nurturer is closely tied to her mediating role between nature and culture. She ventures into the bush of her birth

to find firewood and brings it back to fuel the palace kitchen. The *nakiya* sweet she prepares for the prince functions to link her dual natural and human identities in his mind. The dates are nature's food. They are eaten raw but contain the seed which, grown into a tree, brings the hero back to his human realm. And milk too is a natural product which the Hausa normally ferment and add to other foods. Figuratively, Laɓo's nurturing and life-giving roles merge.

34   Laɓo's function as the source of life is somewhat altered from the image of the *malam*'s daughter or 'Yal Baturiya. Each of these earlier heroines equilibriated an imbalanced marriage by giving birth to her husband's child, despite the obstacles he established. Each son so perfectly resembled his father that he was forced to acknowledge the child's mother as his wife—a wife whose life-giving power outweighed his efforts to deny her marital and (for 'Yal Baturiya) royal status. In narrative terms, the sons express a man's dependency on his wife to reproduce his family line and sustain Hausa culture. The birth of the children also mediates the narrative conflicts, transforming marital conflict into domestic harmony.

35   The Laɓo tale portrays her prince's dependency in terms of his own person, although her life-giving power is still the source of her ability to achieve a balanced marriage. Rather than producing a new life, Laɓo resurrects the prince himself. His dependency and transformation mirror her own. Earlier he was the cultural figure who enticed her away from nature's space toward marriage and a permanent cultural identity. She in turn performs the same function for him. He is incompletely acculturated until he too merges with nature and the supernatural and returns a composite character. He is resurrected as nature's creature, and only through Laɓo's actions does he become a properly acculturated human ruler. They are balanced and interdependent, not only as woman and man but also as nature's and culture's respective offspring. Expressed in other stereotypes, this is not a tale of "civilized" man taming an "earth mother" or of "civilized" woman socializing a "man of the wilderness." It is both these dramas at once, and woman's source of power to assure this domestic and cosmic balance is her life-giving potential.

36   A final *tatsuniya* portrays a royal wife of natural and supernatural origins who explicitly challenges her royal mate's political power. This is the tale of the Squash Girl, who publicly kills her king when he claims that he is greater than she. In a graphic demonstration of her own life-giving power, she then resurrects him.

37   The version discussed here, performed by Baba Ladi in Mirria Niger, is a veritable political satire (Stephens 1981:447–76). Like storytellers everywhere, Hausa *tatsuniya* performers weave their narratives from familiar plot sequences. But Baba Ladi, an emir's daughter and wife, performed beneath the shadows of the palace for women and children of multiple royal connections and added a daring and delightful touch to

her rendition of the tale. She named her characters after Mirria's own rulers sitting inside the royal quarters just yards away. Her villainesses were played by the royal wives. Satirizing these privileged women, she fictitiously beheaded them in retribution for their pompous attitudes. In doing so, she added a unique dimension of humor and immediacy to her narrative, a critique not only of men who underestimate the resources of their female counterparts but of all oppressive rulers.

38   Baba Ladi's story of the Squash Girl illustrates now familiar patterns: the heroine is associated in multiple ways with nature and the supernatural; she demonstrates her superior culinary abilities; she acts out her physiological and cultural ability to perpetuate life.

39   The Squash Girl, like Laɓo, is affiliated with nature and the supernatural where she is born. Her old and barren mother pleads to Allah to bless her with a child, even "if it's no more than a squash" (Stephens 1981:447). And so it is. Following this immaculate conception, she bears a squash.

40   The tie between nature and culture is further developed when the Squash Girl reveals her existence to her mother. The older woman goes out one day, leaving behind the cotton she had teased to make into thread. While she is away, her disguised daughter pops out of her squash and spins the thread. In this way the daughter signals her dual, natural and human identities by transforming a natural product into a cultural article. And she also suggests her supernatural powers by performing this minor miracle.

41   The heroine's link to the supernatural is reinforced when she is alone spinning one day and a Qur'anic student comes by to beg. He is the first human being to see her. Immediately he rushes to the emir to tell his ruler that he alone must marry this exquisite young woman. Off go the king's courtiers to claim her. Despite the old woman's protesting sobs, they cart her squash off to the royal compound.

42   The Squash Girl expresses her nurturing role as a cook at the same time she reveals her stunning human identity. While she is still a squash, the king demands that she and her future co-wives prepare food for a wedding feast. Her old woman attendant despairs, because a squash obviously cannot cook. Cooking food, however, like spinning thread, is work that women do transforming natural products into cultural forms; the girl inside the squash emerges a second time. She sends her attendant off for pots and condiments. All the raw ingredients are placed in the pans, and by morning there has been another miracle. Fragrant pots of porridge *(tuwo)*, the Hausa staple dish, are ready for the ruler. Moreover, the other wives, who have mocked the squash bride, are unable to cook their food. This supernatural event, permitting an exemplary wife to cook while preventing her antagonistic co-wives from doing the same, recalls the tale of the *malam*'s daughter.

43   Once she has fulfilled her traditional nurturing role, the Squash Girl demonstrates the emir's dependence on her life-giving powers. Dazzling everyone in her human form, she promptly challenges her mate,

"Emir, am I greater than you are, or are you greater than I am?"
"No question, I'm greater than you are, Squash Girl."
"Tell all the drummers to stop" (Stephens 1981:469).

44   The emir does so, to no avail. But when his bride looks their way, they disappear. The couple repeats a similar challenge to dispose of the crowd, with the same result. The spectators ignore the husband's command to die, but the Squash Girl obliterates them all. Finally, she destroys the emir too, leaving him headless on the ground.

45   This hybrid heroine is explicitly more powerful than her royal spouse. The root of his dependency is ultimately not so much her power to destroy, but to create. She resurrects first the crowd and then her husband and ruler. He confesses, "You're greater than I am" (Stephens 1981:471). The crowd picks up the chant, her malicious co-wives are beheaded, and a new, stable royal household is established.

46   The Squash Girl plays an even stronger role in her marriage than Laɓo did. The former bestows and nurtures life, and she also destroys it. Metaphorically the dying crowd and emir interpret the implication of a woman's absence from the marriage bond; the implication is no less than the inability of Hausa culture to perpetuate itself.

Conclusion

47   Collectively, the four heroines act out the miracles of reproduction and resurrection in a specific context in these *tatsuniyoyi*. Their physical identities, the spatial movements they make, the actions they perform, and the resolution of their conflicts combine to depict Hausa wives as separate and often superior partners in their marriages. Their royal husbands may be more worldly and active in the community life outside the family compound, but their political power is limited to human dimensions and unable to extend itself beyond a single generation. In contrast, the heroines have close natural and supernatural affiliations by birth, originate from natural spaces, and even have alternative physical identities as natural products or creatures. They often nurture and create life itself as a result of these extracultural qualities. When their politically powerful mates attempt to obstruct their life-giving efforts, the women triumph.

48   These Hausa narratives present marriage as a microcosm of the wider universe. Wives and husbands represent distinct but interdependent domains. Women are natural and supernatural; men are political and cultural. Although the need to socialize natural and supernatural force is portrayed in terms of maidens marrying princes, there is a clear argument that men are not therefore free to dominate completely. To the contrary, 'Yal Baturiya and the Squash Girl explicitly humiliate the men who advance such notions.

49   The narrative spouses are mutually dependent. Each helps to fully socialize the other—whether to change from a squash to a wife or to return from death in the bush to life in the palace. Each is vital to the partnership,

just as natural and supernatural forces interact with cultural activities to produce the Hausa world. However, if one side of these forces sometimes needs to dominate, or at least to direct the other, it is more often the supernatural-natural domain that shapes the human culture rather than the reverse. Man transforms natural products, but without them he would quickly perish. Nature's need for man is not so clearly evident. Similarly, men shape women in important ways, but without women the culture they often seem to dominate would die. *Tatsuniya* performers have long communicated this message in image form.

REFERENCES

Smith, Michael G. "Introduction." *Hausa Tales and Traditions.* Vol. 1. Ed. A. Neil Skinner. London: Frank Cass, 1969.

Skinner, A. Neil. *An Anthology of Hausa Literature.* Zaria, Nigeria: Northern Nigerian Publishing, 1980.

—*Hausa Tales and Traditions: An English Translation of "Tatsuniyoyi na Hausa,"* originally compiled by Frank Edgar. Vol. 1. London: Frank Cass, 1969.

Stevens, Connie L. "The Relationship of Social Symbols and Narrative Metaphor: A Study of Fantasy and Disguise in the Hausa *Tatsuniya* of Niger." 2 vols. Ph.D. diss., University of Wisconsin-Madison, 1981.

Reading for Meaning

1. By what authority does Connie Stephens write her study of the Hausa culture? What kind of knowledge of that culture does she have?

2. Identify the thesis for Stephens's essay about the storytelling tradition as practiced by Hausa women. What evidence supports her thesis? How convincing do you find her examples and explanations?

3. How does Islamic ideology give men the advantage in Hausa culture? In your experience, do men seem to have an advantage?

4. The first group of tales that Stephens analyzes in her essay treats the theme of marital competition. How do the stories affirm a "cosmic balance" between supernatural power (female) and secular authority (male)? Do you find anything in these tales that might compromise Stephens's argument that the female "performers of the Hausa *tatsuniya* . . . argue in a feminist vein"?

5. In the tale of the Squash Girl, what is the significance of her first destroying, then resurrecting, other characters in the tale?

Comparing Texts

In the following excerpt from Italo Calvino's modern fairy tale, "The Canary Prince," the princess (who is never given a name) is kept in a high tower by her evil stepmother. With the help of a good witch, the princess succeeds in turning a prince-admirer into a canary long enough to fly into her window and out again after their encounter. At the point in the story where our text begins, the canary prince, who is now back home, lies ill with seemingly incurable wounds, a victim of a trap set by the evil stepmother. Try to use Connie Stephens's way of analyzing a story as you identify feminist[2] elements in Calvino's story.

1. The princess meanwhile was consumed with longing for her lover. She cut her sheets into thin strips which she tied one to the other in a long, long, rope. Then one night she let herself down from the high tower and set on the hunters' trail. But because of the thick darkness and the howls of the wolves, she decided to wait for daylight. Finding an old oak with a hollow trunk, she nestled inside and, in her exhaustion, fell asleep at once. She woke up while it was still pitch-dark, under the impression she had heard a whistle. Listening closely, she heard another whistle, then a third and a fourth, after which she saw four candle flames advancing. They were four witches coming from the four corners of the earth to their appointed meeting under that tree. Through a crack in the trunk the princess, unseen by them, spied on the four crones carrying candies and sneering a welcome to one another: "Ah, ah, ah!"
2. They lit a bonfire under the tree and sat down to warm themselves and roast a couple of bats for dinner. When they had eaten their fill, they began asking one another what they had seen of interest out in the world.
3. "I saw the sultan of Turkey, who bought himself twenty new wives."
4. "I saw the emperor of China, who has let his pigtail grow three yards long."
5. "I saw the king of the cannibals, who ate his chamberlain by mistake."
6. "I saw the king of this region, who has the sick son nobody can cure, since I alone know the remedy."
7. "And what is it?" asked the other witches.
8. "In the floor of his room is a loose tile. All one need do is lift the tile, and there underneath is a phial containing an ointment that would heal every one of his wounds."
9. It was all the princess inside the tree could do not to scream for joy. By this time the witches had told one another all they had to say, so each went her own way. The princess jumped from the tree and set out in the dawn for the city. At the first secondhand dealer's she came to, she bought an old doctor's gown and a pair of spectacles, and knocked at the royal palace. Seeing the little doctor with such scant paraphernalia, the

---

[2] The term "feminist" as used here refers to the belief in the social, political, and economic equality of the sexes.

servants weren't going to let him in, but the king said, "What harm could he do my son who can't be any worse off than he is now? Let him see what he can do." The sham doctor asked to be left alone with the sick man, and the request was granted.

10   Finding her lover groaning and unconscious in his sickbed, the princess felt like weeping and smothering him with kisses. But she restrained herself because of the urgency of carrying out the witch's directions. She paced up and down the room until she stepped on a loose tile, which she raised and discovered a phial of ointment. With it she rubbed the prince's wounds, and no sooner had she touched each one with ointment than the wound disappeared completely. Overjoyed she called the king, who came in and saw his son sleeping peacefully, with the color back in his checks, and no trace of any of the wounds.

11   "Ask for whatever you like, doctor," said the king. "All the wealth in the kingdom is yours."

12   "I wish no money," replied the doctor, "Just give me the prince's shield bearing the family coat-of-arms, his standard, and his yellow vest that was rent and bloodied." Upon receiving the three items, she took her leave.

13   Three days later, the king's son was again out hunting. He passed the castle in the heart of the forest, but didn't deign to look up at the princess's window. She immediately picked up the book, leafed through it, and the prince had no choice but change into a canary. He flew into the room, and the princess turned him back into a man.

14   "Let me go," he said. "Isn't it enough to have pierced me with those pins of yours and caused me so much agony?" The prince, in truth, no longer loved the girl, blaming her for his misfortune.

15   On the verge of fainting, she exclaimed, "But I saved your life! I am the one who cured you!"

16   "That's not so," said the prince. "My life was saved by a foreign doctor who asked for no recompense except my coat-of-arms, my standard, and my bloodied vest!"

17   "Here are your coat-of-arms, your standard, and your vest! The doctor was none other than myself. The pins were the cruel doing of my stepmother!"

18   The prince gazed into her eyes, dumbfounded. Never had she looked so beautiful. He fell at her feet asking her forgiveness and declaring his deep gratitude and love.

19   That very evening he informed his father he was going to marry the maiden in the castle in the forest.

20   "You may marry only the daughter of a king or an emperor," replied his father.

21   "I shall marry the woman who saved my life."

22   So they made preparations for the wedding, inviting all the kings and queens in the vicinity. Also present was the princess's royal father,

who had been informed of nothing. When the bride came out, he looked at her and exclaimed "My daughter!" "What!" said the royal host. "My son's bride is your daughter? Why did she not tell us?"

23 "Because," explained the bride, "I no longer consider myself the daughter of a man who let my stepmother imprison me." And she pointed at the queen.

24 Learning of all his daughter's misfortune, the father was filled with pity for the girl and with loathing for his wicked wife. Nor did he wait until he was back home to have the woman seized. Thus the marriage was celebrated to the satisfaction and joy of all, with the exception of that wretch.

Ideas for Writing

1. Think about a few fairy tales that you remember from your childhood or that seem interesting to you. Find a copy of one of these tales in the library and study the female characters. Based on your reading, what assumptions about women do these stories make? You might note the women's demeanor, speech, and actions. Also consider whether women are in control of their lives or are manipulated by other characters or by supernatural forces.

2. Several writers in this chapter, including Connie Stephens, analyze the purpose art serves in a particular culture. Using several of the readings in this chapter, analyze the function that art can serve in various cultures. You might discuss the similarities or differences you find or explain which purpose seems most important.

CHAPTER 12
THE SPIRITUAL LIFE

First Thoughts

Primeras impresiones

最初的印象

> Religion . . . imposes equally on everyone its own path to the acquisition of happiness and protection from suffering. Its technique consists in depressing the value of life and distorting the picture of the real world in a delusional manner—which presupposes an intimidation of the intelligence. At this price, by forcibly fixing them in a state of psychical infantilism and by drawing them into a mass-delusion, religion succeeds in sparing many people an individual neurosis. But hardly anything more. There are . . . many paths which *may* lead to such happiness as is attainable by men, but there is none which does so for certain. Even religion cannot keep its promise. If the believer finally sees himself obliged to speak of God's "inscrutable decrees," he is admitting that all that is left to him as a last possible consolation and source of pleasure in his suffering is an unconditional submission. And if he is prepared for that, he could probably have spared himself the *détour* he has made.
>
> Sigmund Freud
> *Civilization and Its Discontents*

In the modern world we tend to separate psychology from religion. We like to think that emotional problems have to do with the family, childhood, and trauma—with personal life but not with spirituality. We don't diagnose an emotional seizure as "loss of religious sensibility" or "lack of spiritual awareness." Yet the soul—the seat of our deepest emotions—can benefit greatly from the gifts of a vivid spiritual life, and can suffer when it is deprived of them.

The soul, for example, needs an articulated world-view, a carefully worked-out scheme of values and a sense of relatedness to the whole. It needs a myth of immortality and an attitude toward death. It also thrives on spirituality that is not so transcendent—such as the spirit of family, arising from traditions and values that have been part of the family for generations. . . .

Just as the mind digests ideas and produces intelligence, the soul feeds on life and digests it, creating wisdom and character out of experience. Renaissance Neoplatonists said that the outer world serves as a means of deep spirituality and that the transformation of ordinary experience into the stuff of soul is all-important. If the link between life experience and deep imagination is inadequate, then we are left with a division between life and soul, and such a division will always manifest itself in symptoms.

Thomas Moore
Care of the Soul

The man whom we can with justice call "modern" is solitary. He is so of necessity and at all times, for every step towards a fuller consciousness of the present removes him further from his original *"participation mystique"* with the mass of men—from submersion in a common unconsciousness. Every step forward means an act of tearing himself loose from that all-embracing, pristine unconsciousness which claims the bulk of mankind almost entirely. . . . Only the man who is modern in our meaning of the term really lives in the present; he alone has a present-day consciousness, and he alone finds that the ways of life which correspond to earlier levels pall upon him. The values and strivings of those past worlds no longer interest him save from the historical standpoint. Thus he has become "unhistorical" in the deepest sense and has estranged himself from the mass of men who live entirely within the bounds of tradition. Indeed, he is completely modern only when he has come to the very edge of the world, leaving behind him all that has been discarded and outgrown, and acknowledging that he stands before a void out of which all things may grow.

Carl Jung
"The Spiritual Problem of Modern Man"
Modern Man in Search of a Soul

In its most basic sense, the spiritual life pertains to the nonsecular, intangible life of the spirit. The human spirit is not concerned with material things but rather with a life that connects it to forces greater than itself. That is not to say that spiritual concerns are to be kept separate from the mundane rituals of everyday living. As John Garvey points out in "A Different Kind of Knowing," religion gives us an ethical framework for living our lives, moral principles by which we can act in the world. Spiritual knowledge relies on the intuitive, emotional, and imaginative ways of knowing as opposed to an epistemology derived from scientific, rational, and empirical thinking. For writers like Karl Marx, who called religion "the opiate of the masses," and Sigmund Freud, who viewed religion as a means of directing individual neurosis, the notion of spiritual "knowledge" is a contradiction in terms. Even for believers, the paths to spirituality are, of course, quite varied and can be at odds with one another. In their book *The Spiritual Life: Learning East and West,* John H. Westerhoff and John D. Eusden advise that "all religious doctrines be thought of as metaphors of universal truth." Occasionally, however, the notion of spiritual "truth" can be taken too narrowly. Thomas Moore identifies this tendency as one of the more pressing concerns about the spiritual life:

> It's easy to go crazy in the life of the spirit, warring against those who disagree, proselytizing for our own personal attachments rather than expressing our own soulfulness, or taking narcissistic satisfactions in our beliefs rather than finding meaning and pleasure in spirituality that is available to everyone.

Such "neurotic spirituality," he advises, can be healed by "soul-intelligence, a sensitivity to the symbolic and metaphoric life, community, and attachment to the world."

The readings in this chapter explore the life of the spirit in a variety of ways. Most discuss the spiritual dimension in terms of everyday life and illustrate the way that spiritual concerns lend "deep imagination," profundity, and transcendence to what would otherwise be little more than routine, everyday nothingness. In the first selection "A Different Kind of Knowing: For Those with Ears to Hear," John Garvey argues that religion alone, and not art, provides the spiritual training that enables us to make ethical, moral decisions. The next reading, "Slowly Becoming," is taken from the first chapter of Malidoma Patrice Somé's autobiographical book *Of Water and the Spirit: Ritual, Magic, and Initiation in the Life of an African Shaman.* In this chapter, Somé describes his grandfather's spiritual connection to his people, to his gods, and to Somé himself, whom he instructed in the religious ways of the Dagara people. In "The Bible and Self-Defense: The Examples of Judith, Moses, and David," Rigoberta Menchú, a Quiché Indian woman, writes about the parallels she and her people found between their Indian ancestors and the biblical heroes Judith,[1] Moses, and David. Menchú explains how her people learned to use these important figures from their enemies' religion against those enemies. Wang Bin writes about assumptions that distinguish Christian

---

[1] Judith's story appears in the Apocryphal book (not included in the Hebrew or Protestant Bible) that bears her name.

thinking from the Chinese-Confucian understanding of life. The poem by Federico García Lorca, "Gacela of the Dead Child" argues for a cosmic significance to human pain and suffering. His surrealistic poem makes a space in the heavens for the tragedies of murdered innocence and profound grief. Will Herberg analyzes the peculiar secular religion that he feels is shared by most citizens of the United States. The "doctrine" that most of us hold dear, he argues, amounts to little more than a vague faith in the American way of life.

Writing before Reading

What songs, paintings, or stories have you found especially moving? Have any led you to change your behavior in some way?

A DIFFERENT KIND OF KNOWING: FOR THOSE WITH EARS TO HEAR

John Garvey

John Garvey writes frequently on Christian themes. He is a regular contributor to Commonweal *and has written on such subjects as miracles, gender and the priesthood, and ethical problems inherent in cloning. Garvey wrote "A Different Kind of Knowing" for* Commonweal *in October 1994. In his essay he argues that the Enlightenment and Romanticism have given Western culture the mistaken idea that art implies an ethical or moral system. Only religion, Garvey argues, can instruct us about how we should lead our lives.*

1   One of the most frightening images in the modern world is that of the not uncommon sort of concentration camp guard who could move from the murderous world of the camp—who could witness, even take active part in, the humiliation and murder of other human beings—to his home, where he could put his children to bed with great tenderness, and listen to Mozart, weeping at the beauty of the experience.

2   The connection between perception, sensing, sensibility—the realm of the aesthetic—and the kind of knowledge we can articulate and act upon is not at all clear. But it is essential that we try to understand the connection as deeply as we can. One of the great myths of the Enlightenment

is that education, an acquaintance with art and literature and the great thought of the past, can make us better people and more competent, even more moral, members of society. World War II should have ended the power of that myth, but it lives on despite all the evidence.

3   It is easy to see why it is so seductive, and especially seductive to people who have experienced the great power of art to bring us into the presence of beauty, sometimes so forcefully that it literally takes your breath away. The first time I read Rilke's first *Duino Elegy* or came to the last paragraph in Joyce's *The Dead,* and felt deep stillness and astonishment, I knew that in some way I was changed, that if I didn't betray that moment things would not be the same from now on.

4   This experience is, to be sure, as fuzzy at one end as it is intense at the other. How would things not be the same? What would it mean, not to betray that stillness—only that I should remember it? That might be enough: but simply to have been brought to the edge of mystery seems to be enough, at the aesthetic level, and not nearly enough, at the level of action.

5   The purpose of art is not to make us better people, nor is art a form of moral exhortation. It is in fact possible for great art to participate in great evil, for art to be aesthetically impressive and degrade at the same time. (There is a genuine sadism that informs Picasso's *Weeping Women,* shown recently at the Metropolitan Museum of Art in New York.) I am not referring here to the terrible influence a brilliantly written but perverse novel might have on someone's behavior. What I am interested in is the ability of the Nazi to listen to Bach or to read Rilke, and continue to be a Nazi, with no apparent internal contradiction. I cannot say he is not moved to the same stillness I am. But what do we think we have found there, either of us?

6   This is related to another problem: the behavior of the artists and writers who can move us this way. Dostoevsky was at once capable of writing *The Brothers Karamazov* and of behaving quite boorishly; Tolstoy was often as full of delusion and self-pity as he was capable of brilliant insight. Walker Percy once said that the only two writers he could think of who were also decent people were Chekhov and Eudora Welty.

7   We could say that this is simply a matter of our living in a fallen world, that in all cases Paul's statement remains true: "The good I would do, I do not do." But it is one thing to say that we can fail in our attempts to live decently, to be good; it is another to live with what seems to be a radical disconnection between the realm of the beautiful and any truth worth living for. Is there no insight in Bach, or Rilke; or, if there is, does it have anything to do with the truths we must live by?

8   We need a larger frame, I think. We are still working with some notions that come down to us from the Enlightenment and from the Romantic movement. From the Enlightenment we get the idea that to understand something rationally is to understand it sufficiently. (This is

the mentality that says that theology could be taught as well by an atheist as a believer, to the extent that theology is a consistent intellectual endeavor.) The Romantics, who reacted to the smug certainties of the Enlightenment, have given us the idea that to understand something completely we must understand it emotionally, from within. We have somehow wedded these contradictory ideas in our understanding of moral education. We can't understand the Nazi who weeps at Mozart in the evening and turns on the gas in the morning, because we have been taught to believe that schooling, a deliberate exposure to culture, makes us better people.

9   The place in which the aesthetic and religious are most clearly wedded may be the icon. Many icons are extraordinarily beautiful. Rublev's *Trinity* is an example of the sort of work of art before which you are brought to stillness. But in an important sense, this isn't the point. Some great Orthodox saints prayed before icons which were dreadful, from an artistic and canonical point of view; and some horrible Orthodox live surrounded by lovely icons.

10   An experience cannot, in and of itself, educate us or form us; this is Romantic fallacy. Nor can the application of reason or a set of standards educate us. (This could be called the rationalistic—or canonical—fallacy.) Both must be understood within a greater context.

11   A person who is formed by prayer, by liturgy, by ascetic struggle, will respond to the world differently from someone who is constantly distracted, who never worships, who responds to every desire by yielding to it. And most of us probably live somewhere in between those two poles.

12   The question is not only one of responding to the world differently, but has to do also with our capacity for seeing the world. We bring the formed self—formed either by prayer or by distraction—to how we reason, to how we envision the world. An experience of overwhelming beauty might bring even the most evil person to a kind of stillness, but if the larger context is lacking, if no serious demand has ever been made on that person, it will remain merely an overwhelming aesthetic experience. We have allowed the Enlightenment and the Romantic strains in our culture to limit us: things are understood rationally, or emotionally. We must consider the possibility that one can also understand the world spiritually, that this dimension is not a variant of the subjective realm of the emotions or the objective realm of reason, but has its own objectivity and subjectivity.

13   The objectivity is what Orthodox spirituality means when it speaks of *apatheia*. Kallistos Ware points out that "the 'dispassioned' person, so far from being apathetic, is the one whose heart burns with love for God, for other humans, for every living creature, for all that God has made" (*The Orthodox Way,* Saint Vladimir's Seminary Press, 1981). He quotes Saint Isaac the Syrian: "The heart of such a man grows tender, and he cannot endure to hear of or look upon any injury, even the smallest suffering

inflicted upon anything in creation. Therefore he never ceases to pray with tears even for the dumb animals, for the enemies of truth, and for all who do harm to it, asking that they may be guarded and receive God's mercy. And for the reptiles also he prays with great compassion, which rises up endlessly in his heart after the example of God."

14   The beauty which brings us to stillness, in Bach or in Rublev's *Trinity*, can be understood only if someone has brought this wider living, this truer understanding, to his or her seeing. The idea of right understanding, truer observation, seems elitist in a time which doesn't feel comfortable with hierarchies of any sort, or the idea that there may be a privileged understanding, a kind of knowing more real than another. It is this more real knowing, a knowing different from and more important than reason or emotion, that Jesus pointed to when he said, "He who has ears, let him hear." Without this hierarchy (which Meister Eckhart, among others, certainly knew—he spoke of the "spiritual aristocrat") we are left with the concentration camp guard and the great theologian Karl Barth,[1] both moved to the depths by Mozart, and both equals in the only kinds of understanding our age allows.

Reading for Meaning

1. How is the title to John Garvey's essay designed to catch the reader's interest? Was it successful in getting your attention?
2. What connections does John Garvey make between feeling and acting? Why does Garvey discuss "the behavior of artists and writers"? How is this topic relevant to his essay?
3. According to Garvey, what ideas in the Western tradition have made it difficult for us to understand how Nazis in concentration camps during World War II could cry over a piece by Mozart and then shut hundreds of Jews into the gas chamber the following day?
4. What does Garvey mean by "orthodox spirituality"? Why is this an important term for Garvey?
5. Why does Garvey think there can be no clear connection between art and human behavior? Why might he have felt compelled to write about this subject?

Comparing Texts

1. How does John Garvey's view of art differ from that of André Brink (page 482)?
2. At the beginning of his essay, Garvey mentions Rainer Marie Rilke's first *Duino Elegy* and the final paragraph in *The Dead*, a short story by James Joyce. Use these selections, which are reprinted for you here, to examine Garvey's discussion in paragraphs 3 and 4 of his

---

[1] A Swiss philosopher (1886–1968) opposed to the assimilation of Christianity into modern, secular culture. While a professor of theology in Bonn, he led the opposition against the Nazi takeover of Germany.

essay. How might a reader feel "changed" after reading these works? What does Garvey see as the limitations of literary passages such as these? What feelings do these excerpts evoke in you?

EXCERPT FROM "THE FIRST ELEGY," *DUINO ELEGIES*

Rainer Maria Rilke (1875–1926)

The First Elegy
Who, though I cry aloud,
would hear me in the angel orders?
And should my plea ascend,
were I gathered to the glory
of some incandescent heart,
my own faint flame of being
would fail for the glare.
Beauty is as close to terror
as we can well endure.
Angels would not condescend
to damn our meager souls.
That is why they awe
and why they terrify us so.
Every angel is terrible!
And so I constrain myself and
swallow the deep, dark music
of my own impassioned plea.
Oh, to whom can we turn
in the hour of need?
Neither angel nor man.
Even animals know that we
are not at home here.
We see so little of what
is clearly visible to them.
For us there is only
a tree on a hillside, which we can memorize, or
yesterday's sidewalks, or
a habit which discovered us,
found us comfortable and moved in.
O and night . . . the night!
Wind of the infinite
blowing away all faces.

Within our solitude appears
a nearly lovely god
or goddess, all the
heart is ever apt to meet.
Lovers fare no better,
concealing, by their love,
each other's destiny.
Do you still not understand?
Pour your emptiness
into the breeze—
the birds may soar
more swiftly for it.

FINAL PARAGRAPH FROM "THE DEAD," *THE DUBLINERS*

James Joyce (1882–1941)

A few light taps upon the pane made him turn to the window. It had begun to snow again. [Gabriel] watched sleepily the flakes, silver and dark, falling obliquely against the lamplight. The time had come for him to set out on his journey westward. Yes, the newspapers were right: snow was general all over Ireland. It was falling on every part of the dark central plain, on the treeless hills, falling softly upon the Bog of Allen and, farther westward, softly falling into the dark mutinous Shannon waves. It was falling, too, upon every part of the lonely churchyard on the hill where Michael Furey lay buried. It lay thickly drifted on the crooked crosses and headstones, on the spears of the little gate, on the barren thorns. His soul swooned slowly as he heard the snow falling faintly through the universe and faintly falling, like the descent of their last end, upon all the living and the dead.

Ideas for Writing

1. John Garvey argues that "the purpose of art is not to make us better people, nor is art a form of moral exhortation." To counter Garvey's generalization about art, discuss one or two works of literature that elicited a moral or ethical outrage great enough to change the way things had been done. Be sure to examine the content of these works and show how they inspired change.

2. John Garvey writes from an ethical code based on Christian principles. Are there other sources that offer a moral code by which to live? Be as specific as you can in your discussion.

3. Find a recent issue of *Commonweal* in your local library or college. Look at the table of contents to get an idea of the topics covered in the magazine. Skim a few of the texts, noting

the tone of the articles and the assumptions the writer makes about his or her subject and audience. What can you infer about the audience for the magazine based on your investigation? Are there articles that might interest a non-Christian reader?

Writing before Reading

Have you had any "spiritual" teachers, that is, people whose teaching has focused on religious or philosophical themes rather than strictly practical concerns? Briefly explain who these people are, what they taught you, and how their teaching changed you.

SLOWLY BECOMING
Malidoma Patrice Somé

Malidoma Patrice Somé is a Shaman or holy man of the Dagara people of coastal West Africa. He was born in the village of Dano in the Burkina Faso area of West Africa. The region was then called Upper Volta, the name given it by the French colonialists who controlled the country from 1896 until independence in 1960. When he was five years old, French Jesuit missionaries took Somé from his family with his father's consent. For the next fifteen years, Somé was educated as part of a "native" group of missionaries who, it was thought, would have a better chance of converting the Dagara people to Catholicism. While with the Jesuits, Somé learned about the "temperamental god who forced everyone to live in constant fear of his wrath." At the age of twenty he escaped and returned to his family. After a painful initiation process, he was readopted by the Dagara culture. He later studied in Europe and the United States, earning doctoral degrees from the Sorbonne in Paris and from Brandeis University.

In the introduction to his autobiography, Of Water and the Spirit: Ritual, Magic, and Initiation in the Life of an African Shaman *(1994), Somé explains that Malidoma means "Be friends with the stranger/enemy." In the Dagara culture, names express the "special destiny" of the individual and "describe the task of their bearers and constitute a continual reminder to the child of the responsibilities that are waiting up ahead." For Malidoma Somé, writing his autobiography fulfills the promise of his name: "I am here in the West to tell the world about my people in any way I can, and to* take back to my people the knowledge I gain about this world." His purpose for writing has a larger humanitarian intent as well:

> My elders are convinced that the West is as endangered as the indigenous cultures it has decimated in the name of colonialism. There is no doubt that, at this time in history, Western civilization is suffering from a great sickness of the soul. The West's progressive turning away from functioning spiritual values; its total disregard for the environment and the protection of natural resources; the violence of inner cities with their problems of poverty, drugs, and crime; spiraling unemployment and economic disarray; and growing intolerance toward people of color and the values of other cultures—all of these trends, if unchecked, will eventually bring about a terrible self-destruction.... Unless we as individuals find new ways of understanding between people, ways that can touch and transform the heart and soul deeply, both indigenous cultures and those in the West will continue to fade away, dismayed that all the wonders of technology, all the many philosophical "isms," and all the planning of the global corporations will be helpless to reverse this trend.

Somé currently lives in Palo Alto, California, and is the leader of The Flight of the Hawk Center for the study of contemporary shamanism. He is also the author of Ritual: Power Healing and Community (1993).

Facts about Burkina Faso

Burkina Faso, formerly Upper Volta, has a long and varied history. The area changed from tribal organization to a series of linked kingdoms with the arrival of the Mossi in the eleventh century. A few centuries later the Mossi fought against inclusion in the expanding empires of the Islamic Mali (twelfth to fifteenth centuries) and Songhai (fourteenth to sixteenth centuries). French forces moved into the area in the late nineteenth century and occupied much of West Africa. The area that is now Burkina Faso became part of the French colony of Haut-Senegal-Niger in 1904. Fifteen years later the region known as Upper Volta withdrew from the original group of colonies, and after being reabsorbed by its neighbors in 1932, the country stabilized as Upper Volta in 1947. The colony gained its independence from France in 1960. Upper Volta was renamed Burkina Faso, "The Country of the Incorruptible," in 1984 to mark the break from its colonial past.

The country is mostly savanna and has poor, semiarid soil that can support few crops. Farmers grow drought-resistant millet, sorghum, and peanuts, as well as cassava and rice. Cotton, shea nuts, and sesame are grown for export. Burkina Faso has some forests and woodlands in the center of the country, with desert and arid plains to the north. The people of Burkina Faso (the Burkinab) comprise more than 60 ethnic groups; most adhere to traditional cultural and religious practices. The oral tradition is an important part of the country's national heritage. Twenty percent of the population are Muslims, and a small but educated minority are Roman Catholic. Native peoples have historically resisted both Islam and Christianity in favor of their indigenous faiths. Drought and overpopulation in the south has led approximately 460,000 Burkinab to migrate to the more prosperous nations of Ghana and Ivory Coast in search of work. Roughly 85 percent of these émigrés eventually return to their homeland. The Dagara people, the tribe to which Patrice Malidoma Somé belongs, live in parts of Ghana, the Ivory Coast, and Burkina Faso. They are known for their spiritual and visionary abilities.

1. The story I am going to tell comes from a place deep inside of myself, a place that perceives all that I have irremediably lost and, perhaps, what gain there is behind the loss. If some people forget their past as a way to survive, other people remember it for the same reason. When cultures with contradictory versions of reality collide, children are often the casualties of that contact. So, like many dark children of the African continent, my childhood was short, far too short to be called a childhood. This is perhaps why it has stuck so vividly in my memory. Exile creates the ideal conditions for an inventory of the warehouse of one's past. . . .

2. My grandfather had been my confident interlocutor for as long as I can remember. There is a close relationship between grandfathers and grandchildren. The first few years of a boy's life are usually spent, not with his father, but with his grandfather. What the grandfather and grandson share together—that the father cannot—is their close proximity to the cosmos. The grandfather will soon return to where the grandson came from, so therefore the grandson is bearer of news the grandfather wants. The grandfather will do anything to make the grandson communicate the news of the ancestors before the child forgets, as inevitably happens. My grandfather obtained this news through hypnosis, putting me to sleep in order to question me.

3. It is not only to benefit the grandfather that this relationship with his grandson must exist. The grandfather must also transmit the "news" to the grandson using the protocol secret to grandfathers and grandsons. He must communicate to this new member of the community the hard tasks ahead on the bumpy road of existence.

4. For the Dagara, every person is an incarnation, that is, a spirit who has taken on a body. So our true nature is spiritual. This world is where one comes to carry out specific projects. A birth is therefore the arrival of someone, usually an ancestor that somebody already knows, who has

important tasks to do here. The ancestors are the real school of the living. They are the keepers of the very wisdom the people need to live by. The life energy of ancestors who have not yet been reborn is expressed in the life of nature, in trees, mountains, rivers and still water. Grandfathers and grandmothers, therefore, are as close to an expression of ancestral energy and wisdom as the tribe can get. Consequently their interest in grandsons and granddaughters is natural. An individual who embodies a certain value would certainly be interested in anyone who came from the place where that value existed most purely. Elders become involved with a new life practically from the moment of conception because that unborn child has just come from the place they are going to.

5   A few months before birth, when the grandchild is still a fetus, a ritual called a "hearing" is held. The pregnant mother, her brothers, the grandfather, and the officiating priest are the participants. The child's father is not present for the ritual, but merely prepares the space. Afterward, he is informed about what happened. During the ritual, the incoming soul takes the voice of the mother (some say the soul takes the whole body of the mother, which is why the mother falls into trance and does not remember anything afterward) and answers every question the priest asks.

6   The living must know who is being reborn, where the soul is from, why it chose to come here, and what gender it has chosen. Sometimes, based on the life mission of the incoming soul, the living object to the choice of gender and suggest that the opposite choice will better accommodate the role the unborn child has chosen for him- or herself. Some souls ask that specific things be made ready before their arrival—talismanic power objects, medicine bags, metal objects in the form of rings for the ankle or the wrist. They do not want to forget who they are and what they have come here to do. It is hard not to forget, because life in this world is filled with many alluring distractions. The name of the newborn is based upon the results of these communications. A name is the life program of its bearer.

7   A child's first few years are crucial. The grandfather must tell the grandson what the child said while still a fetus in his mother's womb. Then, he must gradually help him build a connection with his father, who will help him with the hard challenges up ahead. My father used to complain that his life was calamitous because he never knew his grandfather, who disappeared before he was born. Had he known him, my father said, he would never have lost his first family, never spent his youth working in a gold mine or later embraced the Catholic religion with a fervor grander than the one that linked him to his ancestors. His stepbrothers, who knew their grandfather, did not have the kind of restlessness that plagued my father. The frustration of a grandfatherless male child has no cure.

8   In the beginning, the intense intimacy between the grandson and the grandfather might create feelings of jealousy in the father. While a grandfather is alive, the grandchildren do not have much of anything to

learn from their father—until they reach their preadolescent age. And the father knows that. He knows that a conversation between a grandson and a grandfather is a conversation between brothers of the same knowledge group. To know is to be old. In that, the grandson is as old as the grandfather. Consequently, the father is too young to have a part in this relationship between wise men.

9   I used to spend much of my days in the company of my grandfather. He was a man worn out by hard work, who at the age of sixty was virtually a child—weak and sick, yet with a mind still as alert as that of a man in the prime of youth. He also possessed incomparable wisdom stored over the course of half a century of sustained healing and medicine works.

10   Grandfather was thin and tall. Since I had first known him, he always wore the same traditional *boubou*. It had been white when he first got it, but in order to avoid the cost of maintenance, he had changed the white color of the cloth into red, using the juice of some roots that he alone knew the secret of. In use twenty-four hours a day, the boubou was simultaneously his daily outfit, his pajamas, and his blanket. After more than a decade, it had turned into a remnant of himself, blackened by sweat and dirt. Though most of the boubou had fallen off under the weight of filth, it still hung firmly on his shoulders, its general architecture intact. Unlike modern Christianity, which links cleanliness to godliness, Dagara culture holds the opposite to be true. The more intense the involvement with the life of the spirit, the more holy and wise an individual is, the less attention is paid to outward beauty. Grandfather owned a walking stick carved with artistic dexterity, its wood also darkened from long usage. His movements were slow, and I found it easier to be around him than around the other kids, who were older, stronger and more agile than I was. So every day, while everybody was at the farm, I was with Grandfather.

11   Grandfather knew every story ever told or even heard of in the tribe. And at his age he looked as if storytelling were the only thing he could still do with success. He utilized this talent very well since that was the only way he could gain attention. Each time I sat in his lap, he took it as a request for a story, and he would always begin by asking a question.

12   "Brother Malidoma, do you know why the bat sits upside down?"

13   "No. Why?"

14   "Long, long time ago, and I mean long when I say long because that was when animals used to speak to men and men to animals and both to God."

15   "Then why don't animals speak to men anymore?"

16   "They still do, only we have forgotten how to comprehend them!"

17   "What happened?"

18   "Never mind. We're talking about bats, and why they all sit upside down."

19 "Yes. I want to know why they do that."

20 "Well, see, there was a time when Brother Bat died and no one knew who he was. The town crier took his body to the crocodile, saying, 'The jaws of this damn thing look like they were borrowed from a crocodile. I thought he might be your relative or something.'

21 "The crocodile said, 'It's true that this guy's got a mouth like mine, but I ain't got no brother with fur, let alone with wings.'

22 "So, next the town crier took the dead bat to the head of the birds tribe."

23 "And who's that?"

24 "It's Mother Sila, you know, the bird that flies high and shoots herself down like an arrow when she goes to catch her dinner. Mother Sila said, 'This animal looks like it's got good wings and reasonable claws, but I never saw anyone in my family with so few feathers.'

25 "And so, finally the town crier gave up and threw the bat into a ditch. But when Papa Bat found out about this, he was very angry. He rebelled against God and ordered the whole tribe never to look up to God again. Since then bats never turn their faces upward."

26 "Grandfather, this is too sad. Tell me another one."

27 Grandfather never had to be begged. He would tell you a story even without your asking. And the times you asked, he would keep on talking until you "unasked" him.

28 He also knew how to hypnotize you—to speak you to sleep—when he needed to be left alone to do some important work. He never chased a child away from him; in fact, he always thought children were the most cooperative people on earth. One just needed to know how to use their generous services. A sleeping child is even more obedient than a child awake, and so he would often hypnotize one of us, then awaken us into a state where we would be dispatched to run errands for him. Any child seen silently looking for something, who would not respond when you asked, "What are you looking for?" was a sleeping child on an errand for Grandfather. He did not like to request the services of grown-ups because they would grumble and swear the whole time. He always said that the good in a service has little to do with the service itself, but with the kind of heart one brings to the task. For him, an unwilling heart spoiled a service by infecting it with feelings of resentment and anger.

29 Grandfather knew how to talk to the void, or rather to some unseen audience of spirits. Among the Dagara, the older you get the more you begin to notice spirits and ancestors everywhere. When you hear a person speaking out loud, alone, you don't talk to them because he or she may be discussing an important issue with a spirit or an ancestor. This rule applies more to holy elders than to adults in general. When I was with Grandfather, I felt as if there were more people around than could be accounted for. When he knew I was not following his stories, he used

to redirect his speech to these invisible beings. He never seemed bothered by my not listening.

30 Grandfather's respect and love for children was universal in the tribe. To the Dagara, children are the most important members of society, the community's most precious treasures. We have a saying that it takes the whole tribe to raise a child. Homes have doorless entrances to allow children to go in and out wherever they want, and it is common for a mother to not see her child for days and nights because he or she is enjoying the care and love of other people. When the mother really needs to be with her child, she will go from home to home searching for it.

31 When a child grows into an adolescent, he or she must be initiated into adulthood. A person who doesn't get initiated will remain an adolescent for the rest of their life, and this is a frightening, dangerous, and unnatural situation. After initiation, the elders will pick a partner for the young person, someone who is selected for their ability to team up with you in the fulfillment of your life purpose. If one obediently walks their life path, they will become an elder somewhere in their late forties or early fifties. Graduating to this new status, however, depends on one's good track record.

32 A male elder is the head of his family. He has the power to bless, and the power to withhold blessing. This ability comes to him from his ancestors, to whom he is very close, and he follows their wisdom in counseling his large family.

33 Wealth among the Dagara is determined not by how many things you have, but by how many people you have around you. A person's happiness is directly linked to the amount of attention and love coming to him or her from other people. In this, the elder is the most blessed because he is in the most visible position to receive a lot of attention. The child is too, because it "belongs" to the whole community.

34 Some elders are chosen to sit on the village council. There they participate in decision making that affects the entire village. Women have their council separate from men because of their unique roles and responsibilities. Dagara culture is matrilineal—everybody in the village carries the name of their mother. The family is feminine, the house where the family live is kept by a male. The male is in charge of the family security. The female is in charge of the continuity of life. She rules the kitchen, the granaries where food is stored, and the space where meals are taken. The male is in charge of the medicine shrine and of the family's connection with the ancestors. He brings the things that nourish the family, like food.

35 For a full fifty years, my grandfather had been the priest, the leader, and the counselor of a family of over fifty souls. Faced with domestic problems of all kinds, he had had to be tough. Judging from his physical

appearance—muscles still protruding from tired biceps, square shoulders that looked as if they could still carry weight, big chest that seemed to hide massive lungs—one could see that he had been a robust young man capable of sustaining long hours of demanding physical labor. Grandfather's greatest fame, however, came from his spiritual accomplishments. In the village, everyone knew him as the "upside-down arrow shooter." He was one of the people in the tribe whose name made people shudder, for if he wished to destroy an enemy, he would retire to the quiet of his chambers, place an arrow upside down on his bow, and magically hit his target. The arrow would kill whomever or whatever he named, then rematerialize in his chamber ready for more. The slightest scratch from such a weapon is mortal.

36 Other tribes did not dare go into conflict with ours because they did not possess the secret of such deadly magic. Consequently, Grandfather rarely had a chance to demonstrate to the tribe his power in battle. The arrow did have peacetime uses, however. Grandfather used it to protect our family farm from the nocturnal raids of wild beasts. Although he could no longer work the fields, Grandfather could still in this manner contribute to our food supply. He also displayed the upside-down arrow as a persuasive weapon to warn evildoers away from our family, the Birifor.

37 Grandfather was no longer strong enough to walk the six miles between the house and the farm every day, and as far as I can recall, I never saw him go there. Because the people of my tribe practice slash-and-burn agriculture, their fields are often very far away as people keep moving them around year after year to avoid exhausting the soil. I was born too late to know Grandfather as a more vigorous man. When I was a child, he spent his days sitting in the same place in the central yard of the labyrinthine compound that housed our family group. Sometimes he was pensive, calmly and wisely dispatching legal matters without so much as raising his head or the tone of his voice. He had great knowledge of healing matters as well. Without so much as glancing up from the pots that held the food and medicinal items he dispensed, he could tell young people who had physical problems which roots they should dig up and bring back to him in the evening for their cures.

38 At night, when everyone else was asleep, Grandfather would watch over the farm and the compound from his room. Through the use of complex and magical security devices, his thoughts were constantly turned in to the vibration of the farm, and he could always determine whether the fields were being raided by wild animals. The device he used to keep vigil consisted of a clay pot filled with "virgin water," rainfall that had never touched the earth in its fall from the sky. He saw everything that happened throughout the farm by looking into this water. The precision of vision it afforded superseded the simplicity of this device.

39 Grandfather's magical guardianship had enabled our family to always have enough food to eat. Two thirds of the tribe did not share our

surplus and could never put aside enough extra food to avoid the hardship of the hunger season, which ran every year from July to September, when stored food ran out. During this time, a mild famine visited many compounds. Children would stop singing and laughter would vanish from the houses at night. Every morning during that time, a long line of people stood at the door of the Birifor house, waiting for a calabash of grain. Distributing food to all these needy people was another of grandfather's tasks. So, every morning of those misty days of July and August, after he had given orders to the men and women of the family regarding their daily assignments, Grandfather would drag himself to the door of his room. There, he would take all the time he needed to be seated comfortably. I would wait calmly until he was settled, then I would sit on his bony lap. Aided by a woman whose charge it was to measure up the proper amount of millet to be distributed to each of the needy, Grandfather would dispatch his task until shortly after noontime when the heat became unbearable.

40   Usually, at that particular time of the day, I would fall asleep on his lap. He would wake me up later with a song that rang more like a cry—Grandfather's voice was terrible. Then he would say, "Brother Malidoma, my legs can't hold you any longer. Please allow them to breathe too." And still half asleep, I would stand up and wait, wondering what had happened.

41   After the rite of charity, one of the women brought food to Grandfather and me, and we ate together. Grandfather was very frugal. I remember him once explaining to my father that the weight of undigested food closed the body and the mind off from the ability to perceive the surrounding good and bad vibrations. He who ate too much increased his vulnerability. The good taste of food hid the danger it put the body into. Grandfather's philosophy was that food is a necessary evil.

42   For this reason, the attitude toward food in our family was strange. One ate only when absolutely necessary. Grandfather could tell who was eating too much. For children under six, he encouraged food. For adults, he encouraged frugality. He used to rage at certain adolescents who, in his eyes, had no control of their appetite, saying, "Initiation will be a bitter experience when you come of age. Now is the time you must learn to control the drives of your body. Be alert and firm. Do no let the desire for physical satisfactions temper your warriorship. Remember, our ancestors are spirits, they feed only their minds and that is why they can do things beyond our comprehension."

43   When Grandfather started speaking, he did not particularly care whether someone was listening or not. Speaking was a liberating exercise for him, an act of mental juggling. He would sometimes speak for hours, as if he had a big spirit audience around him. He would laugh, get angry and storm at invisible opponents, and then become quiet once more. When he had a real audience, as he did every evening at storytelling time, he would teach us all through his tales. He would speak until

everyone fell asleep, then would rail at us, saying that sleep was a dangerous practice no different from that of eating too much food. For Grandfather, sleep was tribute we pay to the body far too often. He would often say that the body is merely the clothing of the soul and that it is not good to pay too much attention to it, as if it were really us. "Leave your body alone, and it will align itself to the needs of the spirit you are."

44 I loved Grandfather's company, and he loved having me next to him. He used to call me Brother when he had something serious to tell me. Otherwise, he would call me by my tribal name, Malidoma. I asked him once why he called me Brother and he said, "I call you Brother because you are the reincarnation of Birifor, the elder son of my parents, and someone I used to love very much. Birifor's name is now carried by the entire family, and I will tell you why.

45 "Our father, Sabare, was a priest and a hunter. Before he went hunting, he used to give directions to Birifor about running the family, for Sabare would often disappear for months at a time. One day he left and never returned. We waited for a year, then another year, then we decided we should perform the funeral ritual, believing that our father must have been devoured by a wild beast. We planned to celebrate the rite for six days instead of three. The day before the funeral, Birifor and I were sitting on the roof of the house planning the final details when we saw our father coming toward us on a white horse. He was riding so fast the feet of his mount barely touched the ground.

46 "Mesmerized by the sudden vision, we waited in silence. The closer Sabare got, the slower he rode until he stopped just under the big baobab tree in the yard. He dismounted, walked to the ladder, and climbed up to join us. He still wore the same clothes he had the day he left long ago. His bow still hung solid and real on his back, and his quiver and aimer were still there by his left elbow. He was clearly not dead.

47 "The only strange thing was his horse. We knew what a horse looked like, but we didn't have horses here in our region. We couldn't imagine where he had found one. While we were busy wondering about all these things, he arrived on the roof, produced a little bench out of nowhere, and sat down. Instantly, we all sat. We greeted each other and I asked if he needed anything to wet his throat before we talked.

48 "'No,' he said. 'I have come to tell you to abandon your funeral plans. Even though you will not see me again, know that I am not dead, nor will I be for a long time. I have shifted to the other side of existence without going through the door of death, and I have done this for the benefit of the family. Do not, I repeat, do not perform any funeral rite, for my soul does not need rest. Whenever you need me, say these words' (Grandfather never told me what the words were) 'and I will be there. As long as I can come to you, the family will never be in danger, there will always be prosperity, and you will have a world of medicine to share

among you. Do not mourn my absence, for I am present among you without a body.'

49 "Saying this, he stood up and the bench he was sitting on vanished. Ignoring this magical occurrence, he walked straight toward the ladder without saying goodbye. We were so surprised, we couldn't think of anything to do or say. Finally, I gathered all my strength and begged, 'But at least stay with us a day or two. You must tell us where you are and talk to the family about what happened. You know we are all anxious to hear about you.'

50 "His reply came quickly: 'Nonsense! I have already told you what I came to tell you. No more should be said or the thread will be cut between you and me. Know only that where I exist is not on the earth, but in a universe of its own. I see you better from there than I ever could from here. Not a word, not a thought, not a single movement of my family escapes my attention. Now be content and go about your duties, I have spoken.'

51 "Saying this, he climbed down the ladder. We watched him get on his horse and start to ride away. After he had gone a very short distance, he and the horse began mounting up into the sky. Stunned, we watched them rise higher, then vanish.

52 "After that we canceled the funeral. My brother Birifor was installed as priest and family leader, and an era of extreme material and magical prosperity began for us. We discovered the secret of the upside-down arrow, the surveillance of remote areas, and many, many other medicine secrets you will learn later. You see all these people who come to ask us for food. Because of what Sabare has taught us, we have food and they don't. When you grow up, you'll learn about the secrets of the Birifor Magic. Do you want to know them?"

53 "Yes," I said. "I want to know all about the upside-down arrow, I want to be a hunter like Sabare and fly in the sky. But Grandfather, you have not told me why you call me Brother yet."

54 "Yes, that's right," he replied. "So, like I was saying, your other grandfather became the *Baomale,* the healer of the family. But he died in the war against the white man."

55 "What? They killed him?" I inquired anxiously.

56 "No, Brother," Grandfather said mournfully. "The upside-down arrow killed him."

57 "But it was not supposed to," I said, confused.

58 "Yes, Brother, it was not supposed to do that. But someone made a serious mistake. I'll explain all that to you when you grow bigger. Now it's my turn to remind you that I have not answered your question yet. So let me do it now."

59 Grandfather never tackled a question directly. He had the habit of introducing an answer by way of a whole bunch of stories that often

placed the question being asked into a wider context. Your answer would arrive when you were least expecting it, nestled into the middle of a litany of fascinating narrations. Thus one would go away with more than they came for, enriched with fantastic tales.

60   With me it was different. I would keep reminding Grandfather of my question and, at length, he would announce the answer before giving it to me so that I would know when my thirst was being quenched.

61   "After the death of my brother Birifor and the ceremony of investiture that gave me the leadership of this family," Grandfather continued, "my father, Sabare, came to me in spirit and told me that he was ordering Birifor to return to the family. Your sister had already been born then. A year later, your mother became pregnant again, and the baby inside her, whenever he would speak to me, would call me Brother. I knew it was Birifor about to be born again, and that you would be a boy. So I waited for your birth. And since that night when you came to life at dawn near the river, between here and the house of that white devil on the hill, it has been my turn to call you Brother. Now do you understand?"

62   "No," I said. This was a lot to take into my young mind. "If I am Birifor, why do you call me Malidoma? And if I am Malidoma after all, why do my father and other people like the Jesuit priest at the mission on the hill call me Patrice? Between Malidoma, Brother, and Patrice, what is my true name?"

63   "None of them tells the whole story of who you are. However, there is one that almost does, the one your ancestors call you by: Malidoma. Do you know why this is so?"

64   "No, Grandfather, tell me everything." I moved closer to him and hugged him. His clothes exhaled an unbearable smell and I pulled back sharply to avoid suffocation. Noticing this, Grandfather smiled briefly and regarded me gently. He laid his left hand on my forehead, took my right hand in his, and looked up at the sky for a long while before speaking.

65   "You do not like smell of a dirty old man's clothing? You love fragrance, the kind flowers have. Do you know that these sweet fragrances are born from horrible ones? Before it can liberate the sweet part of itself, the flower must rot. You see I have to rot too so that the Birifor family can smell good. This is the order of things."

66   "But Grandfather, you were talking about names and my birth. Now the flower story..."

67   "Yes, the flower story is a little bit of a detour. I do not want to scramble your little growing mind. Now! What was I saying? Oh, yes. Your true name is Malidoma. This is what your ancestors call you. The other names are things like tools that will get you out of trouble later. 'Patrice' was given to you by the Jesuits shortly after your birth. Your parents, as you know, are friends with that white-bearded priest up there on the hill. They seem to like his medicine and the God he serves, and that is why he comes here to visit so often. But let me tell you that a God who would

send people away from their land must be drinking a very strong wine all the time. Long ago that priest changed the names of your parents so they would come to his church more often. I do not know what your parents and the priest do up there, and I don't think I want to know either.

68 "'Patrice' was the name given to you by that priest up there on the hill. Use it whenever you are out of the tribal boundaries. 'Brother' is the name I call you by. Nobody else has claim to it. 'Birifor'—well, nobody will ever again call you that. 'Malidoma' is the name you will start hearing a lot when you become big. So be alert and prompt to answer. You never know what name another person will address you by. This is something you'll have to live with. That's enough for today."

69 It was dark already, and the farmers were returning from their day's work. My mother was the first to arrive, loaded down with a pack of dry wood that she balanced high on her head. To pass through the gate into our courtyard, she had almost to kneel double to avoid hitting the top and sides of the narrow doorway.

70 My mother walked to the middle of the compound yard, tilted her head, and dropped the wood next to the central cooking pot. Relieved of her burden, she breathed deeply, wiped the blinding sweat from her eyes, and unfastened the wide flat carrying basket from her head. My sister entered with her own small load of dry wood—nothing heavy, since she was so small. She had no trouble passing the gate. She was only six years old, but her education had already begun. Every morning she had to follow my mother to the farm and perform the duties of her sex, on a smaller scale.

71 She dropped her load carelessly and went into the kitchen in search of food. Shortly after, my father arrived, always the last to come home. He rode a bicycle that he had brought back from the Gold Coast, where he had spent three and a half years working in the gold mines of Takouradi and Sakoundé. It was a huge English bicycle. He used to call it *gawule*, after the lengthy branches of the ga-tree, which grows in the savanna.

72 This bicycle was a blessing to my father. Thanks to it, he was always the first to arrive at the farm and the last to leave it. I used to watch him ride in, amazed at his dexterity. Balancing his slim form on the narrow iron seat, he rode so elegantly, it seemed there was a conspiracy between him and the bicycle.

73 The machine had lost its brakes shortly after he arrived home from the Gold Coast. To stop it, he always had to jump off as it neared the gateway and run along with it for a while. Then he would park it against the wall of the compound.

74 Father never left the farm until he knew everybody else had gone. Once he was home, one of his responsibilities was to check the seventeen living areas of the compound, where the seventeen families of the Birifor family group live, to make sure that everyone had returned safely. These family groups comprise our clan. The Dagara tribe consists of

roughly ten clans encompassing over half a million people, covering a surface perhaps the size of Massachusetts.*

75   Our living area was the first one he checked. In it lived my parents, Grandfather, my sister, and myself. It was the leading unit, bigger than the other spaces yet containing less than 10 percent of the people a living area that size ordinarily does. That was because half of the rooms in our area were spirit rooms, the sacred shrines of ancestors, and therefore accessible only to Grandfather, my father, and other family heads.

76   Typical family living units consist of two main areas—the men's quarter and the women's quarter—which face each other across the courtyard. In my village, the husband and wife do not share the same bed, and the children take turns sleeping in the lodgings of both parents. The building that housed my mother was called a *zangala*. It was a large oval structure built with mud and wood, with extensions on the side that looked like extra-large closets. This windowless, wigwamlike lodging was always dark. My mother, and every other woman in the village, preferred it that way. Built against the side of the zangala were two little houses, one for the poultry, the other for the goats and sheep. Across from the zangala was my father's quarter, which was more modern in construction and about the size of a three-bedroom apartment. The floors and walls of all of these buildings were sealed with a kind of polish made from mud and liquefied cow dung to avoid the cracking common to mud houses.

77   Between these two quarters was an enclosed courtyard—a large open space for evening and community gatherings. The only entrance to the compound was built into the wall of this courtyard, and next to it was a little hole that served as a door for the dogs and cats. On one side of the courtyard was a kitchen where people made fire and cooked food. The ceiling of this kitchen was black with soot and God knows what else. On the other side, to the left of my father's quarter, was a toilet and a shower room.

78   Lastly, a set of small buildings joined together by a common back wall constituted the quarter of Grandfather and his spirits. Nobody in the compound entered these small buildings without Grandfather's presence, but at night one could hear him conversing with unknown beings. It was from these rooms that he surveyed the farm in the bush six miles away from home.

79   Grandfather's space housed the pharmacy of the entire Birifor clan—an array of roots, daily collected, nightly prepared, to face emergencies of

---

*Today, colonialism, new and old, has displaced them in three different sovereign nations: Ghana, Ivory Coast, and Burkina Faso. In the fifties there were fewer than two hundred and fifty people in my village. There are fewer than two hundred today. The reasons for this are the migration of the youth due to clashes between the old and the new ways of living, starvation because of destructive "modern" farming techniques, and the melancholy of indigenous life.

all sorts. These little dwellings contained the prosperity—spiritual, material, and magical—of the Birifor. Some of these roots were good for physical illness, but most of them were good for illness of the soul. These little buildings held the spiritual destiny of every member of the family. There, each one of us existed in the form of a stone, silent, docile, available. The stones represented the birth certificate of every person in the clan. This is where Grandfather went to examine the physical and spiritual energy fields of the people under his care. Through this magical means, Grandfather could check on each of us at his leisure.

80   He took care of people outside the family too. Strangers used to come now and then to seek medical help, and Grandfather would begin long ceremonial rites that took most of the day. Sometimes the strangers would bring chickens and, speaking breathlessly in an unintelligible magical language, he would cut their throats and direct the spurting blood onto some statues, representing different spirits, carved out of wood or built against the wall. He never tired of rituals. It took me many years to understand the reasons behind these visits and how Grandfather was able to help these strangers.

81   After my father had finished his tour of the family units, he had to make sure that all the domestic animals were where they ought to be. Then he would close them in for the night. Finally, he would close the main gate and secure it from the inside by tying it to an old bicycle pedal fastened to the wall. This "lock" was one of my father's inventions since his return from the Gold Coast.

82   Because my father was such a quiet and rather gloomy man, it was hard to be around him. Grandfather explained to me that this inner conflict had intensified since my father had become a follower of the priest on the hill. His unfocused and taciturn air was the result of the many trips he had made outside the limits of the Dagara tribe early in his youth. "A youth who leaves the village shortly after initiations is vulnerable. He runs the risk of never dying properly," Grandfather always said. My father started traveling when he was fifteen, and never stopped until he was thirty.

83   These conversations between me and my grandfather may sound very "adult," but it is not uncommon for grandchildren to learn about their fathers—and about everybody else—from their grandfathers. Grandfather was always very open toward me. So open that in retrospect it sometimes seems that he even forgot that the life of the person he was constantly analyzing in my presence was that of my own father. Most of what he said about my father did not make sense until I was much older, but I remembered it because he repeated it so often. Grandfather always spoke to me as an equal, perhaps because his belief that I was his brother implied, in some sense, that I already was an adult. Again, this is not an uncommon attitude among the Dagara: it is not unusual to hear someone exclaim in front of a newly born child, "Oh, he looks so old!"

84. So, when I became older, I came to understand more about the nature of the emotional problems that contributed to my father's gloominess and absentmindedness. His first marriage had occurred at the age of twenty after he returned from the Ivory Coast. There he had served as a soldier in the colonial army. From this first marriage twin daughters were born. My father was supposed to perform the ritual that every person who becomes a father of twins must perform. It consists of filling up two clay pots with root juice and burying them at the entrance of the compound. These pots symbolize the link between this pair of humans and the spirits that invited them to come into the family. The original reason for this ritual, as with many others that the Dagara practice, has been lost in oblivion, but people always perform them because their fathers did before them. It is also a very real incentive, borne out by long experience, that those who do not perform these rituals most often meet with disaster. The purpose of ritual is to create harmony between the human world and the world of the gods, ancestors, and nature.

85. My father's adherence to the new Christian faith made him doubt the validity of such rites. Grandfather had warned him whenever he could about the urgency and importance of the ceremony, but because Grandfather was my father's father, he couldn't do the ceremony himself. Each time he would remind his son of his duty, my father would play deaf, neither refusing nor accepting the responsibility. The truth was that he did not want to offend the white priest, appearing like a pagan devil worshiper in his eyes.

86. My father genuinely feared going to hell. As he confided to me much later on, the white priest had told him that the Almighty God would take good care of his newborn twins and that He could do it better than the ancestors. According to the priest, our ancestors had been condemned to eternal hell and were busy burning. They had no time to enjoy sacrifices. I wondered what kind of expression Grandfather wore when he discovered that his own son actually believed this nonsense.

87. As the years passed and the twin girls, Elizabeth and Marguerite, grew without a problem, Father was convinced that the priest had been right. Even though Grandfather continued to remind him of his duties toward his firstborn, nothing could shake his obstinacy. His faith in the Christian religion grew stronger every day. Finally, Grandfather switched from simple warnings to threats. Father began to see himself as a martyr, like those of Uganda who, in the mid-1800s, preferred to die at the hands of their own "pagan" elders rather than deny their faith in God. The Catholic church later canonized these black men as saints. Convinced that his own suffering at the hands of my grandfather meant free passage to heaven, my father endured it gladly.

88. In the meantime, two other children were born to him. The Catholic priest poured water on them immediately and named them Daniel and Pascal. By this time Grandfather had become a lone observer. Because

they were boys, and it was his duty, he secretly gave them Dagara names. Meanwhile, the twin girls grew to the age of initiation. The missionary warned my father against such practices, and Father refused to allow the girls to become initiated, a terrible decision because it doomed them both to being stuck in adolescence for the rest of their lives, bereft of the secret, adult knowledge that initiation would have given them. At this point, Grandfather was tired of struggling with his stubborn son. His grandchildren had grown beyond his protection, and he could only watch helplessly as disaster struck, faster than was possible to take action against.

89   One morning Elizabeth caught a mysterious illness that no one could diagnose. She died at noon before the missionary could give her extreme unction. During her funeral Marguerite died while running wild with grief. The funeral intensified.

90   The sudden death of Marguerite had affected Father beyond repair. Her funeral, however, was brief. People knew what was going on. Twins don't die on the same day. The people in our family asked my father to perform a reconciliation rite, thinking it would delay further disaster until the twin ritual for the girls could be done posthumously. It must have been my father's fate to not listen. Instead, he prayed to the foreign god harder than ever, offering him his pain as a gift. In his confusion, he saw his tragedy as a test sent by the Lord to try his faith. He kept repeating the famous sentence from the Lord's prayer, "Thy will be done."

91   And the Lord's will was done, beyond his expectations. Pascal, the eldest son, expired two weeks after the funeral of Elizabeth and Marguerite. Nobody knew what killed him. He had been playing with his friends and suddenly cried out loudly that he was dying. Julia, the unfortunate mother, died of sorrow during the funeral of her son. She was already too worn out by the shock of the death of her two daughters to endure any more pain. There remained only Daniel and my father. In my imagination I picture my grandfather emitting sounds of immense sorrow and helplessness. The first time he told me this story, my father himself groaned with grief.

92   My father was a stubborn man to have stood his ground through so much destruction. The missionaries could do nothing but counsel him to pray, and then to pray harder, attributing these calamities to the weakness of his faith in God. All during this time, my father told me, the ghosts of his wife and children haunted his dreams with the question, "Why did you do this to us?"

93   After a few days of living in terror of these ghostly visitations, Father went up to the hill to seek the interventions of the priest. He returned home with a terrible empty look, as if his soul had already gone out of his body. The Jesuits had given him the same worn-out counsel: "Keep praying." Ruined by pain, eroded by continuous hopeless effort, he discontinued all social activities and voluntarily ostracized himself for months. The

only time he would leave his quarter was to check that the only survivor of the holocaust was still alive. Daniel did not care. Who would? His soul was gone. No one could save him from the danger his father had exposed him to, and he was old enough to understand this. He awaited helplessly for death, his anger against his own father for the boundless losses he had endured barely hidden. Daniel died many years later while I was away at the mission school.

94   Perhaps my father could not stand all of this, for after a few months he disappeared. Consumed by restlessness, he suddenly fell in love with adventure once again. He went to the Gold Coast, first in the town Takouradi, then to Sakoundé, where he hoped a change of scene could help him rid himself of the pain that had taken hold of his body and soul since the death of his children.

95   He went to work, mining gold for the white man he had sacrificed his children to. Three years later, he returned from the Gold Coast, somewhat healed emotionally, but seriously ill physically. His face was emaciated like an old man's, and his swollen chest grew larger with every breath. His eyes were bloodshot and he looked ghastly, as if he had seen a ghost. He moved like a drunken man, zigzagging randomly. His legs looked more like sticks than limbs, and they struck against each other when he tried to walk.

96   Grandfather tried to tell my father why he was sick, reminding him yet again of his duty toward his children, living and dead. But, as if accursed, my father always answered in the same way, saying he would think about it.

97   My father was proud of the English bicycle he had successfully smuggled into the tribe. He paid more attention to it than to his health, which was deteriorating more every day. He even decided to get married again. I have always wondered on what grounds my mother married someone so ill. Was it because of the English bicycle, or because the presence of Grandfather as head of our family represented hope to her that everything could be put right again? Meanwhile, Father had returned to his religious activities with the white priests as if nothing had happened. But everyone knew that the ancestors never forget.

98   Things continued to go downhill for him until he was incapable of even moving around. He spent his days sleeping and his nights groaning with the pain in his chest, his belly, and his back.

99   Finally, Grandfather had to warn him that he had only a few days left to live unless he performed his duties. Panic-stricken at the idea of dying at a time when he had just married, my father ordered the ceremony of the twins to be performed.

100   Two clay pots were brought and filled with water from the underworld. This water was kept on a special shrine at the entrance of my mother's room. Then my father ceremonially sprinkled ash on the ground

around the compound to keep malintentioned spirits away from the house. Then the ritual proper began. It lasted a whole day. What was normally a simple gesture toward the spirit had now become painfully elaborate because of my father's constant postponements.

101   It was not long after this event that my father began to feel better. His health was improving almost visibly. At the end of the first week he had recovered his ability to move around, and by the end of the following week he decided he was strong enough to return to the farm. His pain had almost entirely disappeared.

102   He developed a better attitude, perhaps because he realized how much death is contained in the way of the white man and his spirituality. He began to hear the ancestors once again. My father still attended Sunday masses, and still maintained friendship with the white-bearded priest on the hill who misled him, but he also listened more carefully to Grandfather now. My sister was born after all this tragedy, and my father performed the proper ceremonies. The happy event revived him and my sister benefited from the joy he took in her. Yet she too was brought to the hill to be baptized.

103   I was born three years after my sister, shortly after the harvest festival. It was dawn and very cold. My birth took place in the open air, halfway between the family house and the white man's hospital. I still wonder what would have happened if I had been born in that modern, sterilized place. My fate surely would have been different. I like to think that perhaps I knew this in the womb and decided to take matters into my own hands by insisting on being born in nature. Was this the reason why, twenty years later, I was able to find my way back home? And I often wonder if coming into this world between the village and the white man's compound has something to do with the feeling I have of being sandwiched between worlds.

104   Like my sister, I was baptized at the mission hill and given the name Patrice. But Grandfather registered me in the family ledger as Malidoma, he who would "be friends with the stranger/enemy." He knew that the bulk of my life was going to be lived outside of the tribe, and that meant countless challenges, all aimed at securing friends. His duty toward me consisted of delivering this bad news to me before he died.

105   Grandfather had also named me Malidoma for reasons pertaining to ancestral law. Because he was the guardian of the house, the link between the dead and the living, he expected his grandson to be recognized by the ancestors. As the first male of my family, my responsibilities had already been predetermined. The first male must be prepared to take charge of the family shrine when his father, the current priest, dies. I found out later that my education had somewhat broken that tradition because, after all, my fate would be to respond to the challenge of being swallowed up by the white man's world.

Reading for Meaning

1. Who are the "ancestors" in the Dagara tribe? Explain their importance to a family and to the tribe in general.

2. Somé explains that in the Dagara culture, "every person is an incarnation . . . So our true nature is spiritual." Give a few examples of how Somé's grandfather illustrates this belief. In your experience, is there a "true nature" that people express? If so, give a few examples. If not, what do people have instead?

3. Write a brief description of the Dagara idea of communal child rearing. How well would that concept work if applied to child rearing in the United States?

4. Describe the characteristics of storytelling in the Dagara culture. Explain the values or morals inherent in a few of the stories told by Somé's grandfather.

5. How do the Dagara people measure wealth? How is wealth defined in the United States? What alternative definitions of wealth are possible?

Comparing Texts

In the excerpt from *Care of the Soul,* which begins this chapter, Thomas Moore describes the danger of depriving the soul of a "vivid spiritual life." How well have members of Somé's family supplied him with knowledge of the spiritual side of life?

Ideas for Writing

1. In the introduction to *Of Water and the Spirit,* the book from which "Slowly Becoming" was taken, Somé discusses the difficulties he had writing an autobiography using a borrowed language:

   > Although I have made great strides in orally communicating in that language [English], it was still very difficult to write this book. One of my greatest problems was that the things I talk about here did not happen in English; they happened in a language that has a very different mindset about reality. . . . From the time I began to jot down my first thoughts until the last word, I found myself on the bumpy road of mediumship, trying to ferry meanings from one language to another, and from one reality to another—a process that denaturalizes and confuses them.

   Take a moment to identify passages in "Slowly Becoming" that express ideas or descriptions of events that might have been difficult to translate into English from "a language that has a very different mindset about reality." Compare the beliefs about reality that Somé describes in these passages with the assumptions you and other people you know generally accept.

2. The worship of ancestors is important in other cultures besides that of the Dagara. Consult library or computer sources on "ancestor worship." Choose one culture to explore, and once you have gathered some information about the people's relationship to their ancestors, describe how one's forebears are honored in this culture. You might also explain why they are venerated and what purpose they might serve.

3. Interview someone you know who has a special relationship with a member of his or her family or community. What is the spiritual or emotional nature of that relationship? What role does each person have in the relationship?

Writing before Reading

What figures, either female or male, have you heard or read about who fought to preserve a way of life or to correct an injustice? What principles seemed to guide them?

THE BIBLE AND SELF-DEFENSE: THE EXAMPLES OF JUDITH, MOSES, AND DAVID[2]

Rigoberta Menchú

Rigoberta Menchú, a Quiché Indian, was born in Chimel, a village in northwestern Guatemala. She lived most of her life under a series of repressive governments that seemed determined to annihilate the native population. A passionate defender of her people's rights, Menchú helped farmers and villagers in their fight against the soldiers who were in the service of both the military government and large landowners. Government soldiers routinely enslaved, murdered, or drove off the indigenous people and took their land. They were responsible for the torture and murder of Menchú's mother, father, and brother. In 1981 Menchú emigrated to Mexico. She was twenty-three years old when she wrote her autobiography, I, Rigoberta Menchú. *The book is a typescript, with few modifications, of the twenty-four hours of taped conversation she had with her translator, Ann Wright, in Paris in 1982. Menchú told her story in Spanish after studying the language for only three years. In the book, she tells the history of her family and her people and describes what her translator, a Latin American woman from Argentina, calls "internal colonialism," an oppression that mestizo populations sometimes impose on natives of Latin America. Rigoberta Menchú was awarded the Nobel Peace Prize in 1992 for her active role in the survival of her people.*

---

[2] Translated by Ann Wright.

Facts about Guatemala

Guatemala is the most populous country in Central America and is thought to have the least equitable distribution of wealth. Half its population are descendants of the Mayan people; the other half, called *ladinos,* have both Mayan and European ancestry. Guatemala gained its independence from Spain in 1821. Following World War II, Guatemala enjoyed a brief period of democracy under President Jacobo Arbenz Guzman who supported the redistribution of land in an attempt to break up the large plantations or *fincas*.[3] The United Fruit Company, a U.S.-based corporation, lost a substantial portion of its land to Guzman's agrarian reform. Under Dwight D. Eisenhower, the Central Intelligence Agency (CIA) helped Colonel Carlos Castillo Armas lead a revolt that overthrew Arbenz. For the next thirty years Guatemala was controlled by a series of military dictatorships, most bent on suppressing the leftist guerrilla movement that defied them. The military regimes of the early 1980s slated thousands of native Guatemalans for "relocation" as part of their war against the guerrilla forces. Rigoberta Menchú is among the 100,000 people who fled to Mexico to avoid "relocation." Assassinations by right-wing political death squads continued into the early 1990s. At the moment, Guatemala has a tenuous hold on the democratic process.

> '... when the strangers who came from the East arrived, when they arrived; the ones who brought Christianity which ended the power in the East, and made the heavens cry and filled the maize bread of the Katún with sadness...'
>
> —Chilam Balam

> 'Their chief was not defeated by young warriors, nor wounded by sons of Titans. It was Judith, the daughter of Marari, who disarmed him with the beauty of her face.'
>
> —The Bible ('Judith')

1   We began to study the Bible as our main text. Many relationships in the Bible are like those we have with our ancestors, our ancestors whose lives were very much like our own. The important thing for us is that we started to identify that reality with our own. That's how we began studying the Bible. It's not something you memorize, it's not just to be talked about and prayed about, and nothing more. It also helped to change the image we had, as Catholics and Christians: that God is up there and that God has a great kingdom for we the poor, yet never thinking of our own reality as a reality that we were actually living. But by studying the scriptures, we did. Take "Exodus" for example, that's one we studied and

---

[3] Large plantations where coffee, sugarcane, bananas, or cotton is grown. Government soldiers in the service of rich landowners frequently arrested Mayans as "vagrants"—because they held no title to the land they cultivated—and forced them to work on the *fincas.*

analysed. It talks a lot about the life of Moses who tried to lead his people from oppression, and did all he could to free his people. We compare the Moses of those days with ourselves, the "Moses" of today. "Exodus" is about the life of a man, the life of Moses.

2   We began looking for texts which represented each one of us. We tried to relate them to our Indian culture. We took the example of Moses for the men, and we have the example of Judith, who was a very famous woman in her time and appears in the Bible. She fought very hard for her people and made many attacks against the king they had then, until she finally had his head. She held her victory in her hand, the head of the King. This gave us a vision, a stronger idea of how we Christians must defend ourselves. It made us think that a people could not be victorious without a just war. We Indians do not dream of great riches, we want only enough to live on. There is also the story of David, a little shepherd boy who appears in the Bible, who was able to defeat the king of those days, King Goliath. This story is the example for the children. This is how we look for stories and psalms which teach us how to defend ourselves from our enemies. I remember taking examples from all the texts which helped the community to understand their situation better. It's not only now that there are great kings, powerful men, people who hold power in their hands. Our ancestors suffered under them too. This is how we identify with the lives of our ancestors who were conquered by a great desire for power—our ancestors were murdered and tortured because they were Indians. We began studying more deeply and well, we came to a conclusion. That being a Christian means thinking of our brothers around us, and that every one of our Indian race has the right to eat. This reflects what God himself said, that on this earth we have a right to what we need. The Bible was our principal text for study as Christians and it showed us what the role of a Christian is. I became a catechist as a little girl and I studied the Bible, hymns, the scriptures, but only very superficially. One of the things Catholic Action put in our heads is that everything is sinful. But we came round to asking ourselves: "If everything is sinful, why is it that the landowner kills humble peasants who don't even harm the natural world? Why do they take our lives?" When I first became a catechist, I thought that there was a God and that we had to serve him. I thought God was up there and that he had a kingdom for the poor. But we realized that it is not God's will that we should live in suffering, that God did not give us that destiny, but that men on earth have imposed this suffering, poverty, misery and discrimination on us. We even got the idea of using our own everyday weapons, as the only solution left to us.

3   I am a Christian and I participate in this struggle as a Christian. For me, as a Christian, there is one important thing. That is the life of Christ. Throughout his life Christ was humble. History tells us he was born in a little hut. He was persecuted and had to form a band of men so that his seed would not disappear. They were his disciples, his apostles. In those

days, there was no other way of defending himself or Christ would have used it against his oppressors, against his enemies. He even gave his life. But Christ did not die, because generations and generations have followed him. And that's exactly what we understood when our first catechists fell. They're dead but our people keep their memory alive through our struggle against the government, against an enemy who oppresses us. We don't need very much advice, or theories, or documents: life has been our teacher. For my part, the horrors I have suffered are enough for me. And I've also felt in the deepest part of me what discrimination is, what exploitation is. It is the story of my life. In my work I've often gone hungry. If I tried to recount the number of times I'd gone hungry in my life, it would take a very long time. When you understand this, when you see your own reality, a hatred grows inside you for those oppressors that make the people suffer so. As I said, and I say it again, it is not fate which makes us poor. It's not because we don't work, as the rich say. They say: "Indians are poor because they don't work, because they're always asleep." But I know from experience that we're outside ready for work at three in the morning. It was this that made us decide to fight. This is what motivated me, and also motivated many others. Above all the mothers and fathers. They remember their children. They remember the ones they would like to have with them now but who died of malnutrition, or intoxication in the *fincas,* or had to be given away because they had no way of looking after them. It has a long history. And it's precisely when we look at the lives of Christians in the past that we see what our role as Christians should be today. I must say, however, that I think even religions are manipulated by the system, by those same governments you find everywhere. They use them through their ideas or through their methods. I mean, it's clear that a priest never works in the *fincas,* picking cotton or coffee. He wouldn't know what picking cotton was. Many priests don't even know what cotton is. But our reality teaches us that, as Christians, we must create a Church of the poor, that we don't need a Church imposed from outside which knows nothing of hunger. We recognize that the system has wanted to impose on us: to divide us and keep the poor dormant. So we take some things and not others. As far as sins go, it seems to me that the concept of the Catholic religion, or any other more conservative religion than Catholicism, is that God loves the poor and has a wonderful paradise in Heaven for the poor, so the poor must accept the life they have on Earth. But as Christians, we have understood that being a Christian means refusing to accept all the injustices which are committed against our people, refusing to accept the discrimination committed against a humble people who barely know what eating meat is but who are treated worse than horses. We've learned all this by watching what has happened in our lives. This awakening of the Indians didn't come, of course, from one day to the next, because Catholic Action and other religions and the system itself have all tried to keep us where we were. But I think that unless a religion springs from within the people themselves, it is a weapon of the system. So, naturally, it wasn't at all difficult for our community to understand all this and the reasons for us to defend ourselves, because this is the reality we live.

4   As I was saying, for us the Bible is our main weapon. It has shown us the way. Perhaps those who call themselves Christians but who are really only Christians in theory, won't understand why we give the Bible the meaning we do. But that's because they haven't lived as we have. And also perhaps because they can't analyse it. I can assure you that any one of my community, even though he's illiterate and has to have it read to him and translated into his language, can learn many lessons from it, because he has no difficulty understanding what reality is and what the difference is between the paradise up above, in Heaven, and the reality of our people here on Earth. We do this because we feel it is the duty of Christians to create the kingdom of God on Earth among our brothers. This kingdom will exist only when we all have enough to eat, when our children, brothers, parents don't have to die from hunger and malnutrition. That will be the "Glory," a Kingdom for we who have never known it. I'm only talking about the Catholic church in general terms because, in fact, many priests came to our region and were anti-communists, but nevertheless understood that the people weren't communists but hungry; not communists, but exploited by the system. And they joined our people's struggle too, they opted for the life we Indians live. Of course many priests call themselves Christians when they're only defending their own petty interests and they keep themselves apart from the people so as not to endanger these interests. All the better for us, because we know very well that we don't need a king in a palace but a brother who lives with us. We don't need a leader to show us where God is, to say whether he exists or not, because, through our own conception of God, we know there is a God and that, as the father of us all, he does not wish even one of his children to die, or be unhappy, or have no joy in life. We believe that, when we started using the Bible, when we began studying it in terms of our reality, it was because we found in it a document to guide us. It's not that the document itself brings about the change, it's more that each one of us learns to understand his reality and wants to devote himself to others. More than anything else, it was a form of learning for us. Perhaps if we'd had other means to learn, things would have been different. But we understood that any element in nature can change man when he is ready for change. We believe the Bible is a necessary weapon for our people. Today I can say that it is a struggle which cannot be stopped. Neither the governments nor imperialism can stop it because it is a struggle of hunger and poverty. Neither the government nor imperialism can say: "Don't be hungry," when we are all dying of hunger.

5   To learn about self-defence, as I was saying, we studied the Bible. We began fashioning our own weapons. We knew very well that the

government, those cowardly soldiers ... perhaps I shouldn't talk of them so harshly, but I can't find another word for them. Our weapons were very simple. And at the same time, they weren't so simple when we all started using them, when the whole village was armed. As I said before, the soldiers arrived one night. Our people were not in their homes. They'd left the village and gone to the camp. They made sure that we hadn't abandoned the village altogether but thought it would be better to occupy it in the daytime. So sometime later, when we weren't expecting them, about fifteen days later, our lookouts saw the army approaching. We were in the middle of building houses for our neighbours. We needed some more huts there. We had two lookouts. One was supposed to warn the community and the other had to delay or stop the soldiers entering. They were aware that they might have to give their lives for the community. At a time like this, if someone can't escape, he must be ready to accept death. The army arrived, and the first two to enter wore civilian clothes. But our children can easily recognize soldiers, by the way they walk, and dress, and everything about them, so the lookouts knew they were soldiers in disguise. They asked the names of certain *compañeros* in the community so they could take them away, kidnap them. One of the lookouts got away and came to warn the village that the enemy was nearby. We asked him if he was sure and he said: "Yes, they are soldiers, two of them. But as I was coming up here I saw others coming, further off, with olive green uniforms." The whole community left the village straight away and gathered in one place. We were very worried because the other lookout didn't appear. They were capable of having kidnapped him. But he did turn up in the end and told us how many soldiers there were, what each one was like, what sort of weapons they had, how many in the vanguard and the rearguard. This information helped us decide what to do, because it was daytime and we hadn't set our traps. We said: "What are we going to do with this army?" They came into the village and began beating our dogs and killing our animals. They went into the houses and looted them. They went crazy looking for us all over the place. Then we asked: "Who is willing to risk their lives now?" I, my brothers and some other neighbours immediately put up our hands. We planned to give the army a shock and to show them we were organised and weren't just waiting passively for them. We had less than half an hour to plan how we were going to capture some weapons. We chose some people—the ones who'd go first, second, third, fourth, to surprise the enemy. How would we do it? We couldn't capture all ninety soldiers who'd come to the village, but we could get the rearguard. My village is a long way from the town, up in the mountains. You have to go over the mountains to get to another village. We have a little path to the village just wide enough for horses ... and there are big rivers nearby so that the path isn't straight. It bends a lot. So we said, "Let's wait for the army on one of those bends and when the soldiers pass, we'll ambush the last one." We knew we were risking our lives but we knew that this example would benefit the village very much because the army would stop coming and searching the village all the time. And that's what we did.

6   We chose a *compañera,* a very young girl, the prettiest in the village. She was risking her life, and she was risking being raped as well. Nevertheless, she said: "I know very well that if this is my part in the struggle, I have to do it. If this is how I contribute to the community, I'll do it." So this *compañera* goes ahead on another path to a place that the army has to pass on their way to the village. That's where we prepared the ambush. We didn't have firearms, we had only our people's weapons. We'd invented a sort of Molotov cocktail by putting petrol in a lemonade bottle with a few iron filings, mixed with oil, and a wick to light it. So if the army got one of us, or if we couldn't do anything else, we'd set fire to them. This cocktail could burn two or three soldiers because it could land on them and burn their clothes. We had catapults too, or rather, they were the ones we'd always used to protect the maize fields from the birds which would come into the fields and eat the cobs when they were growing. The catapults could shoot stones a long way and if your aim is good it lands where you want it to. We had machetes, stones, sticks, chile and salt—all the different people's weapons. We had none of the weapons the army had. The community decided that the young girl who went on ahead would try to flirt with the last soldier and try to make him stop and talk to her. We all had numbers: who would be the first to jump, who would get him off balance, who would frighten him and who would disarm him. Each of us had a special task in capturing the soldier.

7   First came the ones without weapons—they were members of the secret police, soldiers in disguise. Then came the others. The whole troop. They were about two metres away when the last one came. Our *campañera* came along the path. She paid no attention to the others. It was a miracle they didn't rape her, because when soldiers come to our area they usually catch girls and rape them—they don't care who they are or where they're from. The *compañera* was ready to endure anything. When she came to the last soldier, she asked him where they'd been. And the soldier began telling her: "We went to that village. Do you know what's happened to the people?" The *compañera* said: "No, I don't know." And he said: "We've been twice and there's no-one, but we know they live there." Then one of our neighbours jumped onto the path, another came up behind the soldier. My job was to jump onto the path as well. Between us we got the soldier off balance. One of us said: "Don't move, hands up." And the soldier thought there was a gun pointing at his head or his back. Whatever he thought, he did nothing. Another *compañero* said: "Drop your weapon." And he dropped it. We took his belt off and checked his bag. We took his grenades away, his rifle, everything. I thought it was really funny, it's something I'll never forget, because we didn't know how to use it. We took his rifle, his big rifle, and a pistol, and we didn't even know

how to use the pistol. I remember that I took the soldier's pistol away and stood in front as if I knew how to use it but I didn't know anything. He could have taken it off me because I couldn't use it. But, anyway, we led him away at gun point. We made him go up through the mountains so that if the others came back they wouldn't find the path. If they had it would have been a massacre. Two *compañeras* of about forty-five and a fifty-year-old *compañero* had taken part in the ambush. The little *compañera* who'd attracted the soldier was about fourteen.

8   We took the disarmed soldier to my house, taking all the necessary precautions. We blindfolded him so that he wouldn't recognize the house he was going to. We got him lost. We took him a round-about way so that he'd lose his sense of direction. We finally arrived back. I found it really funny, I couldn't stop laughing because we didn't know how to use the gun. We were very happy, the whole community was happy. When we got near the camp, the whole community was waiting for us. We arrived with our captured soldier. We reached my house. He stayed there for a long time. We took his uniform off and gave him an old pair of trousers and an old shirt so that if his fellow soldiers came back—we tried to keep him tied up—they wouldn't know he was a soldier. We also thought that those clothes could help us confuse the other soldiers later on. Then came a very beautiful part when all the mothers in the village begged the soldier to take a message back to the army, telling all the soldiers there to think of our ancestors. The soldier was an Indian from another ethnic group. The women asked him how he could possibly have become a soldier, an enemy of his own race, his own people, the Indian race. Our ancestors never set bad examples like that. They begged him to be the light within his camp. They explained to him that bearing a son and bringing him up was a big effort, and to see him turn into a criminal as he was, was unbearable. All the mothers in the village came to see the soldier. Then the men came too and begged him to recount his experience when he got back to the army and to take on the role, as a soldier, of convincing the others not to be so evil, not to rape the women of our race's finest sons, the finest examples of our ancestors. They suggested many things to him. We told the soldier that our people were organised, and were prepared to give their last drop of blood to counter anything the army did to us. We made him see that it wasn't the soldiers who were guilty but the rich who don't risk their lives. They live in nice houses and sign papers. It's the soldier who goes around the villages, up and down the mountains, mistreating and murdering his own people.

9   The soldier went away very impressed, he took this important message with him. When we first caught him, we'd had a lot of ideas, because we wanted to use the gun but didn't know how. It wasn't that we wanted to kill the soldier because we knew very well that one life is worth as much as many lives. But we also knew that the soldier would tell what he'd seen, what he'd felt and what we'd done to him, and that for us it

could mean a massacre—the deaths of children, women, and old people in the village. The whole community would die. So we said: "What we'll do with this man is execute him, kill him. Not here in the village but outside." But people kept coming up with other ideas of what to do, knowing full well the risk we were running. In the end, we decided that, even though it might cost us our lives, this soldier should go and do what we'd asked him, and really carry through the role he had to play. After about three hours we let him go, in his new disguise. His comrades, the troop of ninety soldiers, hadn't come back for him because they thought he'd been ambushed by guerrillas and they were cowards. They ran off as fast as they could back to town and didn't try to save the soldier left behind. We didn't kill the soldier. The army itself took care of that when he got back to camp. They said he must be an informer, otherwise how could he possibly have stayed and then returned. They said the law says that a soldier who abandons his rifle must be shot. So they killed him.

10   This was the village's first action and we were happy. We now had two guns, we had a grenade, and we had a cartridge belt, but we didn't know how to use them, nobody knew. We all wanted to find someone who could show us but we didn't know where or who, because whoever we went to, we'd be accused of being guerrillas using weapons. It made us sad to open the rifle and see what was inside, because we knew it killed others. We couldn't use it but it was the custom always to keep anything important. A machete that's not being used for instance, is always smeared with oil and wrapped in a plastic bag so it doesn't rust with the damp or the rain. That's what we had to do with the weapons because we didn't know how to use them. From then on the army was afraid to come up to our villages. They never came back to our village because to get there they would have to go through the mountains. Even if they came by plane they had to fly over the mountains. They were terrified of the mountains and of us. We were happy. It was the most wonderful thing that had happened to us. We were all united. Nobody went down to the *finca,* nobody went to market, nobody went down to any other place, because they would be kidnapped. What we did was to go over the mountains, go to other towns where they sell local salt, or rather some black stones which are really salt. I don't know if you only get this type of black stone in Guatemala, it's black and it's salt. It tastes very good, delicious. So we got very large stones and cooked with these so we didn't have to buy salt in the market. The *compañeros* got salt by other means. You find these stones in Sacapúlas, a town in El Quiché. It's rather strange there because it's up on the *Altiplano* where it's cold and yet when you go down a bit, it's warm. It's on a hillside which produces all the fruits you get on the South coast. You get mangoes, water melons, bananas. And that's where you get this salt stone. They sell it but it's very cheap because nobody wants to buy. In Guatemala it's called "Indian salt." We don't eat sugar, we're not used to drinking coffee. Our drink is *atol,* ground

maize made into *atol*. We produce the maize in our own areas and we do it collectively to grow things better and make better use of the land. The landowners were frightened to come near our village because they thought they would be kidnapped now that our village was organised. So they didn't come near us. The landowners went away, and didn't threaten us like before. The soldiers didn't come any more. So we stayed there, the owners of our little bit of land. We began cultivating things so we wouldn't have to go down to town. It was a discipline we applied to ourselves in the village to save lives and only to put ourselves at risk when we had to. My village was organised from this moment on.

11   I couldn't stay in my village any longer because, now that it could carry on its struggle, organise itself and make decisions, my role was not important. There was no room for a leader, someone telling others what to do any more. So I decided to leave my village and go and teach another community the traps which we had invented and which our own neighbours had used so successfully. It's now that I move on to teach the people in another village.

Reading for Meaning

1. Why does Rigoberta Menchú feel that it was necessary to create a "church of the poor"? How was it different from the Catholic Church that had taught her catechism?

2. What does she mean when she says that her people studied the Bible in terms of their own reality? How did they feel it could apply to them?

3. Menchú recounts an incident when the people of her village captured a government soldier, admonished him, and set him free. How does the story illustrate what the Quiché learned from their study of the Bible? What ideas does the story convey about the villagers and the army?

4. How did the villagers' lives change after they kidnapped, then released, the soldier? What role does Menchú play in the organization of her village? Why does she downplay her role as a leader?

5. Somé wrote *Of Water and the Spirit* at least in part to enlighten people of Western cultures about the spiritual values of his people and to suggest that Westerners need to undergo some deep transformation if they are to survive. What does Rigoberta Menchú's purpose for writing seem to be? How well does she achieve this goal?

Comparing Texts

Aung San Suu Kyi writes about her people's struggle against the Burmese military dictatorship in "Freedom from Fear," page 359. Like Rigoberta Menchú, Suu Kyi lost her father in an armed struggle against a dictatorship, the colonial British government during the Burmese fight for independence. Both "Freedom from Fear" and the essay by Menchú were delivered orally before being published in written form. Compare the writing styles and the organization of these selections, paying particular attention to the uniqueness of each.

Ideas for Writing

1. Rigoberta Menchú says that the lives of the Quiché ancestors "were very much like our own." Read selections that you can find from Mayan texts such as the *Popol Vul* or *Chala Balam*. Write an investigation paper in which you explain Mayan beliefs, customs, or way of life recorded in one or more of these texts.

2. Find *I, Rigoberta Menchú* in your local or college library and read a few additional chapters in the book. What does your reading tell you about the type of person the book's author is, her value system, and her links to the Quiché people?

Writing before Reading

Based on your own knowledge of Christianity, what are its core beliefs? After you have read Wang Bin's article "Two Great Traditions," compare your view of Christianity to his. What does he exclude that you included, and what does he discuss that you omitted?

TWO GREAT TRADITIONS
Wang Bin

Wang Bin wrote this article in 1992. It was published in the July/August issue of the Unesco Courier.

Facts about Confucianism and Taoism

Confucianism, based on the teachings of Confucius (551–479 B.C.E.) has dominated the social and political life of China since its inception. Confucius, the Western spelling for *K'ung Fu-tzu* (Master K'ung), was born into a declining aristocratic family. He became a scholar and eventually a teacher and head of his own school. He developed his philosophy in response to the social upheaval that resulted from conflict among China's feudal warlords. According to Confucian doctrine, human beings are inherently social creatures, naturally inclined to follow social conventions or rituals *(li)* that dictate proper behavior in an elaborate social hierarchy. The *Analects (Lun-yü)* of Confucius comprise twenty books or chapters of conversations between Confucius and his disciples. Written as a series of aphorisms, the *Analects* advise the Chinese about how to live a balanced, ethical life; stress the importance of performing social rituals; and proscribe individuals' responsibilities to society and their duties and obligations to family. The authority of the ruler, according to Confucius, comes from heaven, a belief that would become the standard for medieval European kings who, similarly, ruled by divine right. Rulers have their own responsibilities to the people, and if they follow the true way, or Tao, the state will enjoy peace, social order, and prosperity. As a political philosophy, the aim of Confucianism was to produce benevolent rulers and obedient subjects. It became the official religion during the Han dynasty (206 B.C.E.–220 A.C.E.). Candidates for government jobs could qualify only after being tested on their knowledge of the wisdom of Confucius. During the Han era, the metaphysical principles of Yin (female) and Yang (male), and numerological theories of the universe, both based on the I Ching or Book of Changes, became part of Confucian thinking. With the fall of the Han dynasty, Confucianism was replaced by Buddhism and other religions that had come into China. Four hundred years later, with the establishment of the Tang dynasty, Neo-Confucianism became the established state religion. Influenced by the commentary of Mencius on the *Analects* of Confucius, Neo-Confucian philosophy teaches that humans are innately good and that through the intuition of their heart-mind *(hsin),* they will follow a natural pattern *(li)* in any situation. Communist rulers in the twentieth century sought to undermine Confucian influence on Chinese thought. Today, Confucian philosophy survives in Hong Kong and among Chinese living in the West.

The history of Taoism parallels that of Confucianism. Laozi (sixth century B.C.E.) or Lao-Tzu (Master Lao) is credited with writing the Daode Jing or Tao Te Ching, the major text of Taoist thinking. Little is known about the philosopher, and because of the legends that have grown up around him, some scholars question whether there was such a man. If there was an actual Laozi, he was a contemporary of Confucius. Like his popular rival, Laozi saw his philosophy of the Dao or Tao (the way to absolute reality) as a remedy for the social upheaval of his time. The *Tao Te Ching,* like the *Analects* of Confucius, the teachings of the Greek philosopher Socrates (c. 469–399 B.C.E.), and those of Jesus of Nazareth, were the sayings of Laozi written down as remembered by his disciples. Laozi teaches that the ultimate reality is the Dao (Tao), the way of the universe as exemplified in nature. Whereas Confucianism defended conventional values, and the social and political status quo, Laozi challenged accepted values and proposed that *wu wei,* or "nondoing" is the ideal path of life. In other words, one should not act in prescribed, traditional ways but should practice nonaction—action in harmony with nature. Zhuangzi (Chuang tzu) (c. 369–286 B.C.E.) added the idea that oppositions were mere illusions, and no one way may be judged better than another. To avoid the traps and conflicts of material thinking, one must accept change as the only constant, and seek to abolish aggression and desire.

1   This article endeavours to answer a difficult question: How does Christianity differ (beyond purely religious differences) from the Chinese tradition?

Focusing on collective thought patterns, I shall attempt to explore a number of non-religious phenomena that are deeply rooted in Christian doctrines but are notably absent from Chinese intellectual life. It is these phenomena, the article will argue, that not only differentiate Western culture from Chinese culture, but also illuminate the contributions Christianity has made historically to the general development of the human mind.

2	A transcendent deity emerges when the potential believer separates himself or herself mentally from the external world and attempts to establish a system of interpretation capable of affording a final answer to all the mysteries represented by nature. What impresses a Chinese reader of the Bible is not so much the image of God as His relationship to humankind. The notion of "covenant" is particularly difficult for the Chinese mind to grasp. According to Genesis, man, created by God, separates himself from God through the Fall and devotes life-long strivings to an attempt to be reunited with God in another world. The covenant between God and man not only holds out the hope of achieving that ambition but presupposes a separation of man mentally from the Truth, the Good and Beauty, the whole external world pertaining to or created by God. As for visible cosmic nature, God encourages man to subjugate it by exercising "dominion over the fish of the sea, and over the fowl of the air, and over every living thing that moves upon the Earth" (Genesis 1:28).

3	Stripped of its doctrinal content, the covenant reveals a deep-rooted thought pattern whose archetype can be traced back to ancient Greece and serves as a unique link between the pagan tradition and contemporary intellectual life. The characteristic features of this pattern are, on the one hand, the detachment of man (the observer) from the external world (the observed), and on the other a constant effort to achieve the final yet impossible recombination. Ultimately, man is separated from himself as an object of study. No revolution in the West has ever altered this basic thought pattern.

4	The Chinese counterpart to this thought pattern is its precise opposite. In defining man's relationship to the universe, Confucius, Lao Tzu and his modern critics share a single framework: that of man in the universe. The term "universe" refers mainly to cosmic nature in Taoism and to society in Confucianism. (The former finds its fullest expression in artistic creation while the latter has its roots in Chinese political-moral doctrines.) The man-in-the-universe thought pattern has survived many generations of revolutionary change. The overlapping shadows of Confucius and Lao Tzu still guide the thought processes of the Chinese intelligentsia and circumscribe their imagination.

Transcendency versus Immanency

5	When the Chinese and the Western traditions meet, the Chinese mind tends to appreciate the Greeks and to reject Christianity, disregarding the intellectual process which made the transition from paganism to

Christianity possible. To the modern Chinese, passages in the Bible that encourage the conquest of nature might be acceptable. But the results of the separation described above go much farther than the exploitation of cosmic nature and do not form part of the Chinese mental landscape. They include: a persistent quest for the ontological meaning of human existence; a way of verifying the truth, divine or scientific, which in the historical continuum encompasses not merely modern individualism but a deep Christian sense of the individual's soul identified only with God; man's challenge to the Almighty (as in the story of Job); the formula "I think, therefore I am"; the progress from equality before God to equality before the law; a contractual tradition that binds two separate parts: God and man, a King and his subjects, a state and its citizens; and so on. To understand these ideas, the Chinese mind has to adapt to a new perspective.

6   In addition to a mental state preoccupied with the separation of man from God, a sense of transcendency is indispensable to Christian faith. Without it, it would be impossible to conceive of reunion in the other world.

7   As a concept imported from the West, transcendency is frequently used by Chinese scholars as well as Western sinologists to describe Taoism. This conceptual misplacement, a common phenomenon in contemporary Chinese intellectual life, neglects the basic fact that Chinese "transcendency," restricted as it is to the "man-in-the-universe" framework, is totally different from what is meant by transcendency in its strict Western sense.

8   Christian transcendency takes the individual (his soul) as the point of departure as well as the final goal of fulfilment. It rises above objects which reveal themselves to experience and moves towards God or the absolute truth in the other world. It focuses on the fulfilment of the individual and points to the infinite. Chinese "transcendency," on the other hand, requires the individual to transcend himself so as to merge into nature or society. When there is perfect harmony between man and the universe, the absolute truth can be grasped through sense-perception and intuitive reason. To the Chinese mind, the truth is here and to the Christian mind, the truth is there. The two truths are incommensurable, though they may agree on some specific points.

9   The most obvious manifestation of this difference is to be found in theoretical reflection on artistic creation. From Plato on, classical theories of art and literature attribute the source of inspiration to the divine or the supernatural. In modern times some theorists have seen inspiration as originating in the irrational self (the emotions or the subconscious) as opposed to the rational self, thus postulating a microcosm within human nature of the separation of man from God. Both these ideas involve a transcendent movement from one opposite towards the other. Modernism seeks pure truth in life, a truth which, it maintains, has been

polluted and distorted by civilized society. But it remains a truth which is always there, not here.

10 All this contrasts sharply with the way in which the Chinese understand inspiration. In ancient Chinese, there is no such term as inspiration because such an idea is totally absent from Chinese spiritual and intellectual life. However, classical Chinese theories of art and literature do describe a mental state in which the artist suddenly finds himself confronted with a spiritual spark triggered off as a result of the inexplicable harmonization between the artist and his object to be expressed.

11 Scholars of comparative literature who lack philosophical insight have simplified this situation and wrongly described it by attaching to it another Western label, "expressionism" or "empathy." Chinese expressionism, if we must adopt this term, emphasizes a constant reciprocal movement and recognition between subject and object within a shared space, the universe. It is two in one. As for the source of inspiration, the difference might be summarized as inspiration out of ontological transcendency versus inspiration out of cosmological immanence.

12 To illustrate this difference, let us imagine two classical pictures: a Western figure painting and a Chinese wash painting. In the latter, the landscape often occupies almost the whole space with one or several figures relegated into obscurity. A Western connoisseur might misunderstand the overall arrangement as a suppression of individuality. On the other hand, the nimbus around the head of a beautiful medieval or Renaissance figure often puzzles the Chinese mind. The setting is beautiful, so is the figure. But what is the point of that small halo, a visual cliché? A readily found explanation is Western superstition. If only both sides would understand that appreciation of different mysteries demands different perspectives as well as different imaginations! However, from the Chinese point of view, the challenge of Christian transcendency is more than an image of unfamiliar beauty.

What Is versus What-Ought-to-Be

13 When we discuss the Western tradition, we Chinese are often confronted with a seemingly inexplicable dichotomy between the moral man and the intellectual man, a distinction first made by Matthew Arnold who referred to the two elements involved as, respectively, "the forces of Hebraism and Hellenism." This gives the misleading impression that the Greek mind is concerned with "What-Is" while the Christian mind, like that of Confucius, is oriented towards "What-Ought-To-Be." I would argue that What-Is is characteristic of both the Greek and the Christian traditions.

14 Like Aristotle's "substance," God as a category is characterized by three priorities: knowledge priority—God is the Absolute truth or the subject and purpose of understanding; definition priority—God is the definition or the subject in terms of logic while all the others are predicates; and time

priority—God is the Being independent of and determinant of all other beings. Without this combination of epistemology, logic and ontology as a prerequisite, Christian love and good works are meaningless.

15 Modern Chinese intellectuals feel sympathy for Christian charity and works but many of them reject god as a term imagined through superstition. In the past ten years or so many of them have talked loudly about the importance of "transforming the traditional thought pattern," but what they mean by "thought pattern" has turned out to be economic, political or moral ideas. While they have been busy introducing Western ideas to replace Chinese ones, they have actually paid little attention to the thought pattern which supports those ideas. Thus we have a coin with two sides: Cathayan centricity on one side and wholesale Westernization on the other. This is the inevitable result of a three-thousand-year long tradition in which epistemology has yet to come to maturity.

16 Doubtless, Christianity also experienced domination by What-Ought-To-Be. For more than a thousand years, the spirit of the Church ruled the Western mind. It monopolized the interpretation of the Bible and institutionalized the Christian world into a hierarchy of terror. The Reformation was of profound significance in that it removed the Church as the mediator between God and man. When man confronts directly what he believes, he is free to pursue What-Is. Without this spiritual and intellectual liberation, the capitalist spirit and Protestant ethics could not have made a new world. Max Weber should have added two significant points to his analysis of the rise of Protestantism. Firstly, that the re-establishment of What-Is is predetermined by the separation of man from God, which not only gives rise to a religious revolution but nurtures modern epistemology which, in turn, challenges that religion. Secondly, that any faith or ideal, no matter how perfect it is, will inevitably decline in popularity if it is institutionalized into an interpretational hierarchy in order to control freedom of thought. The second point is more than a matter of thought pattern. Its far-reaching significance is a powerful challenge to any type of authoritarian institution.

The Universal

17 The above argument presents Christianity as a challenge to the Chinese mind. It does not imply that Christianity or the West are universal. If they were it would be impossible to explain Chinese prosperity in the past and its predictable possibility in the future. What, then, is the universal? It seems to be a misleading and even dangerous question, similar to "What is God?" or "What is the absolute truth?" A more acceptable formulation is that of unity in diversity. Unity does not mean conformity, nor does diversity mean the coexistence of independent but discrete elements. How can unity in diversity be achieved? I see it as a kind of challenge. It is a mutual exposure to new dimensions and perspectives, a constant discovery of complementary factors in otherness and, finally, a rediscovery of

oneself. It is a dialectical movement towards reciprocal recognition of different traditions and thought patterns. Even if there is no contact for the time being, the challenge remains. Our task is to turn potentiality into actuality. The process is endless. It is in this sense that I take Christianity as a challenge to the Chinese mind.

Reading for Meaning

1. What is the "thought pattern" implied in the Christian discussion of one's relationship to God? How does that pattern differ from the Chinese definition of one's relationship to the universe?

2. In Wang Bin's view, what are the important results of the Western view of the individual's essential separation from the world?

3. How do the Christian and the Chinese definitions of "transcendency" differ?

4. What importance does Wang Bin attribute to the Reformation—a religious movement in Europe that challenged the authority of the Catholic Church—whose beliefs prepared the way for the Protestant religions?

5. How is the notion of artistic "inspiration" reflected in the art of each culture? What does Wang Bin's analysis of Christian thinking suggest are Christianity's contributions "to the general development of the human mind"?

Comparing Texts

1. Reread the excerpt from Thomas Moore's *Care of the Soul* which appears as the second epigraph for this chapter. In what ways do Moore's perceptions of spirituality coincide with either the Chinese or the Christian way of thinking described in Wang Bin's essay?

2. Read the following examples from the *Analects* of Confucius and the Beatitudes of Jesus of Nazareth, as translated in the Cambridge Bible. Compare these texts in terms of their themes, ideas about ethical behavior, assumptions about the universe, the place of human beings in that universe, or the style of these texts.

FROM THE *ANALECTS* OF CONFUCIUS.[4]

Someone asked Confucius how to elevate virtue, purge evil, and clarify confusion. Confucius said, "Good question! Put service first and gain after; is this not elevating virtue? Attack your own evils, not those of others; is this not purging evil? And suppose you forget yourself and affect your relatives because of a temporary fit of anger; is that not confusion?" (12:21)

---

[4] Translated by Thomas Cleary.

Confucius said, "Don't worry about the recognition of others; worry about your own lack of ability." (12:32)

One of the disciples was studying for employment.
Confucius said, "Learn a lot, eliminate the doubtful, and speak discreetly about the rest; then there will be little blame. See a lot, eliminate the perilous, act prudently on the rest; then there will be little regret. When your words are seldom blamed and your actions seldom regretted, employment will be there." (2:18)

Confucius said, "Not cultivating virtue, not learning, not being able to take to justice on hearing it, and not being able to change what is not good: these are my worries." (7:3)

Confucius said of his foremost disciple, "He is wise indeed! He subsists on bare essentials and lives in a poor neighborhood; for other people this would mean intolerable anxiety, but he is consistently happy. Wise indeed is he!" (6:11)

Confucius said, "Be dutiful at home, brotherly in public; be discreet and trustworthy, love all people, and draw near to humanity. If you have extra energy as you do that, then study literature." (1:7)

Confucius said, "I do not teach the uninspired or enlighten the complacent. When I bring out one corner to show people, if they do not come back with the other three, I do not repeat." (7:8)

FROM CHAPTER 5, THE GOSPEL ACCORDING TO ST. MATTHEW

1. And seeing the multitudes, he [Jesus] went up into a mountain: and when he was set, his disciples came unto him:
2. And he opened his mouth, and taught them, saying,
3. Blessed are the poor in spirit: for theirs is the kingdom of heaven.
4. Blessed are they that mourn: for they shall be comforted.
5. Blessed are the meek: for they shall inherit the earth.
6. Blessed are they which do hunger and thirst after righteousness: for they shall be filled.
7. Blessed are the merciful: for they shall obtain mercy.
8. Blessed are the pure in heart: for they shall see God.
9. Blessed are the peacemakers: for they shall be called the children of God.
10. Blessed are they which are persecuted for righteousness' sake: for theirs is the kingdom of heaven.
11. Blessed are ye, when men shall revile you, and persecute you, and shall say all manner of evil against you falsely, for my sake.

12 Rejoice, and be exceeding glad: for great is your reward in heaven: for so persecuted they the prophets which were before you.

Ideas for Writing

1. Wang Bin explains that "To the Chinese mind, the truth is here [i.e., in the natural universe] and to the Christian mind, the truth is there [i.e., in another world beyond this one]." In what ways do Christianity and a Native American religion express a similar dichotomy? To answer this question, you will probably need to find information about the worldview of a particular Native people (e.g., the Navajo, Hopi, Cherokee, Iroquois, or Lakota). Then draw a few comparisons between the beliefs of the Native Americans and those of Christian believers as described by Wang Bin or another reputable writer.

2. Study the following passages from the *Tao-Te Ching*.[5] Write a paper in which you explain the way of thinking (e.g., assumptions about life and the universe) that the selections suggest.

> Existence is beyond the power of words
> To define:
> Terms may be used
> But are none of them absolute.
> In the beginning of heaven and earth there were no words,
>   Words came out of the womb of matter;
>   And whether a man dispassionately
>   Sees to the core of life
>   Or passionately
>   Sees the surface,
>   The core and the surface
>   Are essentially the same,
>   Words making them seem different
>   Only to express appearance.
>   If name be needed, wonder names them both:
>   From wonder into wonder
>   Existence opens.
>
>   19
>
> Rid of formalized wisdom and learning
> People would be a hundredfold happier,
> Rid of conventionalized duty and honor
> People would find their families dear.
> Rid of legalized profiteering
> People would have no thieves to fear.
> These methods of life have failed, all three.
> Here is the way, it seems to me:
> Set people free,

---

[5] Translated by Witter Bynner.

As deep in their hearts they would like to be,
From private greeds
And wanton needs.

32

Existence is infinite, not to be defined;
And, though it seem but a bit of wood in your hand, to carve as you
    please,
It is not to be lightly played with and laid down.
When rulers adhered to the way of life
They were upheld by natural loyalty:
Heaven and earth were joined and made fertile,
Life was a freshness of rain,
Subject to none,
Free to all.
But men of culture came, with their grades and their distinctions;
And as soon as such differences had been devised
No one knew where to end them,
Though the one who does know the end of all such differences
Is the sound man:
Existence
Might be likened to the course
Of many rivers reaching the one sea.

Writing before Reading

What has been your experience with the reading of poetry? Are there poems or lyrics to popular songs that you are particularly fond of that seem to express your feelings well?

GACELA[6] OF THE DEAD CHILD[7]

Federico García Lorca

Federico García Lorca (1898–1936) is Spain's most influential poet and dramatist. Since his execution by Franco's Falangist Civil Guard,

---

[6] One of the traditional forms of Arabic verse that Lorca used frequently.

[7] Translated from the Spanish by Edwin Honig.

García Lorca has enjoyed international acclaim as a poet who embraces surrealism without compromising his portrayal of profound human passions and fears. The son of a wealthy landowner, García Lorca studied law in Granada but soon followed his interest in the arts. In 1919 he joined the circle of the avant-garde writers and artists in Madrid, among them Salvador Dali, Luis Buñuel, and Pablo Neruda. His poetry often relies on traditional ballad forms and frequently takes its inspiration from the passion and folklore of the marginalized Andalusian gypsies. García Lorca treats the elemental and the terrifying in human experience, and his poems are set in a landscape of dreams and transformation. His plays, including Blood Wedding *(1933) and* The House of Bernarda Alba *(1936), are still performed in the United States.*

Facts about Spain

Spain is located on the Iberian Peninsula in the southwestern corner of Europe. The Canary and Balearic Islands are also part of Spain, as are two cities, Ceuta and Melilla, located on the northern coast of Morocco. Spain is composed of the dozens of peoples who have conquered the land and settled there. Their identity has to do with regional differences based on history and culture. Three distinct minorities have a separate ethnic identification: the Basques in the north, the Galicians, mostly in the northwest, and the Catalans, who comprise 16 percent of the population and live on the east coast.

Spain was first inhabited by humans at least 500,000 years ago. Bones of *Homo erectus* have been found northeast of Madrid, and it is likely that the last Neanderthals died in the caves on what is now the island of Gibraltar. Roughly 15,000 years ago, closer relatives from the Stone Age left evidence of their artistic skills as well as their way of life on the walls of caves like Altamira in Santander, Spain. Since Neolithic times, Spain has been settled by Celts, Phoenicians, Greeks, Carthaginians, Romans, Visigoths, Vandals, Arabs, Jews, Syrians, and Berbers. Spain, or Al-Andalus in Arabic, became part of the Islamic world in 718 after the country was conquered by the Muslims of Morocco and the last Visigoth ruler, King Roderick, was defeated in 711. The Islamic expansion was stopped in the north by a group of Visigoths in Pelayo in 722. The rule of the caliph of Cordoba (929–961) produced one of the great periods of Spanish history, a time of intense learning and unprecedented economic prosperity. During this era, much of the West's knowledge of the literature of the ancient world and of scientific advances in the Middle East came into Europe through Moorish Spain. The Islamic presence in Spain ended officially in 1492 when the Muslim kingdom of Granada fell to the Christians, and Spain was once again in Catholic hands. Conquest of the New World began under the Catholic monarchs, Ferdinand II of Aragon and Isabella I of Castile, and continued under their grandson, Charles I, who became Holy Roman Emperor as Charles V of Spain. During the reign of Charles V,

Hernan Cortes laid claim to Mexico (1519–1521) and Francisco Pizarro conquered Peru (1531–1533). Although shipments of gold and silver from the New World caused crippling inflation and exacerbated the tendency of later rulers like Philip II to finance hopeless wars against the Netherlands and England, the Spanish empire boasted the greatest wealth and power in Europe during the sixteenth century. The next hundred years brought economic collapse and religious persecution at the same time that Spain experienced a golden age in literature and the arts produced by the genius of Miguel de Cervantes, Lope de Vega, El Greco, Diego Velazquez, and others. In the twentieth century, conflicts between the leftist forces in the country—workers, peasants, intellectuals, and ethnic minorities—and the right-wing military supported by landowners and the church escalated into the Spanish Civil War (1936–1939), which is generally regarded as Hitler's "experiment." Roughly a million people died in that war, and at the end of three years of bitter fighting, General Francisco Franco and his right-wing Falangist army established a fascist dictatorship. After Franco's death in 1975, Spain became a constitutional monarchy with a parliamentary form of government under King Juan Carlos I.

> Each afternoon in Granada,
> a child dies each afternoon.
> Each afternoon the water sits down
> to chat with its companions.
>
> The dead wear mossy wings.
> Winds clear and cloudy are
> two pheasants in flight through the towers,
> and the day is a wounded boy.
>
> Not a flicker of lark was left in the sky
> when I met you in the caverns of wine.
> Not the crumb of a cloud was over ground
> when you were drowned in the river.
>
> A giant of water sprawled over the hills,
> the valley tumbling with lilies and dogs.
> Through my hands' violet shadow, your body,
> dead on the bank, was an archangel, cold.

Reading for Meaning

1. What themes or ideas does García Lorca weave into his poem?

2. What feelings do the words, sounds, and images of the poem convey?

3. Discuss the effects of the rhythm, pattern of stanzas, and repetition of phrases in García Lorca's poem.

4. García Lorca uses words that are well within most people's understanding. His poetry is unique, however, because he does not rely on common sense, conventional ways of

combining these words, and instead creates combinations that carry us beyond literal levels of thinking and perception. If García Lorca is not appealing to reason and common sense, what does his poetry speak to?

5. How does the supernatural or apocalyptic imagery in "Gacela of the Dead Child" help the reader understand the significance of the child who dies each afternoon?

Comparing Texts

Compare ideas, themes, tone, or poetic techniques in García Lorca's poem and the portion of *The Heights of Macchu Picchu* by Pablo Neruda that appears here.

> From air to air, like an empty net,
> dredging through streets and ambient atmosphere, I came
> lavish, at autumn's coronation, with the leaves'
> proffer of currency and—between spring and wheat ears—
> that which a boundless love, caught in a gauntlet fall,
> grants us like a long-fingered moon.
>
> (Days of live radiance in discordant bodies: steel converted
> to the silence of acid:
> nights disentangled to the ultimate flour,
> assaulted stamens of the nuptial land.)
> Someone waiting for me among the violins
> met with a world like a buried tower
> sinking its spiral below the layered leaves
> color of raucous sulphur:
> and lower yet, in a vein of gold,
> like a sword in a scabbard of meteors,
> I plunged a turbulent and tender hand
> to the most secret organs of the earth.
>
> Leaning my forehead through the unfathomed waves
> I sank, a single drop, within a sleep of sulphur
> where, like a blind man, I retraced the jasmine
> of our exhausted human spring.

Ideas for Writing

1. In what ways does "Gacela of the Dead Child" rely on the transformation of images and the meanings of words?

2. Select several phrases of García Lorca's poem that you find most powerful. What special combination of images, sounds, and ideas contribute to this power?

3. Writer Odysseas Elytis gives the following description of how one should read and appreciate the poetry of García Lorca:

> The crucial thing is not to leaf through a book looking for more or less stylish phrases, but to unite with a power that propels you all the way to the roots of trees,

where you may caress the faces most in pain and circulate through the veins of your fellows like blood. The crucial thing is to be able to travel with the poet through an infinite, raw, enigmatic world—among knifed fruit, mutilated statues and designs of cosmography—with the sensation you felt as a child.

How might Elytis's description apply to the experience of reading "Gacela of the Dead Child"?

4. Do some research on surrealist poetry and find critical commentaries on Spanish surrealism in particular. With the help of these commentaries, analyze the unique elements in the García Lorca poem printed here or any of his poems you find interesting.

Writing before Reading

1. How "religious" do the people you know consider themselves? In what ways do their lives follow or contradict their professed religious principles?

2. How would you describe your own set of principles or religious convictions? What has shaped those convictions, whether religious or secular? How well do they serve you?

THE RELIGION OF AMERICANS AND AMERICAN RELIGION

Will Herberg

Will Herberg was professor of Judaic Studies and social philosophy at Drew University from 1955 until 1977. Herberg wrote frequently about religious issues and his books include Judaic and Modern Man *(1951) and* Existential Theologians *(1958). He was a religious editor for the* National Review *and contributed posthumously to the collection of essays titled* Jewish Perspectives on Christianity *(Autumn 1991). A collection of his essays titled* From Marxism to Judaism: The Collected Essays of Will Herberg *(1989) include his writings about the ties between Christianity and Judaism, moral responsibility in a largely secular world, and connections between religion and politics. Harry J. Austen's biography,* Will Herberg: From Right to Right *(1987), examines Herberg's move from Marxism to the political right and discusses his ideas on various subjects. Herberg's essay "The Religion of Americans and American Religion" is taken from his book,* Protestant-Catholic-Jew *(1955). In that work*

Herberg discussed the "religious revival" of the 1950s from a sociologist's point of view. In "The Religion of Americans and American Religion" Herberg argues that religious and secular tenets in the United States come from the same sources and that the overriding faith in this country is tied to a somewhat vague belief in the American way of life.

Facts about Religion in the United States

Perhaps the most important aspect of religion in the United States, as in Canada and in Western Europe, is the government's attempt to extend religious freedom to all citizens. The Constitution calls for the separation of church and state with the intent of preventing any single religious sect from foisting its beliefs on an unwilling population. The history of religion in the United States does not always show such tolerance. Several religious groups, including Puritans, Presbyterians, Baptists, and other religious dissenters came to the New World in search of religious freedom but were themselves reluctant to grant other denominations the same right. One hundred and sixty-six years after the Puritans settled in Plymouth, Massachusetts, Thomas Jefferson, James Madison, and George Mason wrote the Virginia Statute of Religious Liberty, a document that distinguished the functions of the state from those of the church. When Madison drafted the Bill of Rights (1789), he was guided by ideas set forth in the Virginia statute.

I

1. What do Americans believe? Most emphatically, they "believe in God": 97 per cent according to one survey, 96 per cent according to another, 95 per cent according to a third.[1] About 75 per cent of them...regard themselves as members of churches, and a sizable proportion attend divine services with some frequency and regularity. They believe in prayer: About 90 per cent say they pray on various occasions.[2] They believe in life after death, even in heaven and hell.[3] They think well of the church and of ministers.[4] They hold the Bible to be an inspired book, the "word of God."[5] By a large majority, they think children should be given religious instruction and raised as church members.[6] By a large majority, too, they hold religion to be of very great importance.[7] In all of these respects their attitudes are as religious as those of any people today, or, for that matter, as those of any Western people in recent history.

2. Yet these indications are after all relatively superficial; they tell us what Americans say (and no doubt believe) about themselves and their religious views; they do not tell us what in actuality these religious views are. Nowhere are surface appearances more deceptive, nowhere is it more necessary to try to penetrate beyond mere assertions of belief than in such ultimate matters as religion.

3   We do penetrate a little deeper, it would seem, when we take note of certain curious discrepancies the surveys reveal in the responses people make to questions about their religion. Thus, according to one trustworthy source, 73 per cent said they believed in an afterlife, with God as judge, but "only 5 per cent [had] any fear, not to say expectation, of going [to hell]."[8] Indeed, about 80 per cent, according to another source, admitted that what they were "most serious about" was not the life after death in which they said they believed, but in trying to live as comfortably in this life as possible.[9] And in their opinion they were not doing so badly even from the point of view of the divine judgment: 91 per cent felt that they could honestly say that they were trying to lead a good life, and 78 per cent felt no hesitation in saying that they more than half measured up to their own standards of goodness, over 50 per cent asserting that they were in fact following the rule of loving one's neighbor as oneself "all the way"![10] This amazingly high valuation that most Americans appear to place on their own virtue would seem to offer a better insight into the basic religion of the American people than any figures as to their formal beliefs can provide, however important in themselves these figures may be.

4   But perhaps the most significant discrepancy in the assertions Americans make about their religious views is to be found in another area. When asked, "Would you say your religious beliefs have any effect on your ideas of politics and business?", a majority of the same Americans who had testified that they regarded religion as something "very important" answered that their religious beliefs had no real effect on their ideas or conduct in these decisive areas of everyday life; specifically, 54 per cent said no, 39 per cent said yes, and 7 per cent refused to reply or didn't know.[11] This disconcerting confession of the irrelevance of religion to business and politics was attributed by those who appraised the results of the survey as pointing to a calamitous divorce between the "private" and the "public" realms in the religious thinking of Americans.[12] There is certainly a great deal of truth in this opinion, and we shall have occasion to explore it in a different context, but in the present connection it would seem that another aspect of the matter is more immediately pertinent. *Some* ideas and standards undeniably govern the conduct of Americans in their affairs of business and politics; if they are not ideas and standards associated with the teachings of religion, what are they? It will not do to say that people just act "selfishly" without reference to moral standards of any kind. All people act "selfishly," of course; but it is no less true of all people, Americans included, that their "selfishness" is controlled, mitigated, or, at worst, justified by some sort of moral commitment, by some sort of belief in a system of values beyond immediate self-interest. The fact that more than half the people openly admit that their religious beliefs have no effect on their ideas of politics and business would seem to indicate very strongly that, over and above conventional religion, there is to be found

among Americans some sort of faith or belief or set of convictions, not generally designated as religion but definitely operative as such in their lives in the sense of providing them with some fundamental context of normativity and meaning. What this unacknowledged "religion" of the American people is, and how it manages to coexist with their formal religious affirmations and affiliations, it is now our task to investigate.

II

5   "Every functioning society," Robin M. Williams, Jr. points out, "has to an important degree a *common* religion. The possession of a common set of ideas, rituals, and symbols can supply an overarching sense of unity even in a society riddled with conflicts."¹³ What is this "common religion" of American society, the "common set of ideas, rituals, and symbols" that give it its "overarching sense of unity"? Williams provides us with a further clue when he suggests that "men are always likely to be intolerant of opposition to their central ultimate values."¹⁴ What are these "central ultimate values" about which Americans are "intolerant"? No one who knows anything about the religious situation in this country would be likely to suggest that the things Americans are "intolerant" about are the beliefs, standards, or teachings of the religions they "officially" acknowledge as theirs. Americans are proud of their tolerance in matters of religion: one is expected to "believe in God," but otherwise religion is not supposed to be a ground of "discrimination." This is, no doubt, admirable, but is it not "at least in part, a sign that the crucial values of the system are no longer couched in a religious framework"?¹⁵

6   What, then, is the "framework" in which they *are* couched? What, to return to our original question, is the "common religion" of the American people, as it may be inferred not only from their words but also from their behavior?

7   It seems to me that a realistic appraisal of the values, ideas, and behavior of the American people leads to the conclusion that Americans, by and large, do have their "common religion" and that that "religion" is the system familiarly known as the American Way of Life. It is the American Way of Life that supplies American society with an "overarching sense of unity" amid conflict. It is the American Way of Life about which Americans are admittedly and unashamedly "intolerant." It is the American Way of Life that provides the framework in terms of which the crucial values of American existence are couched. By every realistic criterion the American Way of Life is the operative faith of the American people.

8   It would be the crudest kind of misunderstanding to dismiss the American Way of Life as no more than a political formula or propagandist slogan, or to regard it as simply an expression of the "materialistic" impulses of the American people. Americans are "materialistic," no doubt, but surely not more so than other people, than the French peasant or petty

bourgeois, for example. All such labels are irrelevant, if not meaningless. The American Way of Life is, at bottom, a spiritual structure, a structure of ideas and ideals, of aspirations and values, of beliefs and standards; it synthesizes all that commends itself to the American as the right, the good, and the true in actual life. It embraces such seemingly incongruous elements as sanitary plumbing and freedom of opportunity, Coca-Cola and an intense faith in education—all felt as moral questions relating to the proper way of life.[16] The very expression "way of life" points to its religious essence, for one's ultimate, over-all way of life is one's religion.

9 The American Way of Life is, of course, conceived as the corporate "way" of the American peole, but it has its implications for the American as an individual as well. It is something really operative in his actual life. When in the *Ladies' Home Journal* poll, Americans were asked "to look within [themselves] and state honestly whether [they] thought [they] really obeyed the law of love under certain special conditions," 90 per cent said yes and 5 per cent no when the one to be "loved" was a person belonging to a different religion; 80 per cent said yes and 12 per cent no when it was the case of a member of a different race; 78 per cent said yes and 10 per cent no when it concerned a business competitor—but only 27 per cent said yes and 57 per cent no in the case of "a member of a political party that you think is dangerous," while 25 per cent said yes and 63 per cent said no when it concerned an enemy of the nation.[17] These figures are most illuminating, first because of the incredible self-assurance they reveal with which the average American believes he fulfills the "impossible" law of love, but also because of the light they cast on the differential impact of the violation of this law on the American conscience. For it is obvious that the figures reflect no so much the actual behavior of the American people—no people on earth ever loved their neighbors as themselves as much as the American people say they do—as how seriously Americans take transgressions against the law of love in various cases. Americans feel they *ought* to love their fellow men despite differences of race or creed or business interest; that is what the American Way of Life emphatically prescribes.[18] But the American Way of Life almost explicitly sanctions hating a member of a "dangerous" political party (Communists and fascists are obviously meant here) or an enemy of one's country, and therefore an overwhelming majority avow their hate. In both situations, while the Jewish-Christian law of love is formally acknowledged, the truly operative factor is the value system embodied in the American Way of Life. Where the American Way of Life approves of love of one's fellow man, most Americans confidently assert that they practice such love; where the American Way of Life disapproves, the great mass of Americans do not hesitate to confess that they do not practice it, and apparently feel very little guilt for their failure. No better pragmatic test as to what the operative religion of the American people actually is could be desired.

10   It is not suggested here that the ideals Americans feel to be indicated in the American Way of Life are scrupulously observed in the practice of Americans; they are in fact constantly violated, often grossly. But violated or not, they are felt to be normative and relevant to "business and politics" in a way that the formal tenets of "official" religion are not. That is what makes the American Way of Life the "common religion" of American society in the sense here intended.

11   It should be clear that what is being designated under the American Way of Life is not the so-called "common denominator" religion; it is not a synthetic system composed of beliefs to be found in all or in a group of religions. It is an organic structure of ideas, values, and beliefs that constitutes a faith common to Americans and genuinely operative in their lives, a faith that markedly influences, and is influenced by, the "official" religions of American society. Sociologically, anthropologically, if one pleases, it is the characteristic American religion, undergirding American life and overarching American society despite all indubitable differences of region, section, culture, and class.

12   Yet qualifications are immediately in order. Not for all Americans is this American religion, this "common religion" of American society, equally operative; some indeed explicitly repudiate it as religion. By and large, it would seem that what is resistive in contemporary American society to the American Way of Life as religion may be understood under three heads. First, there are the churches of immigrant-ethnic background that still cherish their traditional creeds and confessions of a sign of their distinctive origin and are unwilling to let these be dissolved into an over-all "American religion"; certain Lutheran and Reformed churches in this country[19] as well as sections of the Catholic Church would fall into this classification. Then there are groups, not large but increasing, that have an explicit and conscious theological concern, whether it be "orthodox," "neo-orthodox," or "liberal"; in varying degrees, they find their theologies at odds with the implied "theology" of the American Way of Life. Finally, there are the ill-defined, though by all accounts numerous and influential, "religions of the disinherited," the many "holiness," pentecostal, and millenarian sects of the socially and culturally submerged segments of our society; for them, their "peculiar" religion is frequently still too vital and all-absorbing to be easily subordinated to some "common faith." All of these cases, it will be noted, constitute "hold outs" against the sweep of religious Americanism; in each case there is an element of alienation which generates a certain amount of tension in social life.

13   What is this American Way of Life that we have said constitutes the "common religion" of American society? An adequate description and analysis of what is implied in this phrase still remains to be attempted, and certainly it will not be ventured here; but some indications may not be out of place.

14   The American Way of Life is the symbol by which Americans define themselves and establish their unity. German unity, it would seem, is felt to be largely racial-folkish, French unity largely cultural; but neither of these ways is open to the American people, the most diverse in racial and cultural origins of any in the world. As American unity has emerged, it has emerged more and more clearly as a unity embodied in, and symbolized by, the complex structure known as the American Way of Life.

15   If the American Way of Life had to be defined in one word, "democracy" would undoubtedly be the word, but democracy is a peculiarly American sense. On its political side it means the Constitution; on its economic side, "free enterprise"; on its social side, an equalitarianism which is not only compatible with but indeed actually implies vigorous economic competition and high mobility. Spiritually, the American Way of Life is best expressed in a certain kind of "idealism" which has come to be recognized as characteristically American. It is a faith that has its symbols and its rituals, its holidays and its liturgy, its saints and its sancta,[20] and it is a faith that every American, to the degree that he is an American, knows and understands.

16   The American Way of Life is individualistic, dynamic, pragmatic. It affirms the supreme value and dignity of the individual; it stresses incessant activity on his part, for he is never to rest but is always to be striving to "get ahead"; it defines an ethic of self-reliance, merit, and character, and judges by achievement: "deeds, not creeds" are what count. The American Way of Life is humanitarian, "forward looking," optimistic. Americans are easily the most generous and philanthropic people in the world, in terms of their ready and unstinting response to suffering anywhere on the globe. The American believes in progress, in self-improvement, and quite fanatically in education. But above all, the American is idealistic. Americans cannot go on making money or achieving worldly success simply on its own merits; such "materialistic" things must, in the American mind, be justified in "higher" terms, in terms of "service" or "stewardship" or "general welfare." Because Americans are so idealistic, they tend to confuse espousing an ideal with fulfilling it and are always tempted to regard themselves as good as the ideals they entertain: hence the amazingly high valuation most Americans quite sincerely place on their own virtue. And because they are so idealistic, Americans tend to be moralistic: they are inclined to see all issues as plain and simple, black and white, issues of morality. Every struggle in which they are seriously engaged becomes a "crusade." To Mr. Eisenhower, who in many ways exemplifies American religion in a particularly representative way, the second world war was a "crusade" (as was the first to Woodrow Wilson); so was his campaign for the presidency ("I am engaged in a crusade . . . to substitute good government for what we most earnestly believe has been bad government"); and so is his administration—a "battle for the republic" against "godless Communism" abroad and against "corruption and materialism"

at home. It was Woodrow Wilson who once said, "Sometimes people call me an idealist. Well, that is the way I know I'm an American: America is the most idealistic nation in the world"; Eisenhower was but saying the same thing when he solemnly affirmed: "The things that make us proud to be Americans are of the soul and of the spirit."

17 The American Way of Life is, of course, anchored in the American's vision of America. The Puritan's dream of a new "Israel" and a new "Promised Land" in the New World, the *"novus ordo seclorum"* on the Great Seal of the United States reflect the perennial American conviction that in the New World a new beginning has been made, a new order of things established, vastly different from and superior to the decadent institutions of the Old World. This conviction, emerging out of the earliest reality of American history, was continuously nourished through the many decades of immigration into the present century by the residual hopes and expectations of the immigrants, for whom the New World had to be really something new if it was to be anything at all. And this conviction still remains pervasive in American life, hardly shaken by the new shape of the world and the challenge of the "new orders" of the twentieth century, Nazism and Communism. It is the secret of what outsiders must take to be the incredible self-righteousness of the American people, who tend to see the world divided into an innocent, virtuous America confronted with a corrupt, devious, and guileful Europe and Asia. The self-righteousness, however, if self-righteousness it be, is by no means simple, if only because virtually all Americans are themselves derived from the foreign parts they so distrust. In any case, this feeling about America as really and truly the "new order" of things at last established is the heart of the outlook defined by the American Way of Life.

18 In her *Vermont Tradition*, Dorothy Canfield Fisher lists as that tradition's principal ingredients: individual freedom, personal independence, human dignity, community responsibility, social and political democracy, sincerity, restraint in outward conduct, and thrift.[21] With some amplification—particularly emphasis on the uniqueness of the American "order" and the great importance assigned to religion—this may be taken as a pretty fair summary of some of the "values" embodied in the American Way of Life. It will not escape the reader that this account is essentially an idealized description of the middle-class ethos. And, indeed, that is just what it is. The American Way of Life is a middle-class way, just as the American people in their entire outlook and feeling are a middle-class people.[22] But the American Way of Life as it has come down to us is not merely middle-class; it is emphatically inner-directed. Indeed, it is probably one of the best expressions of inner-direction in history. As such, it now seems to be undergoing some degree of modification—perhaps at certain points of disintegration—under the impact of the spread of other-direction in our society. For the foreseeable future, however, we may with some confidence expect the continuance in strength of the

American Way of Life as both the tradition and the "common faith" of the American people.

III

19   The American Way of Life as the "common faith" of American society has coexisted for some centuries with the historic faiths of the American people, and the two have influenced each other in many profound and subtle ways. The influence has been complex and reciprocal, to the point where causal priority becomes impossible to assign if indeed it does not become altogether meaningless. From the very beginning the American Way of Life was shaped by the contours of American Protestantism; it may, indeed, best be understood as a kind of secularized Puritanism, a Puritanism without transcendence, without sense of sin or judgment. The Puritan's vision of a new "Promised Land" in the wilderness of the New World has become, as we have suggested, the American's deep sense of the newness and uniqueness of things in the Western Hemisphere. The Puritan's sense of vocation and "inner-worldly asceticism" can still be detected in the American's gospel of action and service, and his consciousness of high responsibility before God in the American's "idealism." The Puritan's abiding awareness of the ambiguity of all human motivations and his insight into the corruptions of inordinate power have left their mark not only on the basic structure of our constitutional system but also on the entire social philosophy of the American people. Nor have other strands of early American Protestantism been without their effect. There can be little doubt that Pietism co-operated with frontier revivalism in breaking down the earlier concern with dogma and doctrine, so that the slogan, "deeds, not creeds," soon became the hallmark both of American religion and of the American Way of Life. These are but aspects of an influence that is often easier to see than to define.

20   The reciprocal action of the American Way of Life in shaping and reshaping the historic faiths of Christianity and Judaism on American soil is perhaps more readily discerned. By and large, we may say that these historic religions have all tended to become "Americanized" under the pervasive influence of the American environment. This "Americanization" has been the product not so much of conscious direction as of a "diffuse convergence" operating spontaneously in the context of the totality of American life. What it has brought, however, is none the less clear: "religious groupings throughout [American] society [have been] stamped with recognizably 'American' qualities," to an extent indeed where foreign observers sometimes find the various American religions more like each other than they are like their European counterparts.

21   Under the influence of the American environment the historic Jewish and Christian faiths have tended to become secularized in the sense of becoming integrated as parts within a larger whole defined by the

American Way of Life." There is a marked tendency," Williams writes in his discussion of the relations of religion to other institutions in the United States, "to regard religion as a good because it is useful in furthering other major values—in other words, to reverse the ends-means relation implied in the conception of religion as an ultimate value."[23] In this reversal the Christian and Jewish faiths tend to be prized because they help promote ideals and standards that all Americans are expected to share on a deeper level than merely "official" religion. Insofar as any reference is made to the God in whom all Americans "believe" and of whom the "official" religions speak, it is primarily as sanction and underpinning for the supreme values of the faith embodied in the American Way of Life. Secularization of religion could hardly go further.

22   As a consequence, in some cases of its own origins, but primarily of the widespread influence of the American environment, religion in America has tended toward a marked disparagement of "forms," whether theological or liturgical. Even the highly liturgical and theological churches have felt the effects of this spirit to the degree that they have become thoroughly acculturated. Indeed, the anti-theological, anti-liturgical bias is still pervasive despite the recent upsurge of theological concern and despite the greater interest being shown in liturgy because of its psychological power and "emotional richness."

23   American religion is (within the limits set by the particular traditions of the churches) non-theological and non-liturgical; it is activistic and occupied with the things of the world to a degree that has become a byword among European churchmen. With this activism has gone a certain "latitudinarianism," associated with the de-emphasis of theology and doctrine: Americans tend to believe that "ethical behavior and a good life rather than adherence to a specific creed, [will] earn a share in the heavenly kingdom."[24] The activism of American religion has manifested itself in many forms throughout our history: in the Puritan concern for the total life of the community; in the passionate championing of all sorts of reform causes by the evangelical movements of the first half of the nineteenth century; in the "social gospel" of more recent times; in the ill-starred Prohibition "crusade"; in the advanced "progressive" attitudes on social questions taken by the National Council of Churches, the National Catholic Welfare Conference, and the various rabbinical associations; in the strong social emphasis of American Protestant "neo-orthodoxy." This activism, which many Europeans seem to regard as the distinguishing feature of American religion, both reflects the dynamic temper of the American Way of Life and has been a principal factor in its development.

24   It is hardly necessary to continue this analysis much further along these general lines. The optimism, moralism, and idealism of Jewish and Christian faith in America are plain evidence of the profound effect of the American outlook on American religion. Indeed, such evidence is amply

provided by any tabulation of the distinctive features of religion in America, and needs no special emphasis at this point.

25   What is perhaps of crucial importance, and requires a more detailed examination, is the new attitude toward religion and the new conception of the church that have emerged in America.

26   Americans believe in religion in a way that perhaps no other people do. It may indeed be said that the primary religious affirmation of the American people, in harmony with the American Way of Life, is that religion is a "good thing," a supremely "good thing," for the individual and the community. And "religion" here means not so much any particular religion, but religion as such, religion-in-general. "Our government makes no sense," President Eisenhower recently declared, "unless it is founded in a deeply felt religious faith—*and I don't care what it is*" (emphasis added).[25] In saying this, the President was saying something that almost any American could understand and approve, but which must seem like a deplorable heresy to the European churchman. Every American could understand, first, that Mr. Eisenhower's apparent indifferentism ("and I don't care what it is") was not indifferentism at all, but the expression of the conviction that at bottom the "three great faiths" were really "saying the same thing" in affirming the "spiritual ideals" and "moral values" of the American Way of Life. Every American, moreover, could understand that what Mr. Eisenhower was emphasizing so vehemently was the indispensability of religion as the foundation of society. This is one aspect of what Americans mean when they say that they "believe in religion." The object of devotion of this kind of religion, however, is "not God but 'religion.' . . . The faith is not in God but in faith; we worship not God but our own worshiping."[26] When Americans think of themselves as a profoundly religious people, whose "first allegiance" is "reserved . . . to the kingdom of the spirit,"[27] this is, by and large, what they mean, and not any commitment to the doctrines or traditions of the historic faiths.

27   With this view of religion is associated a closely analogous view of the church. For America, the celebrated dichotomy of "church" and "sect," however pertinent it may be to European conditions, has only a secondary significance. The concept of the church as the nation religiously organized, established socially, if not always legally, has only an oblique relevance to American reality; and though America does know sects in the sense of "fringe" groups of the "disinherited," it does not understand these groups and their relation to the more conventional churches the way Europe does. An entirely new conception of church and church institutions has emerged in America.

28   It must be remembered that in America the variety and multiplicity of churches did not, as in Europe, come with the breakdown of a single established national church; in America, taking the nation as a whole, the variety and multiplicity of churches was almost the original condition

and coeval with the emergence of the new society. In America religious pluralism is thus not merely a historical and political fact; it is, in the mind of the American, the primordial condition of things, an essential aspect of the American Way of Life, and therefore in itself an aspect of religious belief.[28] Americans, in other words, believe that the plurality of religious groups is a proper and legitimate condition. However much he may be attached to his own church, however dimly he may regard the beliefs and practices of other churches, the American tends to feel rather strongly that total religious uniformity, even with his own church benefiting thereby, would be something undesirable and wrong, indeed scarcely conceivable. Pluralism of religions and churches is something quite axiomatic to the American. This feeling, more than anything else, is the foundation of the American doctrine of the "separation of church and state," for it is the heart of this doctrine that the government may not do anything that implies the pre-eminence of superior legitimacy of one church over another.

29   This means that outside the Old World distinction of church and sect America has given birth to a new type of religious structure—the denomination.[29] The denomination as we know it is a stable, settled church, enjoying a legitimate and recognized place in a larger aggregate of churches, each recognizing the proper status of the others. The denomination is the "non-conformist sect" become central and normative. It differs from the church in the European understanding of the term in that it would never dream of claiming to be *the* national ecclesiastical institution; it differs from the sect in that it is socially established, thoroughly institutionalized, and nuclear to the society in which it is found. The European dichotomy becomes meaningless, and instead we have the nuclear denomination on the one side, and the peripheral sect on the way to becoming a denomination on the other. So firmly entrenched is this denominational idea in the mind of the American that even American Catholics have come to think in such terms; theologically the Catholic Church of course continues to regard itself as the one true church, but in their actual social attitudes American Catholics, hardly less than American Protestants or Jews, tend to think of their church as a denomination existing side by side with other denominations in a pluralistic harmony that is felt to be somehow of the texture of American life.

30   Denominational pluralism, as the American idea of the church may be called, obviously implies that no church can look to the state for its members or support. Voluntarism and evangelism are thus the immediate consequences of the American idea: For their maintenance, for their very existence, churches must depend on the voluntary adherence of their members, and they are therefore moved to pursue a vigorous evangelistic work to win people to their ranks....

31   The denominational idea is fundamental to American thinking about religion, but it is not the last word. Americans think of their various

churches as denominations, but they also feel that somehow the denominations fall into larger wholes which we have called religious communities. This kind of denominational aggregation is, of course, something that pertains primarily to Protestantism and to a lesser degree to Judaism; both have more or less organized denominations which, taken together, form the religious communities. Catholicism, on the other hand, has no such overt inner divisions, but American Catholics readily understand the phenomenon when they see it among Protestants and Jews. Denominations are felt to be somehow a matter of individual preference, and movement between denominations is not uncommon; the religious community, on the other hand, is taken as something more objective and given, something in which, by and large, one is born, lives, and dies, something that . . . identifies and defines one's position in American society.[30] Since the religious community in its present form is a recent social emergent, its relations to the denominations properly so-called are still relatively fluid and undefined but the main lines of development would seem to be fairly clear.

32   When the plurality of denominations comprehended in religious communities is seen from the standpoint of the "common faith" of American society, what emerges is the conception of the three "communions"—Protestantism, Catholicism, Judaism—as three diverse, but equally legitimate, equally American, expressions of an over-all American religion, standing for essentially the same "moral ideals" and "spiritual values." This conception, whatever may be thought of it theologically, is in fact held, though hardly in explicit form, by many devout and religiously sophisticated Americans. It would seem to be the obvious meaning of the title, *The Religions of Democracy*, given to a recent authoritative statement of the Protestant, Catholic, and Jewish positions.[31] "Democracy" apparently has its religions which fall under it as species fall under the genus of which they are part. And in this usage "democracy" is obviously a synonym for the American Way of Life.

33   It is but one more step, though a most fateful one, to proceed from "the religions of democracy" to "democracy as religion" and consciously to erect "democracy" into a super-faith above and embracing the three recognized religions. This step has been taken by a number of thinkers in recent years. Thus, Professor J. Paul Williams has been urging a program of religious reconstruction in which he insists that: "Americans must come to look on the democratic ideal (not necessarily the American practice of it) as the Will of God, or if they please, of Nature. . . . Americans must be brought to the conviction that democracy is the very Law of Life. . . . The state must be brought into the picture; governmental agencies must teach the democratic ideal *as religion* . . . primary responsibility for teaching democracy as religion must be given to the public school, for instance . . ."[32]

34   Professor Horace M. Kallen reaches very much the same conclusion from another direction. "For the communicants of the democratic faith,"

he writes, "it is the religion *of* and *for* religions.... [It is] the religion of religions, all may freely come together in it."[33]

35 It is not our purpose, at this point, to draw the theological implications of this super-religion of "democracy" as the "religion of religions"; it is only necessary to point out that it marks a radical break with the fundamental presuppositions of both Judaism and Christianity, to which it must appear as a particularly insidious kind of idolatry. What is merely implicit and perhaps never intended in the acceptance of the American Way of Life as the "common religion" of American society is here brought to its logical conclusion and made to reveal its true inner meaning.

36 By and large, the "common faith" of American society remains implicit and is never carried to the logical conclusion to which a few ideologists have pushed it. By the great mass of the American people the American Way of Life is not avowed as a super-faith above and embracing the historic religions. It operates as a "common faith" at deeper levels, through its pervasive influence on the patterns of American thought and feeling. It makes no pretensions to override or supplant the recognized religions, to which it assigns a place of great eminence and honor in the American scheme of things. But all the implications are there....

IV

37 The "common faith" of American society is not merely a civic religion to celebrate the values and convictions of the American people as a corporate entity. It has its inner, personal aspects as well; or rather, side by side and in intimate relation with the civic religion of the American Way of Life, there has developed, primarily through a devitalization of the historic faiths, an inner, personal religion that promises salvation to the disoriented, tormented souls of a society in crisis.

38 This inner, personal religion is based on the American's *faith in faith*. We have seen that a primary religious affirmation of the American is his belief in religion. The American believes that religion is something very important for the community; he also believes that "faith," or what we may call religiosity, is a kind of "miracle drug" that can cure all the ailments of the spirit. It is not faith in *anything* that is so powerful, just faith, the "magic of believing." "It was back in those days," a prominent American churchman writes, recalling his early years, "that I formed a habit that I have never broken. I began saying in the morning two words, 'I believe.' Those two words *with nothing added* ... give me a running start for my day, and for every day" (emphasis not in original).[34]

39 The cult of faith takes two forms, which we might designate as introvert and extrovert. In its introvert form faith is trusted to bring mental health and "peace of mind," to dissipate anxiety and guilt, and to translate the soul to the blessed land of "normality" and "self-acceptance." In earlier times this cult of faith was quite literally a cult of "faith healing," best expressed in what H. Richard Niebuhr has described as the "man-centered,

this-worldly, lift-yourself-by-your-own-bootstraps doctrine of New Thought and Christian Science."[35] Latterly it has come to vest itself in the fashionable vocabulary of psychoanalysis and is offering a synthesis of religion and psychiatry.[36] But at bottom it is the same cult of faith in faith, the same promise that through "those two words, 'I believe,' with nothing added," all our troubles will be dissipated and inner peace and harmony restored.

40   The cult of faith has also its extrovert form, and that is known as "positive thinking." "Positive thinking," thinking that is "affirmative" and avoids the corrosions of "negativity" and "skepticism," thinking that "has faith," is recommended as a powerful force in the world of struggle and achievement.[37] Here again it is not so much faith in anything, certainly not the theocentric faith of the historic religions, that is supposed to confer this power—but just faith, the psychological attitude of having faith, so to speak. And here too the cult is largely the product of the inner disintegration and enfeeblement of the historic religions; the familiar words are retained, but the old meaning is voided. "Have faith," "don't lose faith," and the like, were once injunctions to preserve one's unwavering trust in the God from Whom comes both the power to live and the "peace that passeth understanding." Gradually these phrases have come to be an appeal to maintain a "positive" attitude to life and not to lose confidence in oneself and one's activities. "To believe in yourself and in everything you do": Such, at bottom, is the meaning of the contemporary cult of faith, whether it is proclaimed by devout men from distinguished pulpits or offered as the "secret of success" by self-styled psychologists who claim to have discovered the "hidden powers" of man.[38] What is important is faith, faith in faith. Even where the classical symbols and formulas are still retained, that is very often what is meant and what is understood.

41   Such are some major aspects of the social, cultural, and spiritual environment in which religion in America moves and has its being. And religion in America means the three great religious communities, the Protestant, the Catholic, and the Jewish.

REFERENCES

1. *Belief in God:* 97 per cent—"Do Americans Believe in God?", *The Catholic Digest,* November 1952; 96 per cent—Gallup poll, *Public Opinion News Service,* December 18, 1954; 95 per cent—Lincoln Barnett, "God and the American People," *Ladies' Home Journal,* November 1948, p. 37. According to the *Catholic Digest* poll 89 per cent of Americans believe in the Trinity ("How Many in the U.S. Believe in the Trinity?", *The Catholic Digest,* July 1953) and 80 per cent think of Christ as divine ("What We Americans Think of Our Lord," *The Catholic Digest,* August 1953). [Herberg's notes]

2. *Prayer:* 92 per cent answer yes to the question, "Do you ever pray to God?" ("Americans and Prayer," *The Catholic Digest,* November 1953); 90 per cent say they pray, 56 per cent "frequently"—Barnett, "God and the American People," *Ladies' Home Journal,* November 1948, p. 37.
3. *Life after death:* 77 per cent believe in afterlife, 7 per cent don't, 16 per cent don't know—"What Do Americans Think of Heaven and Hell?", *The Catholic Digest,* March 1953; 76 per cent say yes, 13 per cent no, 11 per cent don't know—Gallup poll, *Public Opinion News Service,* December 11, 1944; 73 per cent say yes, 15 per cent no, 12 per cent no opinion—Barnett, "God and the American People," *Ladies' Home Journal,* November 1948, pp. 230–31; 74 per cent believe in life after death—Gallup poll, *Public Opinion News Service,* April 19, 1957.

    Heaven and Hell: 72 per cent believe in heaven, 58 per cent in hell—*The Catholic Digest,* as above; 52 per cent think that "life after death is divided into heaven and hell," though heaven looms larger in their minds than hell—Barnett, "God and the American People," *Ladies' Home Journal,* November 1948, p. 231; 61 per cent believe there is a devil—Gallup poll, *Public Opinion News Service,* April 19, 1957.
4. *Opinion about church and clergymen:* 75 per cent deny the allegation that the church is too much concerned about money—"Is the Church Too Much Concerned About Money?", *The Catholic Digest,* March 1954; 68 per cent regard clergymen as "very understanding," 21 per cent as "fairly understanding"—"How Understanding Are Clergymen?", *The Catholic Digest,* December 1953; clergymen rank at the top in the scale of those who "do most good"—see above, chap. iv, p. 51.
5. *Bible:* 86 per cent regard it as divinely inspired, the "word of God"—"What Do Americans Think of the Bible?", *The Catholic Digest,* May 1954; a survey conducted by the *British Weekly* gives the figure for Americans who regard the Bible as divinely inspired as 86.5 per cent (see *Information Service* [National Council of Churches of Christ], December 27, 1952).
6. *Religious instruction:* 98 per cent say yes—"Do Americans Want Their Children to Receive Religious Instruction?", *The Catholic Digest,* September 1953. *Children raised as church members:* 72 per cent say yes—"How Important Is Religion to Americans?", *The Catholic Digest,* February 1953.
7. *Importance of religion:* 75 per cent regard it as "very important," 20 per cent as "fairly important"—"How Important Is Religion to Americans?", *The Catholic Digest,* February 1953; 69 per cent think that the influence of religion is increasing and 81 per cent believe that religion can answer "most of today's problems"—Gallup poll, *Public Opinion News Service,* April 21, 1957. The religiosity of the American

people appears even more striking when it is contrasted with the much more "skeptical" views held by the British; see the series of comparative surveys conducted by the Gallup organization, *Public Opinion News Service,* April 16, 17, 18, 19, 21, 1957.

8. Barnett, "God and the American People," *Ladies' Home Journal,* November 1948, p. 234.
9. "What the U.S. Thinks of Life Here and Hereafter," *The Catholic Digest,* May 1953.
10. Barnett, "God and the American People," *Ladies' Home Journal,* November 1948, pp. 233, 234, 235.
11. Barnett, "God and the American People," *Ladies' Home Journal,* November 1948, p. 234.
12. See particularly the statement of Father George B. Ford, in Barnett, "God and the American People," *Ladies' Home Journal,* November 1948, p. 237.
13. Robin M. Williams, Jr., *American Society: A Sociological Interpretation* (Knopf, 1951), p. 312.
14. Williams, *American Society,* p. 320 n.
15. Williams, *American Society,* p. 344.
16. When an American tourist comes upon the inadequate sanitary arrangements in certain parts of Europe and discovers what seems to him the careless attitude of the inhabitants in matters of personal hygiene, he is inclined to feel what he experiences not simply as a shortcoming in modern living conveniences but as a *moral* defect, on a par with irreligion, caste rigidity, and the absence of American representative democracy. Cp. the following placard displayed by many restaurants in the midwest: "Sanitation is a way of life. As a way of life, it must be nourished from within and grow as an ideal in human relations."
17. Barnett, "God and the American People," *Ladies' Home Journal,* November 1948, pp. 235–36.
18. Where this "principle" of the American Way of Life is flagrantly violated by local prescription, as in the case of racial attitudes in the south and elsewhere, festering "bad conscience" and a destructive defensive aggressiveness are the result.
19. Discussing the European background of such churches, H. Richard Niebuhr writes: "These churches are doctrinal and liturgical in character, regarding conformity to creed and ritual as the essential requirements of Christianity" (*The Social Sources of Denominationalism* [Holt, 1929], p. 126).
20. See the illuminating account of Memorial Day as an "American sacred ceremony" in W. Lloyd Warner, *Structure of American Life* (Edinburgh, 1952), chap. x. Warner writes: "The Memorial Day ceremonies and subsidiary rites, such as those of Armistice Day, of today, yesterday, and tomorrow, are rituals which are a sacred symbol system which functions periodically to integrate the whole community, with

its conflicting symbols and its opposing autonomous churches and associations.... Memorial Day is a cult of the dead which organizes and integrates the various faiths, ethnic and class groups, into a sacred unity" (p. 214). As to the "saints" of the American Way of Life, Warner quotes a Memorial Day orator: "No character except the Carpenter of Nazareth has ever been honored the way Washington and Lincoln have been in New England. Virtue, freedom from sin, and righteousness were qualities possessed by Washington and Lincoln, and in possessing these qualities both were true Americans, and we would do well to emulate them. Let us first be true Americans" (p. 220). The theological implications of this statement are sensational: Washington and Lincoln, as "true Americans," are credited with the moral and spiritual qualities ("virtue, freedom from sin, and righteousness") traditionally associated with Christ, and we are all urged to "emulate" them!

21. Dorothy Canfield Fisher, *Vermont Tradition* (Little, Brown, 1953).
22. "America is a middle-class country, and the middle-class values and styles of perception reach into all levels except perhaps the fringes at the very top and the very bottom" (David Riesman, *Individualism Reconsidered* [Free Press, 1954], p. 499).
23. Williams, *American Society*, p. 337.
24. Oscar Handlin, *The Uprooted* (Little, Brown, 1951), p. 128.
25. *The New York Times*, December 23, 1952; see also G. Elson Ruff, *The Dilemma of Church and State* (Muhlenberg, 1954), p. 85. Cp. the very similar sentiment expressed by Robert C. Ruark: "Although I am not a practicing religionist, I have a great respect for organized religion, no matter what shape it takes" ("Scoff-religious," *New York World Telegram*, October 10, 1955).
26. Miller, "Piety Along the Potomac," *The Reporter*, August 17, 1954. Mr. Miller continues: "If the object of devotion is not God but 'religion'... then the resulting religiosity may become simply the instrument of more substantial commitments." The most "substantial" commitment of the American people, to which their "religiosity" is instrumental, is the American Way of Life. Once more to quote Mr. Eisenhower: "I am the most intensely religious man I know. Nobody goes through six years of war without faith. A democracy cannot exist without a religious base. I believe in democracy" (*New York Times*, May 4, 1948).
27. Dwight D. Eisenhower, quoted in Paul Hutchinson, "The President's Religious Faith," *The Christian Century*, March 24, 1954.
28. Williams speaks of a "value-consensus in which religious differences are subsidiary to the values of religious liberty" (*American Society*, p. 345).
29. "The Mormons, the Orthodox Jews, and a few small religious communities are religiously organized people, but almost all other religious bodies in the United States, including the Roman Catholic

Church, are neither national churches nor sects; they are commonly known as denominations or 'communions'" (Schneider, *Religion in 20th Century America,* p. 22). Even the groups Schneider mentions as exceptions, insofar as they have become acculturated to American life, would seem to fall into the same pattern.

30. Despite all the instability of American life, fully 96 per cent of Americans were found in 1955 still belonging to the religious community of their birth (see *Public Opinion News Service,* March 20, 1955).

31. Louis Finkelstein, J. Elliot Ross, and William Adams Brown, *The Religions of Democracy: Judaism, Catholicism, and Protestantism in Creed and Life* (Devin-Adair, 1946). One of the clearest expressions of this conception by a layman was voiced by Admiral William F. Halsey, principal speaker at the fifth annual "four chaplains award dinner." "This picture," Admiral Halsey declared, "is symbolic of our national life. Protestant, Catholic, and Jew, each group has given, when called upon, the full measure of devotion in defense of our [American democratic] way of life" (*The New York Times,* February 6, 1955).

32. J. Paul Williams, *What Americans Believe and How They Worship* (Harper, 1952), pp. 71, 78, 368, 374; see the critical review of this book by J. H. Nichols, *The Christian Century,* September 3, 1952. (A strong tendency toward this kind of "religion of democracy" is to be found in Jewish Reconstructionism; see Ira Eisenstein and Eugene Kohn, *Mordecai M. Kaplan: An Evaluation* [Jewish Reconstructionist Foundation, 1952], p. 259. "The religion of the American majority is democracy.... In fact, the religion of public education is a more powerful factor in American life today than that of the churches. The only religion with which the great majority of American youth have ever come in contact is the religion of public education" (Conrad Moehlman, *School and Church: The American Way* [Harper, 1944], pp. ix, x). David Riesman speaks of "new ways of using the school as a kind of community center, as the chapel of a secular religion perhaps" (*Individualism Reconsidered,* p. 211).

33. H. M. Kallen, "Democracy's True Religion," *Saturday Review of Literature,* July 28, 1951.

34. Daniel A. Poling, "A Running Start for Every Day," *Parade: The Sunday Picture Magazine,* September 19, 1954.

35. H. Richard Niebuhr, *The Social Sources of Denominationalism,* p. 104. Niebuhr thus describes this type of religiosity in which the old Puritan spirituality has terminated: "In its final phase, the development of this religious movement exhibits the complete enervation of the once virile force ... the problem of evil [has been] simplified out of existence, and for the mysterious will of the Sovereign of life and death and sin and salvation [has been substituted] the sweet benevolence of a Father-Mother God for the vague goodness of the All. Here the concern for self has been secularized to its last degree; the conflicts of sick souls have been replaced by the struggles of sick

minds and bodies; the Puritan passion for perfection has become a seeking after the kingdom of health and mental peace and its comforts" (p. 105).

36. The most celebrated effort along these lines is undoubtedly Joshua Loth Liebman, *Peace of Mind* (Simon and Schuster, 1946).
37. Norman Vincent Peale, *The Power of Positive Thinking* (Prentice-Hall, 1952).
38. A salesman writes to Normal Vincent Peale in the latter's regular question page in *Look:* "I have lost my faith and enthusiasm. How can I get them back?" To which Dr. Peale replies: "Every morning, give thanks for the new day and its opportunities. Think outgoingly of every prospect you will call on.... Affirm aloud that you are going to have a great day. Flush out all depressing, negative, and tired thoughts. Start thinking faith, enthusiasm and joy ..." ("Norman Vincent Peale Answers Your Questions," *Look,* August 10, 1954). This may be compared with an advertisement for a quite "secular" self-help book in *The New York Times Magazine* for May 8, 1949:

DON'T WORRY
If you don't acknowledge it,
it isn't so!
Develop the Art of Adaptability

Reading for Meaning

1. What exactly does Will Herberg mean when he talks about the "American Way of Life"? Where does he think it originated?
2. What is Herberg's thesis? Where does it appear in his essay? How does the essay's organization support or advance his thesis?
3. Herberg notes several exceptions to those who practice what he calls the "common religion" of Americans. Why does he exempt these groups? Why do you think he felt he ought to mention them?
4. How does the European way of looking at religion differ from the American concept as presented by Herberg?
5. How do religion and democracy work together in the United States? How might this combination make it difficult for Americans to sympathize with people less fortunate than themselves?
6. What support does Herberg offer for his ideas? Evaluate the strengths or weaknesses of his arguments on the basis of supporting examples and explanations.

Comparing Texts

In what ways might Herberg's descriptions of the secularized religion of Americans also apply to Othman's use of Islamic principles in his life in Naguib Mahfouz's chapters from his novel *Respected Sir* (page 257)?

Ideas for Writing

1. Will Herberg paraphrases Dorothy Canfield Fisher's list of the principles that compose the American Way of Life, which Herberg identifies with the "middle-class ethos" in the United States. Choose a few of these "ingredients" and analyze the extent to which they determine the behavior of people you know.

2. Herberg's analysis of religion in the United States was published in 1955. Write an essay in which you discuss either portions of his argument that accurately describe current attitudes and behavior in America or portions that are no longer valid.

APPENDIX A

VINDICATION OF THE RIGHTS OF WOMAN

Mary Wollstonecroft

CHAPTER I
THE RIGHTS AND INVOLVED DUTIES OF MANKIND CONSIDERED

1. In the present state of society it appears necessary to go back to first principles in search of the most simple truths, and to dispute with some prevailing prejudice every inch of ground. To clear my way, I must be allowed to ask some plain questions, and the answers will probably appear as unequivocal as the axioms on which reasoning is built; though, when entangled with various motives of action, they are formally contradicted, either by the words or conduct of men.

2. In what does man's pre-eminence over the brute creation consist? The answer is as clear as that a half is less than the whole, in Reason.

3. What acquirement exalts one being above another? Virtue, we spontaneously reply.

4. For what purpose were the passions implanted? That man by struggling with them might attain a degree of knowledge denied to the brutes, whispers Experience.

5. Consequently the perfection of our nature and capability of happiness must be estimated by the degree of reason, virtue, and knowledge, that distinguish the individual, and direct the laws which bind society: and that from the exercise of reason, knowledge and virtue naturally flow, is equally undeniable, if mankind be viewed collectively.

6. The rights and duties of man thus simplified, it seems almost impertinent to attempt to illustrate truths that appear so incontrovertible; yet such deeply rooted prejudices have clouded reason, and such spurious qualities have assumed the name of virtues, that it is necessary to pursue the course of reason as it has been perplexed and involved in error, by various adventitious circumstances, comparing the simple axiom with casual deviations.

7. Men, in general, seem to employ their reason to justify prejudices, which they have imbibed, they can scarcely trace how, rather than to root them out. The mind must be strong that resolutely forms its own principles; for a kind of intellectual cowardice prevails which makes many men shrink from the task, or only do it by halves. Yet the imperfect conclusions

thus drawn, are frequently very plausible, because they are built on partial experience, on just, though narrow, views.

8   Going back to first principles, vice skulks, with all its native deformity, from close investigation; but a set of shallow reasoners are always exclaiming that these arguments prove too much, and that a measure rotten at the core may be expedient. Thus expediency is continually contrasted with simple principles, till truth is lost in a mist of words, virtue, in forms, and knowledge rendered a sounding nothing, by the specious prejudices that assume its name.

9   That the society is formed in the wisest manner, whose constitution is founded on the nature of man, strikes, in the abstract, every thinking being so forcibly, that it looks like presumption to endeavour to bring forward proofs; though proof must be brought, or the strong hold of prescription will never be forced by reason; yet to urge prescription as an argument to justify the depriving men (or women) of their natural rights, is one of the absurd sophisms which daily insult common sense.

10   The civilization of the bulk of the people of Europe is very partial; nay, it may be made a question, whether they have acquired any virtues in exchange for innocence, equivalent to the misery produced by the vices that have been plastered over unsightly ignorance, and the freedom which has been bartered for splendid slavery. The desire of dazzling by riches, the most certain pre-eminence that man can obtain, the pleasure of commanding flattering sycophants, and many other complicated low calculations of doting self-love, have all contributed to overwhelm the mass of mankind, and make liberty a convenient handle for mock patriotism. For whilst rank and titles are held of the utmost importance, before which Genius "must hide its diminished head," it is, with a few exceptions, very unfortunate for a nation when a man of abilities, without rank or property, pushes himself forward to notice. Alas! what unheard-of misery have thousands suffered to purchase a cardinal's hat for an intriguing obscure adventurer, who longed to be ranked with princes, or lord it over them by seizing the triple crown!

11   Such, indeed, has been the wretchedness that has flowed from hereditary honours, riches, and monarchy, that men of lively sensibility have almost uttered blasphemy in order to justify the dispensations of Providence. Man has been held out as independent of His power who made him, or as a lawless planet darting from its orbit to steal the celestial fire of reason; and the vengeance of Heaven, lurking in the subtile flame, like Pandora's pent-up mischiefs, sufficiently punished his temerity, by introducing evil into the world.

12   Impressed by this view of the misery and disorder which pervaded society, and fatigued with jostling against artificial fools, Rousseau became enamoured by solitude, and, being at the same time an optimist, he labours with uncommon eloquence to prove that man was naturally a solitary animal. Misled by his respect for the goodness of God, who

certainly—for what man of sense and feeling can doubt it!—gave life only to communicate happiness, he considers evil as positive, and the work of man; not aware that he was exalting one attribute at the expense of another, equally necessary to divine perfection.

13   Reared on a false hypothesis, his arguments in favour of a state of nature are plausible, but unsound. I say unsound; for to assert that a state of nature is preferable to civilization, in all its possible perfection, is, in other words, to arraign supreme wisdom; and the paradoxical exclamation, that God had made all things right, and that error has been introduced by the creature, whom He formed, knowing what He formed, is as unphilosophical as impious.

14   When that wise Being who created us and placed us here, saw the fair idea, He willed, by allowing it to be so, that the passions should unfold our reason, because He could see that present evil would produce future good. Could the helpless creature whom He called from nothing break loose from His providence, and boldly learn to know good by practising evil, without His permission? No. How could that energetic advocate for immortality argue so inconsistently? Had mankind remained for ever in the brutal state of nature, which even his magic pen cannot paint as a state in which a single virtue took root, it would have been clear, though not to the sensitive unreflecting wanderer, that man was born to run the circle of life and death, and adorn God's garden for some purpose which could not easily be reconciled with His attributes.

15   But if, to crown the whole, there were to be rational creatures produced, allowed to rise in excellence by the exercise of powers implanted for that purpose; if benignity itself thought fit to call into existence a creature above the brutes,[1] who could think and improve himself, why should that inestimable gift, for a gift it was, if man was so created, as to have a capacity to rise above the state in which sensation produced brutal ease, be called, in direct terms, a curse? A curse it might be reckoned, if the whole of our existence were bounded by our continuance in this world; for why should the gracious fountain of life give us passions, the power of reflecting, only to imbitter our days and inspire us with mistaken notions of dignity? Why should He lead us from love of ourselves to the sublime emotions which the discovery of His wisdom and goodness excites, if these feelings were not set in motion to improve our nature, of which they make a part,[2] and render us capable of enjoying a more

---

[1] Contrary to the opinion of anatomists, who argue by analogy from the formation of the teeth, stomach, and intestines, Rousseau will not allow a man to be a carnivorous animal. And, carried away from nature by a love of system, he disputes whether man be a gregarious animal, though the long and helpless state of infancy seems to point him out as particularly impelled to pair, the first step towards herding.

[2] What would you say to a mechanic whom you had desired to make a watch to point out the hour of the day, if, to show his ingenuity, he added wheels to make it a repeater, etc., that perplexed the simple mechanism; should he urge—to excuse himself—had you not

godlike portion of happiness? Firmly persuaded that no evil exists in the world that God did not design to take place, I build my belief on the perfection of God.

16   Rousseau exerts himself to prove that all *was* right originally: a crowd of authors that all *is* now right: and I, that all will *be* right.

17   But, true to his first position, next to a state of nature, Rousseau celebrates barbarism, and apostrophising the shade of Fabricius, he forgets that, in conquering the world, the Romans never dreamed of establishing their own liberty on a firm basis, or of extending the reign of virtue. Eager to support his system, he stigmatizes, as vicious, every effort of genius; and, uttering the apotheosis of savage virtues, he exalts those to demigods, who were scarcely human—the brutal Spartans who, in defiance of justice and gratitude, sacrificed, in cold blood, the slaves who had shown themselves heroes to rescue their oppressors.

18   Disgusted with artificial manners and virtues, the citizen of Geneva, instead of properly sifting the subject, threw away the wheat with the chaff, without waiting to inquire whether the evils which his ardent soul turned from indignantly, were the consequence of civilization or the vestiges of barbarism. He saw vice trampling on virtue, and the semblance of goodness taking the place of the reality; he saw talents bent by power to sinister purposes, and never thought of tracing the gigantic mischief up to arbitrary power, up to the hereditary distinctions that clash with the mental superiority that naturally raises a man above his fellows. He did not perceive that regal power, in a few generations, introduces idiotism into the noble stem, and holds out baits to render thousands idle and vicious.

19   Nothing can set the regal character in a more contemptible point of view, than the various crimes that have elevated men to the supreme dignity. Vile intrigues, unnatural crimes, and every vice that degrades our nature, have been the steps to this distinguished eminence; yet millions of men have supinely allowed the nerveless limbs of the posterity of such rapacious prowlers to rest quietly on their ensanguined thrones.[3]

20   What but a pestilential vapour can hover over society when its chief director is only instructed in the invention of crimes, or the stupid routine of childish ceremonies? Will men never be wise?—will they never cease to expect corn from tares, and figs from thistles?

21   It is impossible for any man, when the most favourable circumstances concur, to acquire sufficient knowledge and strength of mind to

---

touched a certain spring you would have known nothing of the matter, and that he should have amused himself by making *an experiment* without doing you any harm, would you not retort fairly upon him, by insisting that if he had not added those needless wheels and springs, the accident could not have happened?

[3] Could there be a greater insult offered to the rights of man than the beds of justice in France, when an infant was made the organ of the detestable Dubois?

discharge the duties of a king, entrusted with uncontrolled power; how then must they be violated when his very elevation is an insuperable bar to the attainment of either wisdom or virtue, when all the feelings of a man are stifled by flattery, and reflection shut out by pleasure! Sure it is madness to make the fate of thousands depend on the caprice of a weak fellow-creature, whose very station sinks him *necessarily* below the meanest of his subjects! But one power should not be thrown down to exalt another—for all power inebriates weak man; and its abuse proves that the more equality there is established among men, the more virtue and happiness will reign in society. But this and any similar maxim deduced from simple reason, raises an outcry—the Church or the State is in danger, if faith in the wisdom of antiquity is not implicit; and they who, roused by the sight of human calamity, dare to attack human authority, are reviled as despisers of God, and enemies of man. These are bitter calumnies, yet they reached one of the best of men,[4] whose ashes still preach peace, and whose memory demands a respectful pause, when subjects are discussed that lay so near his heart.

22   After attacking the sacred majesty of kings, I shall scarcely excite surprise by adding my firm persuasion that every profession, in which great subordination of rank constitutes its power, is highly injurious to morality.

23   A standing army, for instance, is incompatible with freedom; because subordination and rigour are the very sinews of military discipline; and despotism is necessary to give vigour to enterprises that one will directs. A spirit inspired by romantic notions of honour, a kind of morality founded on the fashion of the age, can only be felt by a few officers, whilst the main body must be moved by command, like the waves of the sea; for the strong wind of authority pushes the crowd of subalterns forward, they scarcely know or care why, with headlong fury.

24   Besides, nothing can be so prejudicial to the morals of the inhabitants of country towns as the occasional residence of a set of idle superficial young men, whose only occupation is gallantry, and whose polished manners render vice more dangerous, by concealing its deformity under gay ornamental drapery. An air of fashion, which is but a badge of slavery, and proves that the soul has not a strong individual character, awes simple country people into an imitation of the vices, when they cannot catch the slippery graces, of politeness. Every corps is a chain of despots, who, submitting and tyrannising without exercising their reason, become dead-weights of vice and folly on the community. A man of rank or fortune, sure of rising by interest, has nothing to do but to pursue some extravagant freak; whilst the needy *gentleman*, who is to rise, as the phrase turns, by his merit, becomes a servile parasite or vile pander.

---

[4] Dr. Price [Richard Price (1723–91), dissenting minister and moral theologian, liberal advocate of parliamentary reform—M.K.]

25   Sailors, the naval gentlemen, come under the same description, only their vices assume a different and a grosser cast. They are more positively indolent, when not discharging the ceremonials of their station; whilst the insignificant fluttering of soldiers may be termed active idleness. More confined to the society of men, the former acquire a fondness for humour and mischievous tricks; whilst the latter, mixing frequently with well-bred women, catch a sentimental cant. But mind is equally out of the question, whether they indulge the horse-laugh, or polite simper.

26   May I be allowed to extend the comparison to a profession where more mind is certainly to be found—for the clergy have superior opportunities of improvement, though subordination almost equally cramps their faculties? The blind submission imposed at college to forms of belief serves as a novitiate to the curate, who must obsequiously respect the opinion of his rector or patron, if he mean to rise in his profession. Perhaps there cannot be a more forcible contrast than between the servile dependent gait of a poor curate and the courtly mien of a bishop. And the respect and contempt they inspire, render the discharge of their separate functions equally useless.

27   It is of great importance to observe that the character of every man is, in some degree, formed by his profession. A man of sense may only have a cast of countenance that wears off as you trace his individuality, whilst the weak, common man has scarcely ever any character, but what belongs to the body; at least, all his opinions have been so steeped in the vat consecrated by authority, that the faint spirit which the grape of his own vine yields, cannot be distinguished.

28   Society, therefore, as it becomes more enlightened, should be very careful not to establish bodies of men who must necessarily be made foolish or vicious by the very constitution of their profession.

29   In the infancy of society, when men were just emerging out of barbarism, chiefs and priests, touching the most powerful springs of savage conduct, hope and fear, must have had unbounded sway. An aristocracy, of course, is naturally the first form of government. But, clashing interests soon losing their equipoise, a monarchy and hierarchy break out of the confusion of ambitious struggles, and the foundation of both is secured by feudal tenures. This appears to be the origin of monarchical and priestly powers, and the dawn of civilization. But such combustible materials cannot long be pent up; and, getting vent in foreign wars and intestine insurrections, the people acquire some power in the tumult, which obliges their rulers to gloss over their oppression with a show of right. Thus, as wars, agriculture, commerce, and literature, expand the mind, despots are compelled to make covert corruption hold fast the power which was formerly snatched by open force.[5] And this baneful lurking

---

[5] Men of abilities scatter seeds that grow up and have a great influence on the forming opinion; and when once the public opinion preponderates, through the exertion of reason, the overthrow of arbitrary power is not very distant.

gangrene is most quickly spread by luxury and superstition, the sure dregs of ambition. The indolent puppet of a court first becomes a luxurious monster, or fastidious sensualist, and then makes the contagion which his unnatural state spread, the instrument of tyranny.

30 It is the pestiferous purple which renders the progress of civilization a curse, and warps the understanding, till men of sensibility doubt whether the expansion of intellect produces a greater portion of happiness or misery. But the nature of the poison points out the antidote; and had Rousseau mounted one step higher in his investigation, or could his eye have pierced through the foggy atmosphere, which he almost disdained to breathe, his active mind would have darted forward to contemplate the perfection of man in the establishment of true civilization, instead of taking his ferocious flight back to the night of sensual ignorance.

APPENDIX B
INTERNET

Today we live in a "global village." Radio, television, film, and the Internet have made virtually all parts of the world accessible, with the Internet largely responsible for creating this world community. E-mail allows us to communicate with friends and family wherever they may be, and the World Wide Web allows us to "surf" Web sites with information on topics such as history, literature, art, current events, and culture, among others. Like the world we live in, the Internet is complex, interconnected, and exciting; understanding how to use it is essential to operating in the world community. The Internet has proven to be especially valuable as a research tool, and as such, special care must be applied to determine the accuracy of the various sources.

LITERARY RESEARCH

The Internet is particularly useful for literary research. Online you can find information about literary works from a variety of sources and cultural perspectives. This is particularly useful for multicultural texts from a variety of countries, such as those included in this book, because the Internet itself is international. For example, a preliminary search for Geoffrey Chaucer's Canterbury Tales leads to a diverse list of Web sites; you can read the latest literary criticism from Oxford scholars, or, if so inspired, read the Arabic translation of the Canterbury Tales.

SEARCH ENGINES

There are several search engines designed to help you find the information for which you are looking. Knowing what kind of research you are doing allows you to choose among them. Search engines are designed for either broad or specific research.

Specific Topic Searches

Alta Vista (http://www.altavista.com), Excite (http://www.excite.com), Infoseek (http://www.infoseek.com), or Lycos (http://www.lycos.com) are text-indexing tools and are designed for searches in which you have a specific topic rather than a general idea of a subject area you want to research. You use a form on the engine's Web page to enter one or more key words. You click on the enter button and the automated search engine will locate Web pages related to these key words. These search engines are called text-indexing because they use an automated feature to look at the text of the millions of Web pages on the Web and select ones that have a high frequency of your key words appearing in their pages. For example, if you are looking for information about Chaucer and entered that key word, the search engine would return pages in which the word Chaucer was used multiple times. Keyword searching is most useful if you have a more specific topic than "Chaucer." If you enter the word "Chaucer" as a key word in Alta Vista (http://www.altavista.com), for example, you might receive 50,000 hits or pages that include that key word. Obviously, you cannot look at 50,000 Web pages. Instead, you can use the search engines advanced search features that allow you to restrict your search. If you wanted information about electronic texts of Chaucer's Canterbury Tales, for example, you could use those additional words to restrict your search. You could just enter these words in the engine's main search form, but this method is also hit or miss because of the way search engines are programmed. It is better to use the engine's advanced features. The method for advanced search varies from one search engine to another, but each has help screens that will walk you through the process. Generally, the search engine's home page has a hot link called something like "advanced search," "help," or "tips." Follow the links and read the instructions on how to restrict your search.

Subject-Directory Searches

Subject-directory search tools are used for broader research because they allow you to navigate the World Wide Web by subject. If, for example, you wanted access to all of the information available on Chaucer, ranging from his literary work to his effect on medieval society you would use one of these tools. Most of the search engines now have subject tree indexes on their home pages, though you may not see them if you simply click on "search" in your Web browser because that may take you to a shortened version of the search engine's home page. A good one to try is Yahoo (http://www.yahoo.com) because its subject tree is not automated but rather created by Yahoo's staff and people who register their Web pages with the search engine. Perhaps even more useful are the subject tree directories created by libraries such as Librarian's Index to the Internet (http://sunsite.berkeley.edu/InternetIndex), AlphaSearch (http://www.calvin.edu/library/as), and Infomine (http://www.ucr.edu/search/ucr_sshsearch.html). These directories index Web pages selected by university librarians as being particularly useful for research.

When you use a subject-tree index, you select one of a number of general topics that is closest to your area of interest. If you were looking for Chaucer, for example, you might select "English" or "literature," depending on the options offered. After you click on that hot link, you will be presented with another list of links with more specific topics. Again you choose one and click. You continue this process of narrowing your topic until you reach actual Web sites and explore them for useful information related to your general topic.

EXAMPLE: FINDING ELECTRONIC TEXT OF CHAUCER'S "MILLER'S TALE"

Key-Word Searching

If your search is specific and you are looking for an electronic text of "Miller's Tale," then you will pick a text-indexing tool like Infoseek (http://www.infoseek.com) and make use of its advanced search capabilities. Begin by clicking on "advanced search." Infoseek will give you a form that offers options in which you can fill in words which must, should, or should not appear in your search results. (If Infoseek has changed the composition of this form since press time, it will still have specific instructions on how to do an advanced search). If, for example, you fill in the form requiring the words "Chaucer" "Canterbury Tales," and "electronic texts," you will receive a refined list of Chaucer sites that have electronic texts. From this list, you can connect to the University of Virginia Electronic Text Center (http://etext.virginia.edu/mideng.browse.html) which has an electronic version of Chaucer's "Miller's Tale."

If you connect to Alta Vista (http://www.altavista.com), try typing in Chaucer's Canterbury Tales in the search form. Alta Vista will return a list of Web sites related to the Canterbury Tales. Among the first ten sites listed is one designed by a professor at Washington State University's Department of English. He has designed a Web site which, among other things, lists links to Chaucer related sites. One of these is the Litrix Reading Room (www.litrix.com/canterby/cante001.htm) and it has the electronic text of the Canterbury Tales translated into modern English. Included in the list of Canterbury Tales is, of course, the "Miller's Tale." If you would like to see what additional information Alta Vista can provide about the Canterbury Tales, return to the search results page and click on "Advanced Search." You will receive a form which allows you to refine your search, indicating what sub topics to stress.

Subject-Tree Searching

If you would like to try the subject-tree approach to finding electronic texts for the Canterbury Tales, specifically the "Miller's Tale," connect to one of the librarian-generated subject-trees mentioned above, such as the Librarian's Index to the Internet (http://sunsite.berkeley.edu/InternetIndex). Select "literature" and then "full text." Very quickly you can locate the Online Books Page that has links to two sources of online versions of the Canterbury Tales, including one old English version and the modern English version at the Litrix Reading Room mentioned above. You can also explore other Chaucer links by returning to the "literature" page and exploring other links related to Chaucer.

ACCURACY OF SOURCES

The Internet, like any publishing medium, offers texts to readers. Like newspapers, magazines, and books, moreover, Internet texts must be evaluated for credibility and accuracy of sources. Texts on the Internet, however, should be reviewed perhaps even more carefully because anyone with an Internet connection can put up Web pages; there is not necessarily a review mechanism in place to assure quality. Thus, when you use the Internet for literary or other research, be careful to note the sponsoring organization or individual who is responsible for the pages. If the pages are part of a research project at a major university or are authored by an authority in the field, you have some reason to believe they are credible. If you can't tell who is the author or sponsor, or if the author or sponsor is not well known, that doesn't necessarily mean the pages are inaccurate, but it is a good reason to wonder. In addition, subject Internet texts to the same scrutiny you would apply to print texts. For example, does the author cite sources for statistics or other supporting evidence? Is the text a balanced document rather than a one-sided argument? Is the individual or organization selling anything or advocating membership in an organization?

You may intentionally choose to use biased sources from the Internet in your research. Indeed, one of the strengths of the Internet is that individuals and organizations can put forward their ideas without being filtered by traditional media. Just remember that if the author of a text clearly has a persuasive agenda, you should not treat the text as an unbiased source.

APPENDIX C
BIBLIOGRAPHY

The sources listed here provide instructors and students with further information on themes in chapters 5 through 12 of *Crossing Borders: An International Reader.*

CHAPTER 5: FAMILY

Bruchac, Joseph. *Roots of Survival: Native American Storytelling and the Sacred.* Goldon, Colorado: Fulcrum Publications, 1996.

Cho, Lee-Jay and Moto Yada, eds. *Tradition and Change in the Asian Family.* Honolulu: East-West Center: Distributed by the University of Hawaii Press, 1994.

Dickinson, George E. *Understanding Families: Diversity, Continuity, and Change.* 2nd ed. Ft Worth: Harcourt Brace College Publishers, 1995.

Jones, Rachel K. and April Brayfield. "Life's Greatest Joy? European Attitudes toward the Centrality of Children." *Social Forces,* 75 (1997): 1239–1270.

Lewis, Robert A. and Marvin B. Sussman, eds. *Men's Changing Roles in the Family.* New York: Haworth Press, 1986.

Riley, Matilda White, Robert L. Kay, and Anne Foner, eds. *Age and Structural Lag: Society's Failure to Provide Meaningful Opportunities in Work, Family, and Leisure.* New York: J. Wiley, 1994.

Taylor, Robert Joseph, James S. Jackson, and Linda M. Chatters, eds. *Family Life in Black America.* Thousand Oaks, CA: Sage Publications, 1997.

CHAPTER 6: RITES OF PASSAGE

Delaney, Cassandra Halleh. "Rites of Passage in Adolescence." *Adolescence.* 30.120 (1995): 891–898.

Foster, Charles. "On the Trail of a Taboo: Female Circumcision in the Islamic World." *Contemporary Review.* 264.1540 (1994): 244–250.

Frese, Pamela R., ed. *Celebrations of Identity: Multiple Voices in American Ritual Performance.* Westport, Conn: Bergin & Garvey, 1993.

Golding, William. *Rites of Passage.* New York: Farrar, Straus, Giroux, 1980.

Lane, Sandra D. and Robert A. Rubinstein. "Judging the Other: Responding to Traditional Female Genital Surgeries." *Hastings Center Report.* 26.3 (1996): 31–41.

Mahdi, Louise Carus, Nancy Geyer Christopher, and Michael Meade, eds. *Crossroads: The Quest for Contemporary Rites of Passage.* Chicago: Open Court, 1996.

Spivey, Ed Jr. "Wrongs and Rites of Passage: Rituals for Young Men in America." *Sojourners.* 27.3 (1998): 66–67.

Verberg, Peter. "How Other Cultures Have Solved the Teen Dilemma." *Alberta Report/Western Report.* 22.15 (1995) 32–34.

CHAPTER 7: WORKING

Beach, Betty. *Integrating Work and Family Life: The Home-Working Family.* Albany: State University of New York Press, 1989.

Joekes, Susan. "Working for Lipstick? Male and Female Labour in the Clothing Industry in Morocco." *Women, Work, and Ideology in the Third World.* Ed. Haleh Afshar. London; New York: Ravistock Publications, 1985. 183–213.

Kahne, Hilda and Janet Z. Giele, eds. *Women's Work and Women's Lives: The Continuing Struggle Worldwide.* Boulder: Westview Press, 1992.

Lam, Alice. "Equal Employment Opportunities for Japanese Women: Changing Company Practice." *Japanese Women Working.* Ed. Janet Hunter. London; New York: Routledge, 1993.

Macleod, Arlene Elowe. *Accommodating Protest: Working Women, the New Veiling, and Change in Cairo.* New York: Columbia University Press, 1991.

Trompenaars, Alfons. *Riding the Waves of Culture: Understanding Cultural Diversity in Global Business.* 2nd ed. New York: McGraw-Hill, 1998.

CHAPTER 8: CUSTOM AND GENDER ROLES

Allred, Lenna. "Women in a Man's World: American Women in the Vietnam War." *The Vietnam War: Handbook of the Literature and Research.* Ed. James S. Olson. Westport, Conn.: Greenwood Press, 1993.

Barkalow, Carol. *In the Men's House: An Inside Account of Life in the Army by One of West Point's First Female Graduates.* New York: Poseidon Press, 1990.

Blacksmith, E. A. *Women in the Military.* New York: Wilson, 1992.

Food for Our Grandmothers: Writings by Arab-American and Arab-Canadian Feminists. Ed. Joanna Kadi. Boston, MA: South End Press, 1994.

Hendry, Joy. "The Role of the Professional Housewife." *Japanese Women Working.* Ed. Janet Hunter. London; New York: Routledge, 1993.

Holm, Jeanne. *Women in the Military: An Unfinished Revolution.* Novato, CA: Presidio Press, 1992.

Jeffords, Susan and Lauren Rabinovitz eds. *Seeing through the Media: The Persian Gulf War.* New Brunswick, N.J.: Rutgers University Press, 1994.

Jones, David E. *Women Warriors: A History.* Washington: Brassey's, 1997.

McClain, Carol Shepherd, ed. *Women as Healers: Cross-Cultural Perspectives.* New Brunswick: Rutgers University Press, 1989.

Morton, Walt. "Tracking the Sign of Tarzan: Trans-Media Representation of a Pop-Culture Icon" *You Tarzan: Masculinity, Movies, and Men.* Eds. Pat Kirkham and Janet Thumim. New York: St Martin's Press, 1993.

Salas, Elizabeth. *Soldaderas in the Mexican Military: Myth and History.* Austin: University of Texas Press, 1990.

Speier, Hans. "Risk, Security, and Modern Hero Worship." *The Truth in Hell and Other Essays on Politics and Culture.* New York: Oxford University Press, 1989.

CHAPTER 9: THE INDIVIDUAL AND THE GROUP

Jasper, James M. *The Art of Moral Protest: Culture, Biography, and Creativity in Social Movements.* Chicago: University of Chicago Press, 1997.

Kymlicka, Will, ed. *The Rights of Minority Cultures.* Oxford; New York: Oxford University Press, 1995.

Momaday, N. Scott. "The Story of the Arrowmaker: Language and Meaning." *Parabola.* 20.3 (1995): 21–24.

Perkins, Merle L. *Jean-Jacques Rousseau on the Individual and Society.* Lexington: The University Press of Kentucky, 1974.

Peters, Julie and Andrea Wolper, eds. *Women's Rights, Human Rights: International Feminist Perspectives.* New York: Routledge, 1995.

Tibbetts, Alexandra. "Mamas Fighting for Freedom in Kenya." *Africa Today: A Quarterly Review.* 41.4 (1994): 27–47.

Tuan, Yu-fu. *Segmented Worlds and Self: Group Life and Individual Consciousness.* Minneapolis: University of Minnesota Press, 1982.

CHAPTER 10: IMMIGRANTS AND EXILES

Darder, Antonia. *Culture and Difference: Critical Perspectives on the Bicultural Experience in the United States.* Westport, Conn.: Begin & Garvey, 1995.

Faderman, Lillian. *I Begin My Life All Over: The Hmong and the American Immigrant Experience.* Boston: Beacon Press, 1998.

Hein, Jeremy. *From Vietnam, Laos, and Cambodia: A Refugee Experience in the United States.* New York: Twayne Publishers; London: Prentice Hall International, 1995.

Johnson, Kevin R. "Melting Pot" or "Ring of Fire"? Assimilation and the Mexican-American Experience. LatCrit: Latinas/os and the Law: A Joint Symposium by California Law Review and La Raza Law Journal. *California Law Review.* 85 (1997): 1259–1313.

Maciel, David R. and Maria Herrera-Sobek, eds. *Culture Across Borders: Mexican Immigration and Popular Culture.* Tuscon: University of Arizona Press, 1998.

Root, Maria P. P., ed. *Filipino Americans: Transformation and Identity.* Thousand Oaks, CA: Sage Publications, 1997.

CHAPTER 11: THE ARTIST IN SOCIETY

Bright, Brenda Jo and Liza Bakewell, eds. *Looking High and Low: Art and Cultural Identity.* Tucson, AZ: University of Arizona Press, 1995.

Becker, Carol and Ann Wiens, eds. *The Artist in Society: Rights, Roles, and Responsibilities.* Chicago: New Art Examiner Press, 1995.

Read, Herbert Edward, Sir. *Art and Alienation: The Role of the Artist in Society.* New York: Horizon Press, 1967.

Soyinka, Wole. *Art, Dialogue, and Outrage: Essays on Literature and Culture.* 2nd ed. New York: Pantheon Books, 1993.

CHAPTER 12: THE SPIRITUAL LIFE

Creedon, Jeremiah. "God with a Million Faces: Insights into the Growing Trend of Pastiche Spirituality." *Utne Reader.* July–August 1998: 42–49.

Feuerstein, Georg. *Holy Madness: The Shock Tactics and Radial Teachings of Crazy-Wise Adepts, Holy Fools and Rascal Gurus.* New York: Paragon House, 1990.

Hixon, Lex. *Coming Home: The Experience of Enlightenment in Sacred Traditions.* Burdett, N.Y.: Published for the Paul Brunton Philosophic Foundation by Larson Publications, 1995.

Hurston, Zora Neal. *Tell My Horse: Voodoo and Life in Haiti and Jamaica.* Forward by Ishmail Reed. New York: Perennial Library, 1990.

Lerner, Michael. "Spirituality in America." *Tikkun.* 13.6 (1998): 33.

Jackson, Michael. "The Man Who Could Turn into an Elephant: Shape-Shifting among the Kuranko of Sierra Leone." *Personhood and Agency: The Experience of Self and Other in African Cultures.* Papers presented at a symposium of African Folk Models and their application held at Uppsala University August 23–30, 1987. Eds. Michael Jackson and Ivan Karp. Uppsala University, Washington: 1990: 59–78.

Pucci, Idanna. *The Epic of Life: The Balinese Journey of the Soul.* New York: Alfred van der Marck Editions, 1985.

GEOGRAPHICAL INDEX

AFRICA
Burkina Faso: Malidoma Patrice Somé, "Slowly Becoming"   537
Northwest Africa: Connie Stevens, "Marriage in the Hausa *Tatsuniya* Tradition: A Cultural and Cosmic Balance"   513
Senegal: Sembene Ousmane, "The *Bilal's* Fourth Wife" (short story)   316
South Africa: Jenefer Shute, "Sport, African Cultures, Value for Money: A Return to South Africa"   422; André Brink, "The Artist as Insect"   482
Sudan: Nahid Toubia, "Women and Health in Sudan"   221

ASIA
Bali: Margaret Mead, "Children and Ritual in Bali"   101
Burma (Myanmar): Aung San Suu Kyi, "Freedom from Fear"   359
China: Li Zhai, "Role Reversal: The Kind Father and Stern Mother"   131; Hugh Williamson "China's Toy Industry Tinderbox"   263; Wang Bin "Two Great Traditions"   567
Japan: Nicholas Bornoff, "The Marriage-Go-Round"   211; J. E. Thomas, "Culture and the Communal Organisation"   270
Pakistan: Salman Rushdie, "Imaginary Homelands"   408; Ruxana Meer, "Razia Begum in London" (short story)   445

EUROPE
Czechoslovakia: Franz Kafka, "A Hunger Artist" (short story)   492
England: Salman Rushdie, "Imaginary Homelands"   408; Ruxana Meer, "Razia Begum in London" (short story)   445
France: Raymonde Carroll, "Parents and Children"   85
Poland: Czeslaw Milosz "Looking to the West"   52
Russia: Nikita Pokrovsky, "Land of Meaningless Courtesy"   48
Spain: Barbara Kingsolver, "Somebody's Baby"   78; Federico García Lorca, "Gacela of the Dead Child" (poem)   576

LATIN AMERICA AND THE CARIBBEAN
Argentina: Andrea Malin, "Mother Who Won't Disappear"   365
Brazil: Robert Levine with Ellen Wolff, "Social Time: The Heartbeat of Culture"   288

The Caribbean: Nancie Solien Gonzalez, "Household and Family in the Caribbean" 159
Chile: Pablo Neruda, Excerpt from *The Heights of Macchu Picchu* (poem) 398
Guatemala: Rigoberta Menchú, "The Bible and Self-Defense: The Examples of Judith, Moses, and David," as told to Ann Wright 557
Mexico: Octavio Paz, "Mexican Masks" 303; Gloria Anzaldúa, "La Conciencia de la Mestiza: Towards a New Consciousness" 465

DEVELOPING COUNTRIES[1]
Marvin Harris, "Small Things" 29; Paul Harrison, "The Barefoot Businessman" 245

THE MIDDLE EAST
Egypt: Naguib Mahfouz, "Respected Sir," (fiction) 257; Nawal El Saadawi, "Growing Up Female in Egypt" 325
Israel: Nira Yuval-Davis, "Front and Rear: The Sexual Division of Labour in the Israeli Army" 336

NORTH AMERICA
United States: Barbara Kingsolver, "Somebody's Baby" 78; Raymonde Carroll, "Parents and Children" 85; David Elkind, "WAAAH!! Why Kids Have a Lot to Cry About" 168; Martin King Whyte, "Choosing Mates—The American Way" 199; Horace Miner, "Body Ritual Among the Nacirema" 193; Betty Jacobson and Beverly Kaye, "Balancing Act" 238; Gordon Murray "Picking on the Little Guy: In Boyhood and on the Battlefield" 297; James Dubik, "An Officer and a Feminist" 352; Neil Postman, "Defending Against the Indefensible" 375; Dorothy D. Lee, "An Anthropologist Learns from the Hopi" 386; John Garvey, "A Different Kind of Knowing: For Those with Ears to Hear" 521; Will Herberg, "The Religion of Americans and American Religion" 580
African American: Audre Lorde, "The Transformation of Silence into Language and Action" 487
Asian American: Gish Jen, "The Water-Faucet Vision" (short story) 151; David Mura, "Fictive Fragments of a Father and Son" 436; Ruxaxna Meer, "Razia Begum in London" (short story) 445; Francis Fukuyama, "Immigrants and Family Values" 450
Cherokee: Connie May Fowler, "No Snapshots in the Attic: A Granddaughter's Search for a Cherokee Past" 136
Hopi: Dorothy D. Lee, "An Anthropologist Learns from the Hopi" 386
Mexican American: Susan Orlean, "Debuting: Phoenix, Arizona" 180; Gloria Anzaldúa, "La Conciencia de la Mestiza: Towards a New Consciousness" 465
Zuni: Jane M. Young, "The Power of Image and Place" 503

---

[1] Focuses on several areas of the so-called Third World.

RHETORICAL INDEX

Reading selections listed here are sometimes models of a particular rhetorical strategy. Dorothy D. Lee's "An Anthropologist Learns from the Hopi," for example, uses comparison and contrast to develop ideas, while Margaret Mead's "Children and Ritual in Bali" uses illustration as a primary writing strategy. Many selections employ more than one writing strategy and may be found in several categories.

ANALYSIS
Nicholas Bornoff, "The Marriage-Go-Round" 281
Raymonde Carroll, "Introduction to Cultural Misunderstandings" 8
Raymonde Carroll, "Parents and Children" 85
David Elkind, "WAAAH!!: Why Kids Have a Lot to Cry About" 168
Will Herberg, "The Religion of Americans and American Religion" 580
Robert Levine with Ellen Wolff, "Social Time: The Heartbeat of Culture" 288
Margaret Mead, "Children and Ritual in Bali" 101
Czeslaw Milosz, "Looking to the West" 52
Horace Miner, "Body Ritual among the Nacirema" 193
Neil Postman, "Defending Against the Indefensible" 375
Connie Stephens, "Marriage in the Hausa *Tatsuniya* Tradition: A Cultural and Cosmic Balance" 513
J. E. Thomas, "Culture and the Communal Organisation" 270
Martin King Whyte, "Choosing Mates—The American Way" 199
Jane M. Young, "The Power of Image and Place" 503

ANALOGY AND METAPHOR
Gloria Anzaldúa, "La Consiencia de la Mestiza: Towards a New Consciousness" 465
André Brink, "The Artist as Insect" 482
Franz Kafka, "A Hunger Artist" 492
Federico García Lorca, "Gacela of the Dead Child" 576
Naguib Mahfouz, Excerpt from *Respected Sir* 257
Ruxana Meer, "Razia Begum in London" 445
Rigoberta Menchú, "The Bible and Self-Defense: The Examples of Judith, Moses, and David" 557
Czeslaw Milosz, "Looking to the West" 52
Pablo Neruda, excerpt from *The Heights of Macchu Picchu* 398

ARGUMENT AND PERSUASION

Gloria Anzaldúa, "La Consiencia de la Mestiza: Towards a New Consciousness"   465
Nicholas Bornoff, "The Marriage-Go-Round"   281
Raymonde Carroll, "Introduction to Cultural Misunderstandings"   85
James M. Dubik, "An Officer and a Feminist"   352
Francis Fukuyama, "Immigrants and Family Values"   450
John Garvey, "A Different Kind of Knowing: For Those with Ears to Hear"   531
Nancie Solien Gonzalez, "Household and Family in the Caribbean: Some Definitions and Concepts"   159
Marvin Harris, "Small Things"   29
Will Herberg, "The Religion of Americans and American Religion"   580
Barbara Kingsolver, "Somebody's Baby"   78
Neil Postman, "Defending Against the Indefensible"   375
Aung San Suu Kyi, "Freedom from Fear"   359
Nahid Toubia, "Women and Health in Sudan"   221
Martin King Whyte, "Choosing Mates—The American Way"   199
Hugh Williamson, "China's Toy Industry Tinderbox"   567

CAUSE AND EFFECT

David Elkind, "WAAAH!!: Why Kids Have a Lot to Cry About"   168
John Garvey, "A Different Kind of Knowing: For Those with Ears to Hear"   531
Paul Harrison, "The Barefoot Businessman: Traditional and Small-Scale Industry"   245
Andrea Malin, "Mother Who Won't Disappear"   365
Margaret Mead, "Children and Ritual in Bali"   101
Gordon Murray, "Picking on the Little Girl: In Boyhood and in the Battlefields"   297
Aung San Suu Kyi, "Freedom from Fear"   359
Nahid Toubia, "Women and Health in Sudan"   221
Hugh Williamson, "China's Toy Industry Tinderbox"   263
Li Zhai, "Role Reversal: The Kind Father and Stern Mother"   131

CLASSIFICATION

Paul Harrison, "The Barefoot Businessman: Traditional and Small-Scale Industry"   245
Betsy Jacobson and Beverly Kaye, "Balancing Act"   238
Susan Orlean, "Debuting: Phoenix, Arizona"   180
Neil Postman, "Defending Against the Indefensible"   375
Aung San Suu Kyi, "Freedom from Fear"   359
Martin King Whyte, "Choosing Mates—The American Way"   199
Nira Yuval-Davis, "Front and Rear: The Sexual Division of Labour in the Israeli Army"   336

COMPARISON AND CONTRAST
Wang Bin, "Two Great Traditions"   567
Raymonde Carroll, "Parents and Children"   85
James M. Dubik, "An Officer and a Feminist"   352
Barbara Kingsolver, "Somebody's Baby"   78
Dorothy D. Lee, "An Anthropologist Learns from the Hopi"   386
Robert Levine with Ellen Wolff, "Social Time: The Heartbeat of Culture"   288
Czeslaw Milosz, "Looking to the West"   52
Nawal El Saadawi, "Growing Up Female in Egypt"   325
J. E. Thomas, "Culture and the Communal Organisation"   270
Martin King Whyte, "Choosing Mates—The American Way"   199
Nira Yuval-Davis, "Front and Rear: The Sexual Division of Labour in the
    Israeli Army"   336

DEFINITION
Raymonde Carroll, "Introduction to Cultural Misunderstandings"   8
Nancie Solien Gonzalez, "Household and Family in the Caribbean: Some Definitions
    and Concepts"   159
Will Herberg, "The Religion of Americans and American Religion"   580
Betsy Jacobson and Beverly Kaye, "Balancing Act"   238
Susan Orlean, "Debuting: Phoenix, Arizona"   180
Neil Postman, "Defending Against the Indefensible"   375

DESCRIPTION
Nicholas Bornoff, "The Marriage-Go-Round"   281
James M. Dubik, "An Officer and a Feminist"   352
Gish Jen, "The Water-Faucet Vision"   151
Marvin Harris, "Small Things"   29
Franz Kafka, "A Hunger Artist"   492
Federico Garcia Lorca, "Gacela of the Dead Child"   576
Naguib Mahfouz, Excerpt from *Respected Sir*   257
Andrea Malin, "Mother Who Won't Disappear"   365
Margaret Mead, "Children and Ritual in Bali"   101
Ruxana Meer, "Razia Begum in London"   445
Rigoberta Menchú, "The Bible and Self-Defense: The Examples of Judith, Moses,
    and David"   557
Horace Miner, "Body Ritual among the Nacirema"   193
David Mura, "Fictive Fragments of a Father and Son"   436
Pablo Neruda, excerpt from *The Heights of Macchu Picchu*   398
Susan Orlean, "Debuting: Phoenix, Arizona"   180
Sembene Ousmane, "The *Bilal's* Fourth Wife"   316

Jenefer Shute, "Sport, African Cultures, Value for Money: Return to South Africa"   422
Malidome Patrice Somé, "Slowly Becoming"   537
Connie Stephens, "Marriage in the Hausa *Tatsuniya* Tradition: A Cultural and Cosmic Balance   513

EXAMPLE AND ILLUSTRATION
Wang Bin, "Two Great Traditions"   567
Nicholas Bornoff, "The Marriage-Go-Round"   281
André Brink, "The Artist as Insect"   482
Francis Fukuyama, "Immigrants and Family Values"   450
John Garvey, "A Different Kind of Knowing: For Those with Ears to Hear"   531
Marvin Harris, "Small Things"   29
Paul Harrison, "The Barefoot Businessman: Traditional and Small-Scale Industry"   245
Will Herberg, "The Religion of Americans and American Religion"   580
Dorothy D. Lee, "An Anthropoligist Learns from the Hopi"   386
Robert Levine with Ellen Wolff, "Social Time: The Heartbeat of Culture"   288
Andrea Malin, "Mother Who Won't Disappear"   365
Margaret Mead, "Children and Ritual in Bali"   101
Horace Miner, "Body Ritual among the Nacirema"   193
Octavio Paz, "Mexican Masks"   303
Neil Postman, "Defending Against the Indefensible"   375
Salman Rushdie, "Imaginary Homelands"   408
Connie Stephens, "Marriage in the Hausa *Tatsuniya* Tradition: A Cultural and Cosmic Balance"   513
J. E. Thomas, "Culture and the Communal Organisation"   270
Martin King Whyte, "Choosing Mates—The American Way"   199
Jane M. Young, "The Power of Image and Place"   503
Nira Yuval-Davis, "Front and Rear; The Sexual Division of Labour in the Israeli Army"   336

EXPOSITION
Gloria Anzaldúa, "La Conciencia de la Mestiza: Towards a New Consciousness"   465
Wang Bin, "Two Great Traditions"   567
André Brink, "The Artist as Insect"   482
Raymonde Carroll, "Parents and Children"   85
David Elkind, "WAAAH!!: Why Kids Have a Lot to Cry About"   168
Connie May Fowler, "No Snapshot in the Attic: A Granddaughter's Search for a Cherokee Past"   136
Marvin Harris, "Small Things"   29

Paul Harrison, "The Barefoot Businessman: Traditional and Small-Scale Industry"   245
Betsy Jacobson and Beverly Kaye, "Balancing Act"   238
Barbara Kingsolver, "Somebody's Baby"   78
Dorothy D. Lee, "An Anthropologist Learns from the Hopi"   386
Audre Lorde, "The Transformation of Silence into Language and Action"   487
Andrea Malin, "Mother Who Won't Disappear"   365
Rigoberta Menchú, "The Bible and Self-Defense: The Examples of Judith, Moses, and David"   557
Czeslaw Milosz, "Looking to the West"   52
David Mura, "Fictive Fragments of a Father and Son"   436
Gordon Murray, "Picking on the Little Guy: In Boyhood and in the Battlefields"   297
Octavio Paz, "Mexican Masks"   303
Nikita Pokrovsky, "The Land of Meaningless Courtesy"   48
Salman Rushdie, "Imaginary Homelands"   408
Jenefer Shute, "Sport, African Cultures, Value for Money: Return to South Africa"   422
Malidome Patrice Somé, "Slowly Becoming"   537
Connie Stephens, "Marriage in the Hausa *Tatsuniya* Tradition: A Cultural and Cosmic Balance"   513
J. E. Thomas, "Culture and the Communal Organisation"   270
Nahid Toubia, "Women and Health in Sudan"   221
Nira Yuval-Davis, "Front and Rear: The Sexual Division of Labour in the Israeli Army"   336
Li Zhai, "Role Reversal: The Kind Father and Stern Mother"   131

HUMOR, IRONY, AND SATIRE

Gish Jen, "The Water-Faucet Vision"   151
Connie May Fowler, "No Snapshot in the Attic: A Granddaughter's Search for a Cherokee Past"   136
Franz Kafka, "A Hunger Artist"   492
Naguib Mahfouz, Excerpt from *Respected Sir*   257
Horace Miner, "Body Ritual among the Nacirema"   193
David Mura, "Fictive Fragments of a Father and Son"   436
Sembene Ousmane, "The *Bilal's* Fourth Wife"   316
Jenefer Shute, "Sport, African Cultures, Value for Money: Return to South Africa"   422
Hugh Williamson, "China's Toy Industry Tinderbox"   263

INTERVIEW

Susan Orlean, "Debuting: Phoenix, Arizona"   180

NARRATION

Gloria Anzaldúa, "La Consiencia de la Mestiza: Towards a New Consciousness"   465
James M. Dubik, "An Officer and a Feminist"   352
Connie May Fowler, "No Snapshot in the Attic: A Granddaughter's Search for a Cherokee Past"   136
Gish Jen, "The Water-Faucet Vision"   151
Franz Kafka, "A Hunger Artist"   492
Barbara Kingsolver, "Somebody's Baby"   78
Dorothy D. Lee, "An Anthropologist Learns from the Hopi"   386
Federico García Lorca, "Gacela of the Dead Child"   576
Audre Lorde, "The Transformation of Silence into Language and Action"   487
Naguib Mahfouz, Excerpt from *Respected Sir*   257
Ruxana Meer, "Razia Begum in London"   445
Rigoberta Menchú, "The Bible and Self-Defense: The Examples of Judith, Moses, and David"   557
David Mura, "Fictive Fragments of a Father and Son"   436
Gordon Murray, "Picking on the Little Guy: In Boyhood and in the Battlefields"   297
Pablo Neruda, excerpt from *The Heights of Macchu Picchu*   398
Sembene Ousmane, "The *Bilal's* Fourth Wife"   316
Nawal El Saadawi, "Growing Up Female in Egypt"   325
Jenefer Shute, "Sport, African Cultures, Value for Money: Return to South Africa"   422
Malidome Patrice Somé, "Slowly Becoming"   537
Connie Stephens, "Marriage in the Hausa *Tatsuniya* Tradition: A Cultural and Cosmic Balance"   513

PROCESS ANALYSIS

Nicholas Bornoff, "The Marriage-Go-Round"   281
André Brink, "The Artist as Insect"   482
Margaret Mead, "Children and Ritual in Bali"   101
Horace Miner, "Body Ritual among the Nacirema"   193
Gordon Murray, "Picking on the Little Guy: In Boyhood and in the Battlefields"   297
Susan Orlean, "Debuting: Phoenix, Arizona"   180

THEMATIC INDEX

Themes listed here follow the order in which they appear in *Crossing Borders*.

CULTURAL DIFFERENCES
Raymonde Carroll, "An Introduction to Cultural Analysis," "Parents and Children"   8
Marvin Harris, "Small Things"   29
Nikita Pokrovsky, "The Land of Meaningless Courtesy"   48
Czeslaw Milosz, "Looking to the West"   52
Nancie Solien Gonzalez, "Household and Family in the Caribbean: Some Definitions and Concepts"   159
Horace Miner, "Body Ritual among the Nacirema"   193
Nicholas Bornoff, "The Marriage-Go-Round"   281
Robert Levine with Ellen Wolff, "Social Time: The Heartbeat of Culture"   288
Dorothy D. Lee, "An Anthropologist Learns from the Hopi"   386

REARING CHILDREN
Barbara Kingsolver, "Somebody's Baby"   78
Raymonde Carroll, "Parents and Children"   85
Margaret Mead, "Children and Ritual in Bali"   101
David Elkind, "WAAAH!!: Why Kids Have a Lot to Cry About"   168

FAMILY TIES
Li Zhai, "Role Reversal: The Kind Father and Stern Mother"   131
Connie May Fowler, "No Snapshot in the Attic: A Granddaughter's Search for a Cherokee Past"   136
Gish Jen, "The Water-Faucet Vision" (short story)   151
Nancie Solien Gonzalez, "Household and Family in the Caribbean: Some Definitions and Concepts"   159
David Elkind, "WAAAH!!: Why Kids Have a Lot to Cry About"   168
Jenefer Shute, "Sport, African Cultures, Value for Money: Return to South Africa"   422
David Mura, "Fictive Fragments of a Father and Son"   436
Ruxana Meer, "Razia Begum in London"   445

CUSTOMS

Margaret Mead, "Children and Ritual in Bali" 101
Connie May Fowler, "No Snapshot in the Attic: A Granddaughter's Search for a Cherokee Past" 136
Susan Orlean, "Debuting: Phoenix, Arizona" 180
Horace Miner, "Body Ritual among the Nacirema" 193
Martin King Whyte, "Choosing Mates—The American Way" 199
Nicholas Bornoff, "The Marriage-Go-Round" 281
Nahid Toubia, "Women and Health in Sudan" 221
J. E. Thomas, "Culture and the Communal Organisation" 270
Robert Levine with Ellen Wolff, "Social Time: The Heartbeat of Culture" 288
Gordon Murray, "Picking on the Little Guy: In Boyhood and in the Battlefields" 297
Octavio Paz, "Mexican Masks" 303
Sembene Ousmane, "The *Bilal's* Fourth Wife" (short story) 316
Nawal El Saadawi, "Growing Up Female in Egypt" 325
Nira Yuval-Davis, "Front and Rear: The Sexual Division of Labour in the Israeli Army" 336
James M. Dubik, "An Officer and a Feminist" 352
Dorothy D. Lee, "An Anthropologist Learns from the Hopi" 386

WORKING LIFE

Betsy Jacobson and Beverly Kaye, "Balancing Act" 238
Paul Harrison, "The Barefoot Businessman: Traditional and Small-Scale Industry" 245
Naguib Mahfouz, "Respected Sir" (fiction) 257
Hugh Williamson, "China's Toy Industry Tinderbox" 263
J. E. Thomas, "Culture and Communal Organisation" 270
Robert Levine with Ellen Wolff, "Social Time: The Heartbeat of Culture" 288

WOMEN

Sembene Ousmane, "The *Bilal's* Fourth Wife" (short story) 316
Nahid Toubia, "Women and Health in Sudan" 221
Nawal El Saadawi, "Growing Up Female in Egypt" 325
Nira Yuval-Davis, "Front and Rear: The Sexual Division of Labour in the Israeli Army" 336
James M. Dubik, "An Officer and a Feminist" 352
Andrea Malin, "Mother Who Won't Disappear" 365

MEN

J. E. Thomas, "Culture and the Communal Organisation" 270
Gordon Murray, "Picking on the Little Guy: In Boyhood and in the Battlefields" 297

Octavio Paz, "Mexican Masks"   303
Sembene Ousmane, "The *Bilal's* Fourth Wife" (short story)   316

PROTEST AND CONFORMITY
Gordon Murray, "Picking on the Little Guy: In Boyhood and in the Battlefields"   297
Octavio Paz, "Mexican Masks"   303
Sembene Ousmane, "The *Bilal's* Fourth Wife" (short story)   316
Nawal El Saadawi, "Growing Up Female in Egypt"   325
Aung San Suu Kyi, "Freedom from Fear"   359
Andrea Malin, "Mother Who Won't Disappear"   365
Neil Postman, "Defending Against the Indefensible"   375
Dorothy D. Lee, "An Anthropologist Learns from the Hopi"   386
Pablo Neruda, excerpt from *The Heights of Macchu Picchu* (poem)   398

THE OUTSIDER
Connie May Fowler, "No Snapshots in the Attic: A Granddaughter's Search for a Cherokee Past"   136
Salman Rushdie, "Imaginary Homelands"   408
Pablo Neruda, excerpt from *The Heights of Macchu Picchu*   398
Jenefer Shute, "Sport, African Cultures, Value for Money: Return to South Africa"   422
David Mura, "Fictive Fragments of a Father and Son"   436
Ruxana Meer, "Razia Begum in London"   445
Francis Fukuyama, "Immigrants and Family Values"   450
Gloria Anzaldúa, "La Conciencia de la Mestiza: Towards a New Consciousness"   465

THE IMPORTANCE OF THE ARTIST
Salman Rushdie, "Imaginary Homelands"   408
André Brink, "The Artist as Insect"   482
Audre Lorde, "The Transformation of Silence into Language and Action"   487
Franz Kafka, "A Hunger Artist"   492
Jane M. Young, "The Power of Image and Place"   503
Connie Stephens, "Marriage in the Hausa *Tatsuniya* Tradition: A Cultural and Cosmic Balance"   513

RELIGIOUS LIFE
Naguib Mahfouz, "Respected Sir"   257
John Garvey, "A Different Kind of Knowing: For Those with Ears to Hear"   531
Malidoma Patrice Somé, "Slowly Becoming"   537

Rigoberta Menchú, "The Bible and Self-Defense: The Examples of Judith, Moses, and David"   557
Wang Bin, "Two Great Traditions"   567
Federico García Lorca, "Gacela of the Dead Child"   576
Will Herberg, "The Religion of Americans and American Religion"   580

INDEX OF AUTHORS AND TITLES

"An Anthropologist Learns from the Hopi" 386
Anzaldúa, Gloria 465
"The Artist as Insect" 482

"Balancing Act" 238
"The Barefoot Businessman" 245
"The Bible and Self-Defense: The Examples of Judith, Moses, and David," as told to Ann Wright 557
"The *Bilal's* Fourth Wife" 316
Bin, Wang 567
"Body Ritual Among the Nacirema" 193
Bornoff, Nicholas 281
Brink, André 482

Carroll, Raymonde 85
"Children and Ritual in Bali" 101
"China's Toy Industry Tinderbox" 263
"Choosing Mates—The American Way" 199
"Culture and the Communal Organisation" 270

"Debuting: Phoenix, Arizona" 180
"Defending against the Indefensible" 375
"A Different Way of Knowing" 531
Dubik, James M. 352

El Saadawi, Nawal 325
Elkind, David 168

"Fictive Fragments of a Father and Son" 436
Fowler, Connie May 136
"Freedom from Fear" 359

"Front and Rear: The Sexual Division of Labour in the Israeli Army" 336
Fukuyama, Francis 450

"Gacela of the Dead Child" 576
García Lorca, Federico 576
Garvey, John 531
"Growing Up Female in Egypt" 325

Harris, Marvin 29
Harrison, Paul 245
Excerpt from *The Heights of Macchu Picchu* 398
Herberg, Will 580
"Household and Family in the Caribbean" 159
"A Hunger Artist" 492

"Imaginary Homelands" 408
"Immigrants and Family Values" 450

Jen, Gish 151
Jacobson, Betsy and Beverly Kaye 238

Kafka, Franz 492
Kingsolver, Barbara 78

"La Conciencia de la Mestiza: Towards a New Consciousness" 465
"Land of Meaningless Courtesy" 48
Lee, Dorothy D. 386
Levine, Robert with Ellen Wolff 288
"Looking to the West" 52
Lorde, Audre 487

Mahfouz, Naguib 257
Malin, Andrea 365
"The Marriage-Go-Round" 281
"Marriage in the Hausa *Tatsuniya* Tradition: A Cultural and Cosmic Balance" 513
Mead, Margaret 101
Meer, Ruxana 445
Menchú, Rigoberta 557
"Mexican Masks" 303
Milosz, Czeslaw 52
Miner, Horace 193

"Mother Who Won't Disappear" 365
Mura, David 436
Murray, Gordon 297

Neruda, Pablo 398
"No Snapshots in the Attic: A Granddaughter's Search for a Cherokee Past" 136

"An Officer and a Feminist" 352
Orlean, Susan 180
Ousmane, Sembene 316

"Parents and Children" 85
Paz, Octavio 303
"Picking on the Little Guy: In Boyhood and in the Battlefields" 297
Pokrovsky, Nakita 48
Postman, Neil 375
"The Power of Image and Place" 503

"Razia Begum in London" 445
"The Religion of Americans and American Religion" 580
"Respected Sir" 257
"Role Reversal: The Kind Father and Stern Mother" 131
Rushdie, Salman 408

Shute, Jenefer 422
"Slowly Becoming" 537
"Small Things" 29
"Social Time: The Heartbeat of Culture" 288
Solien Gonzalez, Nancie 159
Somé, Malidoma Patrice 537
"Somebody's Baby" 78
"Sport, African Cultures, Value for Money: A Return to South Africa" 422
Stevens, Connie 513
Suu Kyi, Aung San 359

Thomas, J. E. 270
Toubia, Nahid 221
"The Transformation of Silence into Language and Action" 487
"Two Great Traditions" 567

"WAAAH!! Why Kids Have a Lot to Cry About" 168
"The Water-Faucet Vision" 151

Williamson, Hugh 263
"Women and Health in Sudan" 221
Whyte, Martin King 199

Young, Jane M. 503
Yuval-Davis, Nira 336

Zhai, Li 131

CREDITS

Haleh Afshar
Reprinted from *Women, State and Ideology* by Haleh Afshar (Ed.), by permission of the State University of New York Press, © 1987, State University of New York. All rights reserved.

Anne-Marie Ambert
From "An International Perspective on Parenting: Social Change and Social Constructs" by Anne-Marie Ambert from *Journal of Marriage and the Family,* August 1994, Vol. 56, No. 3, p. 529. Reprinted by permission of the National Council on Family Relations and the author.

Gloria Anzaldua
"La Consciencia de la Mestiza" by Gloria Anzaldua from *Borderlands/La Frontera: The New Mestiza,* © 1987 by Gloria Anzaldua. Reprinted by permission of Aunt Lute Books.

James Baldwin
Excerpted from "The Discovery of What It Means to Be an American" © 1959 by James Baldwin. Originally published in The New York Times Book Review. Collected in *Nobody Knows My Name,* published by Vintage Books. Reprinted by arrangement with the James Baldwin Estate.

Wang Bin
"Two Great Traditions" by Wang Bin reprinted by permission from *UNESCO Courier,* July–August 1992.

Nicholas Bornoff
Reprinted with the permission of Pocket Books, a division of Simon & Schuster, Inc. from *Pink Samurai* by Nicholas Bornoff. Copyright © 1991 by Nicholas Bornoff.

Andre Brink
"The Artist as Insect" by Andre Brink reprinted by permission from *UNESCO Courier,* November 1992.

Witter Bynner
Excerpts from "The Way of Life According to Laotzu" from *The Chinese Translations* by Witter Bynner. This edition copyright © 1978 by The Witter Bynner Foundation. Translation copyright 1944 by Witter Bynner. Translation copyright renewed © 1972 by Dorothy Chauvenet and Paul Horgan.

Italo Calvino
Excerpt from "The Canary Prince" in *Italian Folktales: Selected and Retold by Italo Calvino,* copyright © 1956 by Giulio Einaudi editore, s.p.a., English translation by George Martin copyright © 1980 by Harcourt Brace & Company, reprinted by permission of Harcourt Brace & Company.

Raymonde Carroll
From *Cultural Misunderstandings: The French-American Experience* by Raymonde Carroll, translated by Carol Volk. Reprinted by permission of The University of Chicago Press and the author.

Thomas Cleary
From *The Essential Confucius,* translated by Thomas Cleary. Copyright © 1992 by Thomas Cleary. Reprinted by permission of HarperCollins Publishers, Inc.

James M. Dubik
"An Officer and a Feminist" by James M. Dubik as appeared in *Newsweek,* April 27, 1987. Reprinted by permission of the author.

David Elkind
"Waaah! Why Kids Have a Lot to Cry About" by David Elkind from *Psychology Today,* May/June 1992. Reprinted with permission from *Psychology Today Magazine,* copyright © 1992 (Sussex Publishers, Inc.).

Lawrence Ferlinghetti
"Constantly Risking Absurdity" by Lawrence Ferlinghetti, from *A Coney Island of the Mind.* Copyright © 1958 by Lawrence Ferlinghetti. Reprinted by permission of New Directions Publishing Corp.

Elizabeth Warnock Fernea
"Growing up Female in Egypt" by Nawal al-Sa'dawi reprinted from *Women and Family in the Middle East: New Voices of Change,* edited by Elizabeth Warnock Ferna, copyright © 1985. By permission the University of Texas Press.

Connie May Fowler
"No Snapshots in the Attic" by Connie May Fowler. Copyright © 1999 by Connie May Fowler. First appeared in *The New York Times Book Review,* May 22, 1994. Reprinted by permission of The Joy Harris Literary Agency, Inc. From *River Of Hidden Dreams* by Connie May Fowler. Reprinted by permission of Penguin Putnam, Inc.

Francis Fukuyama
"Immigrants and Family Values" by Francis Fukuyama. Reprinted from *Commentary,* May 1993, by permission; all rights reserved.

John Garvey
"A Different Kind of Knowing: For Those with Ears to Hear" by John Garvey from *Commonweal,* October 1994, Vol. 121, No. 17, p. 9. Copyright © 1994 Commonweal Foundation. Reprinted by permission.

Henry Louis Gates, Jr.
"Whose Culture Is It, Anyway? It's Not Just Anglo-Saxon" by Henry Louis Gates, Jr. from *The New York Times,* May 4, 1991. Copyright © 1991 by *The New York Times.* Reprinted by permission.

Nancie Solien Gonzalez
"Household and Family in the Caribbean" by Nancie Solien Gonzalez from *Social and Economic Studies,* Vol. 9, No. 1, 1960, pp. 101–106. Reprinted by permission of the Institute of Social and Economic Research.

Marvin Harris
"Small Things" from *Good to Eat* by Marvin Harris. Reprinted by permission of the author.

Paul Harrison
"The Barefoot Business Man" from *Inside the Third World* by Paul Harrison. Reprinted by permission of The Peters Fraser and Dunlop Group Limited.

Will Herberg
From *Protestant Catholic Jew* by Will Herberg. Copyright © 1955 by Will Herberg. Used by permission of Doubleday, a division of Random House, Inc.

Betsy Jacobson and Beverly Kaye
"Balancing Act" by Betsy Jacobson and Beverly Kaye from *Training & Development,* February 1993, Vol. 47, No. 2, pp. 24–28. Copyright © 1993, Training & Development, American Society for Training & Development. Reprinted with permission. All rights reserved.

Gish Jen
"The Water Faucet Vision" by Gish Jen. Copyright © 1987 by Gish Jen. First published in *Nimrod.* Reprinted by permission of the author.

Carl Jung
From "The Spiritual Problem of Modern Man" by Carl Jung in *Modern Man in Search of a Soul,* translated by W. S. Dell. Reprinted by permission of Routledge.

Franz Kafka
From *The Trial* by Franz Kafka, translated by Willa and Edwin Muir. Copyright 1925, 1935, 1946 by Schocken Books, Inc. Copyright renewed © 1952, 1963, 1974 by Schocken Books, Inc. Copyright © 1937, 1956 by AAK, Inc. Copyright © renewed 1964, 1984 by AAK, Inc. Reprinted by permission of Schocken Books, distributed by Pantheon Books, a division of Random House, Inc. From *The Penal Colony* by Franz Kafka, translated by Willa and Edwin Muir. Copyright © 1948 and renewed 1976 by Schocken Books, Inc. Reprinted by permission of Schocken Books, distributed by Pantheon Books, a division of Random House, Inc.

Barbara Kingsolver
"Somebody's Baby" from *High Tide in Tucson* by Barbara Kingsolver. Copyright © 1995 by Barbara Kingsolver. Reprinted by permission of HarperCollins Publishers, Inc.

Aung San Suu Kyi
"Freedom from Fear" from *Freedom from Fear and Other Writings, Revised Ed.* by Aung San Suu Kyi. Foreword by Vaclav Havel, translated by Michael Aris, Translation copyright © 1991, 1995 by Aung San Suu Kyi and Michael Aris. Used by permission of Viking Penguin, a division of Penguin Putnam, Inc.

Dorothy D. Lee
"An Anthropologist Learns from the Hopi" by Dorothy D. Lee from *Integrity and Compromise: Problems of Public and Private Conscience,* 1957 edited by R. M. MacIver (lectures published by The Institute for Religious and Social Studies). Reprinted by permission.

Robert Levine and Ellen Wolff
"Social Time: The Hearbeat of Culture" by Robert Levine and Ellen Wolff from *Psychology Today,* March 1985. Reprinted with permission from *Psychology Today Magazine,* copyright © 1985 (Sussex Publishers, Inc.).

Frederico Garcia Lorca
"Gacela of the Dead Child" by Frederico Garcia Lorca, translated by Edwin Honig, from *The Selected Poems of Federico Garcia Lorca.* Copyright © 1955 by New Directions Publishing Corp. Reprinted by permission of New Directions Publishing Corp.

Audre Lorde
Reprinted with permission from "The Transformation of Silence in Language and Action" in *Sister Outsider: Essays and Speeches* by Audre Lorde, © 1984. Published by The Crossing Press, P.O. Box 1048, Freedom, CA 95019.

Naguib Mahfouz
From *Respected Sir* by Naguib Mahfouz, translated by Dr. Rasheed El-Enany. Translation copyright © 1986 by Dr. Rasheed El-Enany. Used by permission of Doubleday, a division of Random House, Inc.

Andrea Malin
Andrea Malin. "Mothers Who Won't Disappear." *Human Rights Quarterly,* February 1994: pp. 187–213. Copyright © 1994 The Johns Hopkins University Press. Reprinted by permission.

Margaret Mead and Martha Wolfenstein
From *Childhood in Contemporary Cultures* edited by Margaret Mead and Martha Wolfenstein. Reprinted by permission of The University of Chicago Press.

Ruxana Meer
"Razia Begum in London" by Ruxana Meer as appeared in *Charlie Chan Is Dead,* edited by Jessica Hagedorn.

Rigoberta Menchu
From *I, Rigoberta Menchu* by Rigoberta Menchu, edited by Elisabeth Burgos-Debray, translated into English by Ann Wright. Copyright © Verso, 1984. Reprinted by permission of Verso.

Czeslaw Milosz
"Looking to the West" from *The Captive Mind* by Czeslaw Milos, translated into English by Jane Zielonko. Copyright 1951, 1953 by Czeslaw Milosz. Reprinted by permission of Alfred A. Knopf, Inc.

Horace Miner
"Body Ritual Among the Nacirema" by Horace Miner. Reproduced by permission of the American Anthropological Association from *American Anthropologist* 58:3, June 1956. Not for further reproduction.

Thomas Moore
From *Care of the Soul* by Thomas Moore. Copyright © 1992 by Thomas Moore. Reprinted by permission of HarperCollins Publishers, Inc.

David Mura
"Fictive Fragments of a Father and Son" from *Turning Japanese: Memoirs of a Sensai* by David Mura. Copyright © 1991 by David Mura. Used by permission of Grove/Atlantic, Inc.

Gordon Murray
Gordon Murray. "Picking on the Little Guy." © 1993 Gordon Murray from Abbott, Franklin. *Boyhood, Growing Up Male.* © 1993 Franklin Abbott. Reprinted by permission of The University of Wisconsin Press.

Pablo Neruda
Excerpts from *The Heights of Macchu Picchu* by Pablo Neruda, translated by Nathaniel Tarn. Translation copyright © 1966 and copyright renewed © 1994 by Nathaniel Tarn. Reprinted by permission of Farrar, Straus and Giroux, LLC and Jonathan Cape.

Susan Orlean
"Debuting: Phoenix, Arizona" from *Saturday Night* by Susan Orlean. Copyright © 1990 by Susan Orlean. Reprinted by permission of Alfred A. Knopf, Inc.

Alan Paton
Reprinted with the permission of Scribner, a Division of Simon & Schuster from *Cry, The Beloved Country* by Alan Paton. Copyright 1948 by Alan Paton; copyright renewed © 1976 by Alan Paton.

Octavio Paz
"Mexican Masks" from *Labyrinth of Solitude* by Octavio Paz, translated by Lysander Kemp. Copyright © 1962 by Grove Press, Inc. Used by permission of Grove/Atlantic, Inc.

Ross Petras and Kathryn Petras
"International Business Machines" from *Inside Track* by Ross Petras and Kathryn Petras. Copyright © 1986 by Ross Petras and Kathryn Petras. Reprinted by permission of Random House, Inc.

Neil Postman
"Defending Against the Indefensible" from *Conscientious Objections* by Neil Postman. Copyright © 1988 by Neil Postman. Reprinted by permission of Alfred A. Knopf, Inc.

Rainer Maria Rilke
"The First Elegy" from *The Duino Elegies and the Sonnets to Orpheus* by Rainer Maria Rilke, translated by A. Poulin, Jr. Copyright © 1975, 1976, 1977 by A. Poulin, Jr. Reprinted by permission of Houghton Mifflin Company. All rights reserved.

Salman Rushdie
"Imaginary Homelands" (pp. 9–21), copyright © 1982 by Salman Rushdie from *Imaginary Homelands* by Salman Rushdie. Used by permission of Viking Penguin, a division of Penguin Putnam, Inc. and The Wylie Agency, Inc.

Hanan al-Shaykh
From *Women of Sand and Myrrh* by Hanan al-Shaykh, translated by Catherine Cobham. Translation copyright © 1989 by Hanan al-Shaykh. Used by permission of Doubleday, a division of Random House, Inc.

Jenefer Shute
"Sport, African Cultures, Value for Money: A Return to South Africa" by Jenefer Shute from *Tikkun*, November/December 1992, Vol. 7, No. 6. Reprinted from *Tikkun Magazine,* a bi-monthly Jewish critique of politics, culture, and society. Information and subscriptions are available from Tikkun, 26 Fell Street, San Francisco, CA 94102.

Malidoma Some
From *Of Water and the Spirit* by Malidoma Some. Copyright © 1994 by Malidoma Patrice Some. Used by permission of Putnam Berkley, a division of Penguin Putnam, Inc.

Connie Stephen
"Marriage in the Hausa Tatsuniya Tradition" by Connie Stephen from *Hausa Women in the Twentieth Century* by Catherine Coles and Beverly Mack. Copyright © 1991. Reprinted by permission of The University of Wisconsin Press.

Studs Terkel
From "Working" by Studs Terkel. Reprinted by permission of Donadio & Olson, Inc. Copyright 1974 by Studs Terkel.

J. E. Thomas
"Culture and the Communal Organization" by J. E. Thomas from *Making Japan Work*. Copyright © 1993. Reprinted by permission of Japan Library Knoll House.

Le Thi Diem Thuy
"The Gangster We Are All Looking For" by Le Thi Diem Thuy from *The Massachusetts Review*, 1997. Reprinted by permission of *The Massachusetts Review*, South College, University of Massachusetts, Amherst, MA 01003.

Nahid Toubia
"Women and Health in Sudan" by Nahid Toubia from *Women of the Arab World*. Copyright © 1988. Reprinted by permission of the Zed Books Ltd. and the author.

Peter Verberg
From "How Other Cultures Have Solved the Teen Dilemma" by Peter Verberg from *Alberta Report / Western Report*, March 27, 1995, Vol. 22, No. 15, p. 32. Reprinted by permission of Interwest Publishing.

Martin King Whyte
"Choosing Mates . . . The American Way" by Martin King Whyte from *Society*, March–April 1992, Vol. 29, No. 3, pp. 71–78. Reprinted by permission of Transaction Publishers. Copyright © 1992. All rights reserved.

Hugh Williamson
"China's Toy Industry Tinderbox" by Hugh Williamson from *Multinational Monitor*, September 1994. Reprinted by permission of Essential Information.

Edmund Wilson
Excerpt from "Philocretes: the Wound and the Bow" from *The Wound and the Bow: Seven Studies in Literature* by Edmund Wilson. Copyright © 1970 by Edmund Wilson. Reprinted by permission of Farrar, Straus & Giroux, Inc.

Richard Wright
From *Native Son* by Richard Wright. Copyright 1940 by Richard Wright. Copyright © renewed 1968 by Ellen Wright. Reprinted by permission of HarperCollins Publishers, Inc.

Jane M. Young
"The Power of Image and Place" by Jane M. Young from *Signs of the Ancestors*. Copyright © 1988. Reprinted by permission of The University of New Mexico Press.